STUDY GUIDE

BUSINESS LAW

STUDY GUIDE
Ramona Atkins
Allan Hancock College

BUSINESS LAW
Sixth Edition

Henry R. Cheeseman

PEARSON

Prentice
Hall

Upper Saddle River, New Jersey 07458

VP/Editorial Director: Jeff Shelstad
Executive Editor: Wendy Craven
Project Manager: Kerri Tomasso
Associate Director, Manufacturing: Vincent Scelta
Production Editor & Buyer: Carol O'Rourke
Printer/Binder: Bind-Rite Graphics

Pearson Prentice Hall™ is a trademark of Pearson Education, Inc.

10   9   8   7   6   5   4   3
ISBN 0-13-198500-0

CONTENTS

DEDICATION

In loving memory of my mother,

Delphine M. Atkins

Whose philosophy was "adversity is a challenge to succeed."

ACKNOWLEDGMENTS

Without Professor Cheeseman, there would not be this Study Guide. His legal expertise as well as dedication to putting the main text together is applauded. Additionally, a special thank you to Project Manager Kerri Tomasso for her commitment as well as professionalism and patience in assuring that the study guide came to fruition. Finally, a special thank you to my family for their patience and understanding while work was being completed for this edition.

Ramona A. Atkins, J.D.
Associate Faculty of Business Law
Allan Hancock College, Business Education
Santa Maria, California
ramonaatkins@msn.com

Chapter 1

Legal Heritage and Critical Legal Thinking

Chapter Overview

This chapter discusses the significance of the concept of law and its functions in our society in terms of overseeing the behavior that takes place within it by individuals, businesses, and organizations. Even though the meaning of law is vast, law in general is a set of standards and rules that we justify our actions by and which is the basis of consequences as well as sanctions. The philosophy of law, various schools of thought on its development and the importance of flexibility in its application are also examined. The history and development of our laws and courts along with interpretation as it pertains to technology, growth of commerce and the standards of society are what bring about changes and new laws.

Objectives

Upon completion of the exercises in this chapter, you should be able to:
1. Describe law based upon its function.
2. Recognize and compare the major schools of jurisprudence.
3. Understand and appreciate the history of American law.
4. Distinguish the differences between a law court, equity court and a merchant court.
5. Comprehend the sources of modern law in the United States.
6. Understand and recognize key terminology when briefing a case.
7. Understand how to recognize legal and ethical issues when briefing a case.
8. Have a broader understanding of legal history as well as business developments in cyberspace.

Practical Application

You should be able to understand the basis, development, and need for law as well as flexible interpretation and the framework by which laws are established.

Helpful Hints

You should read each chapter and complete or read the corresponding study guide exercises. Next, a Refresh Your Memory exercise will determine what materials you need to place more emphasis on. The Critical Thinking Exercise that follows will help to assess your ability to analyze and apply the legal concepts you have learned to the facts. Finally, a Sample Quiz consisting of true/false, multiple choice and short answer questions is provided as a means of assessing your mastery of the chapter.

Essentials for a Well-Written Critical Thinking Exercise

Critical Thinking exercises should be approached in a methodical way. Each exercise should be read twice, the first time to get a feel for the facts and determine what is being asked of you, and the second to spot the issues presented. Once you know what the question is asking you to do, you can mark up the facts with a pen and place possible applicable legal terms from the chapter you have just studied next to the fact it pertains to. In order to prepare a well-written answer, it is imperative that you prepare an outline that is organized by either the topic or legal issues that will be discussed. Demonstrate how the facts in your exercise meet the requirements of the legal principle(s) you are discussing.

There are two sides to every story just as there are two sides to every argument. When applicable, give reasoning for both sides. Also, if you are applying case law that you have studied, be sure to show how the case(s) apply to the facts you've been given, based upon the similarity of both scenarios. Further, if the case is not supportive of your analysis, you may indicate this point with a brief explanation and continue with the issues you have strong support for.

Finally, make sure that you have utilized all of the relevant facts and applied the pertinent law in analyzing these facts. Remember, it is your reasoning and application of the main objectives of the chapter that will help to determine your competency of the information given to you. If you approach these types of exercises as challenging, fun, and practical, you will begin to appreciate their usefulness in your everyday life. A sample answer is given at the end of the chapter and is to be used as a guide. Answers will vary based on the law and analysis applied by individual students.

Study Tips

Law is a set of standards and rules that we justify our conduct and actions by and that, which is subject to consequences and sanctions. A law's description is usually made with its function in mind.

Functions of the law include the following:
- To shape moral standards.
- To maintain the status quo.
- To facilitate planning.
- To maximize individual freedom.
- To keep the peace.
- To promote social justice.
- To facilitate orderly change.
- To provide a basis for compromise.

Various scholars have stated their philosophies on the development of the law. There are several schools of jurisprudential thought. You will notice that each adjective describing each school gives you a hint as to the reasoning behind each school's title. For example, the Command School would be easy to remember, as a commander has been defined as a person who holds rank, such as a higher official. As such, it is easy then to remember that the law changes when the ruler (or commander) changes. Additionally, you can remember the main schools of thought by the following mnemonic:

A cranky squirrel commands natural history!

A — The **A**nalytical School asserts that the law is formed by logic.

C — The **C**ritical Legal Studies School does not believe in rules for settling disputes, but applying rules of fairness to each circumstance.

S — The **S**ociological School believes that law is a way to form social behavior and attain sociological goals.

C — The **C**ommand School espouses that the law changes when the ruler changes.

N — The **N**atural Law School maintains that the basis of law should be on morality and ethics.

H — The **H**istorical School believes that changes in societal norms are eventually demonstrated in the law. These scholars rely on precedent to solve modern problems.

Foundation of American Law

The American common law was derived from England and its laws. It is helpful to understand a brief history of how our laws developed.

English Common Law

These laws developed from judge-issued opinions that became precedent for other judges to decide similar cases. Local judges appointed by the king were given the responsibility of administering the law in a uniform manner.

Law Courts

The judges issued their opinions in cases that later set the precedent for deciding the same types of cases. Legal procedure was stressed over merit, and monetary awards were all that was available in a law court.

Equity Courts

A court that is based on fairness when deciding cases

Merchant Courts

A court that dealt with only the law of merchants and their commercial disputes. Eventually this court was combined with the regular court system.

Sources of Law

- Constitution — The supreme law of the land that provided for the structure of the federal government. This structure established the legislative, executive, and judicial branches of government. Those powers not given to the federal government by the Constitution are reserved for the state.

- Treaties — Compacts or agreements between two or more nations that become a part of the Constitution.

- Statutes — A set of state or federal laws that describes conduct that must be followed by those the statute was designed to protect. These laws are organized by topic in code books. An example would be the Uniform Commercial Code.

- Ordinances — Laws that are created and enforced by local governments including counties, school districts, and municipalities. An example would be a traffic law.

- Executive Orders — These are laws that are made by the president or state governors.

- Judicial Decisions — Federal and state issued decisions about individual lawsuits.

The Doctrine of Stare Decisis

A rule of law set forth by higher courts, which becomes precedence for lower court decisions. In addition to the benefit of helping to establish uniformity of law, this doctrine makes it easier for individuals and businesses to determine what the law is.

Key Terms

Plaintiff is the one who originally brings the lawsuit.

Defendant is the party who is being sued or whom the suit is brought against.

Petitioner or Appellant is the party (plaintiff or defendant) who has appealed the decision of the lower court or trial court.

Respondent or Appellee is the party (or person) who must answer the appeal brought by the petitioner or appellant. The respondent or appellee may be either the plaintiff or defendant based on which party is the petitioner.

Essentials for briefing a case

Case name, citation, and the court
Important case facts briefly and concisely stated
Issues presented to the court
Rules of law
Analysis of the facts with incorporation of the law
Conclusion or holding of the court hearing the case

Refresh Your Memory

The following exercise will give you the opportunity to test your memory of the principles given in this chapter. Read the question twice and place your answer in the blanks provided. Review the chapter material for any question that you are unable to answer or remember.

1.   A legally binding guideline that has a consequence for breaking it is known as _____.

2.   Which modern legal philosophy says that promoting market efficiency should be the central goal of legal decision making? The _____.

3.   If Travis wanted to rely on precedent to solve his problem, which jurisprudential school of thought would best serve his goal? _____

4.   An agreement between two or more nations is known as a
     _____.

5.   A law that states you may not mow your lawn before a certain time in the morning is called an _____.

6.   If the president of the United States commanded that all encrypted technology be banned from high   profile, terrorist-inhabited countries, this would be an example of
     _____.

7.   The supreme law of the land is known as the _____.

8.   What is the type of court that bases its decisions on fairness?
     _____

9.   If George is the party bringing a lawsuit against Henry, what is George's title in the lawsuit? _____

10. If Henry decides to appeal the case brought by George, what legal term describes Henry in his appeal? _____

11. George is served with the appellate lawsuit brought by Henry.   What term describes George's role in this suit?
     _____

12. Which court helped to resolve commercial disputes by applying rules based on common trade practices and usage? _____

13. What document is referred to as a living document based on its adaptability?
     _____

14. The doctrine that helped establish uniformity of law is known as
     _____ _____.

15. A case is briefed by determining the issues, and _____ applying the law to the facts.

Critical Thought Exercise

Following the genocide, torture, rape, and murder of thousands of civilians in Rwanda in 1994, sixty-three individuals were tried for genocide and crimes against humanity. Numerous persons were sentenced to life sentences.

Many of those prosecuted objected to being tried outside Rwanda for acts committed within Rwanda. The accused further objected to being prosecuted for acts that were not deemed criminal by their own leaders or national laws.

You are asked to address a large convention sponsored by a nationalist group that argues against any person ever being subjected to criminal punishment by an international court for acts committed within their home country.

Your argument should address the following issues while trying to explain whether or not you feel prosecutions by an international body are lawful and justified:

1. What law is being violated when someone commits a crime against humanity?
2. Who has the authority to enforce laws against genocide and crimes against humanity?
3. Should a citizen of a sovereign nation be subjected to punishment by an international tribunal for acts committed within their home country?
4. Who is responsible for the prosecution of these crimes?

Answer:

_____

_____

_____

_____

_____

_____

_____

_____

_____

_____

_____

_____

_____

_____

_____

_____

_____

_____

_____

_____

_____

_____

Practice Quiz

True/False

1. _____ Advocates of the law and economics theory feel that the appointing of free counsel to prisoners who initiate civil rights cases needs to be abolished, as a prisoner should be able to hire an attorney for free or enter into a contingency-fee arrangement. [p. 9]

2. _____ The Anglo-American common law system is the same as the civil law legal system. [pp. 8-9]

3. _____ Any federal, state, or local law that is in conflict with the U.S. Constitution will be enforceable as each are separate governing bodies. [p. 9]

4. _____ The Analytical School of jurisprudence is based upon what is morally and ethically correct. [p. 7]

5. _____ Decisions that come from administrative agencies are called orders. [p. 10]

6. _____ The English common law served as a basis from which many of our laws were developed. [p. 9]

7. _____ An equity court emphasizes the procedure of a case versus the merits of a case. [p. 8]

8. _____ One of the goals of the Department of Homeland Security is to assist in the recovery in the event of a terrorist attack. [p. 11]

9. _____ The Chancellor's remedies were called legal remedies because they were shaped to emphasize legal procedure. [p. 8]

10. _____ Courts of one jurisdiction are bound by the precedent established by the courts of another jurisdiction. [p. 11]

11. _____ The structure of the United States federal government is comprised of the legislative, executive, and judicial branches, each of which has been granted certain powers. [p. 9]

12. _____ The federal and state courts must follow the precedent established by lower courts. [p. 11]

13. _____ The doctrine of stare decisis promotes uniformity of law within a court system. [p. 11]

14. _____ The president may issue an executive order to prohibit U.S. companies from selling goods or services to a country we are at war with. [p. 10]

Multiple Choice

15. Some of the primary functions of the law in our country are: [p. 4]
    a. promoting social justice, encouraging legal decisions, and interpreting judicial decisions.
    b. facilitating change, providing a basis for compromise, and developing legal reasoning.
    c. keeping the peace, shaping moral standards, minimizing individual freedom.
    d. none of the above.

16. The Sociological School of jurisprudence does not maintain that [p. 7]
    a. the law is a set of rules enforced by the ruling party and the law changes when the ruler changes.
    b. the purpose of law is necessary to achieve social behavior.
    c. the purpose of law is necessary to advance social behavior.
    d. the purpose of law is necessary to shape social behavior.

17. The term codified refers to [p. 10]
    a. statutes enacted by the legislative branches of state and federal governments that are arranged by topic in code books.
    b. a written agreement made between the United States and another nation.
    c. administrative rules and regulations.
    d. all of the above.

18. The term stare decisis means: [p. 11]
    a. to interpret statutes and make a decision.
    b. to predict the legal decision in a case.
    c. to stand by the decision.
    d. to adopt and regulate the conduct of others.

19. Provisions of state-established constitutions are valid unless [p. 9]
    a. they are patterned after the U.S. Constitution.
    b. they have an executive branch of their governments.
    c. they apply to evolving social, technological, and economic conditions.
    d. they conflict with the U.S. Constitution or any valid federal law.

20. Administrative agencies are often referred to as [p. 10]
    a. the law-making branch of government.
    b. the law-deciding branch of government.
    c. the executive order branch of government.
    d. the fourth branch of government.

21. The theory that the main goal of decision making should be to promote market efficiency is derived from: [p. 7]
    a. the Command School.
    b. the Law and Economics School.
    c. the Jurisprudence School.
    d. the Marketing and Advertising School.

22. Which of the following are examples of ordinances? [p. 10]
    a. Indian gaming regulations
    b. federal government regulations
    c. traffic laws, local building codes and zoning laws
    d. all of the above

23. The law of the United States is mainly based on: [p. 9]
    a. federal law.
    b. Roman civil law.
    c. English business law.
    d. English common law.

Short Answer

24. What did the case of *Brown v. Board of Education* involve? [p. 6]
    _____

25. Identify the court that was primarily concerned with fairness. [p. 6]
    _____

26. Give several examples of federal statutes. [p. 10]
    _____
    _____

27. Give several examples of state statutes. [p. 11]
    _____
    _____

28. Jurisprudence can be defined as [p. 6]
    _____
    _____

29. Why will treaties become increasingly more important to business? [p. 10]
    _____
    _____

30. Administrative agencies are created to enforce and interpret statutes. Give two examples of these types of agencies. [p. 10-11]
    _____

31. Which state bases its law on the French civil code? [p. 8]
    _____

32. A judicial decision is [p. 11]
    _____
    _____

33. What is the term given for a rule of law established in a court decision that lower courts must follow? [p. 11] _____

34. What are the two qualities of law as they pertain to the American legal system? [p. 5]

_____ and _____

35. What type of court emphasized legal procedure over merits? [p. 7]

_____

36. What is the application of law to facts using skills of analysis and interpretation in deciding important issues called? [p. 12]

_____

_____

37. What jurisprudential school of thought do realists follow? [p. 7]

_____

38. What types of agencies are the Securities and Exchange Commission and the Federal Trade Commission? [p. 12]

_____

39. When briefing a case, what does the case name usually contain? [p. 13]

_____

_____

40. What should the summary of the courts reasoning exclude? [p. 14]

_____

_____

41. How should issues that are presented in a case to be briefed be asked? [p. 13]

_____

_____

42. What is the holding in a case? [p. 13]

_____

43. What should the holding state? [p. 13]

_____

44. What is an appellate court or supreme court's decision called? [p. 14]

_____

45. What may the rationale for the court's decision be based upon? [p. 14]

_____

_____

46. What is a statute? [p. 10]

_____

47. What is an executive order? [p. 10]

_____

48. What powers does the judicial branch of the federal government have? [p. 9]

_____

_____

Answers to Refresh Your Memory

1. law [p. 13]
2. The Law and Economics School [p. 7]
3. The Historical School [pp. 6-7]
4. treaty [p. 10]
5. ordinance [p. 10]
6. executive order [p. 10]
7. the Constitution [p. 9]
8. equity court [p. 8]
9. plaintiff [p. 12]
10. appellant or petitioner [p. 12]
11. respondent or appellee [p. 12]
12. merchant court [p. 8]
13. The United States Constitution [p. 9]
14. stare decisis [p. 11]
15. analytically [p. 13]

Critical Thought Exercise Model Answer

The Origins of Law

In its most basic form, law is comprised of the rules created by the controlling authority of a society, usually its government. These rules are given legal force and effect and control the actions of the individuals within the society. Most law is created by each society within a country and is referred to as national law. Law that is created by way of treaties, customs, and agreements between nations is international law.

For most countries, national law finds its foundation in the philosophies of legal positivism, which assumes that there is no law higher than the laws created by the government, and legal realism, which stresses a realistic approach that takes into account customary practices and present day circumstances.

In the area of international law, the philosophy of natural law plays an important role. Natural law holds that there is a universal law that is applicable to all human beings that is higher than any law created by an individual society or government. Certain conduct, such as genocide and crimes against humanity are deemed to be without any possible moral justification, regardless of the existence or nonexistence of any national law concerning these types of acts.

When a nation or segment of a society within a nation engages in conduct that violates natural law, it is no defense to this conduct that the government or society advocates or condones the conduct.

Justification for International Criminal Tribunals and an International Criminal Court

The nations of the world have collectively agreed for over 50 years that international courts capable of resolving disputes and addressing crimes against humanity are needed. This need has been filled by the United Nations.

The members of the United Nations consent to the jurisdiction of the international courts as a way to advance their rights in the international arena. Until 1998, the International Court of Justice (ICJ) was the principal judicial organ of the United Nations. The ICJ, located in The Hague, Netherlands, began operating in 1946. The prior court had been in the same location since 1922. In 1998, the International Criminal Court (ICC) was also created.

The ICJ operates under a statute that is part of the Charter of the United Nations. The ICJ lacks power to address situations such as the Holocaust and genocide in Cambodia because it can only hear cases between states. It has no jurisdiction over individuals.

Prior to the formation of the ICC, the United Nations members formed criminal tribunals to address war crimes and crimes against humanity that have been committed during specific periods of time. These tribunals were given authority to prosecute individuals who were responsible for these severe criminal acts.

The overall purpose of these tribunals was to pursue peace and justice in the affected areas. The International Criminal Tribunal for Rwanda was established for the prosecution of persons responsible for genocide and other serious violations of international humanitarian law committed in the territory of Rwanda between 1 January 1994 and 31 December 1994. The tribunal was also authorized to prosecute Rwandan citizens responsible for genocide and other such violations of international law committed in the territory of neighboring States during the same period.

An international criminal court has been called the missing link in the international legal system. The International Court of Justice at The Hague handles only cases between States, not individuals. Without an international criminal court for dealing with individual responsibility as an enforcement mechanism, acts of genocide and egregious violations of human rights often go unpunished. No one was held accountable for the over 2 million people killed by the Khmer Rouge in Cambodia in the 1970s. The same was true for murders of men, women, and children in Mozambique, Liberia, El Salvador, and other countries.

Defining International Crimes

When each instance of genocide or crimes against humanity has taken place, a specific statute had to be created which not only set up the tribunal, but defined the crimes that were to be prosecuted. The jurisdiction of the tribunal only extended to those crimes and that time period covered in the statute.

In the statute establishing the International Criminal Tribunal for Rwanda, specific definitions for genocide, crimes against humanity, and violations of the Geneva Convention were set forth in detail. To address crimes against humanity, the ICTR statute established "...the power to prosecute persons responsible for the following crimes when committed as part of a widespread or systematic attack against any civilian population on national, political, ethnic, racial or religious grounds: (a) Murder; (b) Extermination; (c) Enslavement; (d) Deportation; (e) Imprisonment; (f) Torture; (g) Rape; (h) Persecutions on political, racial and religious grounds; (i) Other inhumane acts." (ICTR Statute, Article 3.)

Need for International Prosecution

Without the international tribunals, those responsible could easily flee to other countries and avoid being held accountable for their acts of genocide. This was particularly true in the case of Rwanda, where the perpetrators simply went across the border into neighboring countries to hide when pursued. They would then reenter Rwanda and continue the killing when they were able. Rwanda was unable to handle the apprehension and prosecution of those responsible because the government of Rwanda had broken down and lacked the power to enforce peace. The need for international prosecution also arises when the controlling government and its leaders are the actual perpetrators, such as in the case of Yugoslavia. The government in power may actually mandate that the criminal acts be carried out as part of an "ethnic cleansing." This was true in both Nazi Germany and in Yugoslavia in the 1990s.

Deterrence and Responsibility for Prosecutions in the Future

Nations agree that criminals should normally be prosecuted by national courts in the countries where the crimes are committed. When the national governments are either unwilling or unable to act to restore peace and seek justice, there needs to be an institution in place to address the horrors of genocide and crimes against humanity. In the past, perpetrators had little chance of being caught, much less prosecuted. The new ICC seeks to create a deterrent effect. Those responsible for murder, terrorism, genocide, and violations of the Geneva Convention will know that they will be pursued throughout the world. Additionally, the loopholes inherent in the tribunal process will be eliminated. The ineffective nature of the ICTR is shown by the fact that the murder of thousands of people from 1995-1999 will go unpunished because the ICTR was only authorized to prosecute those crimes committed in 1994.

Without an international institution to address crimes such as those committed in Rwanda, the perpetrators of the worst crimes in history would go unpunished. The members of the United Nations have decided that they desire the protection afforded by an international criminal court.

Answers to Practice Quiz

True/False

1. True   The Law and Economics School advocates that promoting market efficiency should be the central goal of legal decision making. Further, as per the example, proponents of this theory feel that if a prisoner cannot afford an attorney or be a client on a contingency fee basis, then the case is probably not worth bringing after all.

2. False   In the Anglo-American common law, laws are created by the judicial system along with congressional legislation. Conversely, the civil law system and parliamentary statutes are the sole sources of law. Further, in most civil law countries, the civil law system used only codes or statutes to adjudicate its cases.

3. False   Any federal, state, or local law that conflicts with the U.S. Constitution is unconstitutional and therefore unenforceable.

4. False   The Natural School of jurisprudence is based upon what is morally and ethically correct.

5. True   Administrative agencies have the authority to hear and decide disputes, their decisions of which are called orders.

6. True   Our laws were developed using the English common law as a foundation.

7. False   The Chancery (Equity) Courts inquired into the merits of the case as opposed to placing emphasis on legal procedure. The Equity Court was a place where a person could go if a law court could not give an appropriate remedy.

8. True   Among the Department of Homeland Security's roles regarding terrorists is to assist in the recovery in the event of a terrorist attack.

9. False   The Chancellor's remedies were called equitable remedies because they were shaped to emphasize the merits of a case.

10. False   The courts of one jurisdiction are not bound by the precedent established by the courts of another jurisdiction; however, they may look to one another for guidance.

11. True   The structure of the United States government is comprised of the legislative, executive, and presidential branches, each of which has been granted certain powers.

12. False   Lower courts such as all federal and state courts must follow the precedents established by higher courts such as the U.S. Supreme Court.

13. True   The term stare decisis means "to stand by the decision" which would logically promote uniformity of law within a court system, as businesses and individuals do not have to guess what the law is since the decision has been made.

14. True   If we are at war with another country, the president by virtue of the powers given to the executive branch of government may issue an executive order prohibiting U.S. companies from selling goods or services to that country.

Multiple Choice

15. A   Some of the primary functions of the law in our country are keeping the peace, shaping moral standards, and maintaining individual freedom. A is incorrect because even though we would like for legal decisions to be made, it is not a main function of law. B is incorrect as compromise comes as a result of negotiation as opposed to a function of law. Further, legal reasoning is not a function of the law, but is developed by applying the law to facts. Therefore, C is the best answer.

16. A   Answer A is correct, as it states the theory behind the Command School of jurisprudence, which would not state the theory behind the Sociological School of jurisprudence. The Sociological School maintains that the law is an avenue of attaining and advancing certain sociological goals. As such, answers B, C, and D are incorrect as the questions asks which of the following would *not* be part of the sociological school of jurisprudence.

17. A   This is the correct definition of codified law. B is incorrect as this is a definition of a treaty. C is incorrect as administrative rules and regulations assist in interpreting the statutes that the administrative agencies are authorized to enforce. D is incorrect for the reasons stated above.

18. C   C is correct, as this is the true meaning of this Latin phrase. Answers A, B, and D are wrong as the meaning is incorrectly stated.

19. D   Many state constitutions mirror the United States Constitution. Therefore, answer A is incorrect. Answer B is incorrect as state constitutions establish an executive branch of government. Answer C is a correct statement as it refers to the law and its flexibility toward evolving technological, social, and economic conditions. However, it is incorrect to say that the law is invalid because of these changes. Answer D is correct as the Constitution is the supreme law of the land. The states must follow it as opposed to creating conflicting provisions in their constitutions.

20. D Answer D is correct, as administrative agencies are often referred to as the fourth branch of government. Answer A is incorrect, as it refers to the legislative branch. Answer B is incorrect as it refers to the judicial branch, and answer C is incorrect as it implies the executive branch.

21. B Answer is correct as those such as U.S. Court of Appeals Judge Richard Posner support the theory that when making decisions in business-related cases, illegalities should be found only if it causes the entire market to be less efficient. Answer A is incorrect as the Command School believes that the law changes when the ruling party changes. Answer C is incorrect as jurisprudence is a philosophy or science about how the law was developed. It is within this philosophy that the different major schools were developed. Answer D is incorrect as it has no bearing on the goal of decision making as it pertains to the law.

22. D D is the correct answer as traffic laws, local building codes, and zoning laws are examples of ordinances that can be made by local government bodies including municipalities, cities, etc. Answers A, B, and C are all incorrect as they cannot be made by local government bodies.

23. D D is the correct answer as the law of the United States is primarily based upon English common law. A is incorrect as federal law developed from various laws including English common law.

Short Answer

24. This case challenged the "separate but equal" doctrine as it applied to elementary and high schools.

25. an equity court

26. Examples of federal statutes include antitrust laws, securities laws, labor, bankruptcy, and environmental protection laws.

27. Examples of state statutes include consumer protection laws, partnership laws, worker's compensation laws, and the Uniform Commercial Code.

28. Jurisprudence is defined as the philosophy or science of law.

29. As more agreements are reached between nations, economic relations between these nations will also increase, thereby increasing their importance to business.

30. The Securities and Exchange Commission (SEC) and the Federal Trade Commission (FTC) are two examples of administrative agencies.

31. Louisiana

32. A judicial decision is a court-issued statement of the holding of the case and the basis for reaching the decision in the case.

33. precedent

34. fairness and flexibility

35. law court

36. critical legal thinking

37. the Sociological School

38. administrative agencies

39. the names of the parties in the lawsuit

40. The summary of the court's reasoning should exclude the nonessentials.

41. Issues should be asked in a one-sentence question that is only answerable by a yes or no.

42. The decision reached by the court.

43. The holding should state which party won the lawsuit.

44. an opinion

45. Specific facts, public policy, prior law or other matters.

46. Statutes are written laws with descriptions of behavior that must be followed by covered parties.
47. an order issued by an executive branch member of the government
48. the power to interpret or translate and determine the validity or legality of the law

Chapter 2

COURT SYSTEMS AND JURISDICTION

Chapter Overview

This chapter examines and compares the state court systems and the federal court system. It also provides a clear overview of the types of cases the various courts can hear as well as both state and federal jurisdictional issues. Emphasis is also placed on the meanings associated with Supreme Court decisions. Finally, a clear explanation of the different types of jurisdiction is given.

Objectives

Upon completion of the exercises in this chapter, you should be able to:
1. Compare and contrast the state court systems and the federal court system.
2. Describe and understand the federal court system.
3. Recognize jurisdictional issues and compare the state and federal courts.
4. Comprehend the various types of U.S. Supreme Court decisions.
5. Understand the principle off standing to sue.
6. Recognize issues surrounding issues pertaining to venue.

Practical Application

You should be able to know which is the proper court and system to hear particular cases as well as differentiate between the various types of courts. Further, you should be able to assess when or why a case has been brought in federal court. Additionally, you should have a broader understanding of the various types of U.S. Supreme Court decisions. Finally, you should be able to determine whether an individual has a stake in the outcome of a lawsuit sufficient to have standing to sue, as well as analyze jurisdictional and venue issues surrounding a case.

Helpful Hints

This chapter may be a little confusing, as there appear to be so many different types of courts, all of which hear different types of cases. It is recommended that you diagram the state and federal court systems, branching each of the various courts off of the applicable state or federal court system. Pages 2-3 of your text gives an example of how one diagram can be utilized. You should also place two to four main points next to each type of court. For example, if you are working on the state court systems, in particular the limited-jurisdiction trial court, you may want to note that they are sometimes called inferior trial courts, hear matters that are specialized, and list some of the examples of the types of cases that are heard in this type of court. As you proceed in this manner, you will find that you have created a flow chart of the courts that will be easy to visualize when determining the answers to text and real life situations. Next, review this chapter's study guide, complete the Refresh Your Memory exercise followed by the Critical Thought Exercise and Sample Quiz.

Study Tips

The laws and their development that you became familiar with in Chapter One as well as the court systems you are learning about in this chapter are analogous to the base layer of a specialty cake. It is by knowing the appropriate law and court within the proper court system that you will be able to apply the correct legal principles to situations as they occur. The areas of law in the chapters that follow will provide the upper layers and frosting to this unique cake. The essential ingredients of adhering to the proper time and procedural requirements along with satisfying the essential substantive elements for various legal actions are what provide balance to this legally created pastry if you will.

There are two main court systems to choose from in the United States, the federal and the state court systems. It is important to know which court system has the proper jurisdiction to hear the case that has been prepared. The following list breaks down each court system highlighting some important points to remember about each court system as well as the courts within each system.

State Court Systems

A general fact about the state court systems is that every state as well as the District of Columbia has one. Additionally the majority of states have at least four types of state court systems that are discussed below.

Limited-Jurisdiction Trial Court (Inferior Trial Courts). These trial courts in most cases can hear specialized cases such as those involving family law, probate, traffic matters, juvenile issues, misdemeanors, and civil cases that do not exceed a set dollar amount. An attorney trying a case in this type of court may introduce evidence and illicit testimony. If the case does not result in a favorable outcome for one of the parties to the lawsuit, that party may appeal his/her case to an appellate court or a general-jurisdiction court. Many states also have a small claims court wherein a party on his/her own behalf brings a civil case worth a small dollar amount. If a party in a small claims case loses, then that party may also appeal to the general-jurisdiction trial court or an appellate court.

General-Jurisdiction Trial Court. A general-jurisdiction trial court can be found in every state. The trial testimony and evidence that is preserved on record allow these courts to be called the courts of record. This court hears felonies, cases above a certain dollar amount and cases not heard by the inferior trial courts.

Intermediate Appellate Court. This court hears appeals from trial courts and decides if the trial court erred thereby justifying a reversal or modification of the decision. The entire trial court record or just the important parts of the record may be reviewed. At this level of the court system, a party may not introduce new evidence or testimony. The decision of this appellate court may be appealed to the highest state court.

Highest State Court. The majority of states have a supreme court, which is the highest court in the state court system. The job of a state Supreme Court is to hear appeals from the intermediate appellate court. Once again, no new evidence or testimony is allowed. Once this court has made its decision, it becomes final. However, if there is a question of law, then the state supreme court's decision May be granted review by the U.S. Supreme Court.

Federal Court System

The United States Constitution states that the federal government's judicial power lies with the Supreme Court. In addition to this judicial power, Congress was allowed to establish inferior, or special courts that include the U.S. district courts and the U.S. courts of appeal.

Special Federal Courts. The nature of these courts is to hear limited types of cases such as those involving federal tax laws, law suits against the United States, international commercial disputes, and cases involving bankruptcy.

U.S. District Courts. These courts are the federal courts' general-jurisdiction courts.

U.S. Courts of Appeal. These courts are the intermediate appellate courts of the federal court system. The U.S. courts of appeal hear appeals from the cases already heard by the U.S. district courts. As with the state court systems, no new evidence or testimony may be introduced by a party.

Court of Appeals for the Federal Circuit. Even though this is a United States appellate court, its jurisdiction is special as it is able to review the decisions made in the Patent and Trademark Office, the Court of International Trade, and the Claims Court.

The U.S. Supreme Court. This high court of our land is administered by a president-appointed chief justice and is made up of nine nominated justices. This court hears cases from the federal circuit courts of appeal, from some federal district and special federal courts, as well as the highest state courts. A special note of interest is that a petition for certiorari must be made to the Supreme Court if a petitioner wants his/her case reviewed. If the court decides to review the case, then a writ of certiorari is issued provided there is a constitutional or other important issue involved in the case. Remember, no new evidence or testimony may be introduced at this level.

Federal and State Courts Jurisdiction

In order for a federal court to hear a case, the case must involve a federal question, or diversity of citizenship. It's important to distinguish these two concepts. A case involving a federal question deals with treaties, federal statutes, and the U.S. Constitution. Also, there need not be a set dollar amount to bring this type of case. Compare this to cases involving diversity of citizenship whereby the cases need to be between citizens of different states or a citizen of a country and a citizen of a state or a citizen of a state and a foreign country with the foreign country acting as the plaintiff in a law suit. These types of cases require that the controversy exceed $75,000.00. If the dollar amount isn't met, then the appropriate state court must hear the case.

Court Jurisdiction to Hear a Case

In order to bring a lawsuit, a person must have a stake in the outcome of the lawsuit. This is known as standing.

The court must also have the proper jurisdiction to hear the case. You must be familiar with *subject matter jurisdiction*, *in personam*, *in rem*, and *quasi in rem* jurisdiction. Finally, you must be familiar with the use of the *long-arm statutes* and when they are permitted over nonresidents.

Which court is the proper venue to hear my case?

The law mandates that lawsuits be heard by the court with jurisdiction that is closest to where the incident happened or where the parties live.

Refresh Your Memory

The following exercise will enable you to refresh your memory on the rules and principles presented to you in this chapter. Read each question twice and place your answer in the blanks provided. Review the chapter material for any question you miss or are unable to remember.

1.   What type of court hears civil cases involving small dollar amounts? _____.

2.   What are the two major court systems in the United States? The _____ and _____.

3.   An inferior trial court is also known as a _____.

4.   What types of courts hear felony and civil cases over a certain dollar amount? _____

5.   What types of cases do appellate courts hear? _____.

6.   If Sam Smith loses on appeal within a state court system, where can he appeal the appellate court decision? _____

7.   What types of cases does the supreme court of a state hear? _____

8.   When aren't state supreme court decisions final? _____.

9.   Name four types of decisions that the United States Supreme Court can issue. _____, _____, _____, _____.

10.   What types of questions can federal courts hear? _____ and _____

11.   Fred sees George, a stranger, kicked by Sam while Fred is walking by. Fred is very polite and knows that Sam's actions were wrong. What must Fred show before he brings a lawsuit against Sam for kicking George? _____.

12.   What is the usual means for accomplishing service of process of the summons and complaint? _____.

13.   In order to invoke a state's long-arm statute, what must the nonresident have with the forum state? _____.

14.   A concept that requires lawsuits to be heard by the court with jurisdiction that is nearest the location in which the incident occurred or where the parties reside is known as _____.

15. Garth Hanson, the mayor of Ordinanceville, has been charged with embezzlement of city funds. The local radio station has been providing continuous coverage ever since the story became known. Garth's attorney wants a change of venue. Tell why it should or should not be granted.

_____

_____

16. Which courts have exclusive jurisdiction to hear cases such as bankruptcy, patent, and copyright cases?

_____

17. What is the term that is used when an individual is served a summons within the territorial boundaries of a state called? _____

Critical Thought Exercise

You are a district manager of marketing for Intestine Smart, Inc., a California corporation, makers of Colon Grenade, a colon-cleansing drug. You have negotiated the sale of over 4 million dollars worth of this product from Prescript Co., another California corporation, which operates pharmacies under the names of Col On, Goodstuff Co., and Drugs 2 Go. These pharmacies are located primarily in California, but Prescript Co. has now expanded into 22 states including Utah.

Enticed by a Goodstuff ad in the Utah Free Press for Colon Grenade, Alice Thinstone bought the drug at Goodstuff Co. and used it. Within a week, Thinstone suffered a ruptured colon. Alleging that the injury was caused by Colon Grenade, Thinstone sued Prescript Co. and Intestine Smart in a Utah state court.

You have received a letter from the CEO of Intestine Smart, Ms. Sheila Snob, threatening to fire you and demanding to know why Intestine Smart is being subjected to a lawsuit in Utah, since she has never been informed of any sales of the product to companies outside of California.

Your assigned task is to **_draft a memo to your boss_**, Ms. Snob, and explain to her whether Intestine Smart must respond to the suit and defend against it in Utah. Explain the legal theory and the reasons for your opinion.

Answer:

_____

_____

_____

_____

_____

_____

_____

_____

_____

_____

_____

_____

_____

_____
_____
_____
_____
_____
_____
_____
_____
_____
_____
_____
_____
_____
_____
_____
_____
_____
_____
_____

Practice Quiz

True/False

1. ___ A writ of certiorari is an official notice that the Supreme Court will review one's case. [p. 26]

2. ___ A justice who does not agree with a decision may not file a dissenting opinion, as concurring opinions are the only ones that are valid. [p. 26]

3. ___ Service of process of a complaint is usually accomplished by mail. [p. 29]

4. ___ In rem jurisdiction allows a plaintiff who obtains judgment in one state to try and collect the judgment by attaching property of the defendant located in another state. [p. 29]

5. ___ In order for the state supreme court to fairly decide the appeals that it hears from the intermediate state courts, it must take all of the evidence from the former trial along with any new evidence or testimony into consideration before rendering its decision. [p. 22]

6. ___ The state of Missouri may have jurisdiction over Fred, a resident from Texas if he caused an automobile accident while in Missouri. [p. 30]

7. ___ The limited jurisdiction of special federal courts include cases involving federal tax laws, cases against the United States, bankruptcy, and international commercial disputes. [p. 24]

8. ___ Most states have a federal district court, however the states with smaller populations do not. [p. 24]

9. ___ The Court of Appeals for the Federal Circuit has special appellate jurisdiction to review the decisions of the Patent and Trademark Office as well as the Court of International Trade and the Claims Court. [p. 25]

10. ___ If new evidence is shown at the Supreme Court level, there is a chance that the lower court decision will be overturned. [p. 25]

11. ___ A judge who agrees with the outcome of a case can issue a concurring opinion that explains his or her reasons for deciding the case. [p. 26]

12. ___ Federal and state courts have exclusive jurisdiction to hear cases involving federal crimes, antitrust, bankruptcy, patent, and copyright cases as well as suits against the United States and admiralty cases. [p. 24]

13. ___ A court that handles cases against the United States is said to have exclusive jurisdiction. [p. 28]

14. ___ A forum-selection clause states that any court may hear any dispute concerning torts. [p. 29]

15. ___ The aggravation as well as psychological costs associated with a lawsuit should be taken into consideration when performing a cost-benefit analysis of the lawsuit. [p. 39]

16. ___ A cross-complaint is a legal pleading filed by the plaintiff once the defendant has answered the plaintiff's original complaint. [p. 35]

17. ___ The reason for providing diversity of citizenship jurisdiction was to prevent state court bias against nonresidents. [p. 27]

18. ___ The advantage of having a case that is being reviewed by the Supreme Court is that new evidence as well as testimony is allowed once a party has gotten his or her case this far. [p. 25]

19. ___ Controversies at the state court level must meet or exceed $75,000 before the court can hear them. [p. 27]

20. ___ The majority opinion has the same force of law as a unanimous decision. [p. 26]

21. ___ Plurality of opinion refers to a majority of the justices agreeing to the outcome as well as reasoning for reaching the outcome of a case. [p. 26]

Multiple Choice

22. The appellate court reviews [p. 24]
    a. new evidence.
    b. new testimony.
    c. pertinent parts or the whole trial court record from the lower court.
    d. small claims cases.

23. A party who disputes the jurisdiction of a court can [p. 29]
    a. enter a claim in the forum state's small claims court to recover expenses of the dispute.
    b. make a special appearance in that court to argue against imposition of jurisdiction.
    c. appeal to the state supreme court and ask that the suit be dismissed.
    d. be served a complaint if he or she makes a special appearance in the court to argue against imposition of jurisdiction.

24. When circumstances on the Supreme Court result in a tie vote regarding a case, what is the result? [p. 26]
    a. The lower court's decision is affirmed.
    b. Such votes are precedent for later cases.
    c. The lower court's decision is irrelevant.
    d. none of the above

25. In a case involving concurrent jurisdiction, if the plaintiff brings the case in state court, the defendant can [p. 28]
    a. do nothing and only hope for the best.
    b. let the case be decided by the state court.
    c. not remove the case to federal court because the plaintiff brought the case in state court.
    d. all of the above

26. Which of the following types of cases are subject to exclusive federal jurisdiction? [p, 27]
    a. antitrust
    b. admiralty
    c. bankruptcy
    d. all of the above

27. When is service of process not permitted? [p. 29]
    a. It is not permitted when bringing an appeal.
    b. It is not permitted when a party disputing jurisdiction makes a special appearance in a particular
       court to dispute jurisdiction.
    c. It is not permitted when bringing a case in state court.
    d. all of the above

28. Federal cases are cases that arise under [p. 27]
    a. the state's constitution in which the case was filed.
    b. the U.S. Constitution.
    c. an appellate court's decision.
    d. same state citizenship.

29.   Which of the following types of decisions can the Supreme Court issue? [p. 26]
    a.   a plurality decision
    b.   a tie decision
    c.   a majority decision
    d.   all of the above

Short Answer

30.   A court that hears matters such as probate, family law, and traffic cases is known as a _____ . [p. 21]

31.   What level of court may evidence be introduced and testimony be given? _____ [p. 21]

32.   What is the length of term a federal judge may serve? _____. [p. 23]

33.   What is the length of term a bankruptcy judge may be appointed for? _____ years. [p. 23]

34.   The geographical area served by each court is referred to as a _____ [p. 24]

35.   Where are the federal district courts located? _____ [p. 24]

36.   A plaintiff must have _____ to sue before he/she can bring a lawsuit. [p. 28]

37.   When a court has jurisdiction over the property of a lawsuit, it has _____ jurisdiction. [p. 29]

38.   The jurisdiction over the subject matter of a lawsuit is known as _____ _____ jurisdiction. [p. 27]

Answers to Refresh Your Memory

1.   small claims court [p. 21]
2.   federal court system; the court systems of the 50 states and the District of Columbia [p. 21]
3.   state limited-jurisdictional trial court [p. 21]
4.   general jurisdiction trial courts [p. 21]
5.   They hear appeals from trial courts. [p. 22]
6.   Sam can appeal the appellate court decision to the state's highest court. [p. 22]
7.   appeals from intermediate state courts and certain trial courts. [p. 22]
8.   If there is a question of law that is able to be appealed to the U.S. Supreme Court. [p. 22]
9.   unanimous decision, majority decision, plurality decision, tie decision [p. 26]
10.   federal questions and diversity of citizenship [p. 27]
11.   Fred must show he has standing or a stake in the outcome before he can sue Sam. [p. 28]
12.   personal service [p. 29]
13.   minimum contact [p. 29]
14.   venue [p. 30]

15. If the pretrial publicity may prejudice jurors located in the proper venue, then a change of venue may be requested in order to find a more impartial jury in light of the continuous radio station coverage. [p. 30]
16. federal courts [p.23]
17. service of process [p. 29]

Model Answer to Critical Thought Exercise

To: Ms. Snob
From: Student, District Manager, Intestine Smart Inc.

Re: Response to Lawsuit in Utah State Court

This is a question involving jurisdiction. Jurisdiction is the authority of a court to hear a case. There are three types of jurisdiction: 1) *In personam* whereby the court has jurisdiction over the parties to a lawsuit; 2) *In rem* jurisdiction which is when the court has jurisdiction to hear a case because of jurisdiction over the property involved in the lawsuit; and 3) *quasi in rem* jurisdiction; where jurisdiction is allowed a plaintiff who obtains a judgment in one state to try to collect the judgment by attaching the property of the defendant located in another state.

Even though you were never informed of any sales of Colon Grenade outside of the state of California, we may be required to respond to the suit and defend against it in Utah based on the following reasons:

1) Even though our company wasn't physically located in Utah when Alice Thinstone suffered a ruptured colon, she may apply the principles surrounding the theory set forth in *International Shoe Co. v. Washington,* 326 U.S. 310 wherein the court said that "the Due Process Clause permits jurisdiction over a defendant in any state in which the defendant has 'certain minimum contacts' such that the maintenance of the suit does not offend traditional notions of fair play and substantial justice." Arguably by selling our product to Prescript Co., which operates in 22 states, including Utah, we are receiving the benefit of increased sales, albeit indirectly from Utah resident Alice Thinstone. Further, as was expressed in the court's ruling in *Calder v. Jones*, 465 U.S. 783, 104 S.Ct. 1482, 79 L.Ed.2d 804 (1984), Intestine Smart should "reasonably anticipate being hauled into court" in Utah as it is reasonably foreseeable that Colon Grenade would be sold in different states given the fact that Prescript Co. operates in 22 states, with Utah being one of them. If it is found that Intestine Smart, Inc., had sufficient minimum contacts with the forum State of Utah and that the sale of its product there afforded Intestine Smart the benefits of the laws of the forum state, then we will be required to defend ourselves in a suit in Utah state court.

2) It may be argued that we assumed the risk that our product would be sold to an out-of-state resident as we knowingly and voluntarily negotiated the sale of the Colon Grenade product with Prescript Co., a business operating in several states. Also, we should not be allowed to reap only the benefits of profit from our sales and shirk our corporate ethical responsibility to not harm those to whom our product is sold.

In conclusion, Ms. Snob, it would be in our best interest to respond to the lawsuit filed against us. If we are able to show that there was some other intervening act (such as improper use of Colon Grenade by Ms. Thinstone, some other medical condition that could have had the same result, etc.) responsible for Ms. Thinstone's ruptured colon and that Colon Grenade in no way caused her injury, we may be successful in defending against the suit. We could really secure a feather in our cap if we could demonstrate that despite an alleged forseeability of the injury alleged, the use of Colon Grenade could not have possibly caused the result complained of by Ms.

Thinstone. *(Note: A higher degree of understanding is demonstrated by a student who incorporates the reasoning given in this paragraph, as this material is not addressed until later in the text.)*

Answers to Practice Quiz

True/False

1. True Once a petitioner has filed a petition for certiorari asking the Supreme Court to review his or her case, a writ of certiorari is issued by the Court giving official notice that it will review one's case.

2. False A justice who does not agree with a decision may file a dissenting opinion that sets forth the reasons for his or her dissent.

3. False Service of process is usually in person. Service by mail is an alternative means of accomplishing service of process when doing so in person is not possible.

4. False In rem jurisdiction involves jurisdiction to hear a case because of the jurisdiction over the property of the lawsuit.

5. False Even though the function of a state supreme court is to hear appeals from intermediate state courts and certain trial courts, no new evidence or testimony is heard.

6. True Under the long-arm statute, jurisdiction over those who commit torts within the state is allowed even if the individuals are not residents who were served a summons within the state.

7. True Congress established special limited-jurisdiction courts including the U.S. tax court, U.S. claims court, U.S. Court of International Trade, and the U.S. Bankruptcy Court.

8. False Each state has at least one federal district court, as does the District of Columbia. The more populated states have more than one district court.

9. True The Court of Appeals for the Federal Circuit was established to provide uniformity in the application of federal law.

10. False The Supreme Court hears appeals from the federal circuit of appeals and reviews the lower court record. However, no new evidence or testimony is heard.

11. True A judge who agrees with the outcome of a case can issue a concurring opinion explaining his or her reasons for deciding the case as he or she did.

12. False Only federal courts have exclusive jurisdiction to hear cases involving federal crimes, antitrust, bankruptcy, patent, and copyright cases, as well as suits against the United States and admiralty cases.

13. True Federal courts have exclusive jurisdiction over cases against the United States, as they are the only courts that can hear this type of case.

14. False A forum-selection clause designates a court to hear only disputes concerning the nonperformance of a contract.

15. True The aggravation as well as psychological costs associated with a lawsuit are only two of several factors that should be weighed before bringing or settling a lawsuit. Other factors to examine include the odds of winning or losing, the money that is to be won or lost, managerial time off as well as loss of time by personnel, the effect on the relationship between the parties, the law's provision for prejudgment interest, and the chance of error in the law.

16. False   A cross-complaint is a legal pleading filed by the defendant who believes that he or she has been injured by the plaintiff. The defendant can file a cross-complaint against the plaintiff at the same time he or she files an answer to the plaintiff's complaint.

17. True   Diversity of citizenship was created to prevent state court bias against nonresidents.

18. False   No new evidence or testimony may be heard at the Supreme Court level.

19. False   The $75,000 amount in controversy requirement applies to the federal, not the state court requirements to hear a case.

20. True   The majority opinion becomes precedent for later cases and has the same force of law as a unanimous decision.

21. True   Plurality refers to a majority of justices agreeing to the outcome, but not the reasoning for reaching the outcome of a case.

Multiple Choice

22. C   An appellate court reviews the trial court record to determine if there have been any errors at trial. As such, the appellate court reviews either pertinent parts or the whole trial record from the lower court. Answers A and B are incorrect as no new evidence or testimony is permitted. Answer D is incorrect, as the appellate court does not review small claims cases.

23. B   A party may make a special appearance to dispute jurisdiction and service of process may not take place during this appearance. Answer A makes no sense, as a party who suffers expenses of a lawsuit would ask for the appropriate remedy in his/her prayer for relief of his/her complaint. Further, expenses to the lawsuit may or may not be allowed depending upon the cause(s) of action being brought. Answer C is incorrect as the function of the state supreme court is to hear appeals from intermediate state courts. The facts do not indicate that the issue of jurisdiction was one that had been tried and that a judgment against the party had been made at an intermediate court level. Answer D is incorrect, as a party may not be served with a complaint in court when the purpose of the party being in court is to dispute jurisdiction.

24. A   Answer A is correct as a tie vote regarding a case at the Supreme Court level results in the lower court's decision being affirmed. Answer B is incorrect, as a majority of the justices would have to concur on a case in order for the opinion to act as precedent in later cases. Answer C is incorrect as it makes no sense. Answer D is incorrect for the reasons given above.

25. B   The defendant may let the case be decided by the state court in a case involving concurrent jurisdiction. Answer A is incorrect, as it has no legal application to the question. Answer C is incorrect, as a defendant can remove the case to federal court if a plaintiff brings a case involving concurrent jurisdiction in a state court. D is incorrect for the reasons stated above.

26. D   Answer D is correct, as antitrust, admiralty, and bankruptcy cases are subject to exclusive federal jurisdiction.

27. B   Answer B is correct because service of process is served within the territorial boundaries of the state so it is not permitted when a party is disputing the jurisdiction.

28. B   Answer B is correct, as federal cases are cases that arise under the U.S. Constitution. Answer A is incorrect, as federal cases do not arise under a state's constitution. Answer C is incorrect, as federal cases stem from federal questions or cases involving diversity of citizenship. Answer D is incorrect, as federal cases do not arise as a result of same state citizenship.

29. D   Answer D is correct as the Supreme Court can issue plurality, tie, and majority decisions.

Short Answer

30. limited jurisdiction trial court or inferior trial courts
31. trial courts
32. life
33. 14
34. district
35. Federal courts are located in each state and in the District of Columbia.
36. standing
37. in rem
38. subject matter

Chapter 3

LITIGATION AND
ALTERNATIVE DISPUTE RESOLUTION

Chapter Overview

This chapter examines the pretrial litigation process, as well as the concepts involved with dismissals and pretrial judgments and settlement conferences. Emphasis is also placed on the importance of a cost-benefit analysis when bringing, maintaining, and defending a lawsuit. The pretrial litigation process, court use of e-filings, and the stages of a trial as well as appeal are also explained. Finally, nonjudicial alternatives, such as arbitration and mediation are also discussed.

Objectives

Upon completion of the exercises in this chapter, you should be able to:
1.   Understand the pretrial litigation process.
2   Comprehend the concepts of dismissal and pretrial judgments.
3.   Describe what occurs at a settlement conference.
4.   Recognize the various stages of a trial.
5.   Understand the basics of the appellate process
7.   Be aware of the nonjudicial alternatives such as arbitration and mediation.

Practical Application

You should be able to be familiar with the costs and benefits of bringing and defending a lawsuit.   Additionally, you should have a broader understanding of the pretrial litigation process and the various procedural requirements. You will also become familiar with the reasoning behind dismissals, pretrial judgments, and settlement conferences. Finally, you should be able to understand the sequence of events associated with a trial as well as the option of appeal after the judgment has been rendered. Finally, you will be able to discern whether nonjudicial alternatives may be an option to you depending on the situation that is presented.

Helpful Hints

The prelitigation process is similar to playing a board game, as an individual must proceed through various steps in order to reach a final goal. If you view discovery as a means of determining your opponent's strategy, it will also assist you in reaching the most desirable outcome in a case. Review of this chapter's study sheet and completion of the Refresh Your Memory exercise followed by the Critical Thought Exercise and Sample Quiz are all helpful in committing the various pretrial, trial, and appeal processes.

Study Tips

The laws and their development that you became familiar with in Chapter One as well as the court systems you learned about in Chapter two are analogous to the base layer of a specialty cake. It is by knowing the appropriate law and court within the proper court system that you will be able to apply the correct legal principles to situations as they occur. The areas of law in the chapters that follow will provide the upper layers and frosting to this unique cake. The essential ingredients of adhering to the proper time and procedural requirements along with satisfying the essential substantive elements for various legal actions are what provide balance to this legally created pastry if you will.

Litigation as you know is the process of bringing, maintaining, and defending a lawsuit. It is through the pretrial litigation process that we are able to do just that. The process of discovery enables us to adequately prepare a case. Some of the most common forms of discovery include depositions, interrogatories, the production of documents, and physical and mental examinations. Finally, once a case is set for trial, a variety of methodical steps are enacted to determine liability in a case. Of course, the individual who loses has the option of appeal. Note, should a person determine that litigation is not the best way to handle a situation, there are a variety of alternative dispute resolution choices that may be more suitable to the individual or particular case.

What are the advantages and disadvantages of bringing and defending a lawsuit?

It is very important to consider all of the factors involved when deciding to sue or defend a lawsuit. This is known as the cost-benefit analysis. This is a commonsense decision that can be made by weighing how much money will be won or lost in light of your chances of winning or losing against the costs to litigate, expenses associated with employees being released from work, as well as prejudgment interest provided by the law. Other emotional considerations such as the impact on the relationship of the parties and their reputations as well as the mental aggravation and turmoil that may manifest itself should also be factored in. Further, a caveat of the potential for error in the legal system must not be discarded in balancing whether or not it is wise to bring or defend a lawsuit.

When can a lawsuit be brought?

This refers to federal and state government time limitations regarding the period of time the plaintiff has the right to sue a defendant. Statutes of limitations will vary depending on the type of lawsuit involved.

What is involved in the pretrial litigation process?

The pretrial litigation process is an essential ingredient in the foundational layer of the legal process. You must be familiar with the various important pleadings of complaint, answer, cross-complaint, and reply when initiating and responding to a lawsuit. Additionally, you will need to know about the different types of discovery and what activities both parties may participate in to discover facts of the case from one another as well as witnesses before trial. The primary types of discovery are depositions, interrogatories, production of documents, and physical and mental examinations. Also, a familiarity with the pretrial motions of judgment on the pleadings, and motion for summary judgment should be developed to create an understanding that some lawsuits in whole or in part should not go to trial. Finally, you should be aware of the purpose of a settlement conference and realize that if a settlement is not forthcoming, this tool is important in identifying the main trial issues.

What are the stages of a trial?

A legal trial is much like a performance at a theater. There are those who are performing the case in a methodical fashion from beginning to end. In using this comparison, the program of a trial would read in the following order: jury selection, opening statements, the plaintiff's case, the defendant's case, rebuttal, rejoinder, closing arguments, jury instructions, with the jury deliberation and the entry of judgment acting as the end of the show. The sequel to the trial in a civil case is the appeal, which can be brought by either the plaintiff or the defendant. In a criminal trial, the appeal can only be brought by the defendant. Opening and responding briefs may be filed with the court. The drama of this performance is in the appellate court finding an error of law in the record, in which case the lower court decision will be reversed.

What other choices does a person have?

Sometimes using the court system to resolve disputes results in a great expenditure of money and time. In order to alleviate these concerns, alternative dispute resolution methods are being utilized to resolve disputes rather than using litigation. Some of the alternatives that are available include mediation, conciliation, mini-trial, fact-finding, and a judicial referee.

Refresh Your Memory

The following exercise will enable you to refresh your memory on the rules and principles presented to you in this chapter. Read each question twice and place your answer in the blanks provided. Review the chapter material for any question you miss or are unable to remember.

1.   The process of bringing, maintaining, and defending a lawsuit is known as _____.

2.   The paperwork that is filed with the court to initiate and respond to a lawsuit is called _____.

3.   A plaintiff is the party who _____.

4.   The document the plaintiff files with the court and serves on the defendant to initiate a lawsuit is called a _____.

5.   A court order directing the defendant to appear in court and answer the complaint is called a _____.

6.   The defendant's written response to the plaintiff's complaint that is filed with the court and served on the plaintiff is known as the _____.

7.   What is the name of the pleading filed by the defendant against the plaintiff to seek damages or some other remedy? _____.

8. The act of others to join as parties to an existing lawsuit is known as

     _____.

9. The act of a court to combine two or more separate lawsuits into one lawsuit is known as

     _____.

10. A statute that establishes the period during when a plaintiff must bring a lawsuit against a defendant is known as the _____ of _____.

11. The party who gives his or her deposition is known as a _____.

12. Written questions submitted by one party to another are called _____.

13. A motion a party can make to try to dispose of all or part of a lawsuit before trial is called a _____ motion.

14. A hearing before the trial court in order to facilitate the settlement of a case is called a

     _____ _____.

15. The choice of whether to bring or defend a lawsuit should be analyzed using a _____-_____ analysis.

16. The jury in a jury trial and the judge where there is not a jury trial is known as the _____ of _____.

17. A statement whereby each party's attorney usually summarizes the main factual and legal issues of a case and describes why he or she believes the client's position is valid is called an _____ statement.

18. After the defendant's attorney has completed calling witnesses, the plaintiff's attorney can call witnesses and put forth evidence to _____ the defendant's case.

19. These inform the jury about what law to apply when they decide a case. _____ _____.

20. The official decision of the court is evidenced as the _____ of _____.

Critical Thought Exercise

You are a district manager of marketing for Intestine Smart, Inc., a California corporation, makers of Colon Grenade, a colon-cleansing drug. You have negotiated the sale of over 4 million dollars worth of this product from Prescript Co., another California corporation, which operates pharmacies under the names of Col On, Goodstuff Co., and Drugs 2 Go. These pharmacies are located primarily in California, but Prescript Co. has now expanded into 22 states including Utah.

Enticed by a Goodstuff ad in the Utah Free Press for Colon Grenade, Alice Thinstone bought the drug at Goodstuff Co. and used it. Within a week, Thinstone suffered a ruptured colon. Alleging that the injury was caused by Colon Grenade, Thinstone sued Prescript Co. and Intestine Smart in a Utah state court.

You have received a letter from the CEO of Intestine Smart, Ms. Sheila Snob, threatening to fire you and demanding to know why Intestine Smart is being subjected to a lawsuit in Utah, since she has never been informed of any sales of the product to companies outside of California.

Your assigned task is to ***draft a memo to your boss***, Ms. Snob, and explain to her whether Intestine Smart must respond to the suit and defend against it in Utah. Explain the legal theory and the reasons for your opinion.

Answer:

_____

_____

_____

_____

_____

_____

_____

_____

_____

_____

_____

_____

_____

_____

_____

_____

_____

_____

_____

_____

_____

_____

_____

_____

_____

_____

Practice Quiz

True/False

1. ____ A form of nonjudicial alternative dispute resolution is known as litigation. [p. 34]

2. ____ The major pleadings are the complaint, the answer, and the cross-complaint. [p.34]

3. ____ A default judgment establishes the defendant's liability. [p. 35]

4. ____ A defendant may not assert affirmative defenses. [p. 35]

5. ____ A reply to a cross-complaint need not be filed with the court. [p. 35]

6. ____ One hundred people bought a hair product known as "Full and Hairy." After using it, their hair fell out. They all now want to bring individual lawsuits against the maker of "Full and Hairy." Under the theory of intervention, they will be able to do just that. [p. 36]

7. ____ Technology allows for the electronic filing of pleadings, briefs, and other documents related to a lawsuit. [p. 36]

8. ____ An attorney usually helps with the preparation of the answers to interrogatories. [p. 38]

9. ____ Depositions cannot be videotaped. [p. 38]

10. ____ Depositions are used to preserve evidence. [p. 38]

11. ____ Federal courts and most state court rules allow the court to direct the attorneys or parties to appear before the court for a settlement conference. [p. 39]

12. ____ Less than 10 percent of all cases are settled before they go to trial. [p. 39]

13. ____ Contingency fees range from 20–50 percent of the award of settlement. [p. 39]

14. ____ In a criminal lawsuit, the plaintiff's lawyer works under a contingency fee. [p. 39]

15. ____ The judge sits as a trier of fact in nonjury trials. [p. 39]

16. ____ A cross-complaint is a legal pleading filed by the plaintiff once the defendant has answered the plaintiff's original complaint. [p. 34]

17. ____ If several lawsuits are brought as a result of the same fact situation against the same defendant, the court can consolidate the cases into one if it does not prejudice the parties. [p. 34]

18. ____ A plaintiff will lose his or her right to sue if a lawsuit is not filed within the statute of limitations established for the particular type of lawsuit being brought. [p. 35]

19. ___ A court cannot order another party to submit to a mental or physical examination prior to trial as this would constitute an invasion of privacy. [p. 37]

20. ___ A motion for summary judgment alleges that if all of the facts presented in the pleadings are true, the party making the motion would win the lawsuit when the proper law is applied to these facts. [p. 38]

21. ___ After the trial has been presented, each of the parties attorneys submit documents to the judge that contain legal support for their side of the case. [p. 39]

22. ___ When the defendant's attorney calls additional witnesses and introduces other evidence, this is known as rebuttal. [p. 40]

23. ___ In a civil case, either party can appeal the trial court's decision prior to the final judgment being entered. [p. 41]

24. ___ The Uniform Arbitration Act promotes arbitration of disputes at the state level. [p. 42]

25. ___ Conciliation is a form of mediation in which the parties select an interested third party to be a mediator. [p. 43]

Multiple Choice

26. A summons is issued once [p. 35]
    a. a complaint has been filed with the court.
    b. if there is a problem with one of the pleadings previously filed.
    c. the complaint has been served on the defendant.
    d. a government official looks it over.

27. Once a default judgment has been entered against a defendant, all the plaintiff need do is [p. 35]
    a. assert his or her affirmative defenses.
    b. prove his or her damages in the case.
    c. bring a lawsuit against the defendant.
    d. bring a motion for relief from default judgment, so the plaintiff can have his or her day in court.

28. The bringing, maintaining, and defense of a lawsuit is known as [p. 34]
    a. discovery.
    b. litigation.
    c. a cross-complaint.
    d. a summons.

29. A law that establishes the period within which a plaintiff must bring a lawsuit against the defendant is known as [p. 37]
    a. a statute of limitations.
    b. a complaining period.
    c. an e-filing of pleadings.
    d. all of the above.

30. A deposition is [p. 38]
    a. written testimony given by a party or witness prior to trial.
    b. oral testimony given by a party or witness prior to trial.
    c. a pleading alleging ultimate allegations of fact.
    d. all of the above.

31. The production of documents refers to [p. 38]
    a. written questions submitted by one party to a lawsuit to another party.
    b. physical and mental concerns of the condition of a party to the lawsuit.
    c. the assembly of legal documents.
    d. one party to a lawsuit requesting that the other party produce all documents that are relevant to the case prior to trial.

32. The term rejoinder refers to [p. 40]
    a. when the plaintiff's attorney calls witnesses and puts forth evidence to rebut the defendant's case.
    b. the making of a closing argument by each party's attorney.
    c. the reading of jury instructions to the jury.
    d. the calling of additional witnesses and introduction of other evidence to counter the plaintiff's rebuttal.

33. When a court overturns a verdict based on bias or jury misconduct, this is known as [p. 40]
    a. a judgment on the pleadings.
    b. an entry of judgment.
    c. a judgment notwithstanding the verdict.
    d. all of the above.

34. The responding party in an appeal is known as [p. 42]
    a. the respondent.
    b. the appellant.
    c. the defendant.
    d. the plaintiff.

35. When the parties choose an impartial third party to hear and decide a dispute, this is known as [p. 43]
    a. mediation.
    b. a minitrial.
    c. arbitration.
    d. a judicial referee.

36. One of the provisions of the Federal Arbitration Act is [p. 42]
    a. to reenact the arbitration agreements that existed in English common law.
    b. to eliminate arbitration agreements that call for resolution of disputes that arise under federal statutes.
    c. to provide that arbitration agreements involving commerce are valid, irrevocable, and enforceable contracts, unless some ground exist at law or equity.
    d. to prohibit parties from obtaining court orders that compel arbitration if the other party has failed, neglected, or refused to comply with an arbitration agreement.

37. The role of a judicial referee is to [p. 43]
    a. conduct a private trial and render a judgment.
    b. report his or her findings to the adversaries and recommend a basis for settlement.
    c. act as an interested third party, a conciliator.
    d. to referee judicial sports activities involving court personnel.

38. One means of eliminating the burden of paper pleadings, interrogatories, and other legal documents would be to implement [p. 36]
    a. a shorter statute of limitations thereby requiring those who were serious about filing a lawsuit to do so in a more expeditious manner.
    b. technology for electronic filing including CD-ROMs to manage e-filings of court documents.
    c. shorter forms that would take up less space.
    d. all of the above.

Short Answer

39. Why is it wise to do a cost-benefit-analysis? [p. 39]_____
_____

40. What is an advantage to receiving interrogatories? [p.38]_____
_____

41. The request by one party to another party to produce all documents relevant to the case prior to
    trial is known as the _____ of _____. [p. 38]

42. A motion a party can make to try to dispose of all or part of a lawsuit prior to trial is known as a _____ _____. [p. 38]

43. The jury in a jury trial and the judge where there is not a jury trial is known as the
    _____ of _____. [p. 39]

44. A person chosen as a neutral third party who acts as a conveyor of information between the parties and helps them to try and reach a settlement of the dispute is known as a _____. [p. 43]

45. A process whereby the parties hire a neutral person to investigate the dispute is known as a _____ _____. [p. 43]

46. Which state act promotes the arbitration of disputes? [p. 42]
_____

47. Where do most depositions take place? [p. 37] _____

48. A _____ is issued once a complaint has been filed with the court. [p. 35]

49. The defendant must file an _____once he/she is served with the complaint. [p. 35]

50.   The defendant may assert _____ _____ when answering the plaintiff's complaint. [p. 35]

Answers to Refresh Your Memory

1.   litigation [p. 34]
2.   pleadings. [p. 34]
3.   files a complaint [p. 34]
4.   complaint [p. 34]
5.   summons [p. 35]
6.   answer [p. 35]
7.   cross-complaint [p. 35]
8.   intervention [p. 36]
9.   consolidation [p. 36]
10.   statute of limitations [p. 36]
11.   deponent [p. 37]
12.   interrogatories [p. 38]
13.   pretrial [p. 38]
14.   settlement conference [p. 39]
15.   cost-benefit [p. 39]
16.   trier of fact [p. 39]
17.   opening [p. 40]
18.   rebut [p. 40]
19.   jury instructions [p. 40]
20.   entry of judgment [p.40]

Model Answer to Critical Thought Exercise

To: Ms. Snob
From: Student, District Manager, Intestine Smart Inc.

Re: Response to Lawsuit in Utah State Court

This is a question involving jurisdiction. Jurisdiction is the authority of a court to hear a case. There are three types of jurisdiction: 1) *In personam* whereby the court has jurisdiction over the parties to a lawsuit; 2) *In rem* jurisdiction which is when the court has jurisdiction to hear a case because of jurisdiction over the property involved in the lawsuit; and 3) *quasi in rem* jurisdiction; where jurisdiction is allowed a plaintiff who obtains a judgment in one state to try to collect the judgment by attaching the property of the defendant located in another state.

Even though you were never informed of any sales of Colon Grenade outside of the state of California, we may be required to respond to the suit and defend against it in Utah based on the following reasons:

1) Even though our company wasn't physically located in Utah when Alice Thinstone suffered a ruptured colon, she may apply the principles surrounding the theory set forth in *International Shoe Co. v. Washington,* 326 U.S. 310 wherein the court said that "the Due Process Clause permits jurisdiction over a defendant in any state in which the defendant has 'certain minimum contacts' such that the maintenance of the suit does not offend traditional notions of fair play and substantial justice." Arguably by selling our product to Prescript Co., which operates in 22 states, including Utah, we are receiving the benefit of increased sales, albeit

indirectly from Utah resident Alice Thinstone. Further, as was expressed in the court's ruling in *Calder v. Jones*, 465 U.S. 783, 104 S.Ct. 1482, 79 L.Ed.2d 804 (1984), Intestine Smart should "reasonably anticipate being hauled into court" in Utah as it is reasonably foreseeable that colon grenade would be sold in different states given the fact that Prescript Co. operates in 22 states, with Utah being one of them. If it is found that Intestine Smart, Inc. had sufficient minimum contacts with the forum State of Utah and that the sale of its product there afforded Intestine Smart the benefits of the laws of the forum state, then we will be required to defend ourselves in a suit in Utah state court.

   2) It may be argued that we assumed the risk that our product would be sold to an out-of-state resident as we knowingly and voluntarily negotiated the sale of the Colon Grenade product with Prescript Co., a business operating in several states. Also, we should not be allowed to reap only the benefits of profit from our sales and shirk our corporate ethical responsibility to not harm those to whom our product is sold.

In conclusion, Ms. Snob, it would be in our best interest to respond to the lawsuit filed against us. If we are able to show that there was some other intervening act (such as improper use of Colon Grenade by Ms. Thinstone, some other medical condition that could have had the same result, etc.) responsible for Ms. Thinstone's ruptured colon and that Colon Grenade in no way caused her injury, we may be successful in defending against the suit. We could really secure a feather in our cap if we could demonstrate that despite an alleged forseeability of the injury alleged, the use of Colon Grenade could not have possibly caused the result complained of by Ms. Thinstone. *(Note: A higher degree of understanding is demonstrated by a student who incorporates the reasoning given in this paragraph, as this material is not addressed until later in the text.)*

Answers to Practice Quiz

True/False

1. False   Nonjudicial alternative dispute resolution usually refers to arbitration, mediation or mini-trials, and the like which are designed to avoid litigation.
2. True   The complaint, answer, and cross-complaint are examples of major pleadings.
3. True   A defendant's liability can be established by a default judgment entered against him or her.
4. False   A defendant can assert and should assert affirmative defenses.
5. False   A reply to a cross-complaint must be filed with the court.
6. False   Consolidation allows the court to gather all lawsuits concerning the same matter into one lawsuit, not intervention.
7. True   Pleadings may be filed electronically thanks to technology.
8. True   An attorney usually does help with the preparation of answers to interrogatories that are served on his or her client.
9. False   Depositions can be videotaped.
10. True   Evidence may be preserved through the use of depositions.
11. True   Both federal and most state courts are allowed to direct the attorneys or parties appear for a settlement conference.
12. False   About 90 percent of all cases are settled before they go to trial.
13. True   Contingency fees do range from 20–50 percent of the award of settlement.
14. False   In a civil lawsuit, plaintiff's lawyers work under a contingency fee arrangement. In a criminal lawsuit, the state acts as a plaintiff and has no such fee arrangement agreement.

15. True   In nonjury trials, the judge sits as a trier of fact.

16. False   A cross-complaint is a legal pleading filed by the defendant who believes that he or she has been injured by the plaintiff. The defendant can file a cross-complaint against the plaintiff at the same time he or she files an answer to the plaintiff's complaint.

17. True   The court may consolidate several cases into one when there are several plaintiffs who have filed separate lawsuits resulting from the same set of facts against the defendant.

18. True   A statute of limitations sets forth the time period within which a plaintiff must bring a lawsuit against the defendant. If the plaintiff fails to bring his or her suit within the set time frame, he or she will lose his or her right to sue.

19. False   A court can order another party to submit to a physical or mental examination prior to trial as this is part of the legal process known as discovery. In cases involving the physical or mental condition of a party, the court may order the party to submit to an exam to assess the extent of the party's injuries or condition.

20. False   A motion for summary judgment alleges that there are no factual disputes to be decided by the jury and that the judge should apply the relevant law to the undisputed facts to decide the case. The question as presented describes a motion for judgment on the pleadings.

21. False   The statement as presented is incorrect as the parties usually present trial briefs to the judge that have legal support for their case at the time of trial, not after the trial has been presented.

22. False   It is after the defendant's attorney is through calling witnesses, that the plaintiff's attorney can call witnesses and present evidence to rebut the defendant's case. The answer given pertains more to the concept of rejoinder wherein the defendant's attorney can call additional witnesses and introduce other evidence to counter the rebuttal.

23. False   Though it is true that either party can appeal the trial court's decision in a civil case, it must be done once a final judgment is entered, not prior to the final judgment.

24. True   Approximately half of the states have adopted the Uniform Arbitration Act.

25. True   The statement given is one definition for conciliation.

Multiple Choice

26. A   Answer A is correct, as once a complaint is filed with the court, a summons is issued. Answer B makes no sense. Answer C is an incorrect statement of law, as the complaint cannot be served on the defendant before a summons is issued as the summons gives notice to the defendant that he or she is being sued. Answer D is incorrect, as a government official need not look over the summons in order for a summons to be issued.

27. B   Answer B is correct, as a plaintiff need only prove his or her damages in a case once a default judgment has been entered against a defendant. Answer A is incorrect as a plaintiff's assertion of affirmative defenses would have taken place if a plaintiff was served with a cross-complaint by the defendant and was preparing his or her answer/reply to the same. Answer C is incorrect, as the plaintiff need not repeat his or her litigation against the defendant as the default judgment is indicative of the defendant's liability in the case. Answer D is incorrect, as the defendant would be the party who would want to file a motion for relief from the default judgment, not the plaintiff. The plaintiff would want the default judgment to stand in order to prove the defendant's liability to him or her.

28. B   Litigation is the process of bringing, maintaining, and defending a lawsuit. Answer A is incorrect as discovery is a detailed pretrial procedure that allows both parties to discover facts of the case from the other party and witnesses before trial. Answer C is incorrect as a cross-complaint is a pleading usually filed by a defendant who is now suing a plaintiff who filed the original complaint against him/her. The cross-complaint is usually filed at the same time as the defendant's answer to the plaintiff's complaint. Answer D is incorrect, as a summons is a court order indicating that the defendant must appear before the court and answer the complaint against him/her.

29. A   A statute of limitations is a law that establishes the time period which a plaintiff must bring a lawsuit against the defendant. Answer B in incorrect as there is no such thing as a complaining period. Answer C is incorrect as an e-filing of pleadings refers to the technology that is currently available for electronic filing of pleadings and other legal documents as they pertain to a lawsuit.

30. B   Answer B gives the correct definition of a deposition. Answer A is incorrect as it tries to confuse you by incorporating the written aspect of interrogatories with the oral facet of testimony which is associated with depositions. Answer C is incorrect as it is referring to the pleading known as a complaint. Answer D is incorrect for the reasons given above.

31. D   Answer D states the correct explanation of the discovery form known as production of documents. Answer A is incorrect as this is the definition for interrogatories. Answer B is incorrect as this is the explanation for discovery requesting a party to submit to a physical or mental examination.   Answer C is incorrect, as it does not make sense as applied to the legal aspect of discovery.

32. D   Answer D gives the correct explanation for the term rejoinder. The important aspect to remember is that rejoinder is a term that is used when the defendant is attempting to counter the plaintiff's rebuttal of the defendant's case. Answer A is incorrect as this explains the term rebuttal. Answer B is incorrect as this in an incorrect explanation of the term. Answer C is incorrect as the reading of jury instructions refers to the aspect of the trial that occurs once the closing arguments by each party are completed.

33. C   Answer C gives the correct terminology for a verdict overturned based on bias or jury misconduct. Answer A is incorrect as a motion for judgment on the pleadings is made once the pleadings are complete. In essence it is asking for the judge to dispose of all or part of the lawsuit before trial as compared to overturning a verdict after the trial as in a judgment notwithstanding the verdict. Answer B is incorrect as the entry of judgment refers to the court's official decision of the successful party based upon the verdict, not on overturning the verdict.

34. A Answer A is correct, as the responding party in an appeal is known as the respondent and is also referred to as the appellee. Answer B is incorrect as the appellant is the party who is bringing the appeal. The appellant is also known as the petitioner. Answer C is incorrect as the term respondent is usually used at the appellate level whereas the term defendant is used at the trial court level. Answer D is incorrect as the plaintiff is the party to the original lawsuit who has initiated the action against the defendant.

35. C Answer C is correct, as arbitration is the term that is defined in the question. Answer A is incorrect as a mediator is chosen as a neutral third party to convey information between the parties in an effort to reach a settlement; however, the mediator does not make a decision or an award like an arbitrator does. Answer B is incorrect as the explanation for a minitrial is one in which the attorneys for both parties present their cases to representatives of each party who have been given authority to settle the dispute. Answer D is incorrect as a judicial referee is usually an appointed retired judge who conducts a private trial and then renders a judgment.

36. C Answer C gives one of the correct provisions of the Federal Arbitration Act. Answer A is incorrect as one of the reasons the Federal Arbitration Act was developed was to reverse hostility toward arbitration agreements that were present at English common law. Answer B is incorrect as another purpose of the Federal Arbitration Act was to enforce arbitration agreements that call for the resolution of disputes arising under federal statutes. Answer D is also incorrect as it is contrary to another provision of the Federal Arbitration Act that allows a party to obtain a court order to compel arbitration if the other party has failed, neglected, or refused to comply with an arbitration agreement.

37. A Answer A is correct as the court appointed judicial referee conducts a private trial and then gives his/her judgment. Answer B is incorrect as this gives the definition of a fact finder. Answer C is incorrect as a conciliator is a person who acts as a mediator in a process referred to as conciliation. Answer D is incorrect, as it does not make any sense.

38. B Answer B is correct, as technology is now available for providing electronic filings of pleadings, briefs, and other legal documents. Answer A is incorrect; as even though it may be true that some people would file their claims in a more efficient manner, it would also hamper the time frame that others may need in preparing, filing, and serving their claims, thereby denying their right to be heard. Answer C is incorrect as shorter forms are not feasible in certain types of pleadings, such as interrogatories. Answer D is incorrect based upon the reasons given above.

Short Answer

39. It might not be wise for the plaintiff to sue as there may be a high probability of losing the case. Further, the amount of money to be won or lost may not be worth it, in light of the cost of litigation and lawyer's fees, not to mention the loss of time by managers and other personnel. Additionally, there are psychological and aggravation costs associated with a lawsuit. Finally there is a possibility of error as well as unpredictability of the legal system to consider as well. These are all factors that go into a cost-benefit analysis in deciding whether to bring a lawsuit or not.

40. Interrogatories are written questions given by one party to a lawsuit to another party. One such advantage to receiving this type of discovery is that a party's lawyer may help assist in the preparation of the answers to the questions.

41. production of documents
42. motion for summary judgment
43. trier of fact
44. mediator
45. fact finder
46. Uniform Arbitration Act
47. at the office of one of the attorneys
48. summons
49. answer
50. affirmative defenses

Chapter 4

CONSTITUTIONAL LAW FOR BUSINESS AND ONLINE COMMERCE

Chapter Overview

This chapter details the functions of the United States Constitution as well as provides a solid overview of the legal framework that our government operates under. Emphasis is placed on the concepts of federalism as well as separation of powers and the federal government's power to regulate foreign, interstate, and even local commerce. Additionally, you will gain familiarity with the First Amendment and its application to the Internet. The concepts of substantive and procedural due process, equal protection, and the constitutional limits on e-commerce are also explored.

Objectives

Upon completion of the exercises in this chapter, you should be able to:
1. Recognize the function of the powers granted to the state and federal government.
2. Understand the importance of the Supremacy Clause and its application.
3. Understand the federal government's authority and rationale for regulating interstate commerce.
4. Anaylze and differentiate the protection various types of speech are afforded under the First Amendment.
5. Apply the first amendment freedom of speech protection to situations involving the Internet.
6. Understand the restrictions placed upon the government regarding the Freedom of Religion.
7. Be familiar with the constitutional limits on e-commerce.
8. Analyze and understand substantive and procedural due process.
9. Understand the constitutional standards applicable in equal protection cases.

Practical Application

You should be able to understand the importance of the Commerce Clause as well as the government's reasoning behind regulation of commerce. You should also be able to understand what types of speech are protected as well as the limitations on speech. Further, you should be able to understand and apply the various standards of review in equal protection cases. Finally, it is important to understand the difference between substantive due process and procedural due process.

Helpful Hints

This chapter should be approached in a manner much like you would approach the weighing as well as need for various elements in a scientific laboratory. The chapter begins with a discussion on the powers given to the federal government and those that are reserved for the states. Next, the chapter discusses the creation, need, and function of balancing the three branches of government. The importance and impact of the commerce clause on the government and its place in business are also examined. Further, the limitations on the First Amendment Freedom of Speech based on the type of speech as well as restrictions on the government concerning Freedom of Religion are also discussed. The significant balancing of classification as set forth in a government regulation against governmental standards in equal protection cases are carefully scrutinized as well. As you review the study tips section followed by the various chapter exercises, it is beneficial to weigh the governmental interest against what is being protected.

Study Tips

Constitution of the United States of America

The two major functions that the U.S. Constitution serves are to create the three branches of the federal government (i.e., the executive, legislative, and judicial) and allocate powers to these branches, as well as to protect individual rights by limiting the government's ability to restrict those rights.

Federalism

This refers to our country's form of government. The states and the federal government share powers. Sometimes the federal law and state law conflict. When this happens, the federal law prevails.

Branches of the Federal Government

You should familiarize yourself with the legislative, executive, and judicial branches of government and know what function each branch serves, as well as how each affects one another.

State and Local Government Regulation of Business – "Police Power"

States are able to regulate intrastate and a large amount of interstate business that takes place within its borders. The police power given to the states allows the states to make laws that protect or promote the health, safety, morals, and welfare of its citizens.

Bill of Rights

You should know that the Bill of Rights is the ten amendments to the United States Constitution. Also, the two rights that are heavily emphasized are the Freedom of Speech and the Freedom of Religion as per the First Amendment.

Freedom of Speech

It is important to realize that this freedom extends only to speech and not conduct. You should also familiarize yourself with the types of speech. It is helpful to list them and place the protection each is given next to them. The following demonstrates an easy way to do this.

Political Speech – fully protected

Commercial Speech – An example would be advertising. Speeches used by businesses are subject to time, place, and manner restrictions.

Offensive Speech – Speech that is offensive to a lot of people is also subject to time, place, and manner restrictions.

Unprotected Speech includes dangerous speech, fighting words, defamatory language, child pornography, and obscene speech.

Note that with obscene speech, the states can define the meaning of obscene speech. It has been stated that obscene is where the average person's prurient interest is appealed to, and the work is patently offensive, thereby describing the sexual conduct in accordance with the state law and the work is in need of serious literary, artistic, political, or social value.

Freedom of Religion

The Constitution mandates that the local, state and federal governments be neutral regarding religion.
The two religion clauses in the First Amendment that you should know the difference between are the Establishment Clause, which prohibits the government from establishing a state religion or promoting one religion over another and the Free Exercise Clause. The Free Exercise Clause prevents the government from making laws that inhibit or prohibit people from participating in or practicing their chosen religion.

Commerce

This is a very important term to know. As you may recall, the Commerce Clause of the Constitution has the greatest impact on business than any other clause. In order to fully appreciate as well as understand this importance, you need to know the following:

- The difference between interstate and intrastate commerce is that interstate involves instrumentalities of trade moving across state borders. Compare this to intrastate where commerce is moving within the state.

- The traditional role of government in regulating interstate commerce was to regulate only commerce that moved in interstate commerce. Whereas modernly the federal government may regulate local commerce if it has an impact on commerce as a whole.

- If state law burdens interstate commerce, then the law is declared void and unconstitutional.

The Equal Protection Clause

This clause of the Fourteenth Amendment states that a state cannot "deny to any person within its jurisdiction the equal protection of the laws." Though it primarily applies to state and local governments, it also applies to federal government action as well. You must know the three standards for review of equal protection cases. They are:

1. *Strict Scrutiny*, which is applied when there is a classification that is a suspect class such as race.

2. *Intermediate Scrutiny*, which is applied when the classification is based on a protected class that is not race, such as age and sex.
3. Finally, the *Rational Basis Test* is applied when neither a suspect nor protected class is involved. All that is needed is a justifiable reason for the law trying to be enacted.

The Due Process Clause

This clause is provided for in the Fifth and Fourteenth Amendments as both have a due process clause. The Fifth Amendment applies to the federal government whereas the Fourteenth Amendment applies to state and local government. The crux of this clause is that no individual shall be deprived of life, liberty, or property without due process of law. There are two types of due process, substantive and procedural. Substantive refers to the content of the law. It must be clear, not too broad, and worded in such a way that a "reasonable person" could understand the law in order to obey it. The procedural aspect requires a person be given notice and an opportunity to be heard before his/her life, liberty, or property is taken. Note, within this aspect is the Just Compensation Clause, which states the government must pay to the owner just compensation for taking an individual's property.

Privileges and Immunities Clause

This clause prohibits states from enforcing laws that unduly favor their own residents thereby resulting in discrimination against residents of other states.

Refresh Your Memory

The following exercise will enable you to refresh your memory of the main principles given to you in this chapter. Read each question twice and placed your answer in the blank(s) provided. If you do not remember, go to the next question and come back to the one you did not answer. It is also helpful to look over the section(s) in the study tips again, and then try to answer what you may be having difficulty with.

1. The creation of the three branches of the federal government as well as the powers given to these branches were established in the _____.

2. The federal government is authorized to deal with _____ and _____ affairs.

3. The part of the government that consists of the Supreme Court and other federal courts is the _____ branch.

4. The United States Constitution's system of _____ and _____ prevents any one of the three branches of the federal government from becoming too powerful.

5. The _____ Clause has a greater impact on business than any other provision of the Constitution.

6. _____ commerce refers to commerce that moves between states or that affects commerce between the states.

7. The legal doctrine that states that federal law takes precedence over state or local law is known as the _____ doctrine.

8. Which clause is intended to foster the development of a national market and free trade among the states? _____

9. Under the incorporation doctrine, many of the fundamental guarantees set forth in the Bill of Rights are also applied to _____ and _____ government action.

10. The First Amendment's Freedom of Speech Clause protects _____ and not conduct.

11. _____ speech offends many individuals in society and is subject to time, place, and manner restrictions.

12. Which act allows for the outlawing of junk faxes? _____ _____ Act.

13. A clause that prohibits the government from establishing a state religion or promoting one religion over another is the _____ _____.

14. The _____ _____ prohibits the government from enacting laws that either prohibit or inhibit individuals from participating or practicing their chosen religion.

15. Which clause provides that a state cannot "deny to any person within its jurisdiction the equal protection of the laws?" The _____ _____ clause.

Critical Thought Exercise

Larry Brown is a very religious person and is very active in the anti-abortion movement. While Brown travels the streets of his hometown of Westerfield, Illinois, he plays taped sermons and spiritual music that support his religious and political views. The City of Westerfield enacted an ordinance that prohibited the playing of car sound systems at a volume that would be "audible" at a distance greater than fifty feet. Brown was arrested and convicted for violating the ordinance. Brown appealed his conviction on the grounds that the ordinance violated his right to free speech and free exercise of his religious beliefs. The City of Westerfield countered that noise coming from Brown's car could pose a hazard if he and other drivers were unable to hear emergency vehicles as they approached, and as such, the ordinance was a proper exercise of the police power possessed by the State of Illinois.

Was the playing of sermons by Brown protected by the Free Speech and Free Exercise clauses of the First Amendment to the United States Constitution?

Answer:

_____

_____

_____

_____

_____

_____

_____

_____

_____
_____
_____
_____
_____
_____
_____
_____
_____
_____
_____
_____
_____
_____
_____
_____
_____

Practice Quiz

True/False

1. ____   The Constitution itself allows for amendments to address social and economic changes. [p. 47]

2. ____   The federal government and the fifty state governments share powers. [p. 48]

3. ____   The part of government that is comprised of the president and vice president is the legislative branch. [p. 48]

4. ____   If a state or local law directly or substantially conflicts with a valid federal law, that state or local law is preempted under the Supremacy Clause. [p. 50]

5. ____   The system of checks and balances is a way to apportioning most of the power in the executive branch. [p.48]

6. ____   Those powers not granted to the state government by the Constitution are reserved to the states. [p. 51]

7. ____   A state can regulate an area that the federal government has chosen not to regulate regardless of the burden caused on interstate commerce. [p. 52]

8. ____   The federal government has exclusive power to regulate commerce with foreign nations. [p. 50]

9. ____   Congress may not provide that a specific federal statute exclusively regulates a specific area or activity. [p. 50]

10. ____ Symbolic speech is protected by the First Amendment. [p. 53]

11. ____ A law that is enacted that forbids citizens from not agreeing with those presently in office does not violate the Freedom of Speech. [p. 53]

12. ____ The government cannot limit the time, place, and manner of speech. [p. 53]

13. ____ A statute authorizing a one-minute period of silence in school for meditation or voluntary prayer is invalid as it violates the Establishment Clause. [p. 56]

14. ____ The First Amendment gives only the right to engage in oral and symbolic speech. [p. 53]

15. ____ Under the rational basis test, the court's standard of review is whether the government classification is "reasonably related" to a legitimate government purpose. [p. 57]

16. ____ The standard for review in an equal protection case involving sex or age is that the government classification will be found to be unconstitutional as sex and age are suspect classes. [p. 57]

17. ____ The Fourteenth and Fifth Amendments of the United States Constitution both contain a Due Process Clause. [p. 59]

18. ____ Procedural due process is the only classification that the government must follow. [p. 59]

19. ____ Substantive due process mandates that the laws, statutes, ordinances, and regulations be clear, and not too broad. [p. 59]

20. ____ Time, place, and manner restrictions may be placed on billboards along a state's freeways as long as other forms of advertising are available. [p. 53]

Multiple Choice

21. The Federal Communications Commission can regulate the use of offensive language on television by [p. 53]
    a. limiting such language to time periods when children would be more likely to watch.
    b. limiting such language to only certain words that are mildly offensive to children.
    c. limiting such language to time periods when children would be unlikely to be watching.
    d. all of the above.

22. Which of the following are enacted under a state's police power? [p. 51]
    a. zoning ordinances
    b. property laws
    c. environmental laws
    d. all of the above

23. Edna lives in Missouri but has always dreamed of owning a vacation home in Michigan. Upon moving to Michigan, Edna is told that she will not be allowed to purchase property in Michigan since she is a resident of Missouri. If Edna wants to contest Michigan's law, what would be her best reasoning to strike it down? [p. 59]
    a. The Just Compensation Clause has been violated.
    b. The substantive due process clause has been violated.
    c. The Privileges and Immunities Clause has been violated.
    d. all of the above

24. Intrastate commerce refers to [p. 50]
    a. commerce that crosses state borders.
    b. commerce that occurs within a state.
    c. commerce that occurs across state borders and within a state.
    d. commerce that occurs only in a limited local area.

25. Political speech is an example of [p. 53]
    a. speech that is given limited protection.
    b. speech that has time, place, and manner restrictions.
    c. speech that will incite the overthrow of the government.
    d. speech that is fully protected.

26. Procedural due process requires the government to give [p. 59]
    a. proper notice and a hearing.
    b. clear laws and not be overly broad in what they cover.
    c. punitive damages.
    d. minimal compensation for the taking of property.

27. The Privileges and Immunities Clause prohibits [p. 59]
    a. states from giving the same privileges to out-of-state residents.
    b. prevents out-of-state residents from owning property in other states.
    c. the government from enacting laws that unduly discriminate in favor of their own residents.
    d. federal government from regulating commerce that moves in interstate commerce.

28. Originally, the Bill of Rights limited intrusive action by [p. 52]
    a. the state government only.
    b. the federal government only.
    c. both the state and federal government.
    d. persons 18 years of age and older.

29. The concept that federal law takes precedence over state or local law is known as [p. 49]
    a. checks and balances.
    b. federalism.
    c. the preemption doctrine.
    c. the superior federal clause.

30. Which of the following would not be considered unprotected speech? [p. 53]
    a. dangerous speech
    b. defamatory speech
    c. political speech
    d. obscene speech

Short Answer

31. The Bill of Rights are additions to the _____. [p. 52]

32. The president is not elected by popular vote but instead is selected by the   [p. 48]
    _____ _____.

33. The executive branch of the federal government can enter into treaties with foreign governments only with the advice and consent of the _____ [p. 48]

34. Who has the exclusive power to regulate commerce with foreign nations? [p. 52}
    _____

35. The rational basis test is used in reviewing equal protection cases that do not involve a _____ or _____ class. [p. 57]

36. Offensive speech is subject to _____, _____, and _____ restrictions. [p. 53]

37. The modern rule concerning the federal government's regulation of interstate commerce is that it may regulate activities that _____. [p. 50]

38. Why isn't it discrimination when a college charges out-of-state residents more tuition than for its own residents? [p. 60]
    _____
    _____

39. State laws that unduly burden interstate commerce are _____. [p. 52]

40. What authority does the judicial branch have? [p. 48] _____
    _____

41. The state's police power enables the state of Caledonia to enact laws that promote the public _____, _____, _____, and _____ welfare for the protection of its citizens. [p. 51]

42. Which branch of the government can enter into treaties with foreign governments only with the advice and consent of the senate? The _____ branch. [p. 48]

43. The two separate First Amendment clauses that pertain to religion are the _____ _____ Clause and the _____ Clause. [p. 56]

44. What is the incorporation doctrine? [p. 52]
    _____
    _____

45. When federal statutes do not expressly provide for exclusive jurisdiction, who has jurisdiction, the state or local governments? _____ [p. 49]

46. The rational basis test is used to determine _____.
[p. 57]

47. Advertising is an example of _____ speech. [p. 53]

48. Give three types of unprotected speech. _____, _____,
and _____ [p. 53]

49. Which amendment contains the Free Exercise and Establishment Clause? [p. 57]
_____

50. If the city of Orangeville makes it illegal for persons to shop at stores that the opposite sex
shops at, what will be the outcome of a case that is brought against the city based on the
theory that the law is unconstitutional. Justify your answer. [p. 59]
_____

Answers to Refresh Your Memory

1. U.S. Constitution [p. 48]
2. national; international [p. 48]
3. judicial branch [p. 48]
4. checks and balances [p. 48]
5. Commerce Clause [p. 50]
6. Interstate [p. 50]
7. preemption [p. 49]
8. Commerce Clause [p. 50]
9. state, local [p. 52]
10. speech [p. 53]
11. Offensive [p. 53]
12. Telephone Consumer Protection Act [p. 54]
13. Establishment Clause [p. 56]
14. Free Exercise Clause [p. 56]
15. Equal Protection Clause [p. 57]

Critical Thought Exercise Model Answer

States possess police powers as part of their inherent sovereignty. These powers may be exercised to protect or promote the public order, health, safety, morals, and general welfare. Free Speech that has political content, such as the speech being used by Brown, has traditionally been protected to the fullest extent possible by the courts. Free speech includes the right to effective free speech. Amplification systems can be used as long as the speech does not harass or annoy others in the exercise of their privacy rights at an inappropriate time or in an inappropriate location. Thus, Brown would have greater leeway to play his sermons in a commercial district during the day than he could to blast then in a residential neighborhood at midnight. The Free Exercise Clause provision in the First Amendment to the Constitution prohibits Congress from making a law "prohibiting the free exercise" of religion. The Free Exercise Clause guarantees that a person can hold any religious belief that he or she wants. When religious practices are at odds with public policy and the public welfare, the government can act. Brown has the absolute right to listen to his sermons and preach them to others. However, he cannot engage in this activity if it causes a danger to the safety of others. The question that is not answered by the facts is whether the distance of fifty feet is to prevent annoyance or a danger to drivers upon the streets and highways. Without a showing by Westerfield that music and speech that is audible from fifty feet is actually dangerous to drivers, Brown is free to play his sermons and spiritual music in a manner that is annoying to others.

Answers to Practice Quiz

True/False

1. True   The Unites States Constitution does allow for amendments to address both social and economic changes.
2. True   The sharing of powers by the federal government and the fifty states is known as federalism.
3. False   The part of government that is comprised of the president and vice Ppresident is the executive, not legislative branch.
4. True   Local and state laws are unconstitutional if they conflict with valid federal law.
5. False   The system of checks and balances is a way to balance the powers given to each branch, *not* apportion the power where the executive branch gets the most powers.
6. False   Those powers not granted to the federal government by the Constitution are reserved to the states.
7. False   State and local laws that unduly burden interstate commerce are unconstitutional as they violate the Commerce Clause.
8. True   The Commerce Clause of the Constitution provides for the federal government's regulation of commerce with foreign nations.
9. False   Congress may provide that a specific federal statute exclusively regulates a specific activity or area.
10. True   The First Amendment Freedom of Speech protects the right to engage in written, oral, and symbolic speech.
11. False   This is an example of political speech, which is fully protected, and not subject to government regulation or prohibition.
12. False   The government can limit certain types of speech such as commercial speech and offensive speech to a proper time, place, and manner, thereby giving these types of speech limited protection.
13. True   This type of statute has been held to be invalid as it endorses religion and it violates the Establishment Clause.
14. False   The First Amendment gives the right to engage in oral, symbolic, and written speech.
15. False   Under the rational basis test, the courts will hold the government regulation as being valid and long as there is a justifiable reason for the regulation. Note that it is the intermediate scrutiny test that the courts determine whether the government classification is "reasonably related" to a legitimate government purpose.
16. False   Sex and age are protected classes and as such the standard for review of these protected classes is the intermediate scrutiny test whereby the courts decide whether the government classification is "reasonably related" to a legitimate government purpose. Compare this to race, which is a suspect class that is subject to the strict scrutiny test that finds classifications based on race to be unconstitutional.
17. True   The Due Process Clause of the Fifth Amendment pertains to federal government action and the Due Process Clause of the Fourteenth Amendment pertains to state and local government action.

18. False   The government must follow procedural as well as substantive due process. The procedural refers to the government giving proper notice and a hearing of the legal action before an individual is deprived of life, liberty, or property, whereas the substantive requires that the government make laws that are clear and not too broad.
19. True   Substantive due process has been achieved if a "reasonable person" could understand the law and be able to comply with it. This is accomplished by the laws' clarity and not being overly broad in their scope.
20. True   Time, place, and manner restrictions may be placed on commercial speech.

Multiple Choice

21. C   Answer C is correct as the Federal Communications Commission can regulate the use of offensive language on television by limiting such language to time periods (such as late at night) when children would be unlikely to be watching programs with such content. Answer A is incorrect, as the FCC would not regulate the use of offensive language to times when children would be more likely to watch television with the offensive content. Answer B is incorrect, as the FCC does not categorize whether the offensive language is mild or otherwise, it simply regulates it according to children's viewing times. Answer D is incorrect for the reasons stated above.
22. D   Answer D is correct as zoning laws, property laws, and environmental laws all are enacted under a state's police power.
23. C   Answer C is correct as it prohibits states from enacting laws that unduly discriminate in favor of their residents, which is exactly what Michigan is doing by denying Edna her right to purchase a home in Michigan based on the fact that she is a Missouri resident. Answer A is incorrect, as the Just Compensation Clause relates to the Fifth Amendment and the government having to pay the owner just compensation for taking a homeowner's property which is not the case here. Answer B is incorrect, as the substantive due process clause requires that government statutes, ordinances, regulations, or other laws be clear on their face and not overly broad in scope. Answer D is incorrect for the reasons stated above.
24. B   Answer B is correct, as intrastate commerce is commerce that moves within a state. Answer A is incorrect as this refers to interstate commerce. Answer C is incorrect as it combines the concepts of interstate and intrastate commerce. Answer D is incorrect as it is an incorrect statement of law.
25. D   Answer D is correct, as political speech is an example of speech that the government cannot prohibit or regulate. Answer A is incorrect as political speech is given full protection whereas offensive speech and commercial speech are given limited protection and are subject to time, place, and manner restrictions. Answer B is incorrect based on the same reasoning why answer A was incorrect. Answer C is incorrect as speech that will incite the overthrow of the government is an example of unprotected speech that is not protected under the First Amendment.
26. A   Answer A is correct, as the reasoning behind this form of process is fairness. The government must give proper notice and a hearing of the legal action before there is a liberty or property is required. Answer B is incorrect as this refers to substantive due process and how the government's statutes, ordinances, laws, and regulations are written. Answer C is incorrect as punitive damages are a type of remedy enforced in cases where punishment is being sought or there is a lesson for the defendant to learn. Answer D is incorrect as the Just Compensation Clause of the Fifth Amendment provides that the government must pay the owner just not minimal compensation for taking an individual's property. Minimal compensation would violate all notions of fairness.

27. C   Answer C is correct, as this is the main premise of the Privileges and Immunities Clause. Answer A is incorrect as the Privileges and Immunities Clause encourages nationalism and favors states giving other states the same privileges as its own residents enjoy and benefit from. Answer B is incorrect, as it would unduly discriminate in favor of the state's own residents owning property, which would defeat the concept of nationalism. Answer D is incorrect as the Privileges and Immunities Clause is not applicable to regulation of interstate commerce.

28. B   Answer B is correct, as the Bill of Rights originally limited intrusive action by the federal government. For this reason, answer A is incorrect, as is Answer C. Answer D is incorrect as it makes no sense and it is not a true statement of law.

29. C   Answer C is correct as this concept is one where federal law takes precedence over state or local law. Answer A is incorrect as checks and balances are built into the Constitution to ensure no one branch of the federal government becomes too powerful. Answer B is incorrect as federalism refers to our country's form of government. Answer D is incorrect, as there is no such thing as the superior federal clause.

30. C   Answer C is correct, as answers A, B, and D are all examples of unprotected speech.

Short Answer

31.   U.S. Constitution
32.   electoral college
33.   intermediate scrutiny
34.   the federal government
35.   suspect or protected
36.   time, place, and manner
37.   affect interstate commerce
38.   Because the out-of-state residents are receiving the benefits of the laws of the state in which the college is located in without having to be residents.
39.   unconstitutional
40.   It has the authority to examine the acts of the legislative and judicial branches of government and determine whether these acts are constitutional.
41.   health, safety, morals, and general
42.   executive
43.   Free Exercise Establishment
44.   A doctrine that states that most of the fundamental guarantees contained in the Bill of Rights are applicable to state and local government action.
45.   State and local have concurrent jurisdiction in these cases.
46.   increase competition within the telecommunications industry
47.   the lawfulness of all government classifications that do not involve suspect or protected classes.
48.   dangerous speech, fighting words, defamatory speech
49.   First Amendment
50.   The law will be found void for vagueness and therefore be unconstitutional.

Chapter 5

TORTS AND CYBER PRIVACY

Chapter Overview

This chapter provides a good understanding of the intentional torts against persons as well as property. Additionally, the tort of negligence as well as applicable defenses to this cause of action is explained in a very methodical fashion. The special negligence doctrines such as negligence per se, negligent infliction of emotional distress, and res ipsa loquitur are also examined. Further, the torts of unfair competition, disparagement, and fraud are also discussed. Also, the issue of punitive damages and the doctrine of strict liability are reviewed as well. Finally, cyber torts conducted on the Internet are analyzed and discussed.

Objectives

Upon completion of the exercises in this chapter, you should be able to:
1. Recognize and compare the different types of intentional torts against persons and against property.
2. Understand the elements that are necessary in a cause of action based on negligence and apply those elements to given fact situations.
3. Be familiar with the defenses associated with a negligence action.
4. Understand the special negligence doctrines and how they differ from one another.
5. Understand the business torts of unfair competition and disparagement.
6. Comprehend the elements of fraud.
7. Understand the purposes of punitive damages and the application of punitive damages in lawsuits involving the tort of bad faith.
8. Understand the doctrine of strict liability and its application.
9. Understand cyber torts conducted on the Internet.

Practical Application

You should be able to recognize the various intentional torts as well as negligence and apply the elements associated with each to real life as well as hypothetical situations. Additionally, you should have a greater understanding of the concept of strict liability as well as why and when punitive damages are asked for.

Helpful Hints

This chapter lends itself towards organization in that you can sort the intentional torts by their application to individuals, property, or business. Also, the elements of the tort of negligence are easily remembered if you list the elements vertically and diagram causation horizontally. This is displayed for you in the study tips section of this chapter. Further, the tort of misrepresentation is easily remembered by using the mnemonic given under the study tips section. Once you have these organizational skills mastered for the main sections in this chapter, the other information given is very easy to remember. Many of the cases you will review in this chapter will be easy for you to understand as they pertain to many companies that you may be familiar with.

Study Tips

The first organizational step you should take is to learn the intentional torts based upon their application. You should also be cognizant of some of the fine nuances associated with some of these torts. It is often easier to list the elements of the tort rather than state its technical definition. However, one of the most important things you should remember about the intentional torts as a whole is to look at the fact pattern or case being given to you and determine if the tortfeasor had the intent to do the act. If there is nothing in the facts to indicate this, then maybe the tortfeasor's action could be classified as negligent. If this is the case, then you will have to proceed through the various steps based on the flow chart given under the negligence heading in this chapter. Student learning styles will vary, and as such, both methods are given. The pages that follow will assist you in studying the torts that are discussed in this chapter.

Tort

A tort is a civil wrong for which an individual or business may seek compensation for the injuries that have been caused. Compensation for these injuries may include damages for mental distress, loss of wages, pain and suffering, past and future medical expenses, and in some situations, punitive damages. In a tort situation where the victim dies, a wrongful death action may also be an option.

Intentional Torts Against Persons

Assault – The intentional threat of immediate harm or offensive contact or any action that arouses reasonable apprehension of imminent harm.

Assault list of elements with special nuances
- *intentional*
- *placing of another*
- *in immediate* – Note that future threats are not actionable.
- *apprehension* –The victim must be fearful of what appears to be an inevitable contact. The victim must be aware of the tortuous act. The victim's reaction must be one of fear as opposed to laughter which would negate the element of apprehension.
- *of harmful or offensive contact*

Battery – The intentional, unauthorized harmful or offensive touching of another without consent or legal privilege.

Battery list of elements with special nuances
- *intentional*
- *unauthorized*
- *harmful* or *offensive* – A kiss may be considered offensive by some.
- *touching* – The touching of an accessory such as a purse that is attached to the victim may be enough to satisfy this element.
- *of another*
- *without consent* or *legal privilege* – You should be aware of the merchant's protection statutes, which sometimes have a role in the privilege arena of this tort.

Other interesting notations on battery are that the victim does not have to be aware of the battery in order for the tort to occur. Also, the victim may be sleeping when it happens or have his or her back turned when the battery occurs. Battery and assault can occur together, however, the victim would need to show awareness in order to fully prove the elements of assault.

Transferred Intent Doctrine – When one individual intends to injure one person but instead injures another individual, the law transfers the perpetrator's intent from the person the harm was originally meant for to the actual victim. The actual victim may then bring a lawsuit against the wrongdoer.

False Imprisonment – The intentional mental or physical confinement of another without consent or legal privilege.

False Imprisonment list of elements with special nuances:
- *intentional*
- *mental* or *physical* – An example of mental confinement may be through an assertion of legal authority or by one in a superior position. Physical confinement may include barriers or threats of physical harm.
- *confinement* – Be careful with this element as future threats or moral pressure does not satisfy this element. Also, if there is a reasonable means of escape, this element may be difficult to prove.
- *of another*
- *without consent* or *legal privilege* – This element will be difficult to establish if a merchant is involved. This aspect of tort law is discussed below.

Merchant Protection Statutes – Since many merchants lose thousands of dollars every year from shoplifters, many states have enacted statutes to protect them. These statutes are often referred to as shopkeeper's privilege. There are three important aspects of this type of statute that will absolve a merchant from liability of false imprisonment allegations.

Merchant Protection Statutes nuances
- There must be reasonable grounds for detaining and investigating the shoplifter.
- The suspected shoplifter can be detained for only a reasonable time.
- The investigations must be conducted in a reasonable manner.

Defamation of Character – This tort involves an intentional or accidental untrue statement of fact made about an individual to a third party.

Defamation of Character list of elements with special nuances
- *intentional* or *accidental* – May be overheard accidentally
- *untrue statement of fact* – Be careful as truth is always a defense.
- *published to a third party* – The third party can see or hear the untrue statement.

You should be aware of some of the other important aspects of defamation of character. For example, libel is written defamation and slander is oral defamation. Some types of media such as television and radio broadcasts come under the category of libel, as the courts view them as permanent in nature since the original scripts were composed prior to broadcasting the defamatory content. Also, opinions are not actionable, as it is not considered to be an untrue statement of fact. Finally, public figures such as movie stars, celebrities, and other famous people must show that the statement was knowingly made or with reckless disregard of the statement's falsity. In other words, malice must be shown.

Misappropriation of the Right to Publicity – This tort is an attempt by another to appropriate a living person's name or identity for commercial purposes. A classic example of this would be individuals who sell cheaper versions of a famous performer's concert merchandise.

Invasion of the Right to Publicity – A violation of an individual's right to live his/her life without unwarranted or undesired publicity

Truth is not a defense to this tort, as the fact does not have to be untrue. If the fact is one of public record, this tort cannot be claimed. Examples include wiretapping and reading hand-delivered as well as the e-mail of another.

Intentional Infliction of Emotional Distress
- intentional or reckless
- extreme and outrageous conduct – The conduct must go beyond the bounds of decency.
- by one individual
- against another
- that causes severe emotional distress – Many states require a physical injury, illness, or discomfort. However, states that are more flexible in their interpretation of this element have found that humiliation, fear, and anger will satisfy this element. Some states no longer require that the severity of the emotional distress be shown.

Negligent Infliction of Emotional Distress
   Though this is not an intentional tort, it is being placed here as it is a tort that is not only against individuals, but is one that some courts are recognizing when defendant's negligent conduct causes the plaintiff to suffer severe emotional distress. This tort requires the plaintiff's relative was injured or killed and that plaintiff suffered the severe distress at the same time he or she observed the accident. Some jurisdictions require the plaintiff suffer some sort of physical injury while other states do not mandate this element.

Intentional Torts Against Property

   The two torts in this area are trespass to land, which is real property, and the trespass to personal property, which involves those items that are movable. The tort of conversion is also discussed along with trespass to personal property.

Trespass to Land
- *intentional* – It is not intentional if someone else pushes an individual onto someone else's land.
- *entry onto the land of another without consent* or *legal privilege* –Rescuing someone from danger is not considered trespass. By the same token, remaining on someone's land after the invitation has expired is trespass.

Trespass to Personal Property
- *intentional*
- *injury* or *interference with* – An example of this would be breaking someone else's glass vase.
- *another's enjoyment of his or her personal property*

Conversion of Personal Property

- *intentionally*
- *depriving* a true *owner* of the *use and enjoyment of his or her personal property* – Note that the failure to return borrowed property can satisfy this element.

The rightful owner can bring a cause of action to get the property back. If the property is destroyed or lost, the true owner can recover the property's value.

Negligence

In order to be successful in a negligence cause of action, one must show that a duty of care was owed to the plaintiff, that the defendant breached this duty, that the defendant was the actual and proximate cause of plaintiff's injuries, and that the plaintiff suffered damages.

Duty of Care

You should know the general duty of care which states that we all owe one another a duty of due care so as to not subject others to an unreasonable risk of harm. This duty is based on the reasonable person standard. An example of when this general duty of care is owed is the situation involving an invitee. An invitee is one who is invited onto the land of another for the mutual benefit of both people. The duty of ordinary care is also owed to licensees. A licensee is one who with consent comes onto the land of another for his or her own benefit. An example of a licensee would be an encyclopedia salesperson. Note, an owner does not owe a general duty of care to a trespasser; however, an owner of property does owe a duty not to willfully or wantonly injure a trespasser. Also, children are measured against other children of similar age and experience.

There are certain situations however where a higher standard of care is owed. They involve the professionals, innkeepers, common carriers, taverns and bartenders, social hosts, and paying passengers riding in a vehicle of another.

Professionals are held to the standard of a reasonable professional. Liability is known as malpractice. You should be cognizant of the medical professional who acts as a good Samaritan. Medical professionals are relieved of liability for injury caused by their ordinary negligence when rendering aid to victims in need of emergency care.

Innkeepers owe a duty of utmost care and have to provide security for their guest.

Common carriers also owe a duty of utmost care for their guests.

Taverns and bartenders are liable to third parties who are injured by a patron who was served too much alcohol or who was served alcohol when he/she was already intoxicated. Social hosts are held liable for injuries caused by guests who are served too much alcohol.

The Danger Invites Rescue Doctrine allows those who are injured while going to someone's rescue to sue the person who caused the dangerous situation. Compare this to the fireman's rule where the fireman who is injured while putting out a fire may not sue the person who caused the fire as not only does the job imply that injury may occur, but people would be reluctant to call for help if they thought they might be sued in doing so.

Breach of Duty

If a duty, albeit general and or special, has been established and it is found that the defendant has not acted as a reasonable person would, the court may find a breach of the duty of care.

Causation

It is important to remember that the plaintiff must show that the defendant was the actual (factual) and proximate (legal) cause of the plaintiff's injuries. Further, the defendant must be the direct cause of the plaintiff's injuries. If this cannot be established, plaintiff must show that the injuries that occurred were foreseeable in that it would be the type of injury one would expect from the activity the defendant was engaged in. It is best to diagram this element horizontally in order to remember its nuances. Please see below.

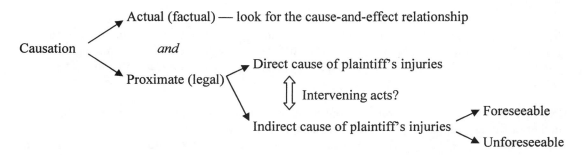

Damages

The plaintiff must have actually suffered an injury or damages.

Defenses

Contributory negligence states that if a plaintiff is partially at fault for causing his or her own injuries, then the plaintiff is barred from recovering damages.

Comparative negligence doctrines assess damages by the plaintiff's percentage of fault. This is known as pure comparative negligence. If, however, the plaintiff is in a jurisdiction that adopts the partial comparative negligence doctrine, then plaintiff must be less than fifty percent negligent in causing his or her injuries. If the plaintiff is over fifty percent negligent, then recovery is barred and the defendant is not liable.

Assumption of the Risk is a defense that states that a defendant may assert indicating that the plaintiff knowingly and voluntarily entered into a risky activity that resulted in injury.

Special Negligence Doctrines

Negligence per se and **res ipsa loquitur** are special negligence doctrines that are important to be aware of as they are special in their establishment of the element of duty as well as assisting in the plaintiff's burden of proof in a negligence case.

Negligence Per Se – This doctrine involves the violation of a statute that proximately causes the plaintiff's injuries. There must be a statute that was enacted to prevent the type of injury suffered by the plaintiff and the plaintiff must be within the class of persons the statute was designed to protect.

Res Ipsa Loquitur – This doctrine means "the thing speaks for itself." This is an important doctrine as there is a presumption of negligence where the plaintiff proves that the defendant had exclusive control of the instrumentality or circumstances that caused the plaintiff's injuries and the injury that the plaintiff suffered wouldn't have ordinarily occurred, "but for" someone's negligence.

Business Torts

Entering into a business or profession without a license can subject the violator to civil and criminal penalties.

Unfair Competition – This tort is also known as palming off whereby one company tries to "palm off" its products as those of a rival. Plaintiff must show the defendant used the plaintiff's symbol, trademark, logo, etc., and that there is a likelihood of confusion as to the product's origin.

Disparagement – This tort involves an untrue statement made by a person or business about another business's reputation, services, products, etc. This tort is also known as product disparagement or trade libel. The defendant must have made the statement intentionally to a third party knowing that what he or she was saying was not true.

False Advertising – When companies use untruthful comparative advertising to compare the qualities of their products to those of their competitors, this is known as false advertising. False and misleading advertising is a violation of part of the federal statute known as the Lanham Act.

Intentional Misrepresentation (Fraud) – This tort lends itself nicely towards a mnemonic that will assist you in remembering its elements. The mnemonic is MIS JD.
M Misrepresentation of material fact that was false in nature
I Intentionally made to an innocent party
S Scienter (knowledge) of the statement's falsity by the wrongdoer
J Justifiable reliance on the false statement by the innocent party
D Damages were suffered by the injured party

Intentional Interference with Contractual Relations – There must be a valid and enforceable contract that a third party knows about. The third party induces one of the contracting parties to breach the contract with the other party.

Breach of Implied Covenant of Good Faith and Fair Dealing – Parties to a contract must adhere to the express terms of a contract and also to the implied term of "good faith." When a party to a contract acts in bad faith, this gives rise to the tort of Breach of Implied Covenant of Good Faith and Fair Dealing.

Punitive Damages – These types of damages are recoverable in torts involving fraud, intentional conduct, and are in addition to actual damages. Punitive damages are awarded not only to set an example for others, but to prevent the defendant from the same or similar conduct in the future and to punish the defendant for his or her actions.

Strict Liability – This is a tort that involves liability without fault if the activity that the defendant is engaged in places the public at risk of injury despite reasonable care being taken. Examples of activities that qualify for this categorization include fumigation, storage of explosives, and blasting. Punitive damages are also recoverable in strict liability cases.

Refresh Your Memory

The following exercise will enable you to refresh your memory on the rules and principles presented to you in this chapter. Read each question twice and place your answer in the blanks provided. Review the chapter material for any question you miss or are unable to remember.

1. Under tort law, what type of lawsuit may be brought by an injured party seeking compensation for a wrong done to him or her or to his or her property? _____

2. The main purpose that punitive damages are awarded is to _____ the defendant.

3. What kind of threat does the tort of assault require in order to be actionable? _____.

4. Which doctrine places the perpetrator's intent from the target to the actual victim of the act? The doctrine of _____ _____.

5. What type of damages may a plaintiff recover in a case based on the tort of appropriation? _____ _____ and an _____

6. Another name for an oral defamatory statement is _____.

7. The tort of appropriation is also known as _____ of the right to _____.

8. Reading someone else's e-mail is an example of the tort of _____ of the right to _____.

9. If Ron sneaks into the operating room where Clair is under anesthesia and thereafter paints body tattoos on her legs while she is sleeping, what tort has probably occurred? _____

10. How long does protection from defamation of character last? _____

11. When proving causation in a negligence action, what are the two types of causation that must be proved before the plaintiff may prevail? _____ in fact and _____ _____.

12. The liability of a professional who breaches his or her duty of ordinary care is known as _____ _____.

13. The term res ipsa loquitur means the _____ _____ ____ _____.

14. Under which doctrine may a rescuer sue the person who caused the dangerous situation that the rescuer has gone to? The _____ _____ _____ doctrine.

15. An original negligent party may raise a _____ event as a defense to liability.

16. In the states that have eliminated the invitee-licensee-trespasser distinction, what type of duty is owed by owners and renters to those who come on their property? _____

17. What does it mean when a person has breached a duty of care?

    _____.

18. If Sam, a hitchhiker, is picked up in the car by Connie and she gets in an accident that causes Sam's injuries, will Connie be liable? Explain.

    _____

19. Liability without fault is known as _____ _____.

20. If a defendant has a duty to avoid an accident and thereafter ignores any warning signs and gets hurt from being in that accident as a result of his or her own contributory negligence, what type of assessment will the court use in deciding the case?

    _____

    _____

Critical Thought Exercise

Chip North is a 22-year-old racing enthusiast who went to a car race at Trona International Speedway. North was excited because he had obtained a seat close to the track near the finish line. North's ticket came with five others in a sealed envelope that was imprinted in a large font with the following:

"WARNING!
Your seating for this event is in a very
DANGEROUS AREA
Debris and fluids from race cars may be ejected or sprayed from the
race surface into your seating area in the event of a crash or malfunction
of a race vehicle. Please ask to change your seating if you do not desire to
ASSUME THE RISK OF SERIOUS INJURY."

The envelope is opened by North's younger brother, who does not pay any attention to the envelope and discards it after removing the tickets. During the race a car crashes into the wall in front of North's seat and sprays him with burning gasoline, causing severe injuries. North sues Trona Speedway for negligence for subjecting him to a known danger by seating him and others so close to the racetrack. Trona Speedway denies any liability based upon the warning on the envelope and the known risk that spectators take when attending a race.

At trial, which side should prevail?

Answer:

_____

_____

_____

_____

_____

_____

_____

_____

_____

_____

_____

_____

_____

_____

_____

_____

_____

_____

_____

_____

_____

Practice Quiz

True/False

1. ___ Alma's threat to Henry that she will beat him up tomorrow is not actionable [p. 65]

2. ___ Carl's pulling of Andrew's chair out from underneath him is considered a battery. [p.66]

3. ___ Edna intended to hit Glenda, but instead hit Frank. Glenda does not have a cause of action against Edna, as she was not the intended victim. [p. 66]

4. ___ An attempt by another person to use a living person's name or identity for commercial purposes is not actionable. [p. 67]

5. ___ Moral pressure is grounds for false imprisonment. [p. 66]

6. ___ The tort of conversion can happen when someone who initially was given possession of personal property fails to return it. [p. 79]

7. ___ A person who is the cause of a car accident because he or she fell asleep while driving is not liable for any resulting injuries caused by his or her carelessness as his or her actions were not intentional. [p. 80]

8. ___ Falsely attributing beliefs or acts to another can form the basis of a lawsuit based on invasion of privacy. [p. 67]

9. ___ Forseeability is the general test of proximate cause. [pp. 74-75]

10. ___ Since there have been an increase in malpractice law suits, almost all states have abolished the Good Samaritan laws that relieve medical professionals from liability for injury caused by their ordinary negligence in such circumstance. [p. 77]

11. ___ A breach of a duty of care is a failure to act subjectively. [p. 72]

12. ___ The fireman's rule provides that a fireman may sue the party whose negligence caused the fire for any resulting injuries from putting out the fire. [pp. 77-78]

13. ___ Under the social host liability rule, a social host is not liable for injuries caused by guests who are served alcohol at a social function. [p. 78]

14. ___ The violation of a statute that proximately causes an injury is negligence per se. [p. 76]

15. ___ If a plaintiff knows of and involuntarily enters into or participates in a risky activity that results in injury, the law acknowledges that the plaintiff assumed the risk involved. [p. 80]

16. ___ Under a jurisdiction that adopts the doctrine of partial comparative negligence, a plaintiff may recover damages that are apportioned according to his or her fault. [p. 81]

17. ___ Good Samaritan laws protect medical professionals from liability for injury caused by their intentional conduct. [p. 77]

18. ___ The tort of intentional misrepresentation is also known as fraud or deceit. [p. 68]

19. ___ Lisa told Ralph that Stella, a famous singer, ate her lunch from the garbage receptacle outside of a famous Hollywood restaurant. The statement was false. Ralph thereafter told the establishment where Stella was currently singing. Thereafter Stella was fired. Since the statement was not in writing such as a newspaper, magazine, or a book, Stella will not be able to sue Ralph. [p. 67]

20. ___ Abel rescued Timmy from a fire deliberately caused by Horace. As a result of the rescue, Abel became injured. Abel may now sue Horace. [p. 78]

Multiple Choice

21. A rule that is applied to even wedding receptions whereby the host is liable for injuries caused by guests who are served alcohol is known as [p. 78]
    a. the danger invites rescue doctrine.
    b. res ipsa loquitur.
    c. the social host liability rule.
    d. battery.

22. Which of the following would the concept of utmost care be best applied to? [p. 78]
    a. a store owner to a passerby on the street
    b. a guest at a small motel in the middle of nowhere
    c. a guest at a large international hotel in Philadelphia
    d. a gas meter reader at a home

23. Which of the following are considered to be superseding or intervening acts that would act as a defense to liability in a negligence cause of action? [p. 79]
    a. a lightening bolt
    b. an avalanche of snow
    c. a crime that causes additional injury
    d. all of the above

24. What would be the best defense Lucy could use if Ethyl knowingly and voluntarily climbed into Lucy's backyard and injured herself on a trampoline that had a sign posted that read, "Warning, Broken…Do Not Use" posted on it? [p. 80]
    a. That Ethyl was intentionally causing Lucy emotional distress.
    b. That Ethyl was not flexible enough to be on the trampoline in the first place.
    c. That Ethyl assumed the risk of injury.
    d. That Ethyl was too heavy for the trampoline to withstand her weight.

25. Under the last clear chance rule, what duty does the defendant have a duty to do? [p. 81]
    a. He or she has a duty to save whoever is in danger.
    b. He or she has a duty to avoid an accident, if at all possible.
    c. He or she does not have a duty.
    d. He or she has a duty to look out for him or herself.

26. If two or more individuals are liable for negligently causing the plaintiff's injuries, both or all can be held liable to the plaintiff if each of their acts is a [p. 74]
    a. proximate cause of plaintiff's injuries.
    b. substantial factor in causing the plaintiff's injuries.
    c. inconsequential cause of plaintiff's injuries.
    d. none of the above

27. A bystander who witnesses the injury or death of a loved one that is caused by another's negligent conduct may bring a cause of action against that individual for [p. 76]
    a. negligent death.
    b. intentional infliction of emotional distress.
    c. battery.
    d. negligent infliction of emotional distress.

28. Liability for a professional who breaches the reasonable professional standard of care is known as [p. 75]
    a. negligence per se.
    b. res ipsa loquitur.
    c. professional malpractice.
    d. social host liability.

29. Joe is determined to be 25 percent negligent in a case he brought against Myra when Myra hit him in the car that she was driving. What dollar amount would Joe recover in a jurisdiction that the jury awarded $100,000 and who applies pure comparative negligence? [p. 81]
    a. Joe would recover nothing as his negligence would be viewed as contributory.
    b. Joe would recover all of the $100,000 that the jury awarded.
    c. Joe would recover $25,000, as he was 25 percent negligent.
    d. Joe would recover $75,000, as his negligence would be a factor in apportioning the dollar amount awarded by the jury.

30. If Dr. Goodman sees Sally D. Victim laying helplessly in the line of traffic and decides to render aid, but, in doing so causes her ankle to be bruised, which statute will relieve him of liability for Sally's injuries? [p. 77]
    a. assumption of the risk
    b. dram shop acts
    c. good Samaritan law
    d. strict liability

31. Which of the following torts would the activities of crop dusting, blasting, and burning fields be best categorized under? [p. 81]
    a. intentional infliction of emotional distress
    b. battery
    c. negligence
    d. strict liability

32. If you invite a friend over for dinner, this person would be considered an [p. 78]
    a. old acquaintance.
    b. invitee.
    c. interested licensee.
    d. intervening event.

33. A person who has no permission or right to be on another's property is known as a [p. 78]
    a. family member.
    b. licensee.
    c. trespasser.
    d. common carrier.

34. Under the doctrine of pure comparative negligence, [p. 81]
    a. the plaintiff must be less than 50 percent responsible for causing his or her own injuries in order to recover damages.
    b. the plaintiff is barred from recovery of damages.
    c. the plaintiff's damages are apportioned according to fault.
    d. the plaintiff's damages are assessed if the plaintiff did not assume the risk.

35. Damages that are awarded to deter the defendant from similar conduct in the future, and to set an example for others as well as punish the defendant are known as [p. 65]
    a. compensatory damages.
    b. nominal damages.
    c. actual damages.
    d. punitive damages.

36. What must a plaintiff suffer in order to recover monetary damages for the defendant's negligence? [p. 81]
    a. ordinary negligence
    b. personal injury or damage to his or her property
    c. emotional distress
    d. extreme and outrageous conduct

37. Jolie, who sells magazines from door to door, would be considered a [p. 78]
    a. very industrious person.
    b. guest.
    c. trespasser.
    d. licensee.

38. Public figures must show actual malice when bringing a cause of action for defamation.
    Which definition best describes what actual malice is? [p. 68]
    a. ordinary negligence
    b. intent to make a false statement
    c. knowing and with reckless disregard for the statement's falsity
    d. a breach of the duty of care

39. Rana owns a dog grooming business which she bought from Sarah. Sarah opened up a dog
    photography studio a few doors down as well as a mobile grooming service. As Sarah
    watched outside of her business door, she kept thinking how she could be doing a better job
    on the dogs and that the dog grooming shop would turn out better cuts and cleaner looking
    dogs if she was still there. Sarah began calling her former customers and told them that
    Rana was bathing their dogs in dirty water. Thereafter, Rana received twenty calls
    indicating that the customers wanted to cancel their appointments. Rana found out about
    what Sarah was saying and she now wants to sue her.
    What is Rana's best cause of action? [p. 68]
    a. breach of the transferred intent doctrine
    b. violation of the merchant protection statute
    c. trade libel.
    d. all of the above

40. The intentional mental or physical confinement of another without consent or legal
    privilege defines which tort? [p. 66]
    a. shopkeeper's privilege
    b. false imprisonment
    c. defamation
    d. misrepresentation

Short Answer

41. Which negligence defense says that a plaintiff who is partially at fault for his or her own
    injury cannot recover against the negligent defendant? [p. 81]

    _____

    _____

42. What duty does Al, the owner of Purple Acres Farm owe to trespassers on his property?
    [p. 70]

    _____

    _____

43. What type of duty is owed to a vacuum cleaner salesperson if they come onto an individual's property? [p. 70]

_____
_____
_____

44. Why are laypersons not trained in CPR not protected by Good Samaritan statutes? [p.77]

_____
_____
_____

45. What is the difference between slander and libel? [p. 67]

_____
_____
_____

46. List the elements for the tort of intentional misrepresentation. [p. 68]

_____
_____
_____

47. What must a plaintiff show in order to succeed in a cause of action for disparagement? [p. 68]

_____
_____
_____

48. Briefly explain the doctrine of transferred intent. [p. 66]

_____
_____
_____

49. Harry was walking down the street in his home town when a bowling ball was dropped from one of the hotel windows and hit him. In order to establish a case based on res ipsa loquitur, what elements must he show? [p. 76]

_____
_____

50. If Fredrick arrives at Eloise's house with the intent to sell her his famous chocolate cheesecake, and a roof shingle falls on his head while he is standing on Eloise's front porch, what duty has Eloise breached? [p.78]

_____

Answers to Refresh Your Memory

1. a civil lawsuit [p. 65]
2. punish [p.65]
3. apprehension [p. 65]
4. transferred intent [p. 66]
5. unauthorized profits; injunction [p. 67]

6. slander [p. 67]
7. misappropriation, publicity [p. 67]
8. invasion of the right to privacy [p. 67]
9. battery [p. 66]
10. until a person dies [p.67]
11. causation in fact, proximate cause [p. 74]
12. professional malpractice [p. 75]
13. thing speaks for itself [p. 76]
14. danger invites rescue [p. 78]
15. superceding [p. 79]
16. Owners and renters owe a duty of ordinary care to all persons who enter upon the property. [p. 78]
17. A failure to act as a reasonable person would act. [p. 72]
18. No, Connie will not be liable under the guest statute. [p. 77]
19. strict liability [p. 81]
20. Courts consider the attentiveness of the parties and the amount of time each had to respond to the situation. [p. 81]

Critical Thought Exercise Model Answer

The tort of negligence occurs when someone suffers injury because of another's failure to exercise the standard of care that a reasonable person would exercise in similar circumstances. The operator of a facility where a sporting event takes place has a duty to provide safe seating for the spectators unless the risk of injury is assumed and accepted by the spectators. Spectators at a baseball game assume the risk that a ball may be hit into the stands and strike them. Spectators at a hockey game do not assume this same risk because pucks are not usually hit high enough over the protective glass to strike spectators. A plaintiff, who voluntarily enters into a risky situation, knowing the risk involved, will not be allowed to recover. This is the defense of assumption of risk. The requirements of this defense are (1) knowledge of the risk and (2) voluntary assumption of the risk. If North had actually been given knowledge of the risk, he may have voluntarily assumed that risk by sitting close to the racetrack. However, six tickets were placed in one envelope that was opened by someone other than North. Trona Speedway cannot argue that North voluntarily assumed a risk for which he was not given notification. The knowledge of risk may be implied from the general knowledge of spectators at a particular type of event, such as baseball. There is no indication that North or any other spectator would know of the danger associated with sitting in a seat for which a ticket was sold. Because North did not assume the risk of being injured by burning gasoline while a spectator at the race, Trona is still liable for negligence.

Answers to Practice Quiz

True/False

1. True   Future threats are not actionable.
2. True   If an injury results, there does not need to be direct physical contact to prove a battery.
3. False   Under the transferred intent doctrine, it is the intent to do the act, not the intent to hit a particular victim that establishes liability.

4. False   Misappropriating a living person's name or identity for commercial gain is actionable under the tort of misappropriation of the right to publicity.

5. False   Moral grounds and threats of future harm are not considered to be false imprisonment.

6. True   When the true owner of property is deprived of the use and enjoyment of his or her personal property by another taking over such property and exercising ownership rights over it, this is known as conversion of personal property. The failure to return borrowed property is also considered conversion.

7. False   The unintentional tort of negligence bases liability for harm on that which is a foreseeable consequence of his or her actions. Therefore, it is foreseeable that injuries may result from a driver who is asleep at the wheel. Under the doctrine of negligence, intent has no applicability.

8. True   Falsely attributing beliefs or acts to another can form the basis of a lawsuit based on invasion of privacy.

9. True   Proximate cause is determined by forseeability, which places a limitation on liability.

10. False   Nearly all states have passed Good Samaritan laws that relieve medical professionals from liability for injury caused by their ordinary negligence in such circumstances.

11. False   A breach of a duty of care is a failure to act as a reasonable person would.

12. False   A fireman may not sue a party whose negligence caused the fire he or she was injured in while putting out the fire.

13. False   A social host is liable for injuries caused by guests who are served alcohol at a social function.

14. True   Violation of a statute that causes injury is negligence per se.

15. False   The plaintiff must know and voluntarily enter into or participate in a risky activity that causes injury before the court will find that the plaintiff assumed the risk involved.

16. False   The doctrine of partial comparative negligence states that a plaintiff must be less than fifty percent responsible for causing his or her injuries in order to recover under this theory.

17. False   Good Samaritan laws only protect medical professionals from liability for their ordinary negligence, not for injuries that are intentionally caused.

18. True   The statement as written is true.

19. False   False, Stella will be able to bring a cause of action for slander for the defamatory statement that Ralph made about her. The untrue statement does not need to appear in a newspaper, magazine, or book.

20. True   Under the "danger invites rescue" doctrine, a rescuer who is injured while going to someone's rescue can sue the person who caused the dangerous situation.

Multiple Choice

21. C   C is the correct answer as the social host liability rule holds that a host is liable for injuries caused by guests who are served alcohol. Further, weddings, birthdays, and the like have been held to fall within the realm of this rule. Answer A is incorrect as the danger invites rescue doctrine pertains to rescuers who are injured while going to someone's rescue and their ability to recover for damages that occurred as a result of the rescue. This doctrine does not apply to the situation as presented in the question. Answer B is incorrect, as res ipsa loquitur is inapplicable since the question has narrowed down who is to be responsible as opposed to determining who is responsible for an act that speaks for itself. Answer D is incorrect as the liability of a social host who serves an individual alcohol who later injures another is not the same as a battery. A battery is the

harmful or offensive touching of another without consent or legal privilege, which has nothing to do with serving someone too much alcohol.

22. C   Answer C is the correct answer as the concept of utmost care is applied on a case-by-case basis. As such, a large international hotel in Philadelphia would owe the utmost care to its guests as it would have more responsibility toward safety in light of its hierarchy in the hotel/inn world. Answer A is incorrect, as a general duty of care is all that is owed by a store owner to a passerby on the street. Answer B is incorrect, because even though a small motel in the middle of nowhere could arguably be said to be an innkeeper, of which a higher duty of care is owed, the reality is that with a larger hotel operation, such as that which was given in C, it would not owe as much care in a motel in the middle of nowhere where perhaps not as many guests stay in the facility. Answer D is incorrect, as a gas meter reader at a home is an invitee onto an individual's land. As such, the only duty that is owed is a general duty of care as opposed to an utmost duty of care.

23. D   Answer D is the correct answer as a person is liable only for foreseeable events. Answers A, B, and C are all superseding, intervening acts that limit or cut off liability thereby provide a defense to liability in a negligence cause of action.

24. C   Answer C is correct as assumption of the risk would be Lucy's best defense since Ethyl knowingly and voluntarily assumed the risk of being injured even after she read the sign that was posted "Warning, Do Not Use" on the trampoline. Answer A is incorrect, as intentional infliction of emotional distress is a cause of action, not a defense. Answers B and D are incorrect as neither of these assertions have a bearing on potential defenses that Lucy may want to use.

25. B   Answer B is correct, as the defendant has a duty to avoid an accident if at all possible under the last clear chance rule. Answer A is incorrect, as there is no such duty to save whoever is in danger under the last clear chance rule. Answer C is incorrect, as the defendant does have a duty as was stated in answer B. Answer D is an incorrect statement of law and is therefore wrong.

26. B   Answer B is the correct answer as two or more individuals can be held liable to the plaintiff if each of their negligent acts is a substantial factor in causing the plaintiff's injuries. Answer A is incorrect as proximate cause is only one of the two types of causation that must be shown before liability can be established. Answer C is incorrect as it is an untrue statement. Answer D is incorrect for the reasons given above.

27. D   Answer D is correct as some jurisdictions have allowed the tort of emotional distress to include the negligent infliction of emotional distress of which the question addresses emotional distress as a result of a negligent act. Answer A is incorrect as death may result from a negligent act; however, there is no such thing as negligent death. Answer B is incorrect as negligent conduct is involved and not intentional. Answer C is incorrect as battery is an intentional tort and the facts indicate that negligent conduct is involved.

28. C   Answer C is correct, as the breach of the reasonable professional standard of care is known as professional malpractice. Answer A is incorrect as negligence per se involves the violation of a statute that was designed to prevent the type of injury suffered. Answer B is incorrect as res ipsa loquitor refers to an instrumentality that was in the control of the defendant that negligently caused another's injuries. Answer D is incorrect as this rule allows for social host liability for injuries caused by guests who are served too much alcohol at a social function.

29. D   Answer D is correct as jurisdictions applying the legal concept of pure comparative negligence apportion the amount of an award based upon the amount of negligence apportioned to the plaintiff. In this case, since Joe was determined to be 25 percent negligent, that amount was deducted from the overall award of $100,000. Hence Joe would be entitled to $100,000 less $25,000 for his negligence, thereby giving him a recovery of $75,000. Answer A is incorrect in a jurisdiction applying principles of pure

comparative negligence. Answer B is incorrect as Joe would not be able to recover all of the $100,000 awarded by the jury, as he is in a jurisdiction applying pure comparative negligence and his negligence was determined to be 25 percent or worth $25,000. Answer C is incorrect as it does not make sense to give Joe $25,000 because he was 25 percent negligent, especially when the jury award was $100,000.

30. C   Answer C is correct, as most states have passed Good Samaritan laws that relieve professionals of liability for injuries caused by their ordinary negligence. If the court finds that Sally's bruised ankle was a result of Dr. Goodman's ordinary negligence, then he will be relieved of liability. Answer A is incorrect as the defense of assumption of the risk has no applicability as Sally did not knowingly and voluntarily assume the risk that her ankle would be bruised by Dr. Goodman. Answer B is incorrect as dram shop acts refer to the civil liability that can be assessed to taverns and bartenders for injuries caused to or by patrons who are served too much alcohol. Answer D is incorrect as strict liability refers to liability without fault. Dr. Goodman's actions would not be considered a hazardous activity to be able to qualify under a strict liability theory.

31. D   Answer D is correct as it provides what many state laws include when a nonpaying guest in an automobile is injured as a result of the driver's ordinary negligence. Answer A is incorrect as this refers to the danger invites rescue doctrine, not the law under a guest statute. Answer B is incorrect as even though it is a true statement under the fireman's rule, it has no applicability under a guest statute. Answer C is incorrect this refers to liability under the social host liability rule and not under a guest statute.

32. B   Answer B is correct as an invitee is one who has been expressly or impliedly invited onto the owner's premises for the mutual benefit of both parties of which dinner would qualify as such. Answer A is incorrect as there are no legal definitions to determine the status of an old acquaintance. Answer C is incorrect as an invitee is one who for his or her own benefit enters onto the property of another with the express or implied consent of the owner. Answer D is incorrect as an intervening event is not a proper description of an individual who has been invited for dinner.

33. C   Answer C is correct, as a trespasser is an individual who does not have consent or legal privilege to enter onto the land of another. Answer A is incorrect as there is not any indication by the vague description weather or not the member had permission to be on the premises. Answer B is incorrect as a licensee usually has express or implied permission to enter onto the land of another. Answer D is incorrect as a common carrier is not an individual and therefore is not applicable to the question.

34. C   Answer C is correct as pure comparative negligence apportions the plaintiff's damages according to the percentage that he or she was at fault. Answer A is incorrect as this defines partial comparative negligence. Answer B is incorrect as this refers to contributory negligence. Answer D is incorrect as the plaintiff's assumption of the risk is a separate defense from comparative negligence.

35. D   Answer D is correct as the question addresses punitive damages. Answer A is incorrect as compensatory damages are given to make the individual whole again. Answer B is incorrect as nominal damages are given as a matter of principle. Answer C is incorrect as actual damages are assessed in terms of what the plaintiff's true injuries were.

36. B   Answer B is correct since even though a defendant's act may have breached a duty of care that was owed to the plaintiff, the plaintiff still needs to show that he or she has suffered an injury. Answer A is incorrect as an individual may not suffer ordinary negligence. Answer C is incorrect as emotional distress is not a requisite in a negligence action. Answer D is incorrect as extreme and outrageous conduct is not an element in a negligence action. However, it may be required in a cause of action for emotional distress.

37. D   Answer D is correct as a magazine salesperson would be considered a licensee since he or she enters onto others' land for his or her own benefit. Though answer A may be true, it is incorrect as there is no basis in law or fact for this answer. Answer B is incorrect as a guest would be an invitee who enters onto another's land for the mutual benefit of both parties. Answer C is incorrect as a trespasser has no implied invitation whereas a licensee does.

38. C   Answer C is correct as it provides the correct definition of malice which defines the required behavior as being more than a mere intentional untrue statement about the plaintiff. Answer A is incorrect as malice has the facet of knowledge associated with it as opposed to negligence, which does not. Answer B is incorrect as a public figure must show a reckless disregard for a statement's falsity, not just a mere intent to make a false statement as would be the case in someone who is not a famous figure or personality. Answer D is incorrect as a breach of the duty of care is an element required in a negligence action not a defamation cause of action.

39. D   Answer D is correct as palming off is another way of phrasing unfair competition, which is what the question describes. Answer A is incorrect as slander is oral defamation, which has nothing to do with the question presented. Answer B is incorrect as libel is written defamation that also has nothing to do with the question presented. Answer C is incorrect as shopkeeper's privilege concerns reasonable grounds, reasonable time, and a reasonable manner for detaining someone on a business premises.

40. B   Answer B is correct as the question provides the correct definition for false imprisonment. Answer A is incorrect as the shopkeeper's privilege may be asserted as a defense to a false imprisonment cause of action not as a definition of false imprisonment as given in the question. Answer C is incorrect as defamation concerns the publishing of a false statement to a third party about another individual, not the mental or physical confinement of another without consent or legal privilege. Answer D is incorrect as misrepresentation is fraud which is associated with the intentional misrepresentation of material fact that is made with knowledge of the statement's falsity and thereafter relied upon by the individual to whom the statement was made.

Short Answer

41. contributory negligence
42. Al owes a duty not to willfully or wantonly injure a trespasser.
43. A duty of ordinary care is owed to licensees, such as a vacuum cleaner salesperson, as he or she is on another's premises for his or her own benefit.
44. Actual cause is the factual cause of plaintiff's injuries whereas proximate cause is the legal cause of the plaintiff's injuries. Proximate cause is based on forseeablity of the injury based upon the defendant's actions.
45. Only medical professionals are protected under the Good Samaritan statutes. This type of statute encourages assistance from medical professional who are trained in medical procedures such as CPR.
46. The elements for the tort of intentional misrepresentation are given below.
    a) A misrepresentation of a material fact is made to the plaintiff.
    b) This misrepresentation was intentionally made.
    c) The defendant had knowledge of the statement's falsity when he or she made it.
    d) The plaintiff justifiably relied upon the misrepresentation.
    e) The plaintiff suffered damages as a result of the misrepresentation.

47. In order to be successful in a cause of action for disparagement, the plaintiff must show:
    a) The defendant made an untrue statement about the plaintiff's products or services, etc.;
    b) the defendant published this untrue statement to another individual; and
    c) the defendant knew the statement that was made was false; and
    d) the defendant made the statement maliciously intending to hurt the plaintiff.
48. The doctrine of transferred intent transfers the wrongdoer's intent from the original target to the actual victim of the act.
49. The plaintiff must show that the defendant had exclusive control of the instrumentality or situation that caused the plaintiff's injury and the injury would not have ordinarily occurred "but for" someone's negligence.
50. The following elements must be shown in order to be successful in a cause of action for Intentional Interference with Contractual Relations:
    a) An enforceable, valid contract between the contracting parties.
    b) The third party must know about the contract.
    c) The third party induced the breach of the contract.

Chapter 6

STRICT LIABILITY AND
PRODUCT LIABILITY

Chapter Overview

This chapter discusses the multiple tort principles that are available to injured parties as a result of defectively made products. Negligence, misrepresentation, and strict liability are the standard causes of action that are available. Many individuals including purchasers, users, lessees, and even innocent bystanders who are injured by a defective product may seek recovery under the legal theory called products liability. This chapter will help you understand how manufactures, sellers, lessors, and others involved with the defective product may be held liable for the injuries caused to others who were injured by the product. Emphasis is placed upon the duties that are required of manufacturers as well as others in the chain of command.

Objectives

Upon completion of the exercises in this chapter, you should be able to:
1. Differentiate between the different legal theories surrounding product liability.
2. Discuss what strict liability is.
3. Determine which parties may be held liable for injuries that are a result of a defective product.
4. Compare and contrast the differences among manufacture, designs and packaging defects.
5. Compare and contrast defects associated with a failure to warn and a failure to provide sufficient instructions.
6. Recognize and be able to state applicable defenses in product liability lawsuits.
7. State and understand what damages are available in a product liability action.
8. Differentiate between contributory and comparative negligence.
9. Discuss the doctrine of market share liability.

Practical Application

You should be able establish a basis for a product liability lawsuit by identifying the different types of legal theories as well as their elements. Additionally you should be able to identify the proper party to assess liability against, identify and apply potential defenses, and be familiar with the types of damages that are available.

Helpful Hints

This chapter is not only a good chapter for reviewing the concepts of negligence and misrepresentation that you learned in the last chapter, but it is also one that you can utilize to build upon your knowledge of torts. It is important to learn the duties that are owed by those who manufacture as well as sell or lease products that are defectively made so that you will be able to select the appropriate cause of action to bring against the proper party. In the Study Tips section that follows, the necessary elements for the causes of action in a product liability lawsuit as well as the proper parties whom suit should be brought against are listed under the same. By studying the causes of action in this manner, it will assist you in committing the entire concept of liability to memory.

Study Tips

Products liability

The liability of manufacturers, sellers, and others for the injuries caused by defective production.

Negligence and Fault

In order to be successful in a negligence action based on products liability, the plaintiff must first establish that a duty was owed and thereafter breached by the defendant. There are several types of duties that are owed, any of which can be breached alone or in combination with the others. These duties as well as who owes the duty (which is listed in parenthesis) include:

- ✓ the duty to assemble the product safely. (the manufacturer)
- ✓ the duty to properly design the product. (the manufacturer)
- ✓ the duty to inspect or test the product. (the manufacturer)
- ✓ the duty to properly package the product. (the manufacturer)
- ✓ the duty to warn of any dangerous propensities that the product may have. (the manufacturer and possibly the retailer and/or wholesaler)

Of course a breach of any of these duties gives rise to a negligence cause of action of which the plaintiff must demonstrate that the defendant was the actual as well as proximate cause of his or her injuries. The interesting part of this aspect is that there may be more than one defendant who is being sued for negligence, and as such, each may assert that the other was a supervening act that breaks the chain of proximate causation thereby making him or her the indirect cause of the plaintiff's injuries.

- ✓ The plaintiff will have a difficult time in proving a negligence cause of action based upon product liability as it is often a challenge determining who was negligent. Any one of the parties that suit will be brought against could have caused the plaintiff's injuries. The potential parties in a negligence cause of action may include the manufacturer, the retailer, a possible wholesaler, and maybe even a repairperson. Any one of these parties could singly or together have caused the plaintiff's injuries.

Misrepresentation

A plaintiff bringing a lawsuit based on misrepresentation will do so because of the fraud associated with the quality of the product. Only those who relied on the misrepresentation and thereafter suffered injury may bring a cause of action under this tort.

- ✓ Though misrepresentation is not the most common cause of action of which to base a product liability action on, it can be utilized if the plaintiff shows the seller or lessor made a misrepresentation concerning the product's quality or did not reveal a defect in the product. Manufacturers, sellers, and lessors are potential defendants for this type of cause of action.

Strict Liability

The basis behind strict liability is to impose liability regardless of whose fault it is. As you learned in the previous chapter, strict liability is often imposed when a defendant is engaged in an ultrahazardous activity. Strict liability is also imposed upon lessors and sellers who are in the business of leasing and selling products. Casual sellers are exempt from the facet of being in the business of leasing and selling products. A casual seller is someone who is not a merchant.

✓ Be careful as strict liability involves products and not services. If the situation involves both, the court will look at the prevalent element in order to determine whether or not strict liability applies.

✓ Who may be liable under a strict liability theory?
All in the Chain of Distribution Are Liable.
All manufacturers, distributors, wholesalers, retailers, lessors, manufacturers of sub-components may be held strictly liable for the injuries caused by the product. Note that if one or more of the parties in the chain of distribution are held liable in a strict liability lawsuit, the parties may seek indemnification by bringing a separate cause of action against the negligent party.

✓ Special notation concerning entrepreneur liability for a defective product - Entrepreneurs may avoid the concern of being named in a product liability lawsuit by taking the cautionary measure of purchasing a products liability insurance policy. This will help minimize or eliminate the costs associated with such a lawsuit. Note that any amount of damages above and beyond what the policy covers will be the responsibility of the business.

✓ Elements in a strict liability cause of action
First, a defect must be shown. Several types of defects exist.

Manufacturing defect – A failure on the manufacturer's part to properly assemble, test, or check the product's quality.

Design defect – This defect involves the application of a risk-utility analysis. The court will weigh the gravity of the danger from the design, the likelihood that injury will result from the design, and the availability as well as expense of producing a safer different design against the utility of the design. The crashworthiness doctrine falls under this category of defect, as the courts have held that automobile manufacturers have a duty when designing automobiles to take into account the possibility of a second collision from within the automobile. A failure to protect occupants from foreseeable dangers may result in a lawsuit based upon strict liability.

Packaging defect – A manufacturer has a duty to design and provide safe packages for their products so that they are either tamperproof or indicate if they have been tampered with. This type of defect has particular application in the pharmaceutical industry.

Failure to warn is viewed as a defect – Manufacturers as well as sellers have a duty to warn users about the dangerous aspects. The warning must be clear and conspicuous on the product. A failure to warn may subject those in the chain of distribution to a lawsuit based on strict liability.

Miscellaneous defects – There are other defects that can give rise to a strict liability cause of action, included of which are the failure to safely assemble a product, failure to provide adequate instructions for the safe use or assembly of a product, failure to adequately test a product or select proper component parts or materials, and failure to properly certify the product.

✓ Defenses to a product liability lawsuit
There are many *defenses* that may have applicability in a product liability lawsuit.

Supervening Event – No liability exists if the product is materially altered or modified after it leaves the seller's possession and the modification or alteration causes the injury.

Generally Known Dangers – If a product is generally known to be dangerous and a seller fails to warn of this, then liability may attach. However, placing a safety feature on a generally known dangerous product may assist in limiting or absolving liability.

Government Contractor Defense – A Government contract must show that the government provided precise specifications for the product and the contract did in fact conform to those specifications. Further that the government was warned by the contractor of any known product defects or dangers.

Assumption of the Risk – Even though a defendant may utilize this defense by showing that the plaintiff knew and appreciated the risk involved and voluntarily assumed the risk, this defense is not widely used.

Misuse of Product – The main aspect the defendant must prove is that the plaintiff has abnormally misused the product and that such misuse was unforeseeable. If the misuse was foreseeable, the seller of the product will remain liable.

Statute of Limitations and Repose – A failure to bring a cause of action within the allowed time frame will relieve the defendant of liability. Many jurisdictions state that the statute of limitations begins to run when the plaintiff suffers an injury. Other states feel this is unfair to the seller and have created statutes of repose that limit the liability a seller has by setting a time frame in terms of years from when the product was initially sold.

Contributory and Comparative Negligence – If a person is found to have been negligent in contributing to his or her own injuries, this will not prevent him or her from recovering in a strict liability cause of action as it would under an ordinary negligence cause of action. Further, the courts have also applied the defense of comparative negligence thereby apportioning the damages based upon the negligence of each of the parties.

✓ Damages in a strict liability action include
  * personal injury with some jurisdictions limiting the dollar amount of the award.
  * property damage, which is recoverable in most jurisdictions.
  * lost income which is recoverable in some jurisdictions.
  * punitive damages are recoverable if the plaintiff can show that the defendant intentionally injured him or her or acted maliciously for his or her safety.

Refresh Your Memory

The following exercise will enable you to refresh your memory on the rules and principles presented to you in this chapter. Read each question twice and place your answer in the blanks provided. Review the chapter material for any question you miss or are unable to remember.

1. Intentional misrepresentation is when a seller or a lessor fraudulently misrepresents the _____ of a product and a buyer is _____ thereby.

2. A person who sells a defective product to a neighbor in a casual sale is not _____ _____ if the product causes injury.

3. In hybrid transactions involving both services and products, the _____ element of the transaction dictates whether strict liability applies.

4. Most jurisdictions have statutorily or judicially extended the protection of strict liability to include _____.

5. Monetary damages that are awarded to punish a defendant who either intentionally or recklessly injured the plaintiff are known as _____damages.

6. Give two ways a product may be defective. _____ and _____.

7. Product design is evaluated by applying a _____-_____ analysis.

8. A defect that occurs when a manufacturer does not provide detailed directions for safe assembly and use of a product is a failure to _____ _____ instructions.

9. A defense that apportions damages based upon the negligence of each of the parties is known as _____ _____.

10. Liability may attach to a seller if a product is generally known to be dangerous and the seller fails to _____ of this danger.

11. Sellers are not strictly liable for failing to warn of generally _____ _____.

12. Products must be designed to protect against _____ misuse.

13. Automobile manufacturers have a duty to take into account the possibility of a second collision within the automobile. This is known as the _____ doctrine.

14. If a product is materially altered or modified after it leaves the seller's possession, then the defense of _____ _____ would be applicable.

15. If a seller or lessor did not reveal a defect in a product, a plaintiff may bring a cause of action based on _____.

Critical Thought Exercise

Bruce Owens bought a Chevrolet Suburban from General Motors Corp. (GMC). Four years later, Owens crashed into the rear of another car while commuting to work. The speed of Owens' vehicle at the time of the crash was estimated to be less than 35 miles per hour. A properly functioning seatbelt will restrain the driver from impacting the steering wheel and the windshield during a crash at 40 miles per hour. During the crash, the seatbelt that Owens was properly wearing broke away from its anchor, causing Owens to be thrust against the steering wheel and into the windshield. Owens received a fractured skull, broken ribs, and a fractured left ankle. Owens sued GMC, Chevrolet, and the dealership that sold the vehicle to him. Owens claimed in his suit that because the seat belt broke, the defendants were strictly liable for his injuries. Investigation determined that the seatbelt anchor was both inadequate to sustain the forces involved in restraining a person during a crash, and had been installed in a manner that increased the likelihood of failure during a crash.

Are the defendants strictly liable to Owens?

Answer:

_____

_____

_____

_____

_____

_____

_____

_____

_____

_____

_____

_____

_____

_____

_____

_____

_____

_____

Practice Quiz

True/False

1. ___ A statute of repose is one that requires an injured person to bring an action within a certain number of years from the time he or she was injured by the defective product. [p. 98]

2. ___ A person who is partially responsible for causing his or her own injuries is said to be contributorily negligent. [p. 98]

3. ___ A supervening event absolves all prior sellers in the chain of distribution from strict liability. [p. 89]

4. ___ Drug manufacturers have a duty to design and provide safe packages for their products. [p. 95]

5. ___ Abnormal misuse of a product no longer relieves the seller of liability. [p. 96]

6. ___ Not everyone in the chain of distribution of a defective product may be held strictly liable for the injuries caused by the product. [p. 89]

7. ___ There must also be privity of contract between the plaintiff and the defendant in a strict liability cause of action. [p. 91]

8. ___ Bystanders are also afforded the protection of strict liability. [p. 91]

9. ___ A plaintiff may not recover property damage in a strict liability action. [p. 91]

10. ___ All of the parties in the chain of distribution of a defective product are liable for any injury caused by the product even though some of the parties are not responsible. [p. 89]

11. ___ To recover for strict liability, the injured party must not only show the product was defective but also who caused the product to become defective. [p. 91]

12. ___ A defect in manufacture may occur when the manufacturer properly tests a product. [p. 91]

13. ___ Cases involving toys designed with removable parts have supported strict liability cases based upon design defects. [p. 92]

14. ___ A manufacturer and dealer may be subject to strict liability if there is a failure to design the automobile to protect occupants from foreseeable dangers caused by a second collision. [p. 94]

15. ___ Drug manufacturers owe a duty to place their products in containers that are easier for children to open. [p. 95]

Multiple Choice

16. Which of the following would apply to a gun manufacturer? [p. 96]
    a. It would need to warn of the dangerous nature of the gun(s) being sold.
    b. It would be strictly liable for selling a dangerous item like a gun, without placing a warning on the gun(s) it manufacturers.
    c. The defense of generally known dangers acknowledges that certain products such as guns are inherently dangerous and are known to the general population to be so.
    d. all of the above

17. A contractor working for the government is [p. 96]
    a. liable for any defect in a product that occurs as a result of specifications provided by the government.
    b. not liable for any defect in a product that occurs as a result of specifications provided by the government.
    c. liable regardless if he or she is working for the government.
    d. liable if he or she is working on airplanes for the government.

18. Which of the following apply to the defense of assumption of the risk [p. 96]
    a. The plaintiff knew and appreciated the risk involved.
    b. The plaintiff voluntarily assumed the risk.
    c. In reality, this defense is narrowly applied by the courts.
    d. all of the above

19. Under the doctrine of comparative negligence, a plaintiff who is contributorily negligent for his or her injuries is responsible for [p. 98]
    a. a small share of the damages.
    b. a proportional share of the damages.
    c. only the property damage that may have resulted.
    d. replacement of part of the product.

20. If a buyer rides a bike for a short distance using only its back wheels and falls backwards and thereafter hits the concrete, under which of the following would the bicycle manufacturer be held liable for? [p. 96]
    a. The manufacturer is relieved of liability as the buyer has misused the bicycle.
    b. The manufacturer is not relieved of liability as the buyer's misuse was foreseeable.
    c. The manufacturer is relieved of liability, as the buyer's use established contributory negligence.
    b. The manufacturer is not liable to the ultimate user or consumer.

21. Which of the following would not be considered a defect in manufacture? [p. 91]
    a. a failure to properly assemble a product
    b. a failure to place a product in tamperproof packaging
    c. a failure to properly test a product
    d. a failure to adequately check the quality of the product

22. A manufacturer that makes a defective product and thereafter discovers the defect must [p. 97]
    a. notify users and purchasers of the defect and correct the defect.
    b. know and appreciate the risk and voluntarily assume the risk.
    c. file a complaint in accordance with its state's statute of limitations.
    d. prove that the plaintiff has abnormally misused the product.

23. Which doctrine establishes a duty of an automobile manufacturer to design an automobile to account for the possibility of harm from a person's body striking something inside the automobile in case of a car accident? [p. 94]
    a. the collision doctrine
    b. the doctrine of res ipsa loquitur
    c. the negligence per se doctrine
    d. the crashworthiness doctrine

24. Who may be able to recover for his or her injuries as a result of a product's defect? [p. 91]
    a. sellers, lessors, and manufacturers
    b. purchasers, lessees, users, or bystanders
    c. anyone who witnesses the defect causing the injuries
    d. all of the above

25. Drug manufacturers owe a duty to [p. 94]
    a. place their products on shelves out of a child's reach.
    b. provide nicely packaged containers for their drugs.
    c. properly design easy to swallow pills.
    d. place their products in containers that cannot be opened by children.

Short Answer

26. Part of assessing the adequacy of a product's design includes considering the gravity of the _____ imposed by the design. [p.93]

27. Handy Dandy makes a meat slicing machine that contains a sharp blade for thin cuts of meat. What must Handy Dandy and those stores who buy the meat slicing machine do? [p. 94]

    _____

    _____

28. Pillco, a major manufacturer of pain relievers has bottled its capsules in plastic, childproof containers, but has failed to seal foil over the bottle's opening. If someone tampers with any of its bottles and a consumer is injured as a result of the way the pills were contained, what might be one basis for a lawsuit against Pillco? [p. 95]

    _____

29. When does the statute of limitations begin to run in a product liability cause of action? [p. 98]

    _____

    _____

30. A person who is partially responsible for causing his or her own injuries is responsible for a _____ share of the damages under a jurisdiction following the theory of comparative fault. [p. 98]

31. All manufacturers, distributors, wholesalers, retailers, lessors, and subcomponent manufacturers involved in a transaction are known as the _____ _____ _____. [p. 89]

32. If an automobile manufacturer fails to design an automobile to protect the passengers from foreseeable dangers caused by a second collision, the _____ and the _____ are subjected to a lawsuit based on strict liability. [p. 94]

33. If Joan's body is slammed into the dashboard of a car she is riding in which just hit another vehicle, and it is determined that her injuries were caused by the jolting within the car, this is referred to as the [p. 94] _____ _____.

34. If Peter leases a boat and the front end is too weighted from the materials used to construct it thereby causing it to sink its first time in the water, Peter may utilize _____ _____ laws in order to recover for the design defect. [p. 89]

35. A _____ and _____ warning placed on the product protects those in the chain of distribution from strict liability. [p. 94]

36. If a computer manufacturer fails to place instructions on how to put together its brand of computer, and a buyer gets injured from overloading the system due to an improperly installed plug, the consumer may claim that the product defect was the manufacturer's _____ to _____ _____ _____. [p. 96]

37. What is the defense that acknowledges that certain products are inherently dangerous and are known to the general population to be so? [p. 96] _____ _____.

38. An abnormally misused product will _____ the seller of product liability if the use was _____. [p. 96]

39. A limitation of a seller's liability to a certain number of years from the date when the product was first sold is known as a _____ of _____. [p. 96]

40. If a bicycle manufacturer discovers that the front tire is not properly mounted or installed due to a bolt that is improperly made, it must _____ the purchasers and _____ of the defect and _____ the defect. [p. 96]

41. Slimy Sid's Sedans, a used car dealer, represents to Donna Dimsy that the car she is about to buy has a better engine than any brand new car she could find. After she purchases it, the engine blows up on the freeway she is driving on, causing massive burns to 70 percent of Donna's body. What tort can Donna base her cause of action against Slimy Sid's Sedans? [p. 89]

_____

_____

42. The statute of repose begins to run when [p. 98]

   _____ .

43. What type of event will relieve a manufacturer of liability in a products liability cause of action? [p. 97] _____ _____ .

44. Michael Lemmone is a car salesperson who sold a new sport utility vehicle to Suzy Victim. He failed to tell Suzy about the vehicle being in a car accident that caused substantial damage to the rear axle and to the transmission. Suzy bought the vehicle relying upon Michael's statement that the vehicle she was buying was in perfect condition. She drove it home on the freeway and the transmission fell out causing Suzy to crash into a ditch on the side of the road. What cause of action may Suzy bring against Michael Lemmone? [p. 89]

   _____

   _____

45. Paul is a worker on an assembly line for a treadmill manufacturer where he is responsible for putting the safety handrails on each machine. The demand for the treadmills has been high and as such, the production line speed has increased dramatically. Paul becomes sloppy trying to keep up with the speed of production and fails to tighten down the safety rail on a machine that Fanny Fitness purchases. Fanny injures herself after losing her balance on the treadmill when the safety handrail detached itself from the machine. What duty has Paul breached? The duty to _____ the _____ carefully. [p. 91]

46. Roger is in a hurry to leave the sewing machine factory where he works and has one more sewing machine to place the bobbin holder in. Since he is unable to find the small type of screw he usually uses, he opts to use a different, less efficient screw to put the bobbin holder in. When Patti purchases the machine and begins to sew, the screw from the bobbin holder pops out and hits Patti in the eye. What type of defect may Patti claim exists in her products liability action? [p. 113]

   _____

   _____

   _____

47. If Marie does not bring a cause of action within the statute of limitations provided by her state, this will _____ the defendant of _____ . [p. 98]

48. Plaintiffs may allege _____ product _____ in one lawsuit for strict liability. [p. 91]

49. Strict liability applies only to _____ , not _____ . [p. 91]

50. Strict liability does not require the injured person prove that the defendant _____ a _____ of _____ . [p. 91]

Answers to Refresh Your Memory

1. quality; injured [p. 89]
2. strictly liable [p. 89]
3. dominant [p. 89]
4. bystanders [p. 91]
5. punitive [p. 91]

6.   manufacture, design [p. 91]   answers will vary
7.   risk-utility [p. 93]
8.   provide adequate [p. 96]
9.   comparative [p. 98]
10.   warn [p. 94]
11.   known dangers [p. 96]
12.   foreseeable [p. 96]
13.   crashworthiness [p. 94]
14.   supervening event [p. 97]
15.   misrepresentation [p 89]

Critical Thought Exercise Model Answer

In order to establish strict liability, Owens must establish the following requirements: (1) *The defendant must sell the product in a defective condition.* The anchor was unable to perform as intended because it was poorly designed and was also installed incorrectly. Either reason makes the product defective. (2) *The defendant was in the business of selling this product.* GMC, Chevrolet, and the dealership are all in the business of selling Suburbans. (3) *The product must be unreasonably dangerous to the user because of its defect.* A vehicle without a safely functioning seatbelt that can properly restrain a passenger during a crash is very dangerous. There is no valid reason for a manufacturer not to install a working seatbelt. (4) *The plaintiff must incur physical injury.* Owens was severely injured. (5) *The defective condition must be the proximate cause of the injury.* We know that Owens was propelled into the steering wheel and windshield because the seatbelt did not restrain him. The speed of the crash was within limits where the seatbelt should have worked properly. (6) *The goods must not have substantially changed from the time of sale to the time of injury.* There are no facts showing any modification to the seatbelt while owned by Owens.

All of the elements needed to establish strict liability for the defective product are present. When a product is defective, as in this case, all defendants in the chain of distribution, from the manufacturer, to the distributor, to the dealer, have joint and several liability for the injury to plaintiff. Owens may recover against all the defendants in this case.

Answers to Practice Quiz

True/False

1. False   This describes a statute of limitations. A statute of repose limits the seller's liability to a certain number of years from the date when the product was first sold.
2. True   A person who is partially responsible for causing his or her own injuries is said to be contributorily negligent.
3. True   A superseding event absolves all prior sellers in the chain of distribution from strict liability.
4. True   Manufacturers of drugs are required to provide packages and containers that are tamper-proof or clearly indicate that they've been tampered with. In other words, they must design and provide safe packages for their products.
5. True   Abnormal misuse of a product does relieve a seller of liability.
6. False   All who are in the chain of distribution are strictly liable. Public policy encourages sellers and lessors to insure against the risk of a strict liability lawsuit.

7. False   Privity of contract is not required between the plaintiff and defendant because strict liability is a tort defense.

8. True   Bystanders are afforded protection in strict liability cases in most state statutes.

9. False   Property damage may be recovered in a majority of jurisdictions.

10. True   Strict liability is imposed irrespective of fault and as such applies to sellers and lessors who are in the business of selling and leasing products.

11. False   The injured party must show that the product was defective; however, he or she need not prove who caused the product to become defective.

12. False   A defect in manufacturer occurs when the manufacturer fails to properly test a product not when the manufacturer properly tests a product.

13. True   Removable parts of toys that could be swallowed by children are among the various types of design defects that have supported strict liability cases.

14. True   The fact that both the manufacturer as well as dealer are in the chain of distribution supports the liability surrounding a design defect under the crashworthiness doctrine.

15. False   Drug manufacturers owe a duty to place their products in containers that cannot be opened by children. These manufacturers are also under a duty to provide packages that are tamperproof or indicative of having been tampered with.

Multiple Choice

16. C   Answer C is correct as the defense of generally known danger does acknowledge that certain products such as guns are inherently dangerous. Answer A is incorrect because it's a generally known danger which the manufacturer does not have to warn the consumer about. Answer B is wrong because a gun manufacturer is not strictly liable for its failure to warn. Answer D is incorrect for the reasons given above.

17. B   Answer B is correct as the government contractor defense provides that a contractor who was provided specifications by the government is not liable for any defect in the product that occurs as a result of those specifications. Answer A is an incorrect statement of law. Answer C is incorrect as it has no application to the government contractor defense. Answer D is incorrect, as it makes no sense whatsoever.

18. D   Answer D is correct, as answers A, B, and C all apply to the defense of assumption of the risk.

19. B   Answer B is correct, as the principle behind comparative negligence is to apportion damages between the plaintiff and the defendant. Answer A is incorrect as this is presuming that the plaintiff's negligence was proportionately less than that of the defendant and that the damages would be reduced only slightly. Answer C is incorrect, as the plaintiff's liability under a comparative negligence statute would include other damages besides property damage as a result of the plaintiff's negligence. Answer D is incorrect as, once again, it is under the assumption that the plaintiff's negligence was as a result of failing to replace a part of the product.

20. B   Answer B is correct, as foreseeable misuse does not relieve the manufacturer of liability and riding a bike on its back wheel would be considered foreseeable misuse by the reasonable person.
Answer A is incorrect because the misuse of the bike was foreseeable. Answer C is incorrect, because regardless of contributory negligence on the part of the buyer, he/she was misusing the bicycle in a foreseeable manner. Answer D is incorrect as it is not a true statement of law.

21. B   Answer B is correct as it describes a defect in packaging as opposed to a defect in manufacture. Answers A, C, and D are incorrect as all state defects in manufacture.

22. A   Answer A is correct as it reiterates what the law requires with regard to notifying consumers and users of defects discovered by the manufacturer. Answer B is incorrect as the explanation for the defense of assumption of the risk does not apply to the duties placed on a manufacturer upon discovery of a defective product it has produced. Answer C is incorrect as the filing of a complaint by a manufacturer who discovered a defect in one of its products is not required to file a complaint as a result of its discovery. Answer D is incorrect as abnormal misuse is a potential defense in a products liability lawsuit, not a requirement of proof upon discovery of a manufacturing defect by the manufacturer.

23. D   Answer D is correct as the crashworthiness doctrine, which is also referred to as the second collision, requires manufacturers to design automobiles with the possibility of a second collision. Answer A is incorrect as being crashworthy and the concept of collision by itself are not synonymous. Answer B is incorrect as res ipsa loquitur means "the thing speaks for itself" and is helpful in establishing negligence in a variety of cases of which the duty to design an automobile taking into account the possibility of harm are contradictory to one another. Answer C is incorrect as negligence per se is also a special negligence doctrine that ha its basis in statutory law that is designed to protect a described class of people against a specific type of act.

24. B   Answer B is correct as purchasers, lessees, users, and bystanders are those who are protected under product liability law. Answer A is incorrect as sellers, lessors, and manufacturers are in the chain of distribution of a product that makes them prone to liability for injuries resulting from a defective product. Answer C is incorrect as witnessing is not the same concept as being injured as a bystander and would therefore not be able to recover based on mere observation of the defect causing injuries. Answer D is incorrect for the reasons given above.

25. D   Answer D is correct as the drug manufacturer has a duty to package its products in tamperproof packaging. Answer A is incorrect, as even though this may be a cautionary measure on the manufacturer's part, it is not a duty that if breached would give rise to a cause of action based on product liability. Answer B is incorrect as the marketing of a manufacturer's drug by use of nicely packaged containers is also not a duty that if breached would give rise to a cause of action based on product liability. Answer C is incorrect as the manufacturer has no duty to properly design easy to swallow pills.

Short Answer

26. danger
27. about the dangerous propensities of their product
28. defect in packaging
29. when the plaintiff suffers injury
30. proportional
31. chain of distribution
32. manufacturer and dealer
33. second collision
34. strict liability
35. proper and conspicuous
36. failure to provide adequate instructions
37. generally known dangers
38. relieve, unforseeable
39. statute of repose
40. notify users and correct
41. intentional misrepresentation
42. the product is first sold

43. intervening event
44. misrepresentation
45. assemble product
46. inadequate selection of component parts
47. relieve liability
48. multiple defects
49. products, services
50. breach of duty of care

Chapter 7

INTELLECTUAL PROPERTY AND INTERNET LAW

Chapter Overview

Intellectual property consists of trade secrets, patents, trademarks, copyrights, and computer law and domain names. The remedies for infringement of the rights that are attached to them are also explored. Additionally, you will become familiar with the protection that is attached to technology based intellectual property.

Objectives

Upon completion of the exercises in this chapter, you should be able to:
1. Explain what intellectual property consists of.
2. Explain the business tort of misappropriating a trade secret.
3. Understand what criminal conduct violates the Economic Espionage Act.
4. Explain the process for obtaining a patent.
5. Discuss how cyber business plans are protected under patent law.
6. Analyze the types of writings afforded protection under copyright laws.
7. Discuss the remedies available for copyright, patent, and trademark infringement.
8. Explain the rights held by computer software designers over their works.
9. Explain the NET Act and its effect on copyright infringement.
10. Explain what changes were made by enacting the Digital Millennium Copyright Act.
11. Compare the differences in trademarks, service marks, and certification marks.
12. Explain what international protection is given to intellectual property rights.

Practical Application

You should be able to distinguish among a copyright, trademark, and patent and determine whether or not an infringement has occurred. Further, you will be more familiar with the various intellectual property acts and what they apply to. This chapter provides a clearer understanding of what is involved in intellectual property and which acts and laws will afford the greatest protection to the creator.

Helpful Hints

The easiest way to study the material is to categorize all of the information and acts in a methodical fashion that is consistent throughout the chapter. The Study Tips section that follows attempts to organize the information for you so that studying becomes more manageable.

Study Tips

Each intellectual topic area is organized in the same fashion so that it becomes habit for you to learn the information in a logical manner. When studying, it will help you to have someone ask you the questions under each heading to determine what you have learned.

Trade Secrets

<u>What is a trade secret?</u> A product, formula, pattern, design compilation of customer data or any other business secret.

<u>What is considered a violation of a trade secret?</u> The defendant, usually an employee, must have obtained the trade secret through unlawful means, such as theft, bribery, etc.

<u>Does an owner of a trade secret have any obligations under the law?</u> Yes, he or she must take all reasonable protections to protect his or her trade secret. If the owner does not protect his or her trade secret, then there is no protection under the law for it.

<u>What laws afford protection of a trade secret?</u>
State unfair competition laws, which may include the Uniform Trade Secrets Act.
The federal Economic Espionage Act of 1996 makes it a federal crime to steal another person's trade secrets.

<u>What may the owner recover if he or she is successful in a trade secret action?</u>
The owner may recover profits, damages, and procure an injunction to stop the offender from using or revealing the trade secret.
Under the Economic Espionage Act, organizations may be fined up to $5 million dollars per criminal act and $10 million if the act benefited a foreign government. Also, individuals may get up to 15 years of prison time per violation increasing to 25 years if the act benefited a foreign government.

Patents

<u>What is required to get a patent?</u> An invention that is novel, useful, and nonobvious.

<u>What types of things can be patented?</u> Processes, machines, improvements of existing machines, compositions of matter, asexually reproduced plants, designs for an article of manufacture, living material invented by a person

<u>How does an individual get a patent?</u> Briefly stated, an individual applies for a patent with the Patent and Trademark Office and is assigned a number. While waiting for approval, the individual may affix the terminology "patent pending" on the thing to be protected.

<u>What other laws are available to help inventors?</u> Under the *American Inventors Protection Act* of 1999, an inventor may file a provisional application with the Patent and Trademark Office pending the final completion and filing of a patent application. The inventor has "provisional rights" for three months pending the filing of a final application.

<u>Federal Law and Patents</u> – The *Federal Patent Statute* protects patented inventions from infringement. There are no state patent laws.

Changes in Patent Laws – In 1994, the General Agreement on Tariffs and Trade extended patent protection from 17 to 20 years. Also, the patent term now begins to run from the date that the application is filed instead of when the patent is issued.

Cyber Business Plans and *financial models* that are used over the Internet are protected by patent law.

Law to be aware of – The *Public Use Doctrine* (also called the one-year "on sale" doctrine) states that a patent may not be granted if the invention was used by the public for more than one year prior to the filing of the patent application. This law encourages timely patent applications.

What may the patent holder recover in a successful patent infringement action? A patent holder may recover money equal to a reasonable royalty rate on the sale of infringed article, damages such as loss of customers, an injunction preventing future infringing action, and an order requiring destruction of the infringing material. If the court finds that the infringement was intentional, then it may award treble the damages.

Copyrights

What can be copyrighted? Only tangible writings that can be physically seen may be copyrighted. This includes books, sermons, greeting cards, jewelry, and glassware.

What is required in order to get a copyright? The work must be the original, tangible work of the author. Notice is not required; however, it is recommended that notice be placed on the work so as to prevent the claim of innocent infringement. Registration with the U.S. Copyright Office is needed as well.

What laws afford protection of an individual's work?
Copyright Term Extension Act of 1998 – This act added 20 years to existing copyrighted work and to future copyrighted works. For individual copyright holders, copyright protection is for the life of the author plus 70 years. For a corporate copyright holder, protection is ninety-five years from the year of first publication or 120 years from the year of creation, whichever is the shorter of the two.

Computer Software Copyright Act – Computer programs were added to the list of tangible items protected by copyright law. It has been held that the creator of a copyrightable software program obtains automatic copyright protection. The *Judicial Improvement Act* allows for the acceptance and recordation of any document relating to computer software. Finally, the *Semiconductor Chip Protection Act of 1984* provides protection of a computer's hardware components, and masks that are used to create computer chips.

The Digital Millennium Copyright Act – This act "prohibits the unauthorized access to copyrighted digital works by circumventing the wrapper or encryption technology that protects the intellectual property." Civil and criminal penalties are imposed under this act. Actual damages, treble damages, attorney's fees, and injunction and statutory damages are some of the remedies available. Criminal penalties in the form of fines and prison time may also be ordered. The level of protection of digital copyrighted works has risen as a result of this act.

The World Intellectual Property Organization prompted the *Copyright Treaty* that "protects computer programs and their data and grants the copyright holders the exclusive right to make their works available on the Internet and other wireless means." The *Phonogram Treaty* gives "performers and producers the exclusive right to broadcast, reproduce, and distribute copies of their performances by any means, including video recording, digital sound, or encryption signal."

The *No Electronic Theft Act (NET act)* provides from criminalizing certain types of copyright infringement. It "prohibits any person from willfully infringing a copyright for either the purpose of commercial advantage or financial gain, or by reproduction or distribution even without commercial advantage or financial gain, including by electronic means where the retail value exceeds $1,000. Up to one year imprisonment and fines up to $100,000 are the penalties for violating this act.

Can work be used even if it is copyrighted? Under the *Fair Use Doctrine,* certain limited, unauthorized use of copyrighted materials is permitted without it being an infringement. Quotations from a review or criticism of a work, brief news report quotations, a small reproduction of a work by a teacher in order to teach a lesson, and reproduction of a work in a judicial or legislative hearing are considered fair use.

What may an individual recover in a successful copyright infringement action? The plaintiff may recover any profit made by the infringer, damages suffered by the plaintiff, an order to impound or destroy the infringing work, an injunction to prohibit future infringement, and statutory damages in lieu of actual damages may be awarded.

Trademarks

What can be trademarked? Marks such as distinctive marks, symbols, names, words, mottos, or slogans can be trademarked. Color may even be trademarked when it is associated with a particular good.

Note the difference between a trademark and other marks, such as a service mark, certification mark, or a collective mark

Service mark – Used to set apart the services of the holder from the competition. *Ex: Weight Watchers*
Certification mark – A mark used to certify that goods are of a certain quality or come from a certain geographical location. *Ex: Santa Maria Tri-Tip Sandwiches*
Collective mark –A mark used by associations or cooperatives, etc. *Ex: Big Brothers of America*

What is the purpose of a trademark? To protect the owner's investment and goodwill in a mark.

What is needed to qualify for protection of a mark? The mark must have acquired secondary meaning and be distinctive. Both of these aspects must be present or the mark will not be protected. A term that becomes descriptive loses its distinction and its protection.

How does an individual register a trademark? Trademarks are registered with the U.S. Patent and Trademark Office in Washington, D.C. The original mark is valid for 10 years and renewable for an unlimited number of 10-year periods. The registered user may use the trademark symbol; however, it is not necessary. Registration is permitted if a mark was in use in commerce or the Individual verifies a good faith intention to use the mark within six months of registration.

<u>What laws protect a trademark?</u>
The *Federal Lanham Trademark Revision Act of 1998* which made it easier to register trademarks, but more difficult to maintain them.

The *Federal Dilution Act of 1995* protects famous marks from dilution. There are three requirements under this act that must be met. The mark must be famous and used for commercial purposes by the other party. Also, the use must cause dilution of the distinctive aspect of the mark. The purpose of this act is to stop those who try to benefit from others monetary and creative efforts in promoting their famous marks. Many situations that call for the use of this act's protection are domain name cases.

The *Agreement on Trade-Related Aspects of International Property Rights* requires that member nations of the WTO must comply with the "international treaties and conventions protecting copyrights in traditional works, computer programs, and digital works, and related intellectual property laws." If one country thinks that another country is not complying with this law, a nation can file a charge with the WTO.

State antidilution statutes allow companies and individuals to register service marks and trademarks in an effort to prevent infringement on and dilution of a mark that has been registered. Local businesses take advantage of registering under the state's protection.

Refresh Your Memory

The following exercise will enable you to refresh your memory on the rules and principles presented to you in this chapter. Read each question twice and place your answer in the blanks provided. Review the chapter material for any question you miss or are unable to remember.

1. What did the Federal Patent Statute of 1952 establish? _____
    _____

2. Which act permits an inventor to file a provisional application with the Patent and Trademark Office (PTO)? _____

3. What is the owner of a trade secret obliged to do? _____
    _____

4. What does the registration of a trademark serve to do? _____
    _____

5. What was the main purpose of enacting the federal Espionage Act of 1996? _____
    _____

6. What was the purpose of Congress enacting the Federal Patent Statute? _____
    _____

7. What three aspects must be present for an invention to be patented? The invention must be
    _____, _____, and _____.

8. Give an example of three things that may be patented. (1) _____
    (2) _____ (3) _____

9.   Under current patent law, when does the patent term begin to run? _____
   _____

10. What does the one-year "on sale" doctrine state? _____
   _____

11. The Semiconductor Chip Protection Act protects _____ that are used to create
   computer chips.

12. When does copyright infringement occur? _____
   _____

13. A doctrine that permits certain limited use of a copyright by someone other than the
   copyright holder without permission is the _____ _____ doctrine.

14. How has the Digital Millennium Copyright Act changed the traditional fair use doctrine?
   _____
   _____

15. The No Electronic Theft Act _____ certain kinds of copyright infringement.

Critical Thought Exercise

   Lindsey and Tony decide to establish an Internet business called Our Business is E-Business (OBE) in Greenport, while enrolled at Green Valley College. The business sells electronic equipment including computers, CD players, home theater systems, and PDAs. The merchandise is high quality, but sales have been in a slump due to competition. They need more sales to keep the business operating. Lindsey and Tony add you as a partner with a one-third interest for your investment of $20,000. Lindsey comments that if all the students who were listening to the latest hits from artists like Linkin Park, O-Town, and Sheryl Crow would buy a piece of equipment from them, OBE would be an overnight success. Lindsey purchased CDs from twelve popular music artists and establishes a link for listening to this music once an item is purchased from OBE. For every $100 spent on OBE merchandise, the customer can listen to an hour of music for free. Lindsey and Tony have not been making very mush profit on each individual sale, especially since many items sold by OBE are relatively inexpensive, such as remote controls, surge protectors, CD cases, and audio/video cables. As a partner, you are worried that there may be something wrong with using the artist's music to help sell OBE merchandise. You ask Tony and Lindsey to remove the link to the free music from the OBE Internet site. Mainly because sales have increased by 30 percent since the music link was added to the OBE site, they vote against you and insist that the music link remain part of the site unless you can prove to them that it is not in the best interest of OBE to continue with the "free music" offer.
   Prepare a memorandum to your partners on the intellectual property rights that may be involved in your situation and the consequences of any infringement for OBE.

Answer:

_____
_____
_____
_____
_____
_____
_____
_____
_____
_____
_____
_____
_____
_____
_____
_____
_____
_____
_____
_____
_____
_____
_____
_____
_____
_____
_____

Practice Quiz

True/False

1. ____ Design patents are valid for 20 years. [p. 104]

2. ____ The use of copyrighted work in parody or satire is permitted under the fair use doctrine. [p. 109]

3. ____ Names such as Microsoft, Louis Vuitton, and Burger King are protected by patent law. [p. 112]

4. ____ A trademark that becomes a generic name is afforded greater protection as it becomes more distinctive. [p. 114]

5. ___ The lessening of the capacity of a famous mark to identify and distinguish its holder's goods and services is known as dilution. [p. 116]

6. ___ The court is given little leeway in awarding damages where intentional infringement is found. [p. 108]

7. ___ The Patent and Trademark Office must issue a patent within three years after the filing of a patent application unless the applicant engages in dilatory activities. [p. 105]

8. ___ The decision of the PTO regarding a patent is final and may not be appealed. [p. 106]

9. ___ After a copyright period runs out, the work enters the public domain. [p.108]

10. ___ The United States follows the first-to-file-a-patent application rule. [p. 104]

11. ___ Cyber business plans and financial models are subject to patent protection. [p. 104]

12. ___ Copyrightable software programs obtain automatic copyright protection. [p. 107]

13. ___ The copyright holder may still recover for infringement where fair use is found. [p. 108]

14. ___ It is illegal to access copyrighted material by breaking through the digital wrapper that protects the work. [pp. 110-111]

15. ___ If Sam Sly copies a very tiny part of the back of your business law text and places it in his text entitled, "Business Law for Numbskulls!" he will not be held liable as he did not copy the entire work. [p. 108]

16. ___ A mark used to certify that goods and services are of a certain quality is an example of a collective mark. [p. 111]

17. ___ A trademark can be a motto. [p. 112]

18. ___ Color cannot be trademarked. [p. 113]

19. ___ In order for a mark to qualify for federal protection, it must have acquired secondary meaning. [p. 112]

20. ___ The Digital Millennium Copyright Act has raised the level of protection of digitally copyrighted works above that of nondigital copyrighted works. [p. 111]

21. ___ A trademark that becomes a common term for the product line loses its protection under the federal trademark law. [p. 114]

22. ___ A state law that allows persons and companies to register trademark and service marks are antidilution statutes. [p. 116]

23. ___ Bonnie has invented a clothes-sorting machine but is not sure if it will be a big selling item. She places the product in various retail stores for a year and a half and is astounded by how well they have done. Thereafter she decides to seek a patent on her invention. Since she has come up with a novel idea, she will have no problem getting her patent. [p. 106]

24. ___ A service mark is used to differentiate the services of the holder from its competitors. [p. 112]

25. ___ In a cause of action for willful copyright infringement, the court can award damages up to one hundred thousand dollars in lieu of actual damages. [p. 108]

Multiple Choice

26. What happens if Ivan Smartguy invents a new invention on January 1, and allows the public to use his Terrific Robot Cleaning machine and does not file a patent application until March of the following year? [p. 106]
    a. Ivan is still protected under copyright law.
    b. Ivan is protected under business law.
    c. Ivan has lost the right to patent his invention.
    d. Ivan may still patent his invention.

27. Damages for patent infringement include [p. 106]
    a. money damages equal to a reasonable royalty rate on the sale of the infringed articles.
    b. damages for loss of customers.
    c. an injunction against the infringer preventing such action in the future.
    d. all of the above.

28. A trademark is good for [p. 114]
    a. 10 years and can be renewed for one more 10-year period.
    b. 10 years.
    c. 10 years and can be renewed for an unlimited number of 10-year periods.
    d. 20 years plus the life of the creator.

29. What federal act specifically provides protection for trademarks, service marks, and other marks? [p. 111]
    a. the Lanham Trademark Act
    b. the Landon Act
    c. the Mask Work Act
    d. the Sonny Bono Term Extension Act

30. What are the state trademark statutes called? [p. 116]
    a. distinct and secondary meaning statutes
    b. public use doctrine statutes
    c. no electronic theft statutes
    d. antidilution statutes

31. Which of the following would not be protected under copyright laws? [p. 114]
    a. photographs
    b. poems
    c. color
    d. maps

32. The World Intellectual Property Organization extended copyright protection to [p. 119]
    a. inventions used by the public for more than one year.
    b. computer programs and data compilations.
    c. the Sonny Bono Term Extension Act.
    d. tangible writings.

33. What is a mask? [p. 108]
    a. a facial façade to disguise oneself to be recognizable
    b. an original layout of software programs that is used to create a semiconductor chip
    c. an item that has an underlying sheet of computer language
    d. a certificate of recordation of documents pertaining to computer software

34. Shelly operates a small clothing boutique in a rural area. In order to bring in more business, she placed an ad in a neighboring town's newspaper indicating that with every purchase over $25.00, the purchaser would be allowed to read a chapter from the newest teen idol book by I. M. Cool for free. This marketing strategy worked for her as her business tripled. If I.M. Cool is informed of what Shelly is doing, what would be his best theory to pursue against her? [p. 108]
    a. patent infringement
    b. trademark infringement
    c. violation of the Lanham Trademark Act
    d. copyright infringement

35. Which best describes what the court may in its discretion award for willful copyright infringement? [p. 108]
    a. an injunction
    b. profits from the infringement
    c. statutory damages up to $150,000
    d. an order requiring the impoundment and destruction of the infringing works

Short Answer

36. A mark is said to be _____ if it is unique and fabricated. [p. 112]

37. If Robby steals the secret recipe to Chandler's Chunky Cocoa Cookies and opens up his own cookie shop, what should Chandler's cause of action against Robby be based on? [p.108] _____

38. If Chandler finds out that Robby stole his recipe by hacking into his computer files, what federal act will give Chandler the best chance of recovering his economic damages from Robby? [p. 109]
    The federal _____ _____ _____.

39. An electronic connection of millions of computers that support a standard set of rules for the exchange of information is called the _____ _____ _____. [p. 117]

40. The title of the web address **www.barbiesbestbarbeque.com** is known as a [p. 118] _____ _____.

41. When is a copyright created? [p.107]
    _____
    _____

42. What types of things qualify as a trade dress? [p. 113] _____
    _____

43. If Winston Watube sues Tom Teacher for copyright infringement based on Tom's use of Winston's poem to provide an example of iambic pentameter for his class, what is Tom's best defense to a lawsuit brought by Winston? [p. 336]
    _____

44. Burger King's slogan, "Have it your way " is an example of [p. 112] _____

45. The domain name extension .name is used for _____. [p. 118]

46. What eliminated the need to place the word "copyright" or "copr." on copyrighted work? [p. 108] _____

47. Give three examples of tangible writings that are afforded copyright protection. [p. 107]
    _____
    _____
    _____

48. What is meant by the terminology "secondary meaning"? [p. 112] _____

49. Give at least three examples of things that cannot be trademarked. [p. 112]
    _____
    _____
    _____

50. Bonnie, a very intelligent computer user, was short on funds. As such, she decided to crack the wrapper to some work her friend Stan had been developing, to see if maybe she wanted to take it and sell it. Which act makes the cracking of wrappers and selling of technology illegal? [pp. 110-111]
    _____
    _____
    _____

Answers to Refresh Your Memory

1. the requirements for obtaining a patent and protection of patented inventions from infringement [p. 104]
2. the American Inventors Protection Act [p. 106]
3. take all reasonable precautions to prevent that secret from being discovered by others [p. 103]

4.   It serves to give constructive notice that the mark is the registrant's personal property. [p. 111]
5.   It makes it a federal crime to steal another person's trade secrets. [p. 104]
6.   to provide an incentive for inventors to invent, make their inventions public, and protect against infringement [p. 104]
7.   novel, useful, and nonobvious [p. 104]
8.   machines, asexually reproduced plants, processes [p. 104]
9.   It begins to run from the date the application is filed. [p. 104]
10. If an invention was used by the public for more than one year, a patent cannot be granted. [p. 106]
11. masks [p. 108]
12. when a party copies a substantial and material part of another's work without permission [p. 108]
13. fair use [p. 109]
14. It has made it illegal to even access the copyrighted material by breaking through the digital wrapper or encryption technology that protects the work. [p. 111]
15. criminalizes [p. 109]

Critical Thought Exercise Model Answer

To: Tony and Lindsey
From: Your Partner
Re: Possible Copyright Infringement

Copyrights are designed to protect the rights of artists while preserving the public's right to benefit from the works of these artists. Use of copyrighted material is legal only if there is permission from the copyright holder or there is permissible use under the fair use doctrine. The fair use doctrine allows limited use of copyrighted material for a specific purpose, such as education, editorial comment, parody, criticism, news reporting, research, and scholarship. Fair use does not apply to situations where the use is for a commercial purpose. A court will also examine the effect the use will have upon the potential market for the value of the copyrighted material. Because we are using the music to enhance our sales, this is an impermissible commercial use. Though we are not copying the music, we may be liable for contributory infringement if a court finds that we, with knowledge of the infringing activity, induce, cause, or materially contribute to the infringing conduct of another. We are making it possible for customers to have access to a copy of the music. Contributory infringement includes a simple link to a Web site with infringing files on it. Liability extends to both the linking site and the site where the files are located. We are not only linking to copyrighted material but we are knowingly and willingly hosting the files with the intent of distributing the music. The penalties for this activity are up to five years in prison and a fine of $250,000 for the first offense.

A solution to this problem is to obtain a license from the copyright holder that would allow us to use the music with their permission. The license fee will be negotiable and we may be able to obtain it for a very fair price when we explain the limited use and nature of our business. The artist may consider the limited use to be a form of free publicity, much like play time on a radio station. The failure to cease using copyrighted material subjects all three of us to civil and criminal penalties. Failure to cure this infringement violated your fiduciary duty to me as a partner. If you do not immediately get OBE in compliance with 17 U.S.C Section 101 et seq., I will be forced to terminate our partnership.

Answers to Practice Quiz

True/False

1. False   Design patents are valid for 14 years, not 20 years.
2. True   Certain limited unauthorized use of copyrighted materials under the fair use doctrine.
3. False   Names, slogans, and logos such as Microsoft are protected by trademark not patent laws.
4. False   Trademarks that become generic names lose their protection as they become descriptive versus distinctive.
5. True   Dilution is the lessening of the capacity of a famous mark to identify and distinguish its holder's goods and services.
6. False   The court is given discretion to award up to treble damages where intentional infringement is found.
7. True   Under the American Inventors Protection Act, the PTO must issue a patent within three years after the filing of a patent application unless the applicant engages in dilatory activities.
8. False   The decision of the PTO regarding a patent application may be appealed to the U.S. Court of Appeal or the Federal Circuit Court in Washington, DC.
9. True   Work enters the public domain once the copyright period runs out.
10. False The United States follows the first-to-invent rule when granting patent protection of an item or process.
11. True   Many cyber business plans and financial models have received patents and are protected.
12. True   Under the Computer Software Copyright Act, the creator of copyrightable software programs obtains automatic copyright protection.
13. False When fair use is found, the copyright holder may not recover for infringement.
14. True   Under the Digital Millennium Copyright Act, it is illegal to access copyrighted material by breaking through the digital wrapper or encryption technology that protects the work.
15. False The copying does not have to be either word for word or the whole work.
16. False A certification mark is one that says that goods and services are of a certain quality.
17. True   Trademarks can be mottos, symbols, names, distinctive marks, etc.
18. False Color can be trademarked.
19. True   A mark must have acquired secondary meaning and be distinctive to qualify for federal protection.
20. True   Protection is increased for digital copyrighted works.
21. True   Loss of federal trademark protection occurs when a mark becomes descriptive instead of distinctive and hence it is then a common term.
22. True   Antidilution statutes allow companies and persons to register service marks and trademarks.
23. False Bonnie will not be able to get her patent under the one-year "on sale" doctrine as her clothes sorting machine was used by the public for over a year before filing her patent application.
24. True   Different names of the same types of services are differentiated by the types of service marks that they bear.
25. True   The court has discretionary power to award damages ranging from $200 for innocent copyright infringement up to $100,000 for willful infringement in lieu of actual damages.

Multiple Choice

26. C   Answer C is the correct answer as Ivan has lost his right to patent his invention under the one-year "on sale" doctrine. Answer A is incorrect as patents are not protected under copyright law. Answer B is incorrect as it is too broad of an answer to succinctly answer one question. Answer D is incorrect as he may not still patent his invention under the one-year "on sale" doctrine.

27. D   Answer D is the correct answer, as damages for patent infringement include all of those listed in answers A, B, and C.

28. C   Answer C is the correct answer that reflects how long trademark protection is good for. Answers A, B, and D are all incorrect as they do not reflect the correct time periods, and in the case of answer D give a misstatement of law.

29. A   Answer A is the correct answer as the Lanham Trademark Act gives trademarks, service marks, and other marks such as certification marks protection. Answer B is incorrect as there is no such act. Answer C is incorrect as the Mask Work Act pertains to computer chips. Answer D is incorrect as this act extended copyright protection.

30. D   Answer D is the correct answer as state trademark statutes are often called antidilution statutes. Answer A is not correct, as there is no such type of statute. Answer B is incorrect as public use refers to the time frame in which an invention has been used by the public not the terminology for a state trademark statute. Answer C is incorrect as the No Electronic Theft Act has no bearing on the name for the state trademark statutes.

31. C   Answer C is the correct answer as color is protected by trademark laws. Answers A, B, and D are all incorrect as they reflect tangible writings that would be protected under copyright laws.

32. B   Answer B is correct as computer programs and data compilations have now been added to the types of tangible writings that are afforded copyright protection. Answer A is incorrect as copyright protection does not protect inventions. Answer C is incorrect as an act cannot be extended for copyright protection. Answer D is incorrect as tangible writings were protected prior to the extension of including computer programs and data compilations.

33. B   Answer B is correct as it is the original layout of software programs that is used to create a semiconductor chip. Answer A is incorrect, as this description refers to items one would wear to a party. Answer C is an incorrect statement of law. Answer D is incorrect, as certificates of recordation have no bearing on the definition of a mask.

34. D   Answer D is correct as Shelly is making money indirectly from I.M. Cool's book, by offering a free reading with a clothing purchase. Since she did not ask I.M. Cool for permission to use his book, she may be found to have committed copyright infringement. Answer A is incorrect, as the facts do not involve an invention. Answers B and C are incorrect as the facts do not involve a motto, symbol, word, etc., that would indicate that a trademark might be involved.

35. C   Answer C correctly states what the court in its discretion can award for willful copyright infringement in lieu of actual damages. Answers A, B, and D are wrong, as these are general remedies that can be awarded regardless of the copyright infringement being categorized as willful.

Short Answer

36. distinctive
37. copyright infringement
38. No Electronic Theft Act
39. World Wide Web
40. domain name
41. when an author produces his or her work
42. the "look and feel" of a product, a product's packaging, or a service establishment
43. fair use
44. trademark
45. individuals who can use it to register personal domain names
46. the Berne Convention
47. Answers will vary, however examples include books, magazines, musical compositions, lectures, and greeting cards to name a few.
48. when an ordinary term has become a brand name
49. flag of the United States, immoral or scandalous remarks, surnames standing alone (answers will vary)
50. Digital Millennium Copyright Act

Chapter 8

BUSINESS AND
ONLINE CRIMES

Chapter Overview

This chapter gives an insightful presentation of business and online crimes. You will be able to differentiate between a felony and a misdemeanor as well as be able to define the various crimes and elements that help to establish liability for each. Additionally, the chapter provides a thorough overview of criminal procedure from arrest through trial. The Racketeer Influenced and Corrupt Organization Act (RICO), Foreign Corrupt Practices Act, and the safeguards provided in the Fourth, Fifth, Sixth and Eighth Amendments to the U.S. Constitution are also examined. Finally, the law as it pertains to the computer and Internet crimes is reviewed.

Objectives

Upon completion of the exercises in this chapter, you should be able to:
1. Describe the difference between a felony and a misdemeanor.
2. Understand the elements of a crime.
3. Discuss criminal procedure beginning with the arrest and ending with the trial.
4. Explain the difference between crimes against persons and property as well as those involving white-collar crimes and criminal fraud.
5. Be familiar with the Racketeer Influenced and Corrupt Organization Act (RICO), and the Foreign Corrupt Practices Act.
6. Understand the safeguards inherent in the Fourth, Fifth, Sixth and Eighth Amendments to the United States Constitution.
7. Be familiar with the laws affecting the computer and crimes involving the Internet.

Practical Application

You should be able to identify the different types of crimes, including those involving the computer and the Internet as well as identify the elements necessary to establish liability. Further, you should be able to understand and explain the criminal process beginning with the arrest through to trial. In addition, you should be able to access the application of the safeguards that are afforded under the United States Constitution.

Helpful Hints

It is helpful to distinguish between what a felony is versus a misdemeanor. This chapter lends itself toward categorization. It is easier to remember the crimes that are involved if you categorize them based on whether the crimes are against individuals, property, or the computer and Internet. In order to remember the aspects of criminal procedure that accompanies the crime itself, it is helpful to draw a horizontal time line listing the various stages of the criminal process. Further, it is important to be aware of the various statutory acts such as Racketeer Influenced and Corrupt Organization Act and the Foreign Corrupt Practices Act.

Study Tips

Background Information

✓ The United States leads the world in terms of humanity and sophistication in the criminal law system.
✓ In the United States, a person is presumed innocent until proven guilty.
✓ Guilt must be established beyond a reasonable doubt.
✓ The United States Constitution gives the accused certain safeguards.

Crime

A crime is a violation of a duty owed to society that has legal consequences and which requires the individual to make amends to the public.

Sources of Criminal Law

✓ Statutes are the main source.
✓ Penal codes – These are detailed, well-defined criminal activities along with punishment for the same if committed.
✓ State and federal regulatory statutes

Parties to a Criminal Action

✓ The government is the plaintiff in a criminal action and is represented by an attorney called a prosecutor.
✓ The accused is the defendant and is represented by a defense attorney. The government will provide a free attorney if the defendant is unable to afford representation.

Important Facts to Know about Felonies

✓ They are the most serious types of crimes.
✓ Crimes that are inherently evil (mala in se) are considered to be felonies.
✓ Crimes such as murder, rape, bribery, and embezzlement are felonies in a majority of jurisdictions.
✓ Imprisonment is the usual punishment; however, the death penalty is imposed in some jurisdictions for the crime of first-degree murder.
✓ Federal law requires mandatory sentencing for certain crimes.
✓ Some states require mandatory sentencing for certain crimes.
✓ A number of statutes provide for the degrees of crime and the penalties for each.

Important Facts to Know about Misdemeanors

✓ They are less serious than felonies.
✓ Crimes that are prohibited by society (mala prohibita) but not inherently evil are categorized as a misdemeanor.
✓ Crimes such as burglary, regulatory statute violations, and robbery are examples of misdemeanors.
✓ These types of crimes have punishments that are less severe than felonies.

✓ Punishment includes imprisonment for less than a year and/or a fine.

Violations Are Neither a Felony nor a Misdemeanor

✓ Examples of a violation include jaywalking and traffic violations. A fine is the only punishment allowable unless a jury trial is granted.

Elements of a Crime

Two necessary elements to be shown when proving a person is guilty of a crime:

Criminal Act

✓ The defendant must have performed the wrongful act. The performance of the wrongful act is also known as the actus reus.
✓ The performing or failure to do a certain act can satisfy this element.
✓ A defendant's thought of doing the crime will not satisfy the criminal act element. The wrongful act must have been carried out.
✓ An interesting notation is that criminal acts can bring about civil law actions that have their basis in tort.

Criminal Intent

✓ The defendant must have the necessary state of mind (specific or general intent) when he/she performed the act. This intent is also referred to as the mens rea.
✓ It is important to differentiate between specific and general intent. Specific intent is demonstrated when the accused intentionally or with knowledge or purposefully performs the prohibited act. General intent is proven where there is a lesser amount of culpability.
✓ The jury may deduce the type of intent based upon the defendant's actions.
✓ There is no crime where there is no mens rea. If the act that was performed was an accident, then mens rea cannot be established.
✓ Strict or absolute liability for a prohibited act means that mens rea is not required. A violation of an environmental statute would be an example where absolute liability would be imposed.

Crimes Affecting Business

The most common crimes that affect business are those given below. It is important for you to be aware of the necessary elements of a particular crime in order to prove that it has or has not been committed. When you are given a certain set of facts, it is important to analyze them and determine their applicability to each of the requisite elements of the crime you are trying to prove.

Robbery

✓ The taking of personal property of another using fear or force.
✓ Note that a pickpocket does not qualify as a robber as there is no fear or force.

Burglary

- ✓ At common law, burglary was the "breaking and entering a dwelling at night" with the intent to commit a felony therein.
- ✓ Compare the common definition to the modern expansion, which includes daytime thefts of offices and commercial buildings. Further, the breaking element is no longer a requirement in many jurisdictions. If there has been an unauthorized entry through an unlocked door or window, this will be sufficient.

Larceny

- ✓ At common law, larceny was the "wrongful and fraudulent taking of another person's personal property."
- ✓ Personal property includes trade secrets, computer programs, tangible property, and other types of business property.
- ✓ Examples of larceny include automobile theft, car stereo theft, and pickpocketing.
- ✓ The perpetrator need not use force or go into a building in order to commit this crime.
- ✓ Some jurisdictions categorize the larceny as either grand or petit based upon the value of the goods that were taken.

Theft

- ✓ In those jurisdictions that do not categorize crimes in terms of robbery, larceny, and burglary, the crimes of this nature are under the heading of theft. These jurisdictions then label the theft as petit or grand depending on the value of the goods taken.

Receiving Stolen Property

- ✓ If a person knowingly receives stolen property with the intent to deprive its rightful owner of that property, they may be found to have committed the crime of receiving stolen property. The stolen property may be personal property, money, stock certificates, or anything tangible.
- ✓ An important notation is that the element of knowledge may be inferred from the circumstances.

Arson

- ✓ The crime of arson at common law was defined as "the malicious or willful burning of the dwelling house of another person."
- ✓ Modernly, the term dwelling includes all buildings including public, commercial, and private ones.

Forgery

- ✓ This crime involves the fraudulent making or alteration of a written document, which affects the legal liability of another person.
- ✓ Examples include falsifying public records and counterfeiting as well as imitating another person's signature on a check or altering the amount of the check. Note, that one spouse may sign his or her spouse's check and deposit it into a joint account without it being designated as forgery. There is no intent to defraud in this situation.

Extortion

- ✓ Extortion involves the obtaining of property of another with or without his or her consent by use of actual or threatened force, violence, or fear.
- ✓ The truth or falsity of the information does not matter.
- ✓ Examples of extortion include when one person threatens another that a piece of information will be exposed unless money or property is given to the extortionist. This is known as blackmail.
- ✓ Extortion of public officials is referred to as extortion "under color of official right."

Credit Card Crimes

- ✓ Many jurisdictions have made it a crime for the misappropriation and use of another person's credit cards.
- ✓ Some states prosecute credit card crimes under their forgery statutes.

Bad Check Legislation

- ✓ A majority of jurisdictions hold that an individual who knowingly makes, draws, or presents a check for which there are insufficient funds in the individual's account to cover the amount of the check has committed a crime.
- ✓ Some jurisdictions require that proof of the intent to defraud be shown.

White-Collar Crimes otherwise known as Crimes Usually Committed by Businesspersons

- ✓ These are usually called white-collar crimes and involve deceit.
- ✓ Embezzlement, criminal fraud, and bribery are examples of white-collar crimes.

Embezzlement

- ✓ A statutory crime involving the fraudulent conversion of property by a person to whom another individual's property was entrusted.
- ✓ Employer's representatives, agents, or employees usually commit this crime.
- ✓ The main element to be aware of is the fact that the property was entrusted to the individual who ultimately absconded with it.

Criminal Fraud

- ✓ This crime is known as false pretenses or criminal fraud or deceit as the accused obtains title to the property through trickery.
- ✓ Included under this crime is the crime of mail and wire fraud. The government will prosecute a suspect if the mail or wires are used to defraud another individual.
- ✓ It is important to be aware of the Identity Theft and Assumption Deterrence Act of 1998. This act makes it a crime for the stealing of another's identity. This crime imposes a penalty of prison sentences from three to twenty-five years. The Federal Trade Commission also appoints a representative to assist in restoring victim's credit and expunging the consequences of the imposter.

Bribery

✓ When one individual gives money, property, favors, or anything of value to another in exchange for a favor in return, this is known as bribery. This is often referred to as a kickback or a payoff.

✓ Intent is an essential element of this crime.

✓ If the offeree accepts the bribe, he or she is then also guilty of the crime.

✓ The offeror can be guilty of the crime without the offeree accepting the bribe.

✓ The Foreign Corrupt Practices Act of 1977 requires firms to keep accurate records as they pertain to foreign transactions. Additionally, American companies may not bribe a foreign official, political party, or candidate in an attempt to influence new business or retention of a continuing business. Knowledge is a key element in making the conduct as described above a crime. Punishment includes fines and imprisonment.

The Racketeer Influenced and Corrupt Organizations Act (RICO)

✓ It is a federal crime to acquire or maintain an interest in or conduct or participate in an "enterprise" through a "pattern" of "racketeering activity."

✓ Examples of racketeering activity include gambling, robbery, arson, deals involving narcotics, bribery, mail fraud, etc.

✓ Punishment includes fines, imprisonment, and forfeiture of any property or business interests that were obtained as a result of the RICO violations.

✓ The government can also seek business reorganization, dissolution, and the dissolution of the defendant's interest in an enterprise as part of civil penalties for RICO violations.

Inchoate crimes

✓ Nonparticipants commit these crimes.

✓ Conspiracy is an inchoate crime, which is defined as two or more individuals who enter into an agreement to commit a crime. An overt act in furtherance of the crime is needed.

✓ Attempt to commit a crime is a crime requiring an act in furtherance but not completion of a crime.

✓ Aiding and abetting the commission of a crime is a crime that occurs when an individual supports, assists, or encourages the commission of a crime.

Corporate Criminal Liability

✓ At common law, the courts held that corporations lacked the mens rea needed to commit a crime.

✓ Modernly, corporations are being held criminally liable for the acts of their managers, employees, and agents. Since imprisonment is not feasible, they are being fined or having their franchise or license taken away.

✓ The corporate officers, employees, or directors are held personally liable for crimes that they personally commit regardless if it was done for personal gain or for the corporation. Further, if a corporate manager fails to appropriately supervise his or her subordinate, the manager may be held criminally liable for the subordinate's criminal activities.

Criminal Procedure

There are several pretrial procedures as well as the trial itself that you need to be familiar with. The pretrial procedure involves the arrest, indictment, arraignment, and plea bargaining.

Arrest

✓ The police must have a warrant based upon probable cause before a person can be arrested. Probable cause has been defined as the existence of objective, articulated facts that would raise in the mind of a reasonable person that a crime has been committed or is about to be committed.

✓ A search without a warrant is allowed when the crime is in progress, those involved in the crime are fleeing from the scene or there is a great chance that the evidence will be destroyed. Probable cause is still required even in the absence of a warrant.

✓ After the accused is arrested, a booking take place. The booking involves the recording of the arrest as well as the standard fingerprinting.

Indictment or Information

✓ The indictment or information involves the formal charges that must be brought against the accused before being brought to trial.

✓ The government evaluates those charged with serious crimes. If there is enough evidence to hold the accused for trial, an indictment is then issued and the accused is held for trial.

✓ For crimes with a lesser magnitude, a judge will determine if there is sufficient evidence to hold the accused for trial. An information is issued upon confirmation that the evidence is sufficient and the accused is then held over for trial.

Arraignment

✓ Once an information or indictment is issued, the accused is informed of the charges against her or him and is requested to enter a plea.

✓ The accused may enter a guilty, not guilty, or nolo contendere plea. If the latter is chosen, the accused does not admit guilt, but agrees to a penalty. Nolo contendere pleas may not be used later on in a civil proceeding. Acceptance of the nolo contendere pleading is optional.

Plea Bargaining

✓ This involves an agreement between the government and the accused whereby the accused admits to a lesser offense in exchange for the government's imposition of a lesser penalty.

✓ The rationale behind plea bargaining is to minimize overcrowding of prisons, avoid trial risks, and to save costs associated with trial.

The Criminal Trial

✓ All jurors must agree unanimously before the accused is found guilty.

✓ The defendant may appeal if he or she is found to be guilty.

✓ Even if one juror disagrees, the accused will not be found guilty.

✓ If the defendant is innocent, the government cannot appeal.

✓ If a unanimous decision does not come to fruition, the jury will be hung in terms of what they decided. The government then has the option of retrying the case before a new jury or judge.

Constitutional Safeguards

✓ The **Fourth Amendment** plays an important role in protecting corporations and persons from *unreasonable searches and seizures* by the government. "It permits people to be secure in their person, houses, papers, and effects." Note that regulated businesses as well as those who are involved in hazardous industries are subject to warrantless searches.

Searches may not go beyond the area specified in the warrant. If evidence is obtained as a result of an unreasonable search or seizure, it will be considered tainted. This evidence may not be used against the accused, but can be used against other individuals.

The "good faith" exception to the exclusionary rule states that illegally obtained evidence may be used against the accused if the police officers that obtained the evidence believed in good faith that they were acting in accordance with a lawful search warrant.

✓ The **Fifth Amendment** states "no person shall be compelled in any criminal case to be a witness against himself."

The *privilege against self-incrimination* is applicable to individuals, not corporations and partnerships. Be aware though that private papers such as personal diaries of businesspersons are protected from disclosure.

✓ **Immunity from Prosecution**
The government consents to not use any evidence given by an individual against that person. Immunity is usually granted when the government wants information from an individual who has asserted his or her Fifth Amendment privilege against self-incrimination. If immunity is granted, the individual loses his or her Fifth Amendment protection.

✓ Fifth Amendment Protection Against **Double Jeopardy**
The Fifth Amendment via its double jeopardy clause states a person may not be tried twice for the same crime. Compare this to where the accused has committed several crimes. The accused may be tried for each of the crimes without being in violation of the double jeopardy rule. Also, if the acts are violations in different jurisdictions, each jurisdiction may try the accused.

The *attorney-client privilege* is provided for in the Fifth Amendment. The Fifth Amendment also recognizes the psychiatrist/psychologist-patient privilege, priest/minister/rabbi-penitent privilege, spouse-spouse privilege, and parent-child privilege.

✓ Sixth Amendment Right to a **Public Jury Trial**

The Sixth Amendment gives the accused the right to be tried by an impartial jury, to cross-examine witnesses against the accused, to have a lawyer's assistance and to have a speedy trial.

✓ Eighth Amendment Protection against **Cruel and Unusual Punishment**
This amendment protects the accused from abusive or torturous punishments.

✓ **Accountant-Client Privilege**
Many states have enacted statutes that have created an accountant-client privilege. This law states that an accountant may not be called as a witness against a client. Note that there is no federal law that provides for the accountant-client privilege.

Federal Antiterrorism Act of 2001

✓ Congress enacted this act to help the government in prevention and detection of terrorist activities and with the investigation and prosecution of terrorists.

✓ Special Intelligence Court – This part of the act provides authorization for the issuance of expanded wiretap orders and subpoenas.

✓ Nationwide Search Warrant – Instead of using the traditional warrant that specified certain areas that a search warrant was good for, the act now provides for a nationwide search warrant to gather evidence of terrorist activities.

✓ Roving Wiretaps – Any person suspected of involvement in terrorism may have a roving wiretap placed on the use of multiple telephones, including cellular phones, in order to monitor their activities. Former law required separate permission for each telephone that was used.

✓ Sharing Information – Evidence that is obtained by the multiple government agencies such as the Federal Bureau of Investigation, Central Intelligence Agency, etc., may share with one another. Prior law restricted what information was being shared.

✓ Detention of Noncitizens – A nonresident of the United States may be detained for up to seven days if he or she is suspected of terrorist activities. If an individual is a threat to national security, he or she may be held for up to six months. Nonresidents who raise revenue to support terrorist activities and organizations may be deported.

✓ Bioterrorism Provision – Biological or chemical weapons may only be used for peaceful purposes. Possession for any other use is illegal.

✓ Anti-Money Laundering Provision – This aspect provides for the discovery, tracing, and impounding of bank accounts that are being used to fund terrorist activities. The banks are required to divulge information regarding sources of large overseas bank accounts. Failure to do so will result in sanctions or forfeiture of the banks' licenses to do business.

Refresh Your Memory

The following exercise will enable you to refresh your memory on the rules and principles presented to you in this chapter. Read each question twice and place your answer in the blanks provided. Review the chapter material for any question you miss or are unable to remember.

1. There is no crime if the requisite _____ _____ cannot be proven.

2. A _____ crime is one that imposes criminal liability without a finding of mens rea.

3. The term actus reus means _____ _____.

4. The term mens rea means _____ _____.

5. An injured party may bring a civil _____ action against a wrongdoer who has caused the party injury during the commission of a criminal act.

6. The two elements that must be shown for a person to be found guilty of most crimes are criminal _____ and criminal _____.

7. When the police obtain an arrest warrant, it usually must be based upon _____ _____.

8. The charge of having committed a crime based on the judgment of the magistrate is known as the _____.

9. One of the most common forms of _____ is signing another person's signature to a check or changing the amount of the check.

10. Obtaining title to property through trickery is known as _____ _____.

11. The crime of embezzlement is typically committed by an _____ _____.

12. The wrongful and fraudulent taking of another person's personal property is the definition for the crime of _____.

13. Extortion of a public official is called extortion _____ _____ ____ _____ _____.

14. The Fourth Amendment protects the rights of the people from _____ _____ and seizure by the _____.

15. The _____ _____ clause of the Fifth Amendment protects persons from being tried twice for the same crime.

16. The Sixth Amendment provides the right to a _____ _____ trial.

17. The _____ Amendment protects against cruel and unusual punishment.

18. The _____ _____ _____ of 2001 assists the government in detecting and preventing terrorist activities and prosecuting businesses.

19. A plea of ____ _____ means that the accused agrees to the imposition of a penalty but does not admit guilt.

20. Crimes that involve cunning and deceit and that are prone to be committed by businesspersons are referred to as _____ _____ crimes.

Critical Thought Exercise

Build-Rite Construction Company of Santa Maria, Jamaica, receives a copy of an invoice for $160,000 of supplies from Hayward Lumber. Tom Cheat, owner of Build-Rite, notices that the invoice states that the company name is Build-Right Contractors and gives the company office address as Santa Maria, California. The invoice contains three different account numbers that Cheat discovers are all assigned to Build-Right. Cheat pays the invoice but does nothing to correct the account numbers. During the next 14 months, Cheat has his employees order over

$800,000 worth of materials from Hayward Lumber via the Internet, using the account numbers assigned to the California company. When the bills come due each month, Build-Right pays for the materials sent to Build-Rite, thinking that they have been shipped to one of their own construction sites. Cheat builds over 200 luxury vacation homes in Jamaica and has the funds from the sale of the homes sent to his accounts in the Bahamas, where his brother runs a one-person bank. The credit of Build-Right is ruined when they discover the misuse of their account numbers and refuse to pay the balance of over $300,000 charged to their accounts. Several banks pull their funding of Build-Right projects and equipment is seized. Build-Right has to temporarily lay off 180 employees.

What crime, if any, has been committed by Tom Cheat or his company? Who may be prosecuted? What law will apply? What steps should Build-Right take to help it recover financially and prevent this from happening again in the future?

Answer:

_____

_____

_____

_____

_____

_____

_____

_____

_____

_____

_____

_____

_____

_____

_____

_____

_____

_____

_____

_____

_____

_____

_____

_____

Practice Quiz

True/False

1. ____   The main difference between embezzlement as opposed to robbery, burglary, and larceny is that the stolen property was entrusted to the embezzler. [p. 131]

2. ___ The payment of bribes to private individuals or businesses is known as a kickback or a payoff. [p. 132]

3. ___ The maximum penalty for mail, wire, and Internet fraud is three years. [p.133]

4. ___ Money laundering is a misdemeanor. [p.134]

5. ___ The Fourth Amendment protects corporations and individuals from unreasonable searches and seizures. [p. 135]

6. ___ If the defendant is not found guilty, he or she may appeal. [p. 129]

7. ___ A person can be compelled to give testimony against him or herself. [p. 138]

8. ___ The stealing of automobiles and car stereos are considered to be larceny. [p. 130]

9. ___ The crime of commercial bribery encourages the payment of bribes to private persons and businesses. [p. 132]

10. ___ The fraudulent conversion of property by a person to whom the property was entrusted is known as embezzlement. [p. 131]

11. ___ A client cannot raise the attorney-client privilege. [p. 139]

12. ___ Under the exclusionary rule, evidence that is tainted cannot be prohibited from introduction at a trial or administrative proceeding against the person searched. [p. 135]

13. ___ Any confessions or statements obtained from a suspect before he or she is read his or her Miranda rights may be excluded from evidence at trial. [p. 138]

14. ___ The government may grant partial immunity. [p.139]

15. ___ If the same criminal act violates the laws of two or more jurisdictions, each jurisdiction may try the accused. [p. 139]

16. ___ One of the guarantees provided for in the Sixth Amendment is the right to confront the witnesses against the accused. [p. 139]

17. ___ The Eighth Amendment prohibits capital punishment. [p. 139]

18. ___ Crimes involving cunning and deceit as opposed to force are referred to as white-collar crimes. [p. 131]

19. ___ Protection against self-incrimination applies only to natural persons who are accused of crimes. [p. 138]

20. ___ When a magistrate finds that there is enough evidence to hold the accused for trial, he or she will issue an indictment. [p. 128]

21. ___ Corporate directors, officers, and employees can be held individually liable for crimes that they personally commit, whether for personal benefit or on behalf of the corporation. [pp. 134-135]

22. ___ The government may deny immunity from prosecution if a suspect asserts his or her Fifth Amendment privilege against self-incrimination. [p. 138]

23. ___ Under modern law, arson includes the burning of all types of private, commercial, and public buildings. [p. 130]

24. ___ Misdemeanors are crimes that are mala in se because of their inherently evil nature. [p. 125]

25. ___ The crime of forgery has been committed if one spouse signs the other spouse's payroll check for deposit in a savings account or joint checking account at the bank. [p. 131]

Multiple Choice

26. Which of the following are true regarding felonies? [p. 125]
    a. Some states require mandatory sentencing for specified crimes.
    b. Many states define different degrees of crime.
    c. Serious violations of regulatory statutes are also felonies.
    d. all of the above

27. When is specific intent found to exist? [p. 126]
    a. where the accused purposefully commits a prohibited act
    b. where the accused intentionally commits a prohibited act
    c. where the accused with knowledge commits a prohibited act
    d. all of the above

28. Booking can best be described as [p. 127]
    a. the substantial likelihood that someone committed or is about to commit a crime.
    b. the procurement of an arrest warrant based on probable cause.
    c. an administrative procedure for recording the arrest, fingerprinting, and so on.
    d. none of the above

29. When an accused is asked to enter a plea, he or she can plead [p. 129]
    a. guilty.
    b. not guilty.
    c. nolo contendre.
    d. all of the above

30. Which crime means to obtain property from another, with or without his or her consent induced by actual or threatened force, violence, or fear? [p. 130]
    a. forgery
    b. extortion
    c. receiving stolen property
    d. larceny

31. If Samantha obtains title to June's car through deception or trickery, which crime has she committed? [p. 133]
    a. embezzlement
    b. mail fraud
    c. false pretenses
    d. misrepresentation

32. If Bob Builder writes a large check to Ivan, a building inspector, in an effort to get Ivan to ignore exposed asbestos, a building code violation, which crime has Bob Builder committed? [p. 133]
    a. violation of the exclusionary rule
    b. credit card fraud
    c. criminal fraud
    d. bribery

33. In order to be liable for the crime of criminal conspiracy, what must take place? [p. 133]
    a. the harboring of one of the criminals after he or she committed the crime
    b. an overt act in furtherance of the agreed upon crime
    c. a wrongful and fraudulent taking of another person's personal property
    d. intent to permanently deprive another person of his or her personal property

34. Which of the following pertains to the Federal Antiterrorism Act? [p. 138]
    a. A nationwide search warrant to obtain evidence of terrorist activities was created.
    b. The act permits roving wiretaps on a person suspected of involvement in terrorism.
    c. The federal government has the authority to detain a nonresident in the United States for up to seven days without filing charges against that person.
    d. all of the above

35. Which amendment guarantees the right of the accused to be tried by an impartial jury of the state or district in which the accused crime was committed as well as to be able to cross-examine the witnesses against the accused, to have an attorney's assistance, and to have a speedy trial? [p. 139]
    a. the Fifth Amendment
    b. the Fourth Amendment
    c. the Sixth Amendment
    d. the Eighth Amendment

Short Answer

36. Entry through an unlocked door is sufficient under the modern law definition of [p. 130] _____.

37. What are the two elements that must be proven for a person to be found guilty of most crimes? [pp. 125-126]

    _____

38. Who has the burden of proof if a person is charged with a crime? [p. 124]

    _____

39.   What types of things are not protected from disclosure under the Fifth Amendment? [p. 138]

_____

40.   Give three examples of privileges that exist under the Fifth Amendment. [p. 139]

_____
_____
_____

41.   What is the definition for the crime of robbery? [p. 130] _____

_____

42.   What is required for the crime of receiving stolen property? [p. 130] _____

_____

43.   Mr. Sly convinces Suzy Sweet to withdraw all of her money and invest in his water well that he claims to bottle as the water of youth. He has Suzy believe that her investment will triple in a month. Mr. Sly takes her money and flees the country to live in Barbados. What crime has Mr. Sly committed? [p. 133] _____

44.   What does the Fourth Amendment protect persons and corporations from? [p. 137]

_____
_____
_____

45.   How may an accused be prosecuted twice or more without violating the double jeopardy clause of the Fifth Amendment? [p. 139]

_____
_____
_____

46.   What is the definition of a crime? [p. 124] _____

47.   What does a plea of nolo contendere mean? [p. 129]

_____
_____
_____

48.   What is a hung jury? [p. 129]

_____
_____
_____

49.   What is the good faith exception to the exclusionary rule? [p. 136]

_____
_____
_____

50.   What is the attorney-client privilege? [p. 139]

_____
_____

Answers to Refresh Your Memory

1.   mens rea [p. 126]
2.   non-intent [p. 126]
3.   guilty act [p. 125]
4.   evil intent [p. 126]
5.   tort [p.126]
6.   act, intent [pp. 125-126]
7.   probable cause [p. 127]
8.   information [p. 128]
9.   forgery [p. 131]
10.   criminal fraud [p. 133]
11.   employer, employee, agents, or representatives [p. 131]
12.   larceny [p. 130]
13.   extortion "under color of official right" [p. 131]
14.   unreasonable search, government [p. 135]
15.   double jeopardy [p. 139]
16.   public jury [p. 139]
17.   Sixth [p. 139]
18.   Federal Antiterrorism Act of 2001 [p. 138]
19.   nolo contendere [p. 129]
20.   arraignment [p. 129]

Critical Thought Model Answer

Obtaining title to property through deception or trickery constitutes the crime of theft by false pretenses. This crime is commonly referred to as fraud. When the fraud is accomplished by the use of mails or wires, a federal offense has taken place. Because Cheat assumed the identity of Build-Right, the offense of identity theft may have been committed. The use of new technology, especially computers and the Internet, make this offense hard to prevent and extremely damaging to the victim. To combat such fraud, Congress passed the Identity Theft and Assumption Deterrence Act of 1998. Identity theft is a federal felony punishable by a sentence of up to 25 years. The act also appoints the Federal Trade Commission to help victims restore their credit and erase the impact of the imposter.

Cheat may be both criminally and civilly liable under the Racketeer Influenced and Corrupt Organization Act (RICO). RICO makes it a federal crime to acquire or maintain an interest in, use income from, or conduct or participate in the affairs of a criminal enterprise through a pattern of racketeering activity. The commission of two or more enumerated crimes within a ten-year period establishes the pattern of activity. The enterprise can be a corporation, partnership, sole proprietorship, business, or organization. The Build-Rite construction company suffices as a criminal enterprise. The use of the Internet previously created a problem if wires were not used for transmission of the fraudulent communication. The statutes concerning wire fraud have been amended to include Internet activity within the definition of wire fraud. If the profits from the building of the condominiums had been invested in or maintained by Build-Rite, the assets would have been subject to forfeiture.

Unfortunately, the funds have been transferred to a bank in the Bahamas. The Bahamas have joined the Cayman Islands as a location where the bank secrecy laws protect the identity and amount of account deposits. The assets of Build-Rite are subject to forfeiture as are the proceeds sent to the Bahamas. Cheat is liable for multiple criminal offenses, if he can be apprehended. The employees of Build-Rite will incur criminal liability only if they knew that the account numbers were being misused. To remedy the situation, Build-Right should create a secure electronic signature for all account transactions. They can insist that all orders over a certain amount be confirmed by a separate e-mail with a password. The FTC should be consulted for advice and help in getting equipment released and credit with the banks restored.

Answers to Practice Quiz

True/False

1. True   Embezzlement differs from robbery, burglary, and larceny in that the stolen property was entrusted to the embezzler.
2. True   A payoff or kickback exists when payment of bribes are made to private persons or businesses.
3. False   The maximum penalty for mail, wire, and Internet fraud is twenty years, not three years.
4. False   Money laundering is now a federal crime.
5. True   The Fourth Amendment protects the rights of the people from unreasonable searches and seizures.
6. False   If the defendant is found not guilty, he or she would be innocent and have no need for an appeal.
7. False   Under the Fifth Amendment, a person cannot be compelled to give testimony against him or herself.
8. True   The stealing of automobiles and car stereos are considered to be larceny.
9. False   The crime of commercial bribery prohibits, not encourages the payment of bribes to private persons and businesses.
10. True   Embezzlement is most commonly committed by an employer's employees, agents or representatives, thus to people whom property is entrusted. The embezzlement occurs when the entrusted individual(s) convert the property.
11. False A client can raise the attorney-client privilege.
12. False Tainted evidence can be prohibited from introduction at a trial or administrative hearing if it is against the accused; however, this tainted evidence may be used against other individuals.
13. True   The Supreme Court requires that the Miranda rights be read to a criminal suspect before he or she is interrogated. The Fifth Amendment privilege against self-incrimination cannot be utilized unless a suspect is aware of this right.
14. True   Partial grants of immunity may be made by the government.
15. True   If the laws of two or more jurisdictions are violated by the same act, each jurisdiction may try the accused.
16. True   The Sixth Amendment guarantees criminal defendants the right to cross-examine and confront witnesses against the accused.
17. False The Eighth Amendment protects against cruel and unusual punishment but does not prohibit capital punishment.
18. True   White-collar crimes are often those which involve cunning and deceit as opposed to force.
19. True   Artificial persons such as corporations may not assert the protection against self-incrimination, as it applies only to natural persons who are accused of crimes.
20. False A grand jury determines if there is enough evidence and issues an indictment whereas a magistrate (a judge) will determine if there is sufficient evidence to hold the accused for trial of usually lesser crimes. Thereafter the magistrate will issue an nformation.

21. True   Even though the common law held that corporations did not have the criminal mind to be held criminally liable, modern courts have expanded a corporation's criminal liability for acts of their employees, agents, and managers. Additionally, the employees, agents, and managers can be held individually liable for crimes they personally commit.

22. False   The government may offer immunity from prosecution in cases where the suspect has asserted his or her Fifth Amendment privilege against self-incrimination. The policy behind this offer is for the government to obtain information that will lead to the prosecution of other more important criminal suspects.

23. True   At common law, the definition of arson was the malicious or willful burning of the dwelling of another person. Under the modern definition, all types of private, commercial, and public buildings are included.

24. False   Misdemeanors are mala prohibita because they are not inherently evil but are prohibited by society, unlike felonies, which are mala in se because of their inherently evil nature.

25. False   Though forgery happens if a written document is fraudulently made or altered, one spouse signing another spouse's payroll for deposit into a joint savings or checking account is not forgery.

Multiple Choice

26. D.   Answer D is correct as the statements contained in answers A, B, and C are all true regarding felonies.

27. D   Answer D is correct as specific intent is found to exist where the accused purposefully, intentionally, and with knowledge commits a prohibited act.

28. C.   Answer C is correct as it properly describes what a booking is. Answer A is incorrect as this is a brief description of probable cause which would have to be present before an arrest and a booking. Answer B is incorrect as the procurement of an arrest warrant would also have to occur before a booking could occur. Answer D is incorrect as answer C was the accurate description of a booking.

29. D.   Answer D is correct as answers A, B, and C all state what an accused may plead when entering his or her plea.

30. D.   Answer B is correct as extortion involves the procurement of another's property with or without their consent, induced by an improper use of actual or threatened force, fear, or violence. Answer A is incorrect as forgery involves the fraudulent making or altering of a written document that alters the legal liability of another person. Answer C is incorrect as receiving stolen property is where an individual knowingly receives stolen property and intends to deprive the rightful owner of that property. Answer D is incorrect as larceny is the intentional taking and carrying away of the personal property of another without consent or legal privilege. Notice that with the crime of larceny there is no force as there can be with the crime of extortion.

31. C.   Answer C is correct as false pretenses involves obtaining title to property through deception or trickery. Answer A is incorrect as embezzlement is the fraudulent conversion of property by a person to whom the property is entrusted. Answer B is incorrect as the facts do not indicate that the mail was used to defraud June. Answer D is incorrect because even though misrepresentation has an element of deceit to its cause of action, this is a tort, and further, title to property is not always the result of the misrepresentation.

32. D. Answer D is correct as bribery is defined as one person giving money, property, favors, or anything else of value to another for a favor in return. In this example, Bob gave Ivan a check in exchange for Ivan's noncompliance with the building code. Answer A is incorrect as the exclusionary rule pertains to tainted evidence that is inadmissible. Answer B is incorrect as credit card fraud entails the misappropriation and use of some one else's credit cards. The question has nothing to do with credit cards. Answer C is incorrect as criminal fraud involves obtaining title to property through deception or trickery.

33. B. Answer B is correct as conspiracy is defined as two or more persons entering into an agreement for an unlawful purpose, of which an overt act must be taken in furtherance of the crime. Answer A is incorrect as this refers to aiding and abetting, of which the harboring of one of the criminals after the crime was committed would be an accessory after the fact. Answers C and D are incorrect as both refer to the crime of larceny.

34. C. Answer C is correct as a hung jury is one that could not come to a decision about the defendant's guilt one way or the other. Answer A is incorrect as it is an incorrect statement of law. Answer B is incorrect as being found not guilty has nothing to do with a hung jury. Answer D is incorrect as this statement describes a finding of guilt, versus the inability to come to a decision with respect to the guilt of a defendant.

35. C. Answer C is correct as the Sixth Amendment provides for an accused to be tried by an impartial jury of the state, etc. Answer A is incorrect as the Fifth Amendment provides an accused with the privilege against self-incrimination. Answer B is incorrect as the Fourth Amendment protects against unreasonable searches and seizures. Answer D is incorrect as the Eighth Amendment protects against cruel and unusual punishment.

Short Answer

36. burglary
37. criminal act, criminal intent
38. the government
39. corporations and partnerships
40. psychiatrist/psychologist-patient privilege, priest/minister/rabbi-penitent privilege, spouse-spouse privilege (Answers will vary)
41. Robbery is the taking of personal property from another by the use of fear or force.
42. It is a crime for a person to (1) knowingly receive stolen property, and (2) intend to deprive the rightful owner of that property.
43. false pretenses
44. Generally, the government does not have the right to search business premises without a search warrant.
45. If the same criminal act violates the laws of two or more jurisdictions, each jurisdiction is free to prosecute the accused without violating the double jeopardy clause.
46. Any act done by an individual in violation of those duties that he or she owes to society and for the breach of which provides that the wrongdoer shall make amends to the public.
47. The accused agrees to the imposition of a penalty but does not admit guilt.
48. a jury that cannot come to a unanimous decision about the defendant's guilt.
49. This exception allows illegally obtained evidence to be introduced against the accused if the police officers who conducted the unreasonable search reasonably believed that they were acting pursuant to a lawful search warrant.
50. The attorney-client privilege is invoked when a client tells his or her attorney about his or her case without fear that the attorney will be called as a witness against his or her client.

Chapter 9

NATURE OF TRADITIONAL
AND ONLINE CONTRACTS

Chapter Overview

There are a variety of circumstances which an individual will enter into a contractual situation in his or her lifetime. This chapter is intended to provide you with a broad overview of the different types of contracts, the requirements for contract formation, the sources of contract law, and technology's role in contract law.

Objectives

Upon completion of the exercises in this chapter, you should be able to:
1. Define what a contract is.
2. Describe the necessary elements to form a valid contract.
3. Distinguish between a bilateral and unilateral contract.
4. Differentiate between an implied-in-fact contract and an express contract.
5. Describe and distinguish the difference between an executed and executory contract.
6. Describe the differences among valid, void, voidable, and unenforceable contracts.
7. Define what a quasi-contract is and when it applies.
8. Discuss equity and its applicability to contracts.
9. Recognize the important role that the Uniform Computer Information Transaction Act plays in the creation and enforcement of cyberspace contracts and licenses.
10. Discuss the importance of the United Nations Convention on Contracts for the Sale of International Goods (CISG).

Practical Application

You should be able to determine whether or not a contract has been formed, as well as the type of contract that is involved. You should also be able to recognize whether or not equity will play a role in the situation you are assessing. Finally, you should be more aware of the difficulties that individuals face when entering into electronic contracts and the licensing of computer information as well as the importance of the Uniform Computer Information Transaction Act in these matters.

Helpful Hints

This chapter lends itself toward organization. As you attempt to learn the area of contract law, it is first helpful to know what a contract is as well as the necessary requisites for its formation. Then it is beneficial to list the various types of contracts along with an example of each to help you remember and differentiate between them. As you study various fact situations, it is especially important in contract law that you read the hypotheticals and or cases line by line, being careful to examine the facts as they may or may not be controlled by the contract principles that you have learned. In contract law, slight variations in wording or sequence of events can change the outcome.

Study Tips

The following study tips have been organized in a manner that will assist you in easily learning the concepts involved in this chapter.

Contract

- Defined: An agreement between two or more parties that is enforceable in equity or a court of law.

- Parties to a contract: The offeror who is the one making the offer, and the offeree who is the individual to whom the offer is made.

- Requirements to have a valid contract: In order to have a valid contract, there must be:
    1. An offer and acceptance, both of which equate to an agreement.
    2. Consideration that is a legally sufficient bargained-for exchange. Be careful with this element, as gift promises, moral obligations, past consideration, and illusory promises are considered insufficient consideration.
    3. Contractual capacity to enter into the contract. This is another area to watch for issues in, as minors, intoxicated individuals, and those who have been adjudged insane may not have the requisite capacity to understand the nature of the transaction they are entering into.
    4. Lawful object. Contracts to accomplish illegal goals are contrary to public policy and are void. An example of this would be a contract entered into to kill another individual in order to receive an insurance policy's proceeds.

- Sources of Contract Law: There are three sources of contract law. They are as follows:
    1. Common law of contracts – This law was developed from early court decisions that eventually became precedent for subsequent decisions. Many of the principles developed under the common law are still the same today.
    2. Uniform Commercial Code (UCC) – The purpose of this law is to establish a uniform system of commercial law in the United States. It is important to note that the UCC takes precedence over common law.
    3. Restatement (Second) of Contracts – Though this compilation of contract law principles is law, it is used more often as a guide due to its statutory nature as opposed to law.

- Types of Contracts: There are a variety of contracts, each of which have differences that you must be aware of.
    1. *Bilateral contract* – This type of contract involves a promise for a promise. For example, "I promise to wash your car if you promise to take me to the movies." Acceptance is in the form of a promise.
    2. *Unilateral contract* – This type of contract involves a promise for performance. For example, "If you mow the lawn, I will pay you $10.00." There is no contract until the offeree performs the requested act of mowing the lawn. Acceptance is in the form of performance.
    3. *Express contract* – Simply stated, these are either oral or written agreements between two parties. An example would be an oral agreement to buy someone's radio and a written agreement to buy someone's home.

4. ***Implied-in-fact contracts*** – This type of contract is implied on the conduct of the parties. There are certain requirements that must be met before a court will find that this type of contract exists. These requirements are:
   - The plaintiff gave services or property to the defendant.
   - The plaintiff expected compensation for the property or services. In other words the property or services were not gifts.
   - Even though the defendant could have refused to accept the property or services given by the plaintiff, he or she did not.
5. ***Objective Theory of Contracts*** applies to both express and implied-in-fact contracts – It does not matter whether or not the contract is express or implied-in-fact; the court will still apply the reasonable person standard. This means, would a reasonable person conclude that the words and conduct of the parties as well as surrounding circumstances were enough to demonstrate that the parties intended to create a contract? Subjective intent is irrelevant as it is the objective intent based on the reasonable person standard that will be examined.
6. ***Quasi-contracts*** – The term quasi-contract is an equitable one and is also known as implied-in-law contract. The Court will create a contract even though there is not an actual contract between the parties, if the plaintiff provided goods or services to the defendant without compensation. Further reinforcement for the creation of a quasi-contract exists when it is shown that it would be unjust not to require the defendant to pay for the benefit received.
7. ***Formal contracts*** – A formal contract is one requiring a special method or form to create it. Some examples of formal contracts are contracts under a state's wax seal, a recognizance for example in the form of a bond, negotiable instruments as per the Uniform Commercial Code, and letters of credit which are also governed by the Uniform Commercial Code.
8. ***Informal contracts*** – All contracts that do not require a special form or method to create are considered informal contracts.
9. ***Valid contract*** – A valid contract is one that meets all of the required elements to establish a contract.
10. ***Void contract*** – A void contract is one that does not have any legal affect.
11. ***Voidable contract*** – A voidable contract is one that enables one party to avoid his or her contractual obligations. Examples of where this situation may exist absent certain exceptions are contracts entered into by minors, insane individuals, intoxicated persons, those acting under undue influence, duress, or fraud, and where there is a mutual mistake.
12. ***Unenforceable contract*** – If there is a legal defense to the enforcement of the contract, the contract is unenforceable. An example of this would by if a writing such as the case with the purchase of real estate is required to be in writing as per the Statute of Frauds.
13. ***Executed contract*** – If both parties have performed their required obligations under the contract, the contract is said to be executed.
14. ***Executory contract*** – If only one side has fully performed his or her obligations of the contract, the contract is said to be executory.

- <u>Equity Court and Contracts</u> – The equity courts of England developed a set of rules whose foundation was premised on fairness, moral rights, and equality. Equity principles were applied when the remedy at law was not adequate or in the interest of fairness, equitable principle had to be applied.

- Importance of the Uniform Computer Information Transactions Act (UCITA) – This act targets a majority of the legal issues that are faced when conducting e-commerce over the Internet. Since a majority of the states have adopted some or all of the act, it is anticipated to become the foundation for the creation and enforcement of cyberspace licenses and contracts.

- Importance of The United Nations Convention on Contracts for the International Sale of Goods – The CISG is important because it incorporates rules from all of the prominent legal systems. It is substantially similar to the Uniform Commercial Code. This is another reason that Americans conducting overseas business should be familiar with its provisions.

Refresh Your Memory

The following exercise will enable you to refresh your memory on the rules and principles presented to you in this chapter. Read each question twice and place your answer in the blanks provided. Review the chapter material for any question you miss or are unable to remember.

1. An agreement between two or more parties that is enforceable by a court of law or equity is a _____.

2. The _____ is the party who makes an offer and the _____ is the party to whom the offer is made.

3. Parties who are adjudged insane do not have _____ capacity.

4. Contracts that accomplish illegal objects are _____.

5. List three sources of contract law. (1) _____,
(2) _____, and (3) _____.

6. The parties' consent to create a contract must be _____.

7. If the offeror's offer can be accepted only by the performance of an act, the contract is _____.

8. A comprehensive statutory scheme that includes laws that cover aspects of commercial transactions is known as the _____ _____ _____.

9. The Restatement Second of Contracts is often used for _____ in contract disputes.

10. The intent to enter into an implied-in-fact or express contract is judged by the _____ _____ standard.

11. A contract that requires a special form or method of creation is known as a _____.

12. If a contract does not equate to a formal contract, it is called an _____ contract.

13. Equity courts based their decisions on _____.

14. The purpose of the Uniform Commercial Code was to _____
_____.

15. The equitable doctrine of _____ allows a court to award monetary damages to a plaintiff for providing services or work to a defendant even though the parties did not have an actual contract between them.

Critical Thought Exercise

      Ricky Boggs, a 27-year-old country singer, was severely injured in an automobile accident. Boggs was airlifted by Bishop County Air Ambulance to Bishop Trauma Center for surgery and treatment. Boggs slipped into a coma and after seven weeks was transported to Bishop County Extended Care Hospital. Boggs remained in the hospital for fourteen months before he died without ever having regained consciousness. The total charges assessed by Bishop County for the care of Boggs exceeded $370,000.00. After he died, Bishop County sued the Boggs estate to recover the expenses of the air ambulance, trauma treatment, surgery, hospital stay, and extended care.

      Was there a contract between Bishop County and Boggs? If so, how much can Bishop County recover from the estate?

Answer:

_____

_____

_____

_____

_____

_____

_____

_____

_____

_____

_____

_____

_____

_____

_____

_____

_____

Practice Quiz

True/False

1. ____ The UCITA creates uniform legal rules for the formation and enforcement of electronic contracts and license. [p. 149]

2. ___ No act or performance is necessary to create a unilateral contract. [p. 149]

3. ___ The doctrine of equity is never applied in contract cases. [p. 153]

4. ___ A contract that has not been fully performed by either or both sides is an executory contract. [p. 152]

5. ___ A contract that cannot be enforced because of a legal defense is unenforceable. [p. 152]

6. ___ The reasonable person standard uses a hypothetical reasonable person when concluding whether the parties intended to create a contract. [p. 148]

7. ___ Certain contracts need to be in writing and in a certain form. [p. 146]

8. ___ The Uniform Commercial Code usually takes precedence over the common law of contracts. [p. 147]

9. ___ Negotiable instruments do not need any special formalities or language for their creation. [p. 151]

10. ___ A contract is voidable where at least one party has the option to avoid his or her contractual obligations. [p. 152]

11. ___ A void contract is one that does not meet all of the essential elements to establish a contract. [p. 152]

12. ___ An executed contract is one that has been fully performed on both sides. [p. 152]

13. ___ A contract will not be implied by law regardless of the unjust enrichment of one of the parties. [p. 151]

14. ___ A contract that is inferred from the conduct of the parties is known as an implied-in-fact contract. [p. 150]

15. ___ A formal contract does not require a special form or method of creation. [p. 151]

16. ___ In order for the CISG to apply, the buyer and seller must have their places of business in different countries. [p. 154]

17. ___ If consent to a contract is gained by duress, undue influence, or fraud, the court will find there has been no genuineness of assent. [p. 146]

18. ___ A contract may still be created if the offer is not accepted. [p. 146]

19. ___ The parties to a contract may voluntarily perform a contract that is unenforceable. [p. 146]

20. ___ In an equitable action, there is no right to a jury trial. [p. 153]

Multiple Choice

21. If no contract exists and yet monetary damages may be awarded to a plaintiff for provided work or services to the defendant, which of the following theories may the court use to prevent unjust enrichment to that defendant? [p. 151]
    a. quasi-contract
    b. There is no remedy, as all contracts need to be in writing.
    c. The court would apply the unilateral contract doctrine.
    d. The court would apply the bilateral contract doctrine.

22. Which of the following would be considered to be a formal contract? [p. 152]
    a. a check
    b. a letter of credit
    c. a recognizance
    d. all of the above

23. A voidable contract is [p. 152]
    a. one that meets all of the essential elements to establish a contract.
    b. a nullity.
    c. one in which one or both parties have to option to avoid their contractual obligations.
    d. none of the above

24. A contract to commit a crime is [p. 152]
    a. valid.
    b. void.
    c. voidable.
    d. informal.

25. The Uniform Computer Information Transaction Act will be useful in acting as [p. 149]
    a. a quasi-contract.
    b. the reasonable person standard.
    c. the basis for establishing legally sufficient consideration.
    d. the basis for the creation and enforcement of cyberspace contracts and licenses.

26. An oral agreement to purchase a neighbor's gardening tools is an example of [p. 150]
    a. an implied-in-fact contract.
    b. an express contract.
    c. an executory contract.
    d. a void contract.

27. If Cathy and Central Properties prepare their own lease agreement for an apartment that Cathy is renting, this contract would be considered [p. 151]
    a. a voidable contract.
    b. an informal contract.
    c. a formal contract.
    d. an obligatory contract.

28. In the situation where Judy Smith angrily offers to sell her neighbor Roger Jones a piece of land located in the next town for $150,000, the type of contract that has been formed is [p. 148]
    a. a valid contract as all essential elements have been met.
    b. a subject contract as Judy intended to sell Roger the land for a set price.
    c. no contract as the offer was made in anger.
    d. an objective contract as both Judy and Roger were willing to enter into a contract.

29. If Joe's Car Dealership sells Jim a car and Jim pays Joe's Car Dealership for the car, the type of contract the parties entered into would be [p. 152]
    a. an executed contract.
    b. an executory contract.
    c. an informal contract.
    d. implied-in-fact contract.

30. An offer to create a unilateral contract can be revoked by the offeror except [p. 150]
    a. when the Uniform Commercial Code applies.
    b. when the offeror's intent is based on the reasonable person standard.
    c. when there is a nondisclosure agreement.
    d. when the offeree has begun or has substantially completed performance.

Short Answer

31. Give two defenses that may be raised to the enforcement of contracts. [p.146]

    _____

    _____

    _____

32. A contract is created if an offer is [p. 146]_____.

33. Gift promises are not considered supported by valid [p. 146] _____ .

34. There is no unilateral contract until the _____ performs the requested act. [p. 149]

35. If there is any ambiguity in determining whether a contract is unilateral or bilateral in nature, it is presumed to be a _____contract. [p. 149]

36. If Cassie tells her son Rex that she will give him everything she owns if he loves her the rest of her life, would a valid contract exist between the two? [p. 151]

    _____

    _____

37. Jan Ruiz, a business owner, says to Mary Munoz, a decorator, "If you promise to wallpaper my waiting room by December 1, I will pay you $600.00." Mary promises to do so. What type of contract has been created? [p. 149]

    _____

38. Dr. Kurt Crandall says to Collin Jones, a contractor, "If you promise to have the extra rooms to my office built and ready to see patients by May 5, I will pay you $25,000." What type of contract may have been created? [p. 149]

_____

_____

39. Which act is expected to become the basis for the creation and enforcement of cyberspace contracts and licenses? [p. 149]

_____

40. What type of contract is formed where Anthony says to Paul, "I will give you $10,000 if you help my friend Joe rob A & B liquor"? [p. 149]

_____

_____

41. Why is the Uniform Commercial Code important to the law of contracts? [p. 147]

_____

_____

42. Why was the Uniform Computer Information Transactions Act developed? [p. 149]

_____

_____

43. If Alan has painted George's entire house except for the front door, may George revoke his offer to pay Alan for painting his house? [p. 150]

_____

_____

44. What type of agreement exists where the agreement between the parties has been inferred from their conduct? [p. 150] _____

45. What does the objective theory of contracts hold? [p. 148]

_____

_____

_____

46. Article 2 of the Uniform Commercial Code prescribes a set of uniform rules for the creation and enforcement of contracts for [p. 147] _____ .

47. When is a quasi-contract imposed? [p. 151]

_____

48. What is the result if both parties to a contract avoid their contractual obligations? [p. 152]

_____

_____

Answers to Refresh Your Memory

1. contract
2. offeror; offeree

3.   contractual
4.   void
5.   Contracts
6.   genuine
7.   unilateral
8.   Uniform Commercial Code
9.   guidance
10.   reasonable person
11.   formal contract
12.   informal
13.   fairness
14.   create a uniform system of law among the 50 states
15.   quasi-contract

Critical Thought Exercise Model Answer

For parties to have an express contract, the terms of the agreement must be fully and explicitly stated in words, either oral or written. If there is no express agreement, an implied-in-fact contract may be created in whole or in part from the conduct of the parties, rather than their words. In this case, Boggs was unconscious, so he never manifested an assent to any agreement to pay for services, either by his words or conduct. In this type of situation, a plaintiff may have to rely upon a theory of quasi-contract. A Quasi-contract is a fictional contract imposed on parties by a court in the interests of fairness and justice. Quasi-contracts are usually imposed to avoid unjust enrichment of one party at the expense of another. Society wants medical personnel to come to the aid of injured persons without regard to the existence of a contract before services are rendered. This is especially true in an emergency situation where life may be in jeopardy. Though Boggs never consented to an agreement, it would be unfair for Bishop County to render medical treatment to Boggs to save his life and then receive no compensation. Boggs would then be unjustly enriched at the expense of Bishop County. The amount of recovery, however, is not dependent upon the charges assessed by the county. Because Boggs was never able to bargain for the amount or extent of services, the court will only allow Bishop County to recover the reasonable value of the medical services rendered. The $370,000.00 in bills will be scrutinized by the court and reduced if they exceed a reasonable cost for Boggs' treatment.

Answers to Practice Quiz

True/False

1. True   The UTICA handles most of the legal issues that are encountered while conducting e-commerce over the Internet.
2   False   A unilateral contract is one in which the offeror's offer can be accepted only by the performance of an act by the offeree; hence, a promise for an act is a unilateral contract.
3   False   The doctrine of equity is sometimes applied in contract cases.
4. True   A contract that has not been fully performed by either or both sides is an executory contract.
5. True   A legal defense can prevent a contract from being enforced.
6. True   When considering whether the parties intended to create a contract, the use of a hypothetical reasonable person is used to apply the reasonable person standard.
7. True   The law mandates certain contracts to be in writing and in a certain form.

8. True   The Uniform Commercial Code usually does take precedence over the common law of contracts.

9. False   Negotiable instruments do require a special form and language for their creation.

10. True   Where at least one party has the option to avoid his or her contract obligations, the court will find that the contract is voidable.

11 True   A void contract is one that has not met the essential elements to establish a contract, and as such, has no legal effect. A valid contract on the other hand is one that meets the essential elements to establish a contract.

12. True   If both parties have performed each of their obligations to the contract, the contract is said to be executed.

13. False   Under the theory of quasi-contract, a contract will be implied by laws in order to prevent unjust enrichment.

14. True   The parties' conduct can result in a contract.

15. False   A formal contract does in fact require a special form or method of creation.

16. True   The CISG does apply to contracts for the international sale of goods, provided that the buyer and seller have their places of business in different countries.

17. True   The consent of the parties to form a contract must be genuine. If there is undue influence, duress, or fraud, then the genuineness of assent is negated.

18. False   No contract is formed if the offer is not accepted.

19. True   Even though an unenforceable contract exists where there is a legal defense to its enforcement, the parties may still voluntarily perform the unenforceable contract.

20. True   In an equitable action, a judge decides the issue, not a jury.

Multiple Choice

21. A   Answer A correctly states the applicable theory of quasi-contract, wherein a plaintiff may be awarded monetary damages for work or services provided to the defendant even though no contract exists between the parties. Answer B is an incorrect statement of law and is therefore wrong. Answers C and D are both incorrect, as there is no such doctrines per se.

22. C   Answer C correctly defines a bilateral contract as it is a promise for a promise. Answer A is incorrect as this is the definition of a unilateral contract. Answer B is incorrect as the way it is phrased could imply either a bilateral or a unilateral contract. Answer D is incorrect as a promise for an offer could imply a unilateral contract.

23. C   Answer C correctly states the true definition of a voidable contract. Answer A is incorrect as this describes what a valid not a voidable contract is. Answer B is incorrect as a nullity describes a void contract. Answer D is incorrect for the reasons given above.

24. B   Answer B is correct as a contract to commit a crime has no legal effect and is therefore void, as though no contract had ever been created. Answer A is incorrect as contracting to commit a crime is not a lawful object, which would make the contract void. Answer C is incorrect as a contract is only voidable when one party has the option of performing or not performing. In the situation where the main object of the contract is to commit a crime, this option is not available. Answer D is incorrect as an informal contract is one that does not qualify as a formal contract. A contract to commit a crime is not a contract at all and as such would not fall under either the formal or informal categorization of contracts.

25. D   Answer D is correct as it succinctly states the purpose of the Uniform Computer Information Transaction Act. Answer A is incorrect as a quasi-contract is an equitable remedy that is enforced to prevent unjust enrichment. Further, the UCITA does not need to be present in order to enforce a quasi-contract. Answer B is incorrect as the UCITA was not designed to define the reasonable person standard. Answer C is incorrect as even though the act will help address issues such as consideration in the formation of cyberspace contracts, that is not the sole purpose or issue to be addressed by the act.

26. B   Answer B is correct as this is a primary example of an oral, express contract. Answer A is incorrect as implied-in-fact contracts are implied from the conduct of the parties. The facts are silent as to any conduct, but instead state that there was an oral agreement. Answer C is incorrect as an executory contract is one that is not fully performed by one or both of the parties. There is nothing in the facts that would indicate nonperformance by either or both parties. Answer D is incorrect as a void contract is one that has no legal effect and is against public policy. In the example given, purchasing a neighbor's gardening tools is not a crime nor is it against public policy.

27. B   Answer B is correct as the facts state that Cathy and Central Properties prepared their own lease agreement, which indicates that no special form or method of creation was necessary in order to make the agreement. Answer A is incorrect as the facts do not indicate a potentially voidable contract situation as would possibly be the case if a minor, intoxicated, or insane person was involved. Answer C is incorrect as simple contracts such as leases, service contracts, and sales contracts usually do not qualify as formal contracts, whereas contracts under seal, negotiable instruments, recognizances, and letters of credit are examples of formal contracts.

28. C   Answer C is correct as contracts made in anger negate the intent to create a contract when the reasonable person standard is applied. Answer A is incorrect because even though all of the elements to form a valid contract appear to be present, a reasonable person would conclude that because Judy Smith was angry when she offered to sell her land to Roger, she did not intend to enter into a contract with him. Answer B is incorrect as this answer makes no sense, since there is no such thing as a subject contract. Answer D is incorrect as Judy's anger makes her intent to enter into the contract with Roger questionable.

29. A   Answer A is correct as Joe's Car Dealership and Jim have both fully performed their obligations under the contract. Answer B is incorrect as an executory contract exists where the contract is not fully performed by one or both parties. Answer C is incorrect as an informal contract refers to the fact that no special form or method of creation is necessary. Answer D is incorrect as the facts are not indicative of a contract that is inferred from conduct, but instead give details of the parties agreement.

30. D   Answer D is correct as generally an offer to create a unilateral contract may be revoked at anytime prior to the offeree's performance of the requested act, unless the offeree has begun or substantially completed performance. Answer A is incorrect as application of the Uniform Commercial Code has no significance regarding when a unilateral contract may be revoked. Answer B is incorrect as the reasonable person standard is irrelevant in terms of when revocation may take place. Answer C is incorrect as nondisclosure agreements are entered into for the purpose of protecting an invention or trade secret or things of that nature that one of the parties does not want disclosed. Nondisclosure agreements have no relevance in terms of the period of time for revocation.

Short Answer

31. genuineness of assent; writing and form
32. accepted
33. consideration
34. offeree
35. bilateral
36. Probably not, as moral obligations such as loving one's mother would not be construed as bargained-for consideration that is legally sufficient.
37. A bilateral contract was created the moment that Mary promised to wallpaper the waiting room.
38. Dr. Crandall's offer created a unilateral contract whereby the offer can be accepted only by the contractor's performance of the requested act.
39. the Uniform Computer Information Transactions Act (UTICA)
40. A void contract as entering into a contract to commit a crime has no legal effect.
41. It helps to establish a uniform system of commercial law among the 50 states.
42. It was developed to establish uniform legal rules for the formation and enforcement of electronic contracts and licenses.
43. No, George may not revoke his offer as Alan has substantially completed the entire house with the exception of the front door.
44. implied-in-fact contract
45. This theory holds that the intent to enter into an implied-in-fact contract or an express contract is judged by the reasonable person standard.
46. the sale of goods
47. It is imposed where one party confers a benefit on another who keeps the benefit and it would be unjust not to require that person to pay for the benefit received.
48. Both parties are released from their contractual obligations.

Chapter 10

AGREEMENT

Chapter Overview

The previous chapter discussed the requirements for the formation of a contract as well as the various types of contracts. This chapter expands upon the requirement of agreement. You will learn what constitutes a valid offer as well as the various ways that an offer can be terminated. Offers such as rewards, advertisements, auctions, and counteroffers are also discussed. Additionally, you will discover the many ways that an acceptance can be effectuated with special attention being paid to the mailbox rule. Finally, the author gives a clear explanation of nondisclosure agreements.

Objectives

Upon completion of the exercises in this chapter, you should be able to:
1. Define offer and acceptance.
2. List the requirements of an offer.
3. List the terms that can be implied in a contract.
4. Discuss the requirements of special offers such as rewards, advertisements, and auctions.
5. Explain what a counteroffer is as well as its impact.
6. Discuss the various ways an offer may be terminated.
7. Define what an option contract is.
8. Describe what the mailbox rule is and how it is applied.
9. Explain the importance of nondisclosure agreements.

Practical Application

You should be able to recognize whether or not a valid offer has been made and whether or not the essential terms are included within it. You should also be able to determine whether an offer has been properly terminated or if the mailbox rule applies. Finally, with your basic knowledge, you should be able to draft a simple offer by utilizing the information contained in this chapter.

Helpful Hints

Each chapter, especially in the area of contracts builds on one another. As such, it is vital that you understand the information given in each chapter and know how to apply it to given fact situations. Your initial analysis of a potential contract should begin with the offer. You should use a mental checklist of what is required to establish a valid offer. If one of the elements is missing, then ask yourself whether there is a rule of law that may apply to satisfy that missing element. Next, you should determine whether or not you are examining a special offer such as a reward, an advertisement, auction, or counteroffer. Once again, quickly review your mental checklist on any special rules that may apply to these types of offers. Before you proceed any further, look at the facts and assess whether or not the offer has been terminated. Next, has there been an acceptance to the offer you have analyzed? If so, you need to address the issue of whether the acceptance was proper. Examine whether the offer specified a means of acceptance, the time for acceptance, method of communication, and the mailbox rule. The Study Tips section that follows gives easy to remember lists of what is required for the aspects of this chapter.

Study Tips

Agreement

Definition: The manifestation by two or more persons of the substance of a contract. It requires an *offer* and an *acceptance*.

Offer

Definition as per Section 24 of Restatement (Second) of Contracts: "The manifestation of willingness to enter into a bargain, so made as to justify another person in understanding that his assent to that bargain is invited and will conclude it."

Requirements

- The offeror must objectively intend to be held to the offer. Remember objective intent is gauged against a reasonable person in the same or similar circumstances.
    a. Were mere preliminary negotiations going on between the parties? If the offeror is asking a question as opposed to making a statement of intent to bargain, it is probably an invitation to make an offer and not indicative of the offeror's present intent to contract.
    b. Was the offer made in anger, jest, or undue excitement? If any of these exist, the objective intent is missing and the offer cannot result in a valid contract.
    c. Offers made as an expression of opinion are not enforceable promises.
- The offer's terms must be definite or reasonably certain.
    a. Were the terms clear so that the offeree was able to accept or reject the terms of the offer?
    b. Did the offer contain an identification of the parties, identification of the subject matter, the consideration to be paid, and the time for performance? If the answer is yes, then the offer will probably be considered definite and certain.
    c. Were there any implied terms?
        Common Law: If any of the terms were missing, the offer would fail.
        Modern Law: There is more leniency, as the court will supply a missing term if a reasonable term can be implied, such as for price and time or performance.
- The offer has to be communicated to the offeree. Without communication, there can be no acceptance.

Special Types of Offers

Advertisements

- These are treated as invitations to make an offer.
- The exception to it being an invitation is if the offer is definite or specific that it is obvious that the advertiser had the present intend to be bound by the advertisement, then it will be considered to be an offer.

Rewards

- An offer to pay a reward is an offer to form a unilateral contract.
- The two requirements to accept a reward are that the offeree had knowledge of the reward before completing the requested act and he or she performed the requested act.

Auctions

- Usually a seller uses an auctioneer to offer to sell his or her goods.
- Auctions are with reserve as they are usually considered an invitation to make an offer. The seller can withdraw his or her goods from the sale and refuse the highest bid.
- Note, that if the auction is without reserve, the seller must accept the highest bid and cannot take his or her goods back.

Termination of an Offer by the Parties

An offer may be terminated by the parties by revoking the offer, rejecting the offer, or by a counteroffer made by the offeree. These three means of terminating an offer are discussed below.

Revocation of An Offer by the Offeror

- At common law, the offeror could revoke his or her offer any time before the offeree accepted.
- The revocation may be express or implied by the offeror or a third party.
- The majority of states rule that the revocation is not effective until it is received.
- Revocation of an offer made to the public may be revoked by communicating in the same way that the offer was made for the same length of time.
- Prevention of revocation by the offeror is accomplished through an option contract. The offeree usually pays the offeror money to keep the offer open for an agreed-upon period of time. During this period of time the offeror agrees not to sell the subject matter of the offer to anyone else. Keep in mind that death or incompetency does not terminate the option contract unless it was a personal service contract.

Rejection of an Offer by the Offeree

- The rejection may be express or implied by the offeree's conduct.
- The rejection is not effective until it is received.
- An acceptance by the offeree after the offeree has rejected the offer is construed as a counteroffer.

Counteroffer by the Offeree

- It terminates the original offer.
- It creates a new offer that the original offeror is now free to accept or reject.

Termination of the Offer by Operation of Law

An offer may be terminated by operation of law in several situations. It can be terminated by destruction of the subject matter or by death or incompetency of the offeror or offeree, by a supervening illegality, or by lapse of time.

Destruction of the Subject Matter

- The offer is terminated if the subject matter of the offer is destroyed through no fault of either party before the offer is accepted.
- An example of this would be if a boat that was listed for sale sank and was unable to be recovered, the offer would automatically terminate

Death or Incompetency of the Offeror or Offeree

- Death of either the offeror or offeree terminates the offer.
- Incompetency of the offeror or offeree terminates the offer.
- Notice of the death or incompetency is not a requirement.
- Death or incompetency will not terminate an option contract unless it was a personal service contract.

Supervening Illegality

- If the object of the offer is made illegal before the offer is accepted, the offer terminates. For example, if a bog frog becomes an endangered species after an offer is made for its sale to pet stores, but before the pet stores accept, the offer is terminated.
- Many times statutes are enacted that make the object of the offer illegal.

Lapse of Time

- The offer sometimes limits the time in which it can be accepted.
- The time begins to run from the time it is actually received by the offeree and extends until the stated time period ends.
- If no time is stated in the offer, then the offer terminates within a "reasonable time" and on a case-by-case basis.
- If an offer is made over the telephone or face to face, then the offer usually terminates after the conversation.

Acceptance

Defined: Simply stated, an acceptance is an outward manifestation of assent to be bound by the terms of the offer as assessed by the reasonable person standard.

Basic Facts about Acceptance

- Only the offeree can accept the offer to create a contract.
- If an offer is made to more than one person, each person has the power to accept the offer.
- If an acceptance is made by one party, it terminates the offer as to the other individuals to whom the offer was made.
- If a joint offer has been made, the offer must be accepted jointly.

Mirror Image Rule

- This rule states that the offeree must accept the offeror's terms. The acceptance must be unequivocal.
- Grumbling acceptances do form contracts.
- Acceptances, however, that add conditions to them are not unequivocal and thus fail.

Silence as Acceptance

- The general rule is that silence is not held to be an acceptance despite the offeror stating it is.
- There are several exceptions to the general rule.
    a. Where the offeree by his words intended his silence to mean acceptance.
    b. A signed agreement by the offeree allowing continued delivery until notice was given. For example, if Sid continued to buy crafts from a monthly craft club then his silence would indicate acceptance until he notifies the craft club that he wants to discontinue his membership.
    c. Prior course of dealings by the parties where silence is construed as an acceptance.
    d. The offeree accepts the benefit of goods or services given by the offeror even though the offeree had the opportunity to reject the services or goods.

Time and Method of Acceptance

Mailbox Rule

- This rule is also known as the acceptance-upon-dispatch rule.
- Acceptance is effective when it is placed in the mailbox, or dispatched, even if it gets lost along the way.
- The rule does not apply if a rejection is sent first and then an acceptance is mailed.
- The acceptance has to be properly dispatched. In other words, it has to be properly addressed, packaged, and have proper postage applied. Under common law, if the acceptance wasn't properly dispatched, it wasn't effective unless received by the offeror.

Mode of Acceptance

- The usual rule is that the offeree must accept by an authorized mode of communication.
- The offer can state how it is to be accepted. This is called express authorization.
  Note: If the offeree uses a different means to communicate his or her acceptance instead of the means stipulated to be the parties, then the acceptance is ineffective.

- Implied authorization may apply where it is customary in similar transactions between the parties, or prior dealings or usage of trade. Implied authorization will be allowed "by any medium reasonable in the circumstances." Section 30 of the Restatement Second.

Nondisclosure Agreements

"Nondisclosure agreements swear the signatory to secrecy about confidential ideas, trade secrets, and other nonpublic information revealed by the party proffering the NDA." Traditionally, nondisclosure agreements were used by professionals such as lawyers and bankers who were involved in large corporate deals. However, today they are being used by individuals who believe they have a great idea and want to share it with others such as a partner or a banker, but who do not want their idea revealed. Should a breach of a nondisclosure agreement occur, an individual may sue for breach of contract.

Refresh Your Memory

The following exercise will enable you to refresh your memory on the rules and principles presented to you in this chapter. Read each question twice and place your answer in the blanks provided. Review the chapter material for any question you miss or are unable to remember.

1. The offeree has the power to create an agreement by _____.

2. The terms of an offer must be definite or reasonably _____.

3. In what type of auction does the seller retain the right to refuse the highest bid and withdraw the goods from sale? _____

4. How may offers made to the public be revoked? _____ _____

5. Which theory is used in determining whether the parties intended to enter into a contract? The _____ _____ of contracts.

6. If Homer asked Ernie, "Would you be interested in selling your car to me?" Would this be a valid offer?
   _____
   _____

7. Under the modern law of contracts, which two terms of an offer may be implied? _____ and _____ _____ _____

8. _____ are usually viewed as invitations to make an offer.

9. What type of auction provides that the seller must accept the highest bid and cannot withdraw the goods from sale? An _____

10. An offer is terminated if the offeree _____ it.

11. A _____ by the offeree terminates the offeror's offer and creates a new offer at the same time.

12. The offer terminates by operation of law if the _____ _____ of the offer is destroyed through no fault of either party before its acceptance.

13. The offeree's acceptance must be _____.

14. Under the mailbox rule, acceptance is effective upon _____.

15. Usually an offeree must accept an offer by an _____ means of communication.

16. What ways may an offer be rejected? _____
    _____

17. What happens if the subject matter of an offer is destroyed by a fire? _____
    _____.

18. When the offeree must accept the terms as stated in the offer, this is known as the
    _____ _____ _____.

Critical Thought Exercise

Gus Vincent sent invitations to a number of potential buyers to submit bids for the mineral rights to his 2,000-acre parcel in upstate New York on the outskirts of the City of Hudson. Seven bids were received, including the highest bid from International Mining and Cement Company, LTD. (IMC). Vincent then decided to hold onto the land for a few more years and never responded to any of the bidders. IMC claimed that a contract had been formed by submission of its winning bid and sued Vincent for breach of contract.

Did a contract exist?

Answer:

_____
_____
_____
_____
_____
_____
_____
_____
_____
_____
_____
_____
_____
_____
_____
_____
_____

Practice Quiz

True/False

1. ___ An equivocal acceptance is a legal acceptance. [p. 165]

2. ___ Silence is an acceptance if prior dealings between the parties indicate that silence means acceptance. [p. 165]

3. ___ A counteroffer is effective when received. [p. 163]

4. ___ Under modern law, the court will not imply terms in a contract. [p. 158]

5. ___ An offer may be accepted even though it has not been communicated. [p. 159]

6. ___ Generally speaking, time of performance can be implied even if it is a term that is not present. [p. 158]

7. ___ An advertisement is considered an offer if it is so definite or specific that it is obvious that the advertiser has the present intent to be bound by the terms of the ad. [p. 159]

8. ___ An auction with reserve is not considered an invitation to make an offer. [p. 161]

9. ___ On April 1, Kevin commented to Monica that he would like to offer her his summer home on the lake for $2,000. She immediately accepted, where he thereafter started laughing. Her acceptance formed a contract. [p. 158]

10. ___ Rejection of an offer is effective upon receipt. [p. 162]

11. ___ Price may be implied if it is missing in a contract if there is a market or source from which to determine the price of the item or service. [p. 158]

12. ___ If a snowmobile being purchased by Sam is destroyed after Jan makes the offer but before Sid accepts the offer, the offer is terminated. [p. 163]

13. ___ Frank's Used Cars places an ad in the local newspaper for a 1969 Mustang, Vehicle Identification Number V12340987, price $10,000. Frank also left his telephone number. Art was the first one to call Frank and told him he would take the 1969 Mustang as advertised. A contract has not been formed. [p. 159]

14. ___ Generally speaking, a grumbling acceptance is a valid, legal acceptance. [p. 165]

15. ___ Dick Smith makes an offer to sell Jan Jones something custom made for $230,000 with the time of performance set for July 1. The subject matter of the offer can be implied. [p. 158]

16. ___ Under the mailbox rule, acceptance is effective upon receipt. [p. 165]

17. ___ Nondisclosure agreements are no longer enforceable. [p. 167]

18. ___ Unilateral contracts may only be accepted by the offeree's performance. [p. 160]

19. ___ Implied authorization cannot be implied from prior transactions between the parties. [p. 166]

20. ___ If Holly gives Nancy $500.00 to keep Nancy's offer to sell her French horn open for an agreed-upon time period of one month, this would be option contract. [p. 164]

Multiple Choice

21. The manifestation of willingness to enter into a bargain, so made as to justify another person in understanding his assent to that bargain is invited and will conclude it, is the definition of [p. 157]
   a. an offer.
   b. a rejection.
   c. a revocation.
   d. none of the above.

22. A car dealer tells his customer that he feels the car she is interested in buying is the best car on his lot and will probably give her a lifetime of happiness. If the customer buys the car and immediately has problems, the customer may [p. 160]
   a. enforce the car dealer's promise.
   b. return the car for her money back.
   c. not enforce the promise.
   d. none of the above

23. An offer of a reward must be accepted by [p. 160]
   a. writing a letter to the offeror.
   b. one having knowledge of the reward before doing the requested act, and performing the requested act.
   c. everyone having an interest in the subject matter of the reward.
   d. Implication.

24. When a seller at an auction refuses to sell the goods, it is known as [p. 161]
   a. playing hardball.
   b. being stubborn.
   c. an auction with reserve.
   d. a quasi-contract.

25. Ray is selling his rare vase at an auction without reserve. Who will get the vase? [p. 161]
   a. Walter bids $12,600.
   b. Ralph bids $17,500.
   c. Pablo bids $4,000
   d. Sally bids $18,000.

26. Two ways to terminate an offer by operation of law are [p. 163]
   a. by rejection and revocation.
   b. death or incompetency of the offeror or offeree.
   c. rewards and auctions.
   d. intoxication and incapacity.

27. The ABC Corporation mailed an offer of employment to Ernest. The offer stated that acceptance of the job was to be by certified mail. Ernest was so elated about the idea of working for the ABC Corporation that he flew to the city where ABC was located and hand delivered his acceptance within the time stated in the offer. Has a contract been formed between ABC and Ernest? [p. 166]
    a. No, because Ernest used an unauthorized means of communication to give his acceptance.
    b. Yes, as an offeree may accept an offer by an unauthorized means of communication.
    c. No, because the Restatement (Second) of Contracts permits implied authorization by "any medium reasonable in the circumstances."
    d. Yes, because adherence to the comity principle requires that ABC respect the law that Ernest is applying.

28. In order for an offer to be effective, which elements must be established? [p. 158]
    a. The offeror must objectively intend to be bound by the offer.
    b. The terms of the offer must be definite and reasonably certain.
    c. The offer must be communicated to the offeree.
    d. all of the above

29. Implied authorization for acceptance of an offer may be [p. 166]
    a. inferred by properly addressing and packaging and dispatching the acceptance.
    b. expressly stating that acceptance is not effective until received.
    c. inferred from prior dealings, trade usage, or what is customary from similar transactions.
    d. by stipulation that acceptance must be by specified means.

30. Mrs. Sweet, the president of Sweetest Things Corporation, puts an offer to sell the packaging division in writing to Mr. Baker but does not send it. Thereafter, Mrs. Baker stops in to visit Mrs. Sweet and notices the written offer on Mrs. Sweet's desk. She then goes home and tells Mr. Baker about the offer. Can Mr. Baker accept the offer to buy the packaging division of the Sweetest Things Corporation? [p. 159]
    a. Yes, as Mrs. Baker was acting as a proxy for Mr. Baker.
    b. No, as Mrs. Baker did not tell Mr. Baker all of the particulars of the offer.
    c. Yes, as a wife, Mrs. Baker steps into the shoes of her husband and may convey the message to Mr. Baker.
    d. No, because Mrs. Sweet never communicated the offer to Mr. Baker and therefore there is no offer to be accepted.

Short Answer

31. A theory that says that the intent to contract is judged by the reasonable person standard and not by the subjective intent of the parties is known as the _____ theory of _____. [p. 158]

32. What happens if the terms of an offer are not definite and certain? [p. 158]
    _____
    _____

33. If Teddy puts an offer in an envelope to sell his 1950-style juke box to Marla for $10,000, but fails to send it, what is the result? [p. 159]

_____

_____

34. Sean accidentally leaves his grandfather's top hat in a fancy restaurant he was dining at. He places an ad in the Bradley News Gazette stating, "$500.00 reward for the return of an old, black top hat left in Patrano's Italian Restaurant on March 15, 2007, at approximately 8 p.m. Call 911-555-1212. Dawn, who has not seen the offer, finds Sean's top hat and also notes that there is a phone number on a tag inside of it. She telephones Sean and determines that she has found his top hat. Dawn's friend Sally thereafter tells Dawn that there is a reward for finding the hat as she had seen the ad in the paper and recognized that the number in the newspaper is the same as the number inside of the hat. Is Dawn entitled to the reward money? [p. 160]

_____

_____

35. Give an example of a contract term that can be implied. [p. 158]

_____

_____

36. If Marcia places an ad in the Sunset News Press offering a reward for her lost cat Barney and she lets the ad run for five weeks, what must she do to revoke the ad? [p. 162]

_____

_____

37. If Sue says to Julius, "I think $3,500 is too high for your old truck. I will pay you $2,500 instead." What is the effect of Sue's statement? [p. 163]

_____

_____

38. What is the result if a flood from a broken pipe destroys the bolts of silk fabric Martha was intending to buy? [p. 163]

_____

_____

39. If Omar decides to sell Jane his motor home for $60,000, provided she decides by May 1, and Omar is adjudged insane before Jane makes her decision, what is the effect of Omar's insanity? [p. 163]

_____

_____

40. Acceptance can best be defined as [p. 164]

_____

_____

41. A bilateral contract may be accepted by [p. 164]

_____

42. What does the mirror image rule require? [p. 165]

_____

_____

43. What is an option contract? [p. 164]

_____

_____

_____

44. If Mario offers to sell Jennifer two pallets of freshly picked bananas for $150.00 on Monday, but Jennifer waits for almost a month to accept his offer, what defense does Mario have if he has already sold the two pallets of bananas to someone else? [p. 163]

_____

_____

45. Why is silence usually not considered an acceptance even if the offeror states that it is? [p. 165]

_____

_____

46. Under the common law, what was the effect of an acceptance that was not properly dispatched? [p. 165]

_____

47. What is another name for an offer that stipulates that acceptance must be by a specified means of communication? [p. 166]

_____

48. The statement "I will buy your dining room set for $5,000" is a valid offer because [p. 158]

_____

49. If the price term is missing from an offer, when can it be implied? [p. 158]

_____

_____

50. What is the effect of a supervening illegality on an offer? [p. 163] _____

_____

Answers to Refresh Your Memory

1. accepting the offer [p. 157]
2. certain [p. 157]
3. an auction with reserve [p. 161]
4. by communicating the revocation by the same means used to make the offer [p. 162]
5. objective theory [p. 158]
6. No, it is not a valid offer as it is a preliminary negotiation. [p. 158]
7. price and time for performance [p. 158]
8. Advertisements [p. 159]
9. auction without reserve [p. 161]

10. rejects [p. 162]
11. counteroffer [p. 163]
12. subject matter [p. 163]
13. unequivocal [p. 165]
14. dispatch [p. 165]
15. authorized [p. 166]
16. by the offeree's express words (oral or written) or conduct [p. 162]
17. The offer automatically terminates. [p. 162]
18. mirror image rule [p. 165]

Critical Thought Exercise Model Answer

To have an offer that is capable of acceptance, three elements must be present: (1) There must be a serious, objective intention by the offeror; (2) The terms of the offer must be reasonably certain, or definite, so that the parties and the court can ascertain the terms of the contract; and, (3) The offer must be communicated to the offeree. There appears to be sufficient information in the bid to find definite terms. Sending the request for a bid to IMC fulfilled the communication requirement. The issue centers on whether the request for a bid was accompanied by a serious intent to be bound by the offeror. Intent is not determined by the subjective intentions, beliefs, or assumptions of the offeror. What meaning Vincent attached to his invitation to bid is not relevant. Intent is determined by what a reasonable person in the offeree's position would conclude the offeror's words and actions meant. A request or invitation to negotiate is not an offer. It only expresses a willingness to discuss the matter and possibly enter into a contract after further negotiations. A reasonable person in the position of IMC would not conclude that the invitation evidenced an intention to enter into a binding agreement. As in construction contracts, an invitation to submit a bid is not an offer, and the bidding party does not bind the party who requests bids merely by submitting a bid. The party requesting the bids is free to reject all the bids or not act at all. Vincent was not bound by the bid of IMC merely because it was the highest submitted. Vincent never manifested an intent to be bound by the invitation to bid and he remained free to reject the bid of IMC or simply change his mind and take no action at all.

Answers to Practice Quiz

True/False

1. False   An unequivocal acceptance is a legal acceptance.
2. True   The general rule is that silence is not an acceptance; however, if prior dealings between the parties indicate that silence means acceptance, then the law views it as such.
3. False   A counteroffer is effective when received.
4. False   Modernly courts are more lenient and will imply terms such as price and time for performance. Price will be implied if there is a market or source to determine the price of the item or service. The time for performance will be implied based on what is reasonable under the circumstances.
5. False   An offer cannot be accepted if it is not communicated to the offeree by the offeror or an agent or representative of the offeror.
6. True   Price will be implied if there is a market or source to determine the price of the item or service. The time for performance will be implied based on what is reasonable under the circumstances.

7. True   Generally advertisements are treated as invitations to make an offer. However, if the offer is so definite and specific that it is obvious that the advertiser has the present intent to bind himself or herself to the terms of the advertisement, it will be considered an offer.

8. False   An auction with reserve is an invitation to make an offer. In this situation, the seller keeps the right to refuse the highest bid and may withdraw the goods from sale.

9. False   Offers made in jest such as this one on April 1 (April Fool's Day) do not constitute the requistite objective intent. Further, his laughing after her acceptance also confirms that a reaonsable person would not have taken him seriously.

10. True   A rejection is not effective until it is actually received by the offeror.

11. True   The modern law of contracts merely requires the terms of the offer be "reasonably certain."

12. True   The offer terminates if the subject matter, in this case the snowmobile, of the offer is destroyed through no fault of either party prior to its acceptance.

13. False   The offeree is the only one who has the legal power to accept an offer and create a contract.

14. True   The offeree may feel discontented; a grumbling acceptance is a legal acceptance, as he or she is not adding any conditions to the offer before accepting.

15. True   This is an exception to the general rule that silence usually is not considered acceptance even if the offeror states that it is. If the offeree has indicated that silence means assent, then it will be construed as an acceptance. A classic example is when someone indicates that if you haven't heard from them by a date certain, then go ahead and send the order.

16. False   Under the mailbox rule, acceptance is effective upon dispatch, not receipt.

17. False   Nondisclosure agreements are enforceable. As a matter of fact, if an individual breaches a nondisclosure agreement, suit may be brought against the breaching party for damages.

18. True   Unilateral contracts may only be accepted by the offeree's performance of the required act. Compare this to a bilateral contract where it can only be accepted by an offeree who promises to perform the requested act.

19. False   Implied authorization may be implied from what is customary in similar transactions.

20. True   The ethical based rule provides for each nation to respect other nations' laws.

Multiple Choice

21. A   Answer A is correct as the question defines an offer. Answer B is incorrect as a rejection is performed by the offeree after an offer has been made indicating that he or she is not interested in the offer. Answer C is incorrect as a revocation is performed by the offeror after having made an offer, which in turn would indicate a lack of intent to enter into a bargain. Answer D is incorrect based on the reasons given above.

22. C   Answer C is correct as the car dealer expressed his opinion that he felt the car was the best car on his lot and would probably give her a lifetime of happiness. Traditionally expressions of opinions are not actionable as promises as they do not satisfy the intent requirement of the formation of a contract. Answer A is incorrect for the reason stated above. Answer B is incorrect as her grounds for rescission only appear to be based on the car dealer's opinion, which would not substantiate granting her money back. Answer D is incorrect for the reasons stated above.

23. B   Answer B is correct as it states what is needed in order for an award to be accepted, hence, knowledge of the reward before performing the requested act and the performance of the requested act. Answer A is incorrect, as writing a letter to the offeror is not the proper way to accept an offer of a reward. Answer C is incorrect as everyone having an interest in the subject matter of the reward is not a legally recognized way in which a reward may be accepted. Answer D is incorrect as an offer of a reward may not be accepted by implication.

24. C   Answer C is correct as the bidder is the offeror and the seller is the offeree. The seller may refuse to sell the goods. In such case, the auction is with reserve unless otherwise stated. Answers A and B are incorrect as they do not legally state what an auction where the seller refuses to sell the goods is known as. Answer D is incorrect as a quasi-contract is one that is implied by law which has nothing to do with what the question asked.

25. D   Answer D is correct as Ray must sell his rare vase to Sally for $18,000, as she is the highest bidder. Auctions without reserve require that items being sold be sold to the highest bidder. As such, answers A, B, and C are incorrect as all of these are lower bids than Sally's.

26. B   Answer B is correct as death or incompetency of the offeree or offeror are two ways by operation of law that an offer may be terminated. Answer A is incorrect as rejection and revocation are ways that the parties may terminate an offer. Answer C is incorrect as it does not make any sense. Answer D is incorrect as intoxication and incapacity are defenses to the enforcement of a contract not ways to terminate an offer.

27. A   Answer A is correct as an offer may stipulate that acceptance must be by a specified means of communication, such as registered mail. Further, since Ernest used an unauthorized means of communication by hand delivering his acceptance, the acceptance of employment is not effective even if it is received by the ABC Corporation in a timely manner because the means of communication was a condition of acceptance. Ernest should have accepted by certified mail as stated in the offer from the ABC Corporation. Answer B is incorrect as the general rule states that an offeree must accept an offer by an authorized means of communication, not an unauthorized means of communication. Answer C is incorrect as implied authorization usually applies in circumstances of prior dealings between the parties, or it is implied from what is customary in similar transactions or usage of trade. Accepting employment does not appear to fit within any of the categories given for an implied authorization situation. Answer D is incorrect as the comity principle is an ethical rule that states that nations will respect other nations' laws. This principle does not apply in this particular case.

28. D   Answer D is correct as answers A, B, and C all correctly state the necessary elements to establish a valid offer.

29. C   Answer C is correct as implied authorization may be inferred from prior dealings between the parties, usage of trade, and from what is customary in similar transactions. Answer A is incorrect as this states the proper dispatch rule. Answer B is incorrect as it not only is contradictory in that authorization cannot be implied and expressed at the same time. Further, the general rule regarding acceptance is that it is effective upon dispatch unless there was a stipulation by the parties that acceptance was effective upon receipt. Answer D is incorrect as once again the answer is phrased in contradictory terms to the question. Authorization may not be implied and stipulated to at the same time.

30. D   Answer D is correct as an offer may not be accepted if it is not communicated to the offeree by the offeror or a representative or agent of the offeror. Since Mrs. Sweet did not communicate the offer to Mr. Baker, he cannot accept the offer to buy the packaging division of the Sweetest Things Corporation. Answer A is incorrect as the rule does not apply to representatives or agents of the offeree, but rather representatives or agents of the offeror. Answer B is incorrect as the fact that Mrs. Baker did not tell Mr. Baker all of

the offer's particulars is irrelevant as she cannot communicate the offer to her husband. Answer C is incorrect as, even though she as a manner of speaking may wear the shoes in their family, she may not make the offer to her husband. Mrs. Sweet as the offeror must make the offer to Mr. Baker, the offeree.

Short Answer

31. objective contracts
32. The courts cannot enforce the contract or determine an appropriate remedy for its breach if the terms of the offer are not definite and certain.
33. The offer cannot be accepted if it is not communicated to the offeree.
34. Time for performance can be implied as can price if there is a market or source from which to derive the price of the item or service from.
35. an auction with reserve
36. Marcia must communicate the revocation in the Sunset News Press for five weeks as the general rule is that revocation of offers made to the public must be by the same means and for the same length of time as the original offer.
37. Sue has made a counteroffer that in effect terminated the original offer from Julius and created a new offer.
38. The offer is automatically terminated by operation of law as the subject matter, here the bolts of silk fabric, was destroyed through no fault of either party (flooding from a broken pipe) prior to the offer being accepted.
39. The offer automatically terminates since there is no contract prior to Omar being adjudged insane.
40. a manifestation of assent by the offeree to the terms of the offer in a manner invited or required by the offer as measured by the objective theory of contracts
41. an offeree who promises to perform
42. The mirror image rule requires the offeree to accept the offeror's terms. Acceptance must be unequivocal.
43. An option contract is one in which an offeror is prevented from revoking his or her offer by receiving compensation from the offeree to keep the offer open for an agreed-upon period of time.
44. An offer terminates when a stated time period ends. If no time is stated, an offer terminates after a reasonable time.
45. This rule is intended to protect offerees from being legally held to offers because they did not respond.
46. Under common law, if an acceptance was not properly dispatched, it was not effective until it was actually received by the offeror.
47. express authorization
48. It indicates the offeror's present intent to contract.
49. A price term can be implied if there is a market or source from which to determine the price of the service or item.
50. It terminates the offer.

Chapter 11

CONSIDERATION AND EQUITY

Chapter Overview

This chapter explores the element of consideration, or in lay person's terms, "something of legal value given in exchange for a promise." Upon reviewing this chapter, you will have an in-depth understanding of what is meant by consideration as well as its significance in the formation of a contract. Additionally, the material provided in this chapter will enable you to analyze promises that are not supported by consideration, as well as enforceable promises that are lacking consideration.

Objectives

Upon completion of the exercises contained in this chapter, you should be able to:
1.   Explain the meaning of consideration as applied in a contractual setting.
2.   Understand the meaning of legal value.
3.   Define and identify bargained-for-exchange.
4.   Discuss output and requirements contracts.
5.   Explain when a best efforts contract provision is used.
6.   Describe what an illusory promise is and its impact.
7.   Describe when promises lacking consideration are enforceable.
8.   Explain an accord and satisfaction and the effect it has on the original contract.
9.   Understand and discuss the doctrine of promissory estoppel.

Practical Application

You should be able to recognize whether there is sufficient consideration in a contractual situation to become part of the basis of the bargain between the parties. You should also be able to recognize what type of consideration is being given. Further, if consideration is lacking, you should be able to determine whether it will or will not be enforceable.

Helpful Hints

It will be very beneficial to you to break down the definition of consideration into several parts as well as give an example for each. Additionally, it would be especially helpful to analyze the cases given at the end of the chapter in your text and attempt to apply the contract principles you have learned up to this point.

As you begin to analyze the cases at the end of the chapter, it is important to make a notation of the issues you spot on the case itself. You will do a more thorough job if you analyze the cases line by line. This will enable you to address the legal concerns that may be present in each fact situation. Each contract question should be read twice before being answered. Also, you will find that making an outline of your answer before actually writing it is very useful as it provides a means to organize and prepare a makeshift rough draft before your final response to each question is written.

Study Tips

Consideration

- Defined: "Something of legal value."
  Examples: money, property, forbearance of a right, the provision of services, or anything else of legal value
- Presumption: A written contract is presumed to be supported by consideration.
- Two requirements for consideration
  1. Something of legal value must be given, and
  2. There must be a bargained-for exchange.

  Elaboration of the two requirements:
  - **Legal Value** is established if the promisee suffers a legal detriment or the promisor receives a legal benefit.
  - **Bargained-for Exchange** refers to the exchange that parties engage in that leads to an enforceable contract. Gift promises and gratuitous promises by themselves are not enforceable, however if the promissee offers to do something in exchange for either of these two types of promises, then consideration is established.

Output Contracts

The seller agrees to sell all of its production to one buyer.

Requirements Contracts

The buyer contracts to purchase all of the requirements for an item from a single seller. For example, Kurt has an Internet store that he wishes to sell leather purses in. After doing his research, he contacts Abbot, an international wholesaler who gives him the best price of anyone in the market. Kurt and Abbot agree that Kurt will purchase all of his leather purse requirements from Abbot.

Nominal Consideration

This type of consideration is minimal in light of the subject matter of the contract. As such it is not considered legally sufficient in states that recognize the "shock the conscience of the court" standard for determining the adequacy of the consideration.
Example: "I will give you $1.00 for your oceanfront home." One dollar is hardly adequate for an oceanfront home and in most states would "shock the conscience of the court."

Best Efforts Clause

This clause usually states that one or both of the parties will use their best efforts to achieve the objective of the contract. It's important to remember that the courts have held that imposition of the duty to use best efforts is sufficient consideration to make a contract enforceable.

Contracts that Lack Consideration

- **Illegal Consideration**

A contract based on illegal consideration is void. A promise to refrain from doing an illegal act will not be enforceable as illegal consideration is part of the bargained-for exchange.

Example: "If you pay me $5,000, I will not damage your brand new car!"

- **Illusory Promises**

  If the parties enter into a contract, but one or both of them choose not to perform, then consideration will be lacking.

  Example: Fred says to Jim, "I will paint your garage if I feel like it."

- **Moral Obligations**

  The general rule regarding moral obligations is that they lack consideration. The minority rule, however, allows for the enforcement of moral obligations.

  Example: Deathbed promises or contracts based on affection and love are promises based upon moral obligations.

- **Preexisting Duty**

  If a person promises to perform an act or do something he or she is already under an obligation to do, then the promise is unenforceable because no new consideration has been given. In other words, the individual had a preexisting duty.

  Exception: If a party encounters substantial unforeseen difficulties while performing his or her contractual duties and the parties modify their contract to accommodate these difficulties, no new consideration is necessary.

- **Past Consideration**

  When a party to a contract promises to compensate another for work that has been performed in the past, then the situation involving past consideration exists. A contract must be supported by new consideration in order to be binding.

Settlement of Claims Involving Accord and Satisfaction

- **Accord**

  An accord is an agreement where both parties agree to accept something different in satisfaction of the original contract.

- **Satisfaction**

  Simply stated, this is the performance of the accord.

Promissory Estoppel

The purpose of promissory estoppel is to give a remedy to a person who has justifiably relied upon another's promise, but that person takes back his or her promise. Further, because there is no agreement or consideration, the recipient of the promise cannot sue based on breach of contract. This doctrine estops the promisor from revoking his or her promise and thereby prevents unjust enrichment by the promisor. An injustice would occur if the promise were not enforced.

Refresh Your Memory

The following exercise will enable you to refresh your memory on the rules and principles presented to you in this chapter. Read each question twice and place your answer in the blanks provided. Review the chapter material for any question you miss or are unable to remember.

1.   Written contracts are presumed to be supported by _____.

2.   An unenforceable promise because it lacks consideration is called a _____ promise.

3.   Contracts based on _____ consideration are void.

4.   If Betty and Jane enter into a contract whereby Betty only has to perform if she chooses to do so, this would be classified as an _____ contract.

5.   A deathbed promise is not enforceable because it is one that is
_____.

6.   A contract supported by a promise to refrain from doing an illegal act is considered to be
_____   _____.

7.   A contract that provides that one of the parties only has to perform if he or she chooses to is an example of an _____ _____.

8.   A majority of jurisdictions hold that promises made out of a sense of moral obligation are
_____.

9.   If a person promises to perform an act or do something he or she is already required to do, this is called a _____ _____.

10.   An agreement made by the parties to a contract whereby the parties agree to accept something different in satisfaction of the original contract is known as an _____.

11.   Performance of an accord is known as _____.

Critical Thought Exercise

David Johnson was a well-known businessman in Connecticut and was considering a political career. Johnson desired to enter the race for his local congressional seat. Johnson had a 21-year-old daughter, Stacey, who had studied theater at an Ivy League School and was ready to seek her fame and fortune in movies. When no roles in movies were forthcoming, Stacey was offered a lucrative contract to perform in adult films. David Johnson was afraid that his daughter's pornographic film career would cause great embarrassment to his family and ruin his political career. Stacey would not listen to her father and was anxious to make the adult films. Mr. Johnson offered his daughter $750,000 if Stacey refrained from making any adult films or any other film that involved nudity for a period of ten years. The offer by Mr. Johnson was conveyed to Stacey in a letter. Stacey agreed to her father's offer and stated in a return letter that she would use his promise to motivate her to lead a more moral life. Stacey rejected the offers to make adult films and refrained from making any film wherein she appeared nude for a period of ten years. At the end of ten years, Stacey requested that her father pay the $750,000 as promised.

Mr. Johnson refused to pay the money, stating that Stacey had given him nothing in return for his promise except a promise to be a good person. Mr. Johnson took the position that their agreement lacked legally sufficient consideration.

Was a contract formed that was supported by consideration?

Answer:

_____

_____

_____

_____

_____

_____

_____

_____

_____

_____

_____

_____

_____

_____

_____

_____

_____

_____

_____

_____

Practice Quiz

True/False

1. ___ Past consideration will support a new contract. [p. 175]

2. ___ Chris tells Julie he will stop driving drunk if she gives him $100 a month. This is an enforceable promise. [p. 174]

3. ___ Forbearance of a legal right and refraining from drinking or smoking for a period of time is not forms of consideration. [p. 171]

4. ___ An accord and satisfaction is the same as a compromise. [p. 177]

5. ___ Parties in requirements and output contracts have an obligation to act in good faith. [p. 177]

6. ___ Cyrina, a real estate broker, entered into a contract with Bert that contained a best efforts clause to sell Bert's home. She faithfully showed Bert's house to potential buyers for five of the six-month contract without so much as one offer. Bert now claims that the contract is not enforceable and wants another realtor. Bert will prevail. [p. 177]

7. ___ A contract that imposes a duty to use one's best efforts in achieving the contract's objective is enforceable. [p. 177]

8. ___ The doctrine of promissory estoppel does not prevent the promissory from revoking his or her promise. [pp. 177-178]

9. ___ Lucy's statement to Winnie that she may buy Winnie's house if she feels like it is enforceable. [p. 174]

10. ___ A contract may exist without consideration. [p. 171]

11. ___ A police officer may accept a reward for arresting a criminal. [p. 175]

12. ___ If a party encounters unforeseen difficulties while performing duties under the contract, any modification that is made to the contract must be supported by new consideration. [p. 176]

13. ___ Satisfaction of a new agreement refers to the performance of an accord. [p. 177]

14. ___ Jay promises to pay Kelly an extra $1,000 for the concert she performed in last month. If Jay fails to pay Kelly, then Kelly may enforce the promise. [p. 175]

15. ___ A compromise agreement is another name for an accord. [p. 177]

16. ___ A minority of states will not examine sufficiency of the consideration in a contract between two parties. [p. 171]

17. ___ A promise where one or both parties chooses to perform or not perform is a preexisting duty promise. [p. 174]

18. ___ If John promises to perform an act that he is already under an obligation to do, the promise is unenforceable. [p. 175]

19. ___ A promissory may revoke his or her promise if necessary under the doctrine of promissory estoppel. [p. 177]

20. ___ Mike's threat to graffiti Jeff's house if Jeff doesn't give him money is unenforceable. [p. 174]

Multiple Choice

21. Which of the following would not be viewed as sufficient consideration? [p. 175]
    a. money
    b. property
    c. receiving additional money for a house that was painted two months ago
    d. refraining from drinking for six months.

22. Which of the following are supported by consideration? [p. 175]
    a. deathbed promises
    b. gift promises
    c. contracts made out of moral obligation
    d. all of the above

23. A bargained-for exchange can best be described as [p. 172]
    a. an exchange that parties engage in that leads to an enforceable contract.
    b. unenforceable as the contract lacks consideration.
    c. enforceable as otherwise the property would escheat to the state.
    d. unenforceable as it would be difficult for the court to determine how much love was bargained for in the contract.

24. Modifications of a contract not supported by consideration will be enforced if [p. 175]
    a. the parties have a preexisting duty to perform.
    b. there are substantial unforeseen difficulties.
    c. the parties file the modified contract with a local court.
    d. none of the above.

25. What type of contract exists where the seller agrees to sell all of its production to a single buyer? [p. 177]
    a. a requirements contract
    b. an output contract
    c. a moral obligation contract
    d. an illusory contract

26. What type of contract exists where a buyer contracts to purchase all of what is needed for an item from one seller? [p. 175]
    a. a requirements contract
    b. an output contract
    c. an adhesion contract
    d. an unenforceable contract as the terms are vague and uncertain

27. If Karissa and Monica disagree about what Monica owes Karissa under a contract between the two of them, they may attempt to reach a compromise agreement that is called [p. 177]
    a. an arbitration.
    b. a legal value agreement.
    c. a quasi-contract.
    d. an accord.

28. If Monica pays Karissa the settlement that they agree to under the contract, her performance of rendering the newly agreed-upon amount is called [p. 177]
    a. satisfaction.
    b. welching on an agreement.
    c. a breach of contract as the contract could not be altered or modified.
    d. a best efforts contract.

29. A contract that provides that Waldo only has to clean Margie's swimming pool if he chooses to do so is an [p. 174]
    a. example of best efforts.
    b. example of good faith and fair dealing.
    c. example of past consideration.
    d. example of an illusory promise.

30. A contract is considered supported by legal value if [p. 171]
    a. it is based on a moral obligation.
    b. if the promisor suffers a legal detriment or the promisee receives a legal benefit.
    c. if there is a market or standard to which the court can set a value should it be missing.
    d. the promisee suffers a legal detriment or the promisor receives a legal benefit.

Short Answer

31. If a party seeks to change the terms of an existing contract during the course of its performance, it is _____. [p. 175]

32. If Samantha says to Tito, "Because you were such a good employee, the ABC Company will pay you a $10,000 bonus," this is considered _____ _____ and therefore unenforceable [p. 175]

33. The law imposes an obligation of _____ _____ on the performance of the parties to requirements and output contracts. [p. 177]

34. An _____ is one way to compromise a dispute over what is owing under a contract. [p. 177]

35. Mrs. Henning promised to give her niece $5,000, but then rescinded the promise. What will the result be? [p. 175]

    _____

    _____

36. Elmer said to Jay, "I will graffiti your business unless you give me $350,000." Jay gave Elmer the requested amount of money in exchange for Elmer's implied promise not to graffiti his business. Is the contract enforceable? [p. 174]

    _____

    _____

37. A contract is considered supported by legal value if either one of two things are present. What are they? [p. 171]

    _____

    _____

38. What type of situation allows the parties to modify their contract even though it is not supported by new consideration? [p. 177]

    _____

    _____

39. How would past consideration best be described? [p. 175]

_____

_____

40. If Maria says to Eva, "I will purchase all of the red paint that you have," what kind of contract has she possibly entered into? [p. 177]

_____

41. Contracts based on illegal consideration are _____. [p. 174]

42. In terms of the settlement of claims, what does the term satisfaction mean? [p. 177]

_____

_____

43. When is the doctrine of promissory estoppel used? [pp. 177-78]

_____

_____

44. If Hank agrees to sell all of his canned tuna to Patricia, what type of contract may apply to this situation? [p. 175] _____

45. "I will give you $600," is an example of a _____. [p.172]

46. What type of obligation does the law impose on the performance of the parties to requirements and output contracts? [p. 177] _____

47. Why won't refraining from doing an illegal act serve as a basis for an enforceable contract? [p. 174]

_____

_____

48. If Mrs. French says to Brandon, "If you come to class every day this semester as you are supposed to, I will take you to lunch at the restaurant of your choice," would this be an enforceable promise? Support your answer. [p. 174]

_____

_____

49. What is an illusory promise? [p. 174]

_____

_____

50. A contract must arise from a _____ in order to be enforceable. [p. 172]

Answers to Refresh Your Memory

1. consideration [p. 171]
2. gift promises [p. 172]
3. void [p. 174]
4. illusory [p. 174]

5.   made out of moral obligation [p. 175]
6.   illegal consideration [p. 174]
7.   illusory promise [p. 174]
8.   unenforceable [p. 174]
9.   preexisting duty [p. 175]
10.   accord [p. 177]

Critical Thought Exercise Model Answer

The fact that a party has made a promise does not mean that the promise is enforceable. In contract law, a basis for the enforcement of promises is consideration. Consideration is the value given in return for a promise. It is usually broken into two parts: (1) something of legally sufficient value must be given in exchange for the promise, and (2) there must be a bargained-for exchange. Something of legally sufficient value may consist of (1) a promise to do something that one has no prior legal duty to do, (2) the performance of an action that one is otherwise not obligated to perform, or (3) the refraining from an action that one has a legal right to undertake. Stacey has the legal right to enter into a contract to perform in adult movies. She has suffered a detriment by forfeiting income that she was legally entitled to obtain. The second element of consideration is that it must provide the basis for the bargain that was struck between the parties to the agreement. The consideration given by the promisor must induce the promisee to incur a legal detriment and the detriment incurred must induce the promisor to make the promise. This keeps the promise from being a gift. Stacey was induced to refrain from making adult films by the promise of her father to pay her $750,000. She was anxious to make the films and did not sign the contract offered to her because of Mr. Johnson's promise. Keeping his daughter out of adult films is what induced Mr. Johnson to make his promise to pay her money. Therefore, the agreement between Mr. Johnson and Stacey was supported by legally sufficient consideration. Because Stacey fulfilled the requested act and suffered the detriment requested by Mr. Johnson, he is now legally obligated to pay her $750,000.00.

Answers to Practice Quiz

True/False

1. False past consideration
2. False Promises to refrain from doing an illegal act such as driving drunk are not enforceable as the consideration is illegal.
3. False Forbearance of a legal right and refraining from drinking or smoking for a period of time are special forms of consideration.
4. True An accord and satisfaction is the same as a compromise.
5. True The law imposes an obligation of good faith on the performance of the parties to requirements and output contracts.
6. False Courts generally have held that the imposition of a best efforts duty provides sufficient consideration to make it enforceable. Cyrina will prevail to remain as Bert's realtor for another month, as per the parties original agreement.
7. True A requirement that one or both of the parties use their best efforts in achieving the objective of the contract is sufficient consideration to make the contract enforceable.
8. False The doctrine of promissory estoppel does prevent the promissory from revoking his or her promise.

9. False Lucy's statement would be viewed by a court as being illusory in that it does not indicate a present intent to enter into the contract. Illusory contracts are not enforceable.
10. False A contract may not exist without consideration.
11. False Many statutes prohibit police officers from accepting rewards for arresting criminals as they are already under a preexisting duty to apprehend the criminals as part of their job. Because of this preexisting duty, there is no new consideration being given and any reward that is offered may not be enforced by the police officer.
12. False If a party runs into substantial unforeseen difficulties while performing his or her duties under the contract, the parties may modify their contract to accommodate these unforeseen difficulties even if the modification is not supported by new consideration.
13. True The performance of an accord is called satisfaction.
14. False Jay's offer to pay Kelly additional compensation for the concert she performed last month is viewed as being past consideration and would therefore be unenforceable.
15. True An accord is an agreement whereby the parties agree to accept something different in satisfaction of the original contract and in essence is a compromise.
16. False The majority of states usually do not inquire into the sufficiency of the consideration. However, the minority of jurisdictions will look at the adequacy of the consideration and if it "shocks the conscience of the court," a party will be relieved from his or her duties under the contract.
17. False A promise where one or both parties choose to perform or not perform is an illusory promise.
18. True If John promises to perform an act or do something he is already under an obligation to do, the promise lacks consideration and is unenforceable. This is known as a preexisting duty.
19. False The doctrine of promissory estoppel prevents the promisor from revoking his or her promise.
20. True Mike's threat would be considered illegal consideration and therefore the contract is void and unenforceable.

Multiple Choice

21. C Answer C is correct as receiving additional money for a house that was painted two months ago would be viewed as past consideration, which is unenforceable. Answers A, B, and D are considered sufficient consideration.
22. D Answer D is correct as deathbed promises, gift promises, and contracts made out of moral obligation are not supported by consideration. Therefore, answers A, B, and C are incorrect.
23. A Answer A is correct as bargained-for exchange can be best described as an exchange that parties engage in that leads to an enforceable contract. Answer B is incorrect as it is a false statement. Answer C is incorrect, a bargained-for exchange has nothing to do with the property escheating to the state. Answer D is incorrect as love has nothing to do with what a bargained-for exchange is other than to say that love is generally not accepted as consideration.
24. B Answer B is correct as modifications of a contract not supported by consideration will be enforced if there are substantial unforeseen difficulties. Answer A is incorrect as modifications of a contract have no relation to a preexisting duty to perform. Answer C is incorrect as the filing of modifications with a local court would not validate the contract as modified if it was not supported by consideration. Answer D is incorrect for the reasons given above.

25. B   Answer B is correct as an output contract is where the seller agrees to sell all of its production to a single buyer. Answer A is incorrect as a requirements contract refers to a buyer who contracts to purchase all of the requirements for an item from one seller. Answer C is incorrect as contracts based on moral obligations usually involve promises of love or deathbed promises. Answer D is incorrect as an illusory contract involves one or both parties choosing whether they want to perform or not under the contract.

26. A   Answer A is correct as when a buyer contracts to purchase all of what is needed for an item from a seller, this is called a requirements contract. Answer B is incorrect as output contracts involve the seller agreeing to sell all of its production to a single buyer. Answer C is incorrect as an adhesion contract is an unconscionable one whereby one of the parties is induced by undue influence or duress or fraud to enter into the contract. Answer D is incorrect as despite the appearance of being vague and not definite, courts have recognized these types of requirements contracts with the understanding that the parties have a duty to act in good faith.

27. D   Answer D is correct as an accord is an agreement whereby the parties agree to accept something different in satisfaction of the original contract, and hence compromise. Answer A is incorrect as arbitration is a means in which to settle a dispute by way of a neutral third party. The facts are silent as to whether the contract permits arbitration and if there is another individual involved in resolving the dispute. Answer B is incorrect as there is no such thing as a legal value agreement. Answer C is incorrect as a quasi-contract is an equitable remedy that is sometimes imposed by the court when there isn't a contract. The facts clearly state that there is a contract between Monica and Karissa.

28. A   Answer A is correct as the performance of an accord of the new agreement is called the satisfaction. Answer B is incorrect as it is contradictory to the facts as Monica is paying Karissa what they have agreed to and hence could not be welching on their agreement. Answer C is incorrect as there is nothing in the facts that indicates that the contract could not be altered or modified. Answer D is incorrect as the term best efforts usually refers to a clause, not an entire contract. Further, a best efforts clause is one where the court imposes a duty to act in good faith in the performance of the objective of the contract.

29. D   Answer D is correct as Waldo's option of cleaning or not cleaning Margie's swimming pool is too indefinite to be enforced and is an example of an illusory contract. Answer A is incorrect as the term best efforts refers to the parties' duty to act in good faith in the performance of the objective of the contract. As such, Waldo's option to clean or not to clean would not be an example of one acting in good faith to get Margie's pool cleaned. Answer B is incorrect for the reasons that answer A is incorrect. Answer C is incorrect as there is nothing in the facts to indicate that additional compensation is being given to Waldo for a job that he has already performed.

30. B   Answer B is correct as the modern law of contract provides that a contract is supported by legal value if the promisee suffers a legal detriment or the promissory receives a legal benefit. Answer A is incorrect as moral obligations have been found to have no legal value. Answer C is correct if the price is missing in a contract; however, answer B provides a broader meaning in assisting the court in determining legal value. Answer D incorrectly states who suffers the legal detriment and who receives the legal benefit. The answer as stated has the roles reversed.

Short Answer

31. unenforseeable
32. past consideration
33. good faith
34. accord

35. The niece would have no recourse as it was a gift promise that lacked consideration.
36. No, the contract is void and unenforceable, because it is supported by illegal consideration (extortion is unlawful).
37. The promissory receives a legal benefit, or the promisee suffers a detriment.
38. Where a party encounters substantial unforeseen difficulties while performing his or her contractual duties and a modification to the contract is made to accommodate those difficulties, the modification will be enforced even though there is no new consideration.
39. Past consideration is when a party to a contract promises to pay additional compensation for work done in the past.
40. She has possibly entered into a requirements contract.
41. void
42. the performance of an accord
43. It is used to provide a remedy to a person who has relied on another person's promise, but the other individual takes back his or her promise and is not subject to a breach of contract cause of action because either the agreement or consideration is missing.
44. An output contract may apply to this situation.
45. a gift promise
46. good faith
47. Because refraining from an illegal act is viewed as illegal consideration, any promise attempting to support a contract based on not performing an illegal act will not be enforced.
48. No, because Brandon is under a preexisting duty to come to class every day as he is expected to do that as a student.
49. An illusory promise is one in which one or both parties have the option of performing or not performing an act.
50. bargained-for exchange

Chapter 12

CAPACITY AND LEGALITY

Chapter Overview

This chapter's primary emphasis entails the capacity to enter into contracts as well as the lawfulness of certain contracts. You will learn about the obligations minors, intoxicated and insane individuals have under contracts that they enter into. Additionally, contracts that are contrary to statutes or those that are unconscionable are also examined in this chapter.

Objectives

Upon completion of the exercises contained in this chapter, you should be able to:
1. Describe and recognize situations where the infancy doctrine applies.
2. Explain when minors, intoxicated individuals, and insane individuals are responsible for what they contract for.
3. Describe legal insanity and explain its impact on contractual capacity.
4. Describe intoxication and explain its impact on contractual capacity.
5. Understand and explain illegal contracts that are contrary to statutes.
6. Recognize and explain illegal contracts that are contrary to public policy
7. Describe what a covenant not to compete is and recognize when they are lawful.
8. Explain the use for exculpatory clauses and explain when they are lawful.
9. Explain what an unconscionable contract is and when it is unlawful.

Practical Application

You should be able to determine what an incapacitated individual will be responsible for when entering into a contract. Further, you should be able to determine whether the rules of law regarding the infancy doctrine, legal insanity, and intoxication will have an impact on any contracts that you may enter into. Additionally you should be able to determine whether covenants not to compete as well as any exculpatory clauses are lawful based on the knowledge you should have obtained. Finally, your knowledge should enable you to determine whether or not a contract may be unconscionable, void, or voidable.

Helpful Hints

This chapter lends itself toward simple organization based on who may be involved in a contractual situation as well as what type of clause the parties are concerned with. The rules are very straightforward in this chapter and simple to learn. It is very beneficial to explore the critical legal thinking cases at the end of the chapter in your text as well as answer the Critical Thought Exercise contained herein. The more exposure you have to situations involving capacity and legality, the easier and more recognizable these issues will become for you.

Study Tips

You should start your studying of this chapter by learning that the general presumption is that the law presumes that parties that enter into a contract have the capacity to do the same.

Next, you should examine the contractual situation for any potential capacity issues. These usually involve minors, intoxicated or insane individuals.

Minors

- Who is considered to be a minor?
  <u>Common law</u>: Females under 18 years of age and males under 21 years of age
  Most states have statutes specifying the age of majority.
  Most prevalent age of majority is 18 years old for males and females.
  Any age below the statutory age of majority is called the period of minority.

- Infancy Doctrine – This gives minors the right to disaffirm most contracts they have entered into with adults. It serves as a minor's protection against unscrupulous adults who may want to take advantage of a minor. It is an objective standard.
  - A minor may choose whether or not to enforce the contract. If both parties are minors, both parties have the right to cancel the contract.
  - A minor cannot disaffirm as to part of the contract and affirm as to another part of the contract.

- Disaffirmance
  - A minor may disaffirm a contract in writing, orally, or by conduct.
  - No formalities are needed.
  - It must be done prior to reaching the age of majority or a reasonable time thereafter. Reasonable is assessed on a case-by-case basis.

Restoration and Restitution

If either party has not performed the contract, the minor only needs to disaffirm the contract. If the minor has given consideration to the competent party before disaffirming, the competent party must place the minor in the status quo. In other words, he or she must give the minor back his or her money to make him or her whole again. This is also known as the *competent party's duty of restitution.*

Minor's Duty of Restoration

Upon disaffirmance of the contract, the minor must return the goods to the adult, even if the goods are lost, destroyed, consumed, or have depreciated in value.

Minor's Duty of Restitution

In a majority of states, the minor will be required to put the adult in status quo upon disaffirming the contract if the minor was intentionally or grossly negligent in his or her conduct thereby causing the adult's property to lose value. Some states require the minor to make restitution of the reasonable value of the item when disaffirming any contract.

Minor's Misrepresentation of Age

- At common law the minor would still be able to disaffirm the contract despite the misrepresentation.
- Modernly most states hold the minor must place the adult in the status quo if he or she disaffirms the contract and hence would owe the duties of restoration and restitution to the adult.

Ratification

- Simply defined: To accept.
- How is ratification accomplished? Ratification may be expressed, impliedly, or by conduct.
- Rule of law: A minor may ratify a contract before reaching the age of majority or a reasonable time thereafter. If disaffirmance does not occur in this time frame, it is considered accepted.

Contracts That Are Enforceable Against Minors

- Minors are required to pay for the necessaries of life that they contract for.
- Examples of necessaries: food, clothing, tools of the trade, medical services, education.
- Note that the minor is required to pay the reasonable value of the services or goods.
- Also, statutes exist that make minors liable for certain contracts. Examples of some of these special types of contracts as per the statutes include child support, education, medical, surgical, and pregnancy cares to name a few.

Parents' Liability for Their Children's Contracts

- If the parents have not sufficiently provided for their children's necessaries of life, then they are liable for their children's contracts.
- Exception: If a minor becomes emancipated by voluntarily leaving home and living apart from his or her parents and can support him or herself, then the parents have no duty to support their child. This is looked at on a case-by-case basis.

Mentally Incompetent Persons

- In order for a person to be relieved of his or her duties under a contract, the law mandates that the person have been legally insane at the time he or she entered into the contract.

- Legal insanity defined: Legal insanity is determined by using the *objective cognitive understanding test* which involves determining whether the person was incapable of understanding or comprehending the nature of the transaction.

- The following do not qualify as insanity: delusions, light psychological or emotional problems, or weakness of intellect.

- Impact of being found insane: If an individual is adjudged insane, the contract is void.

- Impact of being insane, but not adjudged insane: The contract is voidable by the insane person. The other party does not have the option to avoid the contract unless that party doesn't have the contractual capacity either.

- The other party must put the insane party back to the status quo. The sane party must also be placed back to the status quo if he or she was unaware of the other party's insane condition.

- Liability of insane people: Under a quasi-contract, insane individuals are liable for the reasonable value for the necessaries of life that they receive.

Intoxicated Individuals

- General rule: Contracts entered into by intoxicated individuals are voidable by that person. Intoxication may be by alcohol or drugs.

- The contract is voidable only if the person was so intoxicated that he or she was incapable of understanding or comprehending the nature of the transaction. Note that some states will only allow the person to disaffirm the contract if he or she was forced to become intoxicated.

- Impact of disaffirming the contract based on intoxication: The intoxicated one must be returned to the status quo. Also, the intoxicated person must return the consideration under the contract, thereby making restitution to the other party and returning him or her to the staus quo.

- Liability of intoxicated individuals: These individuals are liable in quasi-contract to pay the reasonable value for the necessaries that they receive.

Illegality

- The object of a contract must be lawful. If the object is illegal, then the contract is void and unenforceable.

- Illegal contracts

    - **Usury laws** – These laws set an upper limit on the annual rate that can be charged on certain loans. They are enacted to protect borrowers from loan sharks. Consequences for violating these laws include criminal and civil penalties.

    - **Gambling Statutes** – All states have some sort of regulation or prohibition concerning gambling,

    - **Lotteries, wagering, and games of chance** – Consequences for violating these laws also include criminal and civil penalties.

- **Sabbath Laws** – These are also known as blue laws or Sunday laws. They prohibit or limit the carrying on of certain secular activities on Sundays. Only certain states enact these laws.

- **Contracts to commit a crime** – These are void. However, if the object of the contract became illegal after the contract was entered into because of a governmental statute, both parties no longer have to perform under the contract.

- **Licensing Statutes** – All states require that certain occupations and professions be licensed in order to practice. There are two types of statutes to be aware of, regulatory and revenue-raising statutes. The regulatory statutes concern those that protect the public. For example, an unlicensed doctor may not collect payment for services that a regulatory statute requires a licensed person to provide. The revenue-raising statutes are made to raise money for the government. Their purpose is to gather revenue. Protecting the public is not a consideration with this type of statute.

Contracts Contrary to Public Policy

- If the contract has a negative impact on society or impacts public safety or welfare, it is void.

- Example: Immoral contracts may be against public policy, such as a contract that requests sexual favors. Societal beliefs and practices are used as a guide in determining what immoral conduct is.

- Exculpatory Clauses – An exculpatory clause relieves one or both parties from tort liability under a contract. This type of clause can relieve a party from ordinary negligence but not be used in cases of gross negligence, intentional torts, fraud, or willful conduct. Courts do not condone exculpatory clauses unless the parties have equal bargaining power.

- Covenants Not to Compete – These types of ancillary contracts are lawful if reasonableness can be demonstrated based on the line of business protected, the duration of the restriction and the geographical area that is being protected. The court can refuse to enforce it or alter it to make it reasonable if there is a need.

- Effect of Illegality – Generally speaking one cannot enforce an illegal contract. However, there are exceptions to every rule, including this one. Those that may enforce an illegal contract include innocent persons who justifiably relied on the law or fact making the contract illegal or, persons who were induced to enter into a contract to name just a few.

- Unconscionable Contracts – Some contracts are so unfair that they are unjust. The public policy based doctrine of unconscionablility allows the courts to refuse to enforce the contract, refuse to enforce the unconscionable clause but enforce the rest of the contract or limit the application of any unconscionable clause in order to avoid an unconscionable result.

- Requirements to Demonstrate a Contract Is Unconscionable
  - The parties possessed severely unequal bargaining power.
  - The dominant party unreasonably used its unequal bargaining power to obtain unfair contract terms.
  - The subservient party had no reasonable alternative

Refresh Your Memory

The following exercise will enable you to refresh your memory on the rules and principles presented to you in this chapter. Read each question twice and place your answer in the blanks provided. Review the chapter material for any question you miss or are unable to remember.

1. If Kerri and Jess want to enter into a contract for the purchase of Kerri's house, the law presumes that both parties have the requisite _____ to enter into a contract.

2. _____ contracts are unenforceable.

3. What option does a minor have under the infancy doctrine? _____
_____

4. If Tara, a-seventeen-year-old enters, into a contract to buy an $8,000 snow mobile from Pete, and later decides she does not really want the snow mobile, when must she rescind it?
_____

5. Aaron told Bill's Used Boats that he was twenty-one-years-old so that he could buy a boat he had been wanting for quite some time. He was really seventeen years old. After Aaron made one payment on the boat, he decided to disaffirm the contract. What duty or duties does Aaron owe Bill's Used Boats?
_____

6. If Cathy, a minor, ratifies a contract with Harold, what in effect is she doing?
_____
_____

7. What sorts of things are helpful for the court to look at in order to determine what is considered necessary in a minor's life?
_____
_____

8. Contracts that have a negative impact on society or that interfere with the public's safety and welfare are referred to as _____ _____ ____ _____
_____.

9. Why are licensing statutes enacted?
_____
_____

10. Contracts that have a negative impact on society or interfere with public safety and welfare are _____.

11. An exculpatory clause is

    _____.

12. What are some of the factors that the court will consider before they will strike down an exculpatory clause?

    _____

    _____

13. What are the three aspects that the courts will consider in determining whether or not to enforce a covenant not to compete?

    _____

    _____

14. What is meant by the term in pari delicto?

    _____

15. An unconscionable contract is also known as a contract of _____.

Critical Thought Exercise

You manage a small bicycle shop and sell a very good product, with some bikes costing $2,000. A young man comes into your store and wants to buy a mountain bike for $1,200. He has the cash. You are very happy to sell it to him. He tells you that he is an ambitious high school student who is taking classes at the local university and needs a bicycle that is capable of handling the large hills between the high school and college so that he can make it to class.

Two years later, the young man comes into the shop and tells you that yesterday was his eighteenth birthday, and after drinking a great deal of alcohol, he rode his bike down the Cuesta Grade and crashed into a Ford Expedition. He hands you a piece of bent frame and states that this is all that was left of the bicycle when he went back to the accident scene this morning. He asks for his $1,200 back as he now "desires to undue the contract."

Will you agree to the full refund? Why or why not?

Answer:

_____

_____

_____

_____

_____

_____

_____

_____

_____

_____

_____

_____

_____

Practice Quiz

True/False

1. ___ An illegal contract can be enforced by the offeree. [p. 183]

2. ___ The most prevalent age of majority is 18 years of age for both males and females [p. 183]

3. ___ The right of a minor to rescind a contract is based on public policy reasons. [p. 183]

4. ___ Contracts for the necessities of life are exempt from the infancy doctrine. [p. 185]

5. ___ A minor may only disaffirm a contract in writing. [p. 184]

6. ___ In some situations, vocational training is considered a necessity of life. [p. 185]

7. ___ A minor may affirm one part of the contract and disaffirm another part. [p. 184]

8. ___ Ratification relates back to the inception of the contract. [p. 185]

9. ___ The competent party to a contract need not return the minor to status quo if the minor transferred consideration, money, property, or other valuables to the competent party before disaffirming the contract. [p. 184]

10. ___ A minor must put the adult in status quo upon disaffirmance of the contract if the minor's intentional or grossly negligent conduct caused the loss of value to the adult's property. [p. 184]

11. ___ George, who had been drinking martinis all night long, offered to sell Floyd his brand new motor home for $2,000. Floyd accepted. The next day Floyd brought a check for $2,000 to George and wanted the keys and title to the motor home. George did not know what Floyd was talking about. Floyd may enforce the contract. [p. 187]

12. ___ A minor's ratification may be accomplished by express, oral, or written words or implied from the minor's conduct. [p. 185]

13. ___ Minors are obligated to pay for the necessaries of life that they contract for. [p. 185]

14. ___ Minors are not responsible for such things as shelter, clothing, food, or medical services. [p. 185]

15. ___ The court will not consider the minor's lifestyle, age, and status in life in determining what is necessary. [p. 185]

16. ___ When a minor voluntarily leaves home and lives apart from his or her parents, this is known as emancipation. [p. 186]

17. ___ The subjective cognitive understanding test is used to determine legal insanity in most jurisdictions. [p. 186]

18. ___ If a person is insane, but not adjudged insane, the contract he or she has entered into is void. [p. 186]

19. ___ Contracts made while an individual was not legally sane can be disaffirmed. [p. 187]

20. ___ Insane individuals are liable in quasi-contract to pay the reasonable value for the necessaries of life they receive. [p. 187]

Multiple Choice

21. Under the infancy doctrine, which is true with respect to a minor's decision to affirm or disaffirm? [p. 183]
    a. The adult is not bound by a minor's decision.
    b. The adult is only bound by a minor's decision to affirm.
    c. The adult is bound by the minor's decision regardless if he or she affirms or disaffirms.
    d. The adult is only bound by a minor's decision to disaffirm.

22. If Woodrow, who has been a minor for eleven months, tries to disaffirm a contract with Zippy, an adult, what would be the most likely result? [p. 185]
    a. Woodrow may disaffirm the contract because it has not been a year yet.
    b. Woodrow is bound by the contract and the right to disaffirm the contract has been lost.
    c. Woodrow may attempt to ratify the contract.
    d. all of the above

23. Which of the following is true with respect to intoxicated individuals who enter into contracts? [p. 187]
    a. The amount of alcohol or drugs that is necessary to consider a person to be intoxicated enough to disaffirm a contract is judged on a case-by-case basis.
    b. A factor that is looked at are a user's physical characteristics.
    c. Some states allow a person to disaffirm a contract if he or she was forced to become intoxicated.
    d. all of the above

24. Which of the following is not true with respect to gambling? [p. 189]
    a. All states either prohibit or regulate gambling.
    b. States provide criminal and civil liabilities for gambling.
    c. Risk-shifting contracts and gambling are the same.
    d. Games of change are regulated by all states.

25. What is the purpose of an exculpatory clause? [p. 192]
    a. to relieve one or both parties to a contract from tort liability
    b. to relieve one or both parties from fraud
    c. to relieve one or both parties from gross negligence
    d. to relieve one or both parties from recklessness

26. Unconscionability can best be defined as [p. 194]
    a. an act that is done with the other contracting party in mind.
    b. an act to create a lawful contract.
    c. an act to even out the bargaining power between the parties.
    d. There is no single definition for unconscionablility.

27. If Lucy was adjudged insane at the time she entered into a contract with Maile, what obligation if any would Maile have to Lucy? [p. 187]
    a. Maile would have to void the contract with Lucy.
    b. Maile would have no obligation to Lucy.
    c. Maile would have to place Lucy in status quo.
    d. Maile does not have any duty to Lucy.

28. Intoxicated individuals are liable in quasi-contract to pay for [p. 187]
    a. the alcohol or drugs that may be consumed.
    b. the reasonable value for necessaries they receive.
    c. damages and attorneys fees if they lose.
    d. all of the above.

29. Which of the following would not be considered to be an illegal contract? [p. 190]
    a. a higher interest rate than what is allowed by state usury laws
    b. medical services provided by an unlicensed physician
    c. state-operated lottery
    d. insurance that you purchased on your neighbor's car

30. Usury laws were created to [p. 188]
    a. make certain forms of gambling illegal.
    b. protect the public.
    c. raise revenue.
    d. protect unsophisticated borrowers from loan sharks and others who charge outlandish rates of interest.

31. Bob and Francis entered into a contract whereby Bob was to sell Francis green and brown striped tree frogs to sell in Francis' pet store. Thereafter the green and brown striped tree frog became protected under a state statute, which added it to its endangered species list. What impact does the statute have on the contract between Bob and Francis? [p. 188]
    a. It has no impact whatsoever as the parties entered into the contract before the statute was enacted.
    b. It has no impact on the frogs sold after the statute becomes law.
    c. Bob and Francis must adhere to the statute as it was designed to protect the public from unlicensed sellers of tree frogs.
    d. Bob and Francis are discharged from the contract.

32. A statute that states that medical services can only be provided by physicians who have graduated from medical school and passed appropriate board exams would be categorized as a [p. 191]
    a. revenue-raising statute.
    b. Sabbath law.
    c. licensing statute.
    d. contrary to public policy.

33. Which of the following applies to revenue-raising statutes? [p. 191]
    a. They are enacted to raise money for the government.
    b. They are enacted to protect the public.
    c. They prohibit or limit the carrying on of certain secular activities on Sundays.
    d. They have a negative impact on society and interfere with the public's safety and welfare.

34. Contracts are contrary to public policy if [p. 188]
    a. they have a negative impact on society.
    b. they interfere with the public's welfare.
    c. they interfere with the public's safety.
    d. all of the above

35. If Lee remarks to Hanna that her employment will be based upon granting him sexual favors, this type of contract would be considered [p. 188]
    a. voidable as Hanna may assert that Lee is suffering from substantial mental incapacity.
    b. necessary in order for Hanna to obtain her job.
    c. void as it is an immoral contract that is against public policy.
    d. a covenant not to compete for other job opportunities.

Short Answer

36. If Solomon is insane, but not adjudged insane when he and Rudy enter into a contract, Rudy may not _____ the contract. [p. 187]

37. Generally _____ persons cannot recover payment for services that a _____ statute requires a licensed person to provide. [p. 191]

38. Contracts in restraint of trade are held to be _____ [p. 191]

39. If Tanya reaches the age of majority and says nothing about the contract she entered into with Boris as a minor, her silence will be said to have _____ the contract. [p. 185]

40. Albert (a minor) prior to disaffirming his contract with Morri gives Morri $500. What must Morri do? _____[p. 184]

41. What does the revised rule concerning a minor's misrepresentation of age state a minor must do? _____ [p. 184]

42. What sorts of things do the courts consider when determining emancipation for a minor?
    _____
    [p. 186]

43. An immoral contract is _____
    _____.
    [p. 188]

44. What are the two standards that have been developed under the law regarding contracts of mentally incompetent persons? [pp. 186-187]
    _____
    _____

45. Anita Brown sells her croissant shop in Phoenix, Arizona, to Margo Jones and at the time of sale has signed a covenant not to compete. In the covenant, Anita has agreed not to open another croissant shop in Arizona for a 20-year period. Will the covenant be enforced by the courts as written? Be sure to provide justification and support for your answer. [p. 194]

_____

_____

46. What elements must be shown in order to prove that a contract or clause in a contract is unconscionable? [p. 194]

_____

_____

47. Wanda has entered into a contract with Wilma to purchase Wilma's car. On the day that the parties are about to exchange the keys and title to the car for the purchase price, Wanda tells Wilma that she thought she was buying a tractor and does not want the car after all. What will be the probable result if Wilma sues Wanda and Wanda claims that she was insane at the time she entered into the contract with Wanda? [pp. 186-187]

_____

_____

48. Ronald, a seventeen-year-old, purchases several different types of wrenches from Ace Tools. He has purchased these tools on credit with the store as he has just started as an apprentice plumber with his uncle Joe. Ronald's first bill from Ace Tools arrives and he finds that he cannot pay it. He immediately notifies Ace Tools of the situation. Ace Tools wants to enforce the credit agreement against Ronald and they indicate this to him. His response is that he is a minor and does not have to pay for the tools. If Ace Tools attempts to enforce the agreement against Ronald, what is the probable outcome? [p. 185]

_____

_____

49. Peter and Mike were in a bar one day after a long day at work when Peter commented to Mike on how lucky he was to live out of the hustle and bustle of the city. Mike agreed that living on the farm was quite nice; however, he claimed he missed the nightlife of the city. The two co-workers continue to talk, have dinner, and partake in a couple of alcoholic beverages. After a few beers, Mike said to Peter, "You want the country life and I want the city life, I'll sell you my California farm for $50,000." Peter immediately jumped at the offer and accepted. The next day when Peter came up to Mike with proof that he had obtained the necessary financing for Mike's farm, Mike laughed at him and said, "You've got to be kidding, I'm not selling my farm! My wife would have my head! I was too drunk last night to know what I was doing!" If Peter tries to enforce the agreement between the two of him, what factors will be considered in determining whether Mike was intoxicated? Also, what is the majority rule regarding contracts entered into while intoxicated? [p. 187]

_____

_____

_____

_____

_____

50. Charlie is interested in buying Sue's high performance speedboat for $10,000. Sue begins to ask a few questions regarding Charlie's previous experience with this type of watercraft, his means of financing, and finally his age. He indicates to her that he has grown up with speedboats, he has the money from a trust fund, and that he is eighteen years old. Sue, a very trusting individual, lets Charlie purchase the speedboat for the asking price. Charlie immediately takes the boat for a ride on the nearby lake and loses control of the boat due to large branches under the water that could not be seen. The boat crashes into a dock and sustains $5,000 in damages. What must Charlie, who is really only sixteen years old, do if he wants to disaffirm the contract? [p. 184] _____

_____

Answers to Refresh Your Memory

1.   capacity [p. 183]
2.   unconscionable [p. 183]
3.   the option to either enhance or void the contract [p. 183]
4.   within a reasonable time of reaching the age of majority [p. 184]
5.   Aaron, a minor who misrepresented his age, owes Bill's the duty of restoration and restitution when disaffirming a contract. [p. 184]
6.   A minor who ratifies a contract indicates that he/she accepts a contract entered into when he or she was a minor. [pp. 184-185]
7.   The minor's age, lifestyle, and status in life all influence what is considered necessary. [pp. 184-185]
8.   contracts contrary to public policy [p. 188]
9.   They are enacted to protect the public from those who may not have met the state standard for a particular profession. [p. 191]
10.   illegal [p. 188]
11.   It is a clause that relieves one or both parties from the contract. [p. 190]
12.   The court will consider the type of activity involved, the relative bargaining power of the parties, knowledge, experience, and sophistication of each of the parties. [p. 192]
13.   The court will consider the type of business being protected, the geographical area being protected, and the length of time the restriction will be in place. [p. 194]
14.   It refers to when both parties are equally at fault in an illegal contract. [p. 194]
15.   adhesion [p. 194]

Critical Thought Exercise Model Answer

In almost all states, the age of majority for contractual purposes is eighteen years old. With some exceptions, the contracts entered into by a minor are voidable at the option of the minor. For a minor to exercise their option to disaffirm a contract, he or she only needs to manifest an intent not to be bound by the contract. The contract can normally be disaffirmed at any time during minority or for a reasonable time after attaining the age of majority. When a minor disaffirms a contract, all property that he or she has given to the adult as consideration must be returned to the minor. Upon disaffirmance, most states require that the minor need only return the goods or money that were the subject of the contract, provided that the minor still has the goods or money. The minor may disaffirm the contract even if the goods are lost, stolen, damaged, or destroyed. A minor may not disaffirm a contract for necessaries, such as food, clothing, shelter, and medical services. However, the minor remains liable for the reasonable value of the goods used when the goods are deemed a necessary. Transportation is normally not considered a necessary. The young man who purchased the bike told me that he was only in high school. This should have put me, as the agent for the store, on notice that I was dealing with a minor. It is irrelevant that the minor drank alcohol before he crashed the bicycle. I will be obligated to return the total purchase price unless my store is in one of the few states that require the minor to put me in the same position as before the contract. In that state, the minor would only be entitled to a refund of the purchase price minus the cost of the damage to the bicycle. Since the bicycle was destroyed, no refund would be warranted.

Answers to Practice Quiz

True/False

1. False   Illegal contracts are void and cannot be enforced by either party.
2. True   The age of majority is 18 for both males and females.
3. True   The right of a minor to disaffirm or rescind a contract is based on public policy reasons that minors should be protected from the unscrupulous behavior of adults.
4. True   Minors are obligated to pay for the necessaries of life that they contract for.
5. False   A minor may disaffirm a contract orally, in writing or through his or her conduct.
6. True   Vocational training, tools of the trade, and goods and services are sometimes considered necessaries of life.
7. False   A minor may not affirm one part of the contract and disaffirm another part.
8. True   Ratification is retroactive to the time the contract was incepted.
9. False   If the minor has transferred consideration to the competent party before disaffirming the contract, that party must place the minor in status quo.
10. False   A majority of jurisdictions hold that the minor must put the adult in status quo upon disaffirmance of the contract, even if the minor's intentional or grossly negligent conduct cause the loss of value to the adult's property.
11. False   The contract is voidable if the person was so intoxicated when the contract was executed that he or she was unable to understand the nature of his or her transaction.
12. True   Ratification may be accomplished by express, oral, or written words or implied by the minor's conduct.
13. True   Minors are obligated for contracts they enter into involving the necessaries of life.
14. False   Though necessary of life has not been defined by the court, items such as shelter, clothing, food, or medical services are found to be necessaries of life.
15. False   The court will examine the minor's age, status in life, and lifestyle in determining what is necessary.
16. True   Emancipation involves the termination of the parental duty of support, which is judged by a minor's voluntary departure from the home and proof of his or her ability to be self-supporting.
17. False   It is the objective cognitive understanding test that most states utilize in determining legal insanity.
18. False   If no formal ruling has been made to adjudge an individual insane, then the court will find that the contract entered into by one who suffers a mental impairment is voidable.
19. True   A person may disaffirm a contract that he or she entered into while he or she was not legally sane.
20. True   Despite the individual being insane, he or she is still responsible for the necessaries of life that he or she contracts for under a theory of quasi-contract.

Multiple Choice

21. C   Answer C is correct as the adult is bound by the minor's decision regardless if the minor affirms or disaffirms the contract. As such, answers A, B, and D are all incorrect statements of law.

22. B   Answer B is correct as eleven months would be considered more than a reasonable period of time to disaffirm a contract after having reached the age of majority. As such, Woodrow would be bound by the contract. Answer A is incorrect because the fact that it has not been a year yet makes the time frame even more unreasonable and Woodrow would not prevail under this situation either. Answer C is incorrect as ratifying the contract would indicate that Woodrow accepted the terms versus trying to disaffirm or cancel it. Answer D is incorrect based on the reasons given above.

23. D   Answer D is correct as answers A, B, and C are all true with respect to intoxicated individuals who enter into contracts.

24. C   Answer C is correct as there is a distinction that is made between gambling and lawful risk-shifting contracts. The latter often has an insurable interest attached to it, whereas gambling does not. Answers A, B, and D are all true and therefore are all incorrect as the question asked, "Which of the following is not true with respect to gambling?"

25. A   Answer A is the correct answer, as the purpose of an exculpatory clause is to relieve one or both parties to a contract from tort liability. Answers B, C, and D are all incorrect, as exculpatory clauses may not be used to relieve one or both parties from fraud, gross negligence, or recklessness.

26. D   Answer D is correct, as there is no single definition for unconscionability. Answers A, B, and C are therefore incorrect based on the reasoning given for answer D.

27. C   Answer C is correct since the contract is void by virtue of Lucy being adjudged insane, Maile would have to place Lucy in status quo. Answer A is incorrect as the contract is already voided by virtue of Lucy's adjudication of insanity. Answer B is an incorrect statement of law. Answer D is also incorrect as it is an incorrect statement of law.

28. B   Answer B is correct as intoxication does not relieve an individual from paying the reasonable value for the necessaries that they contract for. Answer A is incorrect as alcohol is not considered a necessity. Answer C is incorrect as this is a vague statement that does not indicate exactly what the intoxicated individual may lose. Answer D is incorrect for the reasons given above.

29. C   Answer C is correct as state-operated lotteries are permitted in many states under their gambling statutes. Answers A, B, and D are all forms of illegal contracts, and are therefore the incorrect answers.

30. D   Answer D is correct as usury laws set an upper limit on the annual interest rate that can be charged on certain types of loans. By doing this, it helps to protect unsophisticated borrowers from being taken advantage of by loan sharks and others who charge astronomical rates of interest. Answer A is incorrect as gambling statutes make certain types of gambling illegal, not usury statues. Answer B is incorrect as even though this is a true statement, it does not elaborate on what the public is being protected from and therefore it is not the best answer. Answer C is incorrect as usury laws have no bearing on whether or not revenue is raised. Revenue-raising statutes are separate statutes from usury statutes.

31. D   Answer D is correct as contracts to commit criminal acts are void. However, since the object of Bob and Francis' contract became unlawful under the state statute after their contract was entered into, the parties are discharged from their contract. The contract is not illegal unless Bob and Francis agree to go forward and complete it. Answer A is not correct as it does not matter that they entered into the contract before the object of their contract became illegal. Answer B is incorrect as frogs that are sold after the statute becomes law would be in direct violation of the statute thereby making the contract between the parties an illegal one. Answer C is incorrect as the statute is designed to protect the tree frogs that have been placed on the endangered species list, not to protect the public from unlicensed sellers of tree frogs.

32. C   Answer C is correct as licensing statutes require members of certain professions and occupations to be licensed by the state in which they practice by showing they have the proper schooling, experience, and moral character required by the applicable statute. Answer A is incorrect as revenue-raising statutes are designed to gather revenue not protect the public. Answer B is incorrect as Sabbath laws prohibit or limit the carrying on of certain secular activities on Sundays, of which graduating from medical school and passing appropriate board exams are not included. Answer D is incorrect as graduating from medical school and passing appropriate board exams would have a positive impact on society whereas contracts contrary to public policy would have a negative impact on society, or interfere with the public's safety and welfare.

33. A   Answer A is correct as the main purpose of a revenue-raising statute is to raise revenue. Answer B is incorrect as protection of the public is not a consideration of revenue-raising statutes. Answer C is incorrect as Sabbath laws, not revenue raising statutes, prohibit or limit the carrying on of certain secular activities on Sundays. Answer D is incorrect as this refers to contracts that are contrary to public policy.

34. D   Answer D is correct as answers A, B, and C all describe aspects that describe contracts that are contrary to public policy.

35. C   Answer C is correct as a contract that is based on sexual favors has been held as immoral and against public policy. Answer A is incorrect as there is nothing in the facts that would indicate that Lee might have some sort of mental incapacity to make the contract voidable. Answer B is incorrect as it should never be necessary to grant sexual favors in exchange for obtaining a job. Answer D is incorrect as a covenant not to compete is usually an ancillary agreement between the parties and not the crux of the contract itself. Additionally, there is nothing in the facts that indicates a restriction of the type of business, geographic location, or duration of the restriction to qualify it as a covenant not to compete.

Short Answer

36.   void

37.   unlicensed; regulatory

38.   unlawful.

39.   ratified

40.   Morri must place Albert in status quo by returning his $500.

41.   The revised rule states that a minor who misrepresents his or her age must place the adult in status quo if they disaffirm the contract.

42.   The courts consider such things as getting married, setting up a separate household, or joining the military service in determining whether a minor is emancipated.

43.   one whose objective is the commission of an act that is considered immoral by society

44.   adjudged insane, and insane, but not adjudged insane

45. The covenant probably will not be enforced as written as it is unreasonable in geographic restriction (the entire state of Arizona) as well as in duration (twenty years).

46. In order to show that a clause or contract is unconscionable, it must be shown that: 1) The parties possessed severely unequal bargaining power. 2) The dominant party unreasonably used its unequal bargaining power to obtain oppressive or manifestly unfair contract terms. 3) The adhering party had no reasonable alternative.

47. Wilma's insanity defense may fail as mere weakness of intellect or delusions do not constitute legal insanity. If in a state that utilizes the objective cognitive understanding test, they will apply it and determine if Wilma was incapable of understanding the nature of the transaction. This would be her best argument if indeed she was incapable; otherwise, she may be held to the contract with Wanda.

48. Tools of the trade have been found to be a necessary of life in some situations. Arguably Ronald is an apprentice plumber learning the vocation with his uncle, and as such the tools may be a necessity for his livelihood. So, despite the fact that he is a minor and under different circumstances may have been able to disaffirm the contract based on the infancy doctrine, because they are tools necessary for life, the court would probably hold Ronald to the contract.

49. Since the amount of alcohol that needs to be consumed for a person to become legally intoxicated is viewed on a case-by-case basis, the courts will consider Mike's physical characteristics and his ability to hold alcohol. If Mike is in a jurisdiction that provides that contracts entered into by intoxicated individuals are voidable by that person, the contract may not be enforced against him. However, the contract is voidable only if Mike was so intoxicated when the contract between he and Peter was entered into that he was incapable of comprehending that he was selling his California farm for $50,000. Further, if Mike and Peter are in a jurisdiction that only allows Mike to disaffirm the contract if he was forced to become intoxicated or did so unknowingly, he is out of luck. Mike will then have to sell his farm to Peter as agreed in the bar, especially because there is nothing to indicate that Mike was forced to drink the alcohol.

50. Minors who misrepresent their age must place the adult in status quo if they disaffirm the contract. Since Charlie told Sue that he was eighteen years old when in reality he was only sixteen years old when he entered into the contract, he owes the duties of restoration and restitution. Charlie must return the damaged speedboat plus $5,000 to Sue.

Chapter 13

GENUINENESS OF ASSENT

Chapter Overview

The requirements for creation of a contract as well as agreement, capacity, and consideration have been discussed in the preceding chapters. However, even though an individual may consent to a contract, if his or her assent is not genuine, it may make the contract unenforceable. The emphasis of the issues in this chapter is in the areas of mistake, misrepresentation, duress, and undue influence.

Objectives

Upon completion of the exercises in this chapter, you should be able to:
1. Give an explanation of genuineness of assent.
2. Give an explanation on how mutual mistake of fact excuses performance.
3. Describe and apply the requirements to prove intentional misrepresentation (fraud).
4. Understand and explain the difference between fraud in the inception and fraud in the inducement.
5. Understand and explain by example fraud by concealment or silence.
6. Describe innocent misrepresentation.
7. Differentiate between physical and economic duress.
8. Explain undue influence and its applicability to contracts.

Practical Application

You should be able to recognize whether a mistake as it applies to a contractual situation is a unilateral or a mutual mistake along with the particulars for each. Additionally, you should be able to decide whether or not a fraudulent misrepresentation or the more difficult types of fraud exist and the remedies that are available for the same. Finally you should be able to understand the impact of both physical and economic duress as well as undue influence upon a contractual situation. The information in this chapter will be particularly useful to you in developing a sense of what is genuine assent.

Helpful Hints

The five main areas you should be familiar with are broken down into easy to remember sections in the Study Tips section. Since differentiating between the different types of fraud can be confusing, it is important that you gain exposure to as many cases and examples as possible. The exercises provided for this chapter will help to enhance the exercises given at the end of the chapter in your text.

Study Tips

Genuineness in General

Keep in mind you are studying the areas of mistake, misrepresentation, duress, and undue influence. These areas impact whether or not a party's assent to a contract is genuine or whether other factors influenced his or her consent to enter into the contract in the first place.

Assent

The facts you should know are:
- It must be present to have an enforceable contract.
- It may be accomplished by express words or conduct.

Mistake

Mistakes occur when one or both of the parties have an incorrect belief about the subject matter, value, or some other area of the contract.

Two types of mistake

- Unilateral mistake – This is where one party is mistaken about a material fact concerning the subject matter of the contract.

    1. General rule regarding unilateral mistakes: The mistaken party usually will not be allowed to rescind the contract.

    2. Exceptions to the general rule include:
        - If one party is mistaken and the other party knew or should have known about the mistake, then the mistake is treated like a mutual mistake and rescission is allowed.
        - If a unilateral mistake is made because of a clerical or mathematical error and is not because of gross negligence.
        - The gravity of the mistake makes enforcing the contract unconscionable.

- Mutual mistakes – A mistake made by both parties concerning a material fact that is important to the subject matter of the contract.

    1. General rule regarding mutual mistakes: Either party may rescind the contract if there has been a mutual mistake of a past or existing material fact.

What is considered to be a material fact?

There are several explanations for this question.
First, anything that is significant to the subject matter of the contract.
An ambiguity may also qualify as a mutual mistake of material fact.
An ambiguity is where there is confusion as to the meaning of a word or term in the contract.

Two types of mutual mistakes

- Mutual mistake of fact – The contract may be rescinded because there has been no meeting of the minds between the parties as the subject matter is in dispute.

- Mutual mistake of value – The contract remains enforceable because the subject matter is not in dispute and the parties are only mistaken at to the value.

Fraudulent Misrepresentation

The mnemonic you utilized in Chapter 4 is also applicable here. The mnemonic is MISJD.

<u>M</u> – Misrepresentation of a material fact that was false in nature
<u>I</u> – Intentionally made to the innocent party
<u>S</u> – Scienter (knowledge) of the statement's falsity by the wrongdoer
<u>J</u> – Justifiable reliance on the false statement by the innocent party
<u>D</u> – Damages were suffered by the injured party

Fraudulent misrepresentation as an inducement to enter into a contract – The innocent party's assent is not genuine and the contract is voidable. The remedies that are available are rescission and restitution or enforce the contract and sue for damages.

There are *five types of fraud* you need to become familiar with.
1) **Fraud in the Inception** (also known as fraud in the factum) – The person is deceived on what he or she is signing. The contract is void.
2) **Fraud in the Inducement** – The person knows what he or she is signing, but has been fraudulently induced to enter into the contract. The contract is voidable by the innocent party.
3) **Fraud by Concealment** – Where one party specifically conceals a material fact from the other party.
4) **Silence as Misrepresentation** – One need not divulge all facts to the other party; however, if the nondisclosure would cause death or bodily injury or there is a fiduciary relationship or federal or state statutes require that a fact be disclosed, then fraud may be implied.
5) **Misrepresentation of Law** – The general rule is that this is not actionable as fraud. However, if one party to the contract is a professional who should know what the law is and still intentionally misrepresents the law to a less knowledgeable party, this will be enough to allow rescission of the contract.

Innocent Misrepresentation

This occurs when a party makes a statement of fact that he or she honestly believes is true even though it is not. The injured party may rescind the contract but may not seek damages. This type of misrepresentation is sometimes treated like a mutual mistake.

Duress

There are two types, both of which involve threatening to do a wrongful act unless the other party enters into a contract.

1. Duress via physical harm or extortion or to bring or not drop a criminal lawsuit is the first type. Note, the threat to bring or not drop a civil lawsuit is not duress, unless it's a frivolous suit.

2. Economic duress is the second type, which occurs when one party refuses to continue performing his or her duties unless the other party pays more money and enters into a second contract. The innocent party must show that he or she had no choice but to pay the extra money and succumb to the threat. Economic duress is also known as business compulsion.

Undue Influence

Rescission based on undue influence is allowed if it can be shown that a fiduciary or confidential relationship existed between the parties and the dominant party unduly used his or her influence to persuade the servient party to enter into a contract. This contract is voidable.

Refresh Your Memory

The following exercise will enable you to refresh your memory on the rules and principles presented to you in this chapter. Read each question twice and place your answer in the blanks provided. Review the chapter material for any question you miss or are unable to remember.

1. Give two examples of situations where assent would not be genuine. _____
_____

2. The law allows _____ of some contracts made by mistake.

3. When proving the tort known as fraud, scienter means _____
_____

4. When would justifiable reliance on a misrepresentation of fact not be found?
_____

5. When one party takes specific action to conceal a material fact from another party, this is known as _____ by _____.

6. Give an example when a party to a contract would owe a duty to disclose all the facts to the other party. _____

7. Ken telephones the manager of Your Home Town Electronics store and asks how much the smallest high-density television he sells is, and the manager replies, "Fourteen twenty." Thereafter Ken says, "Put my name on one as I can't pass up a bargain like that!" Ken arrives at the store ready to pay fourteen dollars and twenty cents for the small high-density television set, at which point the manager laughs hysterically and says, "Buddy, you must be joking! The smallest set we have costs one thousand four hundred twenty dollars!" If Ken tries to enforce the contract he claims has been formed against Your Home Town Electronics store, what would Home Town's best defense be? _____
_____
_____

8.   What does a party need to prove in order to establish a cause of action for false misrepresentation? _____

_____

_____

_____

9.   Fraud in the inception is known as _____.

10. If Sheila buys a car from Howard on the representation that it has never had anything major repaired on it and thereafter takes the vehicle to the dealer for a routine check only to discover that it has had three transmissions, what cause of action may Sheila bring against Howard? _____

11. An _____ _____ happens when an individual makes a statement of fact that he or she honestly and reasonably believes to be true, even though it is not.

12. When one party threatens to do a wrongful act unless the other party enters into a contract, this is known as _____.

13. If Bart Brown, a contractor, tells Mary Morris, a homeowner, that he will not finish her room addition on her home unless she agrees to pay him an additional $10,000 and Mary feels pressured to give him the additional compensation, this may be construed as

_____.

14. A threat to bring or drop a civil lawsuit will not be considered duress unless _____

_____.

15. Undue influence happens when one person takes advantage of another person's _____, _____, or _____ weakness and unduly persuades that person to enter into a contract.

Critical Thought Exercise

At Rip-Off Motors, an exotic used car dealership, you are the general manager and Slick is your dishonest salesman. Slick told a potential customer, Dupe, that the Porsche he was interested in purchasing had been driven only 25,000 in four years and had never been in an accident. Dupe hired Grease, a mechanic, to appraise the condition of the car. Grease said that the car probably had at least 75,000 miles on it and probably had been in an accident. In spite of this information, Dupe still thought the car would be a good buy for the price, which was still lower than a Porsche with 75,000 miles. Dupe bought the car and it immediately developed numerous mechanical problems which would cost over $10,000 to repair. Dupe has now come back to Rip-Off Motors and is seeking to have you rescind the contract on the basis of Slick's fraudulent misrepresentations of the car's condition. If you rescind the contract, it will cause the dealership to lose over $13,000.

Write a letter to either:

A) Dupe, if you are refusing to rescind the contract, or

B) Mr. Big, the owner of Rip-Off Motors, if you intend to rescind the contract and suffer the loss.

Explain the reasons for your decision, citing authority for your action.

Answer:

_____

_____

_____

_____

_____

_____

_____

_____

_____

_____

_____

Practice Quiz

True/False

1. ___ An innocent party may recover damages for fraud if he or she can show that the fraud caused economic injury. [p. 202]

2. ___ Contracts involving fraud in the factum are void. [p. 202]

3. ___ If Michael induces Kurt to lend him money as represented by a contract for allegedly starting a new business together, but instead pays for his own household expenses and credit card debt out of it, the contract would be voidable by Kurt. [p. 202]

4. ___ In order to rescind a contract based on undue influence, all that need be shown is that a confidential relationship existed between the parties. [p. 204]

5. ___ When proving economic duress, the duressed party need not show he or she had no alternative but to acquiesce to the other party's threat. [p. 205]

6. ___ A material fact is one that is not very significant to the subject matter of the contract. [p. 200]

7. ___ If Chris fails to tell William about the wobbly frame on a bike he just bought from him and William loses control of the steering on his first ride resulting in a broken leg and collar bone, William may not bring suit under the theory of silence as misrepresentation. [p. 202]

8. ___ John calls Funco Inc. to inquire about one of their arcade games and is told that it costs thirty-two fifty. Thereafter John tells the representative of Funco, "That's a great price. Put my name on it and I'll be right there to pick it up." Upon arrival he is told that the game costs three thousand two hundred and fifty dollars. Despite this fact, John will be able to purchase the arcade game for thirty-two dollars and fifty cents. [p. 200]

9. ___ A misrepresentation of law will not be allowed as a ground for rescission of a contract even if one of the parties to a contract is a professional who should know what the law is and intentionally misrepresents the law to a less knowledgeable contracting party. [p. 203]

10. ___ The innocent party to a contract may rescind the contract based on fraud and obtain restitution or enforce the contract and sue for damages. [p. 202]

11. ___ Justifiable reliance will be found in a cause of action for fraud even if the innocent party knew the misrepresentation was false. [p. 201]

12. ___ An intentional misrepresentation occurs when someone negligently induces another to rely and act on a misrepresentation. [p. 201]

13. ___ An ambiguity happens when a word or term in the contract has only one meaning. [p. 200]

14. ___ A party's misrepresentation of law is actionable as fraud if one party to the contract is professional who should know what the law is and intentionally misrepresents the law to a less sophisticated contracting party. [p. 203]

15. ___ Intent in a cause of action based on fraud may never be inferred from the circumstances. [p. 201]

16. ___ To recover damages for fraud, the innocent party must show economic injury occurred. [p. 205]

17. ___ A mutual mistake of value exists if both parties know the value of the contract but are mistaken as to the subject matter. [p. 200]

18. ___ Predictions or opinions about the future usually do not qualify as a material misrepresentation of fact. [p. 201]

19. ___ Click-wrap licenses are not enforceable contracts. [p. 201]

20. ___ Nondisclosure is a misrepresentation if it constitutes a failure to act in good faith. [p. 2020]

21. ___ A misrepresentation is not actionable unless the innocent party to whom the misrepresentation was made acted upon it. [p. 201]

22. ___ Justifiable reliance may be found in the situation where Ned offers to sell Betty his brand new sport utility vehicle for $1,500 even though it is worth $32,000. [p. 201]

23. ___ The measure of damages for fraudulent misrepresentation is the difference between the value of the property when purchased and the resale value. [p. 202]

24. ___ If George talks Ben into signing what Ben thinks is a receipt for handyman work that has been performed at George's country home, but he really has transferred all of his property to George, Ben would be able to void the contract based on fraud in the inception. [p. 202]

25. ___ Innocent misrepresentation is looked upon as a mutual mistake. [p. 204]

Multiple Choice

26. Michael, a real estate salesperson tells Jane that the home she wants to buy is in mint condition. As Jane tours the second story of the home, she notices as she looks up at the attic's ceiling which happens to be on the same floor as the other bedrooms, that she can see bits of the sky. Upon inquiring about this unusual aspect, the realtor tells her that the roof has shingles that swell shut when it rains and air out when the sky is clear. Since this is Jane's first home purchase, she believes Michael and buys the home. The next time it rains, Jane notices that her silk bedding is soaking wet. As she looks up, there are leak marks on the ceiling. She wants to sue Michael. What cause of action would you recommend under the circumstances? [p. 201]
    a. She may bring a cause of action for specific performance to make Michael perform his end of the bargain.
    b. She may claim that Michael made a mistake and therefore the contract needs to be rescinded.
    c. She may bring a cause of action based on fraud.
    d. She may do all of the above.

27. A cause of action based on rescission can best be described as [p. 199]
    a. an action based on a duty to perform.
    b. one party being mistaken as to the subject matter of the contract.
    c. both parties being mistaken as to the subject matter of the contract.
    d. an action to undo a contract.

28. A mutual mistake of fact can best be described as [p. 201]
    a. a unilateral mistake that is so serious that enforcing the contract would be unconscionable.
    b. a mistake where only one party is mistaken about a material fact regarding the subject matter of the contract.
    c. one in which there is a mutual mistake as to a material fact that is important to the subject matter of the contract.
    d. where one party has knowledge of the falsity of the misrepresentation

29. If Walter threatens to bring a criminal lawsuit against Joshua if Joshua doesn't sign a fencing contract giving Walter the job, this would constitute [p. 205]
    a. a misunderstanding between the parties.
    b. duress.
    c. undue influence over Joshua.
    d. mutual mistake of fact.

30. Which of the following is true regarding undue influence? [p. 204]
    a. One person usually takes advantage of another person's mental, physical, or emotional weakness.
    b. A fiduciary relationship exists between the two parties.
    c. A dominant party must have unduly used his or her influence to persuade the servient party to enter into a contract.
    d. all of the above

31. If a unilateral mistake happens because of a mathematical or clerical error that is not the result of gross negligence, a contract between the parties will [p. 199]
    a. be enforced.
    b. be deemed unconscionable.
    c. not be enforced.
    d. be rewritten to reflect the correct mathematical amount.

32. An innocent party's assent to a contract is not genuine when [p. 199]
    a. the innocent party has made a unilateral mistake.
    b. a fraudulent misrepresentation is used to induce the innocent party to enter into the contract.
    c. the innocent party knew that the misrepresentation was false or so extravagant to be obviously false.
    d. the innocent party has participated in the fraudulent misrepresentation.

33. In a fraudulent misrepresentation cause of action, the element of scienter means [p. 201]
    a. knowledge that the representation was false.
    b. that the representation was made without sufficient knowledge of the truth.
    c. "guilty mind."
    d. all of the above.

34. A misrepresentation is not actionable unless [p. 201]
    a. the innocent party to whom the misrepresentation was made acted upon it.
    b. the measure of damages gives the innocent party the benefit of the bargain.
    c. the innocent party knew the misrepresentation was false or obviously false.
    d. none of the above

35. George, a furniture salesperson, tells Felix that the $1,500 reclining chair he will be buying has a weight sensing gauge in the foam and it will hold a person weighing up to 250 pounds easily. Relying on George's statement, Felix purchases one of the reclining chairs for his 200-pound mother, Iris. When Iris sat in the recliner for the first time, the chair collapsed and Iris hurt herself. Upon inspection of the chair there was nothing more than foam in the seat without any sensing gauges that George had mentioned. What type of fraud has occurred? [p. 202]
    a. fraud in the inception
    b. fraud by concealment
    c. misrepresentation of law
    d. fraud in the inducement

Short Answer

36. What is the general rule regarding unilateral contracts and rescission? [p. 199]

_____

_____

_____

37. When would a threat to drop or bring a civil lawsuit constitute duress? [p. 205]

_____

_____

_____

38. What remedies can an innocent person seek in a cause of action for fraud that has been used to induce another to enter into a contract? [p. 201]

_____

_____

39. What is meant by the term undue influence? [p. 204] _____

_____

40. When might genuine assent be missing in a contract? [p. 199] _____

_____

41. What is an ambiguity? [p. 200] _____

_____

42. When one party takes specific action to hide a material fact from another party, this is known as _____. [p. 202]

43. Kendra visited a garage sale and offered to buy an ugly gray and black quilt with red stitching for $10.00. The owner accepted and was glad to get the quilt out of house. It is later determined that it is a quilt of mourning from the Civil War and worth $50,000. Neither party was aware of this fact at the time of contracting. If the original owner wants to recover the quilt, will she be able to? Be sure to support your reason. [p. 202]

_____

44. Henry and Kevin are at a restaurant where both men run tabs on their purchases. Henry tells Kevin that the slip of paper he has is Kevin's tab and to go ahead and sign it so that Henry can get their bill taken care of in a quicker fashion. Kevin does not read what he is signing and quickly jots his signature on the slip of paper pushed before him. Later Kevin finds out that he has signed over the title to his corvette automobile. What cause of action should Kevin bring against Henry? Be sure to support your answer. [p. 202]

_____

_____

45. If Ralph threatens to punch Albert in the face if Albert does not enter into a contract with Ralph to buy Albert's boat, this is known as _____. [p. 205]

46. What is a mutual mistake of value? [p. 200]

_____

_____

47. Jenna visits the Fine Furniture Store in her town every day. With each visit she sits on a dark blue leather sofa located in the front window of the store. The same sales representative sees her each day and finally asks her if she would like to purchase the sofa. She answers in the affirmative and says she wants that couch as she points between the dark blue leather couch and a silver leather couch next to it. The paperwork is signed and delivery is set for the following day. When the couch arrives, it is the silver leather one that is set up in her living room. She wants to rescind the contract based on a unilateral mistake. Will she succeed in her cause of action? Support your answer. [p. 199]

_____

_____

_____

_____

48. What types of issues might affect an individual's assent to a contract? [p. 200] _____

_____

49. If Brent stops building a room addition on Mona's house unless she gives him an additional $10,000 to complete the job since he underbid it in the first place, this would give rise to a cause of action for [p. 205] _____ _____.

50. A contract is _____ by the innocent party when a fraudulent misrepresentation is used to induce another to enter into a contract. [p. 201]

Answers to Refresh Your Memory

1. mistake, duress, fraudulent misrepresentation (answers will vary) [p. 199]
2. rescission [p. 199]
3. guilty mind [p. 201]
4. if the innocent party knew the misrepresentation was false or so extravagant as to be obviously false [p. 201]
5. fraud by concealment [p. 202]
6. when there is a fiduciary relationship between the contracting parties (answers will vary) [p. 202]
7. Home Town's best defense would probably be that there was a material term (price) that was expressed in an ambiguous way to which Home Town should be allowed to rescind the contract. [p. 200]
8. A party needs to show the following: 1) There was a misrepresentation of material fact. 2) There was an intent to deceive. 3) There was knowledge of the falsity of the statement made to the innocent party. 4) The innocent party justifiably relied on the representation. 5) The innocent party suffered economic injury as a result of the misrepresentation. [p. 201]
9. fraud in the factum [p. 202]
10. fraud by concealment [p. 202]
11. innocent misrepresentation [p. 204]
12. duress [p. 205]
13. economic duress [p. 205]
14. such a suit is frivolous or brought in bad faith [p. 205]
15. mental, physical, or emotional [p. 204]

Critical thought Exercise Model Answer

Dear Mr. Dupe:

    I agree with you that my salesman, Slick, made a misrepresentation to you concerning the mileage and condition of the Porsche you purchased. In order for you to recover damages for the tort of fraud, you must show: (1) a misrepresentation of a material fact; (2) an intent on the part of Slick to deceive you; and, (3) you, the innocent party, must have justifiably relied on the misrepresentation. In our situation, you took the car to an independent mechanic, Grease, who informed you that the car had greater mileage than represented by Slick and had probably been in an accident. You decided that the car was still a good value despite this additional information. You did not rely upon the misrepresentations of my salesman when you purchased the car. As a result, you are not entitled to damages for fraud, nor are you entitled to rescind the agreement.

Yours truly,
General Manager

Answers to Practice Quiz

True/False

1. True   Proof of economic injury is necessary in order for an innocent party to prove fraud.
2. True   If a person is deceived as to what he or she is signing, the contract is void.
3. True   What he or she is signing, the contract is void. The question represents an example of fraud in the inducement of which the contract is voidable by Kurt.
4. False   In addition to a confidential relationship between the parties, the dominant party must have unduly used his or her influence to persuade the servient party to enter into the contract.
5. False   The duresssed party in a cause of action for economic duress must show that he or she had no alternative but to acquiesce to the other party's threat(s).
6. False   A material fact is a fact that is important to the subject matter of the contract.
7. False   William may bring a cause of action under the theory of silence as misrepresentation since Chris's failure to tell William of the wobbly frame resulted in bodily injury, here a broken leg and collarbone.
8. False   Two meanings were obviously applied to the term thirty-two fifty whereby the difference between what each party meant was significant. To quote the language utilized in *Konic International Corp v. Spokane Computer Services, Inc. 708P.2d932 (1985),* "The mutual understanding of the parties was so basic and so material that any agreement the parties thought they had reached was merely an illusion." John will not be able to enforce the agreement.
9. False   The basic rule regarding misrepresentation of law is that it is not actionable as fraud. However, the exception to the rule is that if one of the parties to the contract is a professional who should know what the law is and intentionally misrepresents the law to a less knowledgeable individual, then the misrepresentation will be grounds for rescission.
10. True   The remedy when a fraudulent misrepresentation is used to induce another to enter into a contract is to either rescind the contract and obtain restitution or enforce the contract and sue for damages.
11. False   Justifiable reliance is usually found unless the innocent party was aware of the misrepresentation's falsity or the misrepresentation was so outlandish as to be obviously false.
12. False   An intentional misrepresentation occurs consciously when an individual is attempting to induce another to rely and act upon a misrepresentation, not negligently.

13. False   An ambiguity happens where a word or term of the contract is susceptible to more than one logical interpretation.

14. True   A party's representation of law may be actionable as fraud if one party to the contract is a professional who should know what the law is and intentionally misrepresents the law to a less sophisticated contracting party.

15. False   If a party's assent to a contract is not genuine, the courts will permit the innocent party to avoid the contract. If a party's assent is not genuine, other individuals may get away with claiming mistake, committing fraud, utilizing duress and undue influence to get what they want.

16. True   The innocent party must prove that the fraud caused economic injury. The measure of damages is the difference between the value of the property as represented and the actual value of the property.

17. False   A mutual mistake of value exists if both parties know the subject matter of the contract but are mistaken as to the value of the contract.

18. True   To be actionable as fraud, the misrepresentation must be of a past or existing material fact. Statements of predictions or opinions are usually not a basis for a fraud cause of action.

19. False   Under the Uniform Computer Information Transaction Act, the modern e-commerce view of contracts is that click-wrap licenses are enforceable contracts between software licensors and user licensees.

20. True   Silence as misrepresentation has several exceptions to the general rule that neither party owes a duty to the other to disclose all of the facts of the transaction. However, nondisclosure is a misrepresentation if it equates to a failure to act in "good faith."

21. True   An innocent party to whom a misrepresentation was made must act upon it in order for it to be actionable.

22. False   Betty should know that the statement concerning the price of the brand new sport utility vehicle is false and so way out of line to be true. As such the court probably will not find that Betty justifiably relied upon Ned's statement.

23. False   The measure of damages is the difference between the value of the property as represented and the actual value of the property.

24. True   Since George deceived Ben as to the nature of what he was signing, there is fraud in the inception of which Ben is entitled to void the contract.

25. True   Since the individual making the statement believes it to be true even thought it is not and the individual relying on the mistaken statement believes it to be true, both are mistaken based on the innocent misrepresentation. Therefore, it is often viewed as a mutual mistake.

Multiple Choice

26. C   Answer C is correct as she will be able to bring a cause of action based on fraud since Michael misrepresented a material fact (the swelling shingles) about the roof and its shingles in an effort to get Jane to purchase the home he was trying to sell her. Further, since Jane did buy the home, the element of justifiable reliance was proven. Answer A is incorrect as Jane would not want to make Michael perform his end of the bargain, but rather she wants to rescind the contract with him based on fraud. Answer B is incorrect as a unilateral mistake generally will not rescind a contract. Answer D is incorrect based on the reasoning given above.

27. D   Answer D is correct as the definition of rescission is given as an action to undo a contract. Answer A is incorrect as rescission has nothing to do with a duty to perform. Answer B is incorrect as this answer seems to infer a unilateral mistake which generally is not grounds for rescission. Answer C is incorrect as a mutual mistake at to the value of the subject matter of a contract will not enable a party to rescind a contract.

28. C   Answer C is correct as one in which there is a mutual mistake as to a material fact that is important to the subject matter of the contract. Answer A is incorrect as a mutual mistake is usually not described as a unilateral mistake. Answer B is incorrect, as this answer appears to be describing a unilateral mistake as well. Answer D is incorrect as this answer is geared towards a fraud analysis versus a justification for rescinding a contract depending on the type of mistake that was involved.

29. B   Answer B is correct as Walter is threatening to do the wrongful act of bringing a criminal lawsuit against Joshua unless Joshua gives him the fencing contract. This constitutes duress. Answer A is incorrect as there is nothing in the facts that indicates there is a misunderstanding between the parties. Answer C is incorrect as, even though the facts indicate that Walter was threatening Joshua, there is nothing to indicate that Walter took advantage of Joshua's mental, emotional, or physical weakness nor that the parties had a fiduciary or confidential relationship. Answer D is incorrect as a mutual mistake of fact exists where both parties are mistaken as to the subject matter of the contract of which this theory is not supported by the facts given.

30. C   Answer C is correct as business compulsion is another term for economic duress. Answer A is incorrect as even though economic duress may cause a hardship, it is not referred to as such. Answer B is incorrect as it is a false statement. Answer D is incorrect as a covenant not to compete is an ancillary agreement to a contract not a situation where one individual uses threats to accomplish a contract.

31. C   Answer C is correct as it is one of the exceptions to the general rule that a contract based on a unilateral mistake will not be enforced. Answer A is incorrect as this is one of the exceptions where a contract based on a unilateral mistake will not be enforced. Answer B is incorrect as there is nothing in the facts that would "shock the conscience" of the courts to deem it unconscionable. Answer D is incorrect because as an exception to the general rule of enforcing contracts based on unilateral mistakes, rewriting the contract would be antagonistic to not enforcing the contract based upon the exception.

32. B   Answer B is correct as the use of a fraudulent misrepresentation to induce another to enter into a contract is unenforceable. Answer A is incorrect as the making of a unilateral mistake does not have a bearing on assent unless of course the mistake was based on one of the exceptions to the general rule regarding the enforcement of contracts based on unilateral mistakes. The facts are silent on this point. Answer C is incorrect as acquiescence to false representation is an acceptance that qualifies as an assent since the innocent party knew of the misrepresentation thereby giving the innocent party a chance to make an informed decision. Answer D is incorrect as once again participating in the fraudulent misrepresentation would probably constitute acceptance of the terms being represented and hence genuine assent.

33. D   Answer D is correct as the term scienter means all of the statements given in answers A, B, and C.

34. A   Answer A is correct as an innocent party must act upon a misrepresentation in order for it to be actionable. Answer B is incorrect as the pertinence of the measure of damages is with regard to the requirement that the innocent party must suffer economic injury. It has nothing to do with how damages are measured. Answer C is incorrect as the innocent party's knowledge of the statement's falsity would negate the element of justifiable reliance, which is necessary element in a cause of action for fraudulent misrepresentation. Answer D is incorrect for the reasons given above.

35. D   Answer D is correct as Felix knows that he is signing a purchase agreement to buy a reclining chair for $1,500 of which he was the fraudulently induced to do so by George's representation about that the recliner had a weight sensing gauge in the foam. Answer A is incorrect as fraud in the inception occurs when a person is deceived as to the nature of his or her transaction, which was not the case with this set of facts. Answer B is incorrect as fraud by concealment occurs when one party takes specific action to conceal a fact from another. Answer C is incorrect as the facts do not indicate that there has been a misrepresentation of law, which generally is not actionable as fraud.

Short Answer

36. Generally speaking, the mistaken party will not be permitted to rescind the contract.
37. If the lawsuit is frivolous or brought in bad faith, then a threat to drop or bring a lawsuit will constitute duress.
38. The innocent party may either rescind the contract and obtain restitution or enforce the contract and sue for contract damages.
39. Undue influence is when one individual takes advantage of another person's mental, emotional, or physical weakness and unduly persuades that person to enter into a contract.
40. When a contract is entered into based on mistake, fraud, misrepresentation, or undue influence, the genuineness of assent may be missing.
41. An ambiguity is when a word or term in the contract is susceptible to more than one logical interpretation.
42. fraud by concealment
43. Since it was a mistake of value, the owner may not recover the quilt as the subject matter is not at issue.
44. Kevin should bring a cause of action against Henry based on fraud in the inception as Kevin was deceived by Henry as the nature of his transaction by being told he was signing a restaurant tab.
45. duress
46. A mutual mistake of value happens if both parties know the object of the contract, but are mistaken as to its value.
47. Yes, as the Fine Furniture Store should have known that a mistake was made as Jenna visited the store daily and sat on the blue leather sofa in front of the window every day. Also, the same representative was at the store when she did this. Jenna should not be obligated under the contract as her circumstances satisfy an exception to the general rule that unilateral contracts are enforceable.
48. Mistake, misrepresentation, undue influence, and duress might affect the genuineness of assent in a contract.
49. economic duress
50. voidable

Chapter 14

WRITING AND FORMALITY

Chapter Overview

Once a contract has been established, it is important to examine the subject matter of the contract to determine whether or not the contract was required to be in writing and if there are any issues regarding the proper form that it might have to be in. This chapter explores the Statute of Frauds and which contracts are required to be in writing. Additionally, it discusses if and when prior oral or written agreements between the parties on the same subject matter can be utilized to explain what the parties intended. Explanations of how the court may interpret the parties' contract language as well as whether several documents or references may constitute a contract are also discussed. Finally, the author points out some interesting aspects of international law and compares the United States and Europe to other countries' differing means to adhere signatures onto legal documents.

Objectives

Upon completion of the exercises in this chapter, you should be able to:
1. Describe the contracts that must satisfy the Statute of Frauds.
2. Explain the impact of the failure to adhere to the Statute of Frauds.
3. Discuss how part performance satisfies the Statute of Frauds writing requirement for purchases of land.
4. Explain the application of the Statute of Frauds in situations involving contracts that cannot be performed within one year.
5. Describe what a guaranty contract is.
6. Discuss the need for an agent's contract to be in writing.
7. Explain the sale of goods and the need to satisfy the statute of frauds.
8. Describe and apply the doctrine of promissory estoppel.
9. Understand the parol evidence and its exceptions.
10. Discuss the writing requirements for international contracts.

Practical Application

You will be able to determine which documents comprise a contract based on the expressions used by the parties as well as the location of the documents. Further, you should be able to recognize contractual situations that require the application of the Statute of Frauds and whether or not the writing requirement can be satisfied in the absence of a writing. Also, you should be able to assess whether there are any issues concerning parol evidence and if any exceptions exist.

Helpful Hints

Since most of this chapter concentrates on the Statute of Frauds, it is beneficial to thoroughly understand this concept. A mnemonic has been provided for you to accomplish this objective. Once this primary goal has been fulfilled, the remaining information will be more manageable for you to apply and learn.

Study Tips

Statute of Frauds

<u>General Information</u>
Certain kinds of contracts must be in writing in order to memorialize the significant terms and prevent misunderstanding or fabrications, otherwise known as fraud. The mnemonic given below will help give you an easy way to remember which contracts are required to be in writing. The information that follows the mnemonic is organized in the same order as the mnemonic to provide you with an organized learning method.

<u>M</u>r. <u>D</u>ibbles <u>P</u>laces <u>M</u>any <u>F</u>ancy <u>R</u>eal <u>E</u>state <u>A</u>ds.

Mr.	–	Contracts in consideration of **M**arriage
Dibbles	–	**D**ebt of another
Places	–	**P**art Performance
Many	–	**M**ust be performed within one year
Fancy	–	**F**or goods $500 or more
Real **E**state	–	Transfers of ownership interests in **R**eal **E**state such as mortgages, leases
Ads	–	**A**gency contracts

Contracts in Consideration of Marriage

These types of contracts must be in writing for the most obvious reason, to determine ownership of property and assist in determining benefits and property distribution upon death or dissolution of the same. Also it is important for income tax purposes to know exactly who is a dependent if filing jointly.

Debt of Another

A collateral or guaranty contract occurs where one person agrees to answer for the debts or duties of another individual.

Part Performance

This involves the situation where there is an oral contract for the sale of land or other transfer of interest in real property and there is some sort of partial performance. In order for the partial performance to act as an exception to the Statute of Frauds, many courts require that the purchaser either take possession of the property and pay part of the purchase price or make valuable improvements on the land. If part performance can be shown, the oral contract will be ordered to be specifically performed in order to prevent an injustice.

Must be Performed Within One Year

If a contract cannot be performed by its own terms within one year, it must be in writing. If it can be performed within one year, the contract can be oral.

For Goods $500 or More

The Uniform Commercial Code requires contracts for the sale of goods that cost $500 or more to be in writing in order to be enforceable. Modifications that cause the goods to escalate in price to $500 or more will also need to be in writing.

Real Estate

Contracts that transfer an ownership interest in land must be in writing. This includes mortgages, leases, life estates, and most easements.

Real property includes the land, its buildings, trees, soil, minerals, timber, plants, crops, and permanently affixed things to the buildings (fixtures).

Agency Contracts

Agent's contracts to sell real estate must be in writing under the ***equal dignity rule***.

Electronic Contracts and the Writing Requirement of the Statute of Frauds

- The Electronic Signature in Global and National Commerce Act put electronic contracts on the same level as paper contracts.
- Electronic agreements meet the Statute of Frauds writing requirement.
- The act provides for record retention requirements.

Promissory Estoppel

- Promissory estoppel is also known as equitable estoppel.
- It is an exception to the Statute of Frauds
- It involves an oral promise that is enforceable if three conditions are met.
    1. The promise induces action or forbearance of action by another,
    2. The reliance on the oral promise was foreseeable, and
    3. Injustice can be avoided only by enforcing the oral promise.
- The effect of this doctrine is to estop the promisor from raising the Statute of Frauds as a defense.

Sufficiency of the Writing

Things you should know:
- A contract does not have to be drafted by a lawyer.
- A contract does not have to be formally typed to be binding.
- A contract can be a letter, telegram, invoice, sales receipts, checks, and even handwritings on scraps of paper.
- The contract must be signed by the party to be charged.
- A signature can be a nickname, initial, a symbol, and even the letter 'X.' Also, modernly, a
- Fax may also constitute a signature even though it's a document by electronic means, if the party trying to enforce the contract can demonstrate that the obligation was intentionally incurred.

Japan's Use of a Signature in a Writing

- In Japan, they use a stamp with a set of characters on the end of it. This is called hanko.
- In China it is called chop.
- Hankos and chops are registered with the government.
- The signatures can be made of gold, wood, plastic, ivory, jade, or agate.
- The use of hankos and chops are debated. Some say they promote fraud. Others value the rich tradition and feel it will remain in tact.

Integration of Several Writings

An entire writing does not have to be in one single document in order to be enforceable. Several writings can be combined or *integrated* to form a single written contract. Integration may be accomplished by expressly referring to it in one document that refers to and incorporates another document in it. This is known as *incorporation by reference.*

Interpreting Contract Words and Terms

- The parties may explain the words and terms used in the contract.
- Some contracts contain a glossary that defines the terms and used in a contract.
- If the words and terms are not defined, the courts will interpret using the following standard.
    - Ordinary words – given the meaning as stated in the dictionary.
    - Technical words – given their technical meaning.
    - Specific terms qualify general terms.
    - Typed words prevail over preprinted words.
    - Handwritten words prevail over preprinted and typed.
    - If an ambiguity exists, it will be resolved against the party who drafted the contract.
- If both parties are in the same sort of trade, then the words used in the trade will be given their meaning as per trade usage.
- Interpretation will be to advance the object of the contract.

Parol Evidence Rule

- Parol means word.
- Any words outside of the four corners of the contract are called parol evidence.
- The parol evidence rule states that if a written contract is a complete and final expression of the parties' agreement, any prior oral or written statements that alter, contradict, or are in addition to the terms of the written contract Are inadmissible in any court proceeding concerning the contract.

Refresh Your Memory

The following exercise will enable you to refresh your memory on the rules and principles presented to you in this chapter. Read each question twice and place your answer in the blanks provided. Review the chapter material for any question you miss or are unable to remember.

1. The purpose of the Statute of Frauds is to _____ _____

2. When is the Statute of Frauds asserted in a dispute between the parties? _____ _____

3. What types of personal property become permanently affixed to real property? Be sure to give an example. _____

4. What was the purpose of creating the one-year rule? _____ _____

5. Give examples of writings that can be enforceable as the parties agreement if they contain the essential terms of their agreement. _____ _____

6. What is implied integration? _____ _____

7. What must a purchaser of land under an oral contract do in order for the doctrine of promissory estoppel apply? _____ _____

8. When will contracts for the sale of goods have to be in writing? _____ _____

9. A written contract does not have to be drafted by a _____ or formerly typed in order to be _____.

10. Give three examples of writings that can be enforced as a contract. _____, _____, _____

11. Under the UCC, what is acceptable as a signature? _____ _____ _____

12. Who may affix a signature to a contract. _____

13. What method do the Japanese use for their signature? _____ _____ _____

14. Define the term integration. _____

_____

15. What is meant by the term incorporation by reference? _____

_____

Critical Thought Exercise

On February 1, Professor Herbert was hired by your company's vice president as the company historian at a rate of $1,400 per month for as long as Herbert lived, with $700 to be paid on the first and fifteenth of each month. Herbert was paid regularly for eight months and then the president decided that he didn't like Herbert digging into company history. No further payments were made to Herbert. Herbert claimed that the company had breached the oral contract and brought suit, seeking damages of $1,400 per month for the rest of his life. The company president asserts that the contract is not enforceable because contracts that cannot be performed within one year must be in writing under the Statute of Frauds.

Draft a memorandum to the president advising him as to the applicable law and whether you believe that the company will be able to defend against Herbert's claim based upon the one-year rule.

Answer:

_____
_____
_____
_____
_____
_____
_____
_____
_____
_____
_____
_____
_____
_____
_____
_____
_____
_____

Practice Quiz

True/False

1. ___ The extension of an oral contract might cause the contract to violate the Statute of Frauds. [p. 213]

2. ___ Section 201 of the UCC is the basic Statute of Frauds provision for sales contracts. [p. 214]

3. ___ Usage of trade between the parties is not allowed under the Parol Evidence Rule. [p. 217]

4. ___ The court must let writings between the parties stand. [p. 217]

5. ___ A merger clause is the same thing as an integration clause. [p. 217]

6. ___ A collateral contract for pecuniary gain must be in writing just as if it were the original contract. [p. 213]

7. ___ If the parties to a contract have not defined the words and terms of a contract, the court will void the contract altogether. [p. 216]

8. ___ The Uniform Commercial Code allows several writings to be integrated to form a single written contract. [p. 216]

9. ___ The term parol means that one may be released from prison for good behavior. [p. 217]

10. ___ In Japan individuals often do not use their handwritten signatures to sign legal documents. [p. 215]

11. ___ An implied easement need not be in writing in order to be enforceable. [p. 211]

12. ___ A lease term that is over one year must be in writing under the Statute of Frauds. [p. 212]

13. ___ Merger clauses prevent parol evidence from being introduced to prove fraud, duress, misrepresentation, mistake, or undue influence. [p. 217]

14. ___ Parol evidence will be admissible to show that a contract was void or voidable. [p. 217]

15. ___ Parol evidence may be allowed to explain an ambiguity. [p. 217]

16. ___ Agency contracts to sell real property are one of the few types of contracts that do not need to be in writing. [p. 214]

17. ___ Contracts for the sale of goods for $400 or more need not be in writing. [p. 214]

18. ___ If there is a typographical error in a contract, the court will reform it and allow parol evidence to prove this. [p. 217]

19. ___ A seal may not constitute a signature. [p. 215]

20. ___ A clause that stipulates the contract is a complete integration and the exclusive expression of their agreement is a merger clause. [p. 217]

21. ___ Handwritten words do not prevail over preprinted and typed words in a contract. [p. 216]

22. ___ Incorporation by reference may be accomplished by express reference in one document that refers to and incorporates another document within it. [p. 216]

23. ___ Parol evidence may not be used to fill in a missing price in the contract, as that is the job of the court. [p. 217]

24. ___ A completely integrated contract is viewed as the best evidence in terms of the parties' agreement. [p. 217]

25. ___ The doctrine of part performance is a legal doctrine allowing monetary damages on an oral contract. [p. 211]

Multiple Choice

26. Evan and Gloria, both nonmerchants, enter into an oral contract whereby Gloria agrees to purchase Evan's piano as he has developed severe arthritis and cannot play anymore. He sends her a sloppily written letter with an illegible "e" as his signature setting for the terms of their agreement including the $1,200 sales price. Will Evan's signature be sufficient to satisfy the Statute of Frauds and the Uniform Commercial Code if Evan decides to keep the piano and give it to his granddaughter? [p. 215]
    a. Yes, as Evan's signature need not be his full legal name. As long as the "e" indicates Evan's intent to enter into the contract, it will be sufficient to be binding.
    b. Yes, as long as Gloria's signature appears on the letter as well.
    c. No, because Evan did not sign his full legal name.
    d. No, because Evan really did not intend to sell the piano to Gloria as he wanted to give it to his granddaughter.

27. A clause in a contract that stipulates that it is the complete integration and the exclusive expression of the parties agreement is known as a [p. 217]
    a. promissory estoppel clause.
    b. marital clause.
    c. incorporation by reference clause.
    d. merger clause.

28. Which of the following does the statute of frauds apply to: [p. 211]
    a. mortgages
    b. easements
    c. leases
    d. all of the above

29. James Albertson says to his son Henry and daughter-in-law Grace, "If you quit your jobs in Florida and come take care of me in Texas for six months, I will give you my mansion." Thereafter both Henry and Grace quit their well-paying jobs and move from Florida to Texas to take care of James. They pay off a second mortgage on James's property, move in with James and add a room addition so that James can look out onto the ocean. Six months elapse and Henry and Grace ask James to sign over the deed to the Texas mansion. James laughs and indicates that they do not have any grounds to enforce what they are claiming. What would be Henry and Grace's best theory in order to succeed in a cause of action against James? [p. 211]
    a. an injunction to prevent James from moving from his Texas home
    b. the equitable doctrine of part performance
    c. the integration theory
    d. incorporation of all oral statements by referencing when Henry and Grace moved to Texas

30. Which aspect of the Statute of Frauds is intended to prevent disputes about contract terms that may otherwise occur toward the end of a long-term contract? [p. 212]
    a. the part performance exception
    b. the guaranty contract rule
    c. the one-year rule
    d. goods for $500 or more

31. A collateral or guaranty contract happens where [p. 213]
    a. contracts for the sale of goods costing $500 or more are present.
    b. one person agrees to answer for the debts or duties of another person.
    c. electronic commerce agreements are a secondary means of enforcement to formal contracts.
    d. the most recent agreement of the parties is integrated with the former contract thereby guaranteeing its enforcement.

32. Jane and John enter into a contract for the purchase of Jane's computer, with delivery set for December 15. Upon signing the contract John discovers that a price has not been set. Which rule would best assist the parties for enforcing the contract? [p. 217]
    a. the Kelly Blue Book rule
    b. the promissory estoppel rule
    c. the parol evidence rule
    d. the equal dignity rule

33. Cameron expressly grants to Jennifer the right to use his land to get from her land to the boat dock that is adjacent to the end of his property. If Cameron decides that Jennifer can no longer use his land to get to the boat dock, what must Jennifer show in order to enforce the right to use Cameron's land? [p. 211]
    a. that an easement was created
    b. that she was given a right to use Cameron's land
    c. that the right to use Cameron's land was in writing
    d. all of the above

34. Isabel has brought a cause of action against Murphy for a contract that was induced by fraud. What would Isabel's best argument be in order to void the contract? [p. 217]
    a. an exception to the parol evidence should be validated as it can be utilized for showing that a contract is void or voidable
    b. that Murphy was a scoundrel for tricking her into a fraudulent contract
    c. that the doctrine of promissory estoppel should apply in order to prevent an injustice
    d. none of the above

Short Answer

35. According to the UCC, who must sign a written contract? [p. 215]
    _____
    _____

36. A contract clause that stipulates that it is a complete integration and the exclusive expression of the parties' agreement is a _____ _____. [p. 217]

37. If the Statute of Frauds requires a contract to be in writing, however, despite this requirement the parties have already executed an oral agreement; neither party may seek _____ based on noncompliance with the Statute of Frauds. [p. 210]

38. The doctrine of promissory estoppel prevents the _____ from raising the Statute of Frauds as a defense to the enforcement of an oral contract. [p. 215]

39. Why does a prenuptial agreement have to be in writing? [p. 214]
    _____

40. Briefly define the meaning of fixtures as they pertain to real estate. [p. 211] _____
    _____

41. Give an example of a contract that should be in writing because it will often last longer than a year. [pp. 212-213]
    _____

42. What is the "main purpose" exception to the Statute of Frauds? [p. 213] _____
    _____

43. A _____ is one who agrees to pay the debt if the primary debtor does not. [p. 213]

44. What type of contract has been formed if Stephanie agrees to pay Sally's debt to Visa?
    A _____ contract. [p. 213]

45. If Bert decides to sell his golf cart to Kurt for $800.00, what will be required? [p. 214]
    _____

46. What is the rule that says that agent's contracts to sell property covered by the Statute of Frauds must be in writing to be enforceable? [p. 214] _____

Answers to Refresh Your Memory

1. ensure that the terms of important contracts are not forgotten, misunderstood or fabricated [p. 210]
2. The Statute of Frauds is unusually raised by one party as a defense to the enforcement of the contract by the other party. [p. 211]
3. fixtures An example would be lighting fixtures in a home. [p. 211]
4. The purpose of creating the one-year rule was to prevent disputes about contract terms that may otherwise occur toward the end of a long-term contract. [p. 212]
5. invoices, receipts, telegrams, checks, letters, handwritten agreements written on scraps of paper. [p. 215]
6. Implied integration occurs when an individual places several documents in the same container. [p. 216]
7. The purchaser must pay part of the purchase price as well as take possession of the property or make valuable improvements on the land. [p. 211]
8. The Uniform Commercial Code requires that contracts for the sale of goods costing $500 or more must be in writing in order to be enforceable. [p. 214]
9. lawyer, binding [p. 215]
10. letters, telegrams, checks and sales receipts [p. 215] (answers will vary)
11. A signature may be a person's full legal name, the person's nickname, initials, seal, stamp, a symbol or mark as long as it indicates the person's intent to be bound by the terms of the contract. [p. 215]
12. An authorized agent may affix a signature to a contract. [p. 215]
13. The Japanese use a stamp as their signature, which is composed of a character or a set of characters carved onto the end of a round cylindrical shaped piece held in a person's hand. The Japanese call this a hanko. [p. 215]
14. Integration is the combination of several writings to form a single contract. [p. 216]
15. When integration is made by express reference in one document that refers to and incorporates another document within it, this is known as incorporation by reference. [p. 216]

Critical Thought Exercise Model Answer

Each state has a Statute of Frauds under which certain types of contracts must be in writing to be enforceable. The primary purpose of the statute is to ensure that there is reliable evidence of the existence and terms of certain types of contracts that are deemed important. These types of contracts include those involving interests in land, contracts that cannot by their terms be performed within one year from the date of formation, those that create collateral promised for one person to answer for the debt or duty of another, and contracts for the sale of goods priced at $500 or more. Contracts that cannot, by their own terms, be performed within one year from the day after the contract is formed must be in writing to be enforceable. The test for determining whether an oral contract is enforceable under the one-year rule of the statute is not whether the agreement is likely to be performed within one year from the date the contract was formed but whether performance within a year is possible. When performance within one year is impossible, the contract is unenforceable if it was not in writing. An exception to this "possibility of performance within one year" standard is raised by a lifetime employment contract. Some states rely upon the traditional view that the contract can be performed within one year because a person may die within the first year. The modern view is that a lifetime employment contract anticipates a relationship of long duration, well in excess of one year. These states hold the view that to allow an oral contract for lifetime employment would eviscerate the policy underlying the Statute of Frauds and would invite confusion, uncertainty, and outright fraud. The determination of the enforceability of this oral contract for lifetime employment for Professor Herbert will depend upon whether the jurisdiction adopts the traditional or modern view of the one-year rule.

Answers to Practice Quiz

True/False

1. True   The extension of an oral contract might cause the contract to violate the Statute of Frauds, especially if the contract continues on beyond the one-year rule.
2. True   UCC-201 of the UCC is the basic Statute of Frauds provision for sales contracts.
3. False   Usage of trade between the parties is allowed under the exceptions to the general rule excluding parol evidence.
4. False   The court can reform a contract between the parties in an effort to correct an obvious clerical or typographical error.
5. True   A merger clause is the same as an integration clause, which expressly reiterates the parol evidence rule.
6. False   If the main purpose of a transaction in an oral collateral contract is to provide pecuniary benefit to the guarantor, the collateral contract is treated like an original contract and does not have to be in writing to be enforced.
7. True   The courts will apply standards of interpretation if the parties to a contract have not defined the words or terms of the contract.
8. True   The Uniform Commercial Code does allow several writings to be integrated to form a single written contract.
9. False   The term parol means word.
10. True   The Japanese use a stamp called a *hanko*.
11. True   An implied easement need not be in writing.
12. True   The Statute of Frauds requires leases for a term over one year to be in writing.
13. False   Merger clauses do not prevent the introduction of parol evidence to prove duress, misrepresentation, mistake, or undue influence.
14. True   Parol evidence is admissible to show that a contract is void or voidable.
15. False   Many state Statute of Frauds laws require that agents' contracts to sell real property be in writing to be enforceable.
16. True   The federal law known as the Electronic Signature in Global and National Commerce Act gives an e-signature the same force and effect as a signature written on paper.
17. True   Contracts for the sale of goods under $500.00 need not be in writing.
18. True   The court will allow parol evidence to correct an obvious clerical or typographical error and the court can reform the contract to show the correction.
19. True   A seal may constitute an individual's signature, as the UCC does not require a person's full legal name to appear on the writing.
20. True   This is the explanation for a merger clause, which expressly restates the parol evidence rule.
21. False   Handwritten words do prevail over preprinted and typed words.
22. True   Expressly referring to one document and incorporating it into another document is incorporation by reference.
23. False   Parol evidence may be used to fill in the gaps in a contract if a price term or time for performance term is missing from a written contract.
24. True   A completely integrated contract is viewed as the best evidence of the parties' agreement.

25. False   The doctrine of part performance is an equitable doctrine, which allows the court to order specific performance on an oral contract so that an injustice may be prevented.

Multiple Choice

26. A   Answer A is correct because as long as the illegible "e" indicates Evan's intent to sell Gloria the piano, it can be binding. The signature does not have to be Evan's full legal name. Answer B is incorrect as the Uniform Commercial Code requires the written contract to be signed by the party to be charged. In this case, the party to be charged would be Evan. Gloria's signature is not necessary. Answer C is incorrect based on the reasoning given for Answer A. Answer D is incorrect as the facts do not indicate that he had mixed feelings on who the piano was to go to, but, instead reflect that he intended for Gloria to buy the piano as is evinced by the messy letter that he sent to her.

27. D   Answer D is correct as the question explains what a merger clause is which expressly restates the parol evidence rule. Answers A and B are incorrect as there is no such thing as a promissory estoppel clause or a marital clause. Answer C is incorrect as an incorporation by reference clause refers in one document to another document and incorporates the outside document into the original one.

28. D   Answer D is correct as the Statute of Frauds applies to mortgages, easements, and leases.

29. B   Answer B reflects the best theory that Henry and Grace should utilize against James as the parties' agreement appears to be oral in nature and both Henry and Grace paid off the second mortgage, moved in with James, and added a room onto the property for James to see the ocean. As such, the court will allow the oral contract to be specifically performed in order to prevent an injustice to Henry and Grace. Answer A is incorrect as an injunction is not the remedy that is used in a potential breach of contract cause of action. Answer C makes no sense, as there is nothing in the facts to suggest that there were any documents that were kept together that would imply one contract. Answer D is incorrect as it incorrectly utilizes the term incorporation by reference by associating it with oral statements.

30. C   Answer C is correct as an executory contract that cannot be performed by its own terms within one year of formation must be in writing so as to avoid disputes that may occur toward the end of a long-term contract. Answer A is incorrect as the part performance exception is primarily used in situations involving oral contracts and land. Answer B is incorrect as this refers to answering the debt of another. Answer D is incorrect as the statement does not reflect a measure to prevent disputes but rather states part of a type of contract that needs to be in writing according to the Statute of Frauds.

31. B   Answer B is correct as it correctly states what a collateral or guaranty contract is. Answer A is incorrect as though the goods may in fact cost over $500, there is no dollar amount requirement when it comes to answering for another's debts. Answer C is incorrect as it does not make any sense. Answer D is incorrect as integrating one agreement with another agreement does not necessarily guarantee its enforcement nor does it correctly explain what a collateral or guaranty agreement is.

32. C   Answer C expresses the rule that would help the parties the most as an exception to the parol evidence rule is that if there is a gap such as price in the contract, the court may fill in that price. Answer A is incorrect as there is no such thing as the Kelly Blue Book rule. Answer B is incorrect as the doctrine of promissory estoppel is utilized in oral contract situations where enforcement is necessary to prevent an injustice. The facts indicate that there is a written contract that was signed, and as such promissory estoppel would not be applicable. Answer D is incorrect as the equal dignity rule concerns the requirement that an agents' contract to sell property must be in writing in order to be enforceable.

33. D   Answer D is correct as answers A, B, and C all state what Jennifer must show in order to enforce the right to use Cameron's land.

34. A   Answer A is correct as it provides the best argument for Isabel since an exception to the parol evidence rule is that parol evidence can be admitted to show that a contract was induced by fraud. Answer B is incorrect because even though this might be how Isabel feels, it is a mere accusation verses a legal basis for her cause of action. Answer C is incorrect as the facts are silent as to whether the contract was oral or in writing as well as what the subject matter of the contract is. As such it is nearly impossible to make a determination of the applicability of the doctrine of promissory estoppel.

Short Answer

35.   the party against whom enforcement is sought

36.   a merger clause

38.   rescission

39.   A prenuptial agreement has to be in writing because it defines each other's property.

40.   against whom enforcement is sought

41.   Fixtures are personal property that is permanently adhered to the real property such as the lights on the ceiling in a house.

42.   The "main purpose" exception says that if the main purpose of a transaction and an oral collateral contract is to provide pecuniary benefit to the guarantor, the collateral contract is treated like an original contract and does not have to be in writing to be enforced.

43.   guarantor

44.   guaranty

45.   It will be required to be in writing under the Statute of Frauds as the golf cart costs more than $500.

46.   equal dignity

Chapter 15

THIRD-PARTY RIGHTS
AND DISCHARGE

Chapter Overview

This chapter examines third-party rights under other individual's contracts, more specifically assignees and intended third-party beneficiaries. Additionally it explores conditions to performance and the various ways of discharging the duty of performance. The delegation of contractual duties by mutual agreement, impossibility of performance, and operation of law are also discussed.

Objectives

Upon completion of the exercises contained in this chapter, you should be able to:
1.   Define the meaning of assignment as it pertains to contracts.
2.   Discuss what contracts are assignable.
3.   Define the meaning of delegation of duties and discuss the parties' liability in a delegation.
4.   Define an intended beneficiary and discuss his or her rights under a contract.
5.   Differentiate among a creditor, donee, and incidental beneficiary.
6.   Define a covenant.
7.   Define and differentiate among conditions precedent, conditions subsequent, and concurrent conditions.
8.   Discuss the impact of objective impossibility on a contract.
9.   Discuss the meaning of commercial impracticability and when it applies.
10. Discuss the various ways that contracts are discharged by operation of law.

Practical Application

Upon mastering the concepts in this chapter, you should be able to recognize whether or not a contract may be assigned or delegated and any liabilities that may have been incurred as a result of the assignment or delegation.   Further, you will be able to determine if a third party to a contract has any rights as a beneficiary to the contract. Finally, you should be able to analyze questions and real-life situations concerning the various ways a contract may be discharged by law.

Helpful Hints

Since it is often difficult keeping the parties straight in contracts involving more than two parties, it is helpful to diagram the transaction either in box form as is displayed within your text, or by use of a triangle or any other means that may be useful to you. It is also especially helpful to imagine yourself as the person being given an assignment or right, delegation, or duty. If you substitute yourself into the question or hypothetical, the concepts begin to become clear. Do not get burdened by the titles assignee, assignor, delagatee, delegator, or obligor and obligee.

It is much easier to learn the concept behind the titles first and then the titles. Then the party's actions and its impact will become second nature to you.

Study Tips

It is very important that you become familiar with the terminology expressed in this chapter as it can become confusing.

Vocabulary

Privity of Contract – The state of two specified parties being in contract.

Obligor –The party who owes the duty of performance.
Obligee – The party owed a right under a contract.
Assignor – This is the obligee in disguise as he or she is transferring his or her right under a contract.
Assignee – The party to whom the right has been transferred.
Anti-delegation clause – A clause that prohibits the delegation of duties under the contract. The courts will enforce this clause.
An assignment and a delegation – Where both the rights and duties are transferred under the contract.

Assignment

The transfer of contractual rights by the obligee to another party. No formalities are necessary; however, words to express the intent of the assignor are carefully examined. Words such as transfer, give, and convey have been used to express intent in an assignment.

Rights That May Not Be Assigned Include:

- Personal service contracts are not assignable.
  Exception: A professional athletics contract with a clause that permits the contract to be assigned.

- Assignment of future rights – The general rule is that a person may not assign a currently nonexisting right that he or she is expecting in the future. For example, if Harry was expecting his favorite aunt Linda to leave him her savings account, and Harry tried to assign his expected inheritance to Paul, it would not be a valid assignment. Since Harry does not have a current right to the money, he cannot assign what he does not have.

- Contracts where assignment would materially alter the risk of the obligor – A classic example would be assigning your homeowner's insurance to a friend of yours who cannot afford it.

- Assignment of legal actions – An individual may not assign the right to sue; however, he or she may assign the right to the judgment once it is procured.

Effect of an Assignment

The assignee stands in the shoes of the assignor. The assignor is entitled to performance by the obligor. The assignment extinguishes all rights of the assignor against the obligor.

The assignee must notify the obligor about the assignment and the performance by the obligor must be given to the assignee. If there is no notice given to the obligor, he or she can continue performing under the contract to the assignor. The assignee's only recourse is to sue the assignor for damages.

Rules Used for Successive Assignments

- The American Rule (New York Rule) – The majority of states use this rule, which states that the first assignment in time prevails regardless of notice.

- The English rule – This rule states that the first to give notice prevails.

- The Possession of Tangible Token Rule – Under either the American or English rule, if the assignor makes a successive assignment of a contract right that is represented by a tangible token, such as a savings passbook, stock certificate, etc., the first assignee who receives delivery of the tangible token prevails over subsequent assignees.

If the obligor knows of the assignment but continues to perform to the assignor, the assignee can sue the obligor for payment. He or she will also have to pay to the assignor and to the assignee. Further he or she may sue the assignor for damages.

Anti-assignment and Approval Clauses

- The anti-assignment clause prohibits the assignment of rights under the contract.
- An approval clause is one in which the obligor must approve any assignment.

Delegation of Duties

- A transfer of contractual duties by the obligor to another party for performance.
- Delegator – The obligor who transferred his or her duty.
- Delagatee – The party to whom the duty has been transferred.

Duties That May Not Be Delegated Include

- Personal service contracts that require the discretion, expertise, and the exercise of personal skills.
- Contract whose performance would materially vary if the obligor's duties were delegated.

Effect of Delegation of Duties

- The delegator remains legally liable for the performance of the contract, thereby being subjected to a lawsuit if the delegatee does not perform properly.

- The delegate's liability depends on if there has been a declaration of duties or an assumption of duties. If the word assumption or a similar term is contained in the delegation, then there has been an assumption of duties.

- Compare though, if a delegatee has not assumed the duties under the contract, then this is called a declaration of duties. In the case of a declaration of duties, the delegatee is not obligated to the obligee for nonperformance, and the obligee can only sue the delegator.

Third-Party Beneficiaries

- Third parties who claim rights under contracts are either intended or incidental. The intended beneficiaries are either donee or creditor beneficiaries.

- Intended:
  Donee beneficiary contract – A contract which confers a benefit or gift on an intended third party.
      Donee – The third party to whom the benefit is conferred.
  Creditor beneficiary contract – A contract where a debtor has borrowed money from a creditor to buy an item. The debtor enters into an agreement to pay the creditor back with interest. The debtor thereafter sells the item to another individual before the loan is paid off. The new buyer then promises the debtor that he or she will pay the balance of the loan amount to the creditor.
      Creditor – The party that becomes a beneficiary under the new debtor's contract with another party.

- Incidental beneficiary:
  An incidental beneficiary is one who is incidentally benefited by other people's contracts.

Covenants and Conditions

- Covenant – An unconditional promise to perform.

- Nonperformance of a covenant equals a breach of contract giving the other party the right to sue.

- Condition – A conditional promise is not as definite as a covenant.

- Types of conditions:

  1. Condition precedent – The occurrence or nonoccurrence of an event before a party is obligated to perform under the contract.

     Example: Condition precedent based on satisfaction. There are two tests to determine whether this unique form of condition precedent has been met. They are:

     The personal satisfaction test – This is a subjective test whereby the person is to act in good faith in matters involving personal taste and comfort.

The reasonable person test – This is an objective test that is used to judge contracts involving mechanical fitness and most commercial transactions. This is used when a third person is involved who is used to judge another's work.

Time of performance as a condition precedent:
If a party is not jeopardized by a delay, this will be considered a minor breach. If *"time is of the essence,"* performance by the stated time is an express condition. This will be considered a breach of contract if performance is not rendered by the start date.

2. Condition Subsequent
   This condition exists when a contract provides that the occurrence or nonoccurrence of a certain event automatically excuses the performance of an existing duty to perform.

   In the Restatement (Second) of Contracts, there is no distinction between a condition precedent and a condition subsequent.

3. Concurrent Conditions
   This condition occurs when both parties render performance at the same time.

4. Implied Conditions
   Any of the above conditions may be considered to be express or implied in nature. A condition is implied from the situation surrounding the contract and the parties' conduct.

Discharge of Performance

- There are three ways to discharge a party's duty under a contract. They are by mutual agreement of the parties, by impossibility of performance, or by operation of law.

- **Discharge by agreement** is accomplished by:

  1. Mutual rescission – The parties to a contract can mutually agree to discharge or end their contractual duties.
  2. Substituted contract – The parties can enter into a new contract that revokes and discharges a prior contract.
  3. Novation – This agreement substitutes a new party for one of the original contracting parties. All three must be in unison regarding the substitution.
  4. Accord and Satisfaction – The settlement of a contract dispute where the parties accept something different than originally agreed upon and performance of the same. If an accord is not satisfied when it is due, the injured party may enforce either the accord or the original agreement.

- **Discharge by Impossibility**
  - Discharge by impossibility occurs under the following circumstances:

  - Impossibility of Performance
    This excuse of nonperformance is excused if the contract becomes objectively impossible to perform.

- Examples:
  Death of a promissory in a personal service contract.
  Destruction of the subject matter prior to performance.
  A supervening illegality makes performance of the contract illegal.

- Commercial Impracticability
  This excuse of nonperformance indicates that if an extreme or unexpected development or expense makes it impractical for the promissory to perform, then this excuse may be recognized.

- Frustration of Purpose
  If the object or benefit of the contract is made worthless to the promisor and both parties knew what the purpose was, and the act that frustrated the purpose was reasonably unforeseeable, then this doctrine will excuse the performance of commercial obligations.

- Force Majeure Clauses
  These types of clauses are where the parties agree in their contract as to the events that will excuse nonperformance of the contract. These typical force majeure clause excuses nonperformance caused by natural disasters. Modernly, labor strikes and shortages of materials excuse performance by way of a force majeure clause.

Discharge by Operation of Law

The legal rules that discharge parties from performing their duties under their contracts are as follows:

- Statute of Limitations – The statutory frame in which to bring a lawsuit. The UCC indicates that four years is the time frame to bring a cause of action based on breach of contract.

- Bankruptcy – If the debtor's assets are inadequate to pay all of the creditors' claims, then the debtor receives a discharge of the unpaid debts and is relieved of liability to pay the discharged debts.

- Alteration of Contract – This occurs when a party to the contract intentionally alters the contract's material terms such as price or quantity. The innocent party may discharge the contract or enforce it on its original or modified terms.

Refresh Your Memory

The following exercise will enable you to refresh your memory on the rules and principles presented to you in this chapter. Read each question twice and place your answer in the blanks provided. Review the chapter material for any question you miss or are unable to remember.

1. Explain the meaning of privity of contract. _____
   _____

2. When does the assignee stand in the shoes of the assignor? _____
   _____.

3. What types of defenses may the obligor raise? _____.

4. Which rule provides that the first assignment in time prevails regardless of notice? _____ _____.

5. What is a transfer of contractual duties by an obligor to another party for performance called? _____

6. If Candice does not want her plastic surgeon to be able to substitute another plastic surgeon in his place in the event that he is out of town on the day of her surgery, she may request that an _____ clause be placed in their contract.

7. What is required when the parties want to mutually rescind a contract? _____ _____.

8. When applying the personal satisfaction test, what is required of the person who is given the right to reject the contract? _____

9. What is an approval clause? _____

10. A transfer of contractual duties by the obligor to another party for performance is a _____.

11. A third party who is not in privity of contract but who has rights under the contract against the obligor is an _____ _____.

12. The original creditor who becomes a beneficiary under the debtor's new contract with another party is a _____ _____.

13. An agreement that substitutes a new party for one of the original contracting parties and relieves the existing party of liability on the contract is known as a _____.

14. In order for Ralph to be relieved of his contractual duties under the excuse of impossibility of performance, he must show that the impossibility was _____ in nature.

15. A force majeure clause is one in which the parties may agree _____ _____.

Critical Thought Exercise

The Rocky Mountain Plumbing Company (RMP), which you manage, is very successful and has an excellent reputation. Your business is known for its fairness, prompt performance, and superior work. After a severe earthquake that measured 7.4 on the Richter scale, billions of dollars worth of pipe damage occurred to hundreds of structures within the area serviced by your company. RMP has signed several huge contracts to repair or replace plumbing for government buildings, hospitals, and three hotels owned by Alexis. Each of these contracts will be for $800,000 or more.

You are uncertain if RMP will be able to meet the deadlines set in the contracts as the urgency of the work needing to be done to so many buildings might call for more time.

You have the option of assigning some of the work to Bob's Plumbing, a far less reputable company, or making other arrangements with the county, the hospital district, and Alexis. You are afraid that if you inform people that RMP is unable to perform the contracts on time, it may lose the contracts along with the huge profits they will bring.

Your partners share your skepticism about meeting the deadlines and want to hire Bob's Plumbing immediately without mentioning it to any of the parties involved.

RMP's partners request that you draft a memorandum advising them of the options and risks involved with each option.

Answer:

_____

_____

_____

_____

_____

_____

_____

_____

_____

_____

_____

_____

_____

_____

_____

_____

_____

_____

_____

_____

_____

_____

_____

_____

Practice Quiz

True/False

1. ____ If a lawsuit is not brought during the time period set by statute, an injured party loses his or her right to sue. [p. 233]

2. ____ A legal right that arises out of a breach of contract may be assigned. [p. 223]

3. ____ An assignee takes more rights than the assignor originally had. [p. 223]

4. ____ A condition may be best described as an unconditional promise to perform. [p. 229]

5. ____ A creditor beneficiary may enforce an original contract against the debtor-promisee and enforce the contract against the promisor. [p. 228]

6. ____ A declaration of duties is present when the delegatee has not yet assumed the duties under a contract. [p. 226]

7. ____ When there has been a transfer of both rights and duties under a contract, an assignment as well as delegation has occurred under the contract. [p. 226]

8. ____ Floods, but not earthquakes are excused by what is known as a force majeure clause. [p. 232]

9. ____ Commercial impracticability acts as an excuse for nonperformance of contracts if a foreseeable event makes it practical for the promisor to perform. [p. 232]

10. ____ Courts will often look to see whether the alteration of a contract was intentional and what type of alteration is involved, albeit price, quantity, or some other important term when determining whether the alteration is material enough to allow the innocent party to either discharge the contract or to enforce it. [p. 233]

11. ____ A covenant is a conditional promise to perform. [p. 229]

12. ____ Nonperformance of a convenat is a breach of contract that allows the other party the right to sue. [p. 290]

13. ____ A conditional promise is more definite than a covenant. [p. 229]

14. ____ The personal satisfaction test is a subjective test that requires the use of a third person to determine satisfaction. [p.230]

15. ____ The reasonable person test is an objective test used in situations involving mechanical fitness and commercial contracts. [p. 230]

16. ____ A clause that permits the ABC Corporation to terminate a contract if Sharon Smith does not pass a drug test is an example of a condition subsequent. [p. 230]

17. ____ When each party's absolute duty to perform is conditioned on the other party's absolute duty to perform, this is known as a concurrent condition. [p. 231]

18. ____ An implied-in-fact condition is one that can be implied from the circumstances surrounding a contract and the parties' conduct. [p. 231]

19. ____ Unilateral rescission of a contract does not result in breach as long as notice is given to the other party. [p. 231]

20. ____ If Rod Cool, a famous singer, dies before his New Year's Eve concert, the contract will be discharged based on impossibility of performance. [p. 232]

21. ___ The usual period for bringing a lawsuit based on a breach of contract is one to five years. [p. 233]

22. ___ Commercial impracticability excuses performance under a contract if an unforeseeable event makes it impractical for the promisor to perform. [p. 232]

23. ___ The Uniform Commercial Code provides that the statute of limitations for a breach of a sales or lease contract is one year after the cause of action accrues. [p. 233]

24. ___ If George purposefully changes his hourly rate from $18 per hour to $28 per hour when he walks his paperwork over to Human Resources of the ABC Corporation, this alteration may discharge the contract. [p. 233]

Multiple Choice

25. Which two exceptions allow third parties to acquire rights under other parties' contracts? [p. 222]
    a. a majeure clause and an approval clause
    b. an assignment and a discharge of duties
    c. an assignment and a third-party beneficiary contract
    d. an assignment and a conveyance of personal or real property

26. An obligee who transfers the right to receive performance is called [p. 225]
    a. a delegator.
    b. an assignor.
    c. a delegatee.
    d. a lessor.

27. An assignee is [p. 222]
    a. the party who transfers the right to receive performance.
    b. the party who transfers the right to suspend performance.
    c. the party to whom the right has been transferred.
    d. the party to whom the right has been delegated.

28. Which of the following is an exception which would allow the assignment of personal service contracts? [p. 226]
    a. a plastic surgeon's contract with a patient allowing the transference of his or her duties to any licensed physician in the state in which the surgery is being performed
    b. a poisonous snake handler at a world famous zoo
    c. an auto insurance policyholder wanting to give his or her son the insurance policy
    d. none of the above

29. In order to protect an individual's rights under an assignment, an assignee should [p. 224]
    a. just notify the obligor that an assignment has been made.
    b. notify the assignor that an assignment has been made and that he or she will accept performance from the obligor.
    c. notify the obligor of the assignment and notify the assignor that he or she will not accept performance from the obligor.
    d. notify the obligor that an assignment has been made and indicate to the obligor that performance must be rendered to the assignee.

30. A transfer of contractual duties by the obligor to another party for performance is known as [p. 225]
    a. an assignment of rights.
    b. a delegation of duties.
    c. a declaration of duties.
    d. an assignment and a delegation.

31. Under which of the following would a delegation of duties be acceptable? [p. 226]
    a. if Lionel Richie was scheduled to perform in concert at a local high school but Carrie Underwood appeared instead
    b. if a podiatrist was scheduled to do foot surgery, but instead an oral surgeon came in his or her place to do the surgery
    c. if a famous golfer was scheduled to promote golf balls and a college girl who plays tennis came in his or her place
    d. if a company enters into a contract with another company to send its window washers to do a job may it substitute any of its qualified employees to do the job

32. Tom's Tourist Shop is located on the beach next to where a new high-rise hotel is going in. There are supposed to be sixteen floors to the hotel; however, Charter Construction Company decides to stop building at the thirteenth floor. Since the beginning of the project, the owner of Tom's has noticed a definite increase in business. He knows that once the hotel is complete, his profits will escalate due to the patrons staying at the hotel. Tom decides to bring a cause of action against the Charter Construction Company for breach of contract as he is claiming that his tourist shop was a beneficiary of the hotel and Charter Construction Company contract. What will be the probable result? [pp. 226-228]
    a. Tom will win because his shop is a donee beneficiary under the hotel and Charter Construction Company.
    b. Tom will lose, as his shop is merely an incidental beneficiary as his business unintentionally benefited from the contract just by being located next to the new hotel.
    c. Tom will win because if it were not for Tom, the area surrounding the hotel would be unappealing to tourists.
    d. Tom will lose because he did not give notice of the benefit to Charter Construction.

33. Nonperformance of a covenant entitles the other party to [p. 229]
    a. sue for punitive damages.
    b. sue for breach of contract.
    c. sue for an injunction.
    d. sue for breach of condition.

34. If there has been an extreme or unexpected development expense that makes it impractical for the promisor to perform, this is known as [p. 232]
    a. subjective impossibility.
    b. accord and satisfaction.
    c. commercial impracticability.
    d. frustration of purpose.

Short Answer

35.   An assignment is a [p. 222] _____.

36.   Ralph may not transfer his motorcycle insurance to his roommate Liz because [p. 223]
      _____.

37.   Who owes his or her performance to the assignee? [p. 223] _____

38.   Why would the assignment of Chuck, a professional football player for the Mississippi
      Mohawks, to the St. Louis Rams be valid? [p. 223] _____
      _____

39.   What are the three ways that a party's duty of performance may be discharged?
      [pp. 231-233]
      _____
      _____

40.   The words sell, transfer, and convey as they pertain to contracts might indicate that what
      has taken place? [p. 223] _____

41.   Alice is suing Roger for injuries she sustained when his tractor plowed into the back of her
      small sports car she was driving. She is tired of all of the delays in getting the case to trial
      and assigns her legal action to her best friend Stephanie. Why won't Alice be able to
      assign her legal action to Stephanie? [p.223] _____
      _____

42.   What is the effect of an unconditional assignment of a contract right? [p. 223] _____
      _____

43.   Which rule regarding assignments provides that the first assignee to give notice to the
      obligor prevails? [p. 225] _____

44.   If Sid assigns his savings passbook to Marla and then assigns the same savings passbook to
      Claude but delivers the actual passbook to Claude, who is entitled to the savings account
      and why? [p. 225] _____
      _____

45.   What type of contract language is necessary for there to be an assumption of duties?
      [p. 226] _____

46.   Sarah assigns Abbot the right to collect her lottery proceeds and then Sarah proceeds to
      assign Morgan the same right followed by assigning Greg that same right, but Morgan is
      the first to give notice to the lottery commission. Who will get the lottery proceeds and
      why? [p. 225] _____
      _____

47.   What type of condition is distinguished by the phrase "time is of the essence"? [p. 230]
      _____

48. What type of condition can be inferred from the circumstances surrounding a contract and the parties conduct? [p. 231]_____

_____

49. What is the name of the test that applies to contracts involving personal taste and comfort called? [p. 226] _____

Answers to Refresh Your Memory

1. the state of two specified parties being in a contract [p. 222]
2. when there has been a valid assignment [p. 223]
3. any personal defenses he or she may have against the assignee [p. 223]
4. the American rule (or New York rule) [p. 225]
5. delegation of duties [p. 225]
6. anti-assignment clause [p. 225]
7. The parties must enter into a second agreement that expressly terminates the first agreement. [p. 231]
8. The person given the right to reject the contract must act in good faith. [p. 230]
9. An approval clause is one that permits the assignment of the contract only upon receipt of an obligor's approval. [p. 225]
10. delegation of duties [p. 225]
11. intended beneficiary [p. 226]
12. creditor beneficiary [p. 227]
13. novation [p. 231]
14. objective [p. 232]
15. that certain events will excuse the performance under the contract [p. 232]

Critical Thought Exercise Model Answer

To: RMP Partners
From: Your Partner
RE: Options for performing the contracts

The obligor in a contract must be careful to refrain from informing the obligee that he or she is unable to perform. This may cause the obligee to treat the statement as an anticipatory repudiation and a breach. Therefore, RMP should pursue an option that does not create a breach. It is lawful to transfer the duties under a contract to another party. This delegation of duties does not relieve the party making the delegation of the obligation to perform in the event that the party to whom the duty has been delegated. No special form is required to create a valid delegation of duties. Some duties cannot be delegated, such as when performance depends upon the special skills of the obligor, when the contract expressly prohibits delegation, when special trust has been placed in the obligor, or when performance by a third party will vary materially from that expected by the obligee. These contracts were awarded to us because we are capable of handling the work. This does not mean that Bob's Plumbing is incapable of performing the same duties. RMP would be within its rights to delegate the duties under one or more of the contracts to Bob's Plumbing. RMP would remain liable for any breach of the contract by Bob's Plumbing. Because Bob's Plumbing is a far less reputable company than RMP, we may not want to expose ourselves to greater liability. Another safer option is to enter into a novation with one or more of the obliges and Bob's Plumbing which will allow a new contract to be formed between Bob's Plumbing and an obligee and then extinguish our contract. This will relieve us of any liability under that particular contract, but it will also cause us to lose the profit from the contract and hurt our reputation. Our reputation will be hurt worse if we become embroiled in a contract dispute with the schools and hospital, not to mention a very influential businessperson, Alexis. We should calculate how much of the business we can handle and then approach the parties involved in the smaller contracts and suggest a novation. If the novation is refused, we will then have no choice but to delegate some of the work to Bob's Plumbing.

Answers to Practice Quiz

True/False

1. True   A statute of limitation establishes the time period during which a lawsuit must be brought. If the lawsuit is not brought within this period, the injured party loses the right to sue.
2. True   Legal actions cannot be assigned; however, a legal right that arises out of a breach of contract may be assigned.
3. False   An assignee stands in the shoes of the assignor and as such takes only the rights the assignor originally had.
4. False   A covenant, not a condition is an unconditional promise to perform. A condition is a qualification of a promise that becomes a covenant if it is met.
5. False   The creditor beneficiary may enforce an original contract against the debtor-promisee **or** the promissory, but not both.
6. True   If the delegatee has not assumed the duties under a contract, this delegation of duties is a mere declaration of duties wherein the delegatee is not legally liable to the obligee for nonperformance.
7. True   An assignment and a delegation occurs where there is a transfer of duties and rights under a contract.
8. False   Under a force majeure clause, both flood and earthquakes will excuse the non-performance of a contract.
9. False   Commercial impracticability acts as an excuse for nonperformance of contracts if an unforeseeable (not foreseeable) event makes it impractical (not practical) for the promisor to perform.
10. True   If an intentional alteration is made that is found to be material to the contract, the innocent party may opt to discharge the contract or enforce it.
11 False   A covenant is an unconditional promise to perform.
12. True   A covenant that is not performed gives the other party the right to sue for breach of contract.
13 False   A conditional promise is not as definite as a covenant.
14. False   The personal satisfaction test is a subjective test that involves personal taste and comfort.
15. True   Contracts involving mechanical fitness and most commercial transactions use the reasonable person test which is an objective standard as judged by a third person's satisfaction.
16. True   A condition subsequent exists when a contract states that the occurrence or nonoccurrence of a specific event automatically excuses the performance of an existing duty to perform. Hence, if Sharon Smith does not pass the drug test, the ABC Corporation does not have to employ her.
17. True   Concurrent conditions occur when the parties to a contract must give their performance simultaneously.

18. True   An implied-in-fact condition is one that can be implied from the circumstances surrounding a contract and the parties conduct.

19. False   Unilateral rescission of a contract is equivalent to a breach of that contract. Notice does not have any significance concerning unilateral rescission.

20. True   Impossibility of performance is an objective standard, which indicates "it cannot be done" under the contract. The death of the promisor, here Rod Cool, before the New Year's Eve performance of his contract would be discharge under this rule as this personal service contract, the singing concert cannot be done.

21. True   The parties may agree by way of a force majeure clause that certain events will excuse nonperformance of the contract.

22. True   If an unforeseeable event makes it impractical for the promisor to perform under a contract, then performance will be excused based on commercial impracticability.

23. False   The Uniform Commercial Code provides that a breach of sales or lease contract must be brought within four years after the cause of action accrues.

24. True   Since George intentionally altered a material part of his contract, his hourly pay, the ABC Corporation may choose to either discharge or enforce the contract.

Multiple Choice

25. C   Answer C is correct as assignments and third-party beneficiary contracts allow third parties to acquire rights under other parties' contracts. Answer A is incorrect as a majeure clause involves an agreement between the parties regarding events that will excuse nonperformance under a contract. Further, an approval clause permits the assignment of a contract only upon the receipt of the obligor's approval. Answer B is incorrect as it is only partially correct in stating an assignment. The discharge of duties however is incorrect as this would discharge performance as opposed to acquire a right under another's contract. Answer D is incorrect as once again it is only partially correct with respect to the assignment. However, the conveyance of personal or real property is incorrect in terms of acquiring rights under other parties' contracts.

26. B   Answer B is correct, as an assignor is also an obligee that transfers the right to performance. Answer A is incorrect as a delegator is one who transfers duties under a contract. Answer C is incorrect as a delegatee is one who receives duties under a contract. Answer D is incorrect as a lessor is inapplicable in terms of transferring the right to receive performance.

27. C   Answer C is correct as the party to whom a right has been transferred is referred to as the assignee. Answer A is incorrect as the party who transfers the right to receive performance is the assignor. Answer B is incorrect as there is not a name for a party who attempts to suspend performance nor is this a legally recognized right. Answer D is incorrect as the party to whom the right has been delegated is confusing terminology as it mixes terms associated with assignments and delegations.

28. D   Answer D is correct as none of the above would be considered an exception which would allow the assignment of any of the personal service contracts listed in answers A, B, and C, as they all call for the exercise of personal skill, discretion, and expertise.

29. D   Answer D is correct as the assignee should provide notification to the obligor of the assignment as well as inform the obligor that performance should be made to the assignee. Answer A is incorrect as it is only partially correct, as the obligor would not know whom performance is to be rendered to. Answer B is incorrect as once again notification is only part of what the assignee must do to be protected. Further, acceptance of the performance by the obligor is implied and need not be stated. Answer C is incorrect as even though the notification of the assignment to the obligor will partially

protect the assignee, informing the obligor that the assignee will not accept performance from him or her defeats the purpose of the assignment.

30. B   Answer B is correct as a delegation of duties is a transfer by the parties of the performance of their duties under the contract to other parties. Answer A is incorrect as an assignment involves the transfer of rights, not duties under a contract. Answer C is incorrect as a declaration of duties arises when the delegatee has not assumed the duties under the contract. Answer D is incorrect as there is nothing in the facts that indicate that rights have also been transferred, only duties. Thus, only a delegation has occurred.

31. D   Answer D is correct because any number of window washers could do a job for other companies, whereas answers A, B, and C all could be considered personal service contracts or ones in which the terms of the original contract would be materially altered, in which case, none of them could be delegated.

32. B   Answer B is correct as Tom's Tourist Shop was unintentionally benefited by the hotel and Charter Construction Company contract since there is nothing to indicate at the inception of their contract or thereafter that the parties intended to benefit the shop. Answer A is incorrect as the hotel and the Charter Construction Company did not intend to confer a benefit or gift on Tom's Tourist Shop. Therefore, the shop is not a donee beneficiary. Answer C is incorrect as the appeal of the surrounding area has no bearing on whether Tom should win. Answer D is incorrect as giving notice is not a requirement to receiving benefits especially in a situation involving an incidental beneficiary.

33. B   Answer B is correct as a breach of an unconditional promise to perform, hence a covenant entitles the innocent party to sue. Answer A is incorrect as punitive damages are usually not available in causes of action involving contracts. Answer C is incorrect as the equitable remedy of injunction is more appropriately applied in situations involving tortuous actions verses those concerned with breach of contract. Answer D is incorrect as a covenant is more definite than a condition and the breach of a covenant does not necessarily entitle one to sue for breach of a condition.

34. C   Answer C is correct as commercial impracticability excuses performance if an unforeseeable event makes it impractical for the promisor to perform. Answer A is incorrect as subjective impossibility is not applicable to unforeseeable events. Answer B is incorrect as accord and satisfaction concern a dispute over a contract that is resolved by a new agreement and performance of the same. Accord and satisfaction do not apply to situations involving commercial impracticability. Answer D is incorrect as the doctrine of frustration of purpose excuses the performance of contractual obligations if the object or benefit of the contract is made worthless to a promisor, and both parties knew what the purpose was and the act that frustrated the purpose was reasonably foreseeable.

Short Answer

35.   transfer of contractual rights
36.   The assignment would materially alter the risk or duties of the obligor, which would be the insurance company.
37.   the obligor
38.   because the parties can agree that a personal service contract such as Chuck's playing football may be subject to assignment
39.   A party's duty of performance may be discharged by agreement of the parties, excuse of performance, or by operation of law.
40.   an assignment
41.   because legal actions involving personal rights cannot be assigned

42. It extinguishes all of the assignor's rights including the right to sue the obligor directly for nonperformance.
43. the English rule
44. Claude is entitled to the savings account under the possession of tangible token rule.
45. The word assumption or other similar language is used in a delegation.
46. Morgan will get the lottery proceeds under the English rule, which provides that the first to give notice will prevail when there are successive assignments.
47. "Time is of the essence" is an express condition.
48. An implied-in-fact condition can be inferred from the circumstances surrounding a contract and the parties conduct.
49. the personal satisfaction test

Chapter 16

REMEDIES FOR BREACH OF TRADITIONAL AND ONLINE CONTRACTS

Chapter Overview

This chapter focuses on the differences between the types of performance in a contract as well as the consequences for the same. Additionally, it clarifies the various types of legal damages as well as equitable remedies that are available for breach of contract. The torts associated with contracts along with the consequences of punitive damages are also explained. Finally, with technology becoming an integral of our daily lives, Internet contracts and the breach of the same are also discussed.

Objectives

Upon completion of the exercises in this chapter, you should be able to:
1.   Discuss complete performance in relation to discharging contractual duties.
2.   Explain inferior performance as well as material breach of contract.
3.   Understand the difference among compensatory, consequential, and nominal damages.
4.   Define what liquidated damages are and explain when they are a penalty.
5.   Explain the duty of mitigation of damages.
6.   Discuss the remedy of rescission of a contract.
7.   Discuss the equitable remedies of injunction, quasi-contract, and specific performance.
8.   Explain the torts that are associated with contracts.
9.   Define punitive damages
10.   Analyze breach as it applies to Internet contracts.

Practical Application

You should be able to determine whether a minor or material breach has occurred in a contract as well as what remedies, legal or equitable, may be available for the breach. Further, you will have a better grasp of the requirements that are needed when seeking the equitable remedies of specific performance, injunction, and quasi-contract. Additionally, you will be familiar with the torts that sometimes accompany contracts and whether punitive damages may be an option. Finally, you will have a better understanding of breach as it applies to Internet contracts.

Helpful Hints

It is important that you learn the terminology associated with this chapter in order to know which types of remedies apply to certain situations. Some mnemonics for the equitable remedies of injunction as well as specific performance have been provided for you to assist you in committing what is required for these equitable remedies to memory. The material will be easier to grasp if you list and learn the legal remedies separately from the equitable remedies.

Study Tips

You should begin your study of remedies recognizing that there are three levels of performance of a contract. Each level of performance as well as what is meant by it is given below.

Level 1 – Complete Performance

Complete performance happens when a party to a contract gives performance exactly as outlined in the parties contract. If the contract is fully formed, it is said to be executed. Also, be aware that a contracting party's unconditional and absolute offer to perform will also discharge a party's obligations under the contract.

Level 2 – Substantial Performance

Substantial performance happens when a party to a contract gives performance that only has a little bit left to do before it will be considered completely performed. The nonbreaching party has several options available to him or her. He or she can convince the breaching party to lift his or her performance to completion of the contract. Or, he or she may deduct whatever it costs to repair the defect from the contract price and give the remaining amount under the contract to the breaching party. Finally, if the breaching party has been paid, the innocent party may sue the breaching party to recover the cost of repair.

Level 3 – Inferior Performance: Material Breach

A material breach happens when a party gives inferior performance of his or her contractual obligations so much so that it destroys or impairs the purpose of the contract. The courts will examine each case individually to determine whether the breach is a minor or material breach. The nonbreaching party may rescind the contract and seek restitution of any monies paid under the contract is there has been a material breach. A material breach releases the nonbreaching party from further performance. Another option for the nonbreaching party is to sue for breach of contract and ask for damages.

What about Anticipatory Repudiation?

Anticipatory repudiation happens when one party lets the other party know in advance that either he or she will not perform or may not perform the contractual duties when they come due. The repudiator may expressly state this or his or her conduct may show it. The non-breaching party's obligations are discharged immediately and he or she may sue for breach of contract immediately without waiting for performance to become due.

Damages

The next section categorizes the legal remedies for you, otherwise known as damages. You should be familiar with the differences among compensatory, consequential, liquidated, and nominal damages as well as the requirement for mitigation of the same.

- **Compensatory Damages**

  Purpose ─ to compensate a nonbreaching party for the loss of the bargain. These were designed to "make the person whole again." The court determines how much will be awarded based upon the type of contract involved.

- **Types of contracts and the compensatory damages for the same**:

  Sale of Goods ─ The measure of compensatory damages for a breach of sales contract is the difference between the contract price and the market price at the time and place of delivery of the goods.

  Construction Contracts ─ The amount of compensatory damages available for breach depends upon the status of the construction project itself. In other words, it depends on the stage of completion that the project is in when the breach happens. The contractor may recover the profits that he or she might have made on the contract if the owner breaches before the construction begins.

  Employment Contracts – Recovery based on an employer breaching equals lost wages or salary as compensatory damages. If however the employee breaches, the employer can recover the costs of hiring a new employee plus any salary increase to pay the replacement.

- **Consequential Damages**

  These types of damages are foreseeable damages that happen because of circumstances not related to the contract itself. In order to recover consequential damages, the breaching party must be aware or have reason to know that the breach will cause special damages to the other party.

- **Liquidated Damages**

  Sometimes the parties to a contract agree in advance as to the amount of damages that will be payable in the event of a breach. This is known as liquidated damages. In order for this type of damages to be enforced, it must be shown that the actual damages are difficult or impracticable to determine and the liquidated amount must be reasonable in the circumstances. This is an exclusive remedy regardless of what the actual damages later are assessed as being.

  CAVEAT – A liquidated damages clause is looked upon as a penalty if the actual damages are clearly able to be determined in advance and if the liquidated damages are unconscionable or excessive. When a liquidated damages clause is viewed as a penalty, it is unenforceable.

- **Nominal Damages**

  These damages are awarded based on principle and are usually a very small amount. No real financial loss is suffered when a party brings a suit based upon principle.

Mitigation of Damages

The law places a duty on the nonbreaching party to avoid and reduce the resulting damages. This is referred to as mitigating the damages. A party's duty of mitigation will be based on the type of contract involved.

Enforcement of Remedies

Once a judgment has been rendered, an attempt to collect it is made. If the breaching party fails to satisfy the judgment, then the court may issue a Writ of Attachment or Issue a Writ of Garnishment.

- <u>Writ of Attachment</u> – The writ orders the sheriff to seize the breaching party's property that he or she has in his or her possession and to sell the property to satisfy the judgment. Not all property can be sold depending on the applicable state exemptions.

- <u>Writ of Garnishment</u> – Wages, bank account, and other property owned by the breaching party that is being handled by a third party, such as a bank, must be paid to the non-breaching party. There are limitations on the amount of wages or salary that can be garnished as per federal and state laws.

Rescission and Restitution as Remedies

- <u>Rescission</u> – This is an action to undo a contract where there has been a material breach of contract due to fraud, duress, undue influence, or mistake. The parties must make restitution of the consideration they received under the contract if they are going to rescind it. In other words, they must return the goods, property, money, or other consideration that was received from the other property. Notice of the rescission is a requirement.

Equitable Remedies

If the remedy at law is not adequate, then the equitable remedies of specific performance, quasi-contract and injunction, and reformation may be available so that an injustice may be prevented.

- <u>Specific Performance</u> – This is a discretionary remedy the courts may award if the subject matter is unique and a service contract is not involved. The following mnemonic is a practical application memory device you may use when analyzing whether specific performance applies.

  <u>C</u>athy <u>A</u>lways <u>E</u>ats <u>M</u>uch <u>C</u>andy <u>D</u>uring <u>E</u>aster

  <u>C</u> – Was there a **contract** for unique goods or land between the parties?
  <u>A</u> – The remedy at law was not **adequate.**
  <u>E</u> – The contract may only be **enforced** by this remedy.
  <u>M</u> – The remedy is **mutual**; both the buyer and seller may ask for it.
  <u>C</u> – All **conditions** have been satisfied by the party asking for the remedy.
  <u>D</u> – A discussion of any **defenses** is also brought to light.
  <u>E</u> – A reminder that this is an **equitable** remedy.

- <u>Reformation</u> – This is an equitable remedy that allows the court to rewrite the parties' contract to reflect their true intentions.

- Quasi-Contract — This equitable remedy is an implied-in-law contract often referred to as quasi-meruit. Under this remedy, a party may receive compensation even though there is not an actual enforceable contract due to a failure of the Statute of Frauds or lack of consideration, etc. The reasonable value of materials or service is the recovery that is available in order to prevent unjust enrichment.

- Injunction — An injunction is an equitable remedy that prohibits a person from doing a certain act. The following mnemonic is a practical application memory device that you may use in determining whether an injunction may be sought.

  <u>T</u>ed <u>A</u>lways <u>E</u>njoys <u>P</u>otatoes and <u>H</u>am at <u>D</u>inner

  T — Usually a **tort** is involved which must first be proven.
  A — The remedy at law was not **adequate**.
  E — The tortuous conduct may only be **enforced** by this remedy.
  P — There is a **property** right involved.
  H — A **hardship** will be suffered if this remedy is not enforced.
  D — A discussion of **defenses** is shown if they apply.

Torts Associated with Contracts

If a party demonstrates that a contract-related tort has occurred, tort damages will also be available to a party. These include compensation for pain and suffering, emotional damages, possible punitive damages, and personal injury. The torts in this area include interference with contractual relations and breach of implied covenant of good faith and fair dealing.

- Intentional Interference with Contractual Relations — This occurs when a third party induces a contracting party to breach the contract with another party. Note that a third party will not be held to have induced a breach if the breach already existed between the original parties.

- Breach of Implied Covenant of Good Faith and Fair Dealing — This is implied in certain types of contracts whereby the parties are held to act in "good faith" and deal fairly in also aspects in obtaining the contract's objective. This tort is sometimes called the tort of bad faith.

Punitive Damages

These are usually not recoverable for breach of contract. However, if certain tortuous conduct such as fraud or intentional conduct is associated with the nonperformance of a contract, punitive damages in addition to actual damages may be awarded to punish the defendant. Other purposes of punitive damages are to prevent similar conduct from happening in the future as well as to set an example for other individuals.

Refresh Your Memory

The following exercise will enable you to refresh your memory on the rules and principles presented to you in this chapter. Read each question twice and place your answer in the blanks provided. Review the chapter material for any question you miss or are unable to remember.

1. A contracting party's failure to perform an absolute duty owed under a contract is referred to as a _____ .

2. What are most contracts discharged by? _____
_____

3. When referring to performance, what is meant by the word tender? _____
_____

4. Where there has been a material breach of contract, what may the nonbreaching party do?_____
_____

5. Where there is an anticipatory repudiation, the nonbreaching party's obligations under the contract are _____ immediately.

6. What is meant when someone says that he or she has substantially performed under a contract? _____
_____

7. What two remedies restore the parties to the position they held before the contract?
_____
_____

8. _____ damages help to compensate a nonbreaching party for the loss of the bargain.

9. The compensatory damages for a breach of contract involving the sale of goods is _____
_____

10. What can an employee whose employer has breached an employment contract recover in damages? _____

11. When parties agree in advance to the amount of damages payable upon a breach of contract, this is known as a _____ _____ clause.

12. Cases involving nominal damages are brought based on _____.

13. To mitigate means to _____ or _____.

14. What is the term that means to undo a contract called? _____

15. The term restitution means _____.

Critical Thought Exercise

The Cheersville Fire Department (CFD) entered into a written contract on 2-17-07 with American Emergency Truck Co. (AET) for the purchase of a $290,000.00 ladder/pump truck. The contract set forth a delivery date of September 1, 2007, as insisted upon by CFD. According to CFD Chief Sam Miller, their 1932 pumper truck was not going to last beyond that date and time was of the essence. On August 1, 2007, the CFD truck died and was not able to be repaired. The Cheersville Town Council voted to wait until the new truck arrived on September 1, 2007, instead or renting another old truck from Friendsville Fire District. On August 15, 2007, AET notified CFD that the truck would not be ready for delivery until October 1, 2007. The Town Council again decided to wait without renting another truck. Cheersville notified AET that its truck was out of service and the new truck was desperately needed by September 1, 2007. On September 15, 2007, a major fire damaged the Cheersville School. The fire started in the kitchen and could have easily been controlled with normal fire fighting equipment. The damage to the school was estimated to be approximately $2,800,000.

AET denies any liability. The truck was delivered by AET on October 5, 2007. You are on the Cheersville Town Council and have been assigned the task of drafting a memorandum for the council detailing the following:

1. Whether Cheersville has grounds to sue American Emergency Truck.
2. What damages would be recoverable from AET.
3. What defenses AET may assert.

Answer:

Practice Quiz

True/False

1. ____ All types of performance are treated as minor breaches. [p. 237]

2. ____ The most common award for a breach of contract is an equitable award. [p. 237]

3. ____ There is no clear line between a minor breach and a material breach. [p. 239]

4. ____ An employer may recover the costs to hire a new employee plus any increase in salary paid to the replacement if an employee breaches his or her contract. [p. 241]

5. ____ If liquidated damages are involved, they must be reasonable in the circumstances. [p. 243]

6. ____ A liquidated damages clause may not be considered a penalty regardless of the ability to determine actual damages. [p. 243]

7. ____ A writ of garnishment orders that property that is in the hands of third parties be paid over to the nonbreaching party to satisfy a judgment. [p. 245]

8. ____ Specific performance of personal service contracts is granted because the courts would find it difficult or impracticable to supervise or monitor performance of such a contract. [p. 246]

9. ____ Punitive damages are included in the actual damages awarded by the court and may be kept by the plaintiff. [p. 247]

10. ____ Intentional interference with contractual relations is a contract-based cause of action. [p. 247]

11. ____ The remedy of rescission is available if there has been fraud, undue influence, or mistake involved with regard to the parties' contract. [p. 245]

12. ____ A party may seek the remedy of specific performance for any contract he or she is having difficulty enforcing. [p. 246]

13. ____ Courts often award the remedy of specific performance if the subject matter is unique. [p. 246]

14. ____ An equitable doctrine that allows the court to rewrite the parties' contract to reflect their true intentions is known as reformation. [p. 246]

15. ____ Injunctions are available in contract actions only in limited circumstances [p. 246]

16. ____ A party may seek damages for a breach of the covenant of good faith and fair dealing. [p. 248]

17. ___ Equitable remedies are available regardless of adequate compensation for breach of contract. [p. 246]

18. ___ Tender of performance discharges a party's contractual obligations. [p. 237]

19. ___ Anticipatory breach refers to the excitement of waiting for a breach to occur. [p. 239]

20. ___ The amount of damages recoverable for a breach of a construction contract depends on how much of the contract has been completed. [p. 237]

21. ___ Forseeable damages that arise from circumstances outside the contract are consequential damages. [p. 242]

22. ___ In order to mitigate damages where the employer has breached the contract, the employee must take any employment offered or he or she will also have damages assessed against him or her. [p. 241]

23. ___ In an action for rescission, the rescinding party must give sufficient notice to the breaching party. [p. 245]

24. ___ Consequential damages are an example of an equitable remedy. [p. 242]

25. ___ If Morton and Nathan sign a contract that has a clerical error, and neither one notices it till after the fact, the court will be unable to offer a remedy as it was reasonable that they should have been more careful in reading what they were signing. [p. 246]

Multiple Choice

26. Complete performance of a contract occurs when [p. 237]
    a. a party to the contract gives almost complete performance.
    b. a party to the contract renders performance exactly as required by the contract.
    c. a party to the contract renders inferior performance that destroys the essence of the contract.
    d. a party to the contract is not sure whether he or she can perform the contract or not.

27. Perfecto Home Construction Inc. contracts with Delia Bloom to build her dream home. Perfecto has constructed the home exactly to plan; however, it forgot to put little ceramic knobs on the laundry room cupboards. What type of performance has Perfecto rendered to Delia? [p. 238]
    a. inferior performance
    b. complete performance
    c. substantial performance
    d. no performance

28. Which of the following permits the court to rewrite a contract to express the parties' true intentions? [p. 246]
    a. rescission
    b. restitution
    c. reformation
    d. reconstruction

29. Which of the following elements must be shown in order to establish a cause of action for intentional interference with contractual relations? [p. 247]
    a. A valid enforceable contract must exist between the contracting parties.
    b. The third party must have knowledge of the contract.
    c. The third party is induced to breach the contract.
    d. all of the above

30. A court order that prohibits a person from doing a certain act is [p. 246]
    a. a no trespass order.
    b. prohibitum orderis.
    c. an order for specific performance.
    d. an injunction.

31. The Lemoore Contracting Company agrees to build a racquetball court for Maxine Mills, and the parties sign the $50,000 contract; but, before Lemoore begins, Maxine decides she does not want to ruin her grass with the racquetball court addition. Thereafter she calls and tells Lemoore Contracting that she is canceling the job. If Lemoore brings a suit against Maxine, what might they try to recover? [p. 241]
    a. the difference between the contract price and the market price of the racquetball court at the time and place where the contract was signed
    b. the profits that Lemoore Contracting would have made on the contract
    c. lost wages as compensatory damages
    d. none of the above

32. The Random Engineering Corporation has hired Lisa Sharpe as a robotics engineer to design housekeeper robots. Lisa contracted with Random to give her an initial annual income of $132,000 plus benefits. Additionally, if she can design a microchip to place in the robot which will enable it to garden as well, Random will give Lisa a percentage of the profits and a twelve percent salary increase. Lisa works for Random for two months and Random decides to downsize and use engineers who have been employed with them for twenty or more years to design the housekeeper/gardener robots. Lisa is told she will need to find another place to work. If Lisa brings a lawsuit against Random based on breach of her employment contract, what does she need to do in order to mitigate her damages? [p. 241]
    a. She will need to gather as much information about Random as possible.
    b. She will need to try to find comparable, substitute employment.
    c. She will need to beg to be given a second chance, as she is the best person for the job.
    d. She will need to ask for specific performance based upon her skills and experience.

33. Garage Doors 2 Go purchase $50,000 worth of remote garage openers from Remotes R Us, but they fail to deliver them to Garage Doors 2 Go. Thereafter Garage Doors 2 Go purchases the remotes from another vendor but has to pay $55,000 because the current market price for them has risen. What can Garage Doors 2 Go recover? [p. 241]
    a. nothing, as Garage doors 2 Go is out of luck
    b. $105,000, which represents the hardship for nondelivery
    c. Garage Doors 2 Go may recover $5,000, which represents the market price paid ($55,000) and the contract price ($50,000).
    d. nominal damages

34. Harold, a builder, has breached a construction contract he had with Maude to build her new home. As such, which of the following is a true statement? [p. 241]
   a. Maude is not entitled to any damages should she sue.
   b. Harold may recover the profits he would have made if the owner breaches the contract.
   c. The compensatory damages recoverable for a breach of contract vary with the stage of completion the project is in when the breach occurs.
   d. None of the statements are true.

35. Which of the following would not fall under the category of monetary damages? [p. 246]
   a. compensatory
   b. consequential
   c. liquidated
   d. reformation

Short Answer

36. If there has been inferior performance of a contract, what may the nonbreaching party seek in a court of law? [p. 239] _____
   _____

37. If the Soft Sponge Corporation has breached its contract with its employee Barbara, what is Barbara required to do in terms of mitigating her damages and any employment that is offered to her? [p. 241] _____
   _____

38. What are the three types of performance that are associated with contracts? [p. 237]
   _____, _____, and _____

39. What type of law applies when determining the damages available for a breach of a sales contract involving goods? [p. 241] _____

40. The return of goods, property, money, or other consideration received from the other party to a contract is often referred to as [p. 245] _____.

41. If Shawna wishes to rescind her contract with Elmer, what is she required to do? [p. 245]
   _____

42. If Bob demonstrates a contract-related tort has occurred, what types of tort damages may he recover? [p. 246] _____
   _____

43. Give a purpose for an equitable remedy. [p. 246] _____
   _____

44. Is the cause of action for breach of the implied covenant of good faith and fair dealing considered a tort or a contract cause of action? [p. 248] _____

45. A breach that occurs when a party renders substantial performance of his or her contractual duties is called a _____ _____. [p. 239]

46. What type of damages are recoverable regardless if the breach of contract was minor or material? [p. 240] _____ damages

47. If an owner breaches a construction contract, what type of damages may the contractor recover? [p. 241] _____

_____

48. What factors do the courts consider when viewing whether or not an employee has mitigated his or her damages when seeking substitute, comparable employment after an employer has breached an employment contract? [p. 241]

_____

_____

49. In order to be liable for consequential damages, what must be shown about the breaching party? [p. 242] _____

_____

50. What type of damages may a nonbreaching party sue for where there has been no financial loss as a result of the breach? [p. 244] _____

Answers to Refresh Your Memory

1. breach of contract [p. 237]
2. complete or strict performance [p. 237]
3. Tender is an unconditional and absolute offer by a contracting party to perform his or obligations under the contract. [p. 237]
4. The nonbreaching party may rescind the contract and seek restitution of any compensation paid under the contract to the breaching party. [p. 238]
5. discharged [p. 239]
6. performance by a contracting party that deviates only slightly from complete performance [p. 238]
7. rescission and restitution [p. 245]
8. Compensatory [p. 240]
9. the difference between the contract price and the market price [p. 241]
10. lost wages or salary as compensatory damages [p. 241]
11. liquidated damages [p. 243]
12. principle [p. 244]
13. avoid or reduce [p. 241]
14. rescission [p. 245]
15. to return goods or compensation [p. 245]

Critical Thought Exercise Model Answer

Before either party to a contract has a duty to perform, one of the parties may make an assertion or do an act that indicates they will not perform their obligations under the contract at a future time. This is called an anticipatory repudiation of the contract and is treated as a material breach. The nonbreaching party may immediately bring an action for damages, wait to see if the breaching party changes their name, or may seek specific performance by the breaching party. When AET notifies CFD that it will not be able to deliver the truck as promised, CFD must decide what course of action it will take. The damages that may be sought would be any increase in cost that CFD has to pay to obtain the truck from another seller plus any consequential or incidental damages. In this situation, CFD needs the truck more than it needs money damages. The CFD had a duty to protect the citizens of Cheersville and another truck is not readily obtainable. The truck that was being built for CFD by AET was somewhat unique and failure to perform the contract would create great hardship for CFD. However, CFD had to make an election at the time of the breach, which took place on August 15, 2007. Because CFD failed to elect to pursue specific performance, they will be left with an action for damages. Specific performance is not available at this late point in time because the truck was actually delivered on October 5, 2007. CFD will seek consequential damages for the damage caused to the Cheersville School. AET will be liable for those damages if they were reasonably foreseeable at the time of the breach or fire occurred. CFD had previously notified AET that their truck was old and would not last in service beyond September 1, 2007. CFD again told AET of the urgency when the truck was taken out of service on August 1, 2007. Knowing the need for the truck and the fact that CFD was without a truck after August 1, 2007, AET continued to promise to perform the contract. The damages to the school were probably foreseeable because they are the exact type of damages that would occur if the CFD was without a truck.

AET will have two possible defenses to the contract. The most obvious is that Cheersville failed to fulfill its duty of mitigation of damages. This rule requires the plaintiff to have done whatever was reasonable to minimize the damages caused by the defendant. CFD failed to take any action to mitigate their damages. The city council decided to not rent a replacement truck even after their only truck was taken out of service. Because they failed to mitigate their damages, Cheersville will have their damages reduced by those amounts they could have prevented. In this case, the facts state that the damages to the school could have been minimized if a temporary replacement truck had been obtained. A rental was available from Friendsville and Cheersville failed to mitigate their damages by renting the truck. The second defense that AET may assert is that Cheersville agreed to a modification of the contract when they did not pursue any action when notified of the delay in the delivery date. This defense is weak because Cheersville notified AET that it desperately needed the truck by the original contract date of September 1, 2007. Cheersville did nothing that could be deemed as acquiescence in the request by AET to extend the delivery date. Therefore, no modification of the original agreement was ever accomplished. Cheersville will prevail in their breach of contract suit, but the amount of damages will be relatively small due to Cheersville's failure to mitigate damages.

Answers to Practice Quiz

True/False

1. False   All types of breach are not treated as minor breaches. For example, if there has been substantial performance of a contract and a breach occurs, the breach is treated as a minor breach.
2. False   The most common remedy for a breach of contract is an award for monetary damages.
3. True   There is no clear line between a minor breach and a material breach. A determination is made on a case-by-case basis.
4. True   If the employee breaches the contract, the employer can recover the costs to hire a new employee plus any increase in salary paid to the replacement.
5. True   Liquidated damages must be reasonable in the circumstances.
6. False   A liquidated damages clause is considered a penalty if actual damages are clearly determined in advance or if the liquidated damages are excessive or unconscionable.

7. True   A writ of garnishment order that wages, bank account, or other property of the breaching party that is in the hands of third parties be paid over to the nonbreaching party to satisfy the judgment.

8. False   Specific performance of personal service contracts is **not** granted because the courts would find it difficult or impracticable to supervise or monitor performance of such a contract.

9. False   Punitive damages are **in addition** to actual damages and may be kept by the plaintiff.

10. False   Intentional interference with contractual relations is a tort that arises when a third party induces a contracting party to breach the contract with another party.

11. True   Rescission is an available remedy for a material breach of contract where fraud, undue influence, duress, or mistake is involved.

12. False   Courts have been prone to enforcing the remedy of specific performance in situations involving unique goods or land. Thus, it is not an available remedy for any contract that the parties are having difficulty in enforcing.

13. True   The courts would find it very difficult or impracticable to supervise or monitor the performance of a personal service contract, and as such, specific performance is generally not granted.

14. True   Reformation permits the court to rewrite a contract to express the parties' true intentions.

15. True   Injunctions are available in contract action only in limited circumstances.

16. True   The tort of the implied covenant of good faith and fair dealing allows for the recovery of damages.

17. False   Equitable remedies are available if there has been a breach of contract that cannot be adequately compensated through a legal remedy.

18. True   A party's contractual obligations are discharged by a tender of performance.

19. False   Anticipatory breach occurs when the contracting party informs the other party in advance that he or she will not perform his or her contractual duties when due.

20. True   The damages recoverable for a breach of a construction contract vary depending on the stage of completion the project is in at the time of the breach.

21. True   Consequential damages are foreseeable damages that arise from circumstances outside of the contract.

22. False   Though the employee owes a duty to mitigate damages by finding substitute employment, the employee is only required to accept comparable employment in relation to such factors as rank, status, job description, geographical location, etc.

23. True   The rescinding party is required to give sufficient notice to the breaching party in an action for rescission.

24. False   Consequential damages are foreseeable damages that arise from circumstances outside of the contract and are not an equitable remedy.

25. False   The court can offer the remedy of reformation and rewrite the contract to correct the clerical error to read what the parties originally intended.

Multiple Choice

26. B   Answer B is the correct answer as when a party to a contract renders performance exactly as required by the contract, performance is said to be complete. Answer A is incorrect as rendering performance that is slightly less than perfect is not complete performance. Answer C is incorrect as rendering inferior performance constitutes a material breach of contract, which is not complete performance. Answer D is incorrect as this answer is more reflective of a situation involving anticipatory repudiation where a party indicates that he or she cannot perform a contract versus complete performance where a party has fully performed his or her obligations under the contract.

27. C   Answer C is the correct answer as substantial performance is slightly less than complete performance of which the facts would fit within this description. The lack of ceramic knobs on the laundry room cupboards would qualify as a minor breach as the rest of the house is complete thereby indicating that Perfecto Home Construction Inc. has substantially performed under its contract with Delia Bloom. Answer A is incorrect as inferior performance would indicate that a material breach has taken place which is not the case since most of Delia Bloom's house has been completed with the exception of the ceramic knobs on her laundry room cupboards. Answer B is incorrect as Perfecto Home did not reflect a tender of complete performance as the knobs on the laundry room cupboard still needed to be installed. Answer D is incorrect as Perfecto Home completed almost all of what it was required to do under its contract with Delia Bloom.

28. C   Answer C is correct as the equitable remedy of reformation permits the court to rewrite the parties' contract to reflect the true intentions of the parties. Answer A is incorrect as the remedy of rescission is used when a party wants to undo a contract not rewrite it. Answer B is incorrect as the remedy of restitution involves giving goods or compensation back to a party when a contract has been rescinded. Answer D is incorrect as there is no such remedy as reconstruction.

29. D   Answer D is correct, as answers A, B, and C all must be shown to establish a cause of action for intentional interference with contractual relations.

30. D   Answer D is correct as an injunction is a court order that prohibits a person from doing a certain act. Answers A and B are incorrect as there are no such things as a trespass order or a prohibitum orderis. Answer C is incorrect as an order for specific performance implies that you want a party to perform and continue with the obligations under the contract not prohibit him or her from doing something.

31. B   Answer B is correct as a contractor may recover the profits he or she would have made on the contract if the owner breaches the construction contract before the construction begins. This is exactly what happened in the example. Maxine breached her contract with Lemoore Construction before the building of the racquetball court began. Answer A is incorrect as this answer incorporates the measure of damages for breach of contract for the sale of goods. Answer C is incorrect as the remedy for lost wages is usually applicable in situations involving the breach of employment contracts. Answer D is incorrect for the reasons stated above.

32. B   Answer B is correct as an employee owes a duty to mitigate damages by trying to find substitute employment that is comparable to that which he/she had. Answer A is incorrect as gathering as much information about Random will not assist her in mitigating her damages though it may assist her in the discovery process should she decide to sue. Answer C is incorrect as begging for a second chance will not be a factor that the court will consider in determining whether Lisa has mitigated her damages. Answer D is incorrect as the courts usually do not grant specific performance where contracts of personal service is involved. Arguably, this would be a personal service contract that would be nearly impossible for the court to monitor.

33. C   Answer C is correct, as it clearly states the correct recovery under the UCC (Uniform Commercial Code). Answer A is wrong as it is an untrue statement. Answer B is incorrect as it represents too much compensation. Answer D is wrong as it is nonsensical and absurd.

34. C   Answer C is correct as the compensatory damages recoverable for a breach of a construction contract vary with the stage of completion the project is in when the breach occurs. Answer A is incorrect as it is an untrue statement. Answer B is correct as the question asks what can be recovered if Harold breaches, not Maude, so therefore this answer does not apply. Answer D is incorrect as it is an untrue statement.

35. D   Answer D is correct as reformation is an equitable remedy whereby a court rewrites a contract to express the parties' true intentions. It is usually used to correct clerical errors. Answers A, B, and C are all incorrect as these generally fall under the category of money damages.

Short Answer

36. The nonbreaching party may either (1) rescind the contract and recover restitution or (2) affirm the contract and recover damages.
37. She is required to seek comparable employment.
38. complete, substantial, and inferior
39. the UCC (Uniform Commercial Code)
40. restitution
41. Shawna must give Elmer notice.
42. compensation for personal injury, pain and suffering, emotional distress and possible punitive damages
43. to prevent unjust enrichment
44. a tort
45. minor breach
46. monetary
47. The contractor may recover profits.
48. implied covenant of good faith and fair dealing
49. The breaching party must know or have reason to know that the breach will cause special damages to the other party in order to be liable for consequential damages.
50. nominal damages

Chapter 17

E-CONTRACTS
AND LICENSING

Chapter Overview

This chapter explores e-commerce by giving a thorough explanation of the Internet, the World Wide Web, electronic mail, and domain names. Other important topics that are analyzed are the domain name Anticybersquatting Act, e-contracts and their writing and signature requirements, e-licensing, licensing, and the agreement that is involved with the same as well as a breach of license agreements. Finally, the remedies available to the licensor as well as licensee for the breach of a licensing agreement under UCITA are also assessed.

Objectives

Upon completion of the exercises in this chapter, you should be able to:
1.   Explain the purpose of the Internet and how it applies to the World Wide Web.
2.   Define the meaning of electronic mail.
3.   Discuss the importance and application of domain names.
4.   Discuss the purpose of the Anticybersquatting Act.
5.   Explain the impact of an e-contract and how it is enforced.
6.   Discuss the writing and signature requirements of an e-contract utilizing the Electronic Signature and Global National Commerce Act.
7.   Compare e-licensing to licensing without the Internet.
8   Analyze the breach of a licensing agreement under UCITA.
10.   Discuss the available remedies under UCITA.

Practical Application

You should be able feel comfortable enough with the terminology to be able to apply the concepts associated with e-contracts and licensing to real life situations involving both online as well as the traditional way of accomplishing these tasks.

Helpful Hints

Since this chapter is relatively short in length, the best approach is to become familiar with the terminology, and the application of the same will follow. For some students, the technology-based vocabulary will be relatively easy due to having been exposed to the use of a computer. However, for those who are just beginning their exposure to computers, this chapter will provide you with a good start so that you will be able to apply the various electronic requirements to contracts and licensing.

Study Tips

Each section follows the text, and in essence builds upon one another so that you may get the big picture when applying the terminology and laws to the primary areas of focus, hence contracts, and licensing. When studying, it will help you to have someone ask you the questions under each heading to determine what you have learned.

Uniform Computer Information Transactions Act (UCITA)

<u>How did the Uniform Computer Information Transactions Act come into being?</u> Many legal scholars did not feel that the traditional rules of contract law met the needs of Internet transactions and software and information licensing. As such, the National Conference of Commissioners on Uniform State Laws developed this act for contracts involving computer information transactions and software and information licenses.

The Internet and the World Wide Web

<u>What is the Internet or the Net?</u> It is a collection of millions of computers that provide a network of electronic connections between computers.

<u>What is the history of how the Internet came to be?</u> It began with the U.S. Department of Defense as electronic communications were created for the military for national defense purposes. Thereafter, the National Science Foundation and the federal government's main scientific and technical agency created the Net to aide high-speed communication among research centers at academic and research institutions around the world. Thereafter businesses and individuals followed suit by utilizing the Internet for communication of information and data. What started out as minimal used by only 250 companies in 1989 has boomed into several hundred million computers connected to the Internet in the 2000s.

The World Wide Web

<u>What does it consist of?</u> Millions of computers that support a standard set of rules for the exchange of information called Hypertext Transfer Protocol (HTTP). Web-based documents are formatted using common code language such as Java and Hypertext Markup Language.

<u>What is a Web site?</u> A Web site is composed of electronic documents known as Web pages. Web sites with their own individual unique online addresses and pages are stored on servers all around the world which are operated by Internet Service Providers (ISPs). Individuals may view these sites and pages by using Microsoft Internet Explorer and Netscape Navigator. These pages contain a variety of multimedia content including text images, video, sound, and animation.

<u>What is electronic mail?</u> It is an instantaneous means of communication in the form of electronic writing from one individual to another. Each individual has his or her own unique Web address. In some instances, electronic mail (also known as e-mail) has replaced some paper and telephone correspondence.

Domain Names

<u>What is a domain name?</u> It is a unique name that identifies an individual's or company's Web site.

How does an individual get a domain name? By choosing a name that has not been chosen and registering it with a database like "Whois" or Network Solutions Inc. for example. Upon completion of a registration form and for a minimal payment per year, registration is complete. See pages 255 and 256 of your text for the most commonly used top-level extensions for domain names.

Domain Name Anticybersquatting Act

What is the Domain Name Anticybersquatting Act? It is an act that was promulgated in 1999 to target cybersquatters who register Internet domain names of famous companies and people and hold them hostage by demanding payments of ransom from the famous person or company.

What are the two requirements under the act in order for it to apply? (1) The name must be famous and (2) The domain name must have been registered in bad faith. With respect to requirement number one, trademarked names of famous actors, actresses, singers, and stars etc., apply. As for requirement number two, the courts may consider the extent to which the domain name resembles the holder's name or famous person's name, whether goods or services are sold under the name, the holder's offer to sell or transfer the name, and whether the holder has obtained multiple Internet domain names of famous individuals.

What types of remedies are available for a violation of the act? The court may issue a cease-and-desist order as well as an injunction. Additionally, a plaintiff may opt statutory damages between $1,000 and $300,000 in lieu of proving damages.

E-Contracts

What is needed in order to form an e-contract? All of the same elements necessary to form a regular contract.

How may an individual prove the existence of an e-contract? By printing out the e-mail or Web contract and its prior e-mail or Web negotiations.

What is the writing requirement of an e-contract? The **Electronic Signature in Global and National Commerce Act** recognizes electronic contracts as meeting the writing requirement. However, consumers must consent to receiving electronic records and contracts. Second, consumer must be able to show that they have access to electronic records in order to have met the "receiving electronic records" requirement. Finally, businesses must tell consumers that they have the right to receive hard-copy documents of their transaction.

E-Signatures

Are electronic signatures valid? Under the **Electronic Signature in Global and National Commerce Act,** the *electronic signature or e-signature* is valid. The electronic signature is as valid as a pen-inscribed signature on paper. An e-signature is defined as a digital signature in some electronic method that identifies an individual. Identification of the signature is accomplished by secret password, a smart card, or the likes or by biometric.

E-Licensing

Because of the difficulties associated with forming contracts over the Internet as well as their enforcement, the Uniform Computer Information Transaction Act was created. This act provides as follows:

Uniform Computer Information Transaction Act (UCITA)

- This act provides an exhaustive set of uniform rules that sets the standard for performance and enforcement of computer information transactions. This act creates contract law for the licensing of information technology rights. For purposes of this act, a computer information transaction is an agreement to create, transfer, or license computer information or informational rights. [UCITA Sec.102 (a)(11)]. A state makes UCITA law by way of a state statute. Further, federal law preempts UCITA.

- Consumers are benefited by this act if they make an electronic error in contracting. UCITA provides that consumers are not bound if they learn of the error and tell the other party. Further, the consumer must not derive any benefit from the information. Also, the consumer must deliver all copies of the information to the third party or destroy the information as per the third party's instruction and the consumer must pay all shipping and processing costs of the other party.

- UCITA provides for the limitation of remedies for a breach of contract. They may be limited to return of copies and repayment of the licensing fee or to just the repair and replacement of the nonconforming copies. These limitations are enforceable unless they are found to be unconscionable.

Licensing

What is licensing? An agreement with owners of intellectual property and information rights to transfer limited rights in the property or information to parties for specified purposes and limited duration is a license.

Who are the parties to a license? The parties to a license are the **licensor**, or the one who owns the intellectual property or information rights and obligates him- or herself to transfer rights in the property or information to the licensee. The **licensee** is the party who is given limited rights in or access to the intellectual property of information rights.

What is a licensing agreement? A licensing agreement is a written agreement that expressly states the terms of the parties' agreement in a detailed comprehensive contract.

Breach of License Agreements

Both the licensee and the licensor owe one another a duty to perform the obligations stated in the contract. If either fails to perform as required, there is a breach of contract which gives the non-breaching party certain rights, including the right to recover damages or other remedies.

Remedies

A party cannot recover more than once for the same loss, nor may it be more than the loss caused by the breach.

- <u>Cancellation</u> – The ending of a contract by a contracting party upon the material breach of contract by the other party.

- <u>Licensor's damages</u> – The licensor may sue a licensee who is in breach and seek monetary damages caused by the breach.

- <u>Licensor's right to cure</u> – Under UCITA, a licensor may cure a breach if the time for performance under the contract has not expired, or if it has expired, the licensor had reasonable grounds to feel that the performance would be acceptable and would cure within a reasonable time. Also, if the licensor makes a conforming performance before cancellation by the licensee.

- <u>Licensee's damages</u> – Damages depend on the facts of the situation. The licensee may cover or recover the value of the performance. Remember cover means engaging in a commercially reasonable substitute transaction.

- <u>Licenssee can get specific performance</u> – If this remedy was agreed to in the parties' contract, or if the performance that was agreed upon was unique, then it will be available to the parties.

- <u>Limitation of remedies</u> – The parties may limit which remedies are available in the event of a breach. Limitation of remedies is enforceable unless they are unconscionable.

Electronic Self-Help

Under sections 815 and 816 of UTICA, a licensor can resort to electronic self-help if a breach occurs. Self-help may include activating disabling bugs and time bombs that have been embedded in the software or information that will prevent the licensee from further use of the software or information.
Self-help is only available if:
1) The licensee specifically agrees to the inclusion in the license of self-help as a remedy.
2) Also, the licensor must give at least 15 days' notice before the disabling action.
3) Further, the licensor may not use self-help if it would cause a breach of the peace, risk personal injury, cause significant damage or injury other than the licensee's information, result in injury to the public health or safety, or cause grave harm to national security. Improper use of self-help by the licensor will subject the licensor to damages which cannot be disclaimed.

Refresh Your Memory

The following exercise will enable you to refresh your memory on the rules and principles presented to you in this chapter. Read each question twice and place your answer in the blanks provided. Review the chapter material for any question you miss or are unable to remember.

1. What is the Internet? _____

_____

2. What is a Web site? _____

_____

3. What is e-mail? _____

_____

4. What did the Uniform Computer Information Transaction Act provide for? _____

_____

5. What is a domain name? _____

_____

6. What remedies does the Anticybersquatting Consumer Protection Act provide?

_____.

7. What is a license? _____

_____

8. What does the licensor own? _____

_____

_____

9. What is a licensee? _____

_____

10. Which act enabled electronic signatures to be sufficient to form an enforceable contract?

_____

11. What is the result, if any, if the UCITA provisions are unenforceable?

_____

_____

12. What does it mean to cover? _____

13. What does .com represent? _____

14. What extension is an unrestricted global name that may be used by businesses, individuals, and organizations? _____

15. Who can used the extension .pro? _____ _____

_____

Critical Thought Exercise

The James Co. of New York has been in the business of retail chocolate and confection sales since 1923. As the Internet has developed, James has commenced doing business by e-mail. Mrs. Dubyah communicates with James by numerous e-mails, negotiating the sale of 300 one-pound chocolate Easter eggs. They agree that the price will be $18 per egg and they will be shipped for arrival in Maryland 10 days before Easter. James produces the eggs and ships them in a timely manner. At the last minute, Mrs. Dubyah decides to order her Easter gifts from another company. When the shipment arrives in Maryland, Mrs. Dubyah wants to reject the shipment and order her eggs from her friend in Oklahoma. As the business secretary for Mrs. Dubyah, you are responsible for advising Mrs. Dubyah on business matters and executing her contracts as instructed.

Write a brief memorandum to Mrs. Dubyah, explaining to her your position on whether she can rely upon the Statute of Frauds as a defense to a damages claim by James Co. and whether the shipment should be accepted.

Answer:

_____

_____

_____

_____

_____

_____

_____

_____

_____

_____

_____

_____

_____

Practice Quiz

True/False

1. ____ Most businesses conduct e-commerce using Web sites. [p. 255]

2. ____ The domain name extension .org stands for organic. [p. 255]

3. ____ The parties to a license are the owner and lessee. [p. 259]

4. ____ A model state law that creates contract law for the licensing of information technology rights is known as the Electronic Signature in Global and National Commerce Act. [p. 259]

5. ___ The Anticybersquatting Consumer Protection Act gives owners of trademarks and persons with famous names a new weapon to attack the kidnapping of Internet domain names by cyberpirates. [p. 256]

6. ___ Registration of a domain name is free. [p. 255]

7. ___ Mary has entered into an electronic contract with Watson for the purchase of Watson's motorcycle. Mary authenticates the contract by using an electronic symbol. Mary's means of authentication will be insufficient to constitute a signing. [p. 259]

8. ___ A contract can be formed by operation of electronic agents. [p. 260]

9. ___ Electronic agents usually do not have the ability to evaluate and accept counteroffers or to make counteroffers. [p. 260]

10. ___ The Uniform Electronic Transactions Act was promulgated to establish uniform laws for electronic signatures and electronic records. [p. 259]

11. ___ A party may recover more than once for the same loss under the UCITA. [p. 261]

12. ___ A licensor unfortunately does not have a right to cure a breach of license. [p. 262]

13. ___ Generally speaking, under UCITA, consumers are not bound by their unilateral electronic errors. [p. 261]

14. ___ One of the shortcomings of the Electronic Signature in Global and National Commerce Act is that the act does not provide for verification of digital signatures. [p. 258]

15. ___ A licensor can recover lost profits caused by the licensee's failure to accept or complete performance of the contract. [p. 262]

16. ___ Licensing agreements tend to be very brief and broad in stating the uses granted. [p. 260]

17. ___ Electronic errors by nonconsumers are handled by the common law of contracts or the Uniform Commercial Code. [p. 261]

18. ___ Generally speaking, if the licensor tenders a copy this is a material breach of the licensing agreement, the nonbreaching party must wait and may not refuse the tender as his or her options are extremely limited. [p. 261]

19. ___ If Ryan cancels a license that Victor gave to him, Victor has no right to have all copies of the licensed information returned by Ryan. [p. 262]

20. ___ Electronic self-help can be utilized by activating disabling bombs for those who fail to pay their license fee. [p. 262]

Multiple Choice

21. Which of the following is one of the most widely used means of communication over the Internet? [p. 255]
    a. licensing agreements
    b. electronic mail
    c. chat rooms
    d. all of the above

22. What are the two requirements necessary to show a violation under the Anticybersquatting Consumer Protection Act? [p. 256]
    a. The Internet domain name must be famous and the domain name must be registered within the statutory period.
    b. The Internet domain name need not be famous, just registered and the registration must accompany the proper fee.
    c. The Internet domain name must be famous and the domain name must be registered in bad faith.
    d. The Internet domain name must be famous and the domain name must be registered in good faith.

23. Who is the owner of intellectual property or informational rights who transfers rights in the property or information to the license? [p. 259]
    a. the licensee
    b. the licensor
    c. the obligor
    d. the oblige

24. A software license granting the licensee the right to obtain information in the possession of the licensor is called an [p. 259]
    a. access agreement.
    b. acceptable license.
    c. computer transfer.
    d. limited confirmation contract.

25. Which act places an electronic signature on the same level as a pen-inscribed signature on paper? [p. 258]
    a. the Pen and Paper Act of 2002
    b. the Electronic Paper Act
    c. the Electronic Signature in Global and National Commerce Act
    d. the Electronic Data Base Inscription Act

26. A licensee who has tendered a copy of the license by the licensor is said to have accepted the copy if the licensee [p. 262]
    a. signifies that the tender was conforming.
    b. that his or her acts signify that the tender was conforming.
    c. keeps a copy despite its nonconformity.
    d. all of the above

Short Answer

27. What is the statute of limitations for bringing a cause of action under the UTICA? [pp. 261-262]

_____

_____

28. What is the biggest challenge when someone uses a digital signature? [p. 259]

_____

_____

29. Jeremy licenses a product database from Productdata.com, Inc. for two years to use in his business. However, after only two months of using the database, he receives a court order stating that he must cease and desist use of the product database as it infringes on a copyright that Productsforyou.com holds. If Jeremy sues Productdata.com, Inc., what would be his best theory to sue under? [p. 256] _____

_____

30. What is a licensor liable for if he or she uses electronic self-help improperly? [p. 260]

_____

31. What may an aggrieved party do if he or she thinks that prior to the performance date the other party might not deliver performance when due? [p. 262]

_____

_____

32. What is meant by cancellation as it applies to a breach of contract? [p. 262] _____

_____

33. What is an exclusive license? [p. 260] _____

_____

34. Give an example of a domain name extension that is most commonly used by ISPs, Web-hosting companies, and other businesses that are directly involved in the infrastructure of the Internet. [p. 255] _____

_____

Answers to Refresh Your Memory

1. The Internet is a collection of millions of computers that provide a network of electronic connections between the computers. [p. 254]
2. a combination of Web pages stored on various servers throughout the world [p.255]
3. E-mail is instantaneous communication with another by way of an e-mail address and the Internet. [p. 255]
4. It provided for uniform and comprehensive rules for contracts involving computer information transactions and software information licenses. [p. 254]
5. A domain name is a unique name that identifies an individual's or company's Web site. [p. 255]

6. It provides for the issuance of a cease-and-desist order and injunctions by the court. Monetary damages can also be awarded with the plaintiff opting for damages as provided by statute or he or she may prove his or her damages. [p. 256]
7. a contract that transfers limited rights in intellectual, property, or informational rights
8. an owner of intellectual property or informational rights who transfers rights in the property or information to the licensee [p. 259]
9. a party who is granted limited rights in or access to intellectual property or informational rights owned by a licensor [p. 259]
10. the Electronic Signature in Global and National Commerce Act [p. 258]
11. Any provisions of the UCITA that are preempted by federal law are unenforceable to the extent of the preemption. [p. 259]
12. A licensee's right to engage in a commercially reasonable substitute transaction after the licensor has breached the contract defines what is meant by cover. [p. 263]
13. This extension represents the word *commercial* and is the most widely used extension in the world. [p. 255]
14. .info [p. 255]
15. This extension is available to professionals, such as doctors, lawyers, consultants, and other professionals. [p. 256]

Critical Thought Exercise Model Answer

It is understood that e-mail is a convenient way to negotiate and agree on contract terms and to ultimately agree on a final contract. Assuming that all the elements to establish a valid contact are present, the fact that the contract is communicated by e-mail does not prevent the agreement from being valid and enforceable. In this instance, the subject matter, parties, price, and delivery terms have all been negotiated and agreed upon. While this is a contract for goods exceeding $500 that requires a written contract, there is no reason why the e-mails cannot be printed and used as the required writing. The e-mails will amply demonstrate the parties' intent and desire to enter into the agreement. The ordering of the eggs by Mrs. Dubyah by e-mail will have no less effect than a written letter. Thus, e-mail contracts meet the writing requirements for enforceable contracts.

Mrs. Dubyah is therefore advised to accept the shipment and pay for it as agreed. The Statute of Frauds will not supply a viable defense and it would be unethical for her to cancel the order based merely upon a whim.

Answers to Practice Quiz

True/False

1. True Most businesses conduct e-commerce by using Web sites.
2. False The domain extension .org represents the word *organization,* **not organic,** and is mainly used by nonprofit groups and organizations.
3. False The parties to a license are the licensor and the licensee.
4. False It is the Uniform Computer Information Transactions Act (UCITA) which is a model state law that creates contract law for the licensing of information technology rights.
5. True The Anticybersquatiing Consumer Protection Act gives owners of trademarks and persons with famous names a new weapon to attack the kidnapping of Internet domain names by cyberpirates.
6. False An applicant must complete a registration form and the cost is less than $50 to register a domain name for one year.

7. False   Mary may authenticate her contract with Watson by using the electronic symbol that is attached to, included in, or linked with the record as provided for under the Uniform Computer Information Transactions Act.

8. True   A contract can be formed in any manner showing agreement including the operation of electronic agents.

9. True   Under the Uniform Computer Information Transactions Act, limitations of e-commerce are acknowledged thereby providing that a contract is formed if a person takes action resulting in the electronic agent causing performance or a promise of benefits to the individual.

10. True   This act was designed to provide uniform laws for electronic signatures and electronic records.

11. False   The UDRP requires arbitration of domain name disputes.

12. False   A licensor does have a right to cure under certain circumstances.

13. True   Generally speaking, the UCITA provides that consumers are not bound by their unilateral electronic errors.

14. False   The act does in fact provide three ways to verify a digital signature.

15. True   The licensor may sue and recover from the licensee monetary damages caused by the breach, plus any consequential and incidental damages. A licensor can recover lost profits caused by the licensee's failure to accept or complete performance of the contract.

16. False   Licensing agreements tend to be very detailed and comprehensive contracts.

17. True   Electronic errors by nonconsumers are handled under the common law of contracts or the Uniform Commercial Code, whichever applies.

18. False   If the licensor tenders a copy that is a material breach of the contract, the nonbreaching party to whom tender is made may either (1) refuse the tender, (2) accept the tender, and (3) accept any commercially reasonable units and refuse the rest [UCITA Section 704].

19. False   The licensor, Victor, has the right to have all copies of the licensed information returned by Ryan upon cancellation of the license.

20. True   The activation of disabling bugs, and embedded time bombs can be utilized when a licensee fails to pay his or her license fee.

Multiple Choice

21. B   Answer B is the correct answer as electronic mail is the most widely used means of communication over the Internet. Answer A is incorrect as licensing agreements are not a typical means of communication that are widely used. Answer C is incorrect as even though chat rooms are popular, electronic mail is more widely used. Answer D is incorrect for the reasons given above.

22. C   Answer C correctly states the two requirements in order to prove a violation of the Anticybersquatting Consumer Protection Act. Answers A, B, and D are incorrect as none of these answers state the two necessary requirements under the act.

23. B   Answer B is correct as the owner of informational rights who transfers rights is the licensor. Answer A is incorrect as the licensee receives the rights. Answers C and D do not make sense in this question as even though duties and possible rights might be inferred from the terms obligor and obligee, there is nothing to indicate a license is involved with respect to an obligor and obligee.

24. A   Answer A is correct as an access contract/agreement allows the licensee to access the information for an agreed-upon number of uses. Answers B, C, and D are nonexistent in terms of legal terminology and therefore erroneous.

25. C   Answer C is correct as the Electronic Signature in Global and National Commerce Act places an electronic signature on par with a pen-inscribed signature. Answers A, B, and D are incorrect as these acts do not exist.
26. D   Answer D is correct as answers A, B, and C all indicate acceptance of a copy by the licensee.

Short Answer

27.   The UCITA provides that a cause of action must be commenced within one year after the breach was or should have been discovered, but not more than five years after the breach actually occurred.
28.   The biggest challenge when someone uses a digital signature is making sure he or she is the person he or she claims to be.
29.   Jeremy's best theory would be one based on breach of warranty of noninterference and noninfringement.
30.   A licensor is liable for damages.
31.   The aggrieved party may make a demand for adequate assurance of due performance from the other party.
32.   Cancellation is defined as the termination of a contract by a contracting party upon the material breach of the contract by the other party.
33.   An exclusive license is a license that grants the licensee exclusive rights to use informational rights for a specified duration.
34.   .net

Chapter 18

FORMATION OF
SALES AND LEASE CONTRACTS

Chapter Overview

This chapter focuses on the formation of sales and lease contracts and the requirements for the same. Also, the requirements and exceptions as they pertain to modification, the Statute of Frauds, and parol evidence are explored. Various key sections of the Uniform Commercial Code are also explored in terms of their flexibility as well as applicability to sales and lease contracts.

Objectives

Upon completion of the exercises in this chapter, you should be able to:
1. Discuss what sales contracts are governed by Article 2 of the UCC.
2. Explain lease contracts as governed by Article 2A of the UCC.
3. Analyze and apply good faith and reasonableness as per the UCC.
4. Discuss how sales and lease contracts are formed.
5. Explain the impact of the UCC's gap-filling rules.
6. Explain the UCC's firm offer rule.
7. Explain the UCC's additional terms rule and how to apply it to the "battle of the forms."
8. Discuss the UCC's written confirmation rule.
9. Discuss the requirements for modification in sales and lease contracts.
10. Explain what is considered unconscionable in sales and lease contracts.

Practical Application

You should be able to determine what is necessary as well as acceptable to form valid sales or lease contracts. Further, your studies should provide you with the knowledge you need to modify, explain, or validate either of these types of contracts should the need arise.

Helpful Hints

It is important to remember that basic contract principles also apply to sales and lease contracts, so, in essence, you are not learning all new material. By reviewing the elements of basic contract formation, and adding to it, you will have a better chance at retaining the information. As you study this chapter, keep the Uniform Commercial Code's leniency in mind when forming sales and lease contracts. As a reminder, when you are analyzing a fact situation or a contract, it is advisable to read and analyze each line separately so that you do not miss any potential issues.

Study Tips

This chapter primarily focuses on Article 2 (Sales) and Article 2A (Leases) of the Uniform Commercial Code. It is easiest to study this chapter if you learn the basic scope of each of these articles. Article 2 involves transactions in goods whereas Article 2A involves consumer and finance leases.

Article 2 (Sales)

- You must learn what a sale is. A sale is the passing of title from a seller to a buyer for a price.

- <u>Next, what are goods?</u> Goods are tangible things that are movable at their identification. Be careful in this area, as there are some things that are not considered to be goods. These include money, intangible items, bonds, patents, stocks, and land. Another caveat, things that are severable from the land can be goods.

Services are not covered under Article 2; however, when there is a mixed sale of both goods and services, if the goods dominate the transaction, then Article 2 does in fact apply. Each case involving a mixed sale is examined individually.

Article 2 applies to all sales regardless of a person's status of being or not being a merchant in the transaction. Note though that some sections of Article 2 apply only to merchants as well as express the special rules of duty placed upon merchants.

Article 2A (Leases)

- This article applies to personal property leases, which also involves the formation, performance, and default of leases.

- <u>What is a lease?</u> A lease is the conveyance of the right to the possession and use of the named goods for a set time period in return for certain consideration.

- <u>Who are the parties to a lease?</u> The lessor who is the person who transfers the right of possession and use of the goods under the lease and the lessee who obtains the right to possession and use of goods under a lease.

- <u>What is a finance lease?</u> This involves three parties, the lessor, the lessee, and the vendor (supplier). Here the lessor is not a manufacturer or supplier of goods, but still acquires title to the goods or the right to use and possess in connection with the lease terms.

Formation of Both Sales and Lease Contracts

As with other contracts, both sales and lease contracts require an offer, acceptance, and consideration in order to be properly formed.

Offer

At common law, all necessary terms needed to be in place.
Modernly under the UCC, if a term is left open, the courts will apply the following rules:

Open Terms
The court will look at the parties' intent to make a contract and then determine if there is a reasonably certain basis for giving an appropriate remedy. When open terms are allowed to be read into the contract, this is referred to as gap-filling rules.

Open Price Term
If a price in a contract is missing, the court will imply a "reasonable price" at the time of delivery.

Open Payment Term
In the absence of an agreement on payment terms, payment is due at the time and place where the buyer is to receive the goods.

Open Delivery Term
If there is no agreed-upon place of delivery, then delivery is to take place at the seller's place of business.

Open Time Term
The contract must be performed within a reasonable time if there is no provision in the parties' contract for a set specified time of performance.

Open Assortment Term
This occurs when the buyer is given the option of choosing the goods from an assortment of goods.

Acceptance

At common law and under the UCC, a contract is created when the buyer or lessee sends his or her acceptance to the offeror, not upon receipt.

Acceptance may be accomplished in any manner and by any reasonable medium of acceptance. If a buyer makes an offer, then the seller's acceptance is signified by either the seller's prompt promise to ship or his or her prompt shipment of conforming or nonconforming goods.

Acceptance of the goods by the buyer occurs if after the buyer has a reasonable opportunity to accept the goods, either indicates that the goods are conforming, or signifies that he or she will keep the goods regardless of their nonconformity, or if he or she fails to reject the goods within a reasonable period of time after delivery of the goods.

Accommodation Shipment is Not an Acceptance
A shipment of nonconforming goods is not considered an acceptance if the seller reasonably notifies the buyer that the shipment is being offered as an accommodation to the buyer. An accommodation shipment is considered a counter-offer from the seller to the buyer.

Importance of the Mirror Image Rule

At common law, an offeree's acceptance had to mirror the image of the offer. If additional terms were included, it was considered a counteroffer. The UCC, however, has given flexibility to this rule.

If one or both parties are ***nonmerchants***, any additional terms become ***proposed additions*** to the contract. The proposed additions do not terminate the offer nor does it constitute a counteroffer.

If the offeree's proposed additions are accepted by the offeror, they become part of the contract. If both parties are ***merchants,*** the additional terms become part of the contract unless the acceptance is expressly conditional on assent to the terms of the offer or the additional terms materially alter the terms of the original contract or the offeror notifies the offeree that he or she is rejecting the additional terms.

Consideration

Consideration is also required in the formation of sales and lease contracts. However, unlike common law, the UCC indicates that modification of sales and lease contracts do not require consideration, but they do require the element of ***good faith.***

Statute of Frauds

Goods costing $500 or more and lease payments of $1,000 or more must be in writing. The agreement must be signed by the party to be charged.

Exceptions to the Statute of Frauds – These sales and lease situations do not have to meet the writing requirement of the Statute of Frauds:

   Specially Manufactured Goods
   Admissions in Pleadings or Court
   Part Acceptance

Important Note: If both parties are merchants and one of the parties to the oral contract sends written confirmation within a reasonable time after entering into the contract and the other merchant does not object to the contract within ten days of his or her receipt of the confirmation, then the Statute of Frauds is satisfied.

Modification Required to Be in Writing

If the parties state that the modification must be in writing, then it has to be. However, in general, an oral modification is sufficient if it does not violate the Statute of Frauds.

Parol Evidence

A rule that states that a written contract is the complete and final expression of the party's agreement.

Any prior or contemporaneous oral or written statements to the contract may not be introduced to alter or contradict or add to the written contract.

Exceptions to the Parol Evidence Rule

When the contract's express terms are unclear, the court may consider the course of performance, course of dealing, and usage of trade as outside sources to clarify the terms of the parties' agreement.

Refresh Your Memory

The following exercise will enable you to refresh your memory on the rules and principles presented to you in this chapter. Read each question twice and place your answer in the blanks provided. Review the chapter material for any question you miss or are unable to remember.

1.   Which article of the UCC applies to transactions in goods? _____
_____

2.   Article 2 and Article 2A of the Uniform Commercial Code govern _____.

3.   Which is the only state that has not adopted some version of Article 2 of the UCC? ____
_____.

4.   Bonds and patents are not considered to be tangible _____ under Article 2 of the UCC

5.   The sale of shampoo along with a cut and style at a local beauty salon would be an example of a _____ sale.

6.   A _____ for the sale of goods may be made in any manner sufficient to show _____ including conduct by both parties.

7.   How may an offer for a contract for the sale or lease of goods be formed? _____
_____

8.   If the post office loses an acceptance letter, what happens to the contract? _____
_____

9.   Modification of a sales or lease contract must be in _____ _____.

10.   The inclusion of additional terms in the acceptance is considered a _____.

11.   If one or both parties to a sales contract are both nonmerchants, any additional terms would be considered _____ _____ to the contract.

12.   According to the Statute of Frauds, what types of sales and lease contracts need to be in writing? _____

13.   Part of the _____ rule states that "when a sales or lease contract is evidenced by a writing that is intended to be a final expression of the parties' agreement ... the terms of the writing may not be contradicted by evidence..."

14.   What three situations involving a sales or lease contract will still warrant their enforcement despite the fact that they are not in writing as per the Statute of Frauds? _____
_____

15.   What is the maximum amount of time under the UCC firm offer rule? _____
_____

Critical Thought Exercise

Apex Mattress Company, for whom you are the vice president of material acquisition, entered into an oral agreement with Davis Wool Ranch (DWR), a wool supplier, in which DWR agreed to sell Apex 800 bundles of wool, each weighing 350 pounds. Shortly after your conversation with Dan Davis of DWR, you sent Davis an e-mail confirming the terms of the oral contract. Davis did not respond to the e-mail or offer any objection to the terms stated in the e-mail. When the delivery date arrived four months later, you contacted DWR to finalize the delivery terms. DWR stated that there was no agreement and DWR had sold the 800 bundles to Fluffy-Air Mattress because the price of wool had doubled on the open market since the date of the oral agreement. The board of directors of Apex requests that you inform them of your position in regards to bringing suit against DWR and the likelihood that Apex will prevail.

Write a memo to the board setting forth your position and authority for your conclusion.

Answer:

_____
_____
_____
_____
_____
_____
_____
_____
_____
_____
_____
_____
_____
_____
_____
_____
_____
_____
_____

Practice Quiz

True/False

1. ___ One of the major frustrations of business persons conducting interstate business is that they are subject to the laws of each state in which they operate. [p. 271]

2. ___ Real estate is a tangible good, as an individual may touch the trees, plants, and buildings on it. [p. 272]

3. ___ The sale and removal of a furnace on an individual's property would be considered a sale of goods subject to Article 2 of the UCC. [p. 272]

4. ___ Due to its broad nature, the UCC provides exceptional guidance for deciding mixed sales. [p. 273]

5. ___ Article 4 of the UCC applies to all sales contracts regardless of being a merchant or not. [p. 273]

6. ___ UCC 20104 (1) defines a merchant as a person who by his or her occupation holds himself or herself out as having knowledge or skill peculiar to the goods involved in the transaction. [p. 273]

7. ___ Article 2A of the UCC governs leases of goods. [p. 274]

8. ___ A finance lease is a two-party transaction comprised of a lessee and a supplier. [p. 274]

9. ___ When a contract contains an open assortment term, the buyer must make the selection in good faith and within limits set by commercial reasonableness. [p. 276]

10. ___ Under the UCC, acceptance is limited to either by mail or in person. [p. 277]

11. ___ The UCC provides that in order for an oral modification to be enforceable, it must be in writing if it brings the contract within the Statute of Frauds. [p. 279]

12. ___ If an express term to a contract is not clear, the use of the parties' course of performance may be referenced outside of the contract to determine what the parties intended.
[p. 280]

13. ___ A shipment of nonconforming goods constitutes an acceptance regardless of notification of the accommodation to the buyer. [p. 278]

14. ___ The firm offer rule states that a merchant who offers to buy, sell, or lease goods and gives a separate signed, written assurance that the offer will be held open cannot revoke the offer for the time stated, or if no time is stated, for a reasonable time, not to exceed three months. [p. 276]

15. ___ Common law and the UCC state that a contract is created when the offeree sends an acceptance to the offeror, not when the offeror receives the acceptance. [p. 277]

16. ___ If an order or other offer to buy goods requires prompt or current shipment, the offer is accepted if the seller holds the goods and waits for the buyer to pick them up. [p. 277]

17. ___ An accommodation is a shipment that is offered to the buyer as a concession for the original shipment when the original shipment cannot be filled. [p. 278]

18. ___ Consideration is required for the formation of lease and sales contracts. [p. 277]

19. ___ A modification of a lease or sales contract requires consideration to be binding.
[p. 280]

20. ___ Generally speaking, contracts for specially manufactured goods do not need to be in writing. [p. 279]

21. ___ An offeror who sends a standard form contract as an offer to the offeree may receive the acceptance drafted on the offeree's own form contract. [p. 278]

22. ___ Part acceptance of an oral sales or lease contract that should be in writing is not enforceable. [p. 279]

23. ___ The purpose of the parol evidence rule is to ensure certainty in written sales and lease contracts. [p. 280]

24. ___ Shawndra and Janet entered into a written agreement for the purchase of Shawndra's boat. Janet may be allowed to introduce an oral conversation that took place at the same time as the written agreement whereby Janet claims Shawndra agreed to reupholster the boat's vinyl seats. Janet will be allowed to introduce this oral conversation. [p. 280]

25. ___ Karissa, a lessor, orally contracts to lease 60 video arcade games to Monique and Monique accepts the first 15 tendered by Karissa. Thereafter Monique refuses to take delivery of the remaining 45 arcade games. Monique must pay for the 15 games she originally received and accepted. [p. 279]

Multiple Choice

26. If a sales or lease contract contains specially manufactured goods, it [p.279]
    a. need not be in writing.
    b. needs to be in writing.
    c. can be partially in writing and partially not in writing.
    d. none of the above

27. Examples of things that are severable from real estate and are considered goods are [p. 272]
    a. stocks, patents, bonds.
    b. money, coins.
    c. dental services and legal services.
    d. minerals, structures, and growing crops.

28. Under UCC 2-106(1), a sale consists of [p. 272]
    a. the passing of title from a seller to a buyer for a price.
    b. an ad in the daily newspaper.
    c. answers a and b
    d. the passing of title from a buyer to a seller for a price.

29. Article 2 applies to [pp. 272-274]
    a. merchants.
    b. nonmerchants.
    c. sales contracts.
    d. all of the above.

30. In a finance lease situation, the lessor [p. 274]
    a. selects goods.
    b. acquires title to the goods or right to their possession and use in connection with the terms of the lease.
    c. manufactures goods.
    d. supplies the goods.

31. Which of the following applies to the acceptance of goods? [p. 277]
    a. When the buyer has had a chance to inspect the goods and indicates the goods are conforming, this signifies acceptance.
    b. When the buyer has had a chance to inspect the goods and indicates that he or she will take or retain the goods in spite of their nonconformity, this signifies acceptance.
    c. When the buyer has had a chance to inspect the goods and he or she fails to reject the goods within a reasonable time after tender or delivery, this signifies acceptance.
    d. all of the above

32. Contracts involving a mixed sale are [p. 273]
    a. governed by the UCC if the goods are the predominant part of the transaction.
    b. are not given any guidance by the UCC on how to decide them.
    c. are decided by the courts on a case-by-case basis.
    d. all of the above.

33. An offer to make a sales or lease contract may be accepted   [p. 277]
    a. by a specified manner.
    b. by a specified method of communication.
    c. by any reasonable manner or method of communication.
    d. by both a specified manner and method of communication.

34. If Josephine has had a reasonable opportunity to inspect goods bought from Alma, Josephine may accept the goods by [p. 277]
    a. signifying that the goods do not meet the standard she expected.
    b. signifying that she will not take the goods.
    c. signifying that the goods were perishable in a volatile market.
    d. signifying that the goods are conforming.

35. If both parties to a lease or sales contract are merchants, the Statute of Frauds requirement can be met if [p. 278]
    a. one of the parties to the oral agreement sends a written confirmation within a reasonable time after contracting and the other party does not give written notice of an objection within 10 days of receiving the confirmation.
    b. one of the parties sends an oral confirmation.
    c. one of the parties to the oral agreement sends a written confirmation.
    d. one of the parties has his or her agent or broker send an oral confirmation.

Short Answer

36. The most important point in the battle of the form is that [p. 278]_____
    _____
    _____

37. If one or both parties to a sales contract are nonmerchants, any additional terms are considered [p. 278] _____ _____.

38. Article 5 of the Uniform Commercial Code governs [p. 281] _____

39. What do most banks incorporate in the letters of credit that they issue? [p. 281] _____
_____

40. What was developed to manage the risks in international sales? [p. 281] _____
_____.

41. In a finance lease, the lessor does not _____, _____, or supply the goods. [p. 274]

42. Modification of a sales or lease contract must be made in _____ _____. [p. 279]

43. When express terms are not clear and need interpretation, what three things will the court look at? [p. 280] _____, _____,
_____.

44. An _____ contract is where an offeree pays consideration to keep the offer open. [p. 280]

45. Article 2A of the UCC governs _____. [p. 274]

46. What was the common law rule with regard to revocation of an offer? [p. 276]
_____

47. The _____ _____ _____ is a comprehensive statutory scheme that includes laws that cover most aspects of contract transactions. [p. 271]

48. _____ are tangible things that are moveable at the time of identification to the contract. [p. 272]

49. Under the _____ _____ rule, the offeree's acceptance must be the same as the offer. [p. 276]

50. An accommodation contract is _____
_____.
[p. 278]

Answers to Refresh Your Memory

1. Article 2 [p. 272]
2. govern personal property leases [p. 272]
3. Louisiana [p. 272]
4. goods [p. 272]
5. mixed [p. 273]
6. contract; agreement [p. 275]

7. A contract for the lease or sale of goods may be made in any manner adequate to show agreement. [p. 277]
8. The contract is still valid, regardless if the post office loses the letter. [p. 277]
9. good faith [p. 277]
10. counteroffer [p. 277]
11. proposed additions [p. 278]
12. Contracts for the sale of goods $500 or more and lease contracts involving payments of $1,000 or more must be in writing. [p. 279]
13. parol evidence [p. 280]
14. specially manufactured goods, admissions in pleadings or court, part acceptance [p. 279]
15. three months [p. 276]

Critical Thought Exercise Model Answer

If both parties to an oral sales contract are merchants, the Statute of Frauds requirement can be satisfied if one of the parties to the oral agreement sends a written confirmation of the sale within a reasonable time after making the agreement and the other merchant does not give written notice of an objection to the contract within 10 days after receiving the confirmation. If both merchants are within the United States, UCC section 2-201(2) will control. If one of the merchants is a foreign entity, then the 1980 United Nations Convention on Contracts for the International Sale of Goods (CISG) will apply. Under the CISG, Article 11, an international sales contract "need not be concluded in or even evidenced by writing and is not subject to any other requirements as to form."

When the confirming e-mail was sent to DWR, they did not respond within a ten-day period or voice any objections to the contents of our e-mail. Modernly, an e-mail can serve as a writing. Thus, Apex had a legally binding contract with DWR. The failure of DWR to tender delivery of the 800 bundles of wool on the delivery date put them in breach. The fact that DWR desired to sell the wool for a larger profit hurts their position and helps us because of the requirement that they deal with us in good faith.

Lastly, we will have to obtain the wool from another source and may be required to pay a premium for the wool because of the urgency that we face due to the actions of DWR. We should be able to recover damages in an amount equal to the difference between the contract price and market price at the time we enter into a new contract with a different wool supplier.

Answers to Practice Quiz

True/False

1. True   One of the major frustrations of business persons conducting interstate business is that they are subject to the laws of each state in which they operate.
2. False   Real estate is not a tangible good because it is not movable regardless of what you can touch, albeit trees, plants, or buildings.
3. False   The sale and removal of a furnace would be a sale of real property because its removal would cause material harm. [UCC 2-107 (2)]
4. False   The UCC provides no guidance for deciding cases based on mixed sales.
5. True   Article 2 of the UCC applies to all sales contracts, whether they involve merchants or not.

6. True   Under UCC 2-104(1) a merchant is defined as a person who by his or her occupation holds himself or herself out as having knowledge or skill peculiar to the goods involved in the transaction or a person who deals in the goods of the kind involved in the transaction.
7. True   Article 2A of the UCC governs leases of goods.
8. False   Under the UCC a finance lease is a three-party transaction consisting of a lessor, a lessee, and a supplier.
9. True   The buyer must make the selection in good faith and within the limits of commercial reasonableness.
10. False   The UCC permits acceptance by any reasonable manner or method of communication.
11. True   If the oral modification brings a contract within the Statute of Frauds, it must be in writing to be enforceable.
12. True   The course of the parties' performance may be referenced even though it is outside of the contract, if an express term of the contract is silent.
13. False   A shipment of nonconforming goods does not constitute an acceptance if the seller reasonably notifies the buyer that the shipment if offered only as an accommodation to the buyer.
14. True   UCC 2-205, 2A-205 states the requirements and time limitations of the firm offer rule.
15. True   A contract is created with the offeree sends an acceptance to the offeror. This is true for both common law and the UCC.
16. False   The offer is accepted if the seller promptly promises to ship the goods or promptly ships either conforming or nonconforming goods. The shipment of conforming goods signals acceptance of the buyer's offer.
17. True   An accommodation is a shipment that is offered to the buyer as a replacement for the original shipment when the original shipment cannot be filled.
18. True   Consideration is a necessary requirement in order for a sales or lease contract to be formed.
19. False   UCC 2-209(1), 2A-208(1) state that an agreement modifying a sales or lease contract does not need consideration to be binding.
20. True   The case of specially manufactured goods is a situation in which a contract will be enforceable despite not being in writing if the goods are not suitable for sale or lease to others in the ordinary course of the lessor's or seller's business and the seller or lessor has made commitments for their procurement or a substantial beginning of their manufacture.
21. True   An offeror who sends a standard form contract as an offer to the offeree may receive an acceptance drafted on the offeree's own form contract.
22. False   An oral sales or lease contract that should otherwise be in writing is enforceable to the extent to which the goods have been received and accepted by the buyer or lessee.
23. True   The parol evidence rule was promulgated so that written contracts would evince the parties' final expression of their agreement, thereby leaving no room for doubt.
24. False   The parol evidence rule prevents Janet from introducing her oral conversation with Shawndra, as it would contradict the parties' written agreement. There is nothing in the facts to indicate that the terms of the parties' agreement is not clear on its face. However, if that uncertainty were the case, then the court would look at the course of performance, course of dealing, and usage of trade with respect to the agreement. Further, there is nothing that would indicate that Janet was using the oral agreement to demonstrate fraud, duress, or a mistake. The facts as they stand would not permit the use of parol evidence to be introduced.

25. True   Monique's acceptance of the first fifteen video arcade games from Karissa is a classic example of part acceptance. Even though their contract was not in writing, it is a contract that is enforceable to the extent to which Monique received and accepted the goods from Karissa.

Multiple Choice

26. A   Answer A is correct as UCC 2-201(3) and UCC 2A-201(4), which pertain to specially manufactured goods do not need to be in writing. See page 279 of your text for more details regarding this. Answers B, C, and D are wrong as answers B and C are untrue statements under the above-referenced sections of the UCC.

27. D   Answer D is correct as mineral, structures, and growing crops are severable as per Article 2 of the UCC. Answer A is incorrect as stocks, patents, and bonds are intangible items that do not fall within the UCC's definition of goods. Answer B is incorrect as money and coins also do not fall within the UCC's definition of goods. Answer C is incorrect as contracts for the provision of services are not covered by Article 2 of the UCC.

28. A   Answer A is the correct answer as UCC 2-106(1) states that a sale consists of the passing of title from a seller to a buyer for a price. Answer B is incorrect as it does not apply to the UCC. Answers C and D are wrong for the answers stated above.

29. D   Answer D is correct as Article 2 applies to merchants and nonmerchants and is primarily concerned with sales contracts, thereby making Answers A, B, and C all correct choices.

30. B   Answer B is correct as it correctly states the role of the lessor in a finance situation. Answers A, C, and D are simply incorrect statements.

31. D   Answer D is correct as answers A, B, and C all apply to the acceptance of goods.

32. D   Answer D is correct as all three statements in answers A, B, and C correctly state the law as well as facts concerning a mixed sale.

33. C   Answer C is correct as any reasonable manner or method of communication is a proper way to accept an offer to make a sales or lease contract. Answer A is incorrect as a broad statement such as "specified manner" may not be reasonable. Answer B is incorrect as the statement "by a specified means of communication" may not be reasonable. Answer D is incorrect for the reasons given above.

34. D   Answer D is correct as Josephine's acceptance of the goods after a reasonable inspection may be signified by indicating that the goods are conforming. Answer A is incorrect, as an acceptance would not necessarily include a statement of the goods not meeting the standard she expected. Answer B indicates rejection and not acceptance. Answer C is incorrect as signifying the perishability of goods in a volatile market is not a recognized means of acceptance.

35. A   Answer A is correct as it properly states the law with regard to merchants and the Statute of Frauds. Answer B is incorrect as sending an oral confirmation will not satisfy the Statute of Frauds. Answer C is incorrect as sending a written confirmation is not enough to satisfy the Statute of Frauds. Answer D is incorrect as sending a party's agent or broker with an oral confirmation is also insufficient under the Statute of Frauds.

Short Answer

36. There is no contract if the additional terms so materially alter the terms of the original offer that the parties cannot agree on the contract.
37. proposed additions
38. letters of credit
39. the Uniform Customs and Practices for Documentary Credits (UCP)

40. letters of credit
41. select, manufacture
42. good faith
43. course of performance, course of dealing, usage of trade
44. option
45. leases
46. Offeror could revoke his/her offer any time before acceptance.
47. Uniform Commercial Code
48. goods
49. mirror image
50. a shipment that is offered to the buyer as a replacement for the original shipment when the original shipment cannot be filled

Chapter 19

PERFORMANCE OF SALES
AND LEASE CONTRACTS

Chapter Overview

This chapter provides a clear understanding of sales and destination contracts as well as risk of loss and the passage of title to goods. Emphasis is also placed on the identification of goods. Additionally, it provides a good understanding of sales on approval and how it differs between a sale or return. Further emphasis is placed on insurable interest in goods, good faith purchasers for value, and sales by nonowners.

Objectives

Upon completion of the exercises in this chapter, you should be able to:
1. Explain the difference between a shipment and destination contract and when title passes.
2. Explain the different shipment and delivery terms.
3. Identify who bears the risk of loss when goods are damaged or lost in shipment.
4. Differentiate between a sale on approval and a sale or return.
5. Discuss a sale on consignment.
6. Classify who has an insurable interest in goods.
7. Determine who bears the risk of loss when goods are stolen and resold.
8. Explain the meaning of a good faith purchaser for value.
9. Discuss the different situations involved with sales by nonowners.

Practical Application

You should be able to determine what type of contract has been formed as you analyze the shipping terms. Additionally you should be able to determine who bears the risk of loss in situations involving damaged, lost or stolen, and resold goods. You will have gained a better familiarity with the laws involving consignments, as well as laws concerning good faith purchasers for value.

Helpful Hints

As you peruse the material in this chapter, it is helpful to keep in mind who is receiving the most benefit with regard to the type of contract the parties are entering into. If you remember that the seller begins with the letter "s" and usually will want a shipment (also begins with the letter "s") contract as the carrier that the goods are placed on will then bare the risk of loss. Further, that a buyer will want the contract to be a destination contract as the seller will bear the risk of loss up until the time that the buyer receives the goods.

The remaining rules in this chapter are fairly easy to learn and have been categorized in an order that will make sense as you apply each to any given fact situation. One of the easiest ways to analyze facts in this area is to ask the following questions in the following order.

1) Who are the parties?
2) Have the goods been identified to the contract?
3) Do the parties have a shipment or a destination contract?
4) Who bears the risk of loss in light of the type of contract that exists?
5) What if anything has happened to the goods?
6) Are there any third parties involved?
7) If so, what is their capacity or role in the facts?
8) Are there any special rules of law that apply?

Study Tips

Identification

- This can occur at any time and in any manner.
- If no time is specified, then the UCC will state when it occurs.
- Already existing goods are identified at the contract's inception.
- Goods that are part of a bulk shipment are identified when specific merchandise is separated or tagged.

Shipment contract

- Creation is accomplished in one of two ways:
    1) by using the term shipment contract or
    2) using delivery terms such as F.O.B., F.A.S., C.I.F. or C.& F.
- This requires the seller to ship and deliver goods to the buyer via a common carrier.
- Proper shipping arrangements are required.
- *Title* passes to the buyer at the time and place of shipment.
- *Risk of loss* passes to the buyer when conforming goods are delivered to the carrier.

Destination Contract

- Creation is accomplished in one of two ways:
    1) by using the term destination contract or
    2) using delivery terms such as: F.O.B. *place of destination*, ex-ship, or no-arrival, no-sale contract
- This requires the seller to deliver the goods to buyer's place of business or another specified destination. The seller is also required to replace any goods lost in transit.
- *Title passes* when the seller tenders delivery of the goods at the specified destination.
- *Risk of loss* does not pass until the goods are tendered at the specified destination.

Special Situation Involving Goods That Are Not Moved

Where goods are not required to be moved by the seller, passage of title is dependent upon whether or not document of title is required to be given to the buyer.

If the Seller Is a Merchant – Risk of loss does not pass until the goods are received.

If the Seller Is a Nonmerchant – Risk of loss occurs when there is a *tender of delivery* of the goods.

Sale on Approval

A sale does not occur unless the buyer accepts the goods. The situation presents itself when a merchant allows a buyer to take the goods home for a specified period of time to determine if it meets the customer's needs.

Acceptance is shown by:
1) expressly accepting the goods,
2) failing to notify the seller of buyer's rejection, or
3) use of the goods inconsistently with the purpose of the trial.

Risk of loss and title stay with the seller and do not pass until the buyer accepts the goods. Goods are not subject to buyer's creditor's claims until buyer accepts them.

Sale or Return

The seller delivers the goods to the buyer letting the buyer know that he or she may return them if they are not used or resold within a stated period of time.

If the buyer doesn't return them within a reasonable time, the goods are considered sold.

Risk of loss and title pass when the buyer takes possession of the goods. Buyer's creditors may make claims against the buyer while the goods are in the buyer's possession.

Risk of Loss Involving Breach of Contract Situations

Seller in Breach

Breach occurs when the seller tenders nonconforming goods to the buyer.

If the buyer has the right to reject the goods, the *risk of loss* stays with the seller until the nonconformity or defect is cured or the buyer accepts the nonconforming goods.

Buyer in Breach

Breach occurs where the buyer refuses to take delivery of conforming goods. Also, if the buyer repudiates the contract or otherwise breaches the contract.

The *risk of loss* rests on the buyer for a commercially reasonable time.

Buyer is liable for any loss in excess of insurance covered by the seller.

Risk of Loss in Lease Contracts

The parties may agree who will bear the risk of loss if the goods are lost or destroyed.

If there is no provision, the UCC states that in an ordinary lease, the *risk of loss* stays with the lessor. If it is a finance lease, then the *risk of loss* passes to the lessee. [UCC 2A-219]

If tender of delivery of goods fails to conform to the lease contract, the *risk of loss* stays with the lessor or supplier until acceptance or cure. [UCC 2A-220(1)(a)].

Sales by Nonowners

This category involves individuals who sell goods that they do not have good title to.

Void Title and Lease: Stolen Goods

Where the buyer purchases goods from a thief, title to the goods does not pass and the lessee does not require any leasehold interest in the goods.

The real owner of the goods may reclaim the goods from the buyer or lessee. Title is void.

Voidable Title: Sales or Lease of Goods to Good Faith Purchasers for Value

A seller has voidable title to goods if the goods were obtained by fraud, dishonored check, or impersonation of another person.

An individual with voidable title may transfer good title to goods to a good faith purchaser for value or a good faith subsequent lessee.

Note, a good faith purchaser for value is one who pays consideration or rent for the goods to one he or she honestly believes has good title to those goods. The real owner cannot reclaim the goods from this type of purchaser.

Entrustment Rule

If an owner entrusts the possession of his or her goods to a merchant who deals in the particular type of goods, the merchant may transfer all rights to *a buyer in the ordinary course of business.* The real owner cannot reclaim the goods from this type of buyer.

Refresh Your Memory

The following exercise will enable you to refresh your memory on the rules and principles presented to you in this chapter. Read each question twice and place your answer in the blanks provided. Review the chapter material for any question you miss or are unable to remember.

1.   Article 2 of the UCC allows parties to a sales contract the right to _____ the goods that are not tied to title.

2.   Already existing goods are _____ when the contract is made and names the specific goods sold or leased.

3.   If Zeb has fifty acres of corn that he planted, when is the corn identified?
     _____.

4.   Those goods that are not yet in existence are referred to as _____.

5.   What does the shipping term ex-ship mean?

_____

_____

6.   When does a nonmerchant seller pass the risk of loss to the buyer?

_____.

7.   What is the seller called in a consignment? _____

8.   A shipment contract requires the seller to ship goods _____ to the contract via a _____.

9.   A destination contract requires the seller to _____ conforming goods to a specific destination.

10.   What types of terms signify a destination contract?

_____

_____

11.   Who bears the risk of loss if the goods are stolen or destroyed after the contract date and before the buyer picks up the goods from the seller who is a merchant?

_____

_____

12.   What is meant by the terminology void title?

_____

_____

13.   Give the definition of a bailee.

_____

_____

14.   A type of sale in which there is not an actual sale unless the buyer accepts the goods is a

_____   _____.

15.   How long does the risk of loss rest on a buyer when he or she is in breach?

_____   _____.

Critical Thought Exercise

Bristol Physical Therapy (BPT) contracted with Summit Pools, Inc., for the purchase of a "fully installed portable therapy whirlpool" for the sum of $14,000. The price included all labor and parts but the order form was not itemized. The freight carrier hired by the manufacturer delivered the pool to the parking lot just outside the building occupied by BPT. A receptionist for BPT signed the delivery invoice and immediately called Summit Pools. When the installation crew for Summit Pools arrived five days later to install the whirlpool, it was gone.

In this situation, had the risk of loss of the whirlpool passed from Summit Pools to BPT?

Answer:

_____

_____

_____

_____

_____

_____

_____

_____

_____

_____

_____

_____

_____

_____

Practice Quiz

True/False

1. ___ If Melba contracts to purchase 800 cases of soda from a manufacturer who has 1000 cases of soda, the goods will be identified when the manufacturer explicitly separates the 800 cases. [p. 285]

2. ___ If a destination contract is involved, the parties may choose who bears the risk of loss. [p. 287]

3. ___ If Gordie ships light poles by using the railroad, the goods are presumed to be sent pursuant to a shipment contract. [p. 286]

4. ___ No arrival and no-sale contracts are treated like destination contracts with the seller bearing the risk of loss. [p. 287]

5. ___ The risk of loss in destination contracts does not pass until the goods are tendered to the buyer at a specified destination. [p. 287]

6. ___ In a sale or return contract, the risk of loss and title to the goods pass to the buyer when the goods are in transit. [p. 288]

7. ___ Under a consignment, if a seller fails to file a financing statement, the goods are subject to the claims of the buyer's creditors. [p. 289]

8. ___ The entrustment rule does not apply to leases. [p. 291]

9. ___ If Peter, a silk scarf merchant, has been entrusted with Velma's silk scarves, Peter may transfer all rights in the goods to Eli, a buyer in the ordinary course of business. [p. 291]

10. ___ Marla's Magnificent Creations, a large Oklahoma clothing manufacturer, places the term F.O.B. Atlanta when shipping an order of clothes to Tamara's Boutique in Atlanta, Georgia. Marla's will bear the expense and risk of loss until Tamara's Boutique has the goods tendered upon it. [p. 287]

11. ___ Jared's Fine Jalopy's is a new car dealership in Somewhere, U.S.A. Francine has been allowed to take one of Jared's cars home for three days. This would be considered to be a sale on approval. [p. 288]

12. ___ A sale does not occur in a situation involving a sale on approval until the buyer accepts the goods. [p. 288]

13. ___ In a sale on approval, the risk of loss and title to the goods remains with the buyer. [p. 288]

14. ___ In a sale or return contract, the seller delivers goods to a buyer making it clear that the buyer may not return the goods if they are not used within a stated or reasonable period of time. [pp. 288-289]

15. ___ In a consignment situation, the consignee delivers goods to a consignor to sell. [p. 289]

16. ___ A buyer may breach a sales contract if he or she refuses to take delivery of conforming goods. [p. 290]

17. ___ Betty purchases goods from Slick, a thief who has stolen them. Betty does not acquire title to these goods and Slick does not acquire a leasehold interest in the goods. [p 291]

18. ___ A good faith purchaser or lessee for value is someone who pays insufficient consideration or rent for goods to the person he or she honestly believes has good title to those goods. [p. 291]

19. ___ If Zeus, a seller of aquariums, sells his largest fish tank and filter system to Paul, the risk of loss won't pass until Paul picks up the goods. [p. 287]

20. ___ Ed buys a television from his friend Doug for fair market value. Doug originally had obtained the television with a dishonored check. The appliance store that sold the television may reclaim the television. [p. 291]

21. ___ Cory is short on money and is referred to Pam for buying inexpensive gifts. Cory purchases a diamond bracelet for his girlfriend for pennies on the dollar. Upon further investigation, it is revealed that Pam obtained the diamond bracelet in a jewelry store robbery. The jewelry store may reclaim the diamond bracelet. [p. 291]

22. ___ A buyer in the ordinary course of business is an individual who in good faith and without knowledge that the sale violates ownership or security interest of a third party buys the goods in the ordinary course of business from a person in the business selling goods of that kind. [p. 291]

23. ___ Title to goods passes even if a person steals the goods. [p. 291]

24. ___ Title to goods is voidable if the goods were procured through fraud. [p. 292]

25. ___ The parties may provide in their contract who will bear the risk of loss if the goods are lost or destroyed. [p. 290]

Multiple Choice

26. What determines whether the goods of a consignment are subject to the claims of a buyer's creditors? [p. 289]
    a. the agreement between the consignor and the consingee
    a. whether the consignment had an additional party involved
    b. whether the seller filed a financing statement
    c. whether the seller failed to file a financing statement

27. In a sale or return, what options does the buyer have? [p. 288]
    a. The buyer has no choice but to keep the goods.
    b. The buyer may return all of the goods or any commercial unit of the good.
    c. The buyer may treat the contract as nonexistent.
    d. none of the above

28. If a document of title is required, title passes [p. 286]
    a. when and where the buyer delivers the document to the seller.
    b. when and where the buyer delivers the document to the carrier.
    c. when and where the seller delivers the document to the carrier.
    d. when and where the seller delivers the document to the buyer.

29. What does the term identification of goods mean? [p. 285]
    a. It means that each good has a uniform product code label.
    b. It means that each product has a name of its own.
    c. It means that the goods must be in existence in order to determine what goods are involved.
    d. It means distinguishing the goods named in a contract from the seller's or lessor's other goods.

30. A buyer orders 5,000 toy racecars that light up when pushed along a flat surface. The contract between the parties was a shipment contract. Further, the cars that were shipped were plain racecars that did not have the light-up feature. The toy cars are smashed flat while in transit. Who will bear the risk of loss in this situation? [p. 286]
    a. The buyer will as it is a shipment contract passing the risk of loss to the buyer.
    b. The buyer will as he or she did not purchase insurance to cover potential loss.
    c. The seller will as he or she did not ship conforming goods.
    d. Both the buyer and seller are responsible due to the nature of their transaction.

31. Jacob wants to purchase insurance to protect against financial loss in case the goods that he sells are damaged, destroyed, lost, or stolen. He is told that he must have an insurable interest in the goods. What does this mean? [p. 291]
    a. He must have a valid driver's license with no convictions against him.
    b. He must retain title or have a security interest in the goods.
    c. He must sell the goods to a good faith purchaser for value.
    d. He must not have an insurable interest at the same time as the buyer.

32. If Joe steals an entire shipment of computers that are owned by Computer City and resells them to Computer Land who does not know that they are stolen, Computer City may reclaim the goods from Computer Land because [p. 291]
    a. it found out where the goods were located.
    b. Computer Land was a good faith purchaser for value.
    c. as a seller with an insurable interest in the computers, Computer City is protected.
    d. Joe had no title in the goods and title was not transferred to Computer Land.

33. A seller or lessor has voidable title to goods if the goods were obtained by [p. 293]
    a. fraud.
    b. a dishonored check.
    c. impersonating another person.
    d. all of the above.

34. A person to whom good title can be transferred from a person with voidable title is [p. 291]
    a. a thief.
    b. a lessor.
    c. a good faith purchaser for value.
    d. the real owner.

35. A person to whom a lease interest can be transferred from a person with voidable title is [p. 292]
    a. a good faith purchaser for value.
    b. a lessee.
    c. an insured interested party.
    d. a good faith subsequent lessee.

Short Answer

36. In the case of sales contracts, common law placed the risk of loss of goods on [p. 286]
    _____.

37. What does the shipping term F.O.B. Houghton, Michigan, require the seller to do? [p. 287]_____

38. In a shipment contract, the seller _____ during transportation. [p. 286]

39. Give an example of a document of title. [p. 286]
    _____

40. The shipping term C.I.F. stands for _____, _____, and _____, which are costs that the seller is responsible for. [p. 287]

41. The shipping term F.A.S. requires the seller to deliver and tender the goods
    _____
    _____. [p. 287]

42. When there is no actual sale until the buyer accepts the goods, this is known as a [p. 288]
    _____ ___ _____.

of goods cannot reclaim goods from a [p. 291] _____ _____
A re_____ ___ _____.

43. ___ of an ordinary lease, the risk of loss is kept by the _____. [p. 290]

44. ___ ods are so nonconforming that the buyer has the right to reject them, the risk of ___ ains on the seller until the defect or nonconformity is cured, or the buyer
_____
_____. [p. 290]

___ uyer who breaches a sales contract before the risk of loss would normally pass to him or ___ bears the risk of loss as to which goods? [p. 290]
_____

A holder of goods who is not a seller or a buyer is a _____.
[p. 399]

. Who has title in a lease transaction? [p. 285]
_____

49. What types of terms are needed for the creation of a shipment contract? [p. 287]
_____ and _____

50. Legal, tangible evidence of ownership of goods is known as _____.
[p. 286]

Answers to Refresh Your Memory

1. insure [p. 285]
2. identified [p. 285]
3. When Zeb planted the corn, it became identified. [p. 285]
4. future goods [p. 285]
5. to bear the expense and risk of loss until the goods are loaded from the ship at its port of destination [UCC 2-322(1)(b)] [p. 287]
6. upon "tender of delivery" of the goods [p. 287]
7. a consignor [p. 289]
8. conforming, carrier [p. 286]
9. deliver [p. 287]
10. F.O.B. place of destination, ex-ship, or no-arrival, no-sale contract [p. 287]
11. A merchant-seller bears the risk of loss between the time of contracting and the time that the buyer picks up the goods. [p. 287]
12. a situation in which a thief acquires no title the goods he or she steals. [p. 291]
13. a holder of goods who is not a seller or a buyer [p. 288]
14. sale on approval [p. 288]
15. for a commercially reasonable time [p. 290]

Critical Thought Exercise Model Answer

The goods in this case, a whirlpool, had been delivered to the customer and a rep. of BPT had signed for the shipment. The whirlpool had been placed on BPT's property common carrier. Normally, the risk of loss passes in a shipment contract when the goods placed with the common carrier. In this case, however, the goods are being resold by Sum Pools to BPT. Thus, the risk of loss will not pass to BPT until they have been delivered to L as dictated by the agreement. In this agreement, the goods were to be fully installed as part of contract and there was no separation of the goods from the installation services in the agreemen.

In a mixed goods and services contract, a court will look to see whether the goods or services are the predominant item to be provided. The whirlpool being sold to BPT is considered a portable unit, so the installation services appear to be a secondary purpose in the sales contract. Risk of loss will therefore not pass to BPT until the whirlpool is fully installed as required by the agreement. The theft or loss of the whirlpool unit will fall upon Summit Pools.

Answers to Practice Quiz

True/False

1. True   The identification of goods that are purchased from a larger lot of the same goods are identified upon the purchase being separated from the larger lot.
2. False   The seller bears the risk of loss in a destination contract.
3. True   Unless otherwise agreed, goods that are shipped via a carrier such as a railroad are considered to be part of a shipment contract.
4. False   No arrival and no-sale contracts are the exception to the requirement that the seller bears the risk of loss during transportation of conforming goods.
5. True   Under UCC 2-509(a)(b), the risk of loss does not pass until the goods are tendered to the buyer at the specified destination.
6. False   The risk of loss passes when the buyer takes possession.
7. True   In a consignment situation, if the seller fails to file a financing statement, the goods are subject to the claims of the buyer's creditors.
8. False   The entrustment rule applies to leases.
9. True   UCC 2-403(2) states that if an owner entrusts the possession of his or her goods to a merchant who deals in goods of that kind, the merchant has the power to transfer all rights in the goods to a buyer in the ordinary course of business.
10. True   The shipping term F.O.B. Atlanta indicates that the Oklahoma seller intended to create a destination contract whereby Marla's will have to bear the expense and risk of loss until the goods are tendered at Tamara's Boutique in Atlanta, Georgia.
11. True   In a sale on approval, there is no sale unless and until the buyer accepts the goods.
12. True   In a sale on approval, there is no sale until and unless the buyer accepts the goods.
13. False The risk of loss to the title of the goods remains with the seller in a sale on approval.
14. False The seller delivers goods to a buyer with the understanding that the buyer may return the goods if they are not used or resold within a stated or reasonable period of time under a sale or return contract.
15. False The consignor delivers goods to the consignee to sell.
16. True   A buyer's refusal to take delivery of conforming goods constitutes a breach of contract.
17. True   Where a buyer buys goods or a lessee leases goods from a thief who has stolen them, the purchaser, in this case Betty, does not acquire title to the goods and the lessee, here Slick, does not acquire a leasehold interest in the goods.

18. False   A good faith purchaser for value is someone who pays sufficient (not insufficient) consideration or rent for the goods to the person he or she honestly believes has good title to those goods.

19. True   A merchant-seller such as Zeus bears the risk of loss until Paul, a buyer, picks up the aquarium and filter (goods).

20. False   The appliance store cannot reclaim the television because Ed, the second purchaser, bought the television in good faith and for value.

21. True   The jewelry store may reclaim the diamond bracelet because the second purchaser was not a good faith purchaser for value. Pennies on the dollar would not constitute sufficient consideration for a diamond bracelet.

22. True   This correctly states the meaning of a buyer in the ordinary course of business.

23. False   A thief acquires no title to the goods that he or she steals.

24. True   Fraudulently acquired goods prevent title from passing and as such title is voidable.

25. True   The issue of who will bear the risk of loss may be agreed to in a contract between the parties.

Multiple Choice

26. D   Answer D is correct since if the seller fails to file a financing statement, the goods are subject to the claims of the buyer's creditors. Answer A is incorrect as the agreement between the consignor and buyer is irrelevant as to claims of the buyer's creditors. Answer B is incorrect as it makes no sense. Answer C is incorrect, since if the seller filed a financing statement, then the goods are subject to the claims of the seller's *not* the buyer's creditors.

27. B   Answer B is correct the buyer may return all of the goods or any commercial unit of the goods. Answer A is incorrect, as it is an untrue statement. Answer C is incorrect as it too is a false statement. Answer D is incorrect for the reasons given above.

28. D   Answer D is correct as it correctly states when title passes. Answer A is incorrect as the buyer is not the party who would deliver the document of title. Answer B is incorrect as the buyer would not be delivering the document of title to the carrier. Answer C is incorrect as the seller would not be delivering the document of title to the carrier either.

29. D   Answer D is correct as the identification of goods means "distinguishing the goods named in the contract from the seller's or lessor's other goods." Answers A, B, and C are all incorrect statements as none reflect the true meaning of identification of goods.

30. C   Answer C is correct as the seller bears the risk of loss since he or she shipped nonconforming goods. Answer A is incorrect as despite the fact that a shipment contract would ordinarily shift the risk of loss once the seller placed the goods with a carrier, the fact that the seller shipped nonconforming goods is enough to have the risk of loss remain with the seller. Answer B is incorrect as the fact that the buyer did not purchase insurance to cover the potential loss does not exonerate the seller from the fact that he or she shipped nonconforming goods. Answer D is incorrect as it is an untrue statement, as the buyer does not share in the risk of loss when a seller ships nonconforming goods.

31. B   Answer B is correct as it correctly explains what an insurable interest means. Answer A is incorrect as this answer is referring to insurance one might get for an automobile not with respect to goods being lost, destroyed, or damaged. Answer C is incorrect as selling the goods to a good faith purchaser for value has no bearing on a seller's retention of title and security interest in goods. Answer D is incorrect as both the buyer and seller or lessee and lessor can have an insurable interest in the goods at the same time.

32. D   Answer D is correct as the purchaser, Joe, does not acquire title to goods and the lessee does not acquire any leasehold interest in goods thereby making the title void and the goods subject to reclamation by the real owner, Computer City. Answer A is incorrect as this does not supply the proper reasoning as to why Computer City may reclaim the goods. Answer B is not correct as the rules applicable to stolen goods as is the case with this fact situation are different than that of a seller having voidable title whereby a good faith purchaser for value is involved which in turn precludes the original owner from reclaiming the goods. Answer C is incorrect as the insurable interest would provide reimbursement from the insurance company for the loss of the goods verses the right to reclaim the goods.

33. D   Answer D is correct as answers A, B, and C all correctly state when a seller has voidable title to goods.

34. C   Answer C is correct as a person with voidable title to goods can transfer good title to a good faith purchaser for value. Answer A is incorrect, as good title may not be transferred to a thief. Answer B is incorrect as the person accomplishing the transfer is usually the lessor. Answer D is incorrect as it makes no sense.

35. D   Answer D is correct as a good faith subsequent lessee can acquire a lease interest from a person with voidable title. Answer A is incorrect as the term good faith purchaser for value refers to one paying for goods versus the transferring of a lease interest from a person with voidable title. Answer B is incorrect as it is only partially correct by the terminology lessee. Answer C is incorrect, as it makes no sense that a lease interest could be transferred from an insured interested party with voidable title.

Short Answer

36.   the party who had title to the goods

37.   It requires the seller to arrange to ship goods and put goods in the carrier's possession.

38.   bears the risk of loss

39.   warehouse receipt or bill of lading

40.   cost, insurance and freight

41.   alongside the named vessel or on the dock designated and provided by the buyer

42.   sale on approval

43.   good faith purchaser for value

44.   lessor

45.   accepts the nonconforming goods

46.   to any goods identified to the contract

47.   bailee

48.   Title to the leased goods remains with the lessor or a third party.

49.   The term *shipment* and one of the delivery terms such as *F.O.B., F.A.S., C.I.F*, or *C&F* must be present.

50.   title

Chapter 20

REMEDIES FOR BREACH OF
SALES AND LEASE CONTRACTS

Chapter Overview

The Uniform Commercial Code provides several remedies to an injured party based on a breach of a sales or lease contract. This chapter explores the prelitigation as well as litigation remedies available to an injured party. Additionally, the performance of obligations and options of the remedies that are available for breach of sales and lease contracts are also examined.

Objectives

Upon completion of the exercises in this chapter, you should be able to:
1. Describe the seller's and lessor's obligations under a contract.
2. Distinguish between a shipment and destination contract and determine the risk of loss in each.
3. Discuss the "perfect tender rule."
4. Describe the buyer's and lessee's obligations under a contract.
5. Explain what is meant by assurance of performance
6. Explain anticipatory repudiation and the remedies that are available for the same.
7. Discuss what remedies are available to a seller and lessor if a buyer or lessee breaches the contract.
8. Discuss what remedies are available to a buyer or lessee if a seller or lessor breaches the contract.
9. Define the statute of limitations of any oral or written sales or lease contract.
10. Discuss agreements that could affect the remedies available to a buyer or seller under a contract.

Practical Application

This chapter should enable you to know what types of obligations are expected of you as a buyer or a seller. Additionally it will solidify the remedies that are available to you in the event of a breach of a sales or lease contract if you are a buyer and lessee or a seller and lessor.

Helpful Hints

As with many of the chapters involving the area of contracts, it is helpful to organize your studying around the parties as well as the concepts that pertain to those parties. In this chapter, you are studying the buyer and seller's obligations as well as the remedies available in the event of a breach by the buyer or seller. As such, the study tips section has been created to enable you to learn what each parties obligations are as well as what remedies are available to each of them in the event of a breach.

Study Tips

Seller and Lessor's Obligations

Basic obligation – The seller must tender delivery in accordance with his or her contract terms with the buyer.

Tender of Delivery – There are a few things to remember about this topic:
1) Tender of delivery refers to conforming goods.
2) Seller must give the buyer reasonable notice of the delivery and delivery must be at a reasonable hour and goods must be kept for a reasonable time.
3) Goods must be delivered in one single delivery unless the parties agree to another arrangement.

Place of Delivery – The contract may state where delivery is to take place.
1) The contract may state that the buyer will pick up the goods.
2) If nothing is stated in the contract, the UCC will dictate this term.
3) If no carrier is involved, then delivery is at the seller's or lessor's business.
4) If the parties know the goods are located in another location, then that is the place of delivery.
5) If a carrier is involved, it will depend on if the contract is a shipment or a destination contract.
   a. If it is a *shipment* contract, the seller must deliver the goods to the carrier, obtain proper contract documentation and give the buyer notice.
   b. If it is a *destination* contract, the seller is required to deliver the goods to the buyer's place of business or wherever is designated in the parties' contract. Delivery must be at a reasonable time and in a reasonable manner accompanied with proper notice and documents of title.

Perfect Tender Rule – The seller is under a duty to deliver conforming goods to the buyer.
1) If tender is not perfect, the buyer may:
   a. reject the whole shipment
   b. accept the whole shipment
   c. reject part and accept part of the shipment
2) The parties may also agree to limit the application of the perfect tender rule by doing so in their written contract.
3) If a carrier is involved, the UCC mandates a commercially reasonable substitute be used if the agreed-upon manner of delivery fails or becomes unavailable.
4) If nonconforming goods are delivered, the UCC gives the seller the chance to cure the defective delivery if the time for performance has not expired or the lessor gives the buyer notice that he or she will make a conforming delivery within the time frame stated in the parties' contract.

Installment Contract – One that requires or authorizes the goods to be accepted or delivered in separate lots.

    1) The UCC alters the perfect tender rule by allowing the buyer to reject the entire shipment if the noncomformity substantially impairs the entire contract.

    2) The court will view installment contracts on a case-by-case basis.

Destruction of Goods – If the destruction of goods is not the fault of either party and the goods have been identified to the contract, the contract will be void; but if the goods are partially destroyed, the buyer may then inspect and partially accept the goods or treat the contract as void. If the buyer opts to accept, compensation will be adjusted accordingly.

Good Faith and Reasonableness – These two principles rule the performance of lease and sales contracts. These principles apply to both the buyer and the seller.

Seller's and Lessor's Remedies

The seller and lessors have several remedies available if the buyer or lessee breaches the contract. These remedies are as follows:

Right to Withhold Delivery – Delivery of the goods may be withheld if the seller is in possession of the goods when the buyer or lessee is in breach. If there has been a partial delivery of the goods when the breach occurs, then the seller or lessor may withhold delivery of the remaining part of the goods. A buyer's or lessee's insolvency will also justify a seller's or lessor's withholding of delivery of the goods under the contract.

Right to Stop Delivery of Goods in Transit – Goods are in transit when they are in the carrier's bailee's possession. If a buyer is discovered to be insolvent while the goods are in transit, the seller may stop the goods while in transit.

    If the buyer or lessee repudiates the contract, delivery can be withheld only if it is a carload, a planeload, or a truckload. Notice to the carrier or bailee is required.

    The seller must hold the goods for the buyer after the delivery has been stopped. If the seller resells the goods, the amount received must be credited against the judgment procured against the buyer.

Right to Recover Damages for Breach of Contract – A cause of action to recover damages caused by the breach of contract may be brought where the buyer or lessee repudiates a sales or lease contract or wrongfully rejects tendered goods.

    The measure of damages is the difference between the contract price and the market price at the time and place where the goods were delivered plus incidental damages. If this does not place the seller in a position as though the contract was performed, the seller may recover lost profits that would have resulted from full performance plus an allowance for reasonable overhead and incidental damages.

Right to Cancel the Contract – The seller or lessor may cancel the contract if the buyer or lessee breaches the contract by revoking acceptance of the goods, rejects the contract, or fails to pay for the goods or repudiates all or any part of the contract. The cancellation may apply to the entire contract or to only the affected goods.

<u>Effect of the Cancellation</u> – The seller or lessor who notifies the buyer or lessee of the cancellation is discharged from any further obligations under the contract, and he or she may also seek damages against the buyer or lessee for the breach.

<u>Right to Reclaim Goods</u> – Reclamation refers to a seller or lessor's right to demand the return of goods from the buyer or lessee under certain situations.

<u>Where the buyer is insolvent</u> – Seller has 10 days to demand the return of the goods.

Where the buyer has misrepresented his or her solvency in writing three months before delivery or presents a check that is later dishonored, reclamation may occur at any time.

Requirements of reclamation include:
> Written notice to the buyer or lessee.
> Refraining from self-help if the buyer refuses.
> Use of legal proceedings must be instituted.

<u>Right to Dispose of Goods</u> – If the buyer or lessee breaches or repudiates before the seller or lessor disposes of the goods, then the seller may release or resell goods and recover damages from the buyer or lessee.

Disposition of the goods must be in good faith and in a commercially reasonable manner. Disposition may be as a unit or in parcels and publicly or privately. Notice must also be given.

Damages incurred as a result of disposition are measured by the disposition price and the contract price. Incidental damages may also be recovered.

Unfinished Goods – If a sales or lease contract is breached or repudiated before the goods are finished the seller can:
1) stop manufacturing of the goods and resell them for scrap or salvage value or
2) complete the goods and resell, release, or otherwise dispose of them or
3) recover damages from the buyer or lessee.

<u>Right to Recover the Purchase Price or Rent</u> – The UCC allows a seller to sue the buyer for the purchase price or rent as provided in the parties sale or lease contract. This remedy is available when:
1) The buyer or lessee accepts the goods but does not pay for them when the rent is due.
2) The buyer or lessee breaches the contract after the goods have been identified to the contract and the seller or lessor cannot dispose of or sell the goods.
3) The goods are damaged or lost after the risk of loss passes to the buyer or lessee.

Buyer and Lesee's Obligations

Basic Obligation – If proper tender of delivery is made to the buyer (lessee), the buyer is then
      obligated to accept and pay for the goods as per the parties' contract or as
      mandated by the UCC in the event that there is no contract.

Right of Inspection – Buyer has the right to inspect goods that are tendered, delivered, or
      identified to the contract.
      1) If the goods are shipped, inspection will be at the time the goods arrive.
         If the goods are nonconforming, buyer may reject the goods and not
         pay for them.
      2) Parties may agree as to time, place, and manner of inspection. If there
         Is no agreement, then it must be at a reasonable time, place, and
         manner.
         Reasonableness is determined by common usage of trade, prior course
         dealings, etc. If the goods conform to the contract, buyer pays for the
         inspection. If the goods are nonconforming, the seller pays for the
         inspection.
      3) C.O.D. deliveries are not subject to buyer inspection until the buyer
         pays for the goods.

Payment of the Goods – Goods that are accepted must be paid for when the goods are delivered
      even if the delivery place is the same as the place where the goods are
      shipped.
      1) Goods paid for on credit have a credit period that begins to run from the
         time that the goods are shipped.
      2) Goods may be paid for using any acceptable method of payment unless
         the agreed-upon terms involve cash only. If cash is all that a seller will
         accept from the buyer, then the buyer must be given extra time to
         procure the cash.
      3) Payment by check is conditioned on the check being honored.

Assurance of Performance – If one party has reasonable grounds to believe that the other party
      either will not or cannot perform his or her contractual obligations,
      The other party may demand assurance for performance in writing.
      Also, the aggrieved party may suspend his or her own performance
      if it is commercially practicable to do so until the assurance is forth-
      coming from the potential wrongdoer.

Anticipatory Repudiation – The repudiation of a lease or sales contract by one of the parties
      before the date set for performance.
      1) Simple wavering of performance does not equate to anticipatory
         repudiation.
      2) The aggrieved party may:
         a. await performance for a commercially reasonable time or
         b. treat the contract as breached at the time of the anticipatory
           repudiation.
         Both remedies allow the aggrieved party to suspend performance.

3) An anticipatory repudiation may be retracted before the aggrieved parties performance is due if the aggrieved party has not:
   a. cancelled the contract or
   b. materially changed his or her position or
   c. otherwise stated that the repudiation is viewed as final.
   Repudiation may be made by any method as long as the intent to perform the contract is clearly expressed.

Buyer and Lessee's Remedies

The buyer or lessee also has many remedies available to him or her upon the breach of a sales or lease contract by the seller or lessor. These remedies are as follows:

<u>Right to Reject Nonconforming Goods or Improperly Tendered Goods</u> – If tender of delivery fails, the buyer may:
1) reject the whole,
2) accept the whole or
3) accept any commercial unit and reject the rest.

Note, a buyer who rejects nonconforming goods must identify the defects that are able to be determined by a reasonable inspection. Rejection must be within a reasonable time after delivery and in a reasonable manner. The buyer must also hold the goods for a reasonable period of time.

<u>Right to Recover Goods from an Insolvent Seller or Lessor</u> – If the buyer makes a partial payment to the seller and the seller or lessor becomes insolvent within ten days of the first payment, the buyer or lessee may recover the goods from the seller or lessor. This is called capture.

<u>Right to Obtain Specific Performance</u> – When the remedy at law is inadequate and the goods are unique, the buyer or lessee may ask for specific performance of the sales or lease contract.

<u>Right to Cover</u> – The buyer or lessee may cover if the seller or lessor fails to make delivery of goods or repudiates the contract or the buyer or lessee rightfully rejects the goods or justifiably revokes their acceptance. Renting or purchasing substitute goods accomplish covering.

<u>Right to Replevy Goods</u> – A buyer or lessee may recover scarce goods wrongfully withheld by a seller or lessor by demonstrating that he or she was unable to cover or the attempts to cover will not come to fruition. This remedy is only available as to goods identified to the lease or sales contract.

<u>Right to Cancel the Contract</u> – Failure to deliver conforming goods, repudiation of the contract by the seller, rightful rejection of the goods, or justifiable revocation of goods that were accepted all may enable the buyer to cancel with respect to the affected goods or the whole contract if the breach is material in nature.

<u>Right to Recover Damages for No delivery or Repudiation</u> – The buyer or lessee may recover damages that equate to the difference between the contract price and the market price, along with incidental and consequential damages, less expenses saved if a seller or lessor fails to deliver the goods or repudiates the sales or lease contract.

<u>Right to Recover Damages for Accepted Nonconforming Goods</u> – A buyer may seek to recover damages from any loss as a result of the nonconforming goods accepted from the seller. Incidental damages as well as consequential damages may also be recovered. The buyer must give notice of the nonconformity to the seller within a reasonable time of when the breach should have been discovered.

<u>Statute of Limitations</u> – Under the UCC, an action for breach of any written or oral sales or lease contract must be within four years. The parties can agree to a one-year statute of limitations.

<u>Agreements Affecting Remedies</u>

<u>Preestablished damages</u> – These are called liquidated damages, which act as a substitute for actual damages.

<u>Consequential damages</u> for the breach of sales or lease contract may be excluded or limited unless it would be unconscionable to do so.

Refresh Your Memory

The following exercise will enable you to refresh your memory on the rules and principles presented to you in this chapter. Read each question twice and place your answer in the blanks provided. Review the chapter material for any question you miss or are unable to remember.

1. When a carrier is not involved, where is the place of delivery to where goods can be delivered? _____

2. Under a sales or lease contract, what is the seller or lessor's general obligation? _____

3. Which party has the obligation to accept and pay for the goods? _____.

4. If a contract does not specifically state where the delivery will take place, what is the first thing that is looked at in order to determine the place of delivery? _____ _____

5. If a seller fails to make a proper contract for the shipment of perishable goods, what may the buyer do? _____

6. What is needed in order for a buyer to obtain goods from a carrier? _____ _____

7. If the parties have no agreement respecting the time, place, and manner of delivery, tender must be made at a _____ hour and the goods must _____ _____.

8. If a set of family room furniture to be delivered to the buyer was partially destroyed by fire, what may the buyer choose to do with regard to the goods? _____ _____

9. When may a cure take place? _____
_____

10. Revocation of goods accepted by a buyer or lessee is not effective until _____
_____.

11 A sales contract that requires the seller to deliver the goods to the buyer's place of business or other specified location is a _____ contract.

12. The UCC gives a seller or lessor who delivers nonconforming goods a chance to _____ the nonconformity.

13. What is an installment contract? _____
_____

14. The UCC alters the perfect tender rule concerning _____ contracts.

15. If goods are shipped, the buyer's right to inspection may take place _____ their arrival.

Critical Thought Exercise

Sanco Corporation agreed to sell two seven-ton diesel forklifts to Agro-Star, Inc., for $250,000, with an option to purchase four more at $500,000. The forklifts were to be installed in a produce cooling warehouse according to specific design and performance standards. Sanco did not deliver and Agro-Star covered by purchasing different forklifts from Power Arm Lifts for $200,000, plus an additional $300,000 for testing and development by Power Arm Lifts. Agro-Star also bought the four additional lifts that they needed from Power Arm Lifts for $350,000. At trial, Agro-Star is awarded $250,000, the difference between Sanco's price for the first two forklifts and the cost of the first two Power Arm forklifts.

As an officer in Sanco Corporation, you must decide whether to pay the judgment or pay an additional $20,000 in attorney's fees and appeal the judgment. Will you authorize the appeal? Why? Is it fair for Sanco to receive the benefit of a bargain struck by Agro-Star when they covered?

Answer:

_____
_____
_____
_____
_____
_____
_____
_____
_____
_____
_____
_____

Practice Quiz

True/False

1. ____ A commercial unit is a unit of goods that commercial usage deems a portion for purpose of a sale. [p. 301]

2. ____ If Eb's Furniture Store calls Charlene Jones at 2:00 a.m. to let her know the delivery truck will be at her home in 30 minutes, Charlene must allow Eb to tender delivery of the goods. [p. 297]

3. ____ Sales contracts that require the seller to send goods to the buyer, but not to a particular destination is called a destination contract. [p. 297]

4. ____ The remedy known as cure is specifically defined by the UCC. [p. 298]

5. ____ Under a shipment contract, one thing that the seller must do is put the goods in the carrier's possession and contract for the safe and proper transportation of the goods. [p. 297]

6. ____ In a destination contract, delivery of the goods is to be tendered at the buyer's place of business or shipped to a central warehouse for goods. [p. 297]

7. ____ An example of an installment contract is one in which the buyer orders 100 hats to be delivered in one single installment. [p. 299]

8. ____ A cure may be attempted if the time for performance has expired and the seller or lessor has notified the buyer or lessee of his or her intention to deliver conforming goods within the time stated in the contract. [p. 298]

9. ____ In a situation where a nonconforming installment impairs the value of a contract, the court will decide whether the impairment affects the value of the entire contract or that installment alone. [p. 299]

10. ____ According to the UCC, goods that are accepted by a buyer may be paid for only by check. [p. 301]

11. ____ The parties' prior course of dealing, common usage of trade, and the overall circumstances are factors the court looks at in determining reasonableness with respect to the buyer's right to inspection. [p. 300]

12. ____ Buyers who agree to C.O.D. deliveries are not entitled to inspect the goods before paying for them. [p. 301]

13. ____ Payment is usually due from a buyer where and when the goods are delivered even if the place of delivery is the same place of shipment. [p. 301]

14. ____ The repudiation of a sales or lease contract by one of the parties after the date set for performance is known as anticipatory repudiation. [p. 302]

15. ___ A buyer contracts to purchase 2,500 tires from a tire manufacturer with delivery set for May 1 and partial payment due March 1. In February the buyer learns that automobile sales have decreased by 38 percent and assembly line workers have been laid off in the small plant that he would need the tires in. The tire manufacturer contacts the buyer and wants a written demand for adequate assurance on February 18. The buyer fails to give adequate assurance of performance. The tire manufacturer has no recourse and must now wait until March 1 when partial payment is due before it can do anything. [p. 302]

16. ___ A buyer's insolvency gives the seller and lessor the right to withhold delivery. [p. 302]

17. ___ Delivery of goods may not be withheld if the seller or lesser is in possession of them when the buyer or lessee breaches the contract. [p. 302]

18. ___ The right to withhold delivery of goods is available if the lessee or buyer wrongfully revokes or rejects acceptance of the goods. [p. 302]

19. ___ A seller or lessor that learns of a lessee's or buyer's insolvency while the goods are in transit may not stop delivery of the goods regardless of the size of the shipment. [p. 302]

20. ___ The principles of good faith and commercial reasonableness must be applied if the seller is exercising his or her right to dispose of the goods when a buyer or lessee breaches or repudiates the sales or lease contract before the seller has even delivered the goods. [p. 303]

21. ___ The measure of damages incurred while disposing of goods are defined as the difference between the disposition price and the original contract price. [p. 303]

22. ___ If a buyer or lessee repudiates a lease or sales contract or wrongfully rejects tendered goods, the lessor or seller may not sue to recover the damages caused by the lessee's or buyer's breach. [p. 302]

23. ___ The amount of damages for a wrongful repudiation or rejection of goods is a liquidated amount due to the inability to properly asses damages as a whole. [p. 303]

24. ___ The seller or lessor may not cancel a sales or lease contract by the buyer's or lessee's failure to pay for the goods. [p. 302]

25. ___ A buyer or lessee has an option to reject the whole shipment of goods if the goods or the seller's or lessor's tender of delivery fails to conform to the sales or lease contract in any way. [p. 300]

Multiple Choice

26. The perfect tender rule is altered when [p. 298]
    a. the parties to the sales or lease contract agree to limit the effect of the rule.
    b. the buyer or lessee rejects the whole shipment of goods.
    c. the buyer or lessee rejects part of the shipment of goods.
    d. the buyer or lessee accepts the entire shipment of goods.

27. Rachel contracted for a crystal chandelier from Phoebe, a crystal dealer. Phoebe agrees to deliver the chandelier to Rachel's home. The truck delivering the chandelier breaks down and the chandelier is stolen while the delivery driver has walked away trying to find help. What effect does the theft of the chandelier have on the parties' agreement? [p. 297]
    a. The risk of loss had already passed to Rachel and she is responsible for payment.
    b. The risk of loss remains with Rachel, but she can get her insurance to cover the damage.
    c. The risk of loss is shared between both parties as the situation involved a thief, which requires both parties to share the cost of the damages.
    d. The risk of loss had not yet passed to Rachel, and as such, the contract is voided and she
        does not have to pay for the chandelier.

28. Under the UCC, payment for goods may be by [p. 301]
    a. check, credit card, or the like.
    b. cash if the seller demands payment in cash.
    c. a specific form as named in the parties' agreement.
    d. all of the above.

29. Which of the following would provide the best remedy for Ali, who has contracted for an 1868 hope chest from a seller of antiques who has breached his end of the bargain? [p. 305]
    a. Her best remedy is to seek compensatory damages.
    b. Her best remedy is to seek an injunction to prevent the seller from selling it to someone else.
    c. Her best remedy is to seek a decree of specific performance.
    d. She should seek all of the above remedies.

30. Barbara has accepted a dining room table and chairs from Fast Frank's Furniture; however, two of the chairs have different colored upholstery on them. Though Barbara recognizes this, she needs all the seating room she can get, as she's hosting a large dinner party for her bosses at the company she works for. Which of the following is true with respect to any remedy Barbara may get? [p. 307]
    a. Barbara has accepted the nonconforming goods, and therefore has no recourse against Fast Frank's Furniture.
    b. Barbara has the right to get angry until Fast Frank's Furniture fixes the problem.
    c. Barbara may recover damages caused by the breach or deduct the damages from any part of the purchase price or rent still due under the contract.
    d. none of the above

31. Which of the following are true with respect to the remedies available to the parties to a sales or lease contract? [pp. 305-308]
    a. Any agreed-upon remedies between the parties are in addition to those provided by the UCC.
    b. If the parties agree that the remedies they have chosen are exclusive and the exclusive remedy fails, then any remedy under the UCC may be had.
    c. The parties may agree to a liquidated damages clause, which is a substitute for actual damages.
    d. all of the above

32. If Jaclyn's Fine Vases begins manufacture of 50 vases, all of which have a sculpted form of sea life on them, and the buyer, a tourist shop on the ocean, goes out of business before the goods are finished, Jaclyn, the seller may choose to   [p. 306]
    a. open up the buyer's business and try to sell the vases herself.
    b. stop manufacturing the goods and resell them for scrap or salvage value.
    c. use self-help in reclaiming what is due her under the parties' agreement.
    d. obtain an injunction against the buyer to prevent him or her from contracting with her again.

33. A buyer enters into a sales contract to purchase a rare pink diamond ring with a platinum band for $1.3 million. When the buyer tenders payment, the seller refuses to sell the rare ring to the buyer. What type of action may the buyer bring in order to get the ring? [p. 305]
    a. The buyer may bring an action for damages.
    b. The buyer is out of luck and will have to find another jeweler.
    c. The buyer may bring an equity action to obtain a decree of specific performance from the court ordering the seller to sell the ring to the buyer.
    d. The buyer may bring an action in tort for embezzlement.

34. A buyer or lessor who rightfully covers may sue the seller or lessor to recover [p. 306]
    a. the difference between the cost of cover and the contract price or rent.
    b. incidental damages.
    c. consequential damages less expenses saved.
    d. all of the above.

35. The measure of damages a buyer or lessor may recover for a seller's or lessor's failure to deliver the goods is [p. 306]
    a. an equitable decree of specific performance.
    b. the difference between the contract price and the market price at the time the buyer or lessee learned of the breach.
    c. the difference between the market price and the contract price at the time the buyer or lessee learned of the breach.
    d. a set amount that is preestablished by using a liquidated damages clause.

Short Answer

36. If Nina feels that Quinn's statements and actions indicate that Quinn probably will not perform his end of the contract that he has with Nina, she may treat this as an [p. 308]
    _____ _____.

37. What sort of proof is necessary for the court to find that an unconscionable contract exists between two parties to a contract? [p. 308]_____

38. With regard to the statute of limitation for a breach of any written or oral sales or lease contract, what may the parties agree to do? [p. 308]
    _____

39. A sales contract requires the seller to deliver 80 silk tablecloths to a buyer. When the buyer inspects the delivered goods, it is discovered that 79 tablecloths conform to the contract and one tablecloth does not conform. If the buyer accepts the nonconforming tablecloth, what if any recourse does the buyer have against the seller? [p. 307] _____

_____

_____

40. How are the terms good faith and reasonableness applied to a contractual setting? [p. 300]

_____

41. Give an example of an installment contract. [p. 299] _____

_____

42. Janel wants to inspect ten purses she had shipped by way of C.O.D. May she do this? Why or why not? [p. 301]

_____

_____

43. If a buyer pays for goods by check, payment is conditional upon _____
_____ when it is presented to the bank for payment. [p. 301]

44. What is a commercial unit? [p. 301] _____

45. List at least two things that must occur in order for a revocation by the buyer to be effective. [p. 301]

_____

_____

46. When may an adequate assurance of due performance be demanded of one party by the other party? [p. 307] _____

47. If the repudiation impairs the value of the contract to the aggrieved party, it is called
_____ _____. [p. 308]

48. What remedy is available to a seller when a buyer or lessor when the buyer or lessee repudiates or breaches his or her contract before the seller has delivered the goods? [p. 303]

_____

_____

49. Give examples of incidental damages. [p. 303] _____

50. If a buyer or lessee breaches a contract by rejecting or revoking acceptance of goods, what may the seller or lessee do? [p. 304] _____

Answers to Refresh Your Memory

1. seller's or lessor's place of business [p. 297]
2. to transfer and deliver goods to the buyer or lessee [p. 296]
3. the buyer or lessee [p. 296]
4. whether or not a carrier is involved

5. The buyer may rightfully reject the goods if they spoil during transit. [p. 297]
6. appropriate document of title provided by the seller [p. 297]
7. reasonable, be kept available for a reasonable period of time [p. 297]
8. Buyer or lessee may inspect the goods and then choose either to treat the contract as void or to accept the goods. [p. 299]
9. if the time for performance has not expired and the buyer is given notice [p. 298]
10. The seller or lessor is notified. [p. 300]
11. destination [p. 297]
12. cure [p. 298]
13. An installment contract is one that requires or authorizes the goods to be delivered in separate lots. [p. 299]
14. installment [p. 298]
15. after [p. 300]

Critical Thought Exercise Model Answer

Yes, I will authorize the appeal. Under UCC 2-715, the remedy of cover allows the buyer, on the seller's breach, to purchase the goods, in good faith and within a reasonable time, from another seller and substitute them for the goods due under the contract. If the cost of cover exceeds the cost of the contract goods, the breaching seller will be liable to the buyer for the difference, plus incidental and consequential damages.

In our case, the cost of the contracted forklifts was to be $750,000. Agro-Star had to pay only $550,000 for the forklifts, plus the incidental damages of $300,000 for further testing and development. By exercising their right of cover, Agro-Star only suffered damages of $100,000. The cost of the appeal is only $20,000 and we will likely have the award reduced by $150,000.

It is both fair and ethical for us to take advantage of the cover rule. The purpose of contract damages is to put the nonbreaching party in the same position they would have been if the breach had not occurred. Damages awarded after the nonbreaching party has covered make the buyer whole while avoiding a punitive result to the seller.

Answers to Practice Quiz

True/False

1. False A commercial unit is a unit of goods that commercial usage deems is a single whole for purpose of sale.
2. False Charlene does not have to allow Ed the opportunity to fulfill his obligation in that tender must be at a reasonable hour, of which 2:00 a.m. would not be considered reasonable for a furniture delivery.
3. False Sales contracts that require the seller to send the goods to the buyer, but not to a specifically named destination are called shipment contracts.
4. False Cure is not defined by the UCC.
5. True The safe and proper transportation of goods as well as putting the goods in the carrier's transportation is one of the obligations of a seller.
6. False Tender of delivery in destination contracts is either the buyer's place of business or other place specified in the parties' contract.
7. False An installment contract is a contract that requires or authorizes goods to be delivered and accepted in separate lots.

8. False The UCC gives a lessor or seller an opportunity to cure nonconforming goods if the time for performance has not expired and the seller or lessor notifies the buyer or lessee of his or her intention to make a conforming delivery within the contract time.
9. True Under UCC 2-612 , 2A-510, the court must determine whether the nonconforming installment impairs the value of the entire contract or that installment.
10. False Goods may be paid for in any manner currently acceptable in the ordinary course of business. Examples of payment include check, credit card, or the like.
11. True The court will consider common usage of trade, prior course of dealings between the parties, and other types of similar factors in determining reasonableness as it pertains to a buyer's right to inspection.
12. False Buyers are not entitled to inspection of goods before paying for them when they have agreed to cash on delivery (C.O.D.) deliveries.
13. True The place in which goods are delivered, even if it is the same as the place of shipment, is the place where payment is due from the buyer.
14. False Repudiation of a lease or sales contract by one of the parties prior to the date set for performance is known as anticipatory repudiation.
15. False The buyer does have recourse as he or she may suspend performance and treat the sales contract as repudiated.
16. True A buyer's insolvency gives the seller and lessor the right to withhold delivery.
17. False Delivery of the goods may be withheld if the lessor or seller is in possession of them when the lessee or buyer is in breach of the contract.
18. True If the buyer or lessee wrongfully rejects or revokes acceptance of the goods, then the seller has the right to withhold delivery of the goods.
19. False The delivery can only be stopped if it is a truckload, planeload, carload, or larger express freight shipment.
20. True If the seller or lessor is exercising his or her right to dispose of the goods when the lessee or buyer breaches or repudiates the lease contract before the seller has even delivered the goods, then the principles of good faith and reasonableness must be applied.
21. False Damages incurred on disposition of goods are the difference between the disposition price and the contract price.
22. False The seller or lessor may sue to recover the damages caused by the buyer's or lessee's breach if a lessee or buyer repudiates a sale or lease contract or wrongfully rejects tendered goods.
23. False This is a proper statement of damages for a wrongful repudiation or rejection of goods.
24. False If a buyer or lessee breaches a contract by failing to pay for goods, the seller or lessor may cancel a sales or lease contract.
25. True One of the options a buyer or lessee has if the goods or the seller's or lessor's tender of delivery fails to conform is that he or she may reject the whole shipment.

Multiple Choice

26. A Answer A is the correct answer as the UCC alters the perfect tender rule when the parties agree to limit the effect of it or in cases involving a substitution of carriers. Answers B, C, and D are all incorrect answers as they pertain to the buyer's remedies in certain situations.

27. D Answer D is the correct answer as the risk of loss had not passed to Rachael. The contract is voided and she does not have to pay for the chandelier. Answer A is incorrect as the facts are indicative of a destination contract wherein a buyer does not assume the risk of loss until the goods are delivered. Here the goods were not delivered as the chandelier was stolen. Answer B is incorrect as once again, the risk of loss had not passed. Further, the fact that she has insurance, though a nice benefit, does not assist in the allegation of the risk of loss passing to her, as it did not. Answer C is incorrect as it is a misstatement of law.

28. D Answer D is the correct answer as the UCC provides for payment of goods by all of the means given in answers A, B, and C.

29. C Answer C is the correct answer as specific performance is the equitable remedy available when the subject matter is unique, which clearly an 1868 hope chest is. Answers A and B are incorrect as these are legal remedies that do not apply when the subject matter is unique. Answer D is incorrect for the reasons given above.

30. C Answer C is the correct statement of law. Answer A is incorrect as her acceptance of nonconforming goods does not prevent her from recovery of the damages caused by the breach. Answer B is incorrect as this statement does not reflect a legal or equitable remedy. Answer D is incorrect for the reasons given above.

31. D Answer D is the correct answer as answers A, B, and C are all true statements regarding remedies that are available to parties of a sales or lease contract.

32. B Answer B is the correct answer as the UCC provides for cessation of the manufacturing of goods where the buyer or lessee has breached or repudiated the contract before the goods are finished. Answer A is incorrect as this is not an option under the UCC where unfinished goods are involved. Answer C is incorrect as self-help is also not an option that the seller or lessor has under the UCC. Answer D is incorrect as an injunction would not be a proper remedy for a sales contract situation.

33. C Answer C is the correct answer as the good, here a rare pink diamond with a platinum band, is unique and the remedy at law would be inadequate. Therefore, the buyer or lessee may obtain specific performance of the sales or lease contract. Answer A is incorrect as damages would not be an adequate remedy in light of the unique nature of the good Answer B is incorrect as it is an untrue statement. Answer D is incorrect as embezzlement is not a proper cause of action to bring in light of the facts, as the parties involved do not have an employer/employee relationship and the facts state that the parties have a contract to purchase a good (the ring) the fact of which would not establish any element necessary for the tort of embezzlement.

34. D Answer D is the correct answer as answers A, B, and C all state the remedies available to a buyer or seller who rightfully covers.

35. B Answer B is the correct answer as a buyer may recover the difference between the contract price and the market price at the time the buyer learns of the breach when a seller or lessor fails to deliver the goods. Answer A is incorrect as the remedy of specific performance does not involve damages. Answer C is incorrect as it is worded backwards of the true remedy as stated in answer B. Answer D is incorrect as liquidated damages would need to be in the parties' agreement and as such liquidated damages is not a standard measure of damages that is available to buyers and lessors who want to bring a cause of action against sellers and lessees for a failure to deliver goods.

Short Answer

36. anticipatory repudiation
37. that the parties had substantially unequal bargaining power
38. The parties may agree to reduce the limitations period to one year.
39. remedies
40. The concept of good faith and reasonableness also refers to the "spirit" of the contract with the underlying theory being that the parties are more apt to perform properly if their conduct is to be judged against these principles.
41. As per UCC 2-513(3), Janel is not entitled to inspect the purses she had shipped via C.O.D.
42. A C.O.D. shipment is one in which the buyer agrees to pay cash on delivery of the goods.
43. the check being honored
44. A commercial unit is a unit of goods that commercial usage deems is a single whole for purposes of sale.
45. It must be shown that the goods are nonconforming and the nonconformity substantially impairs the value of the goods to the buyer or lessee.
46. An adequate assurance of performance may be demanded of a party if one party to the contract has reasonable grounds to believe that the other party either will or cannot perform his or her contractual obligations.
47. anticipatory repudiation
48. The seller or lessor may resell or release the goods and recover damages from the buyer or lessee.
49. Incidental damages include reasonable expenses in stopping delivery, transportation charges, storage charges, sales commission, and the like.
50. A seller or lessor may cancel the contract.

Chapter 21

SALES AND LEASE
WARRANTIES

Chapter Overview

This chapter focuses on the different types of warranties as well as clear examples for each. Among the warranties that are discussed are the express warranty, implied warranty of merchantability, and the implied warranty of fitness for a particular purpose. Further, it provides a concise understanding of the special warranties of title and possession as well as the remedies that are available for breach of the various warranties. Also disclaimers and their lawfulness are examined.

Objectives

Upon completion of the exercises in this chapter, you should be able to:
1.   Distinguish between an express warranty and an implied warranty.
2.   Recognize the difference between expressions that become the basis of the bargain versus statements of opinion.
2.   Discuss the damages recoverable for breach of warranty.
3.   Discuss the implied warranty of merchantability.
4.   Discuss the implied warranty of fit for human consumption.
5.   Explain the implied warranty of fit for a particular purpose.
6.   Recognize warranty disclaimers and determine their lawfulness.
7.   Explain the requirements of warranty disclaimers and the limitation of liability clauses in software licenses.
8.   Discuss the importance of the Magnuson-Moss Warranty Act and its impact on consumer goods.
9.   Distinguish the difference among warranty of good title, warranty of no security interest, warranty of no infringements, and warranty of no interference.

Practical Application

You will be able to recognize the various types of warranties as they exist within a transaction. Additionally, you will be able to assess whether or not a warranty has been breached. Further, you should be able to recognize disclaimers and determine whether or not they are lawful as well as the impact of limitation of liability clauses on software licenses.

Helpful Hints

It is helpful to understand that there are three categories of warranties. That is to say that there is an oral, express, and implied warranty. Further, as you study warranties, it is helpful to not only keep them organized according to the type of warranty it is, but, to keep an example of each type in mind so that the material can be kept clear.

Study Tips

Consumers have often been taken advantage of in their daily transactions. Initially one of the only protections afforded a consumer was *Caveat Emptor*, which in Latin means, "Buyer Beware." However, various Uniform Commercial Code laws have been developed thereby establishing certain warranties as being applicable to the sales of goods and certain lease transactions. A warranty is like insurance to a consumer in that it is a way to make sure that goods meet certain standards.

Special Warranties of Title and Possession

- **Good Title**
  General Rule: Sellers of goods warrant that they have valid title to the goods
  Exception: If there is a disclaimer involved, good title is not warranted.

- **No Security Interests**
  General Rule: Sellers of goods automatically warrant that the goods they sell are delivered free of any encumbrances, liens, or third-party security interests.

- **No Infringements**
  General Rule: A lessor or seller who is a merchant who regularly deals in goods of the kind leased or sold automatically warrants that the goods are delivered free of any third-party patent, copyright, or trademark claim. This is known as the warranty against infringements.
  Exception: If the parties agree otherwise.

Warranties of Quality

- General Rule: The goods meet certain standards of quality and are warranted expressly or impliedly.

No Interference

- General Rule: In a lease transaction, the lessor warrants that no person holds a claim or interest in the goods that arose from an act or omission of the lessor that will interfere with the lessee's enjoyment of his or her leasehold interest.

Express Warranties

Creation: Express warranties are created when a seller or lessor affirms that the goods he or she is selling or leasing meet certain criteria of quality, performance, description, or condition.
Usual Form: These warranties are found in brochures, ads, catalogs, diagrams, etc.
Basis of the Bargain: If the warranty was a contributing factor that induced the buyer to buy the product or the lessee to lease the product, this is called the basis of the bargain.

Special Notations: Retailers are responsible for express warranties made by manufacturers of goods it sells.
But, manufacturers are not liable for express warranties made by

wholesalers and retailers unless the manufacturer ratifies or authorizes the warranties.

Statements of Opinion: Puffing or statements of opinion do not create an express warranty. In order to be an express warranty, it must qualify as an affirmation of fact.

Affirmation of Value: An affirmation of value does not create an express warranty.

Implied Warranties

Implied Warranty of Merchantability
Requirements: The goods must be fit for the ordinary purpose for which they are used.
The goods must be adequately contained, packaged, and labeled.
The goods must be of a kind, quality, and quantity with each unit.
The goods must conform to any promise or affirmation of fact made on the container or label.
The quality of the goods must pass without objection in the trade.
Fungible goods must meet a fair average or middle range of quality.

Implied Warranty of Fitness for Human Consumption (a warranty within the implied warranty of merchantability)
Application: This warranty applies to food and drink consumed on or off the premises.
Foreign Substance Test: Used to determine whether food products are unmerchantable. A food product is unmerchantable if a foreign object in a product causes injury to an individual.
Consumer Expectation Test: Merchantability is tested based on what the average consumer would expect to find in his or her food products.

Implied Warranty of Fitness for a Particular Purpose
Application: Applies to both merchant and nonmerchant sellers and lessors.
Explained: A warranty that comes about where a seller or lessor warrants that the goods will Meet the buyer's or lessee's expressed needs.

Overlapping and Inconsistent Warranties
Express and implied warranties may exist within the same transaction
The intent of the parties determines which warranty dominates if the warranties that overlap are inconsistent.

Warranty Disclaimers

- Defined: Statements that negate implied and express warranties.

- Disclaimer of Implied Warranties: This is accomplished by words such as *without fault, as is, etc.* This is primarily good for used products.

- Disclaimer of Implied Warranty of Merchantability – This can be oral or written, but must use the term merchantability. Example: *"There are no warranties that extend beyond the description on the face hereof."*

- Disclaimer of Implied Warranty of Fitness for a Particular Purpose – Disclaimer can be accomplished by using general language without using the word fitness, but it must be in writing.

- Special Notation: There are no implied warranties with regard to any defects that an examination of the goods would have revealed.
  Requirement: The disclaimer must be conspicuous to a reasonable person.

- Unconscionable Disclaimers – The court has three options when the clause is unconscionable:
  1) refuse to enforce the unconscionable clause;
  2) refuse to enforce the entire contract; or
  3) limit the application of the clause.

  Factors in deciding unconscionability: Bargaining power of the parties, sophistication, education, and whether the contract was offered on a "take it or leave it" basis.

General disclaimer of warranty provisions and limitation of liability clauses in software contracts include:
  Limited warranty
  Customer's remedies
  No other warranty
  No liability for consequential damages

Third-Party Beneficiaries of Warranties

- Common Law: The parties had to be in privity of contract in order to have rights.

- Modern Law: The UCC limits the doctrine of privity thereby giving a third party the option of choosing three alternative provisions for liability to third parties.

Damages for Breach of Warranty

- The buyer or lessee may sue the seller or lessor for compensatory damages.

- Compensatory damages are equal to the difference between the value of the goods as warranted and the actual value of the goods accepted at the time and place of acceptance.

Statute of Limitations

- The UCC has a four-year statute of limitations. The parties may agree to reduce the statute of limitations to not less than one year.
- The statute begins to run upon tendering the goods to the buyer or lessee.
- Exception: If the warranty extends to the future performance of the goods. An example of this would be an extended warranty on an automobile.

Magnuson Moss Warranty Act

General Information: This act involves written warranties as they pertain to consumer products. If the product exceeds ten dollars and an express warranty is made, then the warranty must be labeled as "full" or "limited."

Full Warranty – The warrantor must guarantee free repair or replacement of the defective product as well as the time limit of the warranty. Additionally, the warranty must be conspicuous and able to be understood.

Limited Warranty – A limitation of the scope of the warranty is placed on the product. Also, the warranty must be conspicuous and able to be understood.

Damages – Under the act, a consumer may recover damages, attorney's fees, and costs. The consumer must go through the act's arbitration procedure first before taking legal action.

Limitation of Disclaiming Implied Warranties – The act modifies the state law of implied warranties by forbidding sellers or lessors who make express written warranties from disclaiming or modifying implied warranties of merchantability or fitness for a particular purpose. Time limits may be placed on implied warranties but the time limits must correspond to that of the written warranties.

Refresh Your Memory

The following exercise will enable you to refresh your memory on the rules and principles presented to you in this chapter. Read each question twice and place your answer in the blanks provided. Review the chapter material for any question you miss or are unable to remember.

1.   Why are express warranties made? _____
_____

2.   What warranty is implied that sold or leased goods are fit for the ordinary purpose for which they are sold or leased, and other assurances? _____
_____

3.   What test determines merchantability based on foreign objects that are found in food? ___
_____

4.   What does the warranty of no security interests hold? _____
_____

5.   What is a warranty against infringement? _____
_____

6.   Which act concerns written warranties relating to consumer products? _____
_____.

7.   What is a warranty against interference? _____
_____

8. When are manufacturers liable for express warranties made by wholesalers and retailers?

   _____

   _____

9. When may buyers and lessees recover for breach of an express warranty? _____

   _____

10. The statement "This boat has barely been driven 500 miles" is an _____ warranty.

11. Give at least two standards that must be met under the implied warranty of merchantability.

    _____

    _____

12. Which warranty applies to food and drink consumed on or off premises? _____

    _____

13. If five-year-old Bobby Brown cuts his mouth on a piece of metal found in pudding, which test will the court apply to determine if the pudding is unmerchantable? _____

    _____

14. With respect to the merchantability of food products, what is expected of those who prepare food? _____

    _____

15. Who does the implied warranty of fitness for a particular purpose apply to? _____

    _____

Critical Thought Exercise

Bob French, an engineer with Worldwide Construction, travels to Accu-Steel Company in Pennsylvania for the purpose of buying steel cable made by Accu-Steel to help support the upper decks of a new football stadium that Worldwide is building in California. The representative of Accu-Steel reviews the plans for the stadium and sells its recommended cable to Worldwide. The stadium is built using the cable selected by Accu-Steel.

During an exciting football game, the upper deck collapses onto the lower deck due to the inability of the cable to support the weight load. Worldwide Construction now faces suit from thousands of plaintiffs injured or killed in the collapse. Assuming that the steel cable was not defective in either its design or manufacturing process, does Worldwide have a cause of action against Accu-Steel?

Answer:

_____

_____

_____

_____

_____

_____

_____

_____

_____

_____

_____

_____

_____

Practice Quiz

True/False:

1. ____ A food product is unmerchantable if a foreign object in that product causes injury to that person. [p. 317]

2. ____ The buyer's reliance on a seller's or lessor's skill and judgment and purchases or leases of goods is not necessary when establishing that an implied warranty of fitness for a particular purpose applied to a given situation. [p. 317]

3. ____ Centralville Inc. owns a fleet of limousines. A thief steals one of them and sells it to Evan, an entrepreneur who just started his limousine business. Evan does not know that the limousine is stolen. Centralville Inc. has reclaimed the stolen limousine from Evan. Evan is out of luck and cannot recover against the thief for breach of warranty of title. [p. 321]

4. ____ A warranty of no security interest is an implied warranty that the goods have third-party security interests, liens, and encumbrances that automatically come with the goods when they are delivered. [p. 321]

5. ____ Blake sells his efficient weed picking machine called the Weed-O-Rama to a national home and garden retailer. One day while purchasing plants for his garden, Christopher Mills discovers the machine for sale. Thereafter he claims as well as proves that he has a trademark and patent on it. Since the home and garden retailer paid valuable consideration for the tool, Christopher is out of luck. [p. 321]

6. ____ If Katherine tells Taylor that her guitar is worth $7,500, this statement will become part of an express warranty for the sale of the guitar. [p. 314]

7. ____ Express warranties may be made by mistake. [p. 313]

8. ____ Unless there is a showing to the contrary, all statements by the seller or lessor before the time of contracting are not presumed to be part of the basis of the bargain. [p. 314]

9. ____ Statements of opinion such as "This is the best house you will every buy" create an express warranty. [p. 314]

10. ____ One of the standards for the implied warranty of merchantability is that they be adequately contained, packaged, and labeled. [p. 315]

11. ____ Grocery stores, restaurants, fast-food chains, and vending operators come within the purview of the warranty of fitness for human consumption. [p. 317]

12. ____ The foreign substance test is used to find out whether food products are from a foreign country or not, based on the ingredients found in the food. [p. 317]

13. ____ Most of the states have adopted the consumer expectation test in determining the merchantability of food products. [p. 317]

14. ____ Size as well as placement of warnings on products is no longer significant so long as the two are located somewhere on the product. [p. 319]

15. ____ The terminology *"with all faults"* refers to the fact that there are no implied warranties associated with a particular product. [p. 319]

16. ____ Warranties may be disclaimed as well as limited. [p. 319]

17. ____ The courts construe conspicuous as being speculative when it comes to what a manufacturer may tell a consumer. [p. 319]

18. ____ A warranty of no interference is one in which the lessor warrants that no person holds a claim or an interest in the goods that arose from an act or omission of the lessor that will interfere with the lessee's enjoyment of his or her leasehold interest. [p. 321]

19. ____ Software licenses are reluctant to place warranty disclaimers and liability limiting clauses in their packaging. [p. 319]

20. ____ An express warranty may be created by an item's description such as Santa Maria style tri-tip meat. [p. 313]

21. ____ Disclaimers of warranty are required to be in writing. [p. 319]

22. ____ The Magnuson-Moss Warranty Act applies to all goods regardless of cost. [p. 320]

23. ____ The Magnuson-Moss Warranty Act provides for the creation of implied warranties. [p. 320]

24. ____ In order for a full warranty to have effect, the warrantor must limit the scope of its warranty in some way. [p. 319]

25. ____ In a limited warranty, the warrantor must guarantee free repair or replacement of the defective product. [p. 319]

Multiple Choice

26. Under which warranty do sellers of goods automatically warrant that the goods that they sell are delivered free from any third-party liens, or encumbrances that are unknown to the buyer? [p. 313]
    a. good title
    b. the doctrine of caveat emptor
    c. warranty of no security interests
    d. warranty against infringements

27. The implied warranty of merchantability does not apply to which of the following? [p. 316]
    a. leases by nonmerchants
    b. sales by nonmerchants
    c. casual sales
    d. all of the above

28. The warranty of quiet possession is also referred to as [p. 321]
    a. a well-kept secret.
    b. warranty of no interference.
    c. possession without public knowledge.
    d. all of the above.

29. Express warranties are created when [p. 314]
    a. a seller or lessor affirms that the goods that are being sold or leased meet certain standards of quality or condition.
    b. a seller or lessor affirms that the goods that are being sold or leased do not meet certain standards of quality or condition.
    c. it is expected by the parties conduct.
    d. none of the above

30. Which of the following statements is true concerning the "basis of the bargain"? [p. 314]
    a. The UCC does not define the term.
    b. All statements prior to the time of contracting become part of the basis of the bargain.
    c. All post-sale statements that modify the contract are part of the basis of the bargain.
    d. all of the above

31. The statement "This gold necklace is worth more than money can pay" creates [p. 314]
    a. an affirmation of value.
    b. an implied warranty.
    c. no warranty.
    d. a statement of warranty.

32. The statement "This tractor has only been driven 1,500 miles" creates [p. 314]
    a. statement of opinion.
    b. an express warranty.
    c. a puffing remark.
    d. an affirmation of mileage.

33. The implied warranty of merchantability does not apply to [p. 315]
    a. sales by merchants.
    b. sales by a person having a garage sale.
    c. leases by merchants.
    d. a vacuum cleaner salesperson.

34. Which of the following has been incorporated into the implied warranty of merchantability? [p. 317]
    a. the warranty of fitness for human consumption
    b. the warranty of good title
    c. the warranty of no security interests
    d. the warranty against infringement

Short Answer

35 If a party wants to disclaim the implied warranty of merchantability, he or she must specifically mention the term _____. [p. 319]

36. What language might Lydia use if she wants to disclaim the implied warranty of fitness for a particular purpose? [p. 319] _____
_____

37. Ben would like to sell his cherry red motorcycle "as is." In effect what is Ben doing by using these words in an ad? [p. 319] _____

38. Why do software licenses have warranty disclaimers? [p. 319] _____
_____

39. Give an example of an automatic warranty from a merchant who regularly deals in goods of the kind sold or leased. [p. 321] _____

40. What is the warranty that is being breached when an individual transfers goods without the proper title called? [p. 321] _____

41. Give some examples of some forms of express warranties. [p. 313] _____
_____

42. Jacob's Collapsible Ladders placed the following language on its ladders, "There are no warranties that extend beyond the description on the face hereof." What does this indicate to the consumer? [.p 319] _____
_____

43. A warranty by the seller or lessor that goods meet certain criteria of quality is a _____
_____ of _____. [p. 314]

44. An affirmation that goods meet certain standards of quality, performance, description, or condition creates an _____ warranty. [p. 313]

45. A seller's statement of _____ does not create an express warranty. [p. 313]

46. Tell why the implied warranty of merchantability would not apply when a neighbor sells a fish tank to another neighbor. [p. 315] _____

_____

47. Why would an apple pie with a seed in it still be considered merchantable? [p. 317]

_____

48. Which test have most states adopted in order to determine the merchantability of food products? [p. 317] _____

49. Which test do some states use to determine whether food products are unmerchantable? [p. 317] _____

Answers to Refresh Your Memory

1. to entice consumers and others to buy or lease their products [p. 313]
2. implied warranty of merchantability [p. 315]
3. foreign substance test [p. 317]
4. This warranty holds that goods are delivered free from any third-party security interests, liens, or encumbrances known to the buyer. [p. 321]
5. It is a warranty that the goods are delivered free from any third-party patent, trademark, or copyright claim. [p. 321]
6. the Magnuson-Moss Warranty Act [p. 320]
7. a warranty by the lessor that no person holds a claim or interest in the goods that came about from an act or omission of the lessor that will interfere with the lessee's enjoyment of his or her leasehold interest [p. 321]
8. if the manufacturer authorizes or ratifies the warranty [p. 314]
9. Buyers and lessors may recover for breach of an express warranty if the warranty was a contributing factor that induced the buyer to purchase the product or to lease the product to the lessee. [p. 315]
10. express [p. 314]
11. The goods must be fit for the ordinary purposes for which they are used. The goods must be adequately packaged, contained, and labeled. [p. 315] (answers will vary)
12. the implied warranty of fitness for human consumption [p. 317]
13. the foreign substance test [p. 317]
14. A consumer would expect that a food preparer would remove all foreign objects from the food. [p. 317]
15. It applies to both merchant and nonmerchant sellers and lessors. [p. 317]

Critical Thought Exercise Model Answer

An implied warranty of fitness for a particular purpose arises under UCC 2-315 when the buyer's purpose or use for goods is expressly or impliedly known by the seller and the buyer purchases the goods in reliance on the seller's selection of the goods. Accu-Steel was informed of the express purpose for which the steel cable was being bought. Accu-Steel sold the cable to Worldwide that it recommended for the job. Accu-Steel may also be liable to Worldwide and the injured plaintiffs based upon a theory of product liability founded upon Accu-Steel's negligence. Due care must be used by the manufacturer in designing the product, selecting materials, using the appropriate manufacturing process, assembling and testing the product, and placing adequate warnings on the label or product. Accu-Steel selected the size of the cable to be produced. By failing to select a thicker and stronger cable, Accu-Steel was negligent and is liable to those persons who were foreseeable victims of its failure to perform its duties in a reasonable manner. Accu-Steel knew that the cable was going to be used in a stadium where spectators would be the end consumer.

Answers to Practice Quiz

True/False

1. True A food product is unmerchantable if a foreign object in that product causes injury to a person.
2. False The buyer or lessee relies on the seller's or lessor's skill and judgment and purchases or leases the goods. [UCC 2-315, 2A-213]
3. False Evan can recover against the thief for implied warranty of good title as the thief impliedly warranted that he or she had good title to the limousine and that the transfer of title to Evan was rightful.
4. False The warranty of no security interest automatically warrants that they are delivered free from any third-party security interests, not that the goods have a third-party security interest.
5. False Christopher may notify the home and garden retailer that they can no longer use the Weed-O-Rama without his permission except for a fee. The home and garden retailer may rescind its contract with Blake based on the no infringement warranty.
6. False A lessor warrants that no person holds an interest or a claim in the goods, not that a person does hold an interest in the goods.
7. True Express warranties may be made by mistake.
8. False All prior, concurrent, and postsale statements are presumed to be part of the basis of the bargain unless there is something contradictory in nature.
9. False Puffing or commendations of goods does not create an express warranty.
10. True The lessor or seller of goods is a merchant with respect to the goods of that kind, of which the goods must be adequately contained, packaged, and labeled accordingly.
11. True Restaurants, fast-food outlets, and grocery stores as well as vending machine operators do come within the purview of the implied warranty of fitness for human consumption.
12. False The foreign food substance test is used to determine whether food is unmerchantable based on objects that are found in the food.
13. False A majority of the states have adopted the consumer expectation test to determine whether food products are merchantable.
14. True Warnings must be conspicuous and noticeable to the reasonable person.
15. True Such terms as *with all faults* or *as is*, or other language that makes it clear to the buyer that there are no implied warranties, may be considered expressions to connote a disclaimer.
16. True Warranties may be disclaimed or limited.
17. False Speculative products have nothing to do with conspicuous as it relates to warnings and this chapter. This type of question is referred to as a red herring.
18. True When goods are leased, the lessor warrants that no person holds a claim or an interest in the goods that arose from an act or omission of the lessor that will interfere with the lessee's enjoyment of his or her leasehold interest.
19. False Most software licenses do contain warranty disclaimer and limitation on liability clauses in their packaging.

20. True   An express warranty can be created when the seller or lessor indicates that the goods will conform to any description of them, such as Santa Maria style tri-tip refers to the special cut of meat that the seller claims will conform to that cut.

21. False   Disclaimers may be both written or oral.

22. False   It applies if the cost of the good is more than $10 and the warrantor selects the option of making an express warranty.

23. False   The Magnuson-Moss Warranty Act covers written warranties.

24. False   To be considered a full warranty, the warrantor must guarantee free repair or replacement of the defective product.

25. False   In a limited warranty, the scope of a full warranty is limited in some way.

Multiple Choice

26. C   Answer C is the correct answer as the warranty of no security interests provides that the goods that are sold are free from any third-party security interest, liens, or encumbrances that are unknown to the buyer. Under this warranty, this is automatically done by the seller. Answer A is incorrect as sellers of goods warrant that the title they possess is good and that the transfer of title is rightful. Answer B is incorrect as the doctrine of caveat emptor simply means "Let the buyer beware." Answer D is incorrect as this warranty involves a lessor who is a merchant dealing in the goods of the kind that are being leased or sold, which automatically warrants that the goods are delivered free of any third-party trademark, copyright, or patent claims.

27. D   Answer D is the correct answer as answers A, B, and C all correctly state what the implied warranty of merchantability does not apply to, that is it does not apply to sales or leases by nonmerchants or casual sales.

28. B   Answer B is the correct answer as the warranty of quiet possession is referred to as the warranty of no infringement. Answers A and C are incorrect, as they make no sense. Answer D is incorrect for the reasons given above.

29. A   Answer A is the correct answer as express warranties can be made as an assurance of the fulfillment of a goods standards or quality by the seller or lessor to the buyer or lessee. Answer B is incorrect, as this would act more as a disclaimer if a seller or lessor affirmed that the goods do not meet certain criteria or quality.

30. D   Answer D is the correct answer as answers A, B, and C are all correct statements regarding the basis of the bargain.

31. A   Answer A is the correct answer as it is an affirmation of value, which does not create any warranty under UCC 2-313(2). Answer B is incorrect, as statements that involve affirmation of value do not create an express warranty. Answer C is incorrect because, even though it is true, it does not specifically state what is created as answer A does. Answer D is a false statement and therefore not correct.

32. B   Answer B is the correct answer as the statement is an affirmation of fact, which creates an express warranty. Answer A is incorrect as it is not a statement of opinion as it is factual as opposed to puffing with regard to the quality of the product. Answer C is incorrect based on the reasoning given with regard to answer A. Answer D is incorrect as there is no legal basis known as an affirmation of mileage.

33. B   Answer B is the correct answer as nonmerchants are not included in the provisions related to the implied warranty of merchantability. Answer A is incorrect as the implied warranty of merchantability does apply to merchants. Answer C is incorrect as the implied warranty of merchantability also applies to leases by merchants. Answer D is incorrect as a vacuum cleaner salesperson would be a merchant to whom the implied warranty of merchantability would apply based on his or her status of being a merchant.

34. A Answer A is the correct answer as the UCC incorporates the implied warranty of fitness for human consumption into the implied warranty of merchantability. Answer B is incorrect as the warranty of good title stands on its own merit without being incorporated into another warranty. Answer C is incorrect as this is an automatic warranty that also stands on its own merit. Answer D is incorrect as this is also an automatic warranty that is not incorporated as a subcategory of another warranty.

Short Answer

35. merchantability
36. Lydia may want to use the terminology "There are no warranties that extend beyond the description on the face hereof."
37. Ben's placing a disclaimer on his motorcycle
38. to limit the licensor's liability if the software malfunctions
39. warranty against infringements
40. warranty of good title
41. brochures, illustrations, ads, blueprints (answers will vary)
42. The language is sufficient to disclaim the fitness warranty.
43. warranty of quality
44. express
45. opinion
46. The warranty of merchantability would not be applicable, as it does not apply to casual sales.
47. It would still be considered merchantable because a reasonable consumer would expect to find an apple seed in an apple pie, as that would not be a foreign substance to the product.
48. the consumer expectation test
49. the foreign substance test

Chapter 22

CREATION OF NEGOTIABLE INSTRUMENTS

Chapter Overview

This chapter focuses on the different types of negotiable instruments as well as their creation and the transfer of the same. Additional attention is given to nonnegotiable contracts, transfer of negotiable instruments by assignment and negotiation, as well as the various types of indorsements.

Objectives

Upon completion of the exercises in this chapter, you should be able to:
1.   Differentiate between a negotiable and a nonnegotiable instrument.
2.   Discuss drafts and checks as well as name the parties to these instruments.
3.   Explain promissory notes and certificates of deposit as well as name the parties to these
4.   Give the formal requirement of a negotiable instrument.
5.   Differentiate between promises to pay and orders to pay.
6.   Explain the difference between instruments that are payable on a demand and those that are payable at a definite time.
7.   Explain the difference between instruments payable to order and payable to bearer.
8.   Discuss the process for indorsing and transferring negotiable instruments.
9.   Differentiate between blank and special indorsements.
10.   Discuss and apply the imposter rule and the fictitious payee rule.

Practical Application

This chapter will enable you to have a better understanding of negotiable instruments and their importance in conducting your personal as well as business affairs. Further, it will give you the tools that you need in the creation of a negotiable instrument. You will also obtain invaluable knowledge with regard to the different types of indorsements as well as requirements and restrictions for each.

Helpful Hints

Since this chapter involves one form or another of a negotiable instrument, the chance of you having used one or more of these instruments in your lifetime is great. If you keep in mind what you have used or are familiar with in terms of commercial paper, this chapter will be very understandable for you. The best approach is a simple approach. As with other chapters that have had confusing names for the parties involved, it is best to keep the parties separated on a sheet of paper to be able to view how they differ. The more you expose yourself to hypotheticals in this area, the easier the material becomes. Also, if you imagine yourself in one or more of the party's positions, it becomes easier.

Study Tips

Negotiable Instruments

Importance: Commercial paper aids in conducting personal and business affairs.

Three functions:
Negotiable instruments act as a substitute for money. An example is a check.
Negotiable instruments may also act as a credit device.
Negotiable instruments also may serve as a record-keeping device for preparing tax returns, etc.

Types of Negotiable Instruments

Draft – A three-party instrument that is an unconditional written order by one party that orders a second party to pay money to the third party. The parties involved are the drawer, the drawee, and the payee. Note that the drawee is also known as the acceptor because of his or her obligation to pay the payee instead of the drawer.

> Drawer – The customer who writes (draws) the check.
> Drawee – The financial institution upon which the check is written.
> Payee – The party to whom the check is written.

Promissory Note – An unconditional written promise by one party to pay money to another party.

> Maker – This is the borrower who makes the promise to pay.
> Payee – This is the lender to whom the promise is made.

> Collateral – Sometimes the lender needs security known as collateral when a promissory note is made.

> Examples of promissory notes: Mortgage notes, which are notes that are secured by real estate.
> Collateral notes are notes that are secured by personal property.

Certificates of Deposit – A specially created note that is created upon a depositor depositing monies at a financial institution in exchange for the institution's promise to pay the deposited amount back with an agreed-upon amount of interest after a set period of time.

Creation of a Negotiable Instrument

In order to create a negotiable instrument in compliance with UCC 3-104(a), the following must be present and must appear on the face of the instrument:
It must be in writing. – This involves permanency and the writing must be portable.
It must be signed by the maker or drawer. – The UCC is broad with this requirement. Symbols, typed, printed, lithographed, rubber-stamped, or other mechanical signatures are allowed.
It must be an unconditional promise or order to pay. – Mere debt acknowledgement is not sufficient for this requirement.

It must state a fixed amount of money. – The principal amount of the instrument has to be on the face of the instrument. Note, money is a "medium of exchange authorized or adopted by a foreign or domestic government as part of its currency." [UCC 1-201(24)]

It must not require any undertaking in addition to the payment of money.

It must be payable on demand or at a definite time. – Payable on demand instruments are created by language such as "payable on sight," or "payable on demand." Checks are an example of payable on demand instruments. Payable at a definite time are called time instruments.

It must be payable to order or to bearer.

Nonnegotiable Contracts

If a promise or order to pay does not meet the requirements discussed under negotiable instruments, then it is a nonnegotiable contract. A nonnegotiable contract is enforceable under contract law.

Transfer by Assignment or Negotiation

After issuance, negotiable instruments may be transferred to subsequent parties either by negotiation or assignment. The transferee's rights will depend on how the transfer was effectuated. There are two main types:

Transfer by Assignment – It transfers contract rights of the assignor (transferor) to the assignee (transferee). An assignment results when there has been a transfer of a nonnegotiable instrument.

Transfer by Negotiation – Negotiation is defined as the transfer of a negotiable instrument by a person other than the issuer.

Indorsements

Defined – The signature of a signer (not the maker, drawer, or acceptor) that is put on an instrument to negotiate it to another person. The signature may be by itself, state an individual to whom the instrument is to be paid, or be with other words.

Indorser – The one who indorses the instrument.
Indorsee – The payee named in the instrument.

Types of Indorsements

Blank– No indorsee is given and it creates bearer paper.

Special indorsement – It contains the indorser's signature and it indicates the person to whom the indorser intends the instrument to be payable to. Special indorsements create order paper, which are preferred over bearer paper.

Unqualified indorsement – "An indorsement whereby the indorser promises to pay the holder or any subsequent indorser the amount of the instrument if the maker, drawer, or acceptor defaults on it."
Qualified indorsement – "Indorsements that disclaim or limit liability on the instrument." Note that there is no guaranteed payment of the instrument by the qualified indorser if the maker,

drawer, or acceptor defaults on the instrument. These types of indorsements are often used by individuals signing instruments in the capacity as a representative.

Nonrestrictive indorsement – This is an indorsement without conditions or instructions attached to the payment of the funds.

Restrictive indorsement – An indorsement with an instruction from the indorser.
There are two restrictive indorsements you should be familiar with as provided for under UCC 3-206.

Indorsement for Deposit or Collection – This is an indorsement that establishes the indorsee, the indorser's collecting agent. For example: "for deposit only."

Indorsement in Trust – An indorsement for the benefit or use of the indorser or another individual.

Misspelled or Wrong Name

If the payee or indorsee name is misspelled, the payee or indorsee in the negotiable instrument may indorse the instrument in the misspelled name, the correct name or both.

Multiple Payees or Indorsees

If two or more than persons are listed as indorsees or payees on a negotiable instrument and are listed jointly, both indorsements are needed to negotiate the instrument. Example: Payable to Joe and Jan Smith requires both Joe's and Jan's signatures.
If the instrument indicates that one or the other may negotiate the instrument, then each person's signature is sufficient to negotiate the instrument. Example: Payable to Ann or Mark Jones would allow either Ann's or Mark's signature.
If a *virgule* (which is a slash mark) is used, then the negotiable instrument may be paid in the alternative. Example: Maile Price/Winnie Simms indicates that either person may individually negotiate the instrument.

Forged Instrument

The general rule is that unauthorized indorsements are inoperative as the indorsement of the person who signed it. The loss is born by the party accepting the forged instrument. There are two exceptions, the imposter rule and the fictitious payee rule.

Imposter rule – The drawer or maker is liable on the instrument to any person who in good faith pays the instrument or takes it for value or for collection.

The fictitious payee rule – A drawer or maker is liable on an unauthorized or forged indorsement of a fictitious payee rule.

Refresh Your Memory

The following exercise will enable you to refresh your memory on the rules and principles presented to you in this chapter. Read each question twice and place your answer in the blanks provided. Review the chapter material for any question you miss or are unable to remember.

1.   What three functions do negotiable instruments serve? _____ _____ _____

2.   A drawer of a draft is _____,

3.   Who is the party who receives the money from a draft? _____

4.   What is a draft that is payable at a designated future date called? _____.

5.   What is unique about a check? _____ _____

6.   Why is a trade acceptance considered a three-party instrument? _____ _____

7.   A drawer's unconditional order to a drawee to pay a payee is known as an _____ _____.

8.   When creating a negotiable instrument, which requirement is intended to ensure free transfer of the instrument? _____ _____

9.   How must a fixed amount of a negotiable instrument be paid? _____

10.   What does a prepayment clause in an instrument allow? _____ _____

11.   What is the result when the drawer or maker does not make the instrument payable to a specific payee? _____

12.   What is a lender asking for when it requires the maker of a note to post security for the repayment of the note? _____

13.   What is an unconditional written promise by one party to pay money to another party called? _____

14.   What is the party who makes a promise to pay called? _____

15.   A lender is also known as a _____ .

Critical Thought Exercise

The Gold Coast Investment Group (IG) is building a large office building that it is financing itself through its banking arm, Gold Coast Bank (GCB). When payments for the final phase of the building come due, GC issues checks to the contractors with a condition on the front of the check that states:

> ***"This instrument valid only after a permit to occupy the building is granted by all governmental agencies from which a permit is mandatory."***

Ace Construction deposits the check with its bank, First City Bank. The occupancy permits are not issued by the city or county entities where the building is located. When presented with the checks by First City Bank, GCB refuses to honor them.

Ace Construction then brings suit against First City Bank, GCB, and IG.

Should GCB be compelled to pay the checks presented to it by First City Bank on behalf of Ace Construction? Was it ethical for IG to place a condition upon the negotiation of the instrument?

Answer:

_____
_____
_____
_____
_____
_____
_____
_____
_____
_____
_____
_____
_____
_____
_____
_____
_____
_____

Practice Quiz

True/False

1. ___ The phraseology "I wish you would pay" is sufficient to create an unconditional order for the drawee to pay a payee. [p. 333]

2. ___ A maker or drawer is liable on a negotiable instrument signed by an authorized agent. [p. 333]

3. ____ To be a negotiable instrument, a writing must contain either an unconditional order to pay or an unconditional promise to pay. [p. 333]

4. ____ The party who makes the promise to pay is the borrower. [p. 331]

5. ____ Examples of collateral that may be used as security against repayment of a note to a lender include cars, homes, or other property. [p. 331]

6. ____ A CD is an order to pay. [p. 331]

7. ____ A CD is a two-party instrument. [p. 331]

8. ____ Notes are often named after the security that underlies the note. [p. 331]

9. ____ Lithographed, rubber-stamped, and other mechanical means of signing instruments are recognized as valid by the UCC. [p. 333]

10. ____ Oral promises qualify as negotiable instruments because they are clearly transferable as well as fraud free. [p. 332]

11. ____ The term signature is broadly defined under the UCC thereby allowing any symbol executed or adopted by a party with a present intent to authenticate the writing. [p. 333]

12. ____ A note that requires the maker to pay a stated amount of money and perform some type of service is negotiable. [p. 336]

13. ____ Instruments that are payable upon an uncertain act or event are also negotiable. [p. 336]

14. ____ The UCC expressly provides that an instrument may state that it is payable in foreign money. [p. 338]

15. ____ Christy executes a note that promises to pay Ed in goods or services. A negotiable instrument has been created. [p. 335]

Multiple Choice

16. Negotiable instruments serve which function? [pp.327-328]
    a. as a substitute for money
    b. as a credit device
    c. as a record-keeping device
    d. all of the above

17. A drawer of a draft is the [p. 328]
    a. person to whom the check is made payable.
    b. person who issues the draft.
    c. person to whom the draft is made payable.
    d. person who owes money to the drawer.

18. To qualify as a negotiable instrument under the UCC, the writing must [p. 332]
    a. contain an unconditional promise to pay.
    b. contain an unconditional order to pay.
    c. contain an unconditional promise or order to pay.
    d. none of the above

19. A draft's or check's unconditional order for the drawee to pay must [p. 333]
    a. be more than an authorization or request to pay.
    b. be precise.
    c. contain the word pay.
    d. all of the above

20. A promise or order to pay may include [p. 333]
    a. authorization or power to protect collateral.
    b. a vague amount.
    c. a conditional promise to perform.
    d. an immobile writing.

21. An extension clause is [p. 337]
    a. a clause that allows the borrower more time to secure a loan.
    b. allows the maturity date of the loan to extend to some time in the future.
    c. allows the acceleration of the borrower's payments
    d. all of the above.

22. A trade acceptance is [p. 329]
    a. a distinct form of a draft drawn on a financial institution.
    b. a draft payable at a designated future date.
    c. the party who writes an order for a draft.
    d. a sight draft that arises when credit is extended by a seller to a buyer with the sale of goods.

23. Which of the following must a negotiable instrument have? [p. 332]
    a. It must be in writing.
    b. It must be an unconditional promise or order to pay.
    c. It must be payable on demand or at a definite time.
    d. all of the above

24. Which of the following makes a promise nonnegotiable? [p. 334]
    a. if the promise states an express condition to payment
    b. if the promise is subject to or governed by another writing
    c. if the rights or obligations with respect to the promise or order are stated in another writing.
    d. all of the above

Short Answer

25. Why is the drawee called the acceptor of the draft? _____
    _____[p. 328]

26. The language "pay on February 3, 2009," or "pay 180 days after date" creates what type of draft? _____ [p. 328]

27. If Whitney lists her 2006 Corvette as security against repayment of a note, what is this type of security called? _____ [p. 331]

28. If an instrument has to be payable with interest, how must the amount of interest being charged be expressed? _____ [p.335]

29. Why aren't instruments payable in commodities, goods, services, and the like negotiable instruments? _____

_____
[pp. 335-336]

30. What does the UCC require tin terms of how negotiable instruments are made payable? _____ [p. 334]

31. If an instrument states that it is payable in foreign currency, how can this be satisfied in the United States? _____ [p. 338]

32. Give examples of instruments that can be but aren't always payable on demand. _____
_____ [p. 336]

33. What can't a promise or an order to pay state? _____
_____ [p. 337]

34. The party who must pay the money stated in a draft is called the _____ [p. 328]

35. A two-party negotiable instrument that is an unconditional written promise by one party to pay money to another party is a _____ [p. 330]

Answers to Refresh Your Memory

1. substitute for money, act as credit devices, act as record-keeping devices [pp. 327-328]
2. the party who writes an order for a draft [p. 328]
3. the payee of the draft [p. 328]
4. time draft [p. 328]
5. It is drawn on a financial institution and payable on demand. [p. 329]
6. Because the seller is both the drawer and the payee. The buyer whose credit is extended is the drawee. [p. 329]
7. order to pay [p. 333]
8. the portability requirement [p.332]
9. in money [p. 335]
10. It permits the maker to pay the amount due prior to the due date of the instrument. [p. 337]
11. bearer paper [p. 335]
12. collateral [p. 331]
13. a promissory note [p. 330]
14. a maker [p. 331]
15. a payee [p. 331]

Critical Thought Exercise Model Answer

The general rule is that the terms of the promise or order must be included in the writing on the face of a negotiable instrument. UCC 3-104(a) requires that the terms must also be unconditional. The terms cannot be conditioned on the occurrence or nonoccurrence of some other event or agreement.

By placing the condition on the face of the instrument, IG prevented the checks from being valid negotiable instruments. Both First City Bank and GCB would be within their rights to refuse to honor the checks. A promise to pay that is conditional on another event, such as the issuing of the occupancy permits, is not negotiable because the risk of the other event not occurring would fall on the person who held the instrument. A conditional promise like the one placed on the check by IG is subject to normal contract law.

IG will not have made payment on the required contractual installments and may now be in breach of contract. Ace Construction will be able to recover against IG for failure to meet its contractual obligations unless the occupancy permits were a condition of payment contained in the parties' original contract.

The placing of the condition upon the face of the check by IG appears to be unethical. If the condition were not part of its contract with Ace, it would be unethical to attempt to unilaterally modify the terms of their agreement. If the purpose of placing the condition on the check were to cause the checks to be dishonored and thus delay payment, this would also be unethical. IG would be employing a trick to avoid lawful payment, which may damage Ace Construction when it is unable to meet its financial obligations.

Answers to Practice Quiz

True/False

1. True   "I wish you would pay" is not sufficient because it lacks a direction to pay.
2. True   A maker or drawer is liable on a negotiable instrument signed by an authorized agent.
3. True   To be a negotiable instrument under the requirements of UCC 3-104(a), a writing must contain either an unconditional order to pay (draft or check) or an unconditional promise to pay (note or CD).
4. True   A party who makes a promise to pay is the maker of a note (i.e., the borrower).
5. True   Security against repayment of the note that lenders often require may include cars, homes, or other security.
6. False   A CD is a promise to pay, not an order to pay.
7. True   A CD is a two-party instrument.
8. True   Notes are often named after the security that underlies the note.
9. True   Lithographed, rubber-stamped, typed, printed, and other mechanical means of signing instruments are recognized as valid by the UCC.
10. False   Oral promises do not qualify as negotiable instruments because they are not clearly transferable in a manner that will prevent fraud.
11. True   The UCC is very liberal when defining the meaning of signature, which may include symbols, marks, etc.
12. False   If a note required the maker to pay a stated amount of money and perform some type of service, it would not be negotiable.
13. False   Instruments that are payable upon an uncertain act or event are not negotiable.
14. True   The UCC expressly provides that an instrument may state that it is payable in foreign money [UCC 3-107].

15. False   A note that contains a promise to pay in goods or services is not a negotiable instrument because the value of the note would be difficult to determine at any given time.

Multiple Choice

16. D   Answer D is the correct answer as answers A, B, and C all state the functions that negotiable instruments serve.

17. B   Answer B is the correct answer as a person who issues the draft is the drawer of the draft. Answer A is incorrect as this states the definition of a payee. Answer C is incorrect as this is also the definition of a payee. Answer D is incorrect as this states the definition of the drawee.

18. C   Answer C is the correct answer as the writing must contain either an unconditional order or promise to pay. Answer A is incorrect as this is not the only requirement that the UCC allows in determining whether an instrument is negotiable. Answer B is incorrect for the same reasoning given with regard to answer A. Answer D is incorrect based on the reasoning given above.

19. D   Answer D is the correct answer as answers A, B, and C all correctly state what a draft's or check's unconditional order must contain.

20. A   Answer A is the correct answer as it correctly states what is allowed under the UCC 3-104. Answer B is incorrect as vague amounts are not allowed; fixed amounts of money are. Answer C is incorrect as the instrument must contain an unconditional promise. Answer D is incorrect as it makes no sense.

21. B   Answer B is the correct answer as it correctly expresses what an extension clause is, hence it allows the maturity date of an instrument to extend to some future date. Answer A is incorrect as the loan is already in place with an extension clause. Answer C is incorrect as an extension clause does not allow for the acceleration of the borrower's payments. As such this is not a true statement. Answer D is incorrect for the reasons given above.

22. D   Answer D is the correct answer as a sight draft arises when credit is extended with the sale of goods. Answer A is incorrect as this describes a check. Answer B is incorrect as this describes a time draft. Answer C is incorrect as this answer describes a drawer of a draft.

23. D   Answer D is the correct answer as answers A, B, and C are all reflective of all of the items necessary for a negotiable instrument to be valid.

24. D   Answer D is correct as the answers given in answers A, B, and C all make a promise nonnegotiable.

Short Answer

25. because his or her obligation changes from that of having to pay the drawer to that of having to pay the payee
26. a time draft
27. collateral
28. as a fixed or variable rate
29. Instruments that are fully or partially payable in a medium of exchange other than money are not negotiable.
30. to the bearer or to order
31. The currency can be satisfied by the equivalent U.S. dollars.
32. notes, CDs, and drafts
33. It cannot state any undertaking in addition to money.
34. drawee of a draft
35. promissory note

Chapter 23

TRANSFERABILITY AND HOLDER IN DUE COURSE

Chapter Overview

In the previous chapter, you learned about the various types of negotiable instruments as well as their creation and the ability to transfer the same. This chapter expands on the concept of commercial paper being a substitute for money by exploring the liability of parties on negotiable instruments, as well as the requisites that must be satisfied in order to be deemed a holder in due course. Further, you will learn the defenses that can be raised against the imposition of liability as well as what is involved in discharging liability.

Objectives

Upon completion of the exercises in this chapter, you should be able to:
1. Explain transfer by assignment.
2. Discuss transfer by negotiation.
3. Discuss the process for indorsing and transferring negotiable instruments.
4. Differentiate between blank and special indorsements.
5. Discuss and apply the imposter rule and the fictitious payee rule.
6. Explain the meaning of a holder and a holder in due course.
7. Discuss and apply the requisites for becoming a holder in due course.
8. Explain what is meant by taking for value.
9. Define taking in good faith.
10. Understand what is meant by taking without notice of defect.
11. Discuss the shelter principle.

Helpful Hints

This chapter continues to expand upon the concepts associated with the negotiable instruments, with clear explanations concerning assignments, transfer by negotiation, and negotiating order and bearer paper. Further, there is an emphasis on the various types of indorsements and the necessary requirements for qualifying as a holder in due course. Since this chapter lays out a list of requirements that are necessary to be a holder in due course as well as requirements for each of the elements contained within the basic definition, it is especially helpful to make use of lists. To facilitate your studies in this area, the study tips section has been organized so that you will be able to easily refer to the lists when analyzing the case studies or hypotheticals presented to you.

Study Tips

Transfer by Assignment

An assignment is the transfer of rights under a contract. Assignments result when a nonnegotiable contract is transferred. The assignee (transferee) only acquires the rights that the assignor (transferor) possessed. All defenses that could be raised against the assignor can now be raised against the assignee.

Transfer by Negotiation

Negotiation is the transfer of a negotiable instrument by a person other than the issuer. The person to whom the instrument has been transferred is known as the holder. If the holder is found to be a holder in due course, he or she receives the rights of the transferor and may obtain even greater additional rights. A holder in due course (HDC) has greater rights as he or she is not subject to some of the defenses that may have been raised against the transferor.

Negotiating Order Paper

Order paper is described as an instrument that is negotiated by (1) delivery and (2) indorsement.

Negotiating Bearer Paper

Bearer paper is defined as an instrument that is negotiated by delivery; indorsement is not necessary. Further, bearer paper is not payable to a specific payee or indorsee.

Converting Order and Bearer Paper

An instrument can be converted from order paper to bearer paper and vice versa until eventually the instrument is paid. [UCC 3-109] The end result is dependent upon the indorsement placed on the instrument at the time of each subsequent transfer.

Indorsement

An indorsement is the signature of a signer that is placed on an instrument. The signer cannot be the maker, a drawer, or an acceptor. The indorsement can be (1) by itself, (2) name an individual to whom the instrument is to be paid, or (3) be accompanied by other words. Indorsements are usually paid on the back of the instrument. If there is a lack of space to indorse the instrument, the indorsement may be placed on a separate piece of paper (an allonge) affixed to the instrument. *An interesting notation is that indorsements are necessary to negotiate order paper, but they are not required to negotiate bearer paper [UCC 3-201 (b)].*

Types of Indorsements

Blank – No indorsee is given and it creates bearer paper.

Special indorsement – It contains the indorser's signature and it indicates the person to whom the indorser intends the instrument to be payable to. Special indorsements create order paper, which are preferred over bearer paper.

Unqualified indorsement – "An indorsement whereby the indorser promises to pay the holder or any subsequent indorser the amount of the instrument if the maker, drawer, or acceptor defaults on it."

Qualified indorsement – "Indorsements that disclaim or limit liability on the instrument." Note that there is no guaranteed payment of the instrument by the qualified indorser if the maker, drawer, or acceptor defaults on the instrument. These types of indorsements are often used by individuals signing instruments in the capacity as a representative.

Nonrestrictive indorsement – This is an indorsement without conditions or instructions attached to the payment of the funds.

Restrictive indorsement – An indorsement with an instruction from the indorser.
There are two restrictive indorsements you should be familiar with as provided for under UCC 3-206.

    Indorsement for Deposit or Collection – This is an indorsement that establishes the indorsee, the indorser's collecting agent. For example: "for deposit only."

    Indorsement in Trust – An indorsement for the benefit or use of the indorser or another individual.

Misspelled or Wrong Name

If the payee or indorsee name is misspelled, the payee or indorsee in the negotiable instrument may indorse the instrument in the misspelled name, the correct name or both.

Multiple Payees or Indorsees

If more two or more persons are listed as indorsees or payees on a negotiable instrument and are listed jointly, both indorsements are needed to negotiate the instrument. Example: Payable to John and Sarah Smith requires both John's and Sarah's signature.

If the instrument indicates that one or the other may negotiate the instrument, then each person's signature is sufficient to negotiate the instrument. Example: Payable to Ann or Mark Jones would allow either Ann's or Mark's signature.

If a *virgule* (which is a slash mark) is used, then the negotiable instrument may be paid in the alternative. Example: Maile Price/Winnie Simms indicates that either person may individually negotiate the instrument.

Forged Instrument

The general rule is that unauthorized indorsements are inoperative as the indorsement of the person who signed it. The loss is borne by the party accepting the forged instrument. There are two exceptions, the imposter rule and the fictitious payee rule.

| **Holder** | *versus* | **Holder in Due Course** |

Defined: A person in possession of an instrument that is payable to bearer or an identified person who is in possession of an instrument payable to person.

Defined: A holder who takes an instrument for value, in good faith, and without notice that is defective or is overdue.

Requisites for Being a Holder in Due Course

The individual must be a holder of a negotiable instrument that was taken:

1. **for value** (as elaborated on in UCC 3-303)
   a. if the holder performs the agreed-upon promise.
   b. acquires a security interest or lien on the instrument.
   c. takes the instrument in payment of or as security for an antecedent claim.
   d. gives a negotiable instrument as payment.
   e. gives an irrevocable obligation as payment.

2. **in good faith**
   a. which means honesty in fact.
   b. Honesty is a subjective test as judged by the circumstances and only applies to the holder.

3. **without notice of defect**
   a. means that a person cannot be a holder in due course is he or she knows that the instrument is defective in any way.
   b. Defect can be construed as
      1. it being overdue.
      2. it has been dishonored.
      3. it contains an unauthorized signature or has been altered (the red light doctrine).
      4. there is a defense against it.

4. **Other important information**
   - A holder may not be a holder in due course if at the time of negotiation to the holder it was forged or altered, casting doubt on its authentication.
   - Payees usually are not considered to be holders in due course because of their knowledge of claims or defenses against the instrument.

Shelter Principle

The shelter principle involves a holder who does qualify as a holder in due course in his or her own right but becomes a holder in due course if he or she obtains the instrument through a holder in due course. The rules that apply to being a holder in due course under the shelter principle are as follows:

- The holder does not have to qualify as a holder in due course in his or her own right.
- The holder must acquire the instrument from a holder in due course or be able to trace his or her title back to a holder in due course.
- The holder must not have been a party to a fraud or illegality affecting the instrument.
- The holder cannot have notice of a defense or claim against the payment of the instrument.

Refresh Your Memory

The following exercise will enable you to refresh your memory on the rules and principles presented to you in this chapter. Read each question twice and place your answer in the blanks provided. Review the chapter material for any question you miss or are unable to remember.

1.   An _____ is the transfer of rights under the contract.

2.   _____ is the transfer of a negotiable instrument by an individual other than the issuer.

3.   The signature of a signer that is placed on an instrument to negotiate it to another person is an _____.

4.   A _____ in _____ _____ is a holder who takes an instrument for value, in good faith, and without notice that is defective or is overdue.

5.   When an individual takes an instrument honestly believing in the conduct of the transaction, he or she is said to be a holder taking it in _____ _____.

6.   Give an example of when a person may not qualify as a holder in due course. _____ _____.

5.   Steve, a thief, steals a negotiable instrument and transfers it to Cindy. Cindy is unaware that the instrument is stolen. Since Cindy meets the good faith test, she will qualify as a _____ _____ _____ _____.

7.   What is the red light doctrine? _____ _____

8.   What is indicated when an instrument has not been paid when due? _____ _____

9.   A virgule used in between names in a negotiable instrument indicates that _____ _____

9.   When an instrument has been presented for payment and payment has been refused, it is _____.

10.   Jana has misspelled Marsha's name in a negotiable instrument. How should Marsha indorse the instrument? _____ _____

11.   What is needed to indicate that either of two indorsements is sufficient to negotiate an instrument? _____.

12.   When does an assignment of a nonnegotiable contract occur? _____ _____

13. What determines whether the proper method of negotiation has taken place? _____
_____

14. Order paper may best be described as _____.

15. Liability on a negotiable instrument that is imposed on a party only when the party primarily liable on the instrument defaults and fails to pay the instrument when due is known as _____ _____.

Critical Thought Exercise

Betty Smith made out a check to George Bell of Bell Plumbing for $1,500 as a partial payment for plumbing renovation of her kitchen. When it was time for Bell to begin his work, he did not appear, nor could Ms. Smith locate him. Smith immediately ordered her bank to stop payment on the check. Bell had already cashed the check at Redi-Cash. When the check was returned to Redi-Cash marked "payment stopped by account holder," Redi-Cash was contacted by an attorney for Smith who informed Redi-Cash that the plumber did not have a license and that engaging in a contracting trade without a license was a crime. Therefore the contract was void and his client would not honor the check.

As manager of Redi-Cash, will you commence suit against Smith to collect the amount of the check?

Answer:
_____
_____
_____
_____
_____
_____
_____
_____
_____
_____
_____
_____
_____
_____

Practice Quiz

True/False

1. ___ Assignees may not have any defenses brought against them once an assignment has occurred. [p. 342]

2. ___ A holder is the transfer of a negotiable instrument by a person other than the issuer. [p. 343]

3. ___ An instrument may be converted from order paper to bearer paper but not from bearer paper to order paper. [p. 344]

4. ___ A blank indorsement will specify a particular indorsee. [p. 345]

5. ___ A qualified indorsement is one that disclaims or limits liability on the instrument. [p. 347]

6. ___ A special qualified indorsement creates order paper that can be negotiated by indorsement and delivery. [p. 347]

7. ___ A restrictive indorsement restricts the indorsee's rights in some manner. [p. 347]

8. ___ If an instrument reads "pay to Fred Finkle and Wilma Wilson," it means that it is necessary that both persons' indorsements are on the instrument in order to negotiate it. [p. 349]

9. ___ If an instrument is made payable to Susie Samons when the correct spelling of her name is Susie Samonis, a person taking the instrucment for value or collection may require Susie to sign in both the misspelled and correct version of her name. [p. 349]

10. ___ A person may qualify as a holder in due course even if there is a claim to the instrument by another person. [p. 351]

11. ___ The condition of an instrument that has been presented for payment and payment being accepted is termed dishonored. [p. 351]

12. ___ The UCC has eliminated any need for knowing about defects in an instrument and therefore has become more lenient on who can be a holder in due course. [p. 351]

13. ___ The test on whether a holder in due course takes in good faith is an objective one. [p. 351]

14. ___ A holder in due course takes a negotiable instrument free of all claims and most defenses. [p. 349]

15. ___ An indorser may not indorse an instrument so as to make the indorsee his collecting agent. [p. 347]

Multiple Choice

16. A holder is [p. 349]
    a. a person who takes an instrument for value and in good faith.
    b. a person who takes without notice that it is defective or overdue.
    c. a person in possession of an instrument that is payable to bearer or an identified person who is in possession of an instrument payable to that person.
    d. a person who takes a negotiable instrument free of all claims and most defenses.

17. To be classified as a holder in due course, the transferee must [p. 349]
    a. be the holder of a negotiable instrument taken for value.
    b. be the holder of a negotiable instrument in good faith.
    c. be the holder of a negotiable instrument that bears no apparent evidence of forgery.
    d. all of the above

18. If Megan promises to perform but has not done so yet and there has been no value given, Megan is not a [p. 350]
    a. holder in due course.
    b. third-party beneficiary.
    c. holder without value.
    d. none of the above

19. If a time instrument is not paid on its expressed date, then it [p. 351]
    a. becomes effective.
    b. becomes overdue and is defective as to its payment.
    c. is payable on demand.
    d. can be made payable according to business practices.

20. Which of the following falls under the category of indorsements? [p.348]
    a. special
    b. unqualified
    c. blank
    d. all of the above

21. Which type of indorsement does the language "Pay to the order of Simone Reed/s/Mary Timms" indicate? [p. 348]
    a. a special indorsement
    b. a forgery
    c. a holder indorsement
    d. none of the above

22. Which of the following would be considered to be a restrictive indorsement? [p. 349]
    a. an indorsement prohibiting further indorsement
    b. an indorsement for deposit or collection
    c. an indorsement in trust
    d. all of the above

23. Which of the following would be a nonrestrictive indorsement? [p. 349]
    a. "pay to Shawn Muro if he completes construction of my summer house by July 30, 2007" /s/Monica Smith
    b. "pay to Shawn Muro only"/s/Monica Smith
    c. "For deposit only"/s/Monica Smith
    d. Pay to Shawn Muro or order/s/Monica Smith

24. Hugo draws a check on Coast Bank "payable to the order of Lamar Huff." When Lamar presents the check for payment, Coast Bank refuses to pay it. Lamar can collect the amount of the check from Hugo because Hugo is [p. 351]
   a. the maker.
   b. the drawee.
   c. the person who ratified the check.
   d. the drawer.

25. Which of the following is true with respect to a check that is indorsed "pay to Tilly Ruiz only." [p. 347]
   a. The restrictive indorsement will prevent further negotiation.
   b. The indorsement will restrict the indorsee's rights.
   c. The check can still be negotiated to other transferees.
   d. none of the above

Short Answer

26. A holder can covert a blank indorsement into a _____ indorsement by writing any contract consistent with the character of the indorsement over the signature of the indorser in blank. [p. 346]

27. An indorsement is a _____ by the indorser to pay the holder or any subsequent indorser the amount of the instrument if the maker, drawer, or acceptor defaults on it. [p. 346]

28. Unless otherwise agreed, the order and liability of the indorsers is presumed to be
   _____ [p. 347]

29. An assignment is a transfer of _____ under a contract. [p. 342]

30. What does the transferee become if a negotiable instrument has been transferred by negotiation? [p. 343] _____

31. The delivery and indorsement of an instrument that is negotiated is known as _____
   _____ [p. 343]

32. How many payees may drawers, makers, and indorsers make checks, promissory notes, and other negotiable instruments payable to? _____[p. 348]

33. What are the four requirements to qualify as a holder in due course? _____
   _____, _____, _____
   _____, _____[p. 350]

34. What is considered to be a "reasonable time" for presentment of a check? _____
   _____[p. 351]

35. If a maker misses an installment or fails to pay one note in a series of notes, the purchaser of the instrument is on _____ that it is _____[p. 351]

36. Give an example of a trust indorsement. _____ [p. 348]

37. What is a deposit or collection? _____
    _____ [p. 348]

38. What is the result of an indorsee who does not comply with a restrictive indorsement? [p. 348]

    _____

39. When a holder does not qualify as a holder in due course by virtue of his or her own right, but becomes a holder in due course because he or she has obtained the instrument through a holder in due course, this is known as the _____ _____ [p. 352]

40. When qualifying as a holder in due course, who does the good faith requirement apply to? _____[p. 351]

Answers to Refresh Your Memory

1. assignment [p. 342]
2. Negotiation [p. 343]
3. indorsement [p. 344]
4. holder; due course [p. 349]
5. good faith [p. 351]
6. a person who takes a check that has been marked by the payor or bank "payment refused-not sufficient funds"[p. 351]
7. A holder cannot qualify as a holder in due course if he or she has notice that an instrument contains an unauthorized signature or has been altered or that there is any adverse claim against or defense to its payment. [p. 352]
8. that there is some defect in payment [p. 351]
9. that the instrument is payable in the alternative [p. 349]
10. Marsha may indorse the instrument in the misspelled name, the correct name, or both. [p. 349]
11. the word "or" in between the parties' names who are the persons listed as to whom the document is payable to. [p. 349]
12. when the nonnegotiable interest is transferred [p. 342]
13. whether the instrument is order paper or bearer paper [p. 343]
14. An instrument that is payable to a specific payee or indorsed to a specific indorsee is order paper. [p. 343]
15. delivery and indorsement [p. 343]

Critical Thought Exercise Model Answer

A holder of a negotiable instrument is a holder in due course (HDC) pursuant to UCC 3-302 if he or she takes the instrument (1) for value; (2) in good faith; and (3) without notice that it is overdue, that it has been dishonored, that any person has a defense against it or claim to it, or that the instrument contains unauthorized signatures, alterations, or is so irregular or incomplete as to call into question its authenticity. Redi-Cash gave value for the instrument when they cashed it for Bell. The UCC defines good faith as "honesty in fact and the observance of reasonable commercial standards of fair dealing." UCC 3-103(4). It is immaterial whether the transferor acted in good faith. There is nothing in the facts to show that Redi-Cash did anything but act in good faith. There appears to have been nothing that would have put Redi-Cash on notice that

Smith had a defense against the instrument. The fraud, deceit, or illegality of Bell's actions do not keep Redi-Cash from being an HDC.

Unless the instrument arising from a contract or transaction is, itself, made void by statute, the illegality defense under UCC 3-305 is not available to bar the claim of a holder in due course.

Therefore, Redi-Cash should be viewed as an HDC and actually has rights greater than Bell in regards to this negotiable instrument. Smith should be ordered to pay Redi-Cash the $1,500 that Redi-Cash paid for the instrument. Smith will have to seek recourse against Bell.

Answers to Practice Quiz

True/False

1. False   Any defenses to the enforcement of the contract that could have been raised against the assignor can also be raised against the assignee.
2. False   This describes what negotiation is.
3. False   An instrument can be converted from order paper to bearer paper and vice versa..
4. False   A blank indorsement does not specify a particular indorsee.
5. True   Indorsements that disclaim or limit liability on the instrument are called qualified indorsements.
6. True   A special qualified indorsement creates order paper that can be negotiated by indorsement.
7. True   A restrictive indorsement restricts the indorsee's rights in some manner.
8. True   An instrument that has two persons to whom it is payable of which the word and is expressed therein indicates that the instrument is to be paid jointly and as such, both persons' signatures are necessary to negotiate the instrument.
9. True   A virgule is a slash mark in between names, and as such the instrument is payable in the alternative.
10. False   If a person has notice that the instrument is defective, such as another person having a claim in the same instrument, then a person may not qualify as a holder in due course.
11. False   If payment were refused, it would be dishonored, not accepted.
12. False   A person cannot qualify as a holder in due course if he or she has notice that the instrument is defective in certain ways.
13. False   The test for good faith is an objective one, not a subjective one.
14. True   A holder in due course takes a negotiable instrument free of all claims and most defenses.
15. False   An indorser can indorse an instrument so as to make the indorsee his collecting agent.

Multiple Choice

16. C   Answer C is correct as a holder is an identified person who is in possession of an instrument payable to that person or a person in possession of an instrument that is payable to bearer. Answers A and B are incorrect as they each partially state the definition for a holder in due course. Answer D is incorrect as this states a fact with regard to an individual who is a holder in due course.
17. D   Answer D is the correct as answers A, B, and C all state what the transferee must be in order to be classified as a holder in due course.

18. A   Answer A is the correct answer as Megan does not meet the requirements of taking for value and performing the agreed-upon promise as is required in order to be a holder in due course. Answer B is incorrect as it makes no sense since third-party beneficiaries need not perform nor give value per se. Answer C is incorrect as it makes no sense. Answer D is incorrect based on the reasoning given above.

19. B   Answer B is the correct answer as time instruments that are not paid on their expressed due dates become overdue the next day and are indicative of some type of defect in payment. Answer A is incorrect because this is not a true statement. Answer C is incorrect as an instrument that is payable on demand is somewhat opposite of one where a due date is expressed as in the time instrument. Answer D is incorrect as making an instrument payable according to business practices refers to what may be used to determine a reasonable time for payment of other demand instruments as per UU 3-304.

20. D   Answer D is the correct answer as answers A, B, and C are all indorsements as it specifies to whom the indorser intends the instrument to be payable.

21. C   Answer C is the correct answer as it correctly states when an agent will not be held liable for signing on behalf of a principal. Answers A and B are incorrect as these merely state the types of signatures that are acceptable. Answer D is incorrect as the term ambiguous may infer liability of an agent who signs on behalf of a principal as it may cast doubt on the agent's capacity.

22. B   Answer B is the correct answer as primary liability is defined as absolute liability to pay a negotiable instrument, subject to certain real defenses. Answer A is incorrect as secondary liability occurs on a negotiable instrument when the party primarily liable on the instrument defaults and fails to pay with the instrument is due. Answer C is incorrect as there is no principal known as personal liability with respect to payment of negotiable instruments. Answer D is incorrect based on the reasoning given for answer C.

23. D   Answer D is the correct answer as no conditions are attached to the payment of funds. Answers A, B, and C are incorrect as all are conditions on the payment of the transaction.

24. D   Answer D is the correct answer as Hugo as the drawer is secondarily liable on the dishonored check. Answer A is incorrect as makers are usually the borrowers who make the promise to pay, which is not the case in this hypothetical. Answer B is incorrect as Coast Bank would be considered the drawee, as they are the financial institution upon which the check is written. Answer C makes no sense as Hugo cannot accept his own check if he has given it to Lamar Huff.

25. C   Answer C is the correct answer as the check can still be negotiated to other transferees. Answers A and B are false statements. Additionally, the type of restrictive indorsement as expressed in the question is rarely used. Answer D is incorrect for the reasons given above.

Short Answer

26. special
27. promise
28. the order in which they indorse the instrument
29. rights
30. a holder
31. order paper
32. two or more payees or indorsees
33. The person must be a holder of a negotiable instrument (1) for value; (2) in good faith; (3) without notice of defect; and (4) without notice of forgery, alteration, or irregularity.
34. 90 days
35. notice overdue
36. attorneys, executors of estates, real estate agents, etc. (answers will vary)
37. When an indorser deposits a check or other instrument for collection at a bank, this is known as a deposit or collection.
38. He or she is liable to the indorser for all losses that occur because of such noncompliance.
39. shelter principle
40. the holder only

Chapter 24

LIABILITY, DEFENSES, AND DISCHARGE

Chapter Overview

In the previous chapter, you learned about the various types of negotiable instruments as well as their creation and the ability to transfer the same. This chapter expands on the concept of commercial paper being a substitute for money by exploring warranty liability of the parties on negotiable instruments, as well as defenses that can be raised against the imposition of liability and what is involved in discharging liability.

Objectives

Upon completion of the exercises in this chapter, you should be able to:
1.   Discuss signature liability of makers, drawers, drawees, and acceptors.
2.   Discuss what primary liability is and who has primary liability.
3.   Differentiate between primary and secondary liability on negotiable instruments.
4.   Explain how an accommodation party comes about.
5.   Discuss what an agent's signature is and compare the difference between authorized and unauthorized signatures.
6.   Discuss transfer warranties as well as the liability of parties for breaching them.
7.   Discuss the presentment warranties and describe the liabilities for breaching them.
8.   Recognize universal (real) defenses that can be asserted against a holder in due course.
9.   Recognize personal defenses that cannot be asserted against a holder in due course.
10. Explain the Federal Trade Commission rule that prohibits the holder in due course rule in consumer transactions.
11. Explain how liability on a negotiable instrument is discharged.

Practical Application

This chapter will provide you with the understanding that you need to determine if you are a holder in due course of negotiable instruments. Further, you will be aware of any defenses that you may be able to assert, as well as what is involved in discharging liability.

Helpful Hints

This chapter's main focus is on signature, primary, and secondary liability as well as the role of an accommodation party and agent. Forged instruments as well as warranty, transfer, and presentment liability are also discussed in addition to the universal and personal defenses that may arise from the underlying transaction. It is important to realize why certain parties are discharged from liability on negotiable instruments. To assist your studies in this area, the study tips section has been organized so that you will be able to easily refer to the lists when analyzing the case studies or hypotheticals presented to you.

Study Tips

1. Signature Liability

a. A person cannot be held contractually liable on a negotiable instrument unless his or her signature appears on it.

b. A signature on an instrument identifies who is obligated to pay on it.
1. If a signature cannot be identified, parol evidence may be used.
2. Liability does not attach to bearer paper as no indorsement is needed.

c. Signers of instruments may sign in various capacities.
1. makers of notes and certificates of deposit
2. drawers of drafts and checks
3. drawees who accept checks and drafts
4. indorsers who indorse instruments
5. agents who sign on behalf of others
6. accommodation parties

d. Every party that signs a negotiable instrument (except qualified indorsers and agents) is either primarily or secondarily liable.

e. **Signature defined:**
1. The signature on a negotiable instrument can be
   a. any name, word, or mark used in lieu of a written signature
   b. any symbol that is handwritten, typed, printed, stamped, or made in almost any other manner; and
   c. executed or adopted by a party to authenticate the writing
2. Unauthorized signatures of a person on an instrument is effective as that person's signature.
   a. It is effective as the signature of the unauthorized signer in favor of an HDC.
   b. An unauthorized signature may be ratified.

2 Primary Liability

a. Makers of certificates of deposits and promissory notes have what is known as primary liability. The maker unconditionally promises to render the amount stipulated in the note when it is due.

b. No party is primarily liable when a draft or check is issued since these instruments are merely an order to pay.

3. Secondary Liability

a. Secondary liability attaches to the drawers of checks and drafts and unqualified indorsers of negotiable instruments.

b. This is easy to remember, as it's similar to a guarantor of a simple contract.

c. The drawer is obligated to pay if it is an unaccepted draft or check that is dishonored by the drawee or acceptor.

d. **Requirements for secondary liability**
1. The instrument must be properly presented for payment.
2. The instrument is dishonored.
3. Notice of the dishonor is given in a timely manner to the person who is to be secondarily liable on the instrument.

4. **Accommodation Party**

    a.   Defined – A party who signs an instrument and lends his or her credit (and name) to another

          party to the instrument.

    b.   Special notations:

        1. Guarantee of Payment – The accommodation party who signs an instrument is basically guaranteeing payment and is primarily liable on the instrument.

        2. Guarantee of Collection – This arises where the accommodation party guarantees collection rather than payment. Requirement of payment arises only if:

            a.   execution of judgment against the other party has been returned unsatisfied,

            b.   the other party is in an insolvency proceeding or is insolvent,

            c.   the other party is unable to be served with process, or

            d.   it is otherwise obvious that payment cannot be received from the other party. [UCC3-419(d)]

Agent's Signatures

A person may sign an instrument him- or herself or authorize a representative known as an agent to sign on his or her behalf. The representative is the agent and the represented person is the principal.

Authorized Signature

The authorized agent's signature binds the principal regardless if the agent signs the principal's name or the agent's own name.

Personal liability of the agent is dependent on how much information is revealed in the signature. If there is no ambiguity with a signature on behalf of a principal, then the agent has no liability.

If there is an ambiguity in an authorized agent's signature and the agent cannot demonstrate that the original parties to the contract had no intent of holding the agent liable, then the agent is liable. **However, there is an exception:** If the agent signs his or her name as the drawer of a check without indicating the agent's representative status and the check is payable from the account of the principal who is identified on the check, the agent is not liable on the check. [UCC 3-402(c)]

Unauthorized Signature

Defined: A signature made by a purported agent without authority from a purported principal.

How does this situation arise?

1) A person signs a negotiable instrument on behalf of a person for whom he or she is not an agent; or

2) An unauthorized agent exceeds the scope of his or her authority.

What liability does the purported agent have?

1) The purported agent is liable to any person who in good faith pays the instrument or takes it for value.

2) The agent is not liable if the principal ratifies the unauthorized signature.

Forged Instrument

Defined: The forged signature of a payee or holder on a negotiable instrument.

General Rule:
Where an indorsement on an instrument has been forged or is unauthorized, the general rule is that the loss falls on the party who first takes the forged instrument after the forgery.

Exceptions:
1) Where a drawer or maker bears the loss
2) Where an indorsement is forged

Imposter Rule

Impersonating a Payee:

If the imposter forges the indorsement of the named payee, the drawer or maker is liable on the instrument to any person who, in good faith, pays the instrument or takes it for value or for collection.

Posing as an Agent

The imposter rule is inapplicable if the wrongdoer poses as the agent of the drawer or maker.

Warranty Liability of Parties

Basic information – Warranty liability is placed upon a transferor irrespective of whether the transferor signed the instrument or not.

Two types of implied warranties

1. Transfer of warranties – As defined in your main text, "Any passage of an instrument other than its issuance and presentment for payment is considered a **transfer**." There are five warranties that are made when a person transfers a negotiable instrument for consideration. They are:
   a. The transfer of good title to the instrument or authorization to obtain acceptance or payment on behalf of one who does have good title.
   b. All signatures are authentic or authorized.
   c. The instrument has not been altered materially.
   d. No defenses of any party are applicable against the transferor.
   e. The transferor is unaware of any insolvency proceeding against the maker, the acceptor, or the drawer of an unaccepted instrument.
   f. **Special notation** – Instruments other than checks may disclaim transfer warranties with the use of an indorsement such as "without recourse" [UCC3-416 (c)].

2. Presentment Warranties – As defined in your main text, "Any person who presents a draft or check for payment or acceptance makes the following warranties to a drawee or acceptor who pays or accepts the instrument in good faith [UCC 3-417(a)]:
   a. The presenter has good title to the instrument or is authorized to obtain payment or acceptance of the person who has good title.
   b. The material has not been materially altered.
   c. The presenter has no knowledge that the signature of the maker or drawer is unauthorized.

Defenses

There are universal (real) and personal defenses that arise from the underlying transaction concerning the creation of negotiable instruments.

Universal (real) defenses	*versus*	Personal defenses
These can be raised against both holders and holders in due course. If one of these defenses is proven, neither holder nor holder in due course can recover on the instrument.		These can be raised against enforcement of a negotiable instrument by an ordinary holder.
Minority		Breach of contract
Extreme duress		Fraud in the inducement
Mental incapacity		Other personal defenses
Illegality		- mental illness
Discharge in bankruptcy		- illegality of a contract
Fraud in the inception		- ordinary duress or undue influence UCC3-305(a)(ii)
Forgery		-discharge of an instrument by payment or cancellation [UCC 3-602 and 3-604]
Material alteration		

FTC Elimination of Holder in Due Course Status
Concerning Consumer Credit Transactions

The rule puts the holder of due course of a consumer credit contract on the same level as an assignee of a simple contract. The result is the holder of due course of a consumer credit instrument is subject to all of the defenses and claims of the consumer.

This rule applies to consumer credit transactions that includes a promissory note, the buyer signs an installment sales contract that contains a waiver of defenses clause, and the seller arranges consumer financing with a third-party lender.

Discharge

There are several rules that are specified by the UCC on when and how certain parties are discharged from liability on negotiable instruments. The three main ways that will relieve the parties from liability are:
- By payment of the instrument
- By cancellation
    - by any manner or
    - by destroying or mutilating a negotiable instrument with the intent of getting rid of the obligation.
- By impairment of the right of recourse which is accomplished by
    - releasing an obligor from liability or
    - surrendering collateral without the consent of the parties who would benefit by it.

Refresh Your Memory

The following exercise will enable you to refresh your memory on the rules and principles presented to you in this chapter. Read each question twice and place your answer in the blanks provided. Review the chapter material for any question you miss or are unable to remember.

1. What can act as a signature on a negotiable instrument? _____
    _____

2. What type of liability do makers of promissory notes and certificates of deposit have?
    _____

3. A draft or a check is an _____ from a _____ to pay the instrument to a _____
    (or other holder) according to its terms.

4. Acceptance of a draft occurs when the drawee writes the word _____ across the face
    of the draft.

5. Secondary liability is similar to a _____ of a simple contract.

6. What type of liability do unqualified indorsers have? _____ liability.

7. An accommodation party may sign an instrument guaranteeing either _____ or
    _____.

8. A demand for acceptance or payment of an instrument made upon the maker, acceptor,
    drawee, or other payor by or on behalf of the holder is known as _____.

9. When an instrument has been presented for payment and payment has been refused, it is
    _____.

10. A party who signs an instrument for the purpose of lending his or her name (and credit)
    to another party to the instrument is the _____party.

11. When is an accommodation party secondarily liable? _____
    _____

12. A person who has been authorized to sign a negotiable instrument on behalf of another person is an _____.

13. A person who authorizes an agent to sign a negotiable instrument on his or her behalf is known as a _____.

14. A signature that is made by a purported agent without authority from the purported principal is an _____ signature.

15. Liability on a negotiable instrument that is imposed on a party only when the party primarily liable on the instrument defaults and fails to pay the instrument when due is known as _____ _____.

Critical Thought Exercise

Sally Knapp made out a check to Harold Dodd of Dodd Electrical for $1,000 as a partial payment for electrical work in her kitchen. When it was time for Dodd to begin his work, he did not appear, nor could Ms. Knapp locate him. Knapp immediately ordered her bank to stop payment on the check. Dodd had already cashed the check at Quik-Cash. When the check was returned to Quik-Cash marked "payment stopped by account holder," Quik-Cash was contacted by an attorney for Knapp who informed Quik-Cash that the plumber did not have a license and that engaging in a contracting trade without a license was a crime. Therefore the contract was void and his client would not honor the check.

As manager of Quik-Cash, will you commence suit against Knapp to collect the amount of the check?

Answer:

_____
_____
_____
_____
_____
_____
_____
_____
_____
_____
_____
_____
_____

Practice Quiz

True/False

1. ___ An unauthorized signature may not be ratified. [p. 357]

2. ___ Signature liability does not attach to bearer paper because no indorsement is needed. [p. 356]

3. ___ A secondarily liable party cannot be compelled to accept or pay an instrument unless proper notice of dishonor has been given. [p. 359]

4. ___ A debtor cannot seek payment on the instrument directly from the accommodation maker without first seeking payment from the maker. [p. 359]

5. ___ Universal defenses are also called personal defenses. [p. 363]

6. ___ A person who has been authorized to sign a negotiable instrument on behalf of another person is a principal. [p. 360]

7. ___ Signature liability refers to an individual's contractual liability on a negotiable instrument and whether or not his or her signature appears on it. [pp. 356-357]

8. ___ The return of an instrument given to a bank for collection is sufficient notice of dishonor. [p. 359]

9. ___ The signature on a negotiable instrument can only be by name. [p. 357]

10. ___ A holder in due course takes an instrument free from personal defenses but not universal defenses. [p. 363]

11. ___ An agent has no liability if the signature shows unambiguously that it is made on behalf of a principal who is identified in the instrument. [p. 360]

12. ___ Personal defenses cannot be raised against a holder in due course. [p. 365]

13. ___ Fraud in the inducement is not a personal defense that is effective against a holder in due course. [p. 365]

14. ___ Forgery is a real defense to the payment of a negotiable instrument. [p. 364]

15. ___ Discharge in bankruptcy is a personal defense against the enforcement of a negotiable instrument by a holder or a holder in due course. [p. 364]

Multiple Choice

16. Which of the following is one of the most common defenses raised by a party to a
     negotiable instrument? [p. 365]
     a. lack of notice of forgery
     b. violation of the maker's constitutional right to enter into a contract
     c. breach of contract
     d. none of the above

17. When referring to an instrument that has been fraudulently and materially altered, what is
     considered to be a material alteration? [p. 364]
     a. the addition to any part of a signed instrument
     b. the removal of any part of a signed instrument
     c. making changes in the number or relations of the parties
     d. all of the above

18. Which of the following is not a universal defense to the payment of a negotiable
     instrument? [p. 365]
     a. mental incapacity
     b. illegality
     c. fraud in the inducement
     d. all of the above

19. What sorts of things does the court ask about prior to allowing the defense of fraud in the
     inception regarding the payment of a negotiable instrument? [p. 364]
     a. a person's age
     b. a person's experience
     c. a person's education
     d. all of the above

20. Signers of instruments include [p. 356]
     a. drawers of drafts.
     b. drawees who certify checks.
     c. agents who sign on behalf of others.
     d. all of the above.

21. An agent has no personal liability on an instrument he or she signs on behalf of a principal
     if the signature shows [p. 360]
     a. a symbol.
     b. a mark.
     c. unambiguously that it is made on behalf of a principal who is identified in the
         instrument.
     d. ambiguously that it is made on behalf of a principal who is identified in the instrument.

22. Absolute liability to pay a negotiable instrument, subject to certain real defenses is known
     as [p. 357]
     a. secondary liability.
     b. primary liability.
     c. personal liability.
     d. real liability.

23. Liability on a negotiable instrument that is imposed on a party only when the party primarily liable on the instrument defaults and fails to pay the instrument when due is referred to as [p 358]
    a. indorser's liability.
    b. secondary liability.
    c. primary liability.
    d. none of the above.

24. Hugo draws a check on Coast Bank "payable to the order of Lamar Huff." When Lamar presents the check for payment, Coast Bank refuses to pay it. Lamar can collect the amount of the check from Hugo because Hugo is [p. 358]
    a. the maker.
    b. the drawee.
    c. the person who ratified the check.
    d. the drawer.

25. When referring to the imposter rule, who is being impersonated? [p. 361]
    a. the payee
    b. the payor
    c. the principal
    d. the agent

Short Answer

26. Who isn't primarily or secondarily liable on a negotiable instrument that they sign? _____ [p. 356]

27. What does a signature in the lower right corner of a check indicate? _____ _____ [p. 356]

28. What does a signature in the lower right corner of a promissory note indicate? _____ _____ [p. 356]

29. When is a check considered to be accepted? _____ _____ [p. 357]

30. What order are indorsers liable to one another on an instrument? _____ _____ [p. 358]

31. How may a drawer disclaim all liability of a draft? [p. 358]
    _____
    _____

32. What can an accommodation party who pays an instrument recover? _____ _____ [p. 359]

33. When must a bank give notice of a dishonor of an instrument? _____ _____ [p. 359]

34. When doesn't the imposter rule apply? _____
    _____

35. What is a transfer? _____
_____[p. 362]

36. What type of instrument cannot be disclaimed? _____[p. 362]

37. What can be recovered for breach of the presentment warranty? _____
_____[p. 363]

38. What presentment warranties exist when a person presents a draft or check for payment or acceptance? _____[p. 363]

39. What is primary liability? _____
[p. 357]

40. What are the two implied warranties with respect to negotiable instruments?
_____ and _____[p. 362]

Answers to Refresh Your Memory

1. any name, word, or mark used in lieu of a written signature; also, any symbol that is handwritten, typed, printed, stamped, or made in almost any other manner and executed or adopted by a party to authenticate a writing [p. 357]
2. primary liability [p. 357]
3. order, drawer, payee [p. 357]
4. accepted across the face of the draft [p. 357]
5. guarantor [p. 358]
6. secondary [p. 358]
7. payment collection [p. 359]
8. presentment [p. 359]
9. dishonored [p. 359]
10. accommodation [p. 359]
11. When he or she is guaranteeing collection rather than payment of an instrument. [p. 360]
12. agent [p. 360]
13. principal [p. 360]
14. unauthorized [p. 361]
15. secondary liability [p. 356]

Critical Thought Exercise Model Answer

A holder of a negotiable instrument is a holder in due course (HDC) pursuant to UCC 3-302 if he or she takes the instrument (1) for value; (2) in good faith; and (3) without notice that it is overdue, that it has been dishonored, that any person has a defense against it or claim to it, or that the instrument contains unauthorized signatures, alterations, or is so irregular or incomplete as to call into question its authenticity. Quik-Cash gave value for the instrument when they cashed it for Dodd. The UCC defines good faith as "honesty in fact and the observance of reasonable commercial standards of fair dealing." UCC 3-103(4). It is immaterial whether the transferor acted in good faith. There is nothing in the facts to show that Redi-Cash did anything but act in good faith. There appears to have been nothing that would have put Redi-Cash on notice that Knapp had a defense against the instrument. The fraud, deceit, or illegality of Dodd's actions do not keep Quik-Cash from being an HDC.

Unless the instrument arising from a contract or transaction is, itself, made void by statute, the illegality defense under UCC 3-305 is not available to bar the claim of a holder in due course.

Therefore, Quik-Cash should be viewed as an HDC and actually has rights greater than Dodd in regards to this negotiable instrument. Knapp should be ordered to pay Quik-Cash the $1,000 that Quik-Cash paid for the instrument. Knapp will have to seek recourse against Dodd.

Answers to Practice Quiz

True/False

1. False   An unauthorized signature may be ratified.
2. True   Liability does not attach to bearer paper because no indorsement is needed.
3. True   A secondarily liable party cannot be compelled to accept or pay an instrument unless proper notice of dishonor has been given.
4. False   The debtor can seek payment on the instrument directly from the accommodation maker without first seeking payment from the maker.
5. False   Universal defenses are called real defenses.
6. False   A person who has been authorized to sign a negotiable instrument on behalf of another person is an agent not a principal.
7. True   Signature liability is known as contract liability.
8. True   Return of an instrument given to a bank for collection is sufficient notice of dishonor.
9. False   A signature on a negotiable instrument may be by word, name, mark, or any symbol that is handwritten, stamped, typed, or otherwise affixed.
10. True   A holder in due course or a holder through a holder in due course takes the instrument free from personal defenses but not universal defenses.
11. True   The agent has no liability if the signature shows unambiguously that it is made on behalf of a principal who is identified in the instrument.
12. True   Personal defenses cannot be raised against a holder in due course.
13. False Fraud in the inducement is a personal defense that is not effective against a holder in due course.
14. True   Forgery is a universal defense to the payment of a negotiable instrument.
15. False Discharge in bankruptcy is a universal (not a personal) defense against the enforcement of a negotiable instrument by a holder in due course.

Multiple Choice

16. C   Answer C is correct as breach of contract is one of the most common defenses raised by a party to a negotiable instrument. Answer A is incorrect as it makes no sense that a forger would give notice of a forgery. Answer B is incorrect as it is not one of the most common defenses raised by a party to a negotiable instrument if even a defense at all. Answer D is incorrect for the reasons given above.
17. D   Answer D is correct as answers A, B, and C all are considered to be material alterations of an instrument.
18 C   Answer C is the correct answer as fraud in the inducement is a personal not a universal defense. Answers A and B are both incorrect as they are universal (real) defenses. Answer D is incorrect for the reasons given above.
19. D   Answer D is correct, as the court considers all of the factors given in answers A, B, and C.

20. D   Answer D is the correct answer as answers A, B, and C state all who may be signers of instruments.

21. C   Answer C is the correct answer as it correctly states when an agent will not be held liable for signing on behalf of a principal. Answers A and B are incorrect as these merely state the types of signatures that are acceptable. Answer D is incorrect as the term ambiguous may infer liability of an agent who signs on behalf of a principal as it may cast doubt on the agent's capacity.

22. B   Answer B is the correct answer as primary liability is defined as absolute liability to pay a negotiable instrument, subject to certain real defenses. Answer A is incorrect as secondary liability occurs on a negotiable instrument when the party primarily liable on the instrument defaults and fails to pay with the instrument is due. Answer C is incorrect as there is no principal known as personal liability with respect to payment of negotiable instruments. Answer D is incorrect based on the reasoning given for answer C.

23. B   Answer B is the correct answer as secondary liability refers to liability on a negotiable instrument that is imposed on a party only when the party primarily liable on the instrument defaults and fails to pay the instrument when due. Answer A is incorrect as indorsers are secondarily liable on negotiable instruments that they indorse. Answer C is incorrect as primary liability is absolute liability to pay a negotiable instrument, subject to certain real defenses. Answer D is incorrect for the reasons stated above.

24. D   Answer D is the correct answer as Hugo as the drawer is secondarily liable on the dishonored check. Answer A is incorrect as makers are usually the borrowers who make the promise to pay, which is not the case in this hypothetical. Answer B is incorrect, as Coast Bank would be considered the drawee, as they are the financial institution upon which the check is written. Answer C makes no sense as Hugo cannot accept his own check if he has given it to Lamar Huff.

25. D   Answer D is the correct answer as a presentment is a demand for acceptance or payment of an instrument made upon the maker, acceptor, drawee, or other behalf of the holder. Answer A is incorrect as a notice of dishonor refers to the formal act of letting the party with secondary liability to pay a negotiable instrument know that the instrument has been dishonored. Answer B is incorrect as an unqualified indorser is someone who is secondarily liable on negotiable instruments that they indorse. Answer C is incorrect as the red light doctrine refers to a holder having notice of an unauthorized signature or an alteration of an instrument or any adverse claim against or defense to its payment.

Short Answer

26.   qualified indorsers and agents
27.   that the signer is the drawer of the check
28.   when it is certified by a bank
29.   payable on demand
30.   Indorsers are liable to each other in the order in which they indorsed the instrument.
31.   by drawing the instrument "without recourse"
32.   reimbursement from the accommodated party and enforce the instrument against him or her
33.   before midnight of the next banking day following the day that presentment is made.
34.   If the wrongdoer poses as the agent of the drawer or maker, the imposter rule does not apply.
35.   Any passage of an instrument other than its issuance and presentment for payment is considered a transfer.
36   checks

37.   damages which are limited to the amount paid by the drawee less the amount the drawee received or is entitled to receive from the drawer because of the payment plus expenses and interest

38.   (1) The presenter has good title to the instrument or is authorized to obtain payment or acceptance of the person who has good title; (2) The instrument has not been materially altered; and (3) The presenter has no knowledge that the signature of the maker or drawer is unauthorized.

39.   absolute liability to pay a negotiable instrument subject to certain defenses

40.   transfer and presentment warranties

Chapter 25

CHECKS, BANKING, AND WIRE TRANSFERS

Chapter Overview

This chapter is primarily concerned with checks, the most common form of negotiable instrument. In this chapter you will learn about several different kinds of checks as well as the process involved regarding payment and collection of checks through the banking system. Additionally, this chapter explores the duties as well as liabilities of banks and other parties in the collection process along with electronic fund transfers.

Objectives

Upon completion of the exercises in this chapter, you should be able to:
1. Identify the differences among a cashier's check, certified checks, and traveler's checks.
2. Describe the system of processing and collecting checks through the banking system.
3. Explain the effect of postdated and stale checks.
4. Identify when a bank participates in a wrongful dishonor of a check.
5. Explain the liability of parties when a signature or indorsement on a check is forged.
6. Describe the liability of parties when a check has been altered.
7. Explain a bank's midnight deadline for deciding whether or not to dishonor a check.
8. Discuss the requisites of the Expedited Funds Availability Act.
9. Explain the electronic fund transfer system.
10. Explain the term wire transfer and discuss the main provisions of Article 4A of the Uniform Commercial Code.

Practical Application

Whether you are part of a large or small business, or personally transfer funds and pay bills by way of checks or electronic transfers, an understanding of checks and how they are processed is crucial. Since almost everyone will have the opportunity to either have a checking account or purchase one of the various types of checks, this chapter will prove to be an invaluable resource to those who study it. It will provide insight into the banking procedures involving payment and collection of checks as well as assist you in knowing what the banks' duties and other parties' duties and liabilities are in the collection process. Further, you will gain useful information concerning electronic fund transfers.

Helpful Hints

This chapter will be relatively easy for most individuals to learn, since much of what is presented has already been experienced in most individuals' everyday personal and business affairs. In addition to this basic knowledge is an examination of areas where a bank, business, or individual may be liable for improper use or processing of a check. There may be a few terms that you recognize by definition and other terms that you will want to review a little more carefully. Examples of these types of terms include but are not limited to such words as stale checks, incomplete checks, deferred posting, provisional posting, etc. This chapter's high applicability makes it a very interesting learning experience.

Study Tips

Checks

Explained: A substitute for money and also a record-keeping device.
Special Notation: They do not serve a credit function.

The Banking Relationship: Deposits

The customer is the creditor.
The bank is the debtor.
A principal-agent relationship may also be formed whereby the customer is the principal ordering the bank to collect or pay on the check. The bank in turn is the agent that is obligated to follow the customer as principal's order.

The Basics of Banking

Ordinary Checks When a customer goes to a bank, fills out the proper forms along with a signature card, followed by a deposit, the bank issues checks to him or her. Thereafter, the customer uses the checks for his or her purchases. The checks are presented to the bank and paid provided the drawer's signature matches the signature card.

Parties to a Check Drawer – This is the customer with a checking account.
Drawee – This is the bank (or payor) at which the check is drawn.
Payee – The one to whom the check is written.

Indorsement This refers to the holder or payee signing the back of the check. The payee is the indorser and the person to whom the check is indorsed is the indorsee.

Point-of-Sale Terminals The customer's account is immediately debited for the amount of the purchase by using a bank issued debit card to make a purchase.

Direct Deposits and Withdrawals The customer's bank and the payee's bank must belong to the same clearinghouse in order to provide the service of paying recurring payments and recurring deposits.

Pay-by-Internet Customers may pay bills from their account using their PIN number and account number, the amount of the bill to be paid, and the account number of the payee.

Special Checks: Bank checks are special checks. There are certified checks, cashier's checks, and traveler's checks.

Certified checks – With this type of check, the bank agrees in advance to accept the check when it is presented for payment and pay the check out of funds set aside from the customer's account. These types of checks are payable at any time from when they are issued. The bank writes or stamps the word *certified* across the face of an ordinary check thereby certifying it. The date, amount being certified, and the individual certifying the check also are placed on the check. Payment may not be stopped on a certified check.

Cashier's check – This is a bank-issued check where the customer has paid the bank the amount of the check and a fee. The bank guarantees the payment of the check. The bank acts as the drawer and the drawee with the holder as payee. The bank debits its own account when the check is presented.

Traveler's checks – This type of check is a two-party instrument where the bank who issues it is both the drawer and the drawee. An interesting notation about this type of check is that it has two signature lines, one for the purchaser to sign when he or she purchases the checks and the other for the purchaser to sign when he or she uses the check for purchases. This type of check is especially popular among travelers as it serves as a safe substitute for cash, and it is not negotiable until it is signed a second time.

Honoring Checks   The customer of a bank agrees to keep sufficient funds in the account to cover any checks written. If the customer keeps his or her end of this implied agreement, the bank is under a duty to honor the check and charge the customer's (or drawer's) account for whatever amount(s) the check(s) were written for.

Stale Checks   A stale check is one that has been outstanding for more than six months. Under UCC 4-404, the bank is not obligated to pay on a stale check. If the bank does pay it, it may also in good faith charge the drawer's account.

Incomplete Checks   If a drawer fails to provide information on a check, the holder may complete the information and the bank may charge the customer's account the amount of the completed amount. The exception to this is if the bank receives notice that the completion was improper.

Death or Incompetence of a Drawer   Checks may be paid against the accounts of deceased customers on or prior to the date of death for 10 days after the date of death. With regard to incompetent customers, the checks may be paid against their accounts until the bank has actual knowledge of the condition and has had a reasonable chance to act on the information given.

Stop Payment Order   This is an order by a drawer of a check to the payor bank not to pay or certify a check. It may be accomplished orally or in writing; however, if it is oral, the order is good for only fourteen days. If it is in writing, the order is good for six months, and may be renewed in writing for additional six-month periods.

Overdrafts	If a customer does not have sufficient funds in his or her account to cover the amount, the payor bank may either dishonor the check or honor the check and create an overdraft in the drawer's account. In the event of a dishonor, the payor bank notifies the drawer of the dishonor and returns the check to the holder marked insufficient funds. If the holder resubmits the check and there still are insufficient funds in the customer's account, then the holder may seek recourse against the drawer.
Wrongful Dishonor	When the bank fails to honor a check where there are sufficient funds in the drawer's account to pay a properly payable check, it is liable for wrongful dishonor. The bank is liable to the drawer for damages that were proximately caused by the dishonor along with consequential damages and damages that may have resulted from criminal prosecution.

Forged and Altered Checks

Forged signature of the drawer:	The bank is under a duty to verify the drawer's signature by matching the signature on the check with that of the signature card on file at the bank.
	Impact of a forged signature – The instrument is inoperative. The bank cannot charge the customer's account if it pays a check over a forged signature. The bank's recourse is against the party who presented the check provided he or she was not aware of the unauthorized signature. The forger is liable on the check if he or she can be found.
Altered checks:	An unauthorized change in the check that modifies a legal obligation of a party is an altered check. The check may be dishonored by the bank if it discovers the alteration. If an altered check is paid by the bank, the bank may charge the drawer's account for the original tenor (amount) of the check, but not the altered amount.
	The warranty of presentment applies here especially if there has been an alteration in a chain of collection. Each party in the chain may collect from the preceding transferor based on a breach of this warranty.

The Collection Process

The collection process is ruled by Article 4 of the UCC. When an individual receives a check, he or she may go to the drawer's bank or to his or her own bank (known as the **depository bank**). The depository bank must present the check to the payor bank for collection. Banks not classified as a payor or depository bank are **intermediary banks.**

The Federal Reserve System

The Federal Reserve System helps banks to collect on checks. Member banks may submit paid checks to the Federal Reserve Bank for payment. Member banks pay the federal reserve to debit and credit their accounts and to show collection and payment of checks.

Deferred Posting

Deferred posting applies to all banks. This refers to a daily cutoff for posting checks or deposits. Weekends and holidays do not count as business days unless all of the bank's functions are carried on as usual on those days.

Provisional Credits

When a collecting bank gives credit to a check in the collection process prior to its final settlement. Provisional credits may be reversed if the check does not "clear."

Final Settlement

A check is deemed finally settled if the payor bank pays the check in cash, settles for the check without having the right to revoke the settlement, or fails to dishonor the check within certain time periods. UCC 4-215(a)

If the drawer and holder have accounts at the same bank, then the check is called an **"on us"** item. The check is considered paid if the bank fails to dishonor the check by business on the second banking day following the receipt of the check.

If the drawer and holder have accounts at different banks, the check is an **"on them"** item. Each bank must take action prior to its **midnight deadline** following the banking day it received an "on them" check for collection. UCC 4-104(a)(10)

A deposit of money becomes available for withdrawal at the opening of the next banking day following the deposit. UCC 4-215 (a)

Four Legals That Prevent Payment of a Check

1. Receipt of notice of customer's death, bankruptcy, and adjudication of incompentcy.

2. Receipt of court order freezing the customer's account.

3. Receipt of a stop-payment order from the drawer.

4. The payor bank's exercise of its right of setoff against the customer's account.

Failure to Examine Bank Statements in a Timely Manner

Generally banks send monthly statements to their customers. If this does not occur, banks must provide adequate information to allow the customer to be aware of which checks were paid and when and for what amount. If the checks are not given back to the customer, then the bank must keep the checks or copies for seven years.

Customer's duty – To examine the statements promptly and with reasonable care. If an error or forgery is present, the customer must promptly notify the bank.

Liability of Collecting Banks for Their Own Negligence

The collecting bank owes a duty to use ordinary care in presenting and sending a check for collection. A bank is liable only for losses caused by its own negligence. UCC 4-202

Commercial Wire Transfers

A commercial wire transfer involves the transferring of money over one or both of the two main wire systems, the Federal Reserve wire transfer network and the New York Clearing House Interbank Payments System.

Article 4A of the UCC governs wholesale wire transfers. It only applies to commercial electronic fund transfers.

Security procedures that are commercially reasonable should be established.

Refresh Your Memory

The following exercise will enable you to refresh your memory on the rules and principles presented to you in this chapter. Read each question twice and place your answer in the blanks provided. Review the chapter material for any question you miss or are unable to remember.

1. Checks are the most common form of _____.

2. Upon making a _____ into a bank, a creditor-debtor relationship is formed.

3. A _____-_____ relationship is created if a deposit is a check that the bank must collect for the customer or the customer writes a check against his or her account.

4. What types of rules and principles does Article 4 of the UCC regulate? _____ _____

5. Article 4A of the UCC establishes rules that regulate _____ _____.

6. What is a check? _____

7. The _____ is the party to whom a check is written.

8. The _____ is the indorser and the person to whom the check is indorsed is the _____.

9. The _____ on which the check is drawn is the drawee.

10. Give three examples of bank checks. _____, _____, and _____.

11. When a check is certified, the word certified is stamped across the face of the check and the certification also contains the _____, the amount being certified, and the _____ of the person at the bank who certifies the check.

12. _____ are a form of check sold by banks and other issuers that are issued without a named payee and the payee's name is added by the purchaser when they use the check for goods or services.

13. The _____ _____ ____ is a rule that allows banks to fix an afternoon hour of 2:00 P.M. or later as a cutoff hour for the purpose of processing items.

14. An altered check is a check that has been altered without _____ and thus modifies the legal obligation of a party.

15. A forged instrument is a check with a forged drawer's _____ on it.

Critical Thought Exercise

Dave Austin of Austin Imports is an antique dealer who often makes purchases without sufficient funds in his account because he must often act quickly to purchase a one-of-a-kind item before another dealer can take advantage of a very profitable sale price. Austin often postdates checks for the purchases of furniture, art, rugs, and other items that he resells. Austin has a very good relationship with Everglades Bank in Miami, where his main studio is located. The operations officer of Everglades Bank knows that Austin uses postdated checks for purchases approximately 50-75 times per year out of a total of 1,200 checks written on his account.

When the operations officer at Everglades Bank took a position with another bank, four postdated checks totaling $58,000 were negotiated before the written date, causing 47 other checks to be dishonored.

If Austin sues Everglades Bank to recover incidental and consequential damages for wrongful dishonor, will he prevail?

Answer:

_____
_____
_____
_____
_____
_____
_____
_____
_____
_____
_____
_____

Practice Quiz

True/False

1. ____ Checks act as a substitute for money but do not serve a credit function. [p. 372]

2. ____ A drawer is the customer who maintains the checking account and draws checks against the account. [p. 373]

3. ____ Cashier's checks are issued without a named payee. [p. 376]

4. ____ A traveler's check is not a negotiable instrument until signed a second time. [p. 376]

5. ____ The bank does not have to pay on a stale check if it has been outstanding for more than six months. [p. 377]

6. ____ Dave owes Lou $250, and draws a check payable to Lou on Main Bank. Dave signs the check but omits to fill in the amount of the check. Lou fraudulently fills in "$2,500" and presents the check to Main Bank, which pays it. Main Bank may charge Dave's account $2,500. [p. 377]

7. ____ Checks may be paid against the accounts of deceased customers. [p. 378]

8. ____ A stop-payment order on a check may not be done orally. [p. 378]

9. ____ If Mary does not have enough money in her account when a properly presented check is presented for payment, the bank may not dishonor the check and must honor the check and create an overdraft in Mary's account. [p. 379]

10. ____ If Newville Bank does not honor a check when there are sufficient funds in Gill's account to pay a properly payable check, the Newville Bank will be liable for wrongful dishonor, but is not liable for consequential damages. [p. 379]

11. ____ A bank is under a duty to verify the drawee's signature when a check is presented for payment. [p. 380]

12. ____ If a payor bank pays on an altered check, it can charge the drawer's account for the original tenor of the check but not for the altered amount. [p. 380]

13. ____ A payer bank is the bank where the payee or holder has an account. [p. 381]

14. ____ An intermediary bank is a bank in the collection process that is not the depository or payer bank. [p. 381]

15. ____ Under the deferred posting rule, any check or deposit of money received after the cutoff hour is treated as received on the next banking day. [p. 382]

16. ____ An "on us" item refers to the fact that both the drawer and the payee or holder have accounts at the same bank. [p. 382]

17. ____ An "on them" item refers to the fact that a drawer and the payee or holder have accounts at different banks. [p. 382]

18. ____ A deposit of money to an account becomes available for withdrawal immediately following the deposit. [p. 383]

19. ____ The bank's receipt of notice that a customer has died still allows the bank to pay or certify checks drawn on the account on or prior to the date of death and for 10 days after the date of death. [p. 378]

20. ___ When a bank does not return checks to a customer, the bank must retain either the original check or a copy for seven years. [p. 383]

21. ___ One of the benefits of using wire transfers is speed. [p. 384]

22. ___ Article 4A applies to commercial and consumer electronic fund transfers. [p. 384]

23. ___ Debit cards may be used only if the merchant has a point-of-sale terminal. [p. 374]

24. ___ Purchasers of traveler's checks must have an account at the issuing bank. [p. 376]

25. ___ If a bank fails to honor a check when there are sufficient funds in the customer's account to do so, the bank will be liable for wrongful dishonor. [p. 379]

Multiple Choice

26. Which of the following is not true with regard to checks? [p. 372]
    a. Checks act as a substitute for money.
    b. Checks are a good record-keeping device.
    c. Checks serve a credit function.
    d. Checks are the most common form of negotiable instrument.

27. Which of the following are examples of electronic fund transfer systems? [p. 374]
    a. automated teller machines
    b. point-of-sale terminals
    c. direct deposits and withdrawal
    d. all of the above

28. Which of the following is a type of check issued by a bank for which the customer has paid the amount of the check and a fee and the bank guarantees payment of the check? [p. 375]
    a. a cashier's check
    b. a traveler's check
    c. an automatic withdrawal check
    d. a certified check

29. A check that has been outstanding for more than six months is a [p. 377]
    a. cashier's check.
    b. stale check.
    c. dishonored check.
    d. certified check.

30. A stop-payment order is binding for six months if it is [p. 378]
    a. given orally.
    b. given in writing only.
    c. given in writing or given orally if the oral order is confirmed in writing within 14 days.
    d. none of the above.

31. The original amount for which the drawer wrote an altered check is called the [p. 380]
    a. original tenor.
    b. negotiated amount.
    c. forged indorsement.
    d. none of the above.

32. The drawer's failure to report a forged or altered check to the bank within _____ of receiving the bank statement and cancelled checks containing it relieves the bank of any liability for paying the instrument under UCC 4-406(3). [p. 381]
    a. 10 business days
    b. 60 calendar days
    c. six months
    d. one year

33. A bank must take proper action on a check to honor or dishonor it before midnight of the next banking day after receiving the check. This is called [p. 382]
    a. giving provisional credit.
    b. the midnight deadline.
    c. final settlement.
    d. the deferred posting rule.

34. What type of duty does a bank owe in presenting and sending a check for collection? [p. 384]
    a. It owes a duty to inspect.
    b. It owes a special duty of care
    c. It owes a duty to use ordinary care.
    d. It owes a higher duty of care.

35. What type of duty does a customer owe when determining if any payment was unauthorized due to alteration of a check or forged signature? [p. 383]
    a. The customer does not owe any duty whatsoever.
    b. The customer owes a duty to change banks.
    c. The customer owes a duty to promptly examine the statements and determine if payment was unauthorized.
    d. The customer owes a duty to notify the bank of its duty.

Short Answer

36. Article 3 of the UCC establishes the requisites for finding a _____ _____. [p. 372]

37. The checking account holder and writer of the check is the _____ of a check. [p. 373]

38. What does the bank process of certification involve? [p. 375] _____
    _____

39. A bank can be held liable for the amount of the check, expenses, and loss of interest resulting from nonpayment when they fail to honor a _____ check. [p. 375]

40. A bounced check is one that has been _____. [p. 379]

41. A forged instrument is a check with a forged _____ _____. [p.380]

42. An altered check is a check that has been altered without authorization that modifies the _____ _____ of the party. [p. 380]

43. When a collecting bank gives credit to a check in the collection process prior to its final settlement, they are extending _____ _____. [p. 382]

44. When a depository bank physically presents a check for payment at the payor bank instead of depositing an "on them" check for collection, this is called _____. [p. 383]

45. When is the process of posting considered to be complete? [p. 383] _____
_____

46. If Jim wants to write a postdated check to Sue, what must he do to accomplish this under the rules of UCC 4-401(c)? [p. 378] _____
_____

47. Bob, a customer of Louisiana Bank and Trust, passes away on January 1. What is the rule regarding the length of time that his bank may pay or certify checks drawn on his account? [p. 378] _____

48. An overdraft is _____.
[p. 379]

49. River Bank receives a $75,000 deposit from Sam Rich. If River Bank fails to file a Currency Transaction Report (CTR) in order to avoid the reporting requirements, what repercussions might it face for its negligence? [p. 379] _____
_____

50. A stop-payment order is _____. [p. 378]

Answers to Refresh Your Memory

1. negotiable instrument [p. 372]
2. deposit [p. 372]
3. principal-agent [p. 372]
4. It regulates bank deposits and collection procedures for checking accounts offered by commercial banks. [p. 372]
5. the creation and collection of and liability for wire transfers [p. 373]
6. The UCC 3-104(f) defines a check as "an order by the drawer bank to pay a specified sum of money from the drawer's checking account to the named payee (or holder)." [p. 373]
7. payee [p. 373]
8. payee, indorsee [p. 373]
9. bank [p. 373]
10. certified, cashiers, and travelers [p. 374]
11. date, title [p. 375]
12. Traveler's checks [p. 376]
13. deferred posting rule [p. 382]
14. authorization [p. 380]

15. signature [p. 380]

Critical Thought Exercise Model Answer

A bank may charge a postdated check against a customer's account as a demand instrument, unless the customer notifies the bank of the postdating in time to allow the bank to act on the notice before the bank commits itself to pay on the check. If the bank receives timely notice from the customer and nonetheless charges the customer's account before the date on the postdated check, the bank may be liable for any damages incurred by the customer as a result.

Everglades Bank had discussed the use of postdated checks with Austin and permitted his practice of postdating a significant number of checks each year. Everglades Bank will have a difficult time convincing a court that it was not on notice that postdated checks were being written by Austin. However, the UCC makes it clear that the customer must not only give notice that a postdated check has been issued, but must also describe the postdated check with reasonable certainty. Austin never contacted the bank to describe the checks with any certainty. He just relied upon the practice of a prior employee of the bank who examined his checks carefully before charging them to his account. Under the UCC, Everglades Bank has not received notice concerning the specific checks. Therefore, Austin should not prevail in a suit to recover damages caused by having the other 47 checks dishonored.

Answers to Practice Quiz

True/False

1. True   Checks only serve as substitutes for money and as record-keeping devices.
2. True   A payee is the party to whom the check is written. The drawee is the bank.
3. False Traveler's checks are issued without a named payee so that their holder may fill in the payee as he or she makes purchases.
4. True   The purchaser initially signs the traveler's check upon purchases of the same and then must sign the second blank when he or she uses the checks to purchase goods or services.
5. True   The bank is under no obligation to pay on a check that has been outstanding for more than six months.
6. True   Main Bank may in good faith make payment on a completed check and can charge Kami's account the $2,500 unless it has notice that the completion was improper.
7. True   The bank may pay or certify checks drawn on the deceased customer's account on or prior to the date of death for 10 days after the date of the death.
8. False An order to stop payment on a check may be accomplished in writing or orally.
9. False UCC 4-401(a) allows for the payor bank the option to either dishonor the check or honor a check and create an overdraft in the drawer's account if the drawer does not have enough money in his or her account when a properly payable check is presented for payment.
10. False Wrongful dishonor happens when there are sufficient funds in a drawer's account to pay a properly payable check, but the bank does not do so. As such the Newville Bank will be liable for wrongful dishonor and all consequential damages.
11. True A bank is under a duty to verify the drawer's signature when the drawer presents a check to the drawer bank for payment.
12. True The payor bank may charge the drawer's account for the original tenor of the check, but not the altered amount under UCC 3-407, 4-401(d)(1).
13. False The bank where the payee or holder has an account is the depository bank.

14. True   An intermediary bank is a bank in the collection process that is not the depository or payor bank.

15. True   The deferred posting rule allows banks to fix an afternoon hour of 2:00 P.M. or later as a cutoff hour for the purpose of processing items.

16. True   A check that is presented for payment where the depository bank is also the payor bank is an "on us" item.

17. True   When the drawer and payee or holder have accounts at different banks, this is referred to as an "on them" check.

18. False   A deposit of money to an account becomes available for withdrawal the next banking day following the deposit.

19. True   A bank may pay checks drawn against the deceased person's account on or before the date of death.

20. True   The bank must keep either the original checks or legible copies for seven years.

21. True   Most transfers are completed in the same day thereby being a great benefit when conducting business.

22. True   Article 4A governs wholesale wire transfers and applies only to commercial electronic fund transfers.

23. True   Debit cards may only be used if the merchant has a point-of-sale terminal.

24. False   Purchasers of traveler's checks do not necessarily have to have an account at the issuing bank.

25. True   If a customer has sufficient funds in his or her account and the bank fails to honor a check, it will be liable for wrongful dishonor.

Multiple Choice

26. C   Answer C is the correct answer as checks do not serve a credit function. Answers A, B, and D are incorrect as they all true statements with regard to checks.

27. D   Answer D is correct because each of these choices is a valid example of an electronic fund transfer system.

28. A   Answer A is the correct answer as a cashier's check can be purchased from a bank for a fee. The bank then guarantees payment of the check. Answer B is incorrect as traveler's checks are used instead of cash when people are on vacation or on other trips. Answer C is incorrect as once again, there is no such thing as an automatic withdrawal check. Answer D is incorrect because a certified check is one in which the bank agrees in advance to accept the check when it is presented for payment and pay the check out of funds set aside from the customer's account and either placed in a special certified check account or held in the customer's account.

29. B   Answer B is the correct answer as a stale check is one that has been outstanding for six months or more. Answer A is incorrect as a certified check is guaranteed for payment. Answer C is incorrect as a dishonored check lacks sufficient funds in the drawer's account to cover the check amount. Answer D is incorrect because the bank is certifying that the funds remain available from the bank's funds.

30. C   Answer C is correct because it states the two ways that a stop-payment order can become binding on the bank. Answer A is wrong because it does not account for an order in writing. Answer B is incorrect because it does not allow for the oral order with written confirmation. Choice D is incorrect because answer C is correct.

31. A   Answer A is the correct answer as original tenor translates to the original amount for which the drawer wrote the check. Answer B is incorrect because it is not a recognized banking term. Answer C is incorrect because it refers to a signature on a check that is forged. Answer D is incorrect for the reasons stated above.

32. D   Answer D is the correct answer as it states the correct time frame under the controlling UCC section. Answers A, B, and C state incorrect time frames under UCC 4-406(3).

33. B   Answer B is the correct answer as this correctly states the midnight deadline rule. Answer A is incorrect as it relates to giving credit to an account before the midnight deadline pending the bank's review of the item. Answer C is incorrect as it refers to the point in time where all banks in the collecting process have had their opportunity to dishonor the check and the provisional credit has firmed up. Answer D is incorrect as it relates to the cutoff time during a day for the purpose of processing items.

34. C   Answer C is the correct answer as the collecting bank owes a duty to use ordinary care in presenting and sending a check for collection as well as other banking actions in the collection process. Answer A is incorrect as the bank has no such duty with regard to its banking actions. Answer B is incorrect as the bank does not owe a special duty of care with regard to its banking actions in the collection process. Answer D is incorrect based on the reasoning given above.

35. C   Answer C is the correct answer as bank customers are under a duty to promptly examine their bank statements to determine if any payment was unauthorized due to alteration of a check or forged signature. Answer A is incorrect as this is an untrue statement. Answer B is incorrect as the duty to change banks is not a legally recognized duty. Answer D is incorrect as not only is it untrue, but customers normally do not let the bank know of its duty as the bank already knows that it has a duty of ordinary care.

Short Answer

36.   negotiable instrument
37.   drawer
38.   The bank process of certification involves the accepting bank writing or stamping the word certified on the ordinary check of an account holder and setting aside funds from the account to pay the check.
39.   cashier's check
40.   dishonored by a bank due to insufficient funds
41.   drawer's signature
42.   legal obligation
43.   provisional credit
44.   presentment across the counter
45.   It is considered to be complete when the responsible bank officer has made a decision to pay the check and the proper book entry has been made to charge the drawer's account the amount of the check.
46.   Jim must postdate the check to Sue to some date in the future. Also, Jim must give separate written notice to the bank describing the check with reasonable certainty and notifying the bank not to pay the check until the date on the check.
47.   Louisiana Bank and Trust may pay or certify checks drawn on Bob's account on or prior to the date of death for 10 days after the date of Bob's death.
48.   the amount of money a drawer owes a bank after it has paid a check despite insufficient funds in the drawer's account
49.   River Bank may be fined for negligent violations of the currency reporting requirements. Also, willful failure to file reports may subject River Bank to civil monetary penalties, charges of aiding and abetting the criminal activity, and prosecution for violating the money-laundering statutes.
50.   an order by a drawer of a check to the payor bank to not pay or certify a check

Chapter 26

CREDIT AND SECURITY INTERESTS
IN REAL PROPERTY

Chapter Overview

We depend upon credit for our economy to function. Consumers and businesses alike use credit to obtain goods and services. This chapter examines the rights of creditors and debtors under federal and state consumer protection laws. In this chapter, you will explore the repercussions of noncompliance with the recording statutes, as well as the foreclosure process in real estate. Further, you will learn about deficiency judgments, lender liability, and the difference between a surety and a guaranty arrangement. Finally, this chapter gives a good explanation of attachment, garnishment, and execution as well as the difference between a composition agreement and an assignment for the benefit of creditors.

Objectives

Upon completion of the exercises in this chapter, you should be able to:
1. Distinguish between unsecured credit versus secured credit.
2. Describe mortgages and deeds of trust.
3. Explain the repercussions of noncompliance with recording statutes.
4. Discuss how foreclosure comes about and how it is accomplished.
5. Explain what a deficiency judgment is and discuss the effects of an antidifficiency statute.
6. Discuss lender liability.
7. Explain material person's liens.
8. Discuss attachment, garnishment, and execution as they pertain to judgments.

Practical Application

This chapter will provide you with greater insight about the various types of credit along with security interests in real and personal property. Further, you will gain a better understanding of the available remedies associated with personal property transactions. Also, you will have a broader base of knowledge concerning surety and guaranty arrangements as well as remedies associated with the collection of debts.

Helpful Hints

Many items are purchased on credit. The best way to approach this chapter is by differentiating between the main terms such as secured versus unsecured credit, real versus personal property, and surety arrangement versus a guaranty arrangement. Once you have a grasp of these main terms, the remedies that are available become easier to understand and learn. The exercises that follow, as well as the critical thinking exercises located at the end of the chapter in your main text, are very helpful in solidifying the concepts you should be familiar with.

Study Tips

Basic Vocabulary

Debtor – The borrower in a credit transaction.
Creditor – The lender in a credit transaction.

Types of credit:
Unsecured – Credit that does not need any collateral to protect the debt.
Secured – Credit that does need collateral to secure the payment of the loan.

Deficiency Judgment – When a debtor has insufficient collateral to cover the debt, the court will issue an order allowing the creditor to recover other property or income from the defaulting debtor.

Personal Property – This involves tangible property such as furniture, automobiles, and jewelry, and intangible property such as intellectual property and securities.

Vocabulary Relating to Real Property

Mortgage – A property owner borrows money from a creditor who thereafter uses a deed as a means of security (collateral) to secure the repayment of the loan.

Mortgagor – This is the owner-debtor in a mortgage transaction.

Mortgagee – This is the creditor in a transaction involving a mortgage.

Note – A legal instrument that is proof of the borrower's debt to the lender.

Deed of Trust – A legal instrument that evinces the creditor's security interest in the debtor's property that is pledged as collateral.

Land Sales Contract – The transfer and sale of real property in accordance with a land sales contract whereby the owner of the real property agrees to sell the property to a buyer, who assents to pay the asking price to the owner-seller over a stated, agreed period of time. The loan is termed as *"carrying the paper."* If the purchaser defaults, the seller may claim a forfeiture and retake possession of the property. The right of redemption is allowed in many states.

Recording Statute – Law that requires the mortgage or deed of trust to be recorded in the county recorder's office of the county where the real property is located.

Material Person's Lien – When an individual provides contracting or a service toward improvement of real property, their investments are protected by statutory law that allow them to file a material person's lien (also referred to as a mechanic's lien) against the improved real property.

Remedies

Foreclosure – A legal procedure whereby the mortgagee can declare the entire debt due and payable if a debtor defaults on his or her loan.

Deficiency Judgments – As stated above, some states allow a mortgagee to bring a separate legal action to recover a deficiency from the mortgagor.

Antideficiency Statute – Many states prohibit deficiency judgments on mortgages, especially those involving residential property.

Right of Redemption – Many state laws follow the common law, which gives the mortgagor the right to redeem his or her real property after default and before foreclosure. The mortgagor must pay the entire debt including principal, interest, and other costs born by the mortgagee as a result of the mortgagor's default. The mortgagor will obtain title free and clear upon redeeming the property. *Note,* a majority of states allow any party holding an interest in the property may redeem the property during the redemption period.

Refresh Your Memory

The following exercise will enable you to refresh your memory on the rules and principles presented to you in this chapter. Read each question twice and place your answer in the blanks provided. Review the chapter material for any question you miss or are unable to remember.

1. If Henry uses his credit card to purchase a table from Western Furniture Store, he is the _____ and Western Furniture is the _____.

2. There are two basis from which credit may be extended. They are on either an _____ or _____ basis.

3. If Bob is not required to have any security to protect the payment of a debt to Fine Lamps, Inc., then it may be said that Bob has _____ credit.

4. A debtor is judgment proof if the debtor has little or no property or income for a creditor to _____.

5. Collateral is a _____ _____ in the debtor's property that secures payment of a loan.

6. _____ interests in property may be taken in real, personal, or even intangible property.

7. A deficiency judgment is what a creditor recovers in a lawsuit against a debtor when the _____ cannot satisfy the _____.

8. A _____ _____ is a legal procedure by which a secured creditor causes the judicial sale of the secured real estate to pay a defaulted loan.

9. An _____ or _____ lien is one in which a worker in the ordinary course of business works on or provides materials to another person and by statute is allowed to place a lien on the goods until the work or materials are paid for.

10. A _____ is a collateral situation where a property owner borrows money from a creditor who uses a deed as collateral for repayment of the loan.

11. Fred signs a piece of paper that indicates his debt to Union Bank. What is this piece of paper called? It is called a _____.

12. What is a deed of trust? _____

13. What requires the mortgage or deed of trust to be documented in a county office where real property is located? _____ _____

14. Dave fails to pay his monthly mortgage payment on the ranch he is purchasing from Montana Savings and Loan. What legal procedure may Montana Savings and Loan bring against Dave? _____

15. What is an antideficiency statute? _____ .

Critical Thought Exercise

Steve and Bonnie West purchased an old Victorian home outside St. Louis and planned on renovating it and selling it for a profit before moving onto another renovation project. Bonnie's brother, Doug Nixon, did most of the major work on the house and hired trades people to assist in areas that were beyond his expertise. Nixon hired Summit Roofing to replace the old shake roof with a fire resistant composite product that matched the house in color and style. The cost of the new roof is $17,400, including all labor and materials. Steve and Bonnie pay Doug $86,500 for the entire project. Doug failed to pay Summit Roofing and absconded with all the funds.

Steve and Bonnie West entered into a real estate purchase agreement with Lucy Rogers to purchase the home for $515,000. The contract between West and Rogers states that the property is free of all encumbrances and escrow will close in 30 days.

Summit Roofing filed a mechanic's lien against the property. The Wests demanded that Summit Roofing seek payment from Doug Nixon. Summit Roofing gave notice that it was going to foreclose against the property to recover the $17,400 owed to it.

What action should Steve and Bonnie West take to ensure that the sale to Rogers will not be thwarted?

Answer:

_____
_____
_____
_____
_____
_____
_____
_____
_____
_____
_____
_____
_____
_____

Practice Quiz

True/False

1. ___ Artisan's liens are not super-priority liens. [p. 397]

2. ___ If Alex defaults on his mortgage, Mohawk Bank, which holds the note, may not declare the entire debt due and payable immediately, but must wait for a redemption period to pass. [p. 395]

3. ___ States that have antideficiency statutes do not allow deficiency judgments regarding certain types of mortgages. [p. 396]

4. ___ The right of redemption must be exercised before foreclosure. [p. 396]

5. ___ A majority of the states permit the sale of real property by way of land sale contracts. [p. 396]

6. ___ Under a land sale contract, the seller retains title to the property while the purchaser continues to pay the purchase price plus interest. [p. 396]

7. ___ The lienholder must file a notice of lien with the county recorder's office to obtain a material person's lien. [p. 397]

8. ___ When collateral secures payment of a loan, this is called secured credit. [p. 392]

9. ___ Real estate owners cannot create security interests in their property. [p. 392]

10. ___ A deed of trust is a two-party instrument. [p. 393]

11. ___ Under a power of sale, the procedure for the sale is contained in the mortgage or deed of trust. [p. 396]

12. ___ Many states provide a statutory procedure that must be adhered to to foreclose on a land sales contract. [p. 397]

13. ___ Dave, a contractor, files a mechanics' lien against Nancy for laying brick around Nancy's home. Dave may use the improvements as security for payment on the services and materials. [p. 397]

14. ___ The general time frame to foreclose on a lien in all states is always a maximum of six months from the date that the lien is filed. [p. 397]

15. ___ A lien release is a written document signed by a contractor, subcontractor, laborer, or material person demanding to be paid for his or her work. [p. 397]

16. ___ If Smith, a contractor, places a lien on Pope's property, Smith must give notice of the lien to Pope in order for the lien to be perfected as recording with the county recorder is insufficient. [p. 397]

17. ___ Some states allow the mortgagor to redeem real property only for a specified period after foreclosure. [p. 397]

18. ___ Only the mortgagor may redeem the property during the redemption period. [p. 396]

19. ___ Credit that requires collateral that secures payment of the loan is called unsecured credit. [p. 392]

20. ___ Under a note and deed of trust, legal title is with the trustor, and the beneficiary has all of the legal rights to possession of the real property. [p. 393]

Multiple Choice

21. Once a real estate loan is repaid, the trustee files a written reconveyance with the county recorder's office, which transfers title to the real property to the [p. 393]
    a. beneficiary.
    b. mortgagee.
    c. borrower-debtor.
    d. none of the above

22. When a bank fails to record a mortgage in the county recorder's office, the document is not effective against [p. 394]
    a. the mortgagor.
    b. subsequent purchasers of real property.
    c. the borrower-debtor.
    d. the mortgagee.

23. A mortgagor may regain their property that is in default by paying the outstanding principal, interest, and other costs under the [p. 396]
    a. antideficiency statute.
    b. right of redemption.
    c. release of lien.
    d. power of sale.

24. The benefits of a statutory procedure of foreclosing on a land sale contract do not include [p. 397]
    a. the fact that it is a simpler way to foreclose.
    b. the fact that it is less time consuming.
    c. the fact that it is less expensive than foreclosure on a mortgage or deed of trust.
    d. the fact that there is no right of redemption under such a contract.

25. When a borrower defaults on real estate loans and foreclosure proceedings are initiated, the bank or lienholder that will have priority in being paid from the foreclosure sale is the one that [p. 394]
    a. had the largest outstanding balance owed to them.
    b. had the largest original amount on their mortgage or note.
    c. contributed the most to the improvement of the property.
    d. was the first to record their mortgage or deed of trust with the county recorder.

26. Under a deed of trust, once the loan has been repaid in full, the trustee must file a [p. 393]
   a. written reconveyance with the county recorder's office.
   b. written notice of their intent to foreclose on the loan.
   c. release of lien.
   d. none of the above

27. If a mortgagor defaults on a mortgage, the mortgagee can declare the entire debt due and payable [p. 395]
   a. within 60 days.
   b. within 180 days.
   c. within one year.
   d. immediately.

28. Statutes that prohibit deficiency judgments regarding certain types of mortgages, such as loans for the original purchase price of residential property, are called [p. 396]
   a. power of sale statutes.
   b. antideficiency statutes.
   c. redemption statutes.
   d. recording statutes.

29. A two-party instrument that sets forth the security interest in a piece of real property that is executed by the owner-debtor and the creditor is called a [p. 393]
   a. material person's lien.
   b. note and deed of trust.
   c. mortgage.
   d. land sales contract.

30. When a debtor defaults on a mortgage, the mortgagee must name _____ as a defendant in the foreclosure proceeding. [p. 395]
   a. only the debtor
   b. only the mortgagor
   c. only a person who has properly recorded a material person's lien
   d. any party having an interest in the property

Short Answer

31. Credit that does not require any security (collateral) to protect payment of the debt is called [p. 391] _____

32. Collateral is used to [p. 392] _____

   _____

33. Cliff's Concrete contracts with Gus to remove an old driveway and install a new cement driveway and walkway on Gus's property. After Cliff's Concrete has completed the job, Gus refuses to pay for the work because he does not like the color of the concrete work. If Cliff's Concrete decides to place a material person's lien on Gus's home, what four requirements must be met? [p. 397] _____

   _____

   _____

34. What is the major difference between a mortgage and a deed of trust? [p. 393] _____

_____

35. What is a right of redemption? [p. 396] _____

_____

36. A land sales contract is normally used to sell what type of real estate? [p. 396] _____

_____

37. Between a mortgagor and mortgagee, what happens if the mortgagee does not record the mortgage in compliance with the applicable recording statute? [p. 394] _____

_____

38. What happens if a mortgagee is successful in a foreclosure action? [p. 395] _____

_____

_____

39. What may happen if an owner defaults and does not pay a material person's lien? [p. 397]

_____

40. Who holds legal title to real property under a deed of trust? [p. 393]

_____

41. How is a power of sale created? [p. 396] _____

_____

42. What is a deficiency judgment? [p. 396] _____

_____

Answers to Refresh Your Memory

1. debtor, creditor [p. 391]
2. unsecured, secured [p. 392]
3. unsecured [p. 392]
4. garnish [p. 392]
5. security interest [p. 392]
6. Security [p. 392]
7. collateral, loan [p. 392]
8. foreclosure sale [p. 395]
9. artisan, mechanic's [p. 397]
10. mortgage [p. 393]
11. note [p. 393]
12. a legal instrument that gives a creditor a security interest in the debtor's property that is pledged as collateral deed of trust [p. 393]
13. A recording statute requires that the mortgage or deed of trust be recorded in the county recorder's office of the county in which the real property is located. [p. 394]
14. Montana Savings and Loan may bring a foreclosure procedure against Dave. [p. 395]
15. a law prohibiting a mortgagee from recovering the amount that is lacking from the mortgagor's residential property [p. 396]

Critical Thought Exercise Model Answer

Contractors and laborers who expend time and money for materials that are used for improvements upon real property may protect themselves by filing a mechanic's lien against the real property upon which the improvement was made by the contractor or laborer. In order to obtain a mechanic's lien, the contractor will usually have to meet the following requirements to perfect their lien: (1) File a notice of lien with the county recorder's office in the county where the real property is located; (2) The notice must state the amount of the claim, a description of the real property, the name of the property owner, and the name of the claimant; (3) The notice must be filed within the statutory time as set forth in the statute (usually 30-120 days), and; (4) Notice of the lien must be transmitted to the owner of the real property.

Summit Roofing performed actual work upon the West's house and is entitled to file a mechanic's lien if it is not paid. When Nixon absconded with the funds, the Wests may have been defrauded by Nixon, but this does nothing to prevent a proper filing of the lien. The lien will prevent the Wests from conveying clear title and is an encumbrance upon the property. The Wests will be in breach when the date for closing arrives and they are unable to convey clear title to Rogers. The only recourse that the Wests have in this case is to pay Summit Roofing and obtain a release of lien before the escrow closing date. The Wests should be careful to have all the contractors, laborers, and material persons who have worked on their home or supplied materials sign the lien release. The Wests can then proceed against Nixon to recover their $17,400.

Answers to Practice Quiz

True/False

1. False   Mechanic's as well as artisan's liens are termed super-priority liens because they are given priority over any existing lien on the goods.
2. False   Mohawk Bank's right to declare the entire debt due and payable immediately can be enforced through foreclosure proceedings.
3. True   An antideficiency statute prohibits deficiency judgments.
4. True   A mortgagor is given the right to redeem his or her property but cannot do so in part. As such, he or she must pay the full amount owing on the debt, plus interest and costs prior to foreclosure.
5. True   Most states allow the sale and transfer of real property by using land sale contracts.
6. True   While the seller retains title to the property during the period of the contract, the purchaser has the legal right of possession and use of the property, but is responsible for the payment of insurance and taxes.
7. True   The lienholder also must describe the lien, file the notice within the statutory time, and give notice of the lien to the property owner.
8. True   The collateral may secure payment for loans on real property, personal, intangible, and other property.
9. False   Security interests in real estate can be created by the owners of real property.
10. False   The deed of trust and note is a three-party instrument with a trustor, trustee, and a beneficiary.
11. True   The power of sale must be expressly conferred in the mortgage or deed of trust.
12. True   Many states set forth a statutory procedure that must be adhered to when foreclosing on a land sale contract. These procedures ore often easier than foreclosing on a mortgage.

13. True   The brick around Nancy's home would be considered an improvement that Dave may use as security for the payment of his services and materials.
14. False   The statutory period to foreclose on a lien is from six month to two years depending on the jurisdiction the parties are in.
15. False   A lien release is an affidavit attesting to receipt of the payment to contractors, laborers, material persons, etc. One of the purposes of a lien release is to defeat a lien holder's attempt to obtain payment once it has already been paid.
16. True   In general, notice of the lien must be given to the owner of the real property that the lien is being placed on.
17. True   This period is usually six months or one year.
18. False   Any real party in interest, such as a second mortgage holder or another lienholder, may redeem the property during the redemption period.
19. False   Credit that requires security to secure payment of the loan is known as secured credit.
20. False   The trustor has full legal rights to possession of the real property while the legal title to the property is placed with the trustee. The creditor is called the beneficiary.

Multiple Choice

21. C   Answer C is correct as the trustee holds the deed of trust on property being purchased by the debtor. Answer A is incorrect because the beneficiary under the deed of trust was the bank which has now been repaid. Answer B is incorrect because the mortgagee is also the bank under a mortgage, not a deed of trust. Answer D is incorrect because choice C is correct.

22. B   Answer B is the correct answer as an improperly recorded document is not effective against subsequent purchasers of real property or other lienholders or mortgages who do not have any notice of the prior mortgages. Answers A, C, and D are incorrect because the nonrecordation of a mortgage or deed of trust does not affect either the legality of the instrument between the mortgagor and mortgagee or the rights and obligations of the parties. The debtor and the mortgagor are the same person.

23. B   Answer B is the correct answer as common law and several state statutes require that the full amount of the debt, plus interest and costs be satisfied before a property may be redeemed under the right of redemption. Answer A is incorrect as the right of redemption and the underlying concept of an antideficiency statute have nothing to do with one another. Answer C is incorrect as a release of lien pertains to a mechanic's lien, not a mortgage. Answer D is incorrect based on the reasoning given above.

24. D   Answer D is correct as the right of redemption does exist under a land sales contract. All of the statements given in answers A-C state a benefit of utilizing a statutory procedure for foreclosing on a land sale contract.

25. D   Answer D is correct as under a recording statute, the "first in time to record" rule controls. Answers A, B, and C are incorrect because neither the amount of the loan or the purpose of the loan are of any significance. All that matters is which party was the first to properly record their mortgage or deed of trust with the county recorder's office.

26. A   Answer B is correct as it states the correct duty of the trustee when the borrower has paid his loan in full. Answer B is incorrect because a trustee may not foreclose on a mortgage or deed of trust and note that have been paid in full. Answer C is incorrect because a release of lien is filed when payment for improvements to the property has been received from the property owner. Answer D is incorrect because a correct answer is available.

27. D   Answer D is a correct statement of the right of the mortgagee upon default by the mortgagor. The right can be enforced immediately through foreclosure. Answers A, B, and C are incorrect because they state time periods that are not applicable. The mortgagee need not wait for any period of time to commence foreclosure.

28. B   Answer B is correct as the question correctly defines the definition of an antideficiency statute. Answer A is incorrect as this is merely the right of a mortgagee to sell the property to satisfy a defaulted loan. Answer C is incorrect as redemption relates to paying monies owed to the mortgagee to prevent a foreclosure. Answer D is incorrect as a recording statute does not determine the amount or type of loan that can be pursued when a borrower defaults.

29. C   Answer C is correct since the question correctly defines mortgage. Answer A is incorrect as it relates to a security interest for improvements on a property, not a loan. Answer B is incorrect as this is a three-party instrument. Answer D is incorrect because the seller retains title to the property under a land sales contract, not just a security interest.

30. D   Answer D is correct because the mortgagee must take action against all persons who have an interest in the property because they all have the right of redemption. Answers A and B are the same party and must be named in the proceedings, but this answer is incorrect because it fails to cover other parties with an interest in the property. Answer C is incorrect, as it excludes the debtor as a necessary party.

Short Answer

31. unsecured credit

32. secure payment of the loan

33. 1) File a notice of lien with the county recorder's office, 2) The notice must state the amount of the claim, the name of the claimant, the name of the owner, and a description of the real property, 3) The notice must be filed within the specified time period, and 4) Notice of the lien must be given to the owner of the property.

34. A mortgage is a two-party instrument having a collateral arrangement. A deed of trust is a three-party instrument with legal title being placed with the trustee.

35. A mortgagor has the option of exercising his or her right to redemption of the property by paying the full amount of the purchase price, plus interest and other costs.

36. Undeveloped property, farms, and similar types of property such as timberlands and wetlands.

37. Nonrecordation of a mortgage does not affect either the legality of the instrument between the mortgagor and mortgagee or the rights and obligations of the parties.

38. The court will issue a judgment that orders the real property to be sold at a judicial sale. The procedures are mandated by state statute and any surplus from the sale must be paid to the mortgagor.

39. The lien is treated like a mortgage. The lienholder may foreclose on the lien, sell the property, and satisfy the debt plus interest and costs out of the proceeds of the sale. Any surplus must be paid to the owner-debtor.

40. A trustee holds legal title to the property subject to a deed of trust. This is usually a trust corporation.

41. The procedure for the sale must be contained in the mortgage or deed of trust itself.

42. a court judgment allowing a secured lender to recover other income or property from a defaulting debtor if the collateral is insufficient to repay the unpaid loan

Chapter 27

SECURED TRANSACTIONS AND SECURITY INTERESTS IN PERSONAL PROPERTY

Chapter Overview

This chapter elaborates on the concept of security interests as they pertain to the items that are purchased or some other personal property of the debtor. The security interest that is taken by a creditor is known as a secured transaction. You will learn about the creation of security interests as well as the ways to perfect the same by studying these and other rules as presented by Article 9 of the Uniform Commercial Code.

Objectives

Upon completion of the exercises in this chapter, you should be able to:
1. Discuss the concepts in Revised Article 9 of the UCC.
2. Explain how a security interest is created in personal property.
3. Explain how filing a financing statement creates a perfected security interest.
4. Explain how taking possession of collateral perfects a security interest.
5. Discuss the meaning of purchase money security interest.
6. Explain the meaning of floating lien.
7. Discuss priority of claims regarding competing security interests.
8. Explain the difference between surety and guaranty arrangements.
9. Explain the remedies that are available to secured creditors when a debtor defaults.

Practical Application

You will be able to apply the Uniform Commercial Code rules of Article 9 when creating as well as enforcing security interests you may have in personal property. Further, you will become more familiar with the terminology associated with secured transactions. You should also be able to determine the priority among conflicting claims of creditors and whether or not an exception to the perfection-priority rule applies. Additionally, if you are a secured party, you will be more aware of the remedies that are available to you should a debtor default on a security agreement.

Helpful Hints

If you have been in a situation involving a secured transaction, this chapter will be like second nature to you. However, for the individual who is studying this material for the first time, it is advisable to understand the basic vocabulary first and then look upon the remaining materials like building blocks from which to gather and expand the information obtained from Article 9 of the UCC. The first building block that you should familiarize yourself with is that of creation of a security interest in personal property, followed by the floating lien concept. The third building block involves perfecting a secured interest, and then termination followed by the last two building blocks of priority of claims and remedies for the creditor. The following Study Tips section utilizes the building block approach to make your learning easier.

Study Tips

Basic Information and Vocabulary

Article 9 of the Uniform Commercial Code governs secured transactions. When a creditor loans money to a debtor in exchange for the debtor's pledge of personal property as security (collateral), then a secured transaction is created.

Debtor – The party owing payment or some other performance of the secured obligation.

Secured Party – The individual, albeit seller, lender, or other person who holds the security interest.

Security Interest – A personal property interest that secures payment or performance of an obligation.

Security Agreement – The agreement created by the secured party and the debtor that allows for a security interest in personal property.

Collateral – Property, including chattel paper and accounts, that is subject to a security interest.

Secured Transaction
- Two-party secured transaction – Where a seller sells goods to a buyer on credit and keeps a security interest in the goods.
- Three-party secured transaction – Where a seller sells goods to a buyer who has financed the goods.

Vocabulary Relating to Third-Person Liability on a Debt

Surety Arrangement – A situation where a third party promises to be primarily liable with the borrower for the payment of the borrower's debt.

Surety – This is the third person who agrees to be liable in a surety arrangement and in essence acts as a co-debtor and is often called an accommodation party or a cosigner.

Guaranty Arrangement – A situation where a third party promises to be secondarily liable for the payment of another's debt.

Guarantor – This is the third person who agrees to be liable in a guaranty arrangement.

Defenses of a Surety or Guarantor

A surety or guarantor may utilize the same defenses as the principal debtor against the creditor. Possible defenses include fraudulent inducement to enter into the guaranty agreement or surety, duress, and the guarantor's or surety's own bankruptcy or incapacity.

Building Block #1

Creation of a Security Interest in Personal Property

Writing Requirement – In general, security interests must be in writing unless the creditor is in possession of the collateral. The following lists what the writing must contain.
1) The collateral must be clearly described so that it may be easily identified.
2) The writing must state the debtor's promise to pay the creditor as well as the terms of repayment.
3) The writing must state what the creditor's rights are in the event of a debtor's default.
4) The debtor must sign the writing.

Value Requirement – The secured party must give any adequate consideration that will support a simple contract. The debtor must owe a debt to the creditor.

Debtor Has Rights in the Collateral – The debtor must have a present or future right in or the right to possession of the collateral in order to give a security interest in that property.

Attachment – If the writing, value, and debtor's rights in the collateral are met, then the rights of the secured party attach to the collateral and the creditor can satisfy the debt out of the collateral if need be.

Building Block # 2 – The Floating-Lien Concept

This concept has been placed in a category by itself because it deals with security agreements that refer to either property that is acquired after the security agreement is executed or future advances.

After-Acquired Property – This refers to property that the debtor obtains after the execution of the security agreement.

Future Advances – As defined in your main text, this is "personal property of the debtor that is designated as collateral for future loans from a line of credit."

Building Block #3 – Perfecting a Security Interest

Perfection is a legal process that is accomplished by three main methods to establish a secured creditor's rights against the claims of other creditors.

Filing a Financing Statement – This method is the most common way to perfect a creditor's interest. The financing statement must contain the debtor's name and address, as well as the creditor's name and address and a statement that reveals the types of collateral or a description of the items. Further, the secured party may file the security agreement as a financing statement. [UCC 9-402(1)]. The financing statement must be filed with the appropriate state or county office.

Perfection by Possession of Collateral – This method does not require the secured party to file a financing statement if the creditor has possession of the collateral. However, the secured creditor is required to use reasonable care in the collateral's custody and preservation if he or she holds the debtor's property.

Perfection by a Purchase Money Security Interest in Consumer Goods – This method is an interest that a creditor gets automatically when it gives credit to a consumer to purchase consumer goods. Examples of consumer goods include television sets, home appliances, furniture, and the like that are mainly used for family, personal, or household use. Since the creditor does not have to file a financing statement or take possession of the goods, this interest is termed **perfection by attachment** or the **automatic perfection rule.**

Exceptions to the Perfection-Priority Rule

The UCC recognizes several exceptions to the perfection-priority rule.

Purchase Money Security Interest: Inventory as Collateral
"If the collateral is inventory, the perfected purchase money security interest prevails if the purchase money secured party gives written notice of the perfection to the perfected nonpurchase money secured party before the debtor receives possession of the inventory." [UCC 9-312(3)]

Purchase Money Security Interest: Noninventory as Collateral
UCC 9-312 (4) provides that "if the collateral is something other than inventory, the perfected purchase money security interest would prevail over a perfected nonpurchase money security interest in after-acquired property if it was perfected before or within 10 days after the debtor receives possession of the collateral."

Buyers in the Ordinary Course of Business
UCC 9-307(1) provides that "a buyer in the ordinary course of business who purchases goods from a merchant takes the goods free of any perfected or unperfected security interest in the merchant's inventory even if the buyer knows of the existence of the security interest."

Secondhand Consumer Goods
UCC 9-307(2) provides that "buyers of secondhand consumer goods take free of security interest if they do not have actual or constructive knowledge about the security interest, give value, and buy the goods for personal, family, or household purposes. The filing of a financing statement by a creditor provides constructive notice of the security interest."

Building Block #4

This should really be termed tumbling block #4, as once a secured consumer debt has been satisfied, a termination statement must be filed with the same state or county office that the financing statement was filed with. The termination statement must be filed within a month of the debt's satisfaction or within ten days from receipt of the debtor's demand to do so. If the termination statement is not filed, the creditor is liable to the debtor for $100 along with any other losses suffered by the debtor.

Building Block #5 – Priority of Claims

In order to determine which creditor's claim on the same collateral or property takes priority over another, the UCC decides based on whether the claim is secured or unsecured and the time at which secured claims were perfected or attached.

Secured vs. Unsecured Claims – Secured creditors take priority over unsecured creditors.

Competing Unperfected Secured Claims – If there are two or more secured yet unperfected claims to the same collateral exist, then the first to attach takes priority.

Perfected vs. Unperfected – If two or more have a claim or interest in the same collateral, where one is perfected and the other is unperfected, the perfected claim will take priority.

Competing Perfected Secured Claims – When two or more secured parties have perfected security interests in the same collateral, the first to perfect either by filing a financing statement or taking possession of the collateral has priority over the other.

Perfected Secured Claims in Fungible, Commingled Goods – If goods that have a perfected security status associated with them become commingled with other goods that also have perfected security interests to the point where the goods have lost their identity, then security interests will be determined according to the ratio that cost of goods "to which each interest originally attached bears to the cost of the total product or mass."

Building Block #6 – Default and Remedies

Article 9 sets forth the rights, duties, and remedies of the secured party if the debtor defaults. You should know that the parties might define the term default in their security agreement. There are several remedies that a secured party may pursue upon default by the debtor.

Taking Possession of the Collateral
Many secured creditors repossess the goods from the defaulting debtor and then either keep the collateral or sell it and dispose of it to satisfy the debtor's debt. "The secured party must act in good faith and with commercial reasonableness, and with reasonable care to preserve the collateral in his or her possession." [UCC 9-503]

Retention of Collateral
Notice of a secured creditor's intention to repossess and keep the debtor's collateral must be sent to the debtor unless there is a signed written statement renouncing this right. Beware, a secured creditor cannot keep the collateral and must dispose of it if he or she receives a written objection from a person entitled to receive notice within 21 days of the notice being sent or if the debt concerns consumer goods and the debtor has paid 60 percent of the cash price or loan. Here, the secured creditor must dispose of the goods within 90 days after taking possession of them. A consumer may renounce his or her rights under this section. [UCC 9-505(1)]

Disposition of Collateral
A secured creditor in possession of a debtor's collateral may sell, lease, or otherwise dispose of the collateral in a commercially reasonable manner if the debtor is in default. However, the proceeds from the sale must be applied in the order prescribed by UCC 9-504(1) and (2).

Deficiency Judgment
If the proceeds from the disposition of the collateral are insufficient to satisfy the debt, then the secured party may bring a cause of action to recover a deficiency judgment against the debtor. UCC 9-504(2)

Redemption Rights

The debtor may redeem the collateral by paying all obligations secured by the collateral as well as expenses reasonably incurred by the secured party in retaking and holding the collateral along with any attorney's fees and legal expenses provided for in the security agreement and not prohibited by law. [UCC 9-506]

Relinquishment of the Security Interest and Proceeding to Judgment on the Underlying Debt

The secured creditor may proceed to judgment against the debtor to recover on the underlying debt instead of repossessing the collateral.

Security Agreements Covering Real and Personal Property

When a security agreement involves both real and personal property, the secured party may proceed against the personal property as per the provisions in Article 9, or as to both with the rights and remedies provided for by state law. If state law is opted for, Article 9 of the UCC is not applicable.

Refresh Your Memory

The following exercise will enable you to refresh your memory on the rules and principles presented to you in this chapter. Read each question twice and place your answer in the blanks provided. Review the chapter material for any question you miss or are unable to remember.

1. Equipment, vehicles, furniture, computers, clothing, and jewelry are examples of _____ _____ _____.

2. Article 9 of the UCC governs _____ _____.

3. When a creditor extends credit to a debtor and takes a _____ interest in some property of the _____, this is called a secured transaction.

4. A secured party is a _____, _____, or other party in whose favor there is a security interest.

5. Personal property subject to a security interest is called _____.

6. A situation whereby a seller sells goods to a buyer who has obtained financing from a third-party lender who takes a security interest in the goods sold is referred to as a _____-_____ _____.

7. A security agreement is a written document signed by the _____ that creates a _____ interest in personal property.

8. When the creditor has an enforceable security interest against the debtor and can satisfy the debt out of the designated collateral, this is known as _____.

9. A _____ _____ is a security interest that attaches to property that was not originally in the _____ of the debtor when the agreement was executed.

10. After-acquired property is property that a debtor acquires after a _____ _____ is executed.

11. A _____ _____ _____ _____ is an interest a creditor automatically obtains when it extends credit to a consumer to purchase consumer goods.

12. A secured party must file a _____ _____ to end a security interest when the debt has been paid.

13. If two or more secured parties claim an interest in the same collateral but neither has a perfected claim, the first to _____ has priority.

14. Repossession is a right granted to a secured creditor to take possession of the collateral upon _____ by the debtor.

15. A person who acts as a surety is commonly called an accommodation party or _____.

Critical Thought Exercise

Carl Rice and Carpet City, Inc., signed a security agreement with Pacific Ocean Bank for $86,400, plus interest. The collateral for the loan was a commercial truck used for the business run by Rice. The truck had a large hydraulic lift attached to the truck that allowed Rice to load and offload heavy rolls of carpet. Rice and Carpet City defaulted, and the bank took possession of the truck. The bank solicited bids for the truck by word of mouth from other financial institutions, two local furniture stores, and some bank customers. Pacific Ocean Bank sold the truck to a local business for $69,000. The buyer did not need a truck equipped for transporting carpet so they did modifications and repairs totaling $17,000 and sold it two years later for $62,000. Pacific Ocean Bank sued Rice and Carpet City for the difference between the amount due on the loan and the proceeds from the sale. Pacific Ocean Bank did not advertise the truck nor did it contact any carpet stores that might desire to purchase a truck equipped with an integrated hydraulic lift. Rice does not contend that the sale price was wholly unreasonable, only that Pacific Ocean did not use all reasonable means to get the best price.

Should Pacific Ocean Bank be allowed to recover the deficiency from the sale or did it fail to sell the truck in a commercially unreasonable manner, which would preclude recovery by the bank?

Answer:

_____

_____

_____

_____

_____

_____

_____

_____

_____

_____

Practice Quiz

True/False

1. ___ In order to give a security interest in personal property, a debtor need not have possessory or ownership rights to the property. [p. 403]

2. ___ A secured party may obtain a security interest in after-acquired property. [p. 403]

3. ___ The purpose of perfecting a security agreement is to establish the rights of a debtor against other creditors who claim an interest in the collateral. [p. 404]

4. ___ The filing of a financing statement in the proper government office is the most common method of perfecting a creditor's security interest in the debtor's collateral. [p. 404]

5. ___ Even if a creditor has physical possession of the collateral, he or she must file a financing statement to put the rest of the world on notice of their interest. [p. 404]

6. ___ Diane borrows $25,000 from Quick Finance and tells them that they may come and pick up her motor home on Saturday as collateral for the loan. No one from Quick Finance picks up the motor home. Meanwhile, another creditor obtains a lien against Diane. Despite the fact that Quick Finance did not file a financing statement, their interest in the motor home is still perfected thereby preventing the other creditor from recovering the motor home from them. [p. 405]

7. ___ Big Box, a large electronics and computer store, does not need to file a financing statement if they extend credit to Larry, a consumer, when Larry purchases a new plasma television. Once Big Box sells the television under a written security agreement, it obtains a purchase money security interest. [p. 406]

8. ___ If the collateral in a purchase money security interest is a computer that is going to be used in a business, the security interest of the creditor is perfected at the time of purchase. [p. 406]

9. ___ Lew buys four lawnmowers from Regal Mowers. Lenders Bank has a perfected security interest in the inventory of Regal Mowers. Therefore, Lew takes the mowers subject to the perfected security interest in Regal Mower's inventory. [p. 408]

10. ___ Buyers of secondhand consumer goods take free of security interest if they do not have actual or constructive knowledge about the security interest, give value, and buy the goods for personal, household, or family purposes. [p. 408]

11. ___ If the proceeds from the disposition of the collateral are not adequate to satisfy the debt to the secured party, the debtor is relieved of any liability for the deficiency. [p. 410]

12. ___ The debtor may redeem the collateral before the priority lienholder has disposed of it. [p. 410]

13. ___ A secured creditor may not give up his or her security interest in the collateral and proceed to judgment against the debtor to recover the underlying debt. If the collateral is available, the creditor must accept it. [p. 410]

14. ___ Collateral is not subject to a security interest. [p. 402]

15. ___ The term secured party means a seller, lender, or other party in whose favor there is a security interest. [p. 401]

16. ___ If Bob borrows $15,000 from Penny and tells Penny that his delivery truck can be used as security for the loan, this agreement does not have to be in writing even if the truck continues to be used for deliveries. [p. 405]

17. ___ There is not a security agreement if the debtor is not indebted to the creditor. [p. 403]

18. ___ Property that a debtor acquires after a security agreement is executed is called an attachment. [p. 403]

19. ___ Transactions involving real estate mortgages, artisan's or mechanic's liens, liens on wages, and judicial liens are not controlled by Article 9 of the UCC. [p. 403]

20. ___ The terminology perfection of a security interest refers to the establishment of a right of a debtor against creditors who claim an interest in the collateral. [p. 404]

21. ___ In order for a creditor to perfect his or her security interest, he or she must file a financing statement or take possession of the goods unless the creditor extends credit to a consumer to purchase consumer goods under a written security agreement. [p. 406]

22. ___ A creditor need not file a financing statement in order to perfect a security interest in fixtures and motor vehicles because they are consumer goods and the filing is not required by the UCC. [p. 406]

23. ___ The interest that a creditor automatically obtains when it extends credit to a consumer to purchase consumer goods is called a purchase money security interest. [p. 406]

24. ___ A termination statement is a document filed by the debtor that demands that a secured interest be terminated because the collateral is in the possession of the creditor. [p. 407]

25. ___ If two or more secured parties claim an interest in the same collateral but neither has a perfected claim, the most recent creditor to have attached has priority. [p. 407]

Multiple Choice

26. A valid written security agreement must [p. 403]
    a. clearly depict the collateral so that it can be readily identified.
    b. be signed by the debtor.
    c. contain the debtor's promise to repay the creditor, along with terms of repayment and the debtor's signature.
    d. all of the above

27. A security agreement may provide that the security interest attaches to property that was not originally in the possession of the debtor when the agreement was executed. This interest is referred to as [p. 403]
    a. a floating lien.
    b. an artisan's lien.
    c. a mortgage.
    d. a judicial lien.

28. Varoom! is a motorcycle dealer. To finance its inventory of new racing motorcycles and off-road motorcycles, Varoom! borrows money from River Bank and gives the bank a security interest in the inventory. Varoom! sells a racing motorcycle subject to the security interest to Speed Racer, who signs a sales contract whereby he agrees to pay Varoom! for the motorcycle in 48 equal monthly installments. If Varoom! defaults on its payment to River Bank, the bank is entitled to [p. 404]
    a. receive the remaining payments from Varoom!
    b. receive the remaining payments from Varoom! and Speed Racer.
    c. receive the remaining payments from one of Varoom!'s other creditors.
    d. receive the remaining payments from Speed Racer.

29. A future advance is [p. 404]
    a. the resulting assets from the sale, exchange, or disposal of collateral subject to a security agreement.
    b. personal property of the debtor that is designed as collateral for future loans from a line of credit.
    c. property that the debtor acquires after the security agreement is executed.
    d. a security interest in property that was not in the possession of the debtor when the security agreement was executed.

30. When two or more creditors claim an interest in the same collateral or property, the priority of claims is partially determined by [p. 407]
    a. the order in which conflicting claims of creditors in the same collateral are resolved.
    b. whether a secured creditor took possession of the collateral upon the default of the debtor.
    c. whether the claim is unsecured or secured and the time at which secured claims were attached or were perfected.
    d. whether the UCC recognizes an exception to the perfection-priority rule.

31. Wanda purchases a computer on credit from Computer City, a retailer, to be used for personal purposes in her home. Computer City obtains an automatically perfected purchase money security interest in the computer. Computer City fails to file a financing statement and Wanda sells her computer to her friend, Hazel, for cash. Thereafter Wanda defaults on her loan payments to Computer City. What action may Computer City take? [p. 408]
    a. Computer City may recover the computer from Hazel.
    b. Computer City may recover the computer from Wanda.
    c. Computer City cannot recover the computer from Hazel if Hazel had no knowledge of Computer City's security interest.
    d. none of the above

32. In a surety situation, the co-debtor promises [p. 411]
    a. to file a notice of a mechanic's lien with the county recorder's office.
    b. to seek assistance from the World Bank.
    c. to be secondarily liable for the payment of another's debt.
    d. to be liable for the payment of another's debt.

33. One who purchases goods from a merchant and takes goods free of any perfected or unperfected security interest in the merchant's inventory even if he or she is aware of the existence of the security interest is known as a [p. 408]
    a. buyer of secondhand consumer goods.
    b. debtor.
    c. secured party.
    d. buyer in the ordinary course of business.

34. The secured party must notify the debtor in writing about the time and place of any public or private sale or any other intended disposition of the collateral unless [p. 409]
    a. the collateral is consumer goods or the goods are perishable.
    b. the debtor is in default.
    c. the collateral is in the possession of the creditor.
    d. none of the above

35. College Clothing Inc., a retailer, borrows money from Our Town Bank for working capital. In exchange, Our Town Bank gets a security interest in all College Clothing's current and after-acquired inventory. Our Town files a financing statement thereby perfecting its security interest. Subsequently College Clothing purchases new inventory on credit from Korean Clothing Works, a clothing manufacturer. Korean Clothing Works perfects its interest by filing a financing statement and notifies Our Town Bank of this fact prior to delivery of the new inventory. College Clothing Inc. defaults on its loans. Whose lien has priority? [p. 535]
    a. College Clothing Inc.
    b. Korean Clothing Works
    c. Our Town Bank
    d. all of the above

Short Answer

36. A surety is called an accommodation party or a _____. [p. 411]

37. What is a security agreement? [p. 403] _____
    _____

38. What is attachment? [p. 403] _____
    _____

39. Personal property of the debtor that is identified as collateral for future loans from a line of credit is known as a _____ _____. [p. 404]

40. When a creditor perfects a security interest, this establishes the right of a secured creditor against _____ who claim an interest in the collateral. [p. 404]

41. A document filed by a secured creditor with the appropriate government office that constructively notifies the world of his or her security interest in personal property is called a _____ _____. [p. 404]

42. If two or more secured parties claim an interest in the same collateral, but neither has perfected a claim, who has priority? [p. 407] _____

43. List three exceptions to the perfection-priority rule. [p. 408] _____
_____

44. A secured creditor who _____ collateral may propose to retain the collateral in satisfaction of the debtor's obligation. [p. 409]

45. How is the right of redemption accomplished? [p. 410] _____
_____
_____

46. In a guaranty arrangement, the guarantor is _____ liable on the debt. [p. 411]

47. Name three types of goods that can become collateral for a loan. [p. 402] _____
_____

48. If a debtor sells, disposes, or exchanges collateral that is subject to a security agreement, the secured party automatically has the right to receive the _____ of the disposition, exchange or sale. [p. 404]

49. The creditor does not have to file a financing statement if he or she has physical _____ of the collateral. [p. 404]

50. Name three events or conditions that will cause the debtor to be in default under a security agreement. [p. 409] _____
_____

Answers to Refresh Your Memory

1. tangible personal property [p. 401]
2. secured transactions [p. 401]
3. security, debtor [p. 401]
4. seller, lender [p. 401]
5. collateral [p. 402]
6. three-party transaction [p. 402]
7. debtor, security [p. 403]
8. attachment [p. 403]
9. floating lien, possession [p. 403]
10. security agreement [p. 403]
11. purchase money security interest [p. 406]
12. termination statement [p. 407]
13. attach [p. 407]
14. default [p. 409]
15. cosigner [p. 411]

Critical Thought Exercise Model Answer

It is the secured party's duty to the debtor to use all fair and reasonable means to obtain the best price under the circumstances, but the creditor need not use extraordinary means. Under the circumstances of this particular case, the sale may be commercially reasonable even with a lack of advertising. One of the factors to be considered in determining whether the sale was commercially reasonable is the adequacy or insufficiency of the sale price after default. In this case, the truck was sold for far less than the purchaser had invested in its purchase and repair. Though Pacific Ocean may have been able to get a better price for the truck had it advertised the sale to carpet stores, there is no evidence that the sale was conducted in a commercially unreasonable manner. Therefore, Pacific Ocean should recover the full amount of the deficiency.

Answers to Practice Quiz

True/False

1. False   A debtor who does not have possessory or ownership rights to property cannot give a security interest in that property.
2. True   The secured party may obtain a security interest in after-acquired property. After-acquired property is property that the debtor acquires after the security agreement is executed.
3. False   Perfection of a security interest is a legal process that establishes the right of a secured creditor against other creditors who claim an interest in the collateral.
4. True   The filing of a financing statement in the correct government office is the most common method of perfecting a creditor's security interest in collateral.
5. False   If someone who is not the debtor has possession of the property used as collateral, a potential creditor is put on notice that another may have an interest in the debtor's property, thereby eliminating the need to file a financing statement.
6. False   Quick Finance's interest is not perfected because it did not have possession of the motor home.
7. True   Big Box automatically obtained a security interest as a creditor when it extended credit to Larry to purchase goods in its store.
8. False   Since the computer is going to be used in a business, it is equipment, not consumer goods. The creditor does not obtain a purchase money security interest when the purchase is business equipment. A filing statement must be filed to perfect the security interest.
9. False   A buyer who purchases goods from a merchant takes the goods free of any perfected or unperfected security interesat in the merchant's inventory.
10. True   Buyers of secondhand consumer goods take free of security interest if they do not have constructive or actual knowledge about the security interest, give value, and buy the goods for family, personal, or household purposes. If I buy a television from my neighbor and do not know that the store has a security interest in the goods, the store will be unable to recover the goods from me if my neighbor defaults on her loan payments to the store.
11. False The debtor is personally liable to the secured party for the deficiency if the disposition of collateral is insufficient to satisfy the debt to the secured party.
12. True   A debtor or another secured party may redeem the collateral before the priority lienholder has disposed of it, entered into a contract to dispose of it, or discharged the debtor's obligation.

13. False   A secured creditor has the option of proceeding to judgment against the debtor to recover on the underlying debt instead of repossessing the collateral. If this option is chosen, the creditor may relinquish his or her security interest in the collateral.

14. False   Collateral such as goods, accounts, and chattel paper that have been sold are examples of property that are subject to security interests.

15. True   This is a definition for a secured party. If the debtor defaults and does not repay the loan, generally the secured party can foreclose and recover the collateral.

16. False   The oral security agreement is not enforceable if Bob remains in possession of the collateral.

17. True   A security agreement does not exist unless the debtor owes a debt to the creditor.

18. False   Property that the debtor acquires after the security agreement is executed is referred to as after-acquired property.

19. True   Article 9 is inapplicable to real estate mortgage transactions, landlord's liens, liens on wages, artisan's or mechanic's liens, liens on wages, etc. These types of liens are covered by other laws.

20. False   The right of a secured creditor is established by perfection of a security interest against other creditors who claim an interest in the collateral.

21. True   Under the perfection by attachment or automatic perfection rule, a creditor who extends credit to a consumer to purchase a consumer good under a written security agreement obtains a purchase money security interest in the good thereby automatically perfecting the creditor's interest at the time of the sale.

22. False   Under UCC 9-302(1)(d), financing statements must be filed in order to perfect a security interest in fixtures and motor vehicles.

23. True   A creditor's extension of credit to a consumer to purchase a consumer good as per a written security agreement automatically gives the creditor what is known as a purchase money security interest.

24. False   Once a secured consumer debt has been paid, the secured party must file a termination statement with each filing officer with whom a financing statement was filed.

25. False   If two or more secured parties claim an interest in the same collateral but neither has a perfected claim, the first to attach has priority.

Multiple Choice

26. D   Answer D is correct as answers A, B, and C are all correct statements of what must be contained in a valid written security agreement.

27. A   Answer A is correct as the question states the definition of a floating lien. Answers B, C, and D are incorrect because they are types of liens that are not controlled by Article 9 of the UCC which governs secured transactions.

28. D   Answer D is correct as UCC 9-203 provides that if a debtor sells, exchanges, or disposes of collateral subject to a security agreement, the secured party automatically has the right to receive the proceeds of the sale or exchange, or disposition. Here Varoom! sold a motorcycle on an installment basis to Speed Racer. Since Varoom! defaulted on its loan with River Bank, the bank is entitled to collect the proceeds from Varoom!'s motorcycle sale to Speed Racer in order to satisfy the debt. Answer A is incorrect since Varoom! defaulted and is not a viable source for payment. Answer B is incorrect for the reasoning stated in answer A, and the bank may collect from Speed Racer as explained in more detail as per answer D. Answer C is incorrect as River Bank may not collect what Varoom! owes it from one of Varoom!'s other creditors, as they are not party to the security agreement.

29. B   Answer B is correct as collateral for future loans from a line of credit is personal property that may be used as a future advance. Answer A is incorrect as this gives an explanation of what sale proceeds are. Answer C is incorrect as this states the definition of after-acquired property. Answer D is incorrect as this describes what a floating lien is.

30. C   Answer C is correct as the priority of claims involving the same property or collateral is established by viewing whether the claim is secured or unsecured and the time at which the secured claims were perfected or attached. Answer A is incorrect as it makes no sense. Answer B is incorrect as possession has no impact on priority especially if perfection of a creditor's security interest may be accomplished automatically at the time of the sale of goods. Answer D is incorrect as priority of claims may be established without the need for relying on a recognized exception to the perfection-priority rule.

31. C   Answer C is correct because of Computer City's failure to file a financing statement, which would have given notice to Hazel of its interest in the computer. Answer A is incorrect as Hazel did not have notice of Computer City's interest. Answer B is incorrect as Wanda no longer has the computer, since she sold it to Hazel. Answer D is incorrect for the reasons given above.

32. D   Answer D is correct as the surety otherwise known as a co-debtor promises to be liable for the debt of another in a strict surety arrangement. Answer A is incorrect as the filing of a mechanic's lien is irrelevant to a surety arrangement. Answer B is incorrect as the World Bank assists in helping finance international operations not in agreeing to be liable in a surety arrangement. Answer C is incorrect as this describes a guarantor's role in a guaranty arrangement.

33. D   Answer D is correct as this gives the definition of a buyer in the ordinary course of business. Answer A is incorrect as buyers of secondhand consumer goods take free of security interest if they do not have constructive or actual knowledge about the security interest, give value, and buy the goods for household, family, or personal purposes. Answer B is incorrect as a debtor is a party who owes payment or other performance of the secured obligation. Answer C is incorrect as a secured party is a lender, seller, or other party in whose favor there is a security interest.

34. A   Answer A is correct as no notice is needed when the collateral is consumer goods. No notice is needed when the goods are perishable or may decline steadily in value. Answer B is incorrect because a disposition of the collateral would not be taking place unless the debtor was in default. Answer C is incorrect because location of the collateral is not relevant to the issue of notice. Answer D is not correct because A is correct.

35. B   Answer B is correct as the perfected purchase money security interest prevails if the purchase money secured party gives written notice of the perfection to the perfected nonpurchase money secured party before the debtor receives possession of the inventory. UCC 9-312(3). Here Korean Clothing Works notified Our Town Bank before delivery of the inventory and as such its lien has priority. Based on this reasoning, answers A, C, and D are incorrect.

Short Answer

36.   cosigner

37.   A security agreement is the agreement between the debtor and the secured party that creates or provides for a security interest. UCC 1-201 (37)

38.   Attachment is a situation in which the creditor has an enforceable security interest against the debtor and can satisfy the debt out of the designated collateral.

39.   future advance

40.   other creditors

41.   financing statement

42. The first party to attach has priority.
43. purchase money security interest, buyers in the ordinary course of business, secondhand consumer goods
44. repossesses
45. The right of redemption may be accomplished by payment of all obligations secured by the collateral, all expenses reasonably incurred by the secured property in retaking and holding the collateral, and any attorneys' fees and other legal expenses provided for in the security agreement.
46. secondarily
47. consumer goods, equipment used for business, farm products, inventory, fixtures
48. proceeds
49. physical
50. bankruptcy of the debtor, failure to make regular payments when due, breach of the warranty of ownership as to the collateral

Chapter 28

BANKRUPTCY AND THE BANKRUPTCY ABUSE PREVENTION AND CONSUMER PROTECTION ACT OF 2005

Chapter Overview

The Bankruptcy Abuse Prevention and Consumer Protection Act of 2005 substantially amended federal bankruptcy law, making it much more difficult for debtors to escape unwanted debt through bankruptcy. This chapter explores Chapter 7 liquidation bankruptcy as well as Chapter 13 consumer debt adjustment bankruptcy and Chapter 11 business reorganization bankruptcy. Individual debtors as well as businesses often find that they are unable to be responsible for the debts that they have incurred, and as such must rely on the federal bankruptcy laws to free them from their obligations for past debts. You will become more familiar with the procedure involved in filing for bankruptcy as well as creditors' rights, the order of priority for paying creditors, the meaning of an automatic stay in bankruptcy, and voidable transfers and preferential payments.

Objectives

Upon completion of the exercises contained in this chapter, you should be able to:
1. Describe and identify the changes made by the Bankruptcy Abuse Prevention and Consumer Protection Act of 2005.
2. Discuss the procedure for filing for bankruptcy.
3. Explain what is involved in a Chapter 7 liquidation bankruptcy.
4. Explain the meaning of an automatic stay in bankruptcy.
5. Discuss voidable transfers and preferential payments.
6. Be familiar with the order of priority for paying creditors in a Chapter 7 bankruptcy.
7. Be aware of examples of nondischargeable debts in bankruptcy.
8. Explain secured and unsecured rights in bankruptcy.
9. Explain business reorganization as it pertains to a Chapter 11 bankruptcy.
10. Discuss a Chapter 13 consumer debt adjustment bankruptcy.

Practical Application

You should be able to better understand the main purpose of bankruptcy law as well as be familiar with the different types of bankruptcies. Additionally, you will have a clearer understanding of the impact of bankruptcy as well as which creditors take priority with regard to payment of the same.

Helpful Hints

The concepts in this chapter are easier to learn if you keep it simple by learning each of the three types of bankruptcies separately. The study tips section that follows gives you background information, procedures, and little nuances that may be important to know for each kind of bankruptcy. As you will notice, each type of bankruptcy has main points with which you should become familiar. The most important terms are boldly printed.

Study Tips

Two Important Facets of Bankruptcy Law

There are two preliminary aspects of bankruptcy that you should keep in mind. The first is that the law of bankruptcy is federally governed. Secondly, the main purpose of bankruptcy is to free the debtor from cumbersome debts. The 2005 act added a new provision that requires an individual filing for bankruptcy to receive pre-petition and post-petition credit and financial counseling.

Chapter 7 Liquidation Bankruptcy

This is the most common type of bankruptcy and is also referred to as a ***straight bankruptcy***. The debtor's nonexempt property is sold to obtain cash and then the money is distributed to the debtor's creditors. Debts that are not paid are then discharged. Major changes in the bankruptcy code provide that the debtor may not be allowed discharge for debts if the family income exceeds the state's median income. Any party in interest may move to have the petition dismissed. Additionally, under the means test, the court will look to see if the debtor has the ability to pay pre-petition debts out of post-petition income. The formula for the means test is complicated and is set forth on page 430 of your main text.

The procedure to file and maintain a Chapter 7 bankruptcy includes the ***filing of a petition*** by either the debtor (a voluntary petition) or by one or more creditors (an involuntary petition). When a voluntary or involuntary petition is filed, this is known as an ***order for relief***. After the order for relief, the court must call a ***meeting of the creditors*** wherein the debtor is questioned by his or her creditors without a judge being present. At this meeting, a ***permanent trustee*** is elected to be the legal representative of the debtor's estate. The trustee has many duties which include but are not limited to setting aside exempt property, looking into the debtor's finances, investigating the proof of claims, and making reports to the debtor, his or her creditor's, and the court concerning the estate's administration.

An ***automatic stay*** goes into effect upon the filing of an involuntary or voluntary petition. The effect of an automatic stay is that it suspends creditors' actions against the debtor or the debtor's property. It should also be noted that a debtor may have an injunction issued against his/her creditors for activity that is not covered in the automatic stay. However, a creditor does have some recourse against a bankrupt debtor. The secured creditor may seek a ***relief from stay*** in cases where the property is depreciating.

The bankruptcy ***estate*** involves all of the debtor's legal and equitable interests in all types of property, including community property, from the onset of a Chapter 7 bankruptcy proceeding. If the debtor obtains property after he or she files his or her petition, this property usually is not considered to be part of the estate. However, there are certain exceptions, which include but are not limited to inheritance, divorce settlements, and the like if obtained within 180 days of the filing of the petition.

After the 2005 act, the court will engage in the median income and means tests to determine how much debt will be discharged and if the debtor has the ability to pay back part or all of the debt. If the debtor does not meet the median income or means test, their petition may be dismissed or converted to a Chapter 13 repayment plan. Liquidation of all debts is now very difficult for the debtor to obtain.

Additionally, attorneys who represent debtors must *certify the accuracy* of the information contained in the bankruptcy petition and the schedules, under penalty of perjury. Many attorneys have left the practice of bankruptcy law due to the sanctions that can be imposed upon them for mistakes.

Exempt property may be kept by the debtor. The federal exemptions are given on page 424 of your main text. Some state laws also provide for exemptions which are broad in scope. Some states require that the debtor choose between federal or state exemptions or adhere to the state laws.

Bankruptcy courts will now examine transfers of property prior to the filing of the petition to determine if there has been a preferential or fraudulent transfer of property by the debtor. The court may set aside transfers within two years of the petition if they are fraudulent and within ten years if the transfer was to a self-settled trust (where the debtor gets the benefit of the trust).

Distribution of nonexempt property has to be distributed to the debtor's unsecured and secured creditors. The secured creditors take priority over the unsecured creditors. After the property has been distributed to satisfy the claims that are allowed, then the debtor is no longer responsible for the remaining unpaid claims. Only individuals may be given a *discharge.*

Nondischargeable debts are those that are not dischargeable in bankruptcy. Some examples are alimony, child support, and certain fines payable to federal, local, and state authorities. Other examples may be found on page 423 of your main text.

Chapter 11 Reorganization Bankruptcy

Under this type of bankruptcy, the court assists the debtor in reorganizing his or her financial affairs. Individuals, corporations, nonincorporated associations, railroads, and partnerships are able to utilize this type of bankruptcy. Corporations use Chapter 11 bankruptcies the most.

A unique feature about this type of bankruptcy is that the debtor is left to run his or her business while the reorganization proceeding is taking place. The debtor is referred to as a *debtor-in-possession.* The debtor-in-possession has the authority to enter into contracts and operate the business accordingly.

The debtor has a right to file a *plan of reorganization* within 120 days of the *order for relief.* The reorganization plan describes the debtor's proposed new capital structure that indicates the different classes of claims and interests. The creditors and equity holders must be given a court approved *disclosure statement.*

The court must *confirm* the debtor's plan for reorganization in order for it to become effective. Confirmation may be accomplished by giving the different classes of creditors the chance to accept or reject the plan. The court looks at whether the plan is in the best interests of each class of claims, if the plan is feasible, if at least one class has accepted the plan, and whether or not each class of claims and interests is nonimpaired. Confirmation may also be achieved using the *cram-down method.* Under this method, the plan has to be fair and equitable to the impaired class. Remember, the impaired class can be forced to take part in the plan of reorganization.

The debtor is given a *discharge* of all claims that were not a part of the plan of reorganization.

Chapter 13 Consumer Debt Adjustment

Under this plan, the court may oversee the debtor's plan for installment payments of his or her unpaid debts. Chapter 13 is beneficial to both the debtor as well as creditor. The debtor's costs are less under this type of proceeding as well as the fact that he or she may keep more property than is exempt under Chapter 7. The creditors are able to elicit a greater amount of the debts that are owing to them.

The debtor must file a *petition* claiming that he or she is insolvent or not able to pay his or her debts when they are due. A debtor may ask for more time (an *extension*) to pay his or her debts or ask for a *composition* which reduces his or her debts. Subsequent to the filing of the petition, the debtor has to give the court a *list* of his or her creditors, liabilities, and assets. Then there is a *meeting of creditors* where the debtor must be present. A *trustee* is then *appointed* to confirm the plan.

As with a Chapter 7 filing, once a debtor files a petition under Chapter 13, an *automatic stay* is in place regarding liquidation bankruptcy proceedings, creditors' judicial and nonjudicial actions, and creditors' collection activities. The automatic stay is not applicable concerning business debts.

The debtor must file a *plan of payment* within 15 days of filing his or her petition. The plan may not go beyond three years, however, the court may grant a five-year period plan. The debtor must make payments within 30 days of filing his or her plan. If a debtor's circumstances change, then his or her plan may be *modified.*

As with a Chapter 11 bankruptcy, the plan must also be *confirmed* under a Chapter 13 bankruptcy.

When the debtor has made all payments under the plan, the court may *discharge* the debtor from all unpaid debts. Most types of debts are dischargeable except for such things as child support, alimony, and trustee fees. The court will grant a *hardship discharge* if there are unforeseeable circumstances, or the unsecured creditors have been given an amount equal to what they would have received under a Chapter 7 liquidation proceeding or it is not feasible to modify the plan.

Refresh Your Memory

The following exercise will enable you to refresh your memory on the rules and principles presented to you in this chapter. Read each question twice and place your answer in the blanks provided. Review the chapter material for any question you miss or are unable to remember.

1. Allowing creditor claims, deciding preferences, and confirming plans of reorganization are examples of _____ _____ that bankruptcy judges decide.

2. Decisions on personal injury, civil proceedings, and divorce are examples of _____ _____

3. Since federal bankruptcy law discharges the debtor from cumbersome debts, it is in essence giving the debtor a _____ _____ by relieving them from legal responsibility for past debts. With changes made by the 2005 act, a debtor may only get a _____ fresh start.

4. Liquidation bankruptcy is set forth in Chapter ___.

5. Unpaid debts are _____ once a debtor's nonexempt property is sold for cash and the money is given to the creditors.

6. The filing of a _____ commences a Chapter 7 bankruptcy.

7. A voluntary petition under Chapter 7 is filed by the _____.

8. A creditor must allege that the debtor is not paying his or its debts as they become due when the creditor files an _____ _____.

9. An order for relief is an order that occurs upon the filing of either a _____ petition or an _____ involuntary petition.

10. The _____ __ ___ _____ must be called by the court after the court grants an order for relief.

11. A _____ trustee may be elected by the _____ at the first meeting of the creditors.

12. _____ _____ must file a proof of claim that states the amount of their claims against the debtor.

13. The filing of a voluntary or an involuntary petition creates an _____ ____ that suspends certain legal actions by creditors against the debtor or the debtor's property.

14. _____ _____ is property of the debtor that he or she can keep and that does not become part of the bankruptcy estate.

15. Abuse is objectively determined by applying _____ income and _____ tests as established by the 2005 act.

Critical Thought Exercise

Nancy Mills attended two different institutions of higher learning. She received educational loans totaling $22,480. After graduation, Mills was employed, but her monthly take-home pay was less than $1,200. The monthly expenses for herself and her four children were approximately $1,650. Mill's husband had abandoned the family and provided no financial support. Mills received no public assistance and had no possibility to increase her income. A neighbor paid her telephone, water, and gas bills for the two months prior to filing a petition in bankruptcy. Mills also had substantial medical bills and had not been well for months. In her bankruptcy petition, Mills sought to discharge her educational loans.

Are the educational loans owed by Mills dischargeable in bankruptcy? Why was the Bankruptcy Code amended to generally prohibit the discharge of student loans?

Answer:

_____

_____

_____

_____

_____

_____

_____

_____

_____

Practice Quiz

True/False

1. ___ Federal bankruptcy law serves the main purpose of discharging the debtor from his or her onerous debts and gives no relief to creditors. [p. 418]

2. ___ An individual filing for bankruptcy is required to receive pre-petition and post-petition credit and financial counseling. [p. 419]

3. ___ There is no set time frame for filing a proof of claim in a Chapter 7 bankruptcy. [p. 421]

4. ___ Trustees must protect domestic-support creditors under the 2005 act. [p. 422]

5. ___ If secured property is not sufficiently protected during the bankruptcy proceeding, a secured creditor may file a petition for a relief from stay. [p. 423]

6. ___ Gifts and inheritances do not become part of the bankruptcy estate. [p. 424]

7. ___ A debtor may claim only up to $18,450 in equity in property as exempt property under the Bankruptcy Code. [p. 424]

8. ___ Dividends, rents, and interest payments are not considered property of the bankruptcy estate. [p. 424]

9. ___ A bankruptcy court will look at transfers of the debtor's property made up to a year before the filing of the petition to determine if there was a fraudulent transfer. [p. 427]

10. ___ If a transfer of the debtor's property is made to a bona fide good faith purchaser and the transfer is voided, the purchaser must receive the value he or she paid for the property. [p. 426]

11. ___ If the median income and means tests are not met by the debtor, the court has no option but to dismiss the petition. [p. 428]

12. ___ The bankruptcy trustee must act in the best interest of the creditors. [p. 428]

13. ___ The goal of the 2005 act is to deny Chapter 7 discharge to debtors who have the means to pay some of their unsecured debt from post-petition earnings. [p. 428]

14. ___ A state's median income is the average income of all families in the state. [p. 429]

15. ___ The means test determines if the debtor has the means to pay pre-petition debts out of post-petition income. [p. 430]

16. ___ A debtor may be forced to accept a Chapter 13 bankruptcy if abuse is found under a Chapter 7 bankruptcy. [p. 431]

17. ___ A party of interest may not file an objection to the discharge of a debt. [p. 434]

18. ___ A bankruptcy may not be revoked if the discharge is obtained through the fraud of the debtor. [p. 434]

19. ___ Reorganization bankruptcy is governed by Chapter 13 of the Bankruptcy Code. [p. 438]

20. ___ Banks, savings and loan associations, insurance companies, and credit unions are a few of the types of businesses that may not utilize Chapter 11 proceedings. [p. 438]

21. ___ A creditor may involuntarily file a Chapter 13 petition. [p. 435]

22. ___ Though a debtor-in-possession has the authority to operate the debtor's business during the bankruptcy proceeding, the debtor may not enter into contracts, purchase supplies, or incur further debts. [p. 438]

23. ___ Under the Bankruptcy Code, the debtor-in-possession in a Chapter 11 proceeding is given authority to assume or reject executory contracts. [p. 439]

24. ___ The debtor has a right to file a plan of reorganization within the first 120 days after the date of the order for relief. [p. 440]

25. ___ If a class of creditors does not accept the plan of reorganization under a Chapter 11 proceeding, the plan cannot be confirmed. [p. 442]

Multiple Choice

26. A voluntary petition for bankruptcy does not include which of the following? [p. 421]
    a. a list of secured and unsecured creditors
    b. a list of the property owned by the debtor, including exempt property
    c. a statement of the debtor's financial affairs as well as the debtor's income and expenses
    d. a plan for repayments of the debts within one year

27. The filing of either a voluntary petition or an unchallenged involuntary petition constitutes [p. 421]
    a. an order for relief.
    b. a proof of claim.
    c. discharge of all debts.
    d. none of the above

28. To void a transfer or obligation of the debtor that is deemed fraudulent, the court must first find that [p. 427]
    a. the transfer was made or the obligation was incurred by the debtor with the actual intent to hinder, delay, or defraud a creditor.
    b. the debtor received less than a reasonable equivalent in value.
    c. the debtor was insolvent on the date of transfer or when the obligation was incurred.
    d. all of the above

29. A transfer that unfairly benefits the debtor or some creditors at the expense of others is evident when [p. 426]
    a. a debtor transfers property to a creditor within 90 days before filing a petition in bankruptcy.
    b. the transfer is made for a preexisting debt.
    c. the creditor would receive more from the transfer than in a Chapter 7 proceeding.
    d. all of the above

30. Under the 2005 act, if personal property of an individual debtor secures a claim or is subject to an expired lease and is not exempt property, the debtor must choose to do which one of the following? [p. 432]
    a. surrender the personal property
    b. redeem the property by paying the secured lien in full
    c. assume the unexpired lease
    d. any one of the above

31. In order for the court to confirm a Chapter 11 reorganization plan under the cram-down provision over the objection of a class of creditors [p. 442]
    a. at least one class of creditors must have voted to accept the plan.
    b. the plan must be fair and equitable.
    c. the plan must be feasible.
    d. all of the above

32. Which of the following is not true about a proceeding under Chapter 12? [p. 444]
    a. The debtor may be a family fisherman.
    b. A creditor may file an involuntary petition.
    c. The family farmer is a debtor-in-possession who may continue to operate the farm.
    d. The bankruptcy estate also includes property that the debtor acquires after the commencement of the case and before the reorganization plan is completed.

33. The advantages of filing under a Chapter 13 bankruptcy include [p. 435]
    a. the ability to keep more property than is exempt under Chapter 7.
    b. the fact that it is cheaper and there is less compilation involved.
    c. avoidance of having the tag of liquidation attached to the debtor and his or her credit history.
    d. all of the above

34. Who may file a Chapter 13 petition for bankruptcy? [p. 435]
    a. corporations
    b. banks
    c. only individuals with regular income with unsecured debts of less than $307,675 and secured debts of less than $922,975
    d. sole proprietors without debt

35. What type of bankruptcy is Chapter 13 a form of? [p. 435]
    a. It is a form of reorganization bankruptcy.
    b. It is a form of family farmer bankruptcy.
    c. It is a form of liquidation bankruptcy.
    d. It is a form of state court bankruptcy.

Short Answer

36. The granting of bankruptcy gives debtors a _____ _____ by freeing them of some legal responsibility for past debts. [p. 418]

37. An _____ petition is filed by creditors of a debtor. [p. 419]

38. What additional burden does an attorney have under the 2005 act that did not previously exist? [p. 421] _____

    _____

39. The permanent trustee is elected at the _____. [p. 421]

40. The document required to be filed by an equity security holder that states the amount of his or her interest against the debtor is called a _____ _____ _____. [p. 422]

41. Name at least four things that a bankruptcy trustee is empowered to do. [p. 422]

    _____

    _____

42. Who must sign an involuntary petition if there are more than 12 creditors? [p. 419]

    _____

43. The suspension of certain legal actions by creditors against the debtor or the debtor's property when a petition is filed is called an _____ _____. [p. 422]

44. What is relief from stay? [p. 423] _____

    _____

45. Give three examples of property that is exempt from bankruptcy. [p. 424] _____

    _____

46. What is the bankruptcy estate? [p. 424] _____

    _____

47. What is an abusive filing? [p. 429] _____

    _____

48. What is the means test? [p. 430] _____

    _____

49. What does the debtor's plan of reorganization usually contain? [p. 440] _____

    _____

    _____

50. A plan of reorganization must be _____ by the court before it becomes effective. [p. 441]

Answers to Refresh Your Memory

1. core proceedings [p. 418]
2. noncore proceedings concerning the debtor [p. 419]
3. fresh start, partial [p. 418]
4. 7 [p. 428]
5. discharged [p. 423]
6. petition [p. 419]
7. debtor [p. 419]
8. involuntary petition [p. 419]
9. voluntary, unchallenged [p. 421]
10. first meeting of the creditors [p. 421]
11. permanent, creditors [p. 428]
12. Unsecured creditors [p. 421]
13. automatic stay [p. 422]
14. Exempt property [p. 424]
15. median, means [p. 429]

Critical Thought Exercise Model Answer

The restriction against discharge of student loans was designed to remedy an abuse by students, who, immediately upon graduation, would file bankruptcy to secure a discharge of educational loans. These students often had no other indebtedness and could pay their debts out of future wages.

In this case, Mills has truly fallen on hard times. Her monthly income does not meet her usual expenses. The combination of no support from her husband, four in-home dependents, and no prospects for increased income, give rise to a situation where a court could easily find that repayment of the educations loans would create an undue hardship. The restriction against discharge of educational loans was passed by Congress to stop an abuse. The restriction was never intended to prevent a deserving petitioner from getting protection and a fresh start from the bankruptcy court. Mills should be allowed to have all of her debts discharged in bankruptcy to avoid undue hardship.

Answers to Practice Quiz

True/False

1. False The main goal of federal bankruptcy law is to discharge the debtor from burdensome debts while at the same time protecting some of the rights of creditors.
2. True The 2005 act added this provision that requires counseling from an approved nonprofit credit counseling agency.
3. False The proof of claim must be filed in a timely manner which is usually interpreted to mean within six months of the first meeting of creditors.
4. True These creditors include a former spouse and children of the debtor.

5. True   A petition for relief from stay is usually brought by a secured creditor in situations involving depreciating assets where the property is not sufficiently protected during the bankruptcy proceeding.

6. False   Gifts, inheritances, life insurance proceeds, and property from divorce settlements that the debtor is entitled to receive within 180 days after the petition is filed become part of the bankruptcy estate.

7. True   The federal exemptions are adjusted every three years to reflect changes in the Consumer Price Index.

8. False   Earnings from the property of the estate such as the examples given are property of the estate.

9. False   The court will look at transfers up to two years before the filing of the petition.

10. True   The court will pay the bona fide good faith purchaser what was paid for the property and then put the property into the bankruptcy estate.

11. False   The court may also convert the Chapter 7 bankruptcy into a Chapter 13 or Chapter 11 proceeding, forcing the debtor to pay some of their future income over a five-year period to pay off pre-petition debts.

12. False   The trustee acts in the best interest of all the parties, including the debtor and all the creditors.

13. True   The court will steer most debtors into filing for Chapter 13 bankruptcy where they will have to pay some of their pre-petition debt.

14. False   The state median income is that income where half of the state's families have income above the figure and half of the state's families have income below that figure.

15. True   The means test is a new, complicated calculation that establishes a test to determine if the debtor can pay pre-petition debt out of post-petition income.

16. False   The debtor does not have to accept a conversion to Chapter 13, but the court will then dismiss the Chapter 7 petition and the debtor will not get any relief. The debtor will usually agree to convert the case to Chapter 13 proceedings.

17. False   Any party of interest is allowed to file an objection to the discharge of a debt.

18. False   If the discharge is procured through the fraud of the debtor, a party of interest is allowed to bring a motion for revocation of the bankruptcy.

19. False   The main goal of Chapter 11 is to reorganize the debtor with a new capital organization so that it will be able to come through the bankruptcy as a viable concern.

20. True   Chapter 11 is available to individuals, partnerships, corporations, and other business entities, nonincorporated associations, and railroads.

21. False   A petition under Chapter 13 must be voluntarily filed by a debtor with regular income.

22. False   The debtor-in-possession has the power to operate the debtor's business while the bankruptcy proceeding is taking place, including making purchases and entering into contracts. Unsecured creditors are given automatic priority as an administrative expense in bankruptcy.

23. True   An executory contract or unexpired lease has not been fully performed. The debtor, with the court's approval, may reject the contract or lease.

24. True.   The debtor's right to file a plan of reorganization with the bankruptcy court is an exclusive   right that must be accomplished within the first 120 days after the date of the order for relief.

25. False   The plan can still be confirmed by the court, using the Bankruptcy Code's cram-down provision.

Multiple Choice

26. D   Answer D is the correct answer as answers A, B, and C all state what must be contained in a voluntary petition for bankruptcy while answer D is not a requirement.

27. A   Answer A is the correct answer as it is an order that occurs upon the filing of a petition. Answer B is incorrect because it is a form that is submitted by a creditor after the order for relief is issued. Answer C is incorrect because debts are not discharged automatically at the beginning of the proceedings. Answer D is incorrect for the above reasons.

28. D   Answer D is the correct answer as Answers A, B, and C are all requirements to find a fraudulent transfer.

29. D   Answer D is the correct answer as the answers given in choices A, B, and C are all indicative of a transfer that unfairly benefits either the debtor or creditor at the expense of others.

30. D   Answer D is the correct answer as answers A, B, and C all state options that a secured creditor has with respect to the claims that may be made on a debtor's property.

31. D   Answer D is the correct answer as each of the other choices is a correct statement of a requirement under the Bankruptcy Code when a bankruptcy court applies the cram-down provision.

32. B   Answer B is the correct answer as only a voluntary petition may be filed by a family farmer or family fisherman. Answers A, C, and D are all correct statements of requirements for proceedings under a Chapter 12 adjustment of debts of a family farmer or fisherman with regular income.

33. D   Answer D is the correct answer as answers A, B, and C all state the advantages of filing under a Chapter 13 bankruptcy.

34. C   Answer C is the correct answer as it states specifically who may file a Chapter 13 petition for bankruptcy. Answers A and B are incorrect as they may not utilize this type of bankruptcy proceeding. Answer D is incorrect as a sole proprietor without debt would not have a need to file for bankruptcy in the first place.

35. A   Answer A is the correct answer as Chapter 13 is a form of reorganization bankruptcy. Answer B is incorrect as Family Farmer Bankruptcy is provided for in Chapter 12 of the Bankruptcy Code. Answer C is incorrect as liquidation bankruptcy refers to Chapter 7 of the Bankruptcy Code. Answer D is incorrect as there is no state court bankruptcy.

Short Answer

36.   fresh start
37.   involuntary
38.   The attorney must swear under penalty of perjury that he/she has certified the accuracy of the information contained in the bankruptcy petition and the schedules. The attorney is subject to monetary fines and sanctions if there are any factual discrepancies.
39.   meeting of the creditors
40.   proof of interest
41.   take immediate possession of the debtor's property; protect domestic support orders; review all materials filed by the debtor; separate secured and unsecured property; set aside exempt property; investigate the debtor's financial affairs; examine proof of claims; and other items listed on page 422 of the main text
42.   The petition must be signed by at least three creditors if the debtor has more than 12 creditors.
43.   automatic stay

44. relief that is requested by a secured creditor that may be granted by the court if the secured property is not adequately protected during the bankruptcy proceeding

45. Interest up to $2,950 in one motor vehicle; interest in jewelry up to $1,225 that is held for personal use; interest up to $1,850 in value in implements, tools, or professional books used in the debtor's trade. Note that answers will vary. Complete list on page 424 of text.

46. the debtor's property and earnings that comprise the estate of a bankruptcy proceeding

47. a Chapter 7 filing that is found to be an abuse of Chapter 7 liquidation bankruptcy

48. a new test added by the 2005 act that applies to debtors who have family incomes that exceed the state's median income for families of the same size

49. The plan contains the debtor's proposed new capital structure wherein he or she designates the different classes of claims and interests.

50. confirmed

Chapter 29

AGENCY FORMATION
AND TERMINATION

Chapter Overview

This chapter will provide you with a thorough understanding of agency including the important role that it plays in the business world, as well as the creation and termination of an agency relationship. Additionally you will become familiar with the three most common types of employment relationships and how to differentiate among them.

Objectives

Upon completion of the exercises in this chapter, you should be able to:
1.   Describe an agency relationship.
2.   Recognize and define a principal-independent contractor relationship.
3.   Discuss the creation of an express agency versus an implied agency.
4.   Explain the definition of an apparent agency.
5.   Discuss the various ways an agency may be terminated.
6.   Discuss wrongful termination of an agency contract.

Practical Application

You will learn how the different types of agencies are created as well as terminated. You will also be able to recognize an irrevocable agency and whether or not there has been a wrongful termination of an agency contract. Further, you will know the differences among the three main types of employment relationships and the liabilities associated with each. This chapter will be especially useful to anyone in business, because agencies are an essential part of any successful business.

Helpful Hints

Since most of us have been or will be in some sort of employment relationship in our lifetime, this chapter is very easy to apply to either our past employment experiences or our future endeavors. Many of us have been agents and have not realized that fact. You will find this chapter easier to learn if you place yourself in the shoes of the situation you are trying to learn about. Additionally, if you familiarize yourself with the basic terminology given in the Study Tips section that follows, the concepts will become easier and clearer for you to understand.

Study Tips

Basic Terminology

Agency: Section 1(1) of the Restatement (Second) of Agency defines agency as "a fiduciary relationship which results from the manifestation of consent by one person to another that the other shall act in his behalf and subject to his control, and consent by the other so to act."

Principal – A party who employs another individual to act on his or her behalf.

Agent – A party who agrees to act on behalf of another.

Employer-Employee Relationship – An association that results when an employer hires an employee to perform some type of physical service.

Principal-Agent Relationship – A relationship whereby an employee is hired and given the authority to act and enter into contracts on the employer's behalf.

Independent Contractor – A person or business who is not an employee but who is hired by a principal to perform a certain task on his behalf. This person is not controlled by the principal with regard to the performance of the task that he or she is employed to do.

At-will Employee – An employee without an employment contract.

Express Agency – An express agreement between a principal and agent thereby agreeing to enter into an agency agreement with one another.

Exclusive Agency Contract – A distinct contract between the principal and agent whereby the principal agrees not to employ any agent other than the exclusive agent.

Power of Attorney – An agency agreement that expressly gives an agent the authority to sign legal documents on the principal's behalf. The agent in this situation is referred to as an Attorney-in-fact.

Implied Agency – An agency that is inferred from the parties' conduct and where there has not been an express creation of an agency between the principal and the agent.

Apparent Agency – An agency that the principal creates that appears to exist but really does not exist.

Agency by Ratification – An agency that is created by a principal ratifying an agency that is created by an unauthorized act such as the misrepresentation of oneself as another's agent when in fact he or she is not an agent at all.

Wrongful Termination – A violation of the terms of the agency contract thereby resulting in the termination of the agency contract.

Revocation of Authority – The termination of an agency contract by a principal.

Renunciation of Authority – The termination of an agency contract by an agent.

Strategic Alliance – An agreement between two or more businesses from different countries to accomplish a certain purpose or function.

Agency Basics

Capacity – If an individual has the capacity to enter into a contract, then he or she can appoint an agent to act on his or her behalf.

Purpose – The agency must be formed for a lawful purpose.

Three types of employment relationships:

- Employer-Employee Relationship – Where an employer hires an employee to perform some sort of physical service.

- Principal-Agent Relationship – Where an employer hires an employee and gives the employee power to act and enter into contracts on his or her behalf.

- Principal-Independent Contractor Relationship – Persons and businesses who are hired to perform certain tasks on behalf of the principal. The *degree of control* that an employer has over an agent is the determining factor on whether one is an employee or an independent contractor. Other considerations include but are not limited to: *the duration of the agent's employment by the principal, the degree of skill required to complete the task, whether the principal provides the equipment and tools needed in the work, etc*.

Agency Formation

There are four ways that an agency may be formed. They are expressly, impliedly, apparently, and by ratification.

- **Express Agency** – This is the most common type of agency wherein an agent and a principal expressly agree to enter into an agency agreement with one another. It may be oral or in writing. An example of an express agency is a *power of attorney.* The power of attorney may be *general*, thereby giving broad powers to the agent to act in any matters on the principal's behalf, or it may be *special* giving limited powers as provided for in the parties' agreement. *Incidental authority* is implied authority to act in emergency situations and other contingent circumstances in order to protect the principal's property and rights.

- **Implied Agency** – An agency that is created by the parties' conduct. The implied authority of the agent may be given by custom in the industry, the agent's position, or the prior dealing between the parties. There cannot be a conflict between the express and implied authority.

- **Apparent Agency** – An agency by estoppel (or apparent agency) is created when a principal gives the appearance of an agency that in reality does not exist. Upon creation of this type of agency, the principal is bound to contract entered into by the apparent agent while acting within the parameters of the apparent agency.

- **Agency by Ratification** – An agency that is a result of a principal ratifying an unauthorized act by another who represents him or herself as another's agent when the reality is that he or she is not the principal's agent.

Duties Owed by Agent to Principal

Loyalty   – The duty of loyalty is discussed in Chapter 30.

Performance – The agent owes a **duty to perform** the lawful duties stated in the parties' contract. Additionally the agent must meet the standard of reasonable care, skill, and diligence that is implied in all contracts.

Beware, an agent that presents himself or herself as having higher than average skills will be held to a higher standard of performance. For example, a physician who contends that he or she is a plastic surgeon specialist will be held to a reasonable specialist in plastic surgery standard.

Accountability – The agent owes a **duty to keep an accurate accounting** of all transactions performed on behalf of the principal. This means that the agent must keep records of all money that has been spent and all money that has been received during the duration of the agency.

The principal's separate account must be maintained by the agent and the principal's property must be used in an authorized manner.

Notification – The agent owes a **duty of notification** to the principal if the agent learns information that is important to the principal. It is assumed that the principal knows most information that the agent knows. This is called **imputed knowledge.**

The Principal's Duties

The principal's duties may also be stated in the parties' contract or implied by law.
An easy mnemonic to remember the principal's duties is: **C**onnie **R**emembers the **I**ndian **C**oin.

Compensation – The principal owes a **duty to compensate** an agent for the services he or she has provided. If the compensation is not stated in the parties' agreement, then compensation will be based on custom or what is the reasonable value for the agent's services.

Reimbursement – The principal owes a **duty to reimburse** the agent for all expenses the agent has expended from his or her own money if the expenses were authorized and within the scope of the agency and necessary to discharge the agent's duties in carrying out the agency.

Indemnification – The principal owes a **duty to indemnify** the agent for any losses that the agent may suffer due to the principal's misconduct.

Cooperation – The principal owes a **duty to cooperate** with and help the agent in the performance of the agent's duties and the goal of the agency.

Termination of an Agency and Employment Contract

An agency contract may be terminated by an act of the parties or by operation of law. There are four ways to terminate an agency relationship by the actions of the parties.

- **Mutual Agreement** – The parties may mutually agree to terminate their agreement.
- **Lapse of Time** – The agency agreement will end after a certain period of time passes.
- **Purpose Achieved** – The agency ends when the purpose of the agreement is accomplished.
- **Occurrence of a Specified Event** – The agency ends when a specified event in the parties' agreement happens.

There are six ways to terminate an agency relationship by operation of law.

- **Death** – The death of either the agent or principal ends the agency relationship.
- **Insanity** – Insanity of either party ends the agency relationship.
- **Bankruptcy** – If the principal is found bankrupt, the agency is terminated. However, an agent's bankruptcy usually does not end the agency.
- **Impossibility** – The agency ends if circumstances make the agency impossible. The following have been recognized under this method of termination:
  - **Loss or destruction of the subject matter of the agency**
  - **Loss of a required qualification** – For example, a private physician loses his or her license.
  - **A change in the law** – If the agency contains a provision that becomes illegal, the agency contract will end.
- **Changed circumstances** – If there are changed circumstances that lead the agent to determine that the original instructions he or she received from the principal no longer apply, then the agency will be terminated.
- **War** – War between the agent's and principal's countries terminates the agency.

Irrevocable Agencies – These are referred to as agencies coupled with an interest. This type of agency is not ended by death or incapacity of either party and only terminates upon performance of the agent's obligations. It is irrevocable and created for the agent's benefit.

Wrongful Termination of an Agency or Employment Contract – If the principal's or agent's termination of an agency contract breaches the agency contract, then the termination may be considered to be wrongful.

Revocation of Authority – When a principal ends an agency agreement, he or she is terminating the agency agreement by revocation of authority.

Renunciation of Authority – When an agent ends an agency agreement, it is called a renunciation of authority.

Refresh Your Memory

The following exercise will give you the opportunity to refresh your memory of the principles given to you in this chapter. Read the question twice and place your answer in the blanks provided. If you do not remember, go to the next question, and come back to the one you did not answer.

1.   A principal is a party who _____ another individual to act on his or her behalf.

2.   The principal-agent relationship is a _____ relationship.

3.   Individuals who lack contractual capacity cannot appoint an _____.

4.   A _____-_____ relationship is formed when an employer hires an employee and gives that employee authority to act and enter into contracts on his or her behalf.

5.   An agency can be created only to accomplish a _____ purpose.

6.   An independent contractor is a person or business that is not an _____ but is employed by a principal to perform a certain task on his behalf.

7.   If the principal and agent enter into an _____ agency contract, the principal cannot employ any agent other than the _____ agent.

8.   An _____ agency is the most common type of agency.

9.   An express agency agreement used to give an agent the power to sign legal documents is called a _____.

10.   An _____ agency is an agency that arises when a principal creates the appearance of an agency that in actuality does not exist.

11.   An agency by _____ occurs when a person misrepresents himself or herself as another's agent when he/she is not and the purported principal accepts the unauthorized act.

12.   Death, insanity, bankruptcy, and impossibility are four ways to terminate an agency by _____.

13.   If Joe is hired to paint Sue's house and the house burns down before it is painted, the agency is terminated by _____.

14.   If an agency is terminated by _____ _____ ___ _____, the principal is under a duty to give certain third parties notification of the termination.

15.   The duty of _____ includes keeping records of all property and money received and expended during the course of the agency.

Critical Thought Exercise

Dave Polk was a self-employed handyman, doing business under the name Polk Speedy-Fix. From 2000-2007, Polk performed maintenance and repair work for numerous people in Sun City West, Arizona, including Frank and Martha Hamilton. Polk did landscape maintenance, cactus trimming, painting, plumbing, and carpentry. Polk completed a job in May 2007 for the Hamiltons wherein he replaced a toilet and vanity. Polk was then hired to trim a 30-foot-tall palm tree in the Hamiltons' side yard. Polk was paid $20 per hour for his previous jobs by the Hamiltons. Polk was to receive the same rate of pay for trimming the palm tree.

When Polk arrived to trim the palm tree, Mr. Hamilton told him he wanted it trimmed to a height that was approximately the same as the house, along with trimming back the fronds so that they were at least five feet from the homes of both the Hamiltons and their neighbors. Polk took out several saws and two ladders from his repair van. Polk also borrowed a tree trimming saw and a rope from the Hamiltons. When his ladder was unable to reach the top areas of the tree, Polk climbed the tree. Polk fell from the palm tree when the rope broke and he received severe injuries to his back, pelvis, and internal organs. At age 32, he was totally unable to work.

Polk sued the Hamiltons to recover for his injuries, claiming that he was working as an employee at the time of his injuries and was therefore entitled to workers' compensation protection from the Hamiltons. The Hamiltons argued that Polk was an independent contractor.

Was Polk an employee of the Hamiltons or an independent contractor?

Answer:

_____

_____

_____

_____

_____

_____

_____

_____

_____

_____

_____

_____

_____

_____

_____

_____

_____

_____

_____

_____

Practice Quiz

True/False

1. ___ The agent is the party who hires another person to act on his or her behalf. [p. 451]

2. ___ Insane persons and minors cannot appoint agents because they lack contractual capacity. [p. 452]

3. ___ Employees may enter into all contracts once they have been hired by the employer. [p. 452]

4. ___ An auto worker is an employee of the Ford Corporation because he or she performs a physical task. [p. 452]

5. ___ An independent contractor has no authority to enter into contracts on behalf of the principal. [p. 452]

6. ___ When an agent terminates an agency, it is called a revocation of authority. [p. 459]

7. ___ Express agency contracts can be either oral or written. [p. 453]

8. ___ An agent who is hired to be the manager of a store has express authority to hire and fire employees. [p. 453]

9. ___ A principal is estopped from denying the agency relationship exists when the apparent agency is established. [p. 453]

10. ___ If Mary is hired to paint a house for three days, the agency contract does not terminate until the house is painted. [p. 457]

11. ___ Information learned by an agent is not assumed to be known by the principal. [p. 457]

12. ___ If Fred is hired to paint a house for Sue and Fred is just starting when Sue dies, Fred may complete the painting job because he has an agency contract. [p. 458]

13. ___ Nick's agency relationship with Donald to serve as his limo driver is terminated if Nick's driver's license expires. [p. 459]

14. ___ An independent contractor is a person or business who is an employee and who is employed by a principal to perform a certain task on his or her behalf. [p. 452]

15. ___ One of the factors in determining whether an agency by ratification has occurred is if the purported principal accepts the authorized act. [p. 455]

Multiple Choice

16. Which of the following is a type of agency relationship? [p. 453]
    a. express
    b. implied
    c. apparent
    d. all of the above

17. Which one of the following is not a duty owed by an agent to the principal? [p. 456]
    a. duty of performance
    b. duty of indemnification
    c. duty of notification
    d. duty of accountability

18. Joe's Auto Detailing is hired by Helen to wash the four delivery trucks owned by Helen's Market. Helen instructs Joe as to exactly how she wants the trucks washed and watches Joe as he details the vehicles. Joe uses his own supplies and equipment to perform the job. Joe is an [p. 453]
    a. agent.
    b. employee.
    c. independent contractor.
    d. none of the above

19. Which of the following would be considered to be an independent contractor? [p. 452]
    a. a stockbroker
    b. a dentist
    c. a certified public accountant
    d. all of the above

20. Which of the following is not a duty owed by a principal? [p. 455]
    a. duty of performance.
    b. duty of compensation
    c. duty of cooperation
    d. none of the above

21. The parties to an agency contract can terminate the agency contract by [p. 457]
    a. agreement.
    b. the occurrence of a specified act.
    c. achieving the stated purpose of the agency agreement.
    d. all of the above

22. An agency relationship terminates if a situation arises that makes its fulfillment impossible. Which of the following is a circumstance that can lead to termination on the ground of impossibility? [p. 459]
    a. the death of either the principal or the agent
    b. the outbreak of war between the principal's country and the agent's country
    c. a change in the law
    d. all of the above

23. What type of authority can an agent exercise in the event of an emergency? [p. 453]
    a. apparent authority
    b. incidental authority
    c. express authority
    d. implied authority

24. Authority that is derived from the conduct of the parties, custom and usage of trade, or act that is incidental to carrying out the agent's duties is [p. 453]
    a. express authority.
    b. retroactive authority.
    c. obvious authority.
    d. implied authority.

25. If a principal hires a licensed real estate broker to sell his house and the house is sold, when does the agency terminate? [p. 459]
    a. upon finding another real estate broker
    b. upon rejection of the offer to sell the principal's home
    c. on December 31st of the year the house is for sale
    d. upon the sale of the home and payment to the broker of the agreed-upon compensation

Short Answer

26. Agency agreements that are formed for _____ purposes are void and against public policy. [p. 452]

27. The extent of the authority granted to an agent in a principal-agent relationship is governed by any express agreement between the parties and _____ from the circumstances of the agency. [p. 452]

28. A great deal of control over an individual may indicate that what type of relationship exists? [p. 452] _____

29. What is the most common form of agency? [p. 453] _____

30. Whose actions create an apparent agency? [p. 453] _____

31. Give three ways that the parties may terminate an agency relationship. [p. 457] _____
    _____

32. Give at least two ways that an agency relationship may terminate where a situation presents itself and thereby makes its fulfillment impossible. [p. 459] _____
    _____

33. A renunciation of authority is when _____ _____ terminates an agency. [p. 459]

34. What determines whether or not an employee is an agent? [p. 452] _____
    _____

35. What is a professional agent? [p. 452] _____
    _____

36. If an insurance company hires ten bounty hunters to apprehend a wanted felon, when do the agencies terminate? [p. 457] _____
    _____

37. Parties who dealt with an agent must be given _____ notice of termination when the agency is terminated by agreement of the parties. [p. 458]

38. When an agency terminates by operation of law, what type of duty does the principal owe to third parties? [p. 457] _____

39. If the agent continues to perform his or her duties after the principal dies, what is the effect upon the principal's estate? [p. 458] _____

40. What type of notice is usually given by a newspaper announcement upon the termination of an agency? [p. 458] _____

Answers to Refresh Your Memory

1. employs [p. 451]
2. fiduciary [p. 451]
3. agents [p. 452]
4. principal-agent [p. 452]
5. lawful [p. 452]
6. employee [p. 452]
7. exclusive, exclusive [p. 453]
8. express [p. 453]
9. power of attorney [p. 453]
10. apparent [p. 453]
11. ratification [p. 455]
12. operation of law [p. 458]
13. impossibility [p. 459]
14. agreement of the parties [p. 457]
15. accountability [p. 457]

Critical Thought Exercise Model Answer

A court would have to determine Polk's status as to employee versus independent contractor based upon answering several questions.

Did the Hamiltons exercise control over the details of Polk's work? Polk was instructed to trim the tree to an approximate size. The Hamiltons gave no other instructions concerning how the task was to be accomplished.

Was Polk engaged in an occupation or business distinct from that of the Hamiltons? Polk had an ongoing handyman business and accepted work from numerous people. The Hamiltons were not in the home repair or landscape maintenance business.

Is the type of work usually done under the employer's direction or by a specialist without supervision? Tree trimming is a job that requires skill and training. It is not the type of job a homeowner would supervise. The Hamiltons did not supervise Polk.

Does the employer supply the tools at the place of work? Polk had his own van with tools for his jobs. In this case, Polk did borrow a saw and a piece of rope, but this does not appear to be the usual way that Polk accomplishes his tasks.

For how long was Polk employed? Polk was only hired for a limited time until a specific job was completed. He was hired separately for the bathroom work and the tree trimming.

What was the method of payment—periodic or upon completion of the job? Polk was paid an hourly wage, but he was paid by the job instead of receiving a paycheck every week or month.

What degree of skill is required of the worker? Each of the jobs performed by Polk required skill and specialized knowledge. The average homeowner does not have the skill or ability to trim a large tree. A tree trimming service usually performs the cutting back of a large tree.

Polk's status as an independent contractor is borne out by the above analysis. Polk had his own handyman business with his own tools and possessed special skills for accomplishing tasks that are often handled by trades people and specialists. The fact that he was hired for more than one job does not change the fact that he acted as an independent contractor on each job. Therefore, the Hamiltons were under no obligation to purchase workers' compensation insurance for Polk.

Answers to Practice Quiz

True/False

1. False   The party who hires another individual to act on his or her behalf is called the principal.
2. True   Individuals such as insane persons and minors lack contractual capacity and therefore may not appoint an agent. Only a court representative of these people can appoint an agent for the person who lacks capacity.
3. False   An employee may only enter into contracts for his or her employer that are within the scope of his/her employment.
4. True   An employer-employee relationship would be present in the Ford factory example as assembly of an automobile is a physical task.
5. False   Independent contractors may receive authorization from a principal to enter into contracts.
6. False   When an agent terminates an agency, it is called a renunciation of authority.
7. True   Express agency contracts can be either written or oral unless the Statute of Frauds requires a writing.
8. False   The agent will have incidental authority when they have certain implied authority to act.
9. True   When an apparent agent is acting within the scope of the apparent agency, the principal is estopped from denying the agency relationship and is bound to contracts entered into by the agent.
10. False   The agency contract may terminate by lapse of time when a time period is specified.
11. False   Most information learned by an agent in the course of employment is imputed to the principal. That is why the agent has a duty of notification.
12. False   The death of either party in an agency relationship will terminate the agency relationship.
13. True   The loss of a required qualification will terminate the agency.
14. False   An independent contractor is a person or business who is not an employee but who is employed by a principal to perform a certain task on his or her behalf.
15. False   One of the factors in determining whether an agency by ratification has occurred is if the purported principal has accepted the unauthorized act, not the authorized act.

Multiple Choice

16. D   Answer D is correct as answers A, B, and C are each a valid way for an agency relationship to be formed.
17. B   Answer B is correct as it does not state a duty owed by an agent, but sets forth a duty owed by a principal to the agent. Answers A, B, and D are all incorrect as they do state a duty owed by an agent to the principal.
18. C   Answer C is the correct answer as Joe used his own materials and is performing work on a one-time basis. Helen may give her preferences for how the work is performed, but she has no control over Joe. Joe also has an independent business and is not a regular employee of Helen's Market. Answer A is incorrect because Joe is not authorized to enter into contracts on behalf of Helen. Answer B is incorrect because Joe is not an employee whose physical acts are controlled by Helen. Answer D is incorrect because a correct choice is available.

19. D   Answer D is the correct answer as answers A, B, and C all correctly state individuals who would be considered to be independent contractors since they are persons who are not employees but who are hired to perform certain tasks on behalf of a principal.

20. A   Answer A is the correct answer as it does not state a duty of a principal, but a duty owed by an agent to the principal. Answers B and C are incorrect because they do state duties owed by a principal. Answer D is incorrect because a correct answer is available.

21. D   Answer D is the correct answer as Answers A, B, and C all state a way that the parties to an agency contract can terminate the agreement be either their agreement or by their actions.

22. C   Answer C is the correct answer as the passing of a new law that makes the agreed-upon service illegal will make the performance of the agency agreement impossible. Answers A and B are incorrect because they are not examples of an impossibility, but other reasons for termination by operation of law. Answer D is incorrect because Answers A and B are incorrect and there is only one correct answer.

23. B   Answer B is the correct answer as contingencies such as an emergency that may occur in the future regarding the fulfillment of the agency may require implied authority also known as incidental authority to act. Answers A, C, and D are not the types of authority that are incidental to authority originally granted.

24. D   Answer D is the correct answer as implied authority can be inferred from the parties' conduct, custom, and usage of the trade. Answer A is incorrect as express authority is given to the agent by the principal without having to draw inferences from the parties' conduct. Answer B is incorrect as there is no legal basis entitled retroactive authority. Answer C is incorrect as there is also no legal basis entitled obvious authority.

25. D   Answer D is the correct answer as it indicates that the purpose of selling the house has been achieved thereby terminating the agency. Answers A, B, and C do not qualify as examples of acts by the parties that may terminate an agency agreement.

Short Answer

26.   illegal
27.   implied
28.   It may indicate that an employee-employer relationship exists.
29.   express
30.   The principal's actions create an apparent agency.
31.   Lapse of time, mutual agreement, and purpose achieved are three ways that the parties may terminate an agency relationship.
32.   The loss or destruction of the subject matter of the agency and loss of a required qualification are two ways that an agency relationship may terminate if a situation presents itself that makes the agency purpose impossible to fulfill.
33.   an agent
34.   If an employee is given the authority to enter into contracts on behalf of the principal-employer, then the employee is an agent.
35.   an independent contractor who is a professional, such as a lawyer
36.   The agencies with all of the agents end when any one of the agents fulfills the stated purpose. In this instance, when one of the bounty hunters captures the wanted felon.
37.   direct
38.   There is no duty of notification to third parties when an agency terminates by operation of law.
39.   The agent's actions after the principal's death do not bind the principal's estate.
40.   Constructive notice usually involves placing a notice of the termination of the agency in a newspaper that is distributed throughout the community.

Chapter 30

LIABILITY OF PRINCIPALS
AND AGENTS

Chapter Overview

The previous chapter gave you an overview of the creation and termination of an agency as well as the various types of agencies. This chapter expands on what you have learned about agency by discussing the principal's and agent's duties as well as their liability for the breach of the same.

Objectives

Upon completion of the exercises in this chapter, you should be able to:
1. List and discuss the agent's duties to the principal.
2. Describe the effect of an agent's breach of loyalty to the principal.
3. Discuss the principal's and agent's liability when there is a third-party contract involved.
4. Discuss the principal's liability for the agent's tortious conduct.
5. Define the doctrine of respondeat superior.
6. Explain how an independent contract relationship is formed.
7. Explain the principal's liability for an independent contractor's torts.

Practical Application

You will be aware of the duties of both the agent as well as the principal as one day you may be in a position of fulfilling either of the roles. Additionally you will be more cognizant of the liabilities that both the agent and principal face for breach of their respective duties thereby giving you more insight into what is expected of an agent and a principal.

Helpful Hints

Many of the concepts that you will learn in this chapter are filled with common sense. However, in order to remember the duties of the principal and agent as well as the liabilities for breach of the same, it is much easier to not only list them separately, but to commit them to memory by using the suggested mnemonics given in the Study Tips section that follows. Since this chapter is an expansion of the previous chapter, the concepts are easily learned.

Study Tips

The Agent's Duties

The agent's duties are presented in the parties' agency agreement or implied by law.

An easy mnemonic to remember the agent's duties is <u>L</u>oyal <u>P</u>ercy's <u>A</u>ccounting is <u>N</u>oteworthy.

Duties relating to performance, accountability, and notification were discussed in Chapter 29. The study tips from Chapter 29 should be read in conjunction with the material in this chapter.

<u>L</u>oyalty –   The agent owes a duty to be faithful to the principal. The following are examples of breaches of loyalty:
  - An agent is prohibited from **undisclosed self-dealing** with the principal.
  - An agent may not **usurp an opportunity** that belongs to the principal unless upon consideration the principal has rejected it.
  - An agent may **not compete** with the principal during the agency relationship.
  - An agent may not **misuse confidential information** regarding the principal' affairs.
  - An agent may not act for two or more different principals in the same transaction as this is a **dual agency**. The parties may agree to it though.

<u>P</u>erformance –   The agent owes a **duty to perform** the lawful duties stated in the parties' contract. Additionally, the agent must meet the standard of reasonable care, skill, and diligence that is implied in all contracts.

Beware, an agent that presents himself or herself as having higher than average skills will be held to a higher standard of performance. For example, a physician who contends that he or she is a plastic surgeon specialist will be field to a reasonable specialist in plastic surgery standard.

<u>A</u>ccountability – The agent owes a **duty to keep an accurate accounting** of all transactions performed on behalf of the principal. This means that the agent must keep records of all money that has been spent and all money that has been received during the duration of the agency

The principal's separate account must be maintained by the agent and the principal's property must be used in an authorized manner.

<u>N</u>otification –   The agent owes a **duty of notification** to the principal if the agent learns information that is important to the principal. It is assumed that the principal knows most information that the agent knows. This is called **imputed knowledge**.

Contract Liability to Third Parties

Basic Information: If an agent is authorized by the principal to enter into a contract with a third party, then the principal is liable on the contract. In order to determine liability, the classification of the agency must be examined.

Agency Classifications: There are three types of agency classifications. They are the fully disclosed agency, the partially disclosed agency, and the undisclosed agency.

- **Fully Disclosed** – The third party knows who the agent is acting on behalf of. The principal is liable in a fully disclosed agency situation. However, the agent will also be held liable if he or she guarantees that the principal will perform the contract.

- **Partially Disclosed** – The agent's status is disclosed but the principal's identity is undisclosed. Both the principal and agent are liable on a third-party contract. If the agent is made to pay, he or she may seek indemnification from the principal.

- **Undisclosed** – If a third party does not know about the agency or the principal's identity, then an undisclosed agency exists. The principal as well as the agent are liable on a contract with a third party as the agent's nondisclosure makes him a principal to the contract. However, the agent may seek indemnification from the principal if he or she is made to pay on the contract.

Agent Exceeding the Scope of Authority
- An agent who enters into a contract with a third party has in essence warranted that he or she has the authority to do so. However, the principal will not be liable on the contract where the agent has exceeded his or her authority on the contract unless the principal **ratifies** the contract.

Tort Liability to Third Parties

The principal and agent are personally responsible for their own tortious conduct. However, the principal is liable for the agent's conduct if he or she was acting within the scope of his or her authority. The agent, though, is only liable for the torts of the principal if he or she directly or indirectly participates in or abets and aids the conduct of the principal. The factors that are examined in determining whether an agent's conduct was within the scope of his or her employment include:
- Did the principal request or authorize the agent's act?
- Was the principal's purpose being advanced by the agent when the act occurred?
- Was the agent employed to perform the act that he or she completed?
- Was the act accomplished during the time that the time of employment authorized by the principal?

Misrepresentation

- As you may recall, this tort is also referred to as **fraud** or **deceit**.
- The principal is liable for the misrepresentation of the agent if it is made during the scope of his or her employment.
- The third party may rescind the contract with the principal and recover any consideration paid or affirm the contract and recover damages.

Negligence

Liability for negligence is based on the doctrine of **respondeat superior,** which assesses liability based on the employment relationship between the princiapal and agent not on any fault of the principal. However, there are some situations where liability is not clear.

- **Frolic and Detour** – This refers to the situation where an agent performs a personal errand while performing a job for the principal. Negligent acts in this situation are viewed on a case-by-case basis. The court will examine if the detour is minor or substantial.

- **The Coming and Going Rule** – Under common law, a principal is not held liable for injuries caused by employees and agents who are on their way to or from work. This rule holds true regardless if the principal provided the transportation.

- **Dual-Purpose Mission** – This situation refers to when the agent is doing something for him or herself and for the principal. The majority rule holds that both the principal and agent are liable if an injury occurs while the agent is on this sort of mission.

Intentional Torts

If the intentional tort occurs outside of the principal's scope of business, the principal is not liable. The doctrine of vicarious liability applies though in the situation where the agent or employee commits an intentional tort in the scope of his or her employment. The **Motivation Test** and the **Work-Related Test** are applied to determine if the torts were committed within the scope of the agent's employment.

- **The Motivation Test** – If the agent's motivation in performing the intentional tort was the principal's business, then the principal is liable for any injury caused by the tort.

- **The Work-Related Test** – If the intentional tort was performed during a work-related time or space, the principle is liable for any injuries caused by the intentional torts. The motivation of the agent is not considered in the use of this test.

Independent Contractor

As you may recall from the previous chapter, the degree of control that an employer has over an agent is the most important factor in determining whether someone is an employee or an independent contractor. Additional factors include but are not limited to:
- The amount of skill needed to finish the task.
- Whether the principal provides the equipment and tools used in the job.
- Whether payment is by time or by the job.
- Whether the employer controls the means and manner of completing the job.

Liability for Independent Contractor Torts

The general rule is that a principal is not liable for the torts of its independent contractors. However, there are some **exceptions**. They are:

- **Nondelegable Duties** – A principal may not avoid liability by delegating nondelegable duties.
- **Special Risks** – Principals may not avoid strict liability for dangerous activities by assigning them to independent contractors.

- **Negligence in the Selection of an Independent Contractor** – The hiring of an unqualified or knowingly dangerous person who injures someone while on the job will cause the principal to be held liable for such negligent selection of this type of independent contractor.

Refresh Your Memory

The following exercise will enable you to refresh your memory on the rules and principles presented to you in this chapter. Read each question twice and place your answer in the blanks provided. Review the chapter material for any question you miss or are unable to remember.

1. What are four types of breaches of loyalty? _____
_____

2. What is self-dealing? _____
_____

3. An employee who takes the customer list from his/her employer's business and uses it to solicit customers when he/she opens his/her own business has violated the duty of loyalty through _____ ___ _____ _____.

4. A third party can always enforce a contract against _____, regardless of whether the agency is fully disclosed, partially disclosed, or _____.

5. An agent's duty of loyalty is _____ in nature in that he or she is not to act against the principal's interest.

6. An agent may not usurp an opportunity for himself or herself unless _____
_____.

7. If a lawyer represents two clients in a dispute who have adverse interests, the lawyer may not be entitled to any compensation from either client because he or she is snagging in a _____ _____.

8. A third party knows the actual identity of the principal in a _____ _____ agency.

9. If the agent signs his/her name to a contract, "Jim North, Agent," then this will be a _____ _____ agency and _____ will be liable on the contract.

10. What is an undisclosed agency? _____
_____

11. What is a warranty of an agent who enters into a contract on behalf of another party that he or she has the authority to do so? _____

12. If an agent exceeds the scope of his or her authority, the principal is not liable on the contract unless the principal _____ it.

13. A principal is liable for the tortious conduct of an agent who is acting within their _____ ____ _____.

14. What is the name of the rule that says a principal is generally not liable for injuries caused by its agents and employees while they are on their way to or from work? _____

15. Generally, a principal is not liable for the torts of its independent contractors because _____
_____.

Critical Thought Exercise

Earl West works for Dubyah International, an Illinois corporation that sells commercial fixtures and lighting to cities, developers, mall owners, and the government. West is mostly responsible for making sales calls for light poles, light standards, and lighting towers.

West is on the road 40 or more weeks per year and often does not come back to his home or office for three or more months at a time. Over the course of his 17 years of employment with Dubyah, West has had several stretches on the road that last six months or more.

When West is traveling for Dubyah, he often has to shop for food, toiletries, clothing, gifts, and business-related items, such as computer accessories for his laptop computer.

During a sales trip to Indianapolis, Indiana, in March 2006, West found it necessary to wash his laundry and buy an anniversary present for his wife. West went to the mall and then to Suds Town Laundromat to wash his clothes. While wrapping the present on a laundry-folding table, another patron of the Suds Town, Mike, spilled fabric softener on the wrapping paper. West then overloaded a dryer with flammable items, in direct violation of the warnings and rules posted directly above the dryer. This caused a dryer fire. When Mike verbally attacked West for starting the dryer fire, West punched Mike in the eye, causing severe eye damage. Suds Town then burned to the ground due to the dryer fire started by West.

Mike and Suds Town sue Dubyah for the damage caused by West. Dubyah argues that when the events at Suds Town occurred, West was not acting within the scope of his employment, relieving it of all liability.

If you were the judge in this case, what law would you apply and which party would prevail?

Answer:

_____
_____
_____
_____
_____
_____
_____
_____
_____
_____
_____
_____
_____
_____
_____
_____

Practice Quiz

True/False

1. ____ The agent's duty of loyalty does not prevent the agent from doing the same work for himself on the weekend in competition with the principal since the agent is doing the work on his own time. [p. 463]

2. ____ An agent may complete with the principal upon the termination of the agency if the agent has not signed a valid covenant-not-to-compete with the principal. [p. 464]

3. ____ In a partially disclosed agency, the principal is liable for the third-party contract and the agent is relieved of liability because the existence of an agent is known to the third party. [p. 465]

4. ____ The principal is relieved of all liability whenever the agent goes on a frolic and detour and injures a third person. [p. 468]

5. ____ An agent does not create liability for themselves if the principal is disclosed, regardless of how they sign a contract. [p. 464]

6. ____ Ratification occurs when a principal accepts the unauthorized contract entered into by its agent. [p. 466]

7. ____ Misrepresentation, negligence, and intentional torts are the three main areas of tort liability for principals and agents. [p. 467]

8. ____ An innocent misrepresentation occurs when an agent negligently makes a misrepresentation to a third party. [p. 469]

9. ____ A principal is not liable for injuries caused by its agents while they are on their way to or from work. This is referred to as frolic and detour. [p. 468]

10. ____ A principal is not liable for injury caused by its agent when the agent is mailing a package for the principal while on her way home. This is the coming and going rule. [p. 468]

11. ____ If Bob attacks Nelly, his ex-girlfriend, in a jealous rage when she comes into the principal's store where Bob works, the principle is liable for the intentional tort committed by Bob under the motivational test. [p. 468]

12. ____ Lou, an agent who works at principal's bar and restaurant, strikes a patron with a steel club numerous times because Lou is a racist and hates the patron, who is a minority. The agent's motivation in committing an intentional tort is irrelevant in using the work-related test to determine liability. [p. 469]

13. ____ A deceit in which an agent makes an untrue statement that he or she knows is not true is called an innocent misrepresentation. [p. 469]

14. ___ An independent contractor is an agent over which the employer has a substantial degree of control over. [p. 470]

15. ___ The fact that Joe uses his own lawn mower when he cuts the yard in front of Dr. Miller's office is irrelevant in determining whether an individual is an employee or an independent contractor. [p. 470]

16. ___ Principals may avoid strict liability for inherently dangerous activities assigned to independent contractors as they probably are not supplying any tools for these activities and usually have no control over the physical performance by the independent contractor. [p. 472]

17. ___ Mary hires her brother-in-law, Ned, to trim three very large trees on her property. Ned has no tree trimming experience and this is known by Mary. Ned cuts a tree in such a way that it crushes a passing car and severely injures the driver. Mary is not liable for driver's injuries because Ned is an independent contractor. [p. 473]

18. ___ Wes sells real estate for Ace Development. Wes is hired to find some farm land outside Center City for Liz, a developer who builds shopping malls. Wes brokers the sale of his family farm to Liz for a very high price, convincing Liz that the farm cannot be purchased for a lesser amount. Wes has done nothing wrong because Liz was able to buy the real estate she desired. [p. 463]

19. ___ Vince is an assistant foreman for Empire Heating Co. Safe Heating offers Vince a promotion and an increase in salary of $25,000 per year. Vince is expected to bring Empire Heating customers with him to Safe Heating. Vince resigns from Empire Heating and takes the company client list with him. Since Vince is no longer an employee of Empire, he has not violated any duty of loyalty. [p. 464]

Multiple Choice

20. If Gus works for True Painting and is asked by Mike to give an estimate for painting his house, the preparation of an estimate and performing the work by Gus is an example of [p. 463]
    a. self-dealing.
    b. usurping an opportunity.
    c. competing with the principal.
    d. misuse of confidential information.

21. In a partially disclosed agency [p. 465]
    a. the principal is called a partially disclosed principal.
    b. both the principal and agent are liable on third-party contracts.
    c. the nondisclosure may be because the principal instructs the agent not to disclose his or her identity.
    d. all of the above

22. In an undisclosed agency, both the principal and agent are liable on the contract with the third party. This is because [p. 465]
    a. the agent, by not divulging that he or she is acting as an agent, becomes a principal to the contract.
    b. the reliance of the third party upon the reputation of the agent is not relevant.
    c. the third party cannot recover against the agent if the principal fails to perform.
    d. the agent is relieved of all liability if a principal exists.

23. Which of the following would be considered a proper agent's signature in a fully disclosed agency? [p. 464]
    a. Bob Green, by Alice Reed, agent
    b. Alice Reed
    c. Alice Reed, agent
    d. none of the above

24. Which properly states the available tort remedies to an injured third party as a result of the agent's torts? [p. 467]
    a. lost wages
    b. emotional distress
    c. medical expenses
    d. all of the above

25. The law that states that a principal generally is not liable for its agents and employees while they are on their way to or from work is the [p. 468]
    a. frolic and detour rule.
    b. dual-purpose mission rule.
    c. coming and going rule.
    d. intentional tort rule.

26. Attorney Helen asks her secretary, Allen, to drop off some documents at one of her client's home on Allen's way home. Allen negligently injures a Paul, a pedestrian, while on his way to deliver the documents. Who will be liable to the pedestrian? [p. 468]
    a. Allen, the agent is liable to the pedestrian.
    b. The pedestrian is liable for his or her own injuries.
    c. Allen and the pedestrian are equally liable for the pedestrian's injuries.
    d. Helen, the principal is liable to the pedestrian.

27. Ned, a bartender at the Martini Lounge, asked Dave to leave the bar as Dave was getting loud, drunk, and was rude to female patrons. Dave cursed at Ned. Ned responded by striking Dave in the noise with a closed fist, resulting in a broken nose. Who is liable to Dave for his injuries caused by Ned's actions? [p. 468]
    a. Ned is liable to Dave for the injuries he caused.
    b. The Martini Lounge is liable to Dave for the injuries that Ned caused.
    c. Dave deserved the injuries he incurred and is responsible for his own injuries.
    d. A and B are both correct.

28. Suppose Ned the bartender in the previous question saw Dave, a man whom he cannot tolerate due to personal reasons, in the Martini Lounge. Ned is working the night that Dave comes into the bar and decides to punch him just because he is in the establishment. Dave suffers a broken jaw and arm. Who is liable to Dave for his injuries caused by Ned's actions? [p. 469]
    a. The Martini Lounge is vicariously liable for Ned's actions toward Dave.
    b. Dave is responsible for his own injuries as he should not have been in the bar.
    c. Ned is responsible for Dave's injuries.
    d. The Martini Lounge as a business is responsible for Dave's injuries.

29. What is one of the most important factors in determining whether someone is an independent contractor or an employee? [p. 470]
    a. One of the most important factors is whether the doctrine of respondeat superior applies.
    b. One of the most critical factors is the degree of control the employer has over the agent.
    c. One of the key factors is whether the agent committed any intentional torts within a work-related time and space.
    d. all of the above

Short Answer

30. What is a fully disclosed agency? [p. 464] _____
_____

31. What are the three classifications of agencies that establish contract liability to third parties? [p. 464] _____

32. Give at least two examples of what is considered an agent's breach of loyalty. [p. 463]
_____

33. If an agent exceeds the scope of his or her authority, the principal is not liable on the contract unless _____. [p. 466]

34. What is the doctrine of respondeat superior? [p. 467] _____
_____

35. Under the doctrine of respondeat superior, employer liability is based upon what legal theory? [p. 467] _____

36. If Carl stops at a gas station for a drink while making deliveries and injures a motorist while pulling out of the gas station, who is liable for the motorist's injuries caused by Carl's tortious conduct during this frolic and detour? [p. 468] _____
_____

37. What is the rationale used in applying the "coming and going rule"? [p. 468] _____
_____

38. Why aren't principals generally liable for the torts of independent contractors? [p. 471]
_____

39. Acme Air Service hires Fuel Transport to haul jet fuel to its airport facility, and the truck explodes and kills six people because the driver of the truck drove too fast. Is the principal liable for the negligence of the independent contractor? [p. 472] _____

Answers to Refresh Your Memory

1. self-dealing, usurping an opportunity, competing with the principal, misuse of confidential information, and dual agency [p. 463]
2. when the agent directly profits in the transaction for the principal because the agent is paying himself or herself for a service or selling the principal their own property [p. 463] consideration [p. 463]
3. misuse of confidential information [p. 463]
4. principal, undisclosed [p. 464]
5. fiduciary [p. 463]
6. The principal rejects it after due consideration. [p. 463]
7. dual agency [p. 464]
8. fully disclosed [p. 464]
9. partially disclosed, both the agent and the principal [p. 465]
10. an agency in which a contracting third party does not know of either the existence of the agency or the principle's identity [p. 465]
11. implied warranty of authority [p. 466]
12. ratifies [p. 466]
13. scope of authority [p. 466]
14. coming and going rule [p. 468]
15. They do not control the means by which the results are accomplished. [p. 471]

Critical Thought Exercise Model Answer

An employer may be liable for the torts of its employee under the doctrine or respondeat superior. This doctrine imposes vicarious, or indirect, liability on the employer without regard to the fault of the employer for torts committed by an employee in the course or scope of employment. There are several factors that a court will usually consider in deciding whether or not a particular act occurred within the course or scope of employment.

Whether the act was authorized by the employer. West was expected to be on the road making sales calls for long periods of time. Dubyah knew that West had to conduct personal business during sales trips for his employer.

The time, place, and purpose of the act. West was on a sales trip to a city where he was conducting Dubyah's business. The purpose of the act was to clean his laundry so that he could remain on the sales trip for a prolonged period. The overall purpose still favors the employer and would be within the scope of employment, especially when the past employment history and prior lengthy trips are taken into account.

Whether the act was one commonly performed by employees on behalf of their employers. Doing laundry and buying a gift may seem to be very personal tasks unless they are viewed from the broader perspective of the traveling salesperson. It is more economical for Dubyah and allows more sales calls to be made if West says on the road and performs his personal tasks on the road. The overall task or act is that of a sales trip and is clearly within the normal scope of West's duties that he usually performs for Dubyah.

The extent to which the employer's interest was advanced. The reasoning for this factor is the same. Dubyah benefits by having its sales representatives remain on prolonged trips. It is therefore expected that personal business will have to be conducted, allowing the employer to benefit from numerous sales calls to sell its products.

There was no instrumentality (such as an automobile) used for the act in this case, so the fact that an employer did or did not supply the instrumentality that caused an injury is not relevant to this analysis.

Whether the employer had reason to know that the employee would do the act in question and whether the employee had ever done it before. This factor is the most import one for deciding the liability issue. The act of conducting personal business while on the employer's sales trip was obviously an act that had been repeated innumerable times by West over 17 years of employment with Dubyah. Dubyah knew about the long sales trips and apparently was active in creating the situation where personal business had to be conducted while on company trips.

Whether the act involved a serious crime. This factor is the one that draws a distinction between the negligent act of overloading the dryer and causing a fire and the act of striking Mike and severely injuring Mike's eye. The employer is not liable for the intentional torts of employees committed outside the employer's scope of business. However, an employer is liable under the doctrine of vicarious liability for intentional torts of employees committed within the employee's scope of employment. The court will apply either the **motivation test** or the **work-related test**. Under the motivation test, if the employee's motivation in committing the intentional tort is to promote the employer's business, the employer is liable. However, if the employee's motivation in committing the tort was personal, the employer is not liable. Under this rule, Dubyah would not be liable to Mike because West was motivated to conduct personal business, not company business. Under the work-related test, however, the result would be different. If the tort is committed within a work-related time or space, the employer is liable. Since West is working around the clock while on a sales trip, some states would hold the employer, Dubyah, liable for both the damage to Suds Town and the damage to Mike's eye.

Answers to Practice Quiz

True/False

1. False   The agent's duty of loyalty includes a prohibition from competing with the principal during the course of an agency unless the principal agrees.
2. True   Generally agents are prohibited from competing with the principal during the duration of the agency unless the principal agrees. However, if the agent and principal have not entered into a valid covenant-not-to-compete, the agent may compete with the principal once the agency is ended.
3. False   Both the agent and principal are liable on third-party contracts because the third party must rely upon the agent's reputation, integrity, and credit because the principal is not identified.
4. False   If the agent only goes on a minor detour, the principal may remain liable for the tortuous conduct of its agent.
5. False   If the agent fails to disclose the identity of their principal when they sign the contract, they remain liable to the third party on that contract.
6. True   Ratification refers to when a principal accepts an agent's unauthorized contract.
7. True   The three primary areas of tort liability for principals and agents are misrepresentation, negligence and intentional torts.
8. True   When an agent negligently makes a misrepresentation to a third party, innocent misrepresentation occurs.

9. False   This states the coming and going rule. Frolic and detour refers to when agents do things that further their own interest rather than the principal's.

10. False   A dual-purpose mission is one where the agent is acting partly from himself or herself and partly for the principal. The principal remains liable to the third party and the coming and going rule does not apply.

11. False   The principal is not liable for employees' and agent's torts that are committed outside of the principal's scope of business.

12. True   The agent's motivation is not important under the work-related test.

13. False   Fraud or deceit are intentional misrepresentations, not innocent misrepresentations.

14. False   The degree of control that an employer has over his or her agent is a crucial factor in determining whether an individual is an employee or an independent contractor. If an employer has a substantial degree of control over an individual, he or she is probably an employee, whereas if the control is minimal or nonexistent, he or she would probably be classified as an independent contractor.

15. False   If the worker supplies his or her own tools and equipment used in the work for the principal, it is very relevant in that it could indicate the individual is an independent contractor.

16. False   Principals are unable to avoid strict liability for dangerous activities that its independent contractors are assigned to regardless of the independent contractor supplying his or her own tools.

17. False   A principal may be liable for injuries to another person caused by an unqualified or knowingly dangerous independent contractor if the principal was negligent in the selection of the independent contractor. Mary knows that Ned is not qualified. Mary will be liable for the driver's injuries.

18. False   Wes has engaged in self-dealing, which violates his duty of loyalty to Liz.

19. False   Vince has violated his duty of loyalty by misuse of confidential information. An agent is under a legal duty not to disclose or misuse information either during or after the course of the agency.

Multiple Choice

20. B   Answer B is correct as the agent cannot appropriate the opportunity for himself unless the principal rejects it after due consideration. Answer A is incorrect because self-dealing involves secretly selling to the principal. Answer C is incorrect because competing involves an open effort to compete for the same customers. Answer D is incorrect because the agent did not take any information from the principal to misuse.

21. D   Answer D is correct as Answers A, B, and C are all correct statements concerning a partially disclosed agency.

22. A   Answer A is the correct answer because the third party does not know that a principal exists and relies totally upon the reputation of the agent. The third party thinks that the agent is the principal and relies upon this appearance. Answer B is incorrect because reliance upon the reputation of the agent is relevant. Answer C is incorrect because the agent is liable to the third party if the principal fails to perform. Answer D is incorrect because the agent is not relieved of liability when the principal is undisclosed.

23. A   Answer A is the correct answer as Alice Reed's signature clearly indicates that she is acting as an agent for Bob Green, a specifically identified principal. Answer B is incorrect as it indicates only the agent's name. Answer C is incorrect as this signature is indicative of a partially disclosed agency since it only indicates the agent's name. Answer D is incorrect for the reasons stated above.

24. D   Answer D is the correct answer as answers A, B, and C all properly state tort remedies available to an injured party where liability is found.

25. C   Answer C is the correct answer as the question properly states the "coming and going" rule. Answer A is incorrect as the frolic and detour rule refers to a principal's liability based on an agent's detour to run a personal errand that results in injury to another while on assignment for the principal. Answer B is incorrect as the dual-purpose mission rule refers to an agent that is acting partly for himself and partly for the principal. Answer D is incorrect as there is no such thing as the intentional tort rule.

26. D   Answer D is the correct answer as the principal is liable to the pedestrian under the dual-purpose mission rule as Allen was acting partly for himself and partly for his employer. Note that the majority of jurisdictions hold both the principal and agent liable for injuries caused while on this type of mission; however, in light of the choices of answers, answer D is the best answer. Answer A is incorrect as Allen alone would not be liable to the pedestrian in light of the majority rule and the minority rule of holding the principal liable. Answer B is incorrect as there are not enough facts to indicate any type of negligence on the pedestrian's part, nor is there any information to base a contributory or comparative negligence analysis to assess whether the pedestrian may be found liable for his or her own injuries. Answer C is incorrect for the reasoning given to choices A and B above.

27. D   Answer B is the correct answer as Ned committed an intentional tort within a work-related time or space, hence when he was doing his job as a bouncer at a bar. As such, the Martini Lounge would be responsible for any injury, including those incurred by Dave as a result of Ned's actions. Ned is also liable himself for the intentional tort. Answer A is correct as Ned was not merely doing his job of keeping the peace, but exceeded his scope of authority by striking a patron who had only been obnoxious. Hence Ned will also be individually liable for the injuries caused to Dave. Answer C is incorrect as whether or not Dave deserved the injuries is not the issue, but rather who is liable for the injuries he incurred. Further, there are an insufficient amount of facts to determine whether a contributory or comparative negligence analysis would be applicable here. Answer A and B are both correct, making D the correct choice.

28. C   Answer C is the correct answer as Ned's motivation in committing the tort against Dave was personal, not in an effort to promote the Martini Lounge. As such, the Martini Lounge is not liable even if the tort took place during business hours or on business premises. Answer A is incorrect based on the reasoning given for answer C above. Answer B is incorrect as whether or not Dave should have been in the bar is immaterial. The issue hinges on who is liable for the injuries Dave sustained while in another's business establishment. Answer D is incorrect as the injuries were not as a result of the agent's promotion of the principal's business, but instead were personally motivated. Hence, the Martini Lounge is not responsible.

29. B   Answer B is the correct answer as the degree of control is one of the most crucial factors in determining whether someone is an independent contractor or an employee. The less control an employer has over an individual, the more likely he or she is an independent contractor. Answer A is incorrect as the doctrine of respondeat superior refers to vicarious liability during the course and scope of employment, not determining whether someone is an employee or an independent contractor. Answer C is incorrect as an agent's commission of torts during a work-related time or space would only be relevant in assessing liability for injuries caused by those torts, not in determining the status of the individual. Answer D is incorrect based on the reasons given above.

Short Answer

30. an agency in which a contracting third party knows that the agent is acting for a principal and the third party knows the identity of the principal
31. fully disclosed agency, partially disclosed agency, undisclosed agency
32. Usurping an opportunity that belongs to the principal and the misuse of confidential information about the principal's affairs are two examples of an agent's breach of loyalty.
33. The principal ratifies it.
34. a rule that says an employer is liable for the tortious conduct of its employees or agents while they are acting within the scope of its authority
35. The doctrine of respondeat superior is based on the legal premise of vicarious liability, meaning the principal is liable because of his or her employment contract with the agent not due to any fault on his or her part.
36. Under the frolic and detour rule, if the deviation is minor, the principal is liable for injuries caused by the agent's torts. Stopping to get a drink while making deliveries would either be a minor frolic and detour or an expected part of Carl's job, keeping the act within the scope of employment.
37. Since principals do not control where their employees and agents live, they should not be held liable for tortious conduct of agents on their way to and from work.
38. The rationale behind this rule is that principals do not control the means by which the results are accomplished.
39. Principals cannot avoid strict liability for inherently dangerous activities assigned to independent contractors. Hauling jet fuel is a dangerous activity, so Acme Air Service will be liable for the negligence of Fuel Transport.

Chapter 31

EMPLOYMENT AND WORKER PROTECTION LAWS

Chapter Overview

This chapter examines employment contracts and the exceptions to the at-will doctrine that applies to a majority of employment contracts. It also examines the statutes that have been enacted to protect workers. These laws include workers' compensation, minimum wage and overtime pay, occupational safety, pension, immigration, unemployment, Social Security, and other laws that protect employees from unfair treatment.

Objectives

Upon completion of the exercises in this chapter, you should be able to:
1. Discuss the employment at-will doctrine and the public policy exception to its application.
2. Describe how state workers' compensation laws function and the benefits that are available.
3. Explain employer's obligation under OSHA to provide and maintain safe work conditions.
4. Explain how the Fair Labor Standards Act provides for minimum wage and overtime pay.
5. Explain when drug and polygraph testing may be used by employers.
6. Explain the protections provided for employee pensions.
7. Describe how immigration laws affect employers and employees.
8. Understand unemployment compensation benefits and Social Security laws.
9. Describe the rights granted by the Family and Medical Leave Act.
10. Discuss the Consolidated Omnibus Budget Reconciliation Act.
11. Discuss and understand the Immigration Reform and Control Act.

Practical Applications

Upon mastering the material in this chapter, you should be able to recognize the situations where employee rights and protections are applicable and the specific laws that cover a dispute or loss of income. You will understand the limits of the protections and the employee's requirements that must be met to gain protection under the various statutes.

Helpful Hints

Both the employee and employer benefit by a clear understanding of how the various employment protection statutes function. The requirements of some laws apply only to specific employers based upon the qualifying language of the statute. Employees often have requirements of notice and cooperation built into the statute with which they must comply to gain enforcement of their rights. Employers must understand and adhere to the requirements imposed by government regulation in the workplace or they subject themselves to the high costs of law suits and lost production in the workplace.

Study Tips

It is just as important to understand when the employment laws may apply as it is to understand the technical requirements built into the individual statutes. You should develop your understanding of employment laws by organizing the material into general areas.

Employees Protected By Contracts vs. At-Will Employees

An employee who does not have an employment contract is considered an employee at-will. The general rule is that at-will employees can be discharged at any time for any reason. This has been changed by statutes and case law in certain situations. The bulk of this chapter examines the exceptions created to negate the harsh effects of the at-will doctrine.

Statutory exceptions to at-will doctrine

Federal and state statutes protect the overall employment relationship be forbidding discharge in violation of union or collective bargaining agreements. An employer must also refrain from discharging an employee in violation of the Title VII and anti-discrimination laws. When the employee is discharged based upon race, sex, religion, age, handicap, national origin, or other protected classifications, the discharge is unlawful, even if the employee is at-will.

Implied-in-fact exception to the at-will doctrine

An implied-in-fact contract is developed by the conduct of the parties. The employer may issue bulletins or manuals that promise continued employment if the company rules are followed. The employer has removed the at-will condition and replaced it with a contractual understanding of the employment relationship.

Public policy exception to the at-will doctrine

An employee cannot be discharged if the discharge violates public policy. Public policy dictates that an employee will not be fired because they serve as a juror, refuse to violate the law, refuse to distribute dangerous products or goods to consumers, or refuse to commit a tort against another person.

Tort exceptions

The employee can sue for damages for wrongful discharge based upon fraud, defamation, or intentional infliction of emotional distress. If the employee is successful in a tort action, he or she may be able to recover punitive damages.

Drug testing of employees

Pre-employment drug testing is generally upheld by the courts. Incumbent employees can be tested when the employer suspects drug use if there is no prohibition of testing in an employee contract. Government employees can be tested whenever their position has an element of public safety. Some statutes require testing when there is an incident or accident, such as a train wreck.

Protective Statutes

The following statutes and legislative schemes protect both substantive and procedural rights of employees in their dealings with employers.

Workers' Compensation Acts

These acts were enacted to compensate employees for injuries that occurred on the job regardless of fault. The amount of compensation payable to the employee is set by statute. Payment under the workers' compensation statute is the employee's exclusive remedy, meaning that an employee cannot sue his/her employer when he/she is injured on the job.

Workers' Compensation Insurance
Note that states generally require employers to purchase insurance from private insurance companies or state funds to cover workers' compensation claims.

Employment-Related Injury
A claimant must demonstrate that the injury arose out of and in the course of his or her employment before an injury is compensable under workers' compensation. Work-related injuries include those that happen while an employee is actively working, or at a company cafeteria, or while on a business-related lunch. Stress has often been found to be a work-related injury worthy of compensation. Accidents that occur at an off-premises restaurant for a personal lunch are not covered.

Exclusive Remedy
Because workers' compensation is an exclusive remedy, a lawsuit against an employer is not an option for an employee. The exception to this rule exists however where an injury occurs to a worker as a result of an employer's intentional act to injure. In this situation, a worker may sue his or her employer.

Occupational Safety and Health Act

The act was enacted to promote safety in the workplace. It imposes record-keeping and reporting requirements upon the employer. The enforcement arm created by the act is the Occupational Safety and Health Administration (OSHA). OSHA has adopted regulations to enforce the safety standards created by the act. OSHA may inspect places of employment and cite the employer for violations. OSHA violations carry both civil and criminal penalties. OSHA requires both specific duty standards as well as general duty standards that are expected of employers to keep a safe work environment.

Fair Labor Standards Act (FSLA)

The FSLA prohibits child labor and establishes minimum wage and overtime pay requirements.

Child Labor
The FSLA forbids the use of oppressive child labor and makes it unlawful to ship goods produced by businesses that use oppressive child labor.

Regulations defined by the Department of Labor include:

- ❖ Children under age 14 cannot work except as newspaper deliverers.
- ❖ Children ages 14 and 15 may work limited hours in nonhazardous jobs approved by the Department Retirement of Labor (examples: restaurants, gas stations).
- ❖ Children ages 16 and 17 may work unlimited hours in nonhazardous jobs.
- ❖ Persons 18 years and older may work at any job regardless if it is hazardous or not.

Children who are exempt from the above rules include:

- ❖ children who work in agricultural employment, child actors, and performers.

Minimum Wage and Overtime Pay Requirements

The FSLA establishes minimum wage and overtime pay requirements.

Managerial, administrative, and professional employees are exempt from the act's wage and hours provisions.

Covered workers are to receive the minimum wage for their regular work hours and overtime pay for those hours beyond the regular work hours. **Students and apprentices may be paid less than minimum wage as per the Department of Labor.**

Overtime pay is provided to nonexempt employees who work more than 40 hours per week. They receive one and a half times their regular pay for hours in excess of the 40 hours. Each week is treated separately.

Family and Medical Leave Act

The act guarantees workers unpaid time off for medical emergencies. Applies to employers with 50 or more employees. Employee must have worked for at least one year and performed at least 1,250 hours of work during the previous 12-month period. Covers time off for birth or care of child, serious health condition, and care for spouse, parent, or child with a serious health problem. Employee must be restored to their same or a similar position upon their return. **Note, an employer may deny restoration to a salaried employee who is among the highest-paid 10 percent of that employer's employees if the denial is necessary to prevent "substantial and grievous economic injury" to the employer's operations.**

Consolidated Omnibus Budget Reconciliation Act (COBRA)

Provides that employee or his beneficiaries must have the opportunity to maintain group health coverage upon dismissal or death due to certain events. Government employees are covered by the Public Health Service Act.

Employee Retirement Income Security Act (ERISA)

ERISA is designed to prevent fraud and abuses associated with private pension funds. Requires that the pension plan be in writing and name a pension fund manager. ERISA dictates how the pension funds can be invested and sets time limits for when pension rights must vest.

Immigration Reform and Control Act

Forbids employer from hiring illegal immigrants. Employer must examine documents to determine employee's right to work in the country.

Drug Testing and Polygraph Tests

Drug Testing

Drug testing is viewed as a means to increase productivity and decrease liability exposure. Preemployment drug screening has been upheld by the courts due to job applicants' lower expectation of privacy versus that of an incumbent employee. Incumbent employees, however, may be tested for drugs where a reasonable suspicion of impairment is found or following an accident.

Polygraph Testing

The Employee Polygraph Protection Act of 1988 prohibits most private employers from using polygraph tests. Federal and state governments are not covered by the act. Polygraph tests can also be used by private employers when the employee deals with national defense, public health and safety, drug manufacturing, or is involved in theft or espionage. The act sets up procedures that must be followed or penalties may be assessed.

Federal Unemployment Tax Act

Employers must pay unemployment taxes to compensate employees during periods of unemployment. Employee does not receive benefits if they are discharged for misconduct or quit without cause.

Social Security

Under the Federal Insurance Contributions Act (FICA) employees and employers make contributions to the Social Security Fund. The funds are used to pay current recipients of Social Security.

Refresh Your Memory

The following exercise will enable you to refresh your memory of the main points given in this chapter. Read the question twice and place your answer in the blanks provided. If you do not remember the principle, go to the next question and come back to the ones you did not answer.

1.   What does the Statute of Frauds require regarding contracts that cannot be performed within a year? _____.

2.   An employee who has been _____ _____ can sue his or her employer for damages and other remedies.

3.   What are the four exceptions to the employment at-will doctrine?
     _____, _____, _____
     and _____

4.   At common law, what could a worker sue his or her employee for if he or she was injured on the job? _____

5. If an employer does not have workers' compensation insurance, what can an employee sue his or her employee for?

   _____

   _____

6. If Bart slips on a wet floor while in his employer's cafeteria, would he be covered under workers' compensation? Explain your answer. _____

   _____

7. If Cindy's employer defamed her to a mortgage company by making statements that caused her to lose her loan money for a house she was purchasing and thereafter fired her, what are her remedies?

   _____

   _____

8. If the review of a workers' compensation claim is determined to be illegitimate, what may a worker do?

   _____

   _____

9. What record-keeping and reporting requirements are placed on employers under the Occupational Safety and Health Act?

   _____

   _____

10. ERISA is a complex act designed to prevent _____ and other abuses associated with pension funds.

11. COBRA provides that an employee of a private employer or the employee's _____ must be offered the opportunity to continue his or her group _____ insurance after the dismissal or death of the employee or the loss of coverage due to certain qualifying events.

12. The Family and Medical Leave Act guarantees workers _____ time off from work for medical emergencies.

13. The Immigration Reform and Control Act makes it unlawful for employers to hire _____ immigrants.

14. To collect unemployment benefits, applicants must be able and _____ for work and be _____ employment.

15. Under _____, employees and employers must make contributions into the Social Security fund.

Critical Thought Exercise

Sid Frost worked as a merchandising supervisor for Global-Mart, Inc., a large discount store employing over 26,000 people. When Frost suffered his third stroke in April 1999, he took leave from work, which was covered by the Family and Medical Leave Act (FMLA) of 1993. The vice president of personnel for Global-Mart approved the leave. Mike Allen, who had been hired only two months after Frost in 1984, temporarily filled Frost's position. When Frost returned to work, he discovered that Allen had been promoted to senior supervisor and given a $7,000 raise. The senior supervisor position is filled from the supervisor classification based upon seniority. Global-Mart refused to allow Frost to return to his position as a supervisor and demoted him to a senior salesman position that required travel away from home on a weekly basis. Six weeks later Global-Mart fired Frost because he was unable to keep up the schedule required by his position and because his expense account was not timely filed by the end of the month.

Frost sues Global-Mart for violation of the FMLA based upon Global-Mart's failure to promote him to senior supervisor or return him to his prior position. Did Global-Mart violate the FMLA?

Answer:

_____
_____
_____
_____
_____
_____
_____
_____
_____
_____
_____
_____
_____
_____
_____
_____

Practice Quiz

True/False

1. ____ An employee who has been wrongfully discharged can only sue his employer for money damages. [p. 478]

2. ____ Federal and state statutes restrict the application of the employment at-will doctrine. [p. 478]

3. ____ Implied-in-fact contracts develop from the express agreement of the parties. [p. 479]

4. ___ The contents of a company bulletin or handbook may be construed as an implied promise that an employee can only be discharged for good cause. [p. 479]

5. ___ The most used common law exception to the employment at-will doctrine is the public policy exception. [p. 479]

6. ___ Wrongful discharge action can be based on several tort theories. [p. 479]

7. ___ If an employee is successful in a tort action, punitive damages may be awarded. [p. 479]

8. ___ At common law, many injured workers or the heirs of deceased workers were left uncompensated due to the odds that an injured employee may or may not win his or her case against his or her employer. [p. 479]

9. ___ Generally, preemployment drug screening has been upheld by the courts. [p. 483]

10. ___ Private employers are given more leniency when administering polygraph testing to new employees. [p. 484]

11. ___ Drug testing of incumbent employees is upheld due to their lower expectation of privacy. [pp. 483-494]

12. ___ Employers are required to pay for workers' compensation insurance and cannot avoid this requirement by setting aside payments in a self-insured account. [p. 479]

13. ___ An individual's workers' compensation benefit is determined on a case-by-case basis, as some injuries are worse than others. As such, some cases may demonstrate no limits in terms of dollar amounts. [p. 479]

14. ___ Accidents that occur in a company supply room or while in an employer's workroom performing work for an employer are not covered by workers' compensation. [p. 479]

15. ___ If an employer intentionally injures a worker during work hours, the employee's remedy is limited to workers' compensation benefits. [p. 479]

16. ___ The Employee Polygraph Protection Act does not prohibit the use of polygraph tests on government employees. [p. 484]

17. ___ The federal Social Security system provides unlimited retirement and death benefits to certain employees and their dependents. [p. 484]

18. ___ Federal, state, and local governments do not have to comply with the Occupational Safety and Health Act. [p. 480]

19. ___ OSHA citations are subject to only civil penalties. [p. 481]

20. ___ Under the Fair Labor Standards Act, children ages 14 and 15 may work unlimited hours but only in nonhazardous jobs. [p. 481]

21. ___ If an employee works 50 hours one week and only 30 hours the next, he or she is not entitled to any overtime pay because they are only averaging 40 hours per week. [p. 481]

22. ___ Managerial employees are exempt from the Fair Labor Standards Act's wage and hour provisions. [p. 481]

23. ___ Under the FMLA, an employer may require medical proof of claimed serious health conditions. [p. 482]

24. ___ Not only does the Family and Medical Leave Act apply to private employers with 50 or more employees, but it also applies to federal, state, and local governments. [p. 482]

25. ___ Employers covered by the Family and Medical Leave Act are entitled to receive up to 12 weeks of unpaid leave during any 12-month period. [p. 482]

Multiple Choice

26. The termination of an employee will be considered a wrongful discharge if the termination was in violation of [p. 479]
    a. a statute.
    b. an employment contract.
    c. public policy.
    d. all of the above

27. Amy, who has done her job properly, has determined that an implied-in-fact contract may be developed. Where would the most likely place be that formed the basis of her opinion? [p. 479]
    a. an employee handbook
    b. public policy
    c. a written agreement
    d. a union contract

28. The termination of an employee because they refused to copy bootlegged CDs would be a wrongful termination because it violated [p. 479]
    a. a tort exception.
    b. the implied-in-fact contract exception.
    c. the public policy exception.
    d. a statutory exception.

29. Which of the following applies to Employee Retirement Income Security Act pensions? [p. 483]
    a. Pension plans must be in writing.
    b. A pension fund manager must be named.
    c. No more than ten percent of a pension fund's assets can be invested in the securities of the sponsoring employer.
    d. all of the above

30. An employer may not give a polygraph test to an employee if the employer [pp. 483-484]
    a. is a landscaping business and the employee reports that the employer is stealing plants.
    b. deals in matters of national security, such as a defense contractor.
    c. provides security services for the protection of public health and safety, such as guarding electrical power plants.
    d. is a drug manufacturer that hires employees that will have access to drugs.

31. The Employee Polygraph Protection Act requires private employers that are permitted to use polygraph testing to follow certain procedures, including [p. 484]
    a. allowing the employee to return to the same position with the same pay.
    b. giving notice to the person to be tested.
    c. allowing the employee to maintain health insurance after he is discharged.
    d. giving the employee a hearing in front of an administrative law judge.

32. OSHA standards establish rules pertaining to [pp. 480-481]
    a. minimum wage.
    b. amounts of compensation after a work-related injury.
    c. maximum levels for exposure to hazardous chemicals.
    d. age requirements for use of child labor.

33. Employers who establish pension plans for their employees are subject to the record-keeping, disclosure, and other requirements of [p. 483]
    a. COBRA.
    b. ERISA.
    c. FUTA.
    d. FICA.

34. What does the INS Form I-9 attest to once completed? [p. 483]
    a. that an employer has inspected documents of an employee
    b. that an employer has determined that an immigrant is a U.S. citizen
    c. that an employer has determined that an immigrant is qualified to work in this country via a work visa
    d. all of the above

35. Social Security benefits include [p. 484]
    a. survivors' benefits to family members of deceased workers.
    b. the right to continue group health insurance provided by the employer.
    c. the right to take time off for the birth of a child.
    d. payments for a period of time when the employee is temporarily unemployed.

Short Answer

36. At common law, what was allowed in the work place if an employer did not like an employee? [p. 478]

    _____

    _____

37. If Jim is suffering from stress on the job, which act would serve him best for compensation? [p. 479]

    _____

38. Maggie and Elroy, both 14-year-old students, work in an apple field picking apples for Farm Girl Apples. Is Farm Girl Apples in violation of any act? Why or why not? [p. 481]

_____

_____

_____

_____

39. What must the employee prove to receive workers' compensation? [p. 479]

_____

_____

_____

40. What act applies to government employees and is equivalent to COBRA ? [p. 483]

_____

_____

41. What types of liability is a person who fails to submit Social Security taxes subject to? [p. 484]

_____

42. What can OSHA do upon finding a safety violation following an inspection of a place of employment? [p. 480]

_____

43. According to the Fair Labor Standards Act, what type or work can a child under 14 accept? [p. 481]

_____

44. If children cannot work in hazardous jobs, who determines what job is hazardous? [p. 481]

_____

45. To whom may an employer pay less than minimum wage? [p. 481]

_____

46. What pension plans are exempt from coverage under ERISA? [p. 481]

_____

47. What occurs when an employee has a nonforfeitable right to receive pension benefits? [p. 483]

_____

48. What is the prerequisite for an employee to be covered by the Family and Medical Leave Act? [p. 482]

_____

_____

49. Under the Immigration Reform and Control Act of 1986, an employer must attest to what facts before an employee may be hired? [p. 483]

_____

_____

50. How much must a self-employed person contribute to Social Security? [p. 484]

_____

Answers To Refresh Your Memory

1. The contract must be in writing. [p. 478]
2. wrongfully discharged [p. 478]
3. statutory, contract, public policy, and tort [pp. 478-479]
4. negligence [p. 479]
5. damages for work-related injuries [p. 479]
6. Yes, because it was while he was at his company's cafeteria. [p. 479]
7. Cindy can sue under the tort exception to the employment at-will theory. [p. 479]
8. An employee may appeal the decision through the state court system. [p. 479]
9. to place notices in the workplace informing employees of their rights under the act [p. 481]
10. fraud, private [p. 483]
11. beneficiaries, health [p. 483]
12. unpaid [p. 482]
13. illegal [p. 483]
14. available, seeking [p. 484]
15. Federal Insurance Contribution Act [p. 484]

Critical Thought Exercise Model Answer

The FMLA guarantees workers unpaid time off work for medical emergencies. There is little doubt that a stroke is a medical emergency and Global-Mart had approved the leave for Frost. The FMLA will apply to Global-Mart because it has over 50 employees. Under the FMLA, the employer must guarantee employment in the same position or a comparable position when the employee returns to work. Employers who violate the FMLA may be held liable for damages to compensate employees for unpaid wages, lost benefits, denied compensation, and actual monetary losses up to an amount equivalent to the employee's wages for twelve weeks. The employer may also be required to grant a promotion that has been denied. The restored employee is not entitled to the accrual of seniority during the leave period, however. Frost was not returned to his former position when he returned. He was forced to take a demotion, which required travel. Global-Mart violated the FMLA by demoting Frost. The failure to promote Frost may not be a violation because the promotion was based upon seniority and Frost had less seniority than Allen at the time of the promotion. Therefore, Global-Mart should be ordered to return Frost to his prior supervisor position but will not be required to promote him to senior supervisor. Global-Mart will also be required to pay damages for lost wages during the time Frost was not working due to his firing.

Answers to Practice Quiz

True/False

1. False   An employee may also sue his or her employer for other remedies such as reinstatement and back pay.
2. True   These statutes include labor laws that forbid discharge in violation of collective bargaining agreements and discharge that is founded upon discrimination that is prohibited by Title VII.

3. False   Implied-in-fact contracts develop from the conduct of the parties, not an agreement.

4. True   The company handbook or personnel policy manual might mention that employees who do their jobs properly will not be discharged.

5. True   An employee cannot be discharged if such discharge violates the public policy of the jurisdiction, such as firing an employee because they fulfilled their jury duty service.

6. True   An employee can sue for wrongful discharge based upon such tort theories as fraud, intentional infliction of emotional distress, and defamation of character.

7. True   In addition to compensatory and incidental damages, an employer may be assessed punitive damages if the conduct is especially egregious.

8. True   At common law, many workers were left uncompensated as there was no guarantee that they would win their cases against employees for their injuries on the job.

9. True   While present employees may be protected by their employment from drug testing, job applicants can be required to submit to drug testing as part of the application process.

10. False   The Court upheld a Federal Railroad Administration rule that requires blood and urine tests of every employee involved in a "major accident" and permits testing of any worker who violates certain safety rules.

11. True   In addition, the testing of off-duty agents is permitted because of the possibility of bribery and blackmail if an agent is using illegal drugs.

12. False   Employers can either pay for the insurance or become self-insured by setting aside payments in a contingency account.

13. False   Workers' compensation benefits are paid according to preset limits established by statute or regulation.

14. False   Activities such as those occurring at a company cafeteria or while on a business lunch for an employer are covered. As such, accidents that occur in a company's supply or workroom would presumably be considered to have been done in the course of his or her employment and would be entitled to workers' compensation coverage.

15. False   The employee can collect workers' compensation benefits *and* sue the employer.

16. True   The act only covers private employers' use of polygraph tests.

17. False   The federal Social Security system provides **limited** retirement and death benefits to certain employees and their dependents.

18. True   The act applies only to private employers.

19. False   OSHA violations are subject to both civil and criminal penalties.

20. False   Children ages 14 and 15 may work limited hours in nonhazardous jobs that are approved by the Department of Labor.

21. False   The employee is entitled to overtime pay for each hour worked in excess of 40 hours in a week. Each week is treated separately.

22. True   The plan must be in writing to help avoid fraud and the manager has a fiduciary duty to act as a prudent person in managing the fund.

23. True   Under the Family and Medical Leave Act, an employer may require medical proof of claimed serious health conditions.

24. True   Unlike other employee statutes discussed in this chapter, the Family and Medical Leave Act applies to all government employees.

25. True   This 12 weeks of leave can be used for the birth of a child, family illness, or several other reasons set forth in the statute.

Multiple Choice

26. D   Each choice states a correct source for determining whether or not there has been a wrongful discharge upon the violation of the law associated with that source.

27. A   Answer A is the correct choice because a handbook sets forth the expected conduct of the parties and it is from this conduct that a contract is implied. Choice B is incorrect because is a separate way of avoiding the at-will doctrine that is unrelated to implied-in-fact contracts. Choices C and D are incorrect because they are both express agreements, not implied ones.

28. C   Answer C is correct because discharging an employee because they refuse to violate the law for the employer violated public policy. Answers A, B, and D are separate exceptions unrelated to the request of the employer for the employee to do an illegal act.

29. D   Answer D is correct because answers A, B, and C all apply to ERISA pensions. That is, a pension must be in writing and have a manager named. Further, no more than ten percent of a person's funds can be invested in the securities of the sponsoring employer.

30. A   Answer A is correct because a landscaping business does not involve any security or public safety work for which the employer has a genuine safety concern. Choices B, C, and D are incorrect because they are all employment positions that involve issues of public health and safety or national security, thereby allowing the employer to administer a polygraph test.

31. B   B is correct because an employee must be given advance notice when a polygraph test is desired by the employer. Answer A is incorrect because it lists a right granted under the Family and Medical Leave Act. C is incorrect because it states a right under COBRA. D is incorrect because there is no statutory right to an administrative hearing under the EPPA.

32. C   C is correct because it states one type of safety standard set by OSHA. A is incorrect because minimum wage is set by the Fair Labor Standards Act. B is incorrect because workers' compensation is set by state workers' compensation acts. D is incorrect because child labor laws are set forth in the Fair Labor Standards Act.

33. B   B is correct because the Employee Retirement Income Security Act control all aspects of private pensions created by employers for their employees. A is incorrect because COBRA deals with maintaining group health insurance. C is incorrect because FUTA deals with unemployment compensation. D is incorrect because FICA deals with contributions to Social Security.

34. D   D is correct as answers A, B, and C all state what INS Form I-9 attests. Hence, the employer has inspected documents of the employee and has determined that he or she is either a U.S. citizen or otherwise qualified to work in the country.

35. A   Answer A is correct because survivor's rights are part of the compensation plan built into Social Security to help the family of a deceased worker. B is incorrect because continued group health insurance is covered by COBRA, not Social Security. Answer C is incorrect because leave for the birth of a child is covered by the Family and Medical Leave Act. D is incorrect because unemployment compensation is covered by FUTA.

Short Answer

36.   An employer could discharge an employee at any time for any reason.
37.   Workers' Compensation Act
38.   No, because children who work in agricultural employment and child actors and performers are exempt from restrictions imposed by the Fair Labor Standards Act.
39.   The employee must prove that the injury arose out of and in the course of his or her employment.
40.   Public Self Service Act
41.   interest payment, penalties, and possible criminal liability

42. If a violation is found, OSHA can issue a written citation that requires the employer to abate or correct the situation.

43. Children under 14 cannot work except as newspaper deliverers.

44. The Department of Labor determines which occupations are hazardous (e.g., mining, roofing, working with explosives, working with caustic chemicals).

45. The Department of Labor permits employers to pay less than the minimum wage to students and apprentices.

46. Federal, state, and local government pensions are exempt from ERISA coverage.

47. vesting

48. To be covered, the employee must have worked for the employer for at least one year and have performed more than 1,250 hours of service during the previous 12-month period.

49. The employer must fill out INS Form I-9, which attests that the employer has inspected documents of the employee and has determined that he or she is either a U.S. citizen or is otherwise qualified to work in the country.

50. Under the Self-Employment Contribution Act the self-employed individual must contribute an amount to Social Security that is equal to the combined amount contributed by the employer and employee under FICA.

Chapter 32

LABOR LAW

Chapter Overview

When the United States became industrialized in the late 1800s, large corporate employers assumed much greater power than their employees. It was not until the 1930s, during the Great Depression, that state and federal governments began to regulate employment relationships. Legislation granted employees the right to form labor unions and bargain with management for improved working conditions, better pay, and benefits. Further legislation guaranteed the right to strike and picket. This chapter discusses the creation of labor unions and regulation of labor relations.

Objectives

Upon completion of the exercises in this chapter, you should be able to
1.   Explain how a union is formed.
2.   Describe union elections and the consequences of interfering with union elections.
3.   Understand the process of collective bargaining and compulsory subjects of collective bargaining.
4.   Explain the mandates of the Plant Closing Act.
5.   Describe the difference between union and agency shops.
6.   Explain state right-to-work laws.
7.   Describe the rights and procedures associated with the right to strike.
8.   Describe what constitutes an illegal strike.
9.   Describe the right to picket and its limitations.
10. Describe a legal or illegal secondary boycott.

Practical Application

Upon mastering the concepts in this chapter, you should be able to recognize when the conduct involved in a particular labor relationship is legal or illegal. Further, you should be able to recognize the general legal principle that applies to a dispute and understand the likely outcome.

Helpful Hints

When there is a labor dispute, emotions are often frayed and the parties are likely to react impulsively. It is helpful to realize that both state and federal governments and the courts have created a large amount of statutory and case law that will dictate the proper conduct of the parties and the consequences of illegal activity. Examine each statute and case closely for the precise conduct that was either condoned or forbidden. By understanding what conduct triggers which rule of law, you will be more effective in your labor relationships.

Study Tips

It is crucial for you to understand the following rules of law and mandates that must be followed when you are involved in a labor action or negotiations.

Norris-LaGuardia Act. Made it legal for employees to organize.

National Labor Relations Act. Established the right of employees to form, join, and participate in unions. Placed a duty on employers to bargain and deal in good faith with unions.

Labor-Management Relations Act. Expanded the activities that unions were allowed to engage in. Gave employers the right to speak out against the unions. Gave the president the right to enjoin a strike for up to 80 days if the strike would create a national emergency.

Labor-Management Reporting and Disclosure Act. This act regulates internal union affairs related to union elections, who can hold office, and makes union officials accountable for union funds.

Railway Labor Act. This act allows railroad and airline employees to organize and created a mechanism for the adjudication of grievances.

National Labor Relations Board (NLRB). Appointed by the president, the five members of the NLRB oversee union elections, prevent unfair labor practices, and enforces federal labor laws.

Organizing a Union

Section 7 of the NLRA gives employees the right to join together to form a union. Section 7 states that employees shall have the right to self-organization; to form, join, or assist labor organizations; to bargain collectively through representatives of their own choosing; and to engage in other concerted activities for the purpose of collective bargaining or other mutual aid protection.

Types of Union Elections

Contested election – Most union elections are contested by the employer. The NLRB must supervise all contested elections.
Consent election – If management does not contest the election, a consent election may be held without NLRB supervision.
Decertification election – If employees no longer want to be represented by a union, a decertification election will be held. Such elections must be supervised by the NLRB.

Union Selection on Company Property

Employers may restrict solicitation activities to the employees' free time. Areas of solicitation activities may be limited to nonworking areas. Off-duty employees may be barred from union solicitation on company premises and nonemployees may be prohibited altogether from soliciting on behalf of the union anywhere on company property. Employers may dismiss those employees in violation of the rules.

Lechmere v. NLRB (1992). Labor organizers have no right to trespass onto the employer's property to organize the employees when they can have access to the employees via nontrespassory means. Even if it is difficult to contact employees away from work, this does not give the organizers the right to trespass onto the employer's property to pass out leaflets.

Illegal Interference with an Election

Section 8 of the NLRA makes it an unfair labor practice for an employer to interfere with, coerce, or restrain employees from exercising their statutory right to form and join unions. Threats of union closure by employers are considered to be an unfair labor practice.

Section 8(b) of the NLRA prohibits unions from engaging in unfair labor practices that interfere with a union election. If an unfair labor practice is found, the courts or the NLRB may issue a cease-and-desist order or an injunction to restrain unfair labor practices and may set aside an election and order a new election.

Collective Bargaining

The act of negotiating is called collective bargaining. Negotiation between the employer and union must be done in good faith. Subjects of collective bargaining include: **compulsory subjects** (wages, hours, fringe benefits, health benefits, retirement plans, safety rules, etc.); **illegal subjects** such as closed shops and discrimination are illegal and cannot be negotiated; and **permissive subjects** such as size and composition of the supervisory force, location of plants, and corporate reorganizations.

Plant Closing Act

This act covers employers with 100 or more employees, requires employers to give their employees 60 days notice before taking part in plant closings or layoffs. The following actions are encompassed in the act: **plant closings and mass layoffs.**

      Employers are exempt from the notice requirement of this act if:
1) the closing or layoff was as a result of business circumstances that were not reasonably foreseeable as of the time that the notice would have been required.
2) the business was actively seeking capital or business that, if obtained, would have avoided or postponed the shutdown and the employer in good faith believed that giving notice would have precluded it from obtaining the needed capital or business.

Union Security Agreements

There are two types of security agreements:
1) The union shop wherein an employee must join the union within a certain time period after being hired. Those who don't join must be discharged by the employer once notice is given.
2) The agency shop whereby employees do not have to become union members, but they do have to pay an agency fee to the union. Once the union has been notified, employers are required to deduct union dues and agency fees from employees' wages and forward the same to the union.

Strikes and Picketing

If a collective bargaining agreement cannot be reached, union management has the right to recommend that the union call a strike.

Picketing

Picketing usually takes the form of striking employees and union representatives walking in front of the employer's premises carrying signs announcing their strike. Picketing is not lawful if it is accompanied by violence, obstructs customers from entering the employer's place of business, prevents nonstriking employees from entering the employer's premises, or prevents pickups and deliveries at the employer's place of business. An injunction may be sought by the employer if unlawful picketing takes place.

Secondary Boycott Picketing

Picketing an employer's suppliers or customers sometimes pressures an employer. This is known as secondary boycott picketing. This type of picketing is lawful only if the picketing is against the primary employer's products.

Illegal Strikes

The following strikes are illegal and not protected by federal labor law:
    violent strike, sit-down strikes, partial or intermittent strikes, wildcat strikes, strikes
    during the 60-day cooling-off period, strikes in violation of a no-strike clause.

Crossover and Replacement Workers

Workers can elect not to strike or return to work after joining strikers for a period of either. If either of these two options are chosen, the workers are called crossover workers. Once the strike has begun, temporary or permanent replacement workers may be hired. If the new employees are permanent, they do not have to be dismissed when the strike is through.

Employer Lockout

When an employer reasonably anticipates a strike by some of its employees, it may prevent those employees from entering the plant or premises. This is known as an employer lockout.

Internal Union Affairs

A union may be operated by internal union rules that are adopted by the union. Title I of the Landrum Griffin Act gives each union member equal rights and privileges to nominate candidates for union office, vote in elections, and participate in membership meetings. Union members are also permitted to initiate judicial and administrative action.

Union members may be disciplined for participating in activities like walking off the job in a nonsanctioned strike, working for wages below union scale, spying for an employer, or any other activity that is adverse to employer.

Refresh Your Memory

The following exercises will enable you to refresh your memory as to the key principles and concepts given to you in this chapter. Read each question carefully and put your answer in the blanks provided. Review the chapter material for any question you miss or are unable to remember.

1. The relationship between employers and employees changed dramatically when the United States became _____ in the late 1880s.

2. Who were the initial workers that were allowed to belong to the American Federation of Labor?

    _____

3. What organization allowed semiskilled and unskilled workers to become members of the American Federation of Labor?

    _____

4. What did the Norris-LaGuardia Act stipulate?

    _____

5. Which act allowed employees to bargain collectively?

    _____

6. The Labor-Management Reporting and Disclosure Act requires regularly scheduled _____ for union officials by _____ ballot.

7. Managers and professional employees may not belong to _____ formed by employees whom they manage.

8. What percentage of interested employees in a bargaining unit is necessary in order for the NLRB to petition and investigate and set an election date for the joining and formation of a union? _____
    percent

9. If employees no longer want to be represented by a union, a _____ election will be held.

10. If union solicitation is being conducted by fellow employees, an employer may restrict solicitation activities to the employees' _____ time.

11. The NLRA makes it an _____ labor _____ for an employer to interfere with, coerce, or restrain employees from exercising their right to form and join a union.

12. Collective bargaining is

    _____.

13. Under an _____ _____ agreement, employees do not have to become union members, but they have to pay an agency fee.

14. A plant closing is a _____ or _____ shutdown of a single site

that results in a loss of employment of 50 or more employees during any 30-day period.

15. A _____ is a reduction of 33 percent of the employees or at least 50 employees during the 30-day period.

Critical Thought Exercise

When the collective bargaining agreement between the United Pickle and Catsup Makers (Union) and Good Foods Company (Good), the Union called for a strike. Picketers were used to walk in front of 27 grocery stores in the greater Cleveland, Ohio, area and distribute literature. Some of the picket signs said, "Boycott Pickles and Catsup," and "Don't buy Good pickles here, make them at home." Most signs were pre-printed by the Union and stated, "Boycott All Good Products." The majority of pickles and catsup sold by People's Grocery Store and Larry's Supermarket are made by Good. Though customers never saw anyone spray them with catsup, they found their clothing squirted with catsup if they entered People's Grocery Store. Customers refused to enter People's Grocery and Larry's Supermarket because they felt intimidated and are afraid of the unknown catsup squirter. People's and Larry's file suit in federal court seeking injunctions and damages against the Union. Were the activities by the Union illegal?

Answer:

_____

_____

_____

_____

_____

_____

_____

_____

_____

_____

_____

_____

_____

_____

_____

_____

_____

_____

_____

_____

_____

_____

Practice Quiz

True/False

1. ___ Threats of loss of benefits for joining the union are an unfair labor practice. [p. 493]

2. ___ During the Great Depression of the 1930s, several federal statutes were enacted giving workers certain rights and protections. [p. 491]

3. ___ The power of the courts to thwart peaceful union activity was curtailed by the Norris-LaGuardia Act. [p. 491]

4. ___ Most union elections are contested by the employer. [p. 491]

5. ___ The Railway Labor Act covers employees of airline carriers. [p. 491]

6. ___ Union shops do not require employee membership upon being hired. [p. 495]

7. ___ The NLRB oversees union elections. [p. 491]

8. ___ Off-duty employees may not be barred from union solicitation on company premises. [p. 492]

9. ___ If 50 percent of the employees in the bargaining unit are interested in forming a union, the NLRB can be petitioned to investigate and set an election date. [p. 491]

10. ___ The NLRB may issue an injunction to restrain unfair labor practices, but may not issue a cease-and-desist order. [p. 493]

11. ___ An establishment where an employee does not have to join the union but must pay a fee equal to the union dues is known as a union shop. [p. 495]

12. ___ A sit-down strike is lawful where employees sit down outside of their employees business and hold picket signs. [p. 497]

13. ___ Intermittent strikes are illegal as they interfere with an employer's right to operate its facilities at full operation. [p. 497]

14. ___ The 60-day cooling off period is a discretionary period as employees may not come to terms with employers and then must strike according to their union rules. [p. 497]

15. ___ The Plant Closing Act covers employers with more than 25 employees. [p. 494]

Multiple Choice

16. Which of the following prohibits making take-it-or-leave-it proposals? [p. 494]
    a. Norris-LaGuardia Act
    b. Plant Closing Act
    c. the Railway Labor Act
    d. collective bargaining

17. Which act was created that required employers with 100 or more employees to give their employees 60 days notice before engaging in certain plant closings or layoffs? [p. 494]
    a. Worker Adjustment and Retraining Notification Act
    b. Labor-Management Reporting and Disclosure Act
    c. the National Labor Relations Act
    d. all of the above

18. The Landrum-Griffin Act includes a rule that [p. 498]
    a. gives employees the right to form unions.
    b. allows an injunction to be issued to stop unfair labor practices.
    c. makes union officials accountable for union funds and property.
    d. requires a 60-day notice for certain plant closures.

19. The administrative agency created to enforce the Wagner Act (NLRA) is the [p. 491]
    a. NLRB.
    b. AFL.
    c. CIO.
    d. Labor Board of Conciliation and Arbitration.

20. What does the inaccessibility exception to union solicitation on company property apply to? [p. 492]
    a. It applies to employee places within reach of reasonable union efforts.
    b. It applies to such places as logging camps, mining towns, company towns, and other similar places.
    c. It no longer applies as the exception has been repealed.
    d. none of the above

21. If an employer offers incentive bonuses and increased vacation time to his employees right before an election on the acceptance of a new union, this is [p. 493]
    a. within the employer's free-speech rights.
    b. an unfair labor practice.
    c. acceptable under the collective bargaining agreement.
    d. acceptable as long as no threats accompanied the action.

22. The act of negotiating by a union with an employer is called [p. 494]
    a. collective bargaining.
    b. picketing.
    c. a wildcat action.
    d. a secondary boycott.

23. Under a union shop agreement, employees [p. 495]
    a. do not have to become a union members, but they do have to pay an agency fee.
    b. do not have to join the union or pay any dues if they do not desire, because to force the employee to do so would be illegal.
    c. must join the union and pay dues or they will be terminated from employment.
    d. none of the above

24. A wildcat strike takes place when [p. 497]
    a. striking employees continue to occupy the premises of the employer.
    b. individual union members go out on strike without proper authorization from the union.
    c. employees strike part of the day and work part of the day.
    d. striking employees cause substantial damage to the property of the employer.

25. Which of the following are considered to be illegal strikes? [p. 497]
    a. partial strikes
    b. strikes in violation of a no-strike clause
    c. wildcat strikes
    d. all of the above

Short Answer

26. Give an example of what is considered to be an unfair labor practice within Section 8(a) of the NLRA. [p. 493]
    _____

27. What are the three types of union elections? [p. 491] _____,
    _____, _____.

28. The Taft-Hartley Act gives the president the right to seek an _____ against a strike that would create a national _____. [p. 491]

29. The Labor-Management Report and Disclosure Act (Landrum-Griffin Act) regulates _____ union affairs and establishes the rights of union _____. [p. 491]

30. The three main requirements of the Landrum-Griffin Act are: [p. 498]
    (1) _____
    (2) _____
    (3) _____

31. What is the NLRB? [p. 491]
    _____
    _____

32. What are the three main duties of the NLRB? [p. 491] (1) _____
    (2) _____ (3) _____

33. What are things such as closed shops and discrimination considered to be? [p. 494]
    _____ _____

34. What is a bargaining unit? [p. 492]
    _____
    _____

35. Describe where and when these groups may engage in union solicitation activities: [p. 492]
    fellow working employees _____
    _____
    off-duty employees _____
    _____

union management _____
_____

36. What is an unfair labor practice? [p. 493]
    _____
    _____
    _____

37. What two actions are covered by the Plant Closure Act and when do they apply?
    [pp. 494-495]
    _____
    _____
    _____
    _____

38. Name seven things that are proper compulsory subjects of collective bargaining. [p. 494]
    (1) _____ (2) _____ (3) _____ (4) _____
    (5) _____ (6) _____ (7) _____

39. When there is a union or agency shop, what is required of employers in regards to dues and
    fees? What is this requirement called? [p. 495]
    _____
    _____

40. What is secondary boycott picketing? [pp. 496-497]
    _____
    _____
    _____

Answers to Refresh Your Memory

1.   industrialized [p. 490]
2.   silversmiths and artisans [p. 490]
3.   the Congress of Industrial Organizations [p. 490]
4.   that it is legal for employees to organize [p. 491]
5.   the NLRA [p. 491]
6.   elections, secret [p. 491]
7.   unions [p. 491]
8.   30 percent [p. 491]
9.   decertification [p. 492]
10. free [p. 492]
11. unfair, practice [p. 493]
12. the act of negotiating with a union [p. 494]
13. agency shop [p. 495]
14. permanent temporarily [p. 494]
15. mass layoff [p. 494]

Critical Thought Exercise Model Answer

Picketing is a form of lawful protest that can be undertaken by unions during a strike. The picketing is lawful unless it (1) is accompanied by violence, (2) obstructs customers from entering the employer's business, (3) prevents replacement or nonstriking employees from entering the premises, or (4) prevents shipments or deliveries from entering of exiting the premises. If the picketing is unlawful for any of these reasons, the employer may seek an injunction to stop the activity. Picketing of the employer's customers or suppliers is known as secondary boycott picketing. Secondary picketing is lawful only if the union pickets the product or service of the employer. The picketing is illegal if it is directed against the business of the customer or supplier who is not involved in the strike. Good Foods can be lawfully struck by picketing the suppliers and customers of Good Foods. Though the Union may picket both People's Grocery and Larry's Supermarket, the picketers cannot ask customers to not enter the stores or refrain from buying goods in the store that are not produced by Good Foods. The picket signs that are being used are legal for the most part. The only sign that creates a problem is the one that says, "Boycott Pickles and Catsup." This sign is not calling for an exclusive boycott of Good pickles and catsup. Both stores could be selling pickles and catsup made by several manufacturers. This would be asking for a general boycott and would be illegal. The other signs are referring to Good Food products and are a proper form of secondary boycott. The squirting of catsup upon the clothing of customers at People's would allow People's to sue the Union for the tort of intentional interference with a contractual relationship. An injunction could also be issued to stop this from happening again. Failure to honor the injunction would subject the Union to damages for illegal strike activities.

Answers to Practice Quiz

True/False

1. True   Threats or loss of benefits for joining the union are included in Sec 8(a) of the National Labor Relations Act and are considered to be an unfair labor practice.
2. True   The statutes were a reaction to employer abuses during industrialization.
3. True   The act made it legal for employees to organize.
4. True   Most union elections are contested by the employer.
5. True   The Railway Labor Act covers employees of railroad and airline carriers..
6. False   Under a union shop agreement, an employee must join the union within a certain time period (30 days) after being hired.
7. True   The National Labor Relations Act created the NLRB and gave it the responsibility of overseeing all union elections.
8. False   Off-duty employees may be barred from union solicitation on company premises, and nonemployees may be prohibited from soliciting on behalf of the union anywhere on company property.
9. False   Only 30 percent approval within the bargaining unit is needed to petition for an election.
10. False The NLRB may issue a cease-and-desist order.
11. True   The employee must be working, but can only solicit during free time.
12. False In sit-down strikes, striking employees continue to occupy the employer's premises. Such strikes are illegal because they deny the employer's statutory right to continue its operations during the strike.

13. True   This type of strike is illegal because it interferes with the employer's right to operate its facilities at full operation.
14. False   A cooling-off period is mandatory 60 days' notice before a strike can commence.
15. False   The Plant Closing Act only applies to employers with 100 or more employees.

Multiple Choice

16. D   Choice D is correct as collective bargaining requires the duty of good faith bargaining. Choices A, C, and D are labor acts, but they did not address the duty to bargain and deal in god faith.
17. A   Answer A is correct as the Worker Adjustment and Retraining Notification Act covers employers with 100 or more employees, and requires employers to give their employees 60 days notice before engaging in certain plant closings or layoffs. Answers B, C, and D are incorrect as they do not apply to the Worker Adjustment and Retraining Notification Act.
18. C   C is one of the duties imposed by the Landrum-Griffin Act. Choice A is incorrect because that right is contained in the NLRA. Choice B is incorrect because that rule is also contained in the NRLA. Choice D is incorrect because that rule is contained in the Plant Closing Act.
19. A   A is correct because the NLRB was created to enforce the Wagner Act. Answers B, C, and D are not applicable as they were not created to enforce the Wagner Act.
20. B   Answer B is the correct answer as the inaccessibility exception permits employees and union officials to engage in union solicitation on company property if the employees are beyond reach of reasonable union efforts to communicate with them. Answers A and C are false statements and are therefore incorrect. Answer D is incorrect for the reasons given above.
21. B   The correct choice is B because an act that interferes with employees' right to form and join unions is an unfair labor practice. Choice A is incorrect because the employer has no right to influence the employees by anything other than words. Choice C is incorrect because the union has yet to be formed, so there can be no collective bargaining agreement and the parties cannot bargain on illegal subjects. Choice D is wrong because illegal persuasion with increased benefits is an unfair labor practice just as much as the use of threats and intimidation under Section 8(a) of the NLRA.
22. A   A is correct because the act of negotiating a contract or collective bargaining agreement is also called collective bargaining. Choices B, C, and D are incorrect because they all relate to strikes and picketing as part of a strike.
23. C   C is correct as it states the correct definition of a union shop. A is incorrect because it states the definition of an agency shop. Choice B is incorrect because it states the rights of the employee in a right-to-work state where union shops are illegal. Choice D is incorrect because a correct choice, C, is available.
24. B   Answer B correctly defines a wildcat strike. Choice A is incorrect because it defines a sit-down strike. Choice C is incorrect because it defines a partial strike. Choice D is incorrect because it defines a violent strike.
25. D   D is correct because choices A, B, and C all state types of strikes considered to be illegal.

Short Answer

26.   interfering with or coercing or restraining employees from exercising their statutory right to form and join unions
27.   contested, consent, and decertification

28. injunction, emergency
29. internal, members
30. (1) a requirement for regularly scheduled elections for union officials by secret ballot
    (2) a prohibition against ex-convicts and communists from holding union office
    (3) a rule that makes union officials accountable for union funds and property
31. The NLRB is an administrative body comprised of five members appointed by the president and approved by the Senate.
32. The NLRB:
    (1) oversees union elections
    (2) prevents employers and employees from engaging in illegal and unfair labor practices
    (3) enforces and interprets certain federal labor laws
33. illegal subjects
34. A bargaining unit is the group of employees that a union is seeking to represent. The group must be defined before a union election can be held. The bargaining unit can be all the employees from the same company, a group within the company, or like employees from several companies.
35. *Fellow employees* can be restricted to solicitation during their free time, such as lunch hours, and can be restricted to nonworking areas such as the cafeteria, restroom, or parking lot.
    Off-duty employees may be barred from union solicitation on company premises.
    Union Management may be prohibited from soliciting anywhere on company property.
36. An unfair labor practice is any act by an employer that interferes with, coerces, or restrains employees from exercising their statutory rights to form and join unions. It is also any act by the union that interferes with a union election, or used coercion, threats, or intimidation to accomplish union goals.
37. Both actions apply only to employers with 100 or more employees and they can be taken only after a 60-day notice to employees. Plant closings are a permanent or temporary shut-down of a single site that results in a loss of employment of 50 or more employees during any 30-day period. Mass layoffs are a reduction of 33 percent of the employees or at least 50 employees during any 30-day period.
38. (1) wages (2) hours (3) fringe benefits (4) health benefits (5) retirement plans
    (6) work assignments (7) safety rules
39. Union and agency shop employers are required to deduct union dues and agency fees from employees' wages and forward these dues and fees to the union. This requirement is called a check-off provision.
40. A type of picketing where unions try to bring pressure against an employer by picketing his or her suppliers or customers. This type of picketing is often used when the employer has no centralized or main office or plant to picket, such as agricultural businesses. Instead of picketing a cotton field, the union may picket the mill where the cotton is sent or a clothing manufacturer that purchases the cotton.

Chapter 33

EQUAL OPPORTUNITY
IN EMPLOYMENT

Chapter Overview

Prior to the 1960s there was little that an employee could do to address discrimination by the employer in regards to hiring, discharge, promotion, pay, and work assignments. Congress addressed discrimination by passing a comprehensive set of laws that made it actionable to discriminate against a person because of race, sex, religion, national origin, age, or disability. The interpretation of these federal statutes has created a large body of law that has created a much more level playing field in the workplace. The chapter examines the major legislation and the application of these laws by the courts.

Objectives

Upon completion of the exercises in this chapter, you should be able to:
1. Describe the protection provided by Title VII of the Civil Rights Act of 1964.
2. Identify examples of discrimination based upon race, color, and national origin.
3. Describe conduct that creates sex discrimination, including sexual harassment.
4. Recognize how e-mail may be used as evidence of sexual harassment.
5. Discuss the important protections contained in the Equal Pay Act of 1963.
6. Explain how the bona fide occupational qualification (BFOQ) defense works in discrimination cases.
7. Explain the protections provided by the Age Discrimination in Employment Act.
8. Describe the scope of the Americans with Disabilities Act and the protections it affords person with a disability.
9. Define the doctrine of affirmative action and describe how it is used.
10. Describe how the law related to equal opportunity in employment is being applied in Japan.

Practical Application

Antidiscrimination laws set forth mandates for employers and protection for employees that alter the course of conduct of people in the business environment. You should be able to recognize the situations where discrimination is unlawful and instances where a defense to discrimination may apply. This will allow you to make decisions that stay within the requirements set forth by the federal laws.

Helpful Hints

Since most of this chapter concentrates on specific laws and cases that interpret the laws, it is beneficial to know the basic definition or content of each law and understand the examples of how they are applied in the real world. You should focus on the type of conduct that is involved in a situation to determine which area of law is applicable and what actions must be taken to correct the action, if at all possible.

Study Tips

Enforcement of Federal Antidiscrimination Laws

The Equal Employment Opportunity Commission (EEOC) is appointed by the president and is responsible for enforcing the provisions of all the federal laws that address areas of discrimination in the workplace. The EEOC is empowered to not only investigate, but also to issue opinions and directives to offending employers, bring suit against the violator, and even seek injunctive relief to stop the actual conduct that violated a particular law. Though an employee can file suit directly against the employer if the EEOC gives permission, action by the EEOC is the best actions available to force a stop to the illegal conduct.

Title VII of the Civil Rights Act of 1964

Overall, Title VII is the most important piece of legislation ever passed to address discrimination. As such, it provides the authority for the largest number of cases brought to rectify discrimination. The conduct that will trigger a Title VII action will be within the areas of:
- Hiring
- Discharge
- Compensation (rate of pay and classification that affects pay)
- Terms of employment (work schedule, fringe benefits)
- Conditions of the employment (rules, policies, and procedures)
- Privileges granted as part of employment (honorary positions, use of company assets)
- Promotion (not promoted when qualified)
- Work assignment (given less desirable assignments that prevent growth)

If any action on the above list is made by an employer based upon a person's race, color, religion, sex, or national origin; or the employee is limited in any way that deprives them of an opportunity based upon race, color, religion, sex, or national origin, a violation of Title VII has been committed.

Title VII applies to:
- employers with 15 or more employees
- employment agencies
- labor union with 15 or more employees
- state and local governments
- most federal employees
- undocumented aliens

Title VII does not apply to:
- Indian tribes
- tax-exempt private clubs

There are two types of discrimination that Title VII addresses:
- Disparate treatment: employer discriminates against individual
- Disparate impact: employer discriminates against entire protected class

Procedure for bringing Title VII action consists of these steps:
- Private complainant must file complaint with EEOC
- EEOC given opportunity to sue on behalf of complainant
- If EEOC chooses not to sue, issues right to sue letter
- Complainant now has right to sue employer

Remedies for violation of Title VII include:
- Recovery by employee of up to two years' back pay
- If malice or reckless indifference to rights is shown, aggrieved party may recover compensatory and punitive damages
- Statutory damages from $50,000 to $300,000 may be awarded depending upon the size of the employer
- Court may order reinstatement, including seniority rights
- Court may issue injunctions to compel compliance

The **Pregnancy Discrimination Act** was added to Title VII in 1978 to forbid discrimination because of pregnancy, birth, or related medical conditions. The effect that pregnancy or giving birth to a new baby may have upon a woman cannot be raised in a job interview or used as the basis for not offering a position. It also forbids the use of pregnancy, giving birth, or a related medical condition as a basis for making a decision in any of the other employment areas listed above.

Sexual Harassment

Lewd remarks, touching, intimidation, posting pinups, and other verbal of physical conduct of a sexual nature that occur on the job are sexual harassment and violate Title VII. Requesting that an employee has sex with the employer to get hired, receive a promotion, or prevent discharge are all forms of sexual harassment prohibited by Title VII. When the workplace is permeated with discriminatory intimidation, ridicule, and insult, that is sufficiently severe or pervasive to alter the conditions of the victim's employment and create an abusive working environment, Title VII is violated. In evaluating the severity and pervasiveness of sexual harassment, a court will focus on the perspective of the victim and ask whether a "reasonable woman" would consider the conduct to be offensive. Evidence of the offending conduct may come from words, physical acts, e-mails distributed within or outside the office, pictures (including material on computers), jokes, threats, and both employer and employee communications. The court will consider the overall effect that several acts have upon the victim.

Defense to Sexual Harassment

An employer may raise an affirmative defense against liability or damages for sexual harassment by proving that:
1. The employer exercised reasonable care to prevent and correct promptly any sexually-harassing behavior, and
2. The plaintiff employee unreasonably failed to take advantage of any preventive of coercive opportunities by the employer or to otherwise avoid harm

Religious Discrimination

Under Title VII, the employer is under a duty to reasonably accommodate the religious observances, practices, or beliefs of its employees if it does not cause undue hardship on the employer.

Defenses to a Title VII Action

Merit. Employers can select or promote employees based on merit. Thus, a promotion can lawfully be based upon experience, skill, education, and ability tests. A test or condition that has no relevance to the position may not be used to prevent a protected class or individual from qualifying for employment.

Seniority. An employer may maintain a seniority system that rewards long-term employees. The system is lawful unless persons in a position of seniority achieved their position through intentional discrimination in the past.

Bona Fide Occupational Qualification. Employment discrimination based on a protected class (such as sex, but other than race or color), is lawful if it is job related and a business necessity. Hiring only women to work in a women's health spa would be legal but hiring only women for a women's clothing store in the mall would be a violation of Title VII.

Civil Rights Act of 1866

Section 1981 of this act gives all persons equal contract rights. Section 1981 also prohibits racial discrimination and discrimination based upon national origin. Though most discrimination cases are brought under Title VII, there are two good reasons to bring an action under Section 1981: (1) A private plaintiff can bring an action without going through the procedural requirements of Title VII, and (2) there is no limitation period on the recovery of back pay (claimant can only go back two years under Title VII) and no cap on the recovery of compensatory or punitive damages.

Equal Pay Act of 1963

Protects both sexes from pay discrimination based on sex. The act prohibits disparity in pay for jobs that require equal skill, equal effort, equal responsibility, or similar working conditions. If two jobs are determined to be equal and similar, an employer cannot pay disparate wages to members of different sexes.

> *Ex:* Sue is paid $8.50 an hour to climb a 30-foot ladder and clean the light fixtures in the ceilings of the employer's warehouses. Mike is paid $14.00 per hour to climb the same ladder and change burned out light bulbs in the same fixtures that Sue is paid to clean. Sue and Mike are doing jobs that require low skill levels and require the same physical risk. The only basis for the disparate pay is the sex of the employees, making this a violation of the Equal Pay Act.

Criteria That Justify a Differential in Wages*
- Seniority
- Merit
- Quantity of quality of product (commissions)
- A differential based on any factor other than sex (shift differential)

*Note, the employer has the burden of proving these defenses.

Age Discrimination in Employment Act of 1967

The ADEA prohibits age discrimination in all employment decisions, including hiring, promotions, compensation, and other terms and conditions of employment. The Older Worker Benefit Protection Act amended the ADEA to prohibit age discrimination with regard to employee benefits. The ADEA applies to all employees over age 40.

The Americans with Disabilities Act of 1990

The ADA imposes obligations on employers and providers of public transportation, telecommunications, and public accommodations to accommodate individuals with disabilities. Title I of the ADA prohibits employment discrimination against qualified individuals with disabilities in regard to job application procedures, hiring, compensation, training, promotion, and termination. Title I requires an employer to make **reasonable accommodations** to individuals with disabilities that do not cause hardship to the employer. Employers may not inquire into the existence, nature, or severity of a disability during the application process.

Qualified Individual with a Disability

A qualified individual with a disability is a person who, with or without reasonable accommodation, can perform the essential functions of the job that the person desires or holds.

A disabled person is someone who
1) has a physical or mental impairment that substantially limits one or more of his or her major life activities
2) has a record of such impairment, or
3) is regarded as having such impairment

See page 512 of your text for conditions that are covered under the ADA. Note too that recovering alcoholics and former users of illegal drugs are protected whereas a current user of illegal drugs or an alcoholic using alcohol or who is under the influence of alcohol at the workplace is not covered.

Affirmative Action

This is a policy that provides that certain job preferences will be given to minority or other protected class applicants when an employer makes an employment decision. Affirmative action plans will not be upheld when they discriminate against a majority after past discriminatory practices have already been rectified. Additionally, the courts will not allow employers to give a preference to a minority when another employee is far better qualified for a position.

Ex: Bob is white and has both a master's degree and doctorate in psychology. Bob has 25 years of experience in a supervisory position at Major University Psychological Services Center. Keith is black and only has a bachelor's degree. Keith has worked at Major University for only 2 years and has never held any supervisory position. If Keith is hired as the new director of the entire Psychological Services Center because he is black, Bob will have a cause of action under Title VII for racial discrimination.

Reverse Discrimination

Reverse discrimination is also protected under Title VII. Though the courts have held that "this effect is not actionable by members of the majority class who are affected," there is an exception of sorts. If an affirmative action plan is based on preestablished numbers or percentage quotas for hiring or promoting minority applicants, then reverse discrimination is the result whereby the members of the majority may sue under Title VII and recover damages as well as other remedies for the same.

Refresh Your Memory

The following exercise will enable you to refresh your memory of the important rules and concepts set forth in this chapter. Read each question twice and put your answer in the blanks provided. Answer the entire exercise, then review questions and the text in areas you did not remember.

1.   What is the Equal Employment Opportunity Commission responsible for?

      _____

      _____

2.   Title ____ of the _____ _____ ____ of 1964 was intended to eliminate job discrimination.

3.   What type of employers does Title VII apply to?

      _____

4.   What type of damages may a court award against an employer in a case involving an employer's malice or reckless indifference to federally protected rights?

      _____

5.   _____ _____ discrimination occurs when an employer treats a specific individual less favorably because of his/her membership in a protected class.

6.   When is a right to sue letter issued?

      _____

      _____

7.   What is meant by national heritage?

      _____

      _____

8.   Which act protects individuals who are pregnant, experienced childbirth, or other related medical conditions?

      _____

9.   Give an example of sexual harassment.

      _____

      _____

10. What two factors are considered in determining whether or not an individual is subjected to a hostile work environment when establishing a claim for sexual harassment?
_____ and _____

11. What type of conflict usually exists in many religious discrimination cases?
_____

12. Employment discrimination based on a protected class (other than color or national origin) is lawful if it is _____ related and a business _____.

13. Why is the Americans with Disabilities Act considered to be the most comprehensive piece of civil right legislation since the Civil Rights Act of 1964?
_____
_____

14. Give an example of a reasonable accommodation that will not cause an undue hardship to the employer?
_____
_____

15. If an employer is in violation of the Age Discrimination in Employment Act, what must he or she do?
_____
_____

Critical Thought Exercise

Carol Jones was employed with Richmond Components, Inc. (RCI), an electrical engineering and manufacturing company that supplied parts and guidance system development for the United States Air Force. Jones was a public relations and communications manager for RCI at their facility located on Davis Air Force Base for over nine years. Of the 135 employees at the RCI facility at Davis AFB, only 9 women were in professional positions. Employees in the office where Jones worked used e-mail as the major form of communication between employees. Jones was sent sexually explicit material via e-mail, including pictures that had been downloaded from the Internet. Two male engineers in her work area used semi-nude swimsuit pictures as the screensaver on their computer. Pictures of nude women from magazines were cut out and put in her mailbox with notes, such as, "Will you pose like this for us?" When Jones requested that information for press releases be given to her by a stated deadline, she was told to "Go have sex and chill out," along with other sexually demeaning comments about her anatomy. When Jones complained to the vice president in charge of personnel, she was told that she worked in a high-stress 'boys' club" and she had better learn to accept the "give-and-take" environment at RCI. Jones quit her job and filed an action under Title VII. Will she prevail?

Answer:
_____
_____
_____
_____
_____

_____
_____
_____
_____
_____
_____
_____
_____
_____
_____
_____
_____
_____
_____

Practice Quiz

True/False

1. ____ The EEOC is not empowered to bring suit to enforce Title VII of the Civil Rights Act of 1964. [p. 502]

2. ____ Disparate-impact discrimination happens when an employer adopts a work rule that is neutral on its face but is shown to cause an adverse impact on a protected class. [p. 503]

3. ____ A person may elect to sue based on a Title VII violation or file a complaint with the EEOC depending on the amount of time left before the statute of limitations runs. [p. 504]

4. ____ Same-sex discrimination does not violate Title VII but sexual harassment does. [p. 507]

5. ____ Under Title VII, race is considered to be a bona fide occupational job qualification. [p. 508]

6. ____ The right of an employee to practice his or her religion is not absolute. [p. 508]

7. ____ Since age is a protected class, an employer may maintain an employment practice whereby it only hires individuals 50 years of age and older. [p. 511]

8. ____ A differential in wages based on merit is acceptable regardless of identifiable measurement standards. [p. 510]

9. ____ An affirmative action plan must be narrowly tailored to achieve some compelling interest. [p. 513]

10. ___ Title I of the ADA allows the employer to test for an applicant's disabilities. [p. 512]

11. ___ The Equal Pay Act of 1963 covers all levels of private-sector employees. [p. 510]

12. ___ Employers are not required to provide accommodations that would impose an undue burden or that would require significant difficulty or expense. [p. 511]

13. ___ Once a job offer has been made, an employer may require a medical examination, the results of which become public record. [p. 512]

14. ___ Hiring only single male mechanics versus married female mechanics is an example of sex discrimination. [p. 505]

15. ___ Disparate impact discrimination requires the plaintiff to show a causal link between the challenged practice and the statistical imbalance. [p. 503]

16. ___ Undocumented aliens may not bring a Title VII action for employment discrimination. [p. 503]

17. ___ Because of the volume of employees in the United States, equal employment opportunity laws are narrowly interpreted by the federal courts. [p. 502]

18. ___ Seniority systems are lawful if they are not the result of intentional discrimination. [p. 508]

19. ___ Title VII expressly prohibits religious organizations to give preference in employment to individuals of a particular religion. [p. 508]

20. ___ The ADEA covers federal employees with at least 20 employees, labor unions with at least 25 members, and all employment agencies. [p. 511]

Multiple Choice

21. The enforcement of federal antidiscrimination laws is the responsibility of the [p. 502]
    a. OWBPA.
    b. EEOC.
    c. ADEA.
    d. ADA.

22. Which of the following would best prove disparate-treatment discrimination? [p. 503]
    a. statistical data about the employer's employment practices
    b. proof of refusal to hire or promote someone unless he or she has sex with the manager
    c. proof that an employer is treating a specific individual less favorably than others because of that person's color
    d. none of the above

23. Which of the following is true of a BFOQ? [p. 508]
    a. Discrimination based on protected classes is allowed if it is job related.
    b. Discrimination based on protected classes is allowed if it is a business necessity.
    c. Race or color is not encompassed in a BFOQ.
    d. all of the above

24. Which of the following remedies is available in a Title VII action? [p. 504]
    a. back pay
    b. reasonable attorney's fees
    c. fictional seniority
    d. all of the above

25. To bring an action under Title VII, a private complainant must first file a complaint [p. 504]
    a. in federal district court.
    b. in the trial court in the state where they reside.
    c. with the EEOC.
    d. with the Commerce Department.

26 Conduct that creates a hostile work environment includes [p. 506]
    a. a mere offensive utterance.
    b. conduct that is sexually offensive, regardless of whether it unreasonably interferes with an employee's work performance.
    c. conduct that is humiliating.
    d. all of the above

27. Rod is upset because he has been working as a graphics designer for the LMN Corporation for 10 years and is receiving $5.00 less per hour than Kim whom the company just hired. Rod and Kim have equal skill, put in the same amount of effort, have equal responsibility, and work in the exact same work environment. Which of the following is applicable to Rod? [p. 510]
    a. Rod can bring a private cause of action against the LMN Corporation for violating the Equal Pay Act..
    b. Rod may be entitled to back pay and liquidated damages.
    c. The LMN Corporation must increase his wages to eliminate the unlawful disparity of wages.
    d. all of the above

28. Employers can raise a defense to a Title VII action by showing that the discriminatory conduct was based upon [p. 510]
    a. a merit system.
    b. a seniority system.
    c. a bona fide occupational qualification.
    d. all of the above

29. Which factor does not justify a differential in wages under the Equal Pay Act? [p. 510]
    a. protection of a woman's health due to hazardous work conditions
    b. merit, as long as there is some identifiable standard
    c. quantity or quality of product
    d. any factor other than sex, such as night versus day shifts

30. According to the ADA, reasonable accommodations for a disabled employee include [pp. 511-512]
    a. allowing the employee to dictate their work assignment.
    b. providing part-time or modified work schedules.
    c. providing another employee to do the work for the disabled employee.
    d. all of the above.

Short Answer

31. Why are employment decisions covered by section 1981 of the Civil Rights Act of 1866? [p. 510]

    _____

32. What are the two reasons a complainant would bring an action under Section 1981 of the Civil Rights Act of 1866? [p. 510] _____
    and _____

33. Who is exempt from Title I coverage? [p. 511]

    _____

    _____

34. Disparate-impact discrimination is often proven through _____ data about the employer's employment practices. [p. 503]

35. In a case of involving intentional discrimination, what is the cap of recovery of compensatory and punitive damages from employers with 100 or fewer employees? [p. 503] _____

36. Which act will not allow the establishment of mandatory retirement ages for employees? [p. 511]

    _____

37. If an engineer from India is fired from a company because of his accent, to what type of protected class does he belong and why is this correct protected class to allege in his complaint? [p. 504]

    _____

38. If a male applicant is not hired by an airline as a flight attendant because "women are more compassionate towards passengers," he is a victim of _____ _____. [p. 506]

39. Hanging a provocative swimsuit calendar in your office may be _____
    _____. [p. 506]

40. What is affirmative action? [p. 513]

    _____

    _____

    _____

Answers To Refresh Your Memory

1. for enforcing most federal antidiscriminatory laws [p. 502]
2. VII, Civil Rights Act [p. 502]
3. employers with 15 or more employees [p. 503]
4. punitive damages [p. 503]
5. Disparate treatment [p. 503]
6. If the EEOC refuses to file suit on behalf of the claimant, that's when a right to sue letter is issued. [p. 504]

7. refers to a country of a person's ancestors or cultural characteristics [p. 504]
8. the Pregnancy Discrimination Act [p. 505]
9. lewd remarks, job pinups of a sexual nature, etc. Answers will vary [p. 506]
10. frequency and severity [p. 506]
11. a conflict between an employer's work rule and the employee's religious beliefs [p. 508]
12. job, necessity [p. 508]
13. skill, effort, responsibility [p. 511]
14. providing part-time modified work schedules (answers will vary) [p. 511]
15. raise the wages of the discriminated against employee [p. 511]

Critical Thought Exercise Model Answer

Title VII applies to employers with 15 or more employees. With 135 employees at this facility alone, RCI will be covered by Title VII. Title VII prohibits harassment based upon gender in the workplace. Sexual harassment may be based upon lewd remarks, touching, intimidation, posting of sexually explicit pictures, and other unwanted verbal or physical conduct that is sexual in nature. Jones will argue that the activities of her coworkers have created a hostile work environment. To determine if the environment at RCI is hostile, a court will look at all the circumstances. These will include the frequency of the discriminatory conduct; its severity; whether it is physically threatening or humiliating, or a mere offensive utterance, and whether it unreasonably interferes with an employee's work performance. The conduct of the male employees at RCI has created a hostile work environment. The acts are frequent and quite severe. Pictures are deliberately put in Jones's mailbox with notes that ask her to pose nude for fellow employees. Jones is berated verbally with sexual statements when she tries to do her job and get information for press releases. She is subjected to the sexually explicit pictures on computers on a daily basis because they have been installed as screensavers. Finally, there was no effort by RCI to stop or correct the harassment. Jones was told to accept it and no action was taken against the offending employees. Jones should prevail on a claim brought under Title VII for sexual harassment.

Answers to Practice Quiz

True/False

1. False The EEOC is empowered to conduct investigations, interpret statutes, encourage conciliation between employers and employees, and bring suit to enforce the law.
2. True Disparate-impact discrimination occurs when an employer adopts a work rule that is neutral on its face but is shown to cause an adverse impact on a protected class.
3. False To bring an action under Title VII, a private complainant must first file a complaint with the EEOC.
4. False In *Omacle v. Sundowner Offshower Services, Incorporated,* the U.S. Supreme Court held that same-sex discrimination and harassment violated Title VII.
5. False Discrimination based on protected classes (other than race or color) is permitted if it is shown to be a bona fide occupational qualification (BFOQ).
6. True The right of an employee to practice his or her religion is not absolute.

7. False   Because persons under 40 are not protected by the ADEA, an employer can maintain an employment policy of hiring only workers who are 40 years of age or older without violating the ADEA; however, an employer could not maintain an employment practice of hiring only persons 50 years of age and older because it would discriminate against persons aged 40 to 49.

8. False   A justifiable differential in wages based on merit is acceptable as long as there is some identifiable measurement standard.

9. True   To be lawful, an affirmative action plan must be narrowly tailored to achieve some compelling interest.

10. False   Title I of the ADA limits an employer's ability to inquire into or test for an applicant's disabilities.

11. True   The Equal Pay Act of 1963 protects both sexes from pay discrimination and covers all levels of private-sector employees.

12. True   Employers are not obligated to provide accommodations that would impose an undue burden-that is, actions that would require significant difficulty or expense.

13. True   In addition to this, the court will consider whether the employer had an anti-harassment policy and whether the employer had a complaint mechanism in place.

14. True   The prohibition against sex discrimination applies equally to men and women. Sex discrimination is defined as discrimination against a person solely because of his or her gender.

15. True   In order to prevail in a cause of action based on disparate-impact discrimination, the plaintiff must demonstrate a causal link between the challenged practice and the statistical imbalance.

16. False   Any employee of covered employers, included undocumented aliens, may bring actions for employment discrimination under Title VII.

17. False   The comprehensive set of federal laws that eliminated major forms of discrimination were passed to guarantee equal employment opportunity to all employees. These laws have been broadly interpreted by the federal courts.

18. True   Seniority systems are lawful if they are not the result of intentional discrimination.

19. False   Title VII expressly permits religious organizations to give preference in employment to individuals of a particular religion.

20. False   The ADEA covers **nonfederal** employers with at least 20 employees, labor unions with at least 25 members, and all employment agencies.

Multiple Choice

21. B   B is correct because the EEOC is the federal agency that is charged with enforcing federal anti-discrimination laws. Choices A, C, and D are all laws enforced by the EEOC.

22. C   Answer C is the correct answer as disparate-treatment discrimination occurs when an employer treats a specific individual less favorably than others because of that person's race, color, national origin, sex, or religion. Answer A is incorrect as this is more helpful in proving disparate-impact discrimination. Answer B is incorrect as this shows sexual harassment. Answer D is incorrect for the reasons given above.

23. D   Answer D is correct as all of the statements expressed in answers A, B, and C are true of a BFOQ.

24. D   Answer D is correct as all of the above remedies expressed in answers A, B, and C are available in a Title VII action.

25. C   The claimant must file a complaint with the EEOC first. Only after getting a right to sue letter can the private claimant file suit in state or federal court. Choices A and B are incorrect because the complaint process with the EEOC is a prerequisite to an individual filing suit in a trial court. Choice D is incorrect because the EEOC is part of the Department of Labor.

26. C   Choice C is correct because humiliating acts are the type of conduct that create a hostile environment for the employee. Choice A is incorrect because a single offensive utterance is insufficient. Choice B is incorrect because the conduct did not interfere with work performance. Choice D is incorrect because choices A and B are incorrect.

27. D   D is correct because under the Equal Pay Act, disparity in pay for jobs that require equal skill, equal effort, equal responsibility, or similar working conditions is illegal.

28. A   A is correct because women are entitled to take the same risks at work as men. Choices B, C, and D are incorrect because they state three legal exceptions to the Equal Pay Act.

29. B   B is correct because it would be reasonable to allow an employee to work less hours or during certain times of the day if it did not create an undue hardship on the employer. Answers A and C are incorrect because they would create an undue hardship. Choice D is incorrect because it includes choices A and C.

30. B   Answer B is correct as reasonable accommodations under Title I of the ADA include providing part-time or modified work schedules. Answer A is incorrect as there in nothing in the ADA that allows an employee to dictate their work assignment. Answer C is incorrect as the ADA is silent as to whether an employee can do the work of a disabled employee. Answer D is incorrect based on the reason given above.

Short Answer

31.   because the employment relationship is contractual

32   (1) A private plaintiff can bring an action without going through the procedural requirements of Title VII, and (2) there is no cap on the recovery of compensatory or punitive damages.

33.   The United States, corporations wholly owned by the United States, and bona fide tax-exempt private membership clubs are exempt from Title I coverage.

34.   statistical

35.   up to fifty thousand dollars

36.   the Age Discrimination in Employment Act

37.   The discrimination is based upon national origin because speech is one aspect of a person's cultural characteristics, which is part of his/her national origin.

38.   sex discrimination

39.   sexual harassment

40.   Affirmative action is a policy that provides that certain job preferences will be given to minority or other protected-class applicants when an employer makes an employment decision.

Chapter 34

ENTREPRENEURSHIP, SOLE PROPRIETORSHIPS, AND GENERAL PARTNERSHIPS

Chapter Overview

This chapter focuses on the role of the entrepreneur, sole proprietorships, and general partnerships in business. You will learn the advantages as well as disadvantages for operating a business as a sole proprietorship. Additionally you will become aware of the liabilities that a sole proprietor may face. Further, you will learn about general partnerships, their formation, and the rights as
well as duties among the partners. You will also learn that the right to participate in the partnership's management is as important as the right to share in the partnership's profits and losses. Additionally, you will gain familiarity with the duty of loyalty among partners and violation of the same. The duty of care along with the liabilities in contract and tort in addition to the incoming and outgoing partners are also discussed. Finally, you will become aware of how a partnership is terminated and how partners may continue a dissolved corporation

Objectives

Upon completion of the exercises in this chapter, you should be able to:
1. Discuss the role of entrepreneurs in beginning and operating businesses.
2. State the different entrepreneurial forms of conducting business.
3. Explain the meaning of sole proprietorship.
4. Discuss the creation of the sole proprietorship.
5. Explain the meaning of d.b.a.
6. Compare and explain the advantages and disadvantages of operating a business as a sole proprietorship.
7. Discuss the liability of the sole proprietor.
8. Explain what a general partnership is as well as the formation of the same.
9. Discuss the rights and duties among partners.
10. Discuss the duties of care, to inform, and obedience owed by a partner.
11. Explain the duty of loyalty as well as the violations and consequences for the same.
12. Discuss the contract and tort liability of partners.
13. Explain the liability of incoming and outgoing partners.
14. Explain the dissolution and termination of a partnership.
15. Explain the continued operation of a partnership after dissolution of the same.

Practical Application

This chapter will enable you to be more aware of the positive and concerning aspects of operating a business as a sole proprietorship. You will have a greater understanding of the magnitude of the liability associated with conducting business in this manner as well. Further, you will have valuable knowledge that will enable you to make informed decisions regarding the possibility of conducting a business as a partnership. It will also give you insight on the legal duties and ramifications for failing to adhere to the duties expected of a partner under the law.

Helpful Hints

Since the information contained in this chapter focuses on the topics of entrepreneurs and sole proprietorship, as well as general partnerships, the principles are quickly committed to memory. The Study Tips section has been organized in much the same way as the chapter in your text has been presented. Since the information is so concisely written, the concepts will be easy to grasp.

Study Tips

When studying this chapter, it is best to commit the definition of an entrepreneur to memory as well as be familiar with the fact that there are various choices in which to operate an entrepreneur's business organization. Further, if you make a mental check list with duties of partners on one side and rights on the other, the principles associated with general partnerships will readily come to you. This chapter provides an excellent insight into the types of businesses many individuals enter into and also gives a good basis for learning about some of the more complicated businesses that are discussed in the chapters that follow.

Entrepreneur

An individual who creates and operates a new business.

Ways in which to operate a business organization include:

- sole proprietorship
- general partnership
- limited partnership
- corporation
- limited liability company
- franchise
- joint venture

Basic Information

Sole proprietorships are the simplest form of business organization as well as most common form in the United States. A sole proprietorship is not a distinct legal entity.

<u>**Advantages**</u>	<u>**Disadvantages**</u>
1. Easy to form and relatively inexpensive.	1. Access to capital is limited to personal funds plus any loans the proprietor can obtain.
2. The owner can make all management decisions, including hiring and firing.	2. The sole proprietor is held responsible for the business's contracts and torts he/she or any of his or her employees commit in the course of employment.
3. The owner has the right to all profits of the business.	
4. It is easily transferred or sold without anyone else's approval.	

Creation

No state or federal formalities are required.

Some local governments may require that a sole proprietor obtain a license to do business within the city.

Operation of a Sole Proprietorship

A sole proprietorship may conduct itself under the name of the sole proprietor or a trade name.

If a trade name is chosen, it is commonly referred to as **d.b.a.** (*doing business as*). Also, if a d.b.a. is used, most states necessitate the filing of a **fictitious business name statement**. This statement gives the name and address of the applicant, address of the business, and the trade name. Publication of the notice of the trade name is often required.

Personal Liability of Sole Proprietors

- If the sole proprietorship fails, the owner will lose his or her entire contribution of capital.
- The sole proprietor has unlimited personal liability, thereby subjecting his or her personal assets to creditors' claims.

Uniform Partnership Act (UPA)

The Uniform Partnership Act requirements are like the building code requirements of a house in that it is codified partnership law that has been adopted by 48 states. The Uniform Partnership Act details laws concerning formation, operation, and dissolution of basic partnerships. The UPA adopted the *entity theory* of partnership which considers partnerships as separate legal entities that are able to hold title to both real and personal property, and transact business in the partnership name.

Formation

Forming a partnership is akin to laying the foundation of a house and having a blueprint to build the house from. A partnership agreement is like a blueprint, in that it sets forth the terms of the parties' agreement, which includes but is not limited to the following:

- the name of the firm and names of the partners.
- the main partnership office as well as nature and scope of the business.
- the monetary contributions each partner is to be making.
- the distribution of profits and losses among the partners.
- the partners' management duties.
- limitations on the partners' authority to bind the partnership.

Partnerships may be **expressly** formed or **impliedly** formed. There is no necessity to file a partnership's agreement in most states. However, a select few require a general partnership to file **certificates of partnership** with the proper government agency. Partnerships are viewed as **separate legal entities** that can hold title to real and personal property.

General Partnership Requirements

There are four requirements in order to be considered a general partnership. They are:
1. It must be an association of two or more persons.
   a. All partners must be in agreement of each participating co-partner.
   b. Person includes natural persons, partnerships, associations, and corporations.
2. These persons must be carrying on a business.
   a. Co-ownership such as joint tenancy, tenancy by the entireties, and tenancy in common qualify.
   b. A series of transactions conducted over a period of time.
3. These individuals must be operating as co-owners.
   a. Essential to form a partnership.
   b. Co-ownership is evaluated based on the sharing of business profits and management responsibility.
4. The business must be for profit or have a profit motive.

General partners are personally liable for the obligations as well as debts incurred by the partnership.

Property Rights of the Partnership and the Partners

Property rights of the partnership are like fixtures in a home in that all property brought into the partnership on account of the partnership is considered partnership property. A written record of all partnership property should be kept. If a partner dies, the partnership property passes to the remaining partners. However, the value of the deceased partner's share in the partnership passes to his or her heirs. A partner's interest in a partnership is his or her share of the profits and surplus of the partnership.

Assignment of a Partnership Interest

A partner may assign all or part of his or her interest. The assignee may receive the profits which the assigning partner is entitled to. This includes entitlement to rights on liquidation to which the assigning partner is entitled.

Judgment Creditors

A judgment by a creditor against an individual partner entitles the judgment creditor to be paid from the partner's partnership profits by way of a **charging order**. A charging order is similar to having a lien against one's home. It is important to note that judgment creditors do not become partners and are not able to take part in the partnership's management.

Rights and Duties of General Partners

Like roommates or family members in a home, all partners have equal rights in the management of the partnership business. Each partner has a vote. The partners' unanimous consent is required for assignment of the partnership property for creditors' benefit as well as the disposal of the goodwill of the business.

Right to Participate in Management

All partners have equal rights in the conduct and management of the partnership business. Each partner has one vote regardless of the proportional size of his or her capital contribution or share in the partnership profits.

Right to an Accounting

Instead of being allowed to sue one another, partners may bring an **action for an accounting** against the other partners.

Other Important Rights

Partners have the following important rights under the Uniform Partnership Act:
- right to compensation and reimbursement
- right of indemnification
- right to return of advances
- right to return of capital and loans
- right to information
- right to share in profits

Duties of Partners

The duties that partners owe one another and the partnership are:

The Duty of Loyalty Includes:

- The duty not to self-deal.
- The duty not to usurp a partnership opportunity.
- The duty not to compete with the partnership.
- The duty not to make a secret profit from the partnership.
- The duty to keep partnership information confidential.
- The duty not to use partnership property for personal use.

The Duty of Obedience

- This refers to the partners' duties to act in accordance with the partnership agreement.

The Duty of Care

- The duty of care encompasses the duty to use the same level of care and skill a reasonable businessperson would use in the same circumstances.
- Breach of the duty of care is equivalent to negligence.

The Duty to Inform

- Partners must inform their co-partners of all information they possess that concerns the partnership affairs.

Liability to Third Parties

- "General partners are personally liable for contracts entered into on the partnership's behalf."

Tort Liability of Partnerships and Partners

- The liability of the partnership for the torts of its partners, employees, or agents depends on whether or not the person was acting within the ordinary course of the partnership business or with the authority of his or her co-partners. UPA Sections 13 and 14.

- **Joint and Several Liability of Partners** – Partners are jointly and severally liable for torts and breaches of trust regardless of a partner's participation in the act.

- **Liability of Incoming Partners** – A new partner is liable for existing debts and obligations only to the extent of his or her capital contributions. Further, he or she is liable for obligations and debts obtained by the partnership after becoming a partner.

Dissolution of a General Partnership

Termination refers to the dissolution of a partnership. The Uniform Partnership Act at Section 29 defines dissolution as "The change in the relation of the partners caused by any partner ceasing to be associated in the carrying on of the business."

Dissolution may be accomplished by **an act of the parties**, which includes termination of a stated time or purpose, the withdrawal of a partner, the expulsion of a partner, the admission of a partner, or by mutual agreement of the partners.

Additionally, dissolution may be as a result of **an operation of law** such as the death of any partner, the bankruptcy of any partner or the partnership, or an illegality. Further a **judicial decree of dissolution** may dissolve a partnership. This form of dissolution may be appropriate in situations such as the legal insanity of a partner and in extreme medical circumstances of a partner.

Wrongful Dissolution

Finally, a partner may **wrongfully** attempt to **dissolve** the partnership by withdrawing before the expiration of the stated term. If a partner's actions constitute wrongful dissolution of the partnership, he or she is liable for damages caused by the wrongful dissolution.

Requirements for Dissolution of Partnership

Notice

All partners must be given notice of the dissolution. If a partner has not been given notice and he or she enters into a contract on behalf of the partnership, the contract will remain binding on all partners based on the premise of **apparent authority.**

The Uniform Partnership Act at Section 35 requires that third parties be given **notice** if the partnership is dissolved in a manner other than by operation of law. The relationship to the third party is very important.

- If the third party has had actual dealing with the partnership, then ***actual notice***, oral or in writing must be given, or the third party must have obtained notice of the dissolution from another source.

- If the third party has **not** dealt with the partnership, but **has knowledge** of it, **constructive *or* actual notice** must be given. Publication of the notice in a local newspaper where the partnership business was normally conducted is sufficient to satisfy the constructive notice requirements.

- Third parties **without knowledge** of the partnership or who have **not dealt** with the partnership do not need to be given any notice of the dissolution.

Distribution of Assets

Winding up is the process of selling the partnership's assets and distributing the proceeds to fulfill the claims against the partnership. The partners or the court may wind up the partnership. The Uniform Partnership Act at Section 40(b) provides that the debts of a partnership are satisfied in the following order:
- creditors (except partners who are creditors)
- creditor-partners
- capital contributions
- profits

Partners may agree to alter the order of distribution of the assets. If the partnership does not have sufficient means to satisfy the creditors' claims, the partners are personally liable for the obligations and debts of the partnership.

Continuation of a General Partnership after Dissolution

The remaining or surviving partners have the right to continue a partnership after it is dissolved. Despite this right, it is wise for the partners to enter into a continuation agreement detailing the partnership's continuation, amount to be paid to outgoing partners, etc. It is important to note that the creditors of the old partnership become creditors of the new partnership and have equal status with the creditors of the new partnership.

Liability of Outgoing Partners

If a partnership is dissolved because a partner leaves the partnership and the partnership is continued by the remaining partners, the outgoing partner is personally liable for the debts and obligations of the partnership at the time of dissolution. However, the outgoing partner is not liable for any new debts and obligations incurred by the partnership after the dissolution, as long as proper notification of his or her withdrawal from the partnership has been given to the creditor.

Right of Survivorship

Upon the death of a partner, the deceased partner's right in specific partnership property vests in the remaining partner or partners—it does not vest in his or her heirs or next of kin. This is called the right of survivorship. Upon the death of the last surviving partner, the rights in specific partnership property vest in the deceased partner's legal representative. The value of the deceased partner's interest in the partnership passes to his or her beneficiaries or heirs upon his or her death.

Refresh Your Memory

The following exercise will enable you to refresh your memory on the rules and principles presented to you in this chapter. Read each question twice and place your answer in the blanks provided. Review the chapter material for any question you miss or are unable to remember.

1. What duty of care is owed by partners in a partnership? _____
    _____

2. What is an action for an accounting? _____
    _____

3. What does the duty of obedience require of partners? _____
    _____

4. What does the concept of joint and several liability allow third parties to do? _____
    _____

5. What is the result if a third party releases any party of a partnership from liability? _____
    _____

6. What type of liability does a new partner have to an existing partnership? _____
    _____

7. What is a dissolution of a partnership? _____
    _____

8. What is a partner who withdraws from a partnership at will liable for? _____
    _____

9. What happens if a partnership cannot satisfy its creditors' claims upon dissolution?_____
    _____

10. What does dissolution of a partnership terminate? _____
    _____

11. The right to share in the profits of a partnership is considered to be the right to share in the
    _____

12. The UPA covers many problems that arise in the _____, _____
    and _____ of ordinary partnerships.

13. A person who forms and operates a new business by him or herself or with others is an

   _____.

14. If proper notice is not given to a required third party after the dissolution of a partnership, and a partner enters into a contract with the third party, liability may arise on the grounds of

   _____ _____.

15. When a partnership is continued, the old partnership is _____, and a new _____ is created.

Critical Thought Exercise

   Larry and Diane Ortiz own and operate Maria's Restaurant in Houston, Texas. As husband and wife, they operate the restaurant as a sole proprietorship. As part of the advertising plan for Maria's, they participate in several 2-for-1 dinner coupon books and school fundraiser sticker books. An average of 15 2-for-1 coupons are redeemed each week. After Larry Ortiz is struck with a serious illness, the restaurant is sold to Bob Nelson. Nelson files the proper fictitious business name statement with the county and city clerk. The sale of the restaurant did not include the assignment of any contracts entered into prior to the sale by Larry and Diane Ortiz.

   After Nelson remodels the restaurant, he reopens it with a Grand Reopening advertising campaign. Signs stating "New Owners" are posted at the restaurant and the same notice is in each advertisement. When Nelson refuses to honor the 2-for-1 coupons, 24 plaintiffs file suit against Maria's Restaurant and Bob Nelson for breach of contract and fraud.

   Is Bob Nelson liable because he failed to honor coupons for Maria's Restaurant?

Answer:

_____

_____

_____

_____

_____

_____

_____

_____

_____

_____

_____

_____

Practice Quiz

True/False

1. ____ An entrepreneur may operate a new business by himself or herself or cofound the business with others. [p. 519]

2. ____ Entrepreneurs contemplating starting a business have few options when choosing the legal form in which to conduct the business. [p. 519]

3. ____ A sole proprietorship is the most complex form of business organization. [p. 520]

4. ____ The sole proprietor's access to the capital is limited to personal funds plus any loans he or she can obtain. [p. 520]

5. ____ No federal or state governmental approval is required for a sole proprietorship. [p. 520]

6. ____ Operating under a trade name is commonly termed as d.b.a. [p. 520]

7. ____ The sole proprietor has limited personal liability. [p. 520]

8. ____ A general partnership is a voluntary association of two or more persons for carrying on a business as co-owners for profit. [p. 522]

9. ____ An ordinary partnership cannot operate under the names of any one or more of the partners under a fictitious business name. [p. 523]

10. ____ The UPA adopted the entity theory of partnership, which considers partnerships as separate legal entities. [p. 523]

11. ____ The organization or venture must have a profit motive in order to qualify as a partnership. [p. 523]

12. ____ Receipt of a share of business profits is prima facie evidence of a partnership because nonpartners usually are not given the right to share in the business's profits. [p. 523]

13. ____ The agreement to form a partnership may only be written by the parties. [p. 523]

14. ____ Each partner has one vote regardless of the proportional size of his or her capital contribution or share in the partnership's profits. [p. 525]

15. ____ If a partnership agreement provides for the sharing of losses but is silent as to how profits are to be shared, profits are shared according to participation in partnership management. [p. 525]

16. ____ Third parties who have not dealt with the partnership but have knowledge of it must be given either actual or constructive notice of the dissolution. [p. 531]

17. ____ Self-dealing occurs when a partner deals personally with the partnership, such as buying or selling goods or property to the partnership. [p. 526]

18. ____ The partnership books may be kept at a partner's home. [p. 526]

19. ____ A partner is not liable to the partnership for any damages caused by his or her negligence. [p. 526]

20. ____ Partners are liable for errors in judgment regardless if they are honest errors or not. [p. 526]

Multiple Choice

21. An entrepreneur is [p. 519]
    a. an employee of another's business.
    b. an independent contractor.
    c. a person who forms and operates a new business.
    d. all of the above.

22. Which of the following is not a true statement regarding sole proprietorships? [p. 520]
    a. Forming a sole proprietorship is easy and relatively inexpensive.
    b. The sole proprietor is not legally responsible for the business's contracts and torts his or her employees commit in the course of employment.
    c. The sole proprietorship form of doing business does not require any federal or state approval.
    d. The sole proprietor has the right to receive all of the business's profits.

23. Wilma owns and is doing business as Wilma's House of Beauty. Pricilla, one of Wilma's regular customers has Wilma try a new hair color, high sierra brown, on her. Wilma applies   the hair color and sets the timer for fifteen minutes as per the instructions that came with the color. Meanwhile, Wilma's mother Francine calls from Europe and Wilma fails to hear the timer go off. One hour passes, and when Wilma begins to wash Pricilla's hair, large sections begin to fall out leaving her with what looks more like a burned brownie color. If Pricilla brings a lawsuit against Wilma, which of the following may she seek to satisfy her claim of negligence against Wilma and her House of Beauty? [p. 520]
    a. Pricilla may recover a claim against Wilma's home.
    b. Pricilla may recover a claim against Wilma's automobile.
    c. Pricilla may recover a claim against Wilma's bank accounts.
    d. all of the above

24. When is a partner or employee of a partnership liable for torts that cause injury to a third person? [pp. 527-528]
    a. if the act of the partner or employee occurs after normal work hours
    b. if the tort was committed while the person is acting with the ordinary course of partnership business or without the authority of his or her co-partners
    c. a partner is not liable for torts that cause injury to a third person if he or she did not commit the tort
    d. all of the above

25. Which of the following describes a benefit of operating as a sole proprietor? [p. 520]
    a. A sole proprietorship has unlimited liability.
    b. A sole proprietor's access to capital is limited to personal funds and any loans that he or she can obtain.
    c. A sole proprietor has the right to make all management decisions concerning the business.
    d. A sole proprietor is responsible for the torts that his or her employee commits.

26. Wilson, Reggie, and Collin form a partnership to develop land for a housing tract they plan on building. Both Wilson and Collin know that there were old oil wells on the land but Reggie does not. If Reggie becomes upset with Wilson and Collin for failing to inform him of this fact, what would Wilson and Collin's best defense be? [p. 527]
    a. that they did not owe him any duty to inform
    b. that if Reggie wanted to know bad enough, he should have asked him
    c. that even though Reggie didn't have actual knowledge, the knowledge was imputed to him
    d. that there is nothing in the partnership agreement requiring them to inform Reggie of the situation

27. Whitney owns a building that she wants to sell in a booming area of Anywhere, U.S.A. She is also a one-third partner in a partnership called Watchmacallits, which by the way is looking to buy a building. What must Whitney do before she even thinks of selling the building to the partnership? [p. 526]
    a. Whitney must disclose her ownership interest to the partnership.
    b. Whitney need not do anything.
    c. Whitney must hire a real estate agent.
    d. none of the above

28. What can a partner who is made to pay more than his or her proportionate share of contract liability seek against his or her partners who have not paid their share of the loss? [p. 529]
    a. He or she cannot do anything as he or she should have asked the other partners for their share at the time he or she was made to pay.
    b. He or she can seek full compensation of what he or she paid.
    c. He or she cannot do anything until the next liability situation occurs at which time he or she can make those partners who initially did not pay make a payment towards the contract liability.
    d. He or she may seek indemnification from the partnership and from those partners who have not paid their share of the loss.

29. What is a continuation agreement? [p. 531]
    a. an agreement that takes place after dissolution that allows for the partnership to continue business as usual regardless of dissolution
    b. an agreement that expressly sets forth the events that allow for continuation of the partnership, the amount to be paid to outgoing partners and other details
    c. an agreement of ongoing education for each of the partners named in the partnership
    d. all of the above

30. The winding up of a partnership consists of [p. 530]
    a. the liquidation of partnership assets.
    b. the distribution of the proceeds to satisfy claims against the partnership.
    c. reasonable compensation for a surviving partner's services for his or her role in winding up.
    d. all of the above

Short Answer

31. A general partnership may be formed with _____ or ___ formality. [p. 523]

32. Most states require all businesses that operate under a trade name to file a _____ _____ _____ _____ with the appropriate government agency. [p. 520]

33. What was the goal of the Uniform Partnership Act (UPA)? _____ _____[p. 523]

34. The UPA provides that no partner is entitled to _____ for his or her performance in the partnership business. [p. 525]

35. Under the UPA, it is implied that the partners will devote _____ time and _____ to the partnership. [p. 525]

36. A partner who makes a loan to the partnership becomes a _____ of the partnership. [p. 525]

37. A partner may not compete with the partnership without the _____ of the other partners. [p. 526]

38. Partners owe a duty to keep information such as _____, _____ _____ , etc., confidential. [p. 526]

39. Partners owe a duty to _____ their co-partners of all information they possess that is relevant to the affairs of the partnership. [p. 527]

40. Partners of a general partnership have personal liability for the _____ and _____ of the partnership. [p. 527]

41. A release of one partner does not _____ the liability of other partners. [p. 528]

42. After the proceeds are distributed, the partnership automatically _____ [p. 531]

43. What is a tenant partnership? _____ _____[p. 532]

44. Where a partnership agreement provides for the sharing of profits but is silent as to how losses are to be shared, losses are shared _____ _____[p. 525]

45. A partner is entitled to _____ of expenses such as personal, travel, business, and other expenses on behalf of the partnership. [p. 525]

Answers to Refresh Your Memory

1. the same level of care and skill that a reasonable business manager in the same position would use in the same circumstances [p. 526]
2. An action for an accounting is a formal judicial proceeding in which the court is authorized to (1) review the partnership and the partners' transactions and (2) award each partner his or her share of the partnership assets. It results in a money judgment for or against partners, according to the balance struck. [p. 527]
3. The duty of obedience requires the partners to adhere to the provisions of the partnership agreement and the decisions of the partnership. [p. 527]
4. The UPA provides that partners are jointly and severally liable for torts and breaches of trust. [p. 528]
5. If a third party does not name all of the partners, the judgment cannot be collected against any of the partners or the partnership. [p. 529]
6. A new partner who is admitted to a partnership is liable for the existing debts and obligations (antecedent debts) of the partnership only to the extent of his or her capital contribution. [p. 529]
7. the change in the relation of the partners caused by any partner ceasing to be associated in the carrying on of the business [p. 530]
8. He or she is liable for dissolving the partnership. [p. 531]
9. The partners are personally liable for the partnership's debts and obligations [p. 531]
10. The dissolution of a partnership terminates the partners' actual authority to enter into contracts or otherwise act on behalf of the partnership. [p. 530]
11. the right to share in the earnings from the investment of capital [p. 525]
12. formation, operation, and dissolution [p. 523]
13. entrepreneur [p. 519]
14. apparent authority [p. 531]
15. dissolved [p. 531]

Critical Thought Exercise Model Answer

A sole proprietorship has no legal identity separate from that of the individual who owns it. In this case, the 2-for-1 offers were made by Larry and Diane Ortiz. Only Larry and Diane Ortiz can be held liable for not honoring the coupons and fundraiser stickers unless Nelson assumes the liability as part of an assignment and delegation. Bob Nelson did not assume any of the liabilities or assume any of the contracts that had been made with Maria's Restaurant when it was owned by Larry and Diane Ortiz. Bob Nelson did not assume liability for the coupons simply because he chose to use the same name for his restaurant. The sole proprietor who does business under one or several names remains one person. There is no continuity of existence for Maria's Restaurant because upon the sale of the restaurant, the sole proprietorship of Larry and Diane Ortiz ended.

In this case, "Maria's Restaurant" has no legal existence. Bob Nelson did not continue the previous sole proprietorship. He began a new sole proprietorship, that of Bob Nelson, doing business as Maria's Restaurant.

Answers to Practice Quiz

True/False

1. True   An entrepreneur may conduct a business alone or with others.
2. False   Entrepreneurs contemplating starting a business have **many** options when choosing the legal form in which to conduct the business.
3. False   A sole proprietorship is the simplest form of business organization.
4. True   The sole proprietor's access to the capital is limited to personal funds plus any loans he or she can obtain.
5. True   There are no formalities, and no federal or state government approval is required for a sole proprietorship.
6. True   Operating under a trade name is commonly designated as d.b.a. (otherwise known as doing business as).
7. False   The sole proprietor has unlimited personal liability.
8. True   A general partnership or partnership is a voluntary association of two or more persons for carrying on a business as co-owners for profit.
9. False   An ordinary partnership can operate under the names of any one or more of the partners under a fictitious business name.
10. True   The UPA adopted the entity theory of partnership, which considers partnerships as separate legal entities.
11. True   The organization or venture must have a profit motive in order to qualify as a partnership.
12. True   Receipt of a share of business profits is prima facie evidence of a partnership because nonpartners usually are not given the right to share in the business's profits.
13. False The agreement to form a partnership may be oral, written, or implied from the conduct of the parties.
14. True   Each partner has one vote, regardless of the proportional size of his or her capital contribution or share in the partnership's profits.
15. False If a partnership agreement provides for the sharing of losses, but is silent as to how profits are to shared, profits are shared equally.
16. True   Third parties who have not dealt with the partnership but have knowledge of it must be given either actual or constructive notice of dissolution.
17. True   Self-dealing occurs when a partner deals personally with the partnership, such as buying or selling goods or property to the partnership.
18. False The partnership books must be kept at the partnership's principal place of business.
19. True   A partner is liable to the partnership for any damages caused by his or her negligence.
20. False Partners are not liable for honest errors in judgment.

Multiple Choice

21. C   Answer C is the correct answer as a person who forms and operates a new business is an entrepreneur. Answer A is incorrect as an employee of another business would not own and operate that business. Answer B is incorrect as an independent contractor is an individual who has been hired to perform a specific task, not one who forms and operates a new business. Answer D is incorrect for the reasons given above.

22. B   Answer B is correct as the statement as it currently reads is false. A sole proprietor is legally responsible for the business's contracts and torts his or her employees commit in the course of employment. Answers A, C, and D are all true statements regarding proprietorships and are therefore the incorrect.

23. D   Answer D is the correct answer as Pricilla may recover against the business from Wilma's personal assets including her home, automobile, and bank accounts.

24. B   Answer B is the correct answer as the partnership is liable if the act is committed while the person is acting within the ordinary course of partnership business or with the authority of his or her co-partners. Answer A is incorrect as this indicates the act is out of the course and scope of the employment. Answer C is incorrect as partners are equally liable for torts and injuries caused to another regardless if they committed the torts personally or not. Answer D is incorrect for the reasons given above.

25. C   Answer C is the correct answer as holding the exclusive right to make all management decisions, including the hiring and firing of employees, is one of the benefits of operating as a sole proprietor. Answers A, B, and D are all incorrect as they state some of the disadvantages of operating as a sole proprietorship.

26. C   Answer C is the correct answer as the knowledge of the other partners is imputed to Reggie, as though he had actual knowledge. Imputed knowledge has no bearing on whether or not the partnership agreement. Answer A is incorrect as the partners do have a duty to inform. Answer B is incorrect as Reggie's desire to know about certain situations tied to the partnership has nothing to do with what he would know. Answer D is incorrect for the reasons given above.

27. A   Answer A is the correct answer since partners have a fiduciary relationship with one another. There can be no self-dealing. As such, she owes a duty of loyalty and must disclose her ownership interest to the partnership. Answer B is correct as it is untrue based on the reasoning given in answer A. Answer C is incorrect because though hiring a real estate agent regardless of who the building is sold to is a wise business decision, it is not mandatory. Answer D is incorrect based on the reasoning given above.

28. D   Answer D is the correct answer as a partner who is made to pay more than his or her proportionate share of the contract liability may seek indemnification from the partnership and from those partners who have paid their share of the loss. Answer A is incorrect as it is not a true statement. Answer B is incorrect as each partner is equally liable. Answer C is incorrect as it is a ridiculous statement.

29. B   Answer B is the correct answer as it properly describes the essence of a continuation agreement. Answer A is incorrect as no continuation agreement would be needed if the partnership wasn't being dissolved. Answer C is not a correct statement of law. Answer D is incorrect based on the reasoning given above.

30. D   Answer D is the correct answer as the winding up of a partnership consists of all of the statements given in answers A, B, and C.

Short Answer

31.   little; no
32.   fictitious business name statement OR certificate of tradename (both answers are acceptable)
33.   to establish consistent partnership law that was uniform throughout the United States
34.   remuneration
35.   full; service
36.   creditor
37.   permission

38. trade secrets; customer lists
39. inform
40. contracts; torts
41. discharge
42. terminates
43. where a partner is a cofounder with the other partners of the specific partnership
44. in the same proportion as the profits
45. reimbursement

Chapter 35

LIMITED PARTNERSHIPS

Chapter Overview

This chapter provides a further exploration of partnerships, with an emphasis on limited partnerships and their formation as well as the differentiation between limited and general partners. Additionally, this chapter discusses the limited liability partnership and the partners' liability if involved in the same. The process of dissolution as well as winding-up of limited partnerships is also explained.

Objectives

Upon completion of the exercises in this chapter, you should be able to:
1. Discuss what is meant by a limited partnership.
2. Explain the difference between a limited and a general partner.
3. Discuss the requirements for forming a limited partnership.
4. Discuss the defective formation of a limited partnership.
5. Explain the meaning of a foreign limited partnership.
6. Discuss the meaning of a master limited partnership.
7. Differentiate and explain the liability of general and limited partners.
8. Explain limited liability partnership (LLP).
9. Discuss the limited liability of partners of an LLP.
10. Explain the requirements of dissolution and winding-up of limited partnerships.

Practical Application

This chapter will provide you with a wealth of information that will enable you to differentiate between the various types of limited partnerships as well as give you the necessary knowledge of the liability involved in the partnerships discussed herein. For the student who wants to operate a business, the basic partnership explanations will be an invaluable tool in determining the type of business operation that would be best in light of an individual's circumstances.

Helpful Hints

Before beginning this chapter, it is helpful to review the previous study guide chapter on general partnerships, as it provides a solid foundation for this chapter to build upon. It is best to study this material in a methodical fashion in order for the information that is given to be of maximum benefit.

Study Tips

It is important that you learn the difference between a limited partnership and a limited liability partnership.

Limited Partnership

A limited partnership involves general partners who conduct the business and limited partners who invest in the partnership but who do not participate in the management. A corporation may act as a general partner, but is liable only to the extent of its assets.

Revised Uniform Limited Partnership Act (RULPA)

A modern, comprehensive law for the formation, operation, and dissolution of limited partnerships. This law supersedes the ULPA that have adopted it.

Formation of a Limited Partnership

- Creation is informal.
- No public disclosure is required.
- Two or more persons must execute and sign a **certificate of limited partnership** and thereafter file it with the secretary of state if required by state law.
- Items that must be contained in the certificate of limited partnership are on page 537 of your main text.
- The limited partnership is formed upon the filing of the certificate of limited partnership.

Certificate of Limited Partnership

Two or more persons must execute and sign a certificate of limited partnership. In addition to general information (partnership name, business type, address of business, and each partner's address, latest date of partnership dissolution, partner contributions, and any other matters), the certificate of limited partnership must be filed with the secretary of state and if required, the county recorder where the business is being conducted.

Amendments to the Certificate of Limited Partnership

- A limited partnership must be kept current by way of certificates of amendment, which must be filed within 30 days of the happening of certain events.
- A partner's capital contribution changes.
- A new partner's admission.
- A partner's withdrawal.
- A business's continuation after a judicial dissolution to dissolve the partnership.

Name of the Limited Partnership

- A limited partnership may not include the surname of a limited partner unless it is also The surname of the general partner or the business was carried on under that name before the limited partner was admitted to the firm.
- The name may not be deceptively similar to other corporations' names or other limited partnerships' names.

Capital Contributions

General and limited partners' capital contributions may be made in cash, property, services rendered, or a promissory note.

Defective Formation

Defective formation occurs when (1) a certificate of limited partnership is not properly filed, (2) there are defects in a certificate that is filed or (3) some other statutory requirement for the creation of a limited partnership is not met. If there is a substantial defect, persons who thought they were limited partners are then in the position of finding themselves as general partners.

Limited Partnership Agreement

This agreement drafted by the partners describes the rights and duties of the general and limited partners and the conditions concerning operation, termination, and dissolution. If the agreement does not state how the profits and losses are to be shared, then they will be shared based on the value of the partner's capital contribution.

Each limited partner has a right to information regarding the financial condition of the limited partnership. **Note, the limited partnership agreement may state how profits and losses from the limited partnership are to be distributed among the general and limited partners. If no agreement exists, then RULPA states that the profits and losses from a limited partnership are to be shared on the basis of the value of the partner's capital contribution, whereby the limited partner is not liable beyond his or her capital contribution.**

Admission of a new partner

The addition of a partner to an existing limited partnership can only be accomplished by the written consent of all partners. An amendment of the certificate of limited partnership effectuates the admission of the new partner. Withdrawal of a partner can be accomplished as per the certificate of limited partnership, upon the happening of an event, or upon six months' prior notice to each general partner.

Foreign Limited Partnerships

A foreign limited partnership must file an application for registration with the secretary of state before it conducts business with a foreign country. If the application is all in order, a certificate of registration will be issued so that it may transact business with a foreign country.

Master Limited Partnership (MLP)

A limited partnership whose limited partnership interests are traded on organized securities exchanges. The tax benefits in owning an MLP are that MLPs do not pay any income tax, and partnership income and losses go directly onto the individual partner's income tax return. Double taxation is also avoided with an MLP.

Limited Liability Partnership

All partners are given limited liability. Professionals commonly use this type of partnership. A limited partnership must have a minimum of one general partner and one limited partner. Any person may be a limited partner. There is no tax paid at the partnership level.

Participation in Management

General partners have the right to manage the affairs of the limited partnership. However, they relinquish their right to participate in the control and management of the limited partnership. Therefore, there is no right to bind the partnership to contracts or other obligations.

Permissible Activities of Limited Partners

The types of activities a limited partner may participate in without losing his or her limited liability status include: being an agent, employee, contractor of the limited partnership or a general partner, being a consultant or an advisor to a general partner regarding the partnership, or acting as a surety for the limited partnership. Additionally, an individual may approve or disapprove an amendment to the limited partnership and vote on partnership matters.

Dissolution and Winding Up

The affairs of a limited partnership may be dissolved and wound up just like an ordinary partnership. However a certificate of cancellation must be filed with the secretary of state that the limited partnership is organized. The **end of the limited partnership's life, the written consent of limited and genera partners, the withdrawal of a general partner, and the entry of a decree of judicial dissolution** are the events that can cause dissolution of a limited partnership.

Winding Up

A limited partnership's general partners must wind up its affairs once it dissolves itself. RULPA established the order of distribution of partnership assets, beginning with creditors, followed by partners with regard to unpaid distributions, capital contributions, and finally by the remainder of the proceeds.

Liability of General and Limited Partners

General partners have unlimited personal liability for the debts as well as obligations of the limited partnership. Limited partners, however, are only liable for the obligations and debts up to their capital contributions to the limited partnership. Limited partners may be liable on personal guarantees.

Participation in Management by Limited Partners

Limited partners forfeit their right to participate in the management control of the limited partnership. The limited partner is liable only to persons who reasonably believe him or her to be a general partner. RULPA Section 303 (a).

The allowable activities that a limited partner can engage in without losing his or her liability are listed on page 540 of your text.

Limited partners are not solely liable for the obligations or actions of the partnership beyond what is contributed as capital. The exceptions are when there has been a defective formation, participation in management, or if there has been **a personal guarantee. Personal guarantees are required if a creditor will not make the loan based on the limited partnership's own credit history or ability to repay the credit. The creditor may require a limited partner to guarantee the repayment of a loan in order to extend credit to the limited partnership.**

Dissolution of a Limited Partnership

Note that upon the dissolution and the commencement of the winding up of a limited partnership, a certificate of cancellation must be filed by the limited partnership with the secretary of state in which the limited partnership is organized.

Winding Up and the Distribution of Assets

A limited partnership's general partners must wind up its affairs once it dissolves itself. RULPA established the order of distribution of partnership assets, beginning with creditors, followed by partners with regard to unpaid distributions, capital contributions, and finally by the remainder of the proceeds.

Refresh Your Memory

The following exercise will enable you to refresh your memory on the rules and principles presented to you in this chapter. Read each question twice and place your answer in the blanks provided. Review the chapter material for any question you miss or are unable to remember.

1. A limited partnership has two types of partners: (1) _____, who invest capital, manage the business, and are personally liable for partnership debts, and (2) _____ partners who invest capital but do not participate in management and are not personally liable for partnership debts beyond their capital contributions.

2. When is the limited partnership considered to be formed? _____ _____

3. When does defective formation occur? _____ _____

4. Partners of a limited partnership often draft and execute a _____ _____ _____.

5. If there is no agreement as to how profits and losses are to be allocated, what does RULPA provide? _____ _____

6. Once a limited partnership has been formed, when can a new limited partner be added? _____ _____

7. A limited partner is liable as a _____ partner if his or her participation in the control of the business is substantially the same as that of a _____ partner, but the limited partner is liable only to persons who reasonably believed him or her to be a _____ partner.

8. Upon the dissolution and the commencement of the winding up of a limited partnership, a _____ of _____ must be filed by the limited partnership with the secretary of state of the state in which the limited partnership is organized.

9. A limited partnership must _____ up its affairs upon dissolution.

10. After the assets of a limited partnership have been liquidated, the proceeds must be _____.

11. What are some of the tax benefits to owning a limited partnership interest in an MLP? _____

12. What is the trade-off for operating/participating in a limited partnership? _____ _____

13. Name two activities a limited partner may participate in without losing his or limited liability. _____ _____

14. What do banks often require of small businesses wishing to borrow money or obtain an extension of credit? _____ _____

15. The _____ partners of a limited partnership have the same rights, duties, and powers as partners in a _____ partnership.

Critical Thought Exercise

Harris, Nix, and Lewis form a limited partnership for the purpose of hiring and booking motivational speakers for corporate and government training seminars. Harris was a former boxing promoter and will act as the general partner. Nix and Harris contribute $35,000 each and Harris contributes all the furniture and supplies from his current office. A certificate of limited partnership is prepared in a proper and complete manner and filed with the secretary of state. The partnership begins to hire and book motivational speakers and is very successful. Fifteen months later, Harris has a heart attack and is unable to work for several months. Instead of hiring a temporary manager to run the business, Nix completely takes over the day-to-day running of the business. Nix wants to build the business and hire famous speakers. He signs a contract with a famous football coach to give two speeches at a rate of $200,000 each. Harris then returns to work and takes over management duties. Due to poor decisions made by Nix, the partnership is unable to pay the coach after he makes the two speeches. In his suit, the coach alleges that both Harris and Nix are personally liable for the damages caused by the partnerships breach of contract if the damages cannot be satisfied out of partnership assets.

Is Nix personally liable for damages to the coach even though he is only a limited partner?

Answer:

_____

_____

_____

_____

_____

_____

_____

_____

_____

_____

_____

_____

_____

_____

_____

_____

Practice Quiz

True/False

1. ___ The RULPA prohibits a corporation to be the sole general partner of a limited partnership. [p. 537]

2. ___ The creation of a limited partnership is formal and requires public disclosure. [p. 537]

3. ___ A limited partnership must keep its certificate of limited partnership current by filing necessary certificates of amendment at the same offices where the certificate of limited partnership is filed. [p. 537]

4. ___ The firm name of a limited partnership may include the surname of a limited partner if it is also the surname of a general partner or the business was carried on under the name before the admission of the limited partner. [p. 538]

5. ___ Capital contributions of general and limited partners may be in cash, property, services rendered, or promissory notes or other obligations to contribute cash or property or to perform services. [p. 528]

6. ___ General and limited partners must be given equal voting rights. [p. 538]

7. ___ Once registered, a foreign limited partnership may use the courts of the foreign state to enforce contracts and other rights. [p. 539]

8. ___ Failure to register impairs the validity of any act or contract of the unregistered foreign limited partnership. [p. 539]

9. ___ Generally, limited partners have unlimited liability for the debts and obligations of the limited partnership. [p. 540]

10. ___ Upon receiving an application for an extension of credit, the ABC bank refused to extend credit to the Wazzo Limited Partnership. ABC bank may claim the partnership's credit history is the reason for its denial. [p. 541]

11. ___ A limited partnership is dissolved upon the withdrawal of a general partner. [p. 542]

12. ___ General partners of a limited partnership have unlimited personal liability for the debts and obligations of the limited partnership. [p. 542]

13. ___ Defective formation basically means that there has not been substantial compliance in good faith with the statutory retirements to create a limited partnership. [p. 541]

14. ___ A limited partner may engage in any activities on behalf of the limited partnership. [pp. 540-541]

15. ___ Limited partners are not individually liable for the obligations or conduct of the partnership beyond the amount of their capital contribution. [p. 541]

Multiple Choice

16. With regard to the admission of new partners, which of the following is not true? [p. 539]
    a. New general partners can be admitted only with the specific written consent of each partner.
    b. The limited partnership agreement cannot waive the right of partners to approve the admission of new general partners.
    c. The admission of a new partner is effective upon giving notice to the other partners.
    d. none of the above

17. A defective formation of a limited partnership happens when [p. 538]
    a. there are defects in a certificate that is filed.
    b. a certificate of limited partnership is not properly filed.
    c. a statutory requirement for the creation of the limited partnership is not met.
    d. all of the above

18. Before a foreign limited partnership may begin conducting business in a foreign state, it must do which of the following? [p. 539]
    a. It must cause injury to someone in the foreign state so that the court may have jurisdiction over it.
    b. It must initiate litigation in the foreign jurisdiction.
    c. It must file an application for registration with the secretary of state.
    d. It's ownership interest must be traded on organized securities exchanges.

19. A master limited partnership is [p. 540]
    a. a domestic limited partnership in the state in which it is organized.
    b. a foreign limited partnership in all of the states.
    c. a limited partnership whose limited partnership interests are traded on organized securities exchanges.
    d. an unregistered foreign partnership.

20. What do limited partners give up in exchange for limited liability? [p. 540]
    a. They give up their capital investment into the partnership.
    b. They give up their right to participate in the control and management of the limited partnership.
    c. They give up liability only to persons who reasonably believe him or her to be a general partner.
    d. They give up acting as a surety for the limited partnership.

21. If the Bright Balloon Company wants to add Lily as a partner, which of the following is true with respect to the admission of a new partner? [p. 539]
    a. A limited partner can withdraw from a limited partnership only at a time stated in the certificate of limited partnership.
    b. Lily can be added only upon the written consent of all partners of the Bright Balloon Company unless the limited partnership agreement provides otherwise.
    c. Lily cannot be added as the limited partnership agreement has the effect of waiving the right of partners to approve the admission of new general partners.
    d. Lily can be added as a partner upon proof of unequal voting rights.

22. Which of the following correctly expresses the order in which a limited partnership's assets are distributed once the assets have been liquidated? [p. 542]
    a. capital contributions, unpaid distributions, creditors, remainder of the proceeds
    b. creditors of the limited partnership, the remainder of the proceeds, unpaid distributions, capital contributions
    c. creditors of the limited partnership, partners with regard to unpaid distributions first, then capital contributions, with the remainder of the proceeds last
    d. none of the above

23. If Irene and Nicole are attempting to name the partnership that the two want to enter into together, which of the following would be good advice to help them? [p. 538]
    a. Irene and Nicole may use a surname of a general partner.
    b. It is not necessary that the name that they choose contain the actual words, limited partnership.
    c. The name that they choose cannot be the same as or deceptively similar to the names of other limited partnerships and corporations.
    d. The defect of noncompliance with regard to the name will not affect their rights as partners.

24. John is a limited partner in the Healthy For You Food Store. Which activity may John participate in without losing his limited liability? [pp. 539-541]
    a. John may be a consultant or advisor to a general partner regarding the limited partnership.
    b. John may bind the partnership to contracts.
    c. John may participate in the management of the limited partnership.
    d. John may participate in the control of the limited partnership.

25. What type of event would cause a certificate of amendment to be filed? [pp. 537-538]
    a. The admission of a new partner would cause a certificate of amendment to be filed.
    b. A change in a partner's capital contribution would cause a certificate of amendment to be filed.
    c. The withdrawal of a partner would cause a certificate of amendment to be filed.
    d. all of the above

Short Answer

26.	Name at least two things that the certificate of limited partnership must contain. [p. 537]
_____ and _____

27.	What is the purpose of an amendment to the certificate of limited partnership? [p. 537]
_____

28.	Give an example of what types of records the limited partnership must keep. [p. 539]
_____

29.	If an application for registration for transacting business in a foreign state conforms with the law, what will the limited partnership receive that permits the foreign limited partnership to transact business? [p. 539] _____of
_____.

30.	Who must retain first priority when distributing the assets of the partnership? [p. 542]
_____

31.	_____ partners, who invest capital but do not participate in management and are not personally liable for partnership beyond their _____ contribution, is one type of partner in a limited partnership. [p. 536]

32.	What is a domestic limited partnership? [p. 539] _____
_____

33.	If Harry is admitted as a new partner to Smoothies Galore, a limited partnership, what is the time frame in which the amendment must be filed? [p. 537] _____
_____

34.	The Hastings Group, a limited partnership is in existence in Anytown, U.S.A. George wants to file a certificate of limited partnership for a new partnership he and a couple of other individuals are forming. He wants to file his certificate with the name of the limited partnership as The Hasting Group. What problem might he have if the name his partnership has chosen is filed? [p. 538] _____
_____

35.	Which law governs a limited partnership's organization, internal affairs, and the liability of its limited partners? [p. 537] _____
_____

36.	If the Presto Company, a limited partnership organized in Idaho, files an application for registration of its limited partnership in Montana, which state's courts may decide contracts disputes that arise in Montana? [p. 539] _____
_____

37.	Once the dissolution and the initiation of the winding up of a limited partnership have begun, what must be filed by the limited partnership? [p. 542] _____
_____

38. What right allows Judy Jones, a limited partner of the Smooth as Silk Company, to view copies of federal, state, and local income tax returns? [p. 539] _____

_____

39. What type of partner may petition the court to wind up the affairs of a limited partnership? [p. 542] _____

40. Why was the limited liability partnership created? [p. 536] _____

_____

Answers to Refresh Your Memory

1. general partners; limited partners [p. 536]
2. the certificate of limited partnership is filed. [p. 537]
3. (1) a certificate of limited partnership is not properly filed, (2) there are defects in a certificate that is filed, or (3) some other statutory requirement for the creation of a limited partnership is not met [p. 538]
4. limited partnership agreement (also called the articles of limited partnership) [p. 538]
5. RULPA provides that profits and losses from a limited partnership are shared on the value of the partner's capital contribution. A limited partner is not liable for losses beyond his or her capital contribution. [p. 539]
6. only upon the written consent of all partners unless the limited partnership agreement provides otherwise
7. general; general; general [p. 540]
8. certificate of cancellation [p. 542]
9. wind [p. 542]
10. distributed [p. 512]
11. Master limited partnerships do not pay any income tax. The partnership's income as well as losses flow directly onto the individual partner's income tax return. This type of partnership also avoids double taxation of corporate dividends. [p. 540]
12. The limited partners give up their right to take part in the control and management of the limited partnership. [p. 540]
13. A partner may be an agent, an employee, or a contractor of the limited partnership or a general partner. A partner may act as a surety for the limited partnership. [p. 543]
14. Banks will sometime require owners of small businesses to personally guarantee the loan of the business. [p. 541]
15. general; general [p. 539]

Critical Thought Exercise Model Answer

General partners are personally liable to the partnership's creditors. The liability of a limited partner is limited to the capital that he or she contributes to the partnership. A limited partner gains this protection if the requirements for signing and filing the limited partnership certificate are met. In this case the certificate was properly filed. When the partnership began business, both Nix and Lewis had the protection afforded a limited partner.

However, under the Revised Uniform Limited Partnership Act (RULPA), section 303, limited partners only enjoy limited liability as long as they do not participate in management. A limited partner who undertakes management of the partnership's business will be just as liable as a general partner to any creditor who transacts business with the limited partnership and believes, based upon the acts of the limited partner, that the limited partner is a general partner [RULPA, section 303]. In this case, Nix took over complete management and was running the daily affairs of the partnership. With Harris not working at all during the time the contract was signed with the coach, Nix would have appeared to be the general manager and thus, a general partner. Therefore, Nix should be personally liable to the coach for damages for breach of contract. Harris, even though he was not working at the time, will also be personally liable because he is listed as the general partner on the partnership certificate. Lewis is the only partner whose liability to the coach will be limited to his investment in the partnership.

Answers to Practice Quiz

True/False

1. False   The RULPA permits a corporation to be the sole general partner of a limited partnership.
2. True   The creation of a limited partnership is formal and requires public disclosure.
3. True   A limited partnership must keep its certificate of limited partnership current by filing necessary certificates of amendment at the same offices where the certificate of limited partnership is filed.
4. True   The firm name of a limited partnership may not include the surname of a limited partner unless it is also the surname of a general partner or the business was carried on under the name before the admission of the limited partner.
5. True   Under the RULPA, the capital contributions of general and limited partners may be in cash, property, services rendered, or promissory notes or other obligations to contribute cash or property or to perform services.
6. False   General and limited partners may be given unequal voting rights.
7. True   Once registered, a foreign limited partnership may use the courts of the foreign state to enforce contracts and other rights.
8. False   Failure to register neither impairs the validity of any act or contract of the unregistered foreign limited partnership nor prevents it from defending itself in any proceeding in the courts of the foreign state.
9. False   Generally, limited partners have limited liability for the debts and obligations of the limited partnership.
10. True   On some occasions when limited partnerships apply for an extension of credit from a bank, a supplier, or creditor, the creditor will not make the loan based on the limited partnership's own credit history or ability to repay the credit.
11. False   A limited partnership is not dissolved upon the withdrawal of a general partner.
12. True   A limited partnership's general partners have unlimited personal liability for the debts and obligations of the limited partnership.
13. True   Defective formation consists of a lack of substantial compliance in good faith with the statutory requirements to create a limited partnership.
14. True   A limited partner may engage in activities as set forth in the RULPA without losing his or her limited liability. These activities are further clarified on pages 540 and 541 of your text.
15. True   Limited partners are not individually liable for the obligations or conduct of the partnership beyond the amount of their capital contribution.

Multiple Choice

16. C   Answer C is the correct answer as the admission of a new partner need not require the giving of notice to other partners. Answers A, B, and D are incorrect as these statements are true.

17. D   Answer D is the correct answer as answers A, B, and C all state situations in which a defective formation would be the end result of the actions stated.

18. C   Answer C is the correct answer as an application for registration with the secretary of state in the foreign state that the foreign limited partnership wishes to conduct business in must be filed. Answer A is incorrect as it is absurd to think a partnership must cause injury and harm to another in a state before being allowed to conduct business in that state. Answer B is incorrect as initiating litigation in a foreign state in order to transact business not only does not make sense, but also would be a costly and perhaps frivolous endeavor. Answer D is incorrect as there is no requirement of a foreign limited partnership to trade on an organized securities exchange prior to transacting business in a foreign state.

19. C   Answer C is the correct answer as it gives the proper explanation for a master limited partnership. Answer A is incorrect as there is nothing to indicate that this type of partnership could not be foreign as well. Answer B is incorrect as, once again, there is nothing to indicate that this type of partnership is a foreign limited one in all states. Answer D is incorrect as, like other partnerships, it too must go through a registration process.

20. B   Answer B is the correct answer as limited partners do forfeit their right to participate in the control and management of the limited partnership in exchange for limited liability. Answer A is incorrect as a limited partner does not give up his or her capital investment. If that were the case, no one would invest and become a limited partner. Additionally, liability of limited partners would be difficult to assess without something such as the capital investment to measure it by. Answer C is incorrect as it is a false and absurd statement. Answer D is incorrect as there is nothing that automatically implies that a limited partner automatically will act as a surety in exchange for limited liability.

21. B   Answer B is the correct answer as written consent of all partners is required under RULPA at Section 401 in order for Lily to be added as a partner to the Bright Balloon Company. Answer A is incorrect as it addresses the issue of withdrawal of a partner and not admission, which is what the question is concerned with. Answer C is incorrect as it is untrue. Answer D is incorrect, as the proof of unequal voting rights has nothing to do with the requirement of written consent to admit a new partner.

22. C   Answer C is the correct answer as it properly categorizes the order of distribution of a limited partnership's assets upon liquidation. Answers A, B, and D are all incorrect based on the incorrect order and reasoning given as to why answer C is correct.

23. C   Answer C is the correct answer as RULPA Section 102 provides in part that the name of a limited partnership cannot be the same or as deceptively similar to the names of corporations or other limited partnerships. Answer A is not correct in its entirety, as there are restrictions as per RULPA Section 102 that provide for the use of a surname thereby making this answer an incomplete choice. Answer B is incorrect as this is a false statement since the name must contain without abbreviation the words limited partnership. Answer D is incorrect as a defect in the name to be used may affect Irene and Nicole's rights and liabilities.

24. A   Answer A is correct as RULPA Sections 303 (b) and (c) provide for the activity stated in this answer as being one that a limited partner may engage in without losing his or her liability. Answers B, C, and D however are incorrect answers as they all state activities that would affect John's liability thereby making him liable as a general partner.

25. D   Answer D is correct as answers A, B, and C all state events that would cause a certificate of amendment to be filed.

Short Answer

26. name of the partnership and general character of the business (Answers will vary)
27. to keep its certificate of limited partnership current
28. copies of federal, state, and local income tax returns
29. certificate of registration
30. creditors
31. limited capital
32. a limited partnership in the state in which it was formed
33. within 30 days of Harry's admission as a partner
34. The problem that may exist is that the name may be viewed as deceptively similar to an already existing name that bears substantial likeness but for the last letter, thereby elevating the potential for confusion regarding general and liability matters.
35. The law of the state in which the entity is organized governs a limited partnership's organization, internal affairs, and the liability of its limited partners.
36. Montana's state courts may decide contract disputes that arise in Montana as a foreign limited partnership may use the court of a foreign state to enforce contracts and other rights once the limited partnership is registered there.
37. A certificate of cancellation must be filed.
38. The right to information as provided for in RULPA Section 305 gives Judy Jones this right.
39. general partners who have not acted wrongfully or limited partners if there are no general partners
40. It was created for business ventures.

Chapter 36

DOMESTIC AND
MULTINATIONAL CORPORATIONS

Chapter Overview

This chapter explores the formation as well as financing of corporations. Additionally, it explains the difference between publicly held and closely held corporations. Further it examines the various types of stock issues as well as the preferences associated with preferred stock. Other topics that are covered include promoters' liability, S corporations, various issuances of stock as well as preferences that accompany preferred stock, rights of debenture, and bondholders and the organization and operation of multinational corporations. Though a corporation is an unnatural being, it is one of the strongest as well as most important forms of business organization forms in business today.

Objectives

Upon completion of the exercises in this chapter, you should be able to:
1. Discuss the meaning and major characteristics of a corporation.
2. Explain how a corporation is formed.
3. Differentiate between a publicly held corporation and a closely held corporation.
4. Discuss when promoters are liable on preincorporation contracts.
5. Explain what an S corporation is and discuss its tax benefits.
6. Discuss the meaning of common stock and differentiate among authorized, issued, treasury, and outstanding shares.
7. Explain the preferences that are connected with preferred stock.
8. Discuss debenture holder and bondholder rights.
9. Explain the organization and operation of multinational corporations.
10. Discuss the topic of Internet corporate alliances in China

Practical Application

You will have a better understanding of how a corporation is formed and operates. You will also be better aware of the benefits as well as concerns with operating a business as a corporation. Finally, you will have a better appreciation of the impact corporations have on business, the world and our every day lives.

Helpful Hints

Since there is a vast amount of information to learn in this chapter, organization is key to learning the various topics. A corporation is similar to raising a child, in that it starts out small without a name and eventually grows with the help of its family members into a fully functioning being. If you keep in mind that the different aspects of operating a business as a corporation all depend on one another, you will begin to see how the entire picture fits together. The most important key terms and concepts have been typed in bold in the Study Tips section that follows.

Study Tips

General Information

It is important to realize that corporations are **created according to the state laws** where it is incorporated. These laws are vital to a corporation's success as they regulate formation, operation, and the dissolution of corporations. It is beneficial to learn the characteristics associated with a corporation as given below.

A corporation is considered to be **a legal person or legal entity** that is separate and distinct which include the following many interesting characteristics:

- A corporation is an artificial person that is state created.
- A corporation may bring a lawsuit or be sued.
- A corporation may enter into and enforce contracts, hold title to and transfer property.
- A corporation may be found civilly and criminally liable and may have fines assessed or its license revoked.

Other fascinating characteristics that may be attributed to corporations include:

- The shareholders have limited liability to the extent of their contributions.
- Corporate shares are freely transferable by the shareholder.
- Corporations have a perpetual existence if there is no duration stated in the corporation's articles of incorporation.
- Shareholders may voluntarily terminate the corporation's existence.
- Death, insanity, or bankruptcy of a shareholder has no affect on a corporation's existence.
- The shareholders elect the directors who in turn appoint corporate officers to conduct the corporation's daily business.

Classifications of Corporations

Corporations are classified based on **location, purpose**, or **owners**. Private corporations may be for **profit** or **nonprofit**. Nonprofit are created for charitable, educational, scientific, or religious reasons. Note that nonprofit corporations may not distribute any profit to their members, directors, or officers. The **Model Nonprofit Corporation Act** governs nonprofit corporations. **Government-owned** (or public) corporations are formed with a governmental or political reason in mind. The **Revised Model Business Corporation Act (RMBCA)** was promulgated in 1984, wherein it arranged the provisions of the act more logically and made substantial changes in provisions of the model act. Private corporations are created to carry on a privately owned business.

Publicly Held verses Closely Held Corporations

Publicly Held Corporations

These are generally large corporations with hundreds and even thousands of shareholders whose shares are **traded on organized securities markets**. Coca-Cola and Bristol-Myers are examples of publicly held corporations. An **important fact to know** about publicly held corporations is that the **shareholders seldom participate in** this type of corporation's **management**.

Closely Held Corporations

These are **relatively small** corporations whose **shares** are **held by** a few shareholders, mostly comprised of **family, friends, and relatives**. An **important fact to know** and compare to publicly held corporations is that the **shareholders do participate in** a closely held corporation's **management**. Sometimes the shareholders attempt to prevent outsiders from becoming shareholders.

Selecting a State for Incorporating a Corporation

Incorporation may only be in one state even though a corporation may conduct its business in many states. When choosing where to incorporate, the law of the state being considered should be examined. Large corporations look for the state with the most favorable corporate law (e.g., Delaware).

Professional Corporations

These are **formed by professionals**, such as dentists, doctors, lawyers, and accountants. The initials give a clue that it is a professional corporation. You may see the initials **P.C.** for Professional Corporation or **S.C.** for service corporation. This type of corporation is formed like other corporations and has many of the same traits. Its **professional members** are generally **not liable for** the **torts** committed by its **agents or employees**.

Domestic, Foreign, and Alien Corporations

These terms should be somewhat familiar to you in light of the previous chapters, if you have had to study them.

Domestic corporation – A corporation in the state in which it was formed.

Foreign corporation – A corporation in any state or jurisdiction other than the one in which it was formed.

Alien corporation – A corporation that is incorporated in another country.

A Corporation Begins with Promoter's Activities

Now that you are familiar with the different types of corporations, let us study how a corporation begins. It begins with a promoter. **A promoter is an individual or individuals who organizes and starts the corporations**. Additionally he/she or they enter into contracts before the corporation is formed, find investors, and sometimes subject themselves to liability as a result of all that is done.

Promoter's Liability

Promoters enter into contracts such as leases, sales contracts, property contracts, etc. Liability depends on the corporation, keeping the following instances in mind.
- If the **corporation never comes into existence**, then the promoter is solely liable on the contract unless the third party exempts the promoter.
- If the **corporation is formed,** it is liable on the promoter's contract if it agrees to be bound to the contract as per a board of director's resolution.
- The promoter remains liable on the contract unless a **novation** is entered into. A novation is a three-party agreement wherein the corporation assumes the promoter's contract liability with the third party's consent. A novation has the effect of leaving the corporation solely liable on the promoter's contract.

Issues Concerning Incorporation Procedures

An **incorporator** is the person or persons, partnerships, or corporations that are responsible for the incorporation of the corporation.

The **articles of incorporation**, also known as the corporate charter are the basic documents that must be filed with and approved by the state in order to be officially incorporated. The **articles must contain:**
- the name of the corporation
- number of shares the corporation is authorized to issue
- address of the corporation's registered office
- agent for the corporation
- name and address of each incorporator
- duration, regulation of powers, and corporate affairs
- the corporate purpose

Amendments to the articles of incorporation must be filed with the secretary of state after the shareholders approve them.

The organizers must choose a name for the corporation.
- The name must contain the words corporation, company, incorporated, limited, or an abbreviation of any one of these.
- The name cannot contain a word or phrase that states or implies that the corporation is organized for a purpose different than that in the articles of incorporation.
- A trademark search should be conducted to make sure that the name is available for use.
- A domain name search for purposes of Internet use should also be performed.

A general purpose clause should be in a corporation's articles. Some corporations insert a limited purpose clause.

A registered agent must be identified along with a registered office. The purpose of the agent is to have someone be able to accept service of process on behalf of the corporation.

Corporate bylaws are a more exacting set of rules adopted by the board of directors. It contains provisions for managing the business and the affairs of the corporation. The bylaws may also be amended.

An organizational meeting of the first corporate directors must be held upon the filing of the articles of incorporation. The bylaws are adopted, officers elected, and other business transacted at this initial meeting. Additional matters such as ratification of promoter's contracts, approving the form of stock certificates, etc., are also discussed.

A corporate seal is a design affixed by a metal stamp containing the name and date of incorporation.

Corporate status begins when the articles of incorporation are filed. Upon the secretary of state's filing of the articles of incorporation, it is conclusive proof that the incorporators have satisfied all conditions of the incorporation. Note, failure to file the articles of incorporation is conclusive proof that the corporation does not exist.

An **S corporation** has been defined as that which elects to be taxed under Chapter S, thereby avoiding double taxation. Note C, corporations are all other corporations.

Financing the corporation – The sale of equity and debt securities is the most simple way to finance the operation of a corporation. **Equity securities** are stock which represent the ownership rights in the corporation in the form of **common stock** or **preferred stock**.

- **Common stock** – A kind of equity security that represents the residual value of the corporation. The creditors and preferred shareholders receive their interest first. There is no fixed maturity date. Common stockholders may vote on mergers, elect directors, and receive dividends.
- **Par and no par value** – This refers to a value assigned to common shares. Par value is the lowest price for which the shares may be issued. Most shares are no-par shares where no value is assigned to them.
- **Preferred stock** – This is a kind of equity security that is given preferences and rights over common stock. Holders of this type of stock are issued **preferred stock certificates.** The general rule with regard to voting is that this class of stock may not do so, unless there has been a merger or there has been a failure to pay a dividend.
- **Preferences of preferred stock include** dividend preference, liquidation preference, cumulative dividend right, cumulative preferred stock, the right to participate in profits with participating preferred stock and convertible preferred stock.
- **Redeemable preferred stock (also termed callable preferred stock)** allows the corporation to buy back the preferred stock at a future date.

Authorized, Issued, and Outstanding Shares

- **Authorized shares** are the number of shares that are provided for in the articles of incorporation.
- Authorized shares that have been sold are called **issued shares**.
- Repurchased shares are called **treasury shares**.
- Shares of stock that are in the shareholder hands are called **outstanding shares**.

Purchase of Stock and Corporate Debt

- **Consideration to be paid for shares** may include any property or benefit to the corporation as determined by the board of directors.

- **Stock Options and stock warrants** may be offered for sale. A **stock option** is generally given to **top-level managers**. It is the nontransferable right to purchase corporate stock at a set price during an option period. A **stock warrant** is an option that is demonstrated by a **certificate** whereby the holder can exercise the warrant and buy the common stock at a stated price during the warrant period. Warrants are both transferable and nontransferable.

- **Debt Securities** are securities that establish a debtor-creditor relationship in which the corporation borrows money from the investor to whom the debt security is issued.

- **Debenture** – A long-term unsecured debt instrument that is based on the corporation's general credit standing.

- **Bond** – A long-term debt security that is secured by some form of collateral.

- **Note** – A debt security with a maturity of five years or less.

- **Indenture agreement** – A contract between the corporation and the holder that contains the terms of the debt security.

Corporate Powers

A corporation has **express** and **implied powers**. Express powers may be found in the U.S. Constitution, state constitutions, federal statutes, articles of incorporations, bylaws, and resolutions by the board of directors. Corporations may purchase, own, and lease real as well as personal property. They also may borrow money, incur liability, make donations, and perform various other financial functions.

The **implied powers** of a corporation are those that **go beyond** the **express powers** and that allow a corporation to accomplish its corporate purpose.

Ultra Vires Act – This refers to a corporate act that goes beyond its express and implied powers. An injunction as well as damages and an action to enjoin the act or dissolve the corporation are the remedies available for the commission of an ultra vires act.

Dissolution and Termination of Corporations

There are three main ways to dissolve and terminate a corporation. One way is by **voluntary dissolution** which occurs upon recommendation of the board of directors and a majority vote of the shares entitled to vote. Another is by **administrative dissolution** which is an **involuntary dissolution** of a corporation that is order by the secretary of state to comply with certain procedures required by law. The third way is by **judicial dissolution** which occurs when a corporation is dissolved by a court proceeding initiated by the state.

Winding Up, Liquidation, and Termination

Winding-up and liquidation refers to the method by which a dissolved corporation's assets are gathered, liquidated, and then distributed to creditors, shareholders, and other claimants.

Termination is the ending of the corporation that happens only after the winding up of the corporate affairs, the liquidation of its assets, and the distribution of the proceeds to the claimants.

Refresh Your Memory

The following exercise will enable you to refresh your memory on the rules and principles presented to you in this chapter. Read each question twice and place your answer in the blanks provided. Review the chapter material for any question you miss or are unable to remember.

1. What is the only way that corporations may be created? _____
_____

2. Define what a corporation is by elaborating on what it can or cannot do based upon its status as an artificial person. List at least two things. _____
_____

3. What are the differences between the first drafted MBCA and the revised Model Business Corporation Act? _____
_____

4. How many states may a corporation be incorporated in? _____

5. What is a domestic corporation? _____

6. A corporation in any state or jurisdiction other than the one in which it was formed is called a _____ _____.

7. If the Koolone Corporation incorporates in Italy, it would be referred to as an _____
_____.

8. What is the main duty of an incorporator? _____
_____

9. The basic governing documents of a corporation are known as the _____
_____

10. After a novation, what type of liability does a corporation have? _____

_____

11. What meeting must be held by the initial directors of a corporation after the articles of incorporation are filed? _____

12. What is an alien corporation? _____

13. The representation of ownership rights to a corporation which are also called stock are known as _____ _____.

14. What are the articles of incorporation? _____

_____

15. What function do the corporate bylaws serve? _____

_____

Critical Thought Exercise

Gus Hill runs a successful sole proprietorship under the name "Custom Rides." Hill makes custom motorcycles that often sell for over $40,000 each. Hill decides to expand the business and make motorcycles that are more of a standard production. In order to do this, Hill decides to form a corporation and solicit investors through the sale of company stock. Hill contacts an attorney and requests that all of the paperwork necessary for the incorporation be prepared. To prepare for the expanded business that will be done by the corporation, Hill leases a large manufacturing building from LandCo for one year at $12,000 per month. Hill also signs a $175,000 contract with VanTolker Tool Co. for the purchase of equipment and an employment contract with Dirk Dodds, who was hired to serve as plant manager and chief financial officer. Dodds's contract stated that he understood that his $130,000 yearly salary would come from corporate income and that Hill had no ability to pay his salary.

The corporation is formed and all legal filings are complete. Custom Rides immediately begins making payments on all three contracts. Custom Rides, Inc., operates for eight months before poor sales make it unable to meet its financial obligations. LandCo, Dodds, and VanTolker all file suit against Custom Rides, Inc., and Gus Hill personally to recover their contract damages.

Is Gus Hill personally liable for the contracts he signed on behalf of Custom Rides, Inc.?

Answer:

_____

_____

_____

_____

_____

_____

_____

_____

_____

_____

Practice Quiz

True/False

1. ____ An organizational meeting of the initial directors of a corporation must be held after the articles of incorporation are filed. [p. 553]

2. ____ The shareholders of the corporation do not have the absolute right to amend the bylaws even though the bylaws may also be amended by the board of directors. [pp. 552-553]

3. ____ A corporation often sells equity securities and debt securities in order to finance the operation of the business. [p. 555]

4. ____ A common stockholder's investment in the corporation is represented by a common stock certificate. [p. 555]

5. ____ Par share is a value which sets the highest price at which the shares may be issued. [p. 555]

6. ____ The election to form an S corporation may be rescinded by shareholders who collectively own at least a majority of the shares of the corporation. [p. 555]

7. ____ Common stock has a fixed maturity date. [p. 555]

8. ____ Participating preferred stock allows the stockholder to participate in the profits of the corporation along with the common stockholders. [p. 556]

9. ____ Nonconvertible stock is an uncommon type of stock. [p. 556]

10. ____ Authorized shares that have been sold by the corporation are called issued shares. [p. 557]

11. ____ Outstanding shares are those shares that do not have the right to vote. [p. 557]

12. ____ Corporations commonly grant stock option to top-level managers. [p. 557]

13. ____ A corporation has the same basic rights to perform acts and enter into contracts a physical person. [p. 559]

14. ____ Corporations formed under general incorporation laws can engage in certain businesses, such as banking, insurance, or operating public utilities. [p. 559]

15. ____ Implied powers allow a corporation to exceed its express powers in order to accomplish its corporate purpose. [p. 559]

16. ____ The term ultra vires refers to invasion of unwanted spyware concerning corporate Internet transactions. [p. 560]

17. ____ A corporation can be involuntarily dissolved by a judicial proceeding called a judicial dissolution. [p. 560]

18. ___ Termination of a corporation may occur at any time. [p. 560]

19. ___ Dissolution of a corporation impairs the rights and remedies available against the corporation or its directors, officers, or shareholders. [p. 561]

20. ___ The parent corporation usually owns all or the majority of a subsidiary corporation. [p. 561]

21. ___ In a voluntary dissolution, the liquidation is generally conducted by the board of directors. [p. 560]

22. ___ Criminal penalties may be assessed against corporations. [p. 546]

23. ___ The Revised Model Corporation Act helped to provide more consistent and substantial changes in carrying out the initial act of providing a uniform law for the regulation of corporations. [p. 547]

24. ___ Nonprofit corporations may distribute their profit to their members, directors, or officers. [p. 548]

25. ___ Most shares that are issued by corporations are no par shares. [p. 556]

Multiple Choice

26. Which of the following would enable the secretary of state to file an administrative dissolution? [p. 560]
    a. if it failed to file an annual report
    b. if it did not pay its franchise fee
    c. if the period of duration stated in the corporation's articles of incorporation has expired
    d. all of the above

27. Which of the following best describes what a debenture is? [p. 558]
    a. a short-term debt instrument with a maturity of five years or less
    b. a long-term debt security that is secured by some form of property
    c. a long term debt instrument that is based on the corporation's general credit standing
    d. an agreement setting forth the terms of a debt agreement.

28. Which of the following is true with respect to the term par value? [pp. 555-556]
    a. Par share is a value given to common shares by the corporation.
    b. Par share is usually stated in the articles of corporation.
    c. Par is usually the lowest price at which shares may be issued by the corporation.
    d. all of the above

29. Shares that are referred to as being authorized are [p. 557]
    a. shares of stock that are in shareholder hands.
    b. the number of shares provided for in the articles of incorporation.
    c. shares of stock repurchased by the company itself.
    d. stock that permits the corporation to redeem the preferred stock at some future date.

30. An indenture agreement is [p. 558]
    a. a contract between the corporation and the holder that contains the terms of a debt security.
    b. a debt security with a maturity of five years or less.
    c. a long term-debt security that is secured by some form of collateral.
    d. none of the above

31. The term ultra vires refers to [p. 560]
    a. powers beyond express powers that allow a corporation to accomplish its purpose.
    b. an act that is beyond a corporation's express or implied powers.
    c. powers given to the corporation by the U.S. Constitution.
    d. basic rights to perform acts and enter into contracts as a physical person.

32. Bixie Inc. has its principal place of business in the United States and a branch office in Vietnam. Its branch office recently encountered problems with one of its employees, Jon Smith, who became angry with one of the Vietnamese buyers. Jon actually punched the buyer. Which of the following represents an erroneous belief that Bixie Inc. may have about its branch office? [p. 561]
    a. A corporation can conduct business in another country via a branch office.
    b. Bixie's Vietnam branch is a separate legal entity.
    c. Bixie is liable for the contracts of the branch office.
    d. none of the above

33. The ending of a corporation that happens after the winding up of the corporation's affairs is known as [p. 560]
    a. winding up.
    b. judicial dissolution.
    c. voluntary dissolution.
    d. termination.

34. A corporation in the state in which it is formed is a(n) [p. 549]
    a. domestic corporation.
    b. alien corporation.
    c. foreign corporation.
    d. promoter's corporation.

35. Which of the following preferences might preferred stock have? [p. 556]
    a. cumulative dividend rights
    b. liquidation preference
    c. a dividend preference
    d. all of the above

Short Answer

36. The person who organizes and starts a corporation is known as the [p. 550] _____.

37. What are the basic governing documents of a corporation called? [p. 550]

38. Before the articles of incorporation can be amended, what must the board of directors adopt? [p. 551] _____

39. Who do the bylaws of a corporation bind? [p. 553] _____
_____

40. What is a registered agent? [p. 552] _____

41. What is a corporate seal? [p. 553]_____
_____

42. What type of voting rights do common stockholders have? [p. 555] _____
_____

43. What right does a stock option give the recipient? [p. 557] _____
_____

44. What is meant by the terminology issued stock? [p. 557] _____
_____.

45. What are repurchased shares called? [p. 557] _____
_____

46. Why is it a benefit to hold participating preferred stock? [p. 556] _____
_____

47. What is a stock warrant? [p. 558] _____

48. Corporations formed by entrepreneurs with few shareholders who often work for the corporation and manage its day-to-day operations are known as _____ corporations. [p. 559]

49. Dissolution of a corporation that has begun business or issued shares upon recommendation of the board of directors and a majority vote of the shares entitled to vote is known as a _____ dissolution. [p. 560]

50. Which act allows some corporations and their shareholders to avoid double taxation by electing to be an S corporation? [p. 555] _____

Answers to Refresh Your Memory

1. Corporations can only be created according to the laws of the state of incorporation. [p. 546]
2. A corporation is a legal entity that may sue or be sued in its own name, and enter into and enforce contracts as well as hold title to and transfer property. (Answers will vary.) [p. 546]
3. The RMBCA arranges provisions of the act more logically and there are substantial changes in the provisions of the revised act. [p. 547]
4. one [p. 548]
5. A corporation in the state in which it was formed is a domestic corporation. [p. 549]

6. foreign corporation [p. 549]
7. alien corporation [p. 549]
8. to sign the articles of incorporation [p. 550]
9. the articles of incorporation [p 550]
10. The corporation is solely liable on the promoter's contract. [p. 551]
11. organizational meeting [p. 553]
12. A corporation that is incorporated in another country is an alien corporation. [p. 559]
13. equity securities [p. 555]
14. The articles of incorporation are the basic ruling documents of the corporation that must be drafted, filed, and approved by the secretary of state. [p. 550]
15. The bylaws regulate the internal management structure of the corporation. [p. 552]

Critical Thought Exercise Model Answer

Before a corporation is formed, a promoter takes the preliminary steps in organizing the corporation. The promoter makes contracts with investors and third parties. A promoter may purchase or lease property and goods with the intent that it will be sold or transferred to the corporation when the corporation is formed. The promoter may also enter into contracts with professionals whose services are needed. As a general rule, a promoter is held personally liable on preincorporation contracts. A promoter is not an agent when the corporation does not yet exist. If, however, the promoter secures a contracting party's agreement to only hold the corporation liable, then the promoter will not he held liable for any breach. Additionally, the promoter's personal liability continues even after the corporation is formed unless the promoter gains a release of liability from the third party. It does not matter whether or not the contract was made in the name of, or on behalf of, the named corporation.

Hill was acting as a promoter when he entered into contracts with LandCo, VanTolker, and Dodds. The fact that he signed the contracts as a purported agent of Custom Rides, Inc., will have no effect because the corporation had yet to be incorporated. The employment with Dodds is different than the others because Dodds agreed to seek payment only from Custom Rides, Inc., effectively releasing Hill from any personal liability. Even though Custom Rides, Inc., adopted the contracts executed with LandCo and VanTolker, the lack of a formal novation meant that Hill remained personally liable after incorporation. There could not have been a ratification of the preincorporation contracts because there was no principal to ratify the agent's acts at the time the contract was executed. Therefore, Hill will be personally liable to both LandCo and VanTolker.

Answers to Practice Quiz

True/False

1. True   An organizational meeting of the initial directors of a corporation must be held after the articles of incorporation are filed.
2. False   The shareholders of the corporation have the absolute right to amend the bylaws event though the bylaws may also be amended by the board of directors.
3. True   The most common way to finance a corporation's needs is by selling equity securities and debt securities.
4. True   A common stockholder's investment in the corporation is represented by a common stock certificate.
5. False   Par share value is set at the lowest price at which the shares may be issued by the corporation.

6. True   An S corporation's election can be rescinded by shareholders who collectively own at least a majority of the shares of the corporation.
7. False Common stock does not have a fixed maturity date.
8. True   Participating preferred stock allows the stockholder to participate in the profits of the corporation along with the common stockholders.
9. False Nonconvertible stock is more common.
10. True Authorized shares that have been sold by the corporation are called issued shares.
11. False Outstanding shares are issued shares minus treasury shares. These shares have the right to vote.
12. True Corporations commonly grant stock options to top-level managers.
13. True A corporation has the same basic rights to perform acts and enter into contracts as a physical person.
14. False Corporations formed under general incorporation laws cannot engage in certain businesses, such as banking, insurance, or operating public utilities.
15. True Implied powers allow a corporation to exceed its express powers in order to accomplish its corporate purpose.
16. False An act by a corporation that is beyond its express or implied powers is called an ultra vires act.
17. True A corporation can be involuntarily dissolved by a judicial proceeding called a judicial dissolution.
18. False Termination occurs only after the winding up of the corporation's affairs.
19. False The dissolution of a corporation does not impair any rights or remedies available against the corporation, or its directors, or officers, or shareholders.
20. True The parent corporation usually owns all or the majority of a subsidiary corporation.
21. True The board of directors usually carries out the liquidation in a voluntary dissolution.
22. True Criminal penalties may be assessed against corporations in the form of a fine or loss of license, or other sanction.
23. True Substantial changes in carrying out the initial Model Business Corporation Act were enacted in the Revised Model Business Corporation Act.
24. False Nonprofit corporations are prohibited from distributing any profit that they make to their members, directors, or officers.
25. True No par shares have no assigned par value and are the most often issued shares by a corporation.

Multiple Choice

26. D. Answer D is the correct answer as all of the situations stated in answers A, B, and C give the secretary cause to file an administrative solution.
27. C. Answer C is the correct answer as a long-term debt instrument that is based on a corporation's general credit rating. Answer A is incorrect as this describes a note. Answer B is incorrect as this describes a long-term debt security. Answer D is incorrect, as an agreement setting forth the terms of a debt agreement is an indenture agreement.
28. D. Answer D is the correct answer as answers A, B, and C all state true facts regarding the term par value.
29. B. Answer B is the correct answer as authorized shares are the number of shares provided for in the articles of incorporation. Answer A is incorrect as this answer gives the definition for outstanding shares, not authorized shares. Answer C is incorrect as this provides the definition for treasure shares. Answer D is incorrect as it gives the definition for redeemable stock.

30. A. Answer A is the correct answer as an agreement between the corporation and the holder that sets forth the terms of the debt security is an indenture agreement. Answer B is incorrect as this gives the definition of a note. Answer C is incorrect as this gives the definition of a bond. Answer D is incorrect based on the reasoning given above.

31. B. Answer B is the correct answer in that an act that is beyond a corporation's express or implied powers is an ultra vires act. Answer A is incorrect as this gives the definition of implied powers. Answers C and D are incorrect statements of law and are therefore not the right answers.

32. B Answer B is the correct answer as though Bixie is operating a separate branch in a foreign country; it is not a separate legal entity but merely an office. Answers A and C are true statements and therefore incorrect as per the questions. Answer D is incorrect based on the reasoning given above.

33. D. Answer D is the correct answer as termination with respect to corporations is the ending that results from winding up the corporation's affairs. Answer A is incorrect as winding up involves liquidating the corporate assets and it precedes termination. Answer B is incorrect as a judicial dissolution is involuntary and initiated by a judicial proceeding. Answer C is incorrect as a voluntary dissolution is a step toward ending a corporation, but is not the ending itself of the corporation.

34. A. Answer A is the correct answer as a domestic corporation is one in the state in which it is formed. Answer B is incorrect as an alien corporation is one that is incorporated in another country. Answer C is incorrect as a foreign corporation is one in any state or jurisdiction other than the one in which it was formed. Answer D is incorrect as there is no such thing as a promoter's corporation.

35. D. Answer D is the correct answer as answers A, B, and C all list preferences that preferred stock might have.

Short Answer

36. promoter
37. articles of incorporation.
38. a resolution recommending the amendment
39. directors, officers, and shareholders of a corporation
40. an individual or corporation that has the authority to accept service of process on behalf of the corporation
41. a design that contains the name and date of incorporation
42. the right to vote on mergers and other important matters
43. the right to purchase shares of the corporation from the corporation at a stated price for a specified period of time
44. It means shares are sold by the corporation.
45. treasury shares
46. because it allows the stockholder to participate in the profits of the corporation
47. a stock option evidenced by a certificate
48. close
49. voluntary
50. Subchapter S Revision Act

Chapter 37

CORPORATE DIRECTORS, OFFICERS, AND SHAREHOLDERS

Chapter Overview

The previous chapter explored the formation as well as various types of corporations and the characteristics associated with corporations. In this chapter, the rights, duties and liabilities of corporate shareholders, officers, and directors are examined, with an emphasis on the differences in the roles and responsibilities of each.

Objectives

Upon completion of the exercises in this chapter, you should be able to:
1. Discuss the functions of shareholders, directors, and officers in managing the affairs of the corporation.
2. Explain how shareholders' and directors' meetings are called as well as conducted.
3. Differentiate and compare straight and cumulative voting for directors.
4. Discuss the agency authority of officers to enter into contracts on behalf of the corporation.
5. Discuss a director's and officer's duty of care and the business judgment rule.
6. Compare how the differences between the management of closely held corporations and publicly held corporations.
7. Explain the director's duty of loyalty and how it can be breached.
8. Explain directors' and officers' liability insurance and corporate indemnification.
9. Explain what is meant by the corporate veil or alter ego doctrine.

Practical Application

Whether you are a shareholder, a director, officer, or a corporate observer, this chapter will provide you with practical information regarding the internal management structure and its direct impact on one another. This knowledge will provide you with the ability to make educated decisions as may pertain to the basic decisions associated with the management of corporations.

Helpful Hints

Just as it takes a village to raise a child, it takes an entire management structure to mold and develop a corporation. If you keep this analogy in mind as you study the key players in its infrastructure, your learning of this area will be rewarding and insightful. Additionally, if you view the shareholders, directors, and officers like a pyramid with each having different responsibilities that impact the other tiers, you will begin to better understand their importance in keeping the pyramid intact in order to avoid corporate collapse. The most important key terms and concepts have been typed in bold in the Study Tips section that follows.

Study Tips

Shareholders

The shareholders hold a significant position in the corporate pyramid, as they are the **owners** of the corporation. They also **vote** on the directors and other important actions to be taken by the corporation, but cannot bind the corporation to any contract.

Shareholder Meetings

Annual shareholder meetings are held to take actions such as the election of director and independent auditors. Note: there are *special shareholder meetings* that may be conducted to evaluate and vote on significant or emergency issues. Examples include potential mergers, or amendments to the articles of incorporation. Attendance at a shareholder meeting may be by a **proxy,** which is another person who acts as an agent of the shareholder. Proxies must be in **writing** and they are **valid** for **11 months.**

As long as a majority of the shares entitled to vote are present, there will be a *quorum* to hold the meeting. An affirmative vote for elections other than the board of directors is required. However, the election of the directors may be by **straight voting** wherein each shareholder votes the number of shares he or she owns on candidates for the directors positions that are open. The method of **cumulative voting** may also be used in voting for the directors. This method entails a shareholder accumulating all of his or her votes and voting them all for one candidate or dividing his or her votes among many candidates. In essence, a shareholder may multiply the number of shares he or she owns by the number of directors to be elected and then vote the entire amount on a single candidate or apportion the product among contenders. This method is good for minority shareholders. *Supramajority voting requirements* can be made thereby requiring a greater than majority of shares to comprise a quorum or the shareholders' vote.

Voting Agreements – The two types of voting agreements to be concerned with are the voting trust and shareholder voting agreements. In a **voting trust** situation, the shareholders transfer their stock certificates to a trustee who is given the authority to vote the shares. In a **shareholder voting agreement**, two or more shareholders agree on how they will vote their shares.

Proxies

Shareholders who do not attend the shareholder's meeting to vote may vote by proxy. This means that they can appoint another person (as proxy) as their agent to vote at the meeting. The proxy may be directed how to vote or may be given discretion on how to vote the shares. Online or in writing proxies are acceptable. The proxy card is the written document, which is valid for 11 months.

Quorum and Voting Requirement

A quorum is the number of directors required to hold a board of directors' meeting or conduct business of the board.

Shareholder's Rights

Right to Transfer Shares

Shareholders have the right to transfer their shares **under Article 8 of the Uniform Commercial Code.** There are certain restrictions however that the shareholders must be aware of. They concern the right of first refusal and what is known as a buy-and sell agreement. When shareholders do not want certain people to become owners of the corporation, they will often enter into an agreement with another shareholder to prevent new ownership.

The right of first refusal is an agreement that shareholders enter into which grants one another the right of first refusal to purchase shares they are going to sell. Compare this to a buy-and sell agreement whereby the shareholders are required to sell their shares to the other shareholders or the corporation at a price set in the agreement.

Shareholders also Have Preemptive Rights

Preemptive rights give existing shareholders the option of subscribing to new shares being issued in proportion to their current ownership interest. These rights are usually found in the articles of incorporation.

Right to Receive Information and Inspect Books and Records

Shareholders have a right to be up to date about the financial affairs of the corporation and must be given an **annual financial statement**. Further, shareholders have an absolute **right to inspect** the articles of incorporation, bylaws, minutes, and so on within the past three years.

Dividends

Dividends are paid at the discretion of the board of directors. The date that is set prior to the actual payment of a dividend is called a record date. Shareholders on that date are entitled to receive a dividend even if they sell their shares before the payment date.

Shareholder Lawsuits

There are two types of lawsuits a shareholder may bring. The first is a **direct lawsuit** against the corporation. The second is a **derivative lawsuit** wherein the directors are empowered to bring an action on behalf of the corporation. If the corporation does not bring a lawsuit, the shareholders have the right to bring it on the corporation's behalf.

Piercing the Corporate Veil

Generally shareholders are liable for the debts and obligations of the corporation to the extent of their capital contribution. Note though that if the corporation is dominated or misused by the shareholder(s) for improper purposes, the court can disregard the corporate entity theory and hold the shareholders of a corporation personally liable for the corporation's debts and obligations. This is what is meant by *piercing the corporate veil.* This is also called the *alter ego doctrine.* Reasons to pierce the corporate veil include: the corporation not being formed with sufficient capital and lack of separateness between the corporation and its shareholders. This is examined on a case-by-case basis.

Directors

The board of directors makes policy decisions as well as employs the major officers for the corporation. They also make suggestions concerning actions implemented by the shareholders.

Selection of Directors

There are two types of directors, an **inside director** and an **outside director**. An inside director is a member of the board of directors who is also an officer of the corporation. An outside director is a member of the board of directors who is not an officer of the corporation. The **number of directors** is stated in the articles of incorporation, but may be **as little as only one** individual. A **director's term** expires at the next annual shareholders' meeting following his or her election unless the terms are **staggered** so that only a part of the board of directors is up for election each year.

Committees of the Board of Directors

Directors may create committees of the board and give certain powers to those committees. Examples of these committees include the executive committee, audit committee, nominating committee, compensation committee, investment committee, and litigation committee.

The **board may not** delegate the power to declare dividends, initiate actions that require shareholders' approval, appoint members to fill openings on the board, amend the bylaws, approve a merger plan that does not require shareholder approval, or authorize the issuance of shares.

Corporate Officers

Officers have the responsibility of managing the day-to-day operation of the corporation. They also act as agents and hire other officers and employees. The following officers exist in many corporations: president, one or more vice presidents, a secretary, and a treasurer.

Agency Authority of Officers

Officers have the express, implied, and apparent authority to bind the corporation to contract.

Liability of Directors and Officers

Directors and officers owe the **fiduciary duties of obedience, care, and loyalty.** A director or officer must not intentionally or negligently act outside of their authority. If he or she does, he or she is personally responsible for any resulting damages caused to the corporation or its shareholders.

Duty of Care

The **duty of due care** involves an officer's or director's obligation to discharge his or her duties in good faith and with the care of an ordinary prudent person in a like position would use, and in a manner that is in the best interests of the corporation. Examples of breaches a director or officer will be held personally liable for include the failure to make a reasonable investigation in a corporate matter, or the failure to regularly attend board meetings, or properly supervise a subordinate, and failure to keep sufficiently informed of corporate affairs.

The Business Judgment Rule

A director's or officer's duty of care is measured as of the time that he or she makes a decision. Honest mistakes of judgment do not render the director or officer liable.

Reliance on Others

A director is not liable if information he or she relied upon is false, misleading, or unreliable unless the director or officer has knowledge that would cause his or her reliance to be unwarranted.

Dissent to Director's Action

If an individual director dissents to an action taken by a majority of the board of directors, he or she must either resign or register his or her dissent by placing it in the meeting's minutes, filing a written dissent to the secretary, or forwarding his or her dissent by registered mail to the secretary immediately following the meeting.

Duty of Loyalty

Officers and directors are to place their personal interest below that of the corporation and its shareholders.

Usurping a corporate opportunity, self-dealing, competing with the corporation, making a secret profit.

Breaches of this duty include the usurping of a corporate opportunity, self-dealing, competing with the corporation, and disgorgement of secret profits.

Criminal Liability

Officers, directors, employees, and agents are personally liable for crimes that are committed while acting on behalf of the corporation. Punishment includes fines and imprisonment.

Refresh Your Memory

The following exercise will enable you to refresh your memory on the rules and principles presented to you in this chapter. Read each question twice and place your answer in the blanks provided. Review the chapter material for any question you miss or are unable to remember.

1. As a legal entity, what can a corporation be held liable for? _____
   _____

2. In the structure of a corporation, who owns it? _____

3. Why are annual shareholders' meetings held? _____
   _____

4. What is meant by a proxy? _____
   _____

5. What does the record date refer to? _____

6. If a majority of shares entitled to vote are represented at a meeting, this is called a _____ _____.

7. An agreement between two or more shareholders that stipulates how they will vote their shares is called a _____ _____ _____.

8. An arrangement whereby shareholders transfer their stock certificates to a trustee is called a _____ _____.

9. A greater than majority of shares to constitute a quorum of the vote of the shareholders is called a _____ _____ _____.

10. Voting for the election of directors is by the _____ _____ method unless otherwise stated in the corporation's articles of incorporation.

11. A member of the board of directors who is also an officer of the corporation is an _____ _____.

12. A meeting brought by the board of directors to discuss new shares, merger proposals, or hostile takeover attempts is a _____ meeting.

13. The distribution of profits of the corporation to shareholders is known as a _____.

14. Additional shares of stock paid as a dividend is called a _____ _____.

15. What is the main responsibility of the corporations' officers? _____ _____.

Critical Thought Exercise

Ned West was the sole shareholder and president of Westward Co., a corporation that ran truck stops along interstate highways. The corporation did not have its own bank accounts. All business was conducted through West's personal account. All supplies, payroll, debts, and purchases were handled through this one checking account. West also paid all of his personal expenses out of this account. All receipts from the truck stops were deposited into the same account. While the corporation was in business, no directors meetings were ever held. All decisions for the corporation were made solely by West.

For a four-year period, Westward Co. accumulated $187,455 in federal tax liabilities. The government is now seeking to collect the overdue tax payments directly from West. West argues that the government is ignoring his corporate entity.

Can the government pierce the corporate veil in this case and force West to incur personal liability for the taxes owed by Westward Co.?

Answer:

_____
_____
_____
_____
_____

_____

_____

_____

_____

_____

_____

_____

_____

Practice Quiz

True/False

1. ____ Two or more shareholders may enter into an agreement that stipulates how they will vote their shares for the election of director or other matters that require shareholder vote. [p. 569]

2. ____ A selling shareholder need not offer his or her shares for sale to the other parties to the agreement before selling them to someone else. [p. 569]

3. ____ A voting trust agreement must be in writing and cannot exceed ten years. [p. 569]

4. ____ If the corporation fails to bring a lawsuit, shareholders have the right to bring the lawsuit on behalf of the corporation. This is called a subsidiary action. [p. 571]

5. ____ Piercing the corporate veil is a doctrine that is also known as the alter ego doctrine because the corporation has become the alter ego of the shareholder. [p. 571]

6. ____ An outside director is a person who is also an officer of the corporation. [p. 573]

7. ____ Policy decisions of the board of directors include decisions that affect supervision and control of the corporation. [p. 573]

8. ____ The nominating committee approves management compensation which includes stock option plans. [p. 575]

9. ____ The Sarbanes-Oxley Act of 2002 set forth certain responsibilities on a corporation's audit committee. [p. 575]

10. ____ Any one of the six general committees may declare a dividend. [p. 575]

11. ____ The SEC may issue an order prohibiting any person who has committed securities fraud from acting as an officer or a director of a public company. [p. 577]

12. ____ The Sarbanes-Oxley Act permits public companies to make personal loans to their directors or executive officers. [p. 577]

13. ____ Officers are responsible for the day-to-day operation of the corporation. [p. 577]

14. ___ A corporation can ratify an unauthorized act of a corporate officer or agent. [p. 566]

15. ___ The RMBCA forbids officers from relying on information, opinions, reports, or statements presented by officers and employees. [p. 578]

16. ___ Directors and officers who are sued in their corporate capacities may be indemnified by the corporation for the costs of the litigation as well as any judgment or settlements stemming from the lawsuit. [p. 582]

17. ___ Directors and officers are held liable to the corporation or its shareholders for honest mistakes of judgment. [p. 578]

18. ___ An officer or a director who breaches the duty of care is personally liable to the corporation and its shareholders for any damages caused by the breach. [p. 578]

19. ___ Regular meetings of the board of directors can be held without notice. [p. 574]

20. ___ The RMBCA allows board of director meetings to be held via conference calls. [p. 574]

Multiple Choice

21. Which of the following is a true statement concerning a supramajority voting requirement? [p. 568]
    a. These votes are required to approve mergers.
    b. An amendment must be adopted by the number of shares of the proposed increase.
    c. The articles of incorporation or the bylaws of a corporation can mandate a greater than majority of shares to comprise a quorum or the vote of the shareholders.
    d. all of the above

22. Which of the following apply to registering a board of director's dissent? [p. 579]
    a. entering it in the minutes of the meeting of the board of directors
    b. filing a written dissent with the secretary before the adjournment of the meeting
    c. forwarding a written dissent by registered mail to the secretary immediately following the adjournment of the meeting
    d. all of the above

23. Which of the following applies to a derivative action brought by a shareholder? [p. 571]
    a. A shareholder may bring a derivative lawsuit to compel dissolution of the corporation.
    b. A shareholder may bring a derivative lawsuit to enjoin the corporation from committing an ultra vires act.
    c. Any award from a successful derivative lawsuit goes to the treasury.
    d. If a shareholder is successful in a derivative action against the corporation, the award belongs to that shareholder.

24. Which of the following acts would be considered to be unauthorized and a breach of a director's or officer's loyalty? [p. 581]
    a. competing with the corporation
    b. usurping a corporate opportunity
    c. selling the corporation a condominium for its employees use but not telling the corporation that it is owned by either an officer or director
    d. all of the above

25. Alice and Harvey are on the board of directors of the Whizo Corporation. They want to create committees of the board and delegate certain powers to those committees. Which of the following would be the type of committee that Alice and Harvey may create? [p. 575]
    a. the Compensation Committee
    b. the Regular Meeting Committee
    c. the Crime Committee
    d. none of the above

26. What officers do most corporations have? [p. 576]
    a. president, vice president, coordinator
    b. president, one or more vice presidents, secretary, and treasurer
    c. president, vice president, human resource director, treasurer
    d. president, vice president, secretary, and an agent

27. Which of the following expresses the duties that the officers and directors owe to the corporation and its shareholders? [pp. 577-580]
    a. duty of obedience, duty to spend, duty of care
    b. duty of loyalty, duty of care, duty to account properly
    c. duty of loyalty, duty of care, duty of obedience
    d. duty of loyalty, duty to make decisions, fiduciary duty

28. Under the business judgment rule, which choice states what the directors or officers are not liable for? [p. 578]
    a. usurping a corporate opportunity
    b. self-dealing
    c. honest mistakes of judgment
    d. lending trade secrets to corporate competitors

29. If Frank Smith, a director of the Silly Slime Corporation, has usurped a corporate opportunity for himself, what has he done? [p. 580]
    a. Frank has stolen a corporate opportunity for himself.
    b. Frank has purchased a corporate opportunity for himself.
    c. Frank has borrowed a corporate opportunity for himself.
    d. Frank has transferred a corporate opportunity to himself.

30. Which situation least describes when the court will pierce the corporate veil? [p. 571]
    a. When the corporation has been formed with sufficient capitalization.
    b. When there has been a commingling of personal and corporate assets.
    c. When there has been a failure to maintain corporate books and records.
    d. all of the above

Short Answer

31. Shareholders must be provided with an annual _____ statement that contains a balance sheet, an income statement, and a statement of changes in shareholder equity. [p. 570]

32. If a shareholder derivative action is successful, where does any award that is given go? [p. 571] _____

33. What is the right of first refusal as it pertains to stock? [p. 569] _____ _____

34. What is a buy-and-sell agreement? [p. 570]_____ _____

35. What types of information are contained in the annual financial statement that is provided to a corporation's shareholders? [p. 570] _____ _____

36. Actions that require the shareholders' approval are initiated when the board of directors adopts a _____ that approves the transaction and recommends it to the shareholders for their vote. [p. 573]

37. What is a corporation's audit committee responsible for? [p. 575] _____ _____

38. Who can fill a vacancy on the board of directors? [p. 574] _____ _____

39. How many people are needed to comprise a board of directors? [p. 574] _____

40. What is the litigation committee of a corporation responsible for? [p. 575] _____ _____

41. Define the meaning of fiduciary duty. [p. 577] _____

42. Tell what D &O insurance is and what its main purpose is. [p. 582] _____ _____

43. What does indemnification mean as it applies to the corporation? [p. 582]_____ _____

44. What is the criminal penalty imposed upon a corporation? [p. 582] _____ _____

45. When does a director's term of office usually expire? [p. 574] _____ _____

Answers to Refresh Your Memory

1. the acts of the directors and officers and for authorized contracts entered into on its behalf [p. 566]
2. a corporation's shareholders [p. 566]
3. to elect directors, to choose an independent auditor, or to take other actions [p. 567]
4. A proxy is a written document that a shareholder signs authorizing another person to vote his or her shares at the shareholders' meetings in the event of the shareholder's absence. [p. 567]
5. record date [p. 567]
6. quorum [p. 567]
7. shareholder voting agreement [p. 569]
8. voting trusts [p. 568]
9. supramajority voting requirement [p. 568]
10. straight voting [p. 568]
11. inside director [p. 573]
12. special [p. 573]
13. dividend [p. 570]
14. stock dividend [p. 571]
15. The main responsibility of the corporation's officers is to manage the day-to-day operations of the corporation. [p. 576]

Critical Thought Exercise Model Answer

In corporate law, if personal and company interests are commingled to the extent that the corporation has no separate identity, a court may "pierce the corporate veil" and expose the shareholders to personal liability. West mixed all aspects of his personal business with corporate business. All purchases and payroll checks were made from his personal account. There is no way to separate corporate receipts from West's personal funds. In order to prevent a creditor from "piercing the corporate veil" a sole stockholder needs to be careful to preserve the corporate identity. Maintaining separate accounts and detailed records are imperative if corporate identity is to be preserved. West did not attempt to preserve the identity of Westward Co.

Another key factor that favors the government in this case is the failure of Westward Co. to hold directors meetings. The failure of the sole shareholder to comply with statutory corporate formalities demonstrates that the corporate form may be a sham. West never consulted with his directors and made all decisions for Westward Co. by himself. When the corporate business is treated in such a careless and flippant manner, the corporation and the shareholder in control are no longer separate entities, requiring the sole shareholder to assume personal liability to creditors of the corporation. West totally ignored the corporate identity and now the government will be allowed to "pierce the corporate veil." West will be personally liable for the corporation's tax debt.

Answers to Practice Quiz

True/False

1. True   Two or more shareholders may enter into an agreement that stipulates how they will vote their shares for the election of directors or other matters that require shareholder vote.

2. False A selling shareholder must offer his or her shares for sale to the other parties to the agreement before selling them to anyone else.

3. True A voting trust agreement must be in writing and cannot exceed 10 years.

4. False If the corporation fails to bring the lawsuit, shareholders have the right to bring the lawsuit on behalf of the corporation called a derivative action.

5. True The piercing the corporate veil doctrine is also called the alter ego doctrine because the corporation has become the alter ego of the shareholder.

6. False An outside director is a person who sits on the board of directors of a corporation but is not an officer of that corporation.

7. True Policy decisions of the board of directors include such things as supervision and control of the corporation.

8. False The compensation committee approves management compensation, not the nominating committee, which nominates the management slate of directors to be submitted for shareholder vote.

9. True The Sarbanes-Oxley Act of 2002 placed certain responsibilities on a corporation's audit committee.

10. False The power to declare dividends cannot be delegated to committees but must be exercised by the board itself.

11. True The SEC may issue an order prohibiting any person who has committed securities fraud from acting as an officer or a director of a public company.

12. False The Sarbanes-Oxley Act of 2002 prohibits public companies from making personal loans to their directors or executive officers.

13. True Officers are responsible for the day-to-day operation of the corporation.

14. True A corporation can ratify an unauthorized act of a corporate officer or agent.

15. False Under the RMBCA, directors and officers are entitled to rely on information, opinions, reports, or statements including financial statements and other financial data, prepared or presented by officers and employees.

16. True Corporations may provide that directors and officers who are sued in their corporate capacities will be indemnified by the corporation for the costs of the litigation as well as any judgments or settlements stemming from the lawsuit.

17. False Directors and officers are not liable to the corporation or shareholders for honest mistakes of judgment.

18. True A director or officer who breaches the duty of care is personally liable to the corporation and its shareholders for any damages caused by the breach.

19. True Regular meetings of the board of directors can be held without notice.

20. True The RMBCA permits meetings of the board to be held via conference calls.

Multiple Choice

21. D Answer D is the correct answer as answers A, B, and C are all true statements concerning a supramajority voting requirement.

22. D Answer D is the correct answer as all of the procedures listed in answers A, B, and C apply to registering a board of director's dissent..

23. C Answer C is the correct answer as it is the only true statement that applies to a derivative action brought by a shareholder. Answers A, B, and D are all incorrect as they are all statements that apply to a direct lawsuit, not a derivative lawsuit.

24. D Answer D is the correct answer as all of the examples given in answers A, B, and C would constitute a breach of the director's or officer's loyalty.

25.   A   Answer A is the correct answer as Alice and Harvey as members of the board of directors may create a Compensation Committee provided all of the other board members, if any, ratify it. A compensation committee approves management compensation, including bonuses, salaries, stock plans, fringe benefits, etc. Answers B and C are incorrect as these are types of committees that are usually created by a board of directors. Answer D is incorrect based on the reasons given above.

26.   B   Answer B is correct as it properly states the officers that most corporations have. Answer A is incorrect as a coordinator is not an officer. Answer C is incorrect as the human resource director is a member of personnel and not an officer. Answer D is incorrect as an agent is not usually an officer of a corporation.

27.   C   Answer C is the correct answer as it properly states the duties that officers and directors owe to the corporation and its shareholders. Answer A is incorrect as the officers and directors do not owe a duty to spend. Answer B is incorrect as the officers and directors do not owe a duty to account. Answer D is incorrect as the duty to make decisions may be implied; however, this is too broad of a statement to encompass it in the directors' and officers' duties.

28.   C   Answer C is correct as the business judgment rule states that the directors or officers are not liable for honest mistakes in judgment. Answers A, B, and D are all incorrect as they all are activities for which the directors and officers would be held liable for participating in.

29.   A   Answer A is correct as the usurping of a corporate opportunity is akin to stealing the opportunity for oneself. Answer B does not state the correct meaning of usurp, nor do answers C and D. Therefore, answers B, C, and D are all incorrect.

30.   A   Answer A is correct as it is only when the corporation has been formed with thin capitalization that the court will pierce the corporate veil, not with sufficient capitalization. Answers B and C provide good reasons to pierce the corporate veil. Answer D is incorrect based on the reasoning given above.

Short Answer

31.   financial
32.   the corporate treasury
33.   an agreement entered into by shareholders that grant one another the right of first refusal to purchase shares that they are going to sell
34.   It is an agreement entered into by shareholders that requires selling shareholders to sell their shares to the other shareholders of the corporation at the price given in the agreement.
35.   Balance sheets, income statements, and a statement of changes in shareholder equity are the types of information found in an annual financial statement.
36.   resolution
37.   the appointment, payment of compensation, and oversight of public accounting firms employed to audit the company
38.   shareholders or the remaining directors
39.   one or more
40.   The litigation committee reviews and decides whether to pursue requests by shareholders for the corporation to sue persons who have allegedly harmed the corporation.
41.   The board of directors may be removed by any officer.
42.   The duty of loyalty, integrity, honesty, trust, and confidence owed by directors and officers to their corporate employers is what is known as their fiduciary duty.
43.   D & O insurance is directors' and officers' liability insurance that a corporation may purchase to defend an officer or director who has been sued in his or her corporate capacity.
44.   assessment of a monetary fine or the loss of some legal privilege
45.   at the next annual shareholder's meeting following his or her election, unless the terms are staggered

Chapter 38

CORPORATE MERGERS,
TENDER OFFERS, AND
SHAREHOLDER RESOLUTIONS

Chapter Overview

Corporate change is obtained by controlling stockholder votes. Shareholder votes are solicited and voted by proxy. Persons who desire fundamental change in the direction or control of a company often engage in a proxy contest to win over shareholder votes. Another fundamental change may be made by acquiring another company. This may be through a friendly merger of consolidation or by a hostile tender offer. The target company may mount a defense to the takeover. This chapter focuses on all these possible fundamental changes that a corporation may go through.

Objectives

Upon completion of the exercises in this chapter, you should be able to:
1. Explain the process of soliciting proxies.
2. Describe a proxy contest.
3. Understand when a shareholder can insert a proposal in proxy materials.
4. Describe the difference between a consolidation and a merger.
5. Explain the process involved in approving a merger or share exchange.
6. Describe dissenting shareholder appraisal rights.
7. Explain a tender offer.
8. Describe defensive maneuvers to a takeover.
9. Understand the business judgment rule.

Practical Application

For those businesspersons that obtain ownership interests incorporations or choose the corporation as their business form, obtaining or maintaining control of the company is often imperative. It is wise to understand how control of the company may be lost and what efforts can lawfully be made to thwart a proxy battle or hostile takeover.

Helpful Hints

In the corporate environment, mergers, acquisitions, proxy fights, and tender offers are realities that are effectuated only be adhering to the laws and regulations related to these processes and changes. The individual has a greater ability to control his/her financial stake in a corporation if he/she understands his/her rights and duties under the applicable laws. The exercises in this chapter will help you advance your understanding of this area of corporate law.

Study Tips

Before an individual can participate in corporate change and defend his/her investment, he/she must understand the major guiding principles and law that controls the areas of proxy fights, mergers, acquisitions, tender offers, and defenses to corporate takeovers. Understanding the following terms and principles is essential to meaningful participation in any of these corporate events. This short outline and glossary of terms is divided into subject areas.

Proxy Solicitation

proxy voting – shareholders have the right to vote by proxy. A proxy is a means by which a shareholder authorizes another person to represent him or her and vote his or her shares at a shareholders' meeting. This is common in large corporations.

proxy card – a written document signed by a shareholder that authorizes another person to vote the shareholder's shares.

Section 14(a) of the Securities Exchange Act of 1934 gives the SEC the authority to regulate the solicitation of proxies.

proxy statement – anyone soliciting proxies must prepare a proxy statement that fully describes (1) the matter for which the proxy is being solicited, (2) who is soliciting the proxy, and (3) any other pertinent information.

Section 14(a) prohibits misrepresentations or omissions of a material fact in proxy materials.

proxy contests – when shareholders oppose the actions of incumbent directors and management, they may challenge the management in a proxy contest in which both sides solicit proxies.

reimbursement of expenses – because proxy contests can be very expensive, the incumbent management can obtain reimbursement from the corporation if the contest concerns an issue of corporate policy. The dissenting group can get reimbursed only if it wins the proxy contest.

SEC's proxy rules – shareholders who own less than $5 million in stock of a company may communicate with other shareholders without filing proxy solicitation materials with the SEC. Companies seeking proxies must unbundle the propositions so that the shareholders can vote on each separate issue. Performance charts must be included in annual reports. Companies must provide tables in their annual reports that summarize executive compensation.

Mergers and Acquisitions

Mergers, consolidations, share exchanges, and sale of assets are friendly in nature. Both corporations have agreed to the combination of corporations or acquisition of assets.

merger – occurs when one corporation is absorbed into another corporation and ceases to exist. The corporation that continues is the surviving corporation. The other is the merged corporation. Shareholders of the merged corporation receive stock or securities of the surviving corporation.

consolidation – occurs when two or more corporations combine to form an entirely new corporation. Modernly, consolidations are a rarity.

share exchanges – when one corporation (parent corporation) acquires all the shares of another corporation (subsidiary corporation) and both corporations retain their separate legal existence.

required approvals for a merger – a merger requires (1) the recommendation of the board of directors of each corporation and (2) an affirmative vote of the majority of shares of each corporation that is entitled to vote.

articles of merger or share exchange – must be filed with the secretary of state. The secretary of state will then issue a certificate of merger or share exchange to the surviving corporation. If the parent corporation owns 90 percent of the subsidiary corporation, a **short-form merger** procedure may be followed. Approval of shareholders of neither corporation is required for short-form merger. All that is required is approval of the board of directors of the parent corporation.

sale or lease of assets – a corporation may sell, lease, or otherwise dispose of all or substantially all of its property. Such a sale requires (1) the recommendation of the board of directors and (2) an affirmative vote of the majority of the shares of the selling corporation that is entitled to vote.

Dissenting Shareholder Appraisal Rights

Shareholders who object to a proposed merger, share exchange, or sale or lease of all or substantially all of the property of a corporation have a right to have their shares valued by a court and receive cash payment of this value from the corporation.

Williams Act

This act regulates tender offers whether they are made with securities, cash, or other consideration, and establishes certain disclosure requirements and antifraud provisions.

Tender Offer Rules

A tender offer is an offer that an acquirer (tender offeror) makes directly to a target corporation's shareholders in an effort to acquire the target corporation. The shareholders of the target make an individual decision about whether to sell to the tender offeror.

Williams Act – regulates tender offers whether they are made with securities, cash, or other consideration, and establishes certain disclosure requirements and antifraud provisions.

leveraged buyout – the tender offeror uses loans to purchase the stock from the stockholders of the target corporation. These loans, called bridge loans, are usually paid back after assets of the target corporation are sold off. Another source of funds for the tender offeror is the sale of junk bonds, which are risky corporate bonds that pay a higher rate of interest. After the tender offer is completed, the acquiring company is saddled with huge debts. When it merges with the target corporation the resulting company's capital structure consists of a low amount of equity and huge amounts of debt.

Tender offer rules:
1. Offer cannot be closed before 20 days after the commencement of the tender offer.
2. Offer must be extended for 10 days if the tender offer increases the number of shares that it will take or the price it will pay.

3. **Fair price rule** stipulates that any increase in price paid for shares must be offered to all shareholders, even those who have already tendered their shares.
4. **Pro rata rule** requires that shares must be purchased on a pro rata basis if too many. shares are tendered.

Antifraud Provision

Section 14(e) of the Williams Act – prohibits fraudulent, deceptive, or manipulative practices in connection with tender offers.

Fighting a Tender Offer

The incumbent management of a target corporation may desire to oppose a tender offer. Management may engage in a variety of activities to impede or defeat the tender offer. Some of these include:

1. **Persuasion of shareholders** – media campaigns used to oppose the tender offer
2. **Delaying lawsuits** – suits filed alleging antitrust or securities violations to buy time
3. **Selling a crown jewel** – selling an asset that makes the target corporation less attractive
4. **White knight merger** – merger with friendly party that will leave target intact
5. **Pac-Man tender offer** – target makes tender offer for the tender offeror
6. **Adopting a poison pill** – strategy built into articles of incorporation, bylaws, contracts, or leases whereby large payouts or termination of contracts become effective if the corporation changes hands
7. **Issuing additional stock** – issuing more stock makes tender offeror buy more shares
8. **Creating Employee Stock Ownership Plan (ESOP)** – block of stock owned by employees is used to oppose acquirer in proxy fight
9. **Flip-over and flip-in rights plans** – allows stockholders to buy twice the value in stock to make company too expensive to buy
10. **Greenmail and standstill agreements** – target pays premium to get back shares from tender offeror

Business Judgment Rule

Fiduciary duty – the duty the directors of a corporation owe to act carefully and honestly when acting on behalf of the corporation

Business judgment rule – a rule that protects the decisions of the board of directors, who act on an informed basis, in good faith, and in the honest belief that the action taken was in the best interests of the corporation and its shareholders.

State Antitakeover Statutes

These are statutes that enacted by state legislatures that protect corporations incorporated in or doing business in the state from hostile takeovers. They are often challenged as being unconstitutional because they violate the Williams Act and the Commerce and Supremacy Clauses of the U.S. Constitution.

The Exon-Florio Law

The Exon-Florio Law of 1988, as amended by the Byrd-Exon Amendment of 1992, mandates the president of the United States to suspend, prohibit, or dismantle the acquisition of U.S. businesses by foreign investors if there is credible evidence that the foreign investor might take action that threatens to impair the national security.

Refresh Your Memory

The following exercises will enable you to refresh your memory as to the key principles and concepts given to you in this chapter. Read each question carefully and put your answer in the blanks provided. Review the chapter material for any question you miss or are unable to remember.

1. Name two things that corporate shareholders have a right to vote on. _____

_____

2. The proxy holder is often a _____ or an _____ of the corporation.

3. Section 14(a) of the Securities Exchange Act of 1934 prohibits _____ misrepresentations or _____ of material fact in the proxy materials.

4. Shareholder resolutions cannot exceed _____ words.

5. The corporation that continues after a merger is the _____ corporation.

6. A _____ occurs when two or more corporations combine to form an entirely new corporation.

7. A share exchange occurs when a _____ corporation acquires all the shares of the _____ corporation and both corporations retain their separate legal existence.

8. Articles of merger or share exchange must be filed with the _____ ___ _____.

9. If the parent corporation owns 90 percent of the subsidiary corporation, a _____-_____ merger procedure may be followed.

10. Offers whereby each shareholder makes an individual decision about whether to sell his/her shares is known as _____ _____ offers.

11. The _____ Act is an amendment to the Securities Exchange Act of 1934 that regulates _____ offers.

12. The _____ _____ rule stipulates that any increase in price paid for shares under a tender offer must be offered to all shareholders, even those who have already tendered their shares.

13. The use of borrowed money to purchase stock from the shareholders of a target corporation is often referred to as a _____ _____.

14. Mergers with friendly parties that promise to leave the target corporation and/or its management intact are known as _____ _____ mergers.

15. The agreement of the tender offeror to abandon his tender offer and not purchase any additional stock is called a _____ agreement.

Critical Thought Exercise

Blue Cab Co. was merged into Atlantic Cab Corp., with Atlantic being the surviving corporation in the merger. Atlantic did not take over any of the cabs owned by Blue because they were old and in disrepair. Blue Cab was poorly run and owed over $600,000 to Valley Bank for cab purchases. Blue Cab also owed over $60,700 to Fleet Gas Co. for fuel purchased by its employees. Blue Cab is owed $43,000 by Broadway Actors Transportation, Inc. (BAT) for limousine services rendered pursuant to a contract. Blue Cab has already commenced suit against BAT for breach of contract. Valley Bank and Fleet Gas brought a suit against Atlantic for payment of the debts. The board of directors of Atlantic refused to honor the debts of Blue Cab because the purpose in taking over Blue Cab was to eliminate a competitor. Atlantic had no desire to acquire the assets of Blue Cab Co. Atlantic argued that it had never agreed to assume any debt owed by Blue Cab.

What is the effect of the merger and will Valley Bank and Fleet Gas be able to recover breach of contract damages from Atlantic? Can Atlantic maintain the suit against BAT?

Answer:

_____
_____
_____
_____
_____
_____
_____
_____
_____
_____
_____
_____
_____
_____
_____

Practice Quiz

True/False

1. ____ A proxy prohibits other people from voting on their behalf at the shareholders' meeting. [p. 587]

2. ___ Material misrepresentations in proxy materials can result in civil and criminal actions by the Department of Justice. [p. 588]

3. ___ Insurgent shareholders may challenge incumbent management in a proxy contest. [p. 588]

4. ___ The SEC has little to no authority on whether a resolution can be submitted to shareholders. [p. 589]

5. ___ Most shareholder resolutions have a slim chance of being enacted because large-scale investors usually support management. [p. 589]

6. ___ A merger occurs when one corporation becomes separate from another and exists on its own. [p. 590]

7. ___ Consolidations are not used very often today because it is generally advantageous for one of the corporations to survive. [p. 591]

8. ___ A corporation is limited on what it may sell, lease, or otherwise dispose of. [p. 592]

9. ___ If a parent corporation owns 90 percent or more of a subsidiary corporation, a short-form merger procedure may be followed to merge the two corporations. [p. 592]

10. ___ A target corporation is the corporation that is proposed to be acquired in a tender offer situation. [p. 594]

11. ___ A shareholder who has been injured by a violation of Section 14(e) of the Williams Act can sue the wrongdoer for damages. [p. 595]

12. ___ Most tender offers are conservative in their purchases of stock in the target corporation before making an offer just in case it is not accepted. [p. 596]

13. ___ The business judgment rule helps to protect the decisions of the board of directors of a corporation. [p. 597]

14. ___ Antitakeover statutes help protect corporations from tender offers. [p. 598]

15. ___ The Exon-Florio Law mandates the president of the United States to suspend, prohibit, or dismantle the acquisition of U.S. businesses by foreign investors if there is credible evidence that the foreign investor might take action that threatens to impair the "national security." [p. 599]

16. ___ The Exon-Florio law and the regulations that it contains defines "national security" so that there is no doubt as to what is in question. [p. 599]

17. ___ Selling a crown jewel makes the target corporation less attractive to the tender offeror. [p. 596]

18. ___ When objecting to a short-form merger, objecting shareholders may dissent and obtain payment of the fair value of their shares. [p. 593]

19. ___ Two consolidated corporations are called merged corporations and they cease to exist with the new corporation being called a consolidated corporation. [p. 591]

20. ___ In a share exchange, both corporations merge. [p. 591]

Multiple Choice

21. Proxy solicitations are regulated by the Securities and Exchange Act of 1934 under [p. 587]
    a. Section 10(b).
    b. Section 14(a).
    c. Section 14(e).
    d. Section 16(a).

22. A written document signed by a shareholder that authorizes another person to vote the shareholder's shares is a [p. 587]
    a. proxy contest.
    b. proxy statement.
    c. proxy card.
    d. share exchange.

23. A shareholder's proxy can be granted to [p. 587]
    a. only another shareholder.
    b. officers only.
    c. officers or directors only.
    d. anyone.

24. Which of the following states the information that must be contained in a proxy statement? [p. 587]
    a. the matter for which the proxy is being solicited and who is soliciting the proxy
    b. the matter for which the proxy is being solicited and an analysis of the likelihood of success of the proxy contest
    c. the name of the party soliciting the proxy and an analysis of the likelihood of success of the proxy contest
    d. none of the above

25. Which of the following applies to shareholder resolutions? [p. 589]
    a. A shareholder has the right to have the shareholder resolution included in the corporation's proxy materials if it involves a policy issue, relates to corporate business, and doesn't involve the payment of dividends.
    b. Most shareholder resolutions have a slim chance of being enacted.
    c. Shareholder resolutions can cause a corporation to change the way it does business.
    d. all of the above

26. Which best represents who is the winner of a proxy contest? [p. 588]
    a. The side that receives the greatest number of votes wins.
    b. If there are more shareholders than directors, the shareholders win the contest.
    c. The board of directors wins the proxy contest.
    d. The officers win the proxy contest.

27. A transaction in which two corporations combine such that afterwards neither of the combining corporations continues to exist, but that a third corporation is formed is a [p. 591]
    a. merger.
    b. consolidation.
    c. purchase of assets.
    d. share exchange.

28. What is required for an ordinary merger or share exchange? [p. 592]
    a. the recommendation of the board of directors or each corporation
    b. the affirmative vote of the majority of shares of each corporation that is entitled to vote
    c. The approved articles of merger or share exchange must be filed with the secretary of state.
    d. all of the above

29. In a typical situation, a shareholder is allowed to exercise a right of appraisal in conjunction with [p. 593]
    a. regular mergers.
    b. short-form mergers.
    c. sale or lease of substantially all of the corporate assets.
    d. all of the above

30. Jungle Corporation purchases a large bloc of shares in Harvest Corporation as its first step in an attempt to take over Harvest. The management of Harvest immediately purchases a similar size bloc of shares in Jungle and notifies it of Harvest's intent to take over Jungle. This defensive tactic is an example of [p. 596]
    a. a flip-over plan.
    b. selling a crown jewel.
    c. adopting a poison pill.
    d. a Pac-Man tender offer.

Short Answer

31. Give two examples of tactics used by incumbent management in defending against hostile tender offers. [p. 596] _____
    _____
    _____

32. When media campaigns are organized to convince shareholders that a tender offer is not in their best interest, this is known as [p. 596] _____
    _____

33. What is an ESOP? [p. 596] _____
    _____
    _____

34. What is a merger? [p. 590] _____
    _____
    _____

35. Describe what happens in a share exchange. [p. 591] _____

_____

_____

36. What approvals are required for a regular merger? [p. 592] _____

_____

_____

37. What are flip-over and flip-in rights plans? [p. 596]_____

_____

38. When too many shares are tendered, what rule applies? [p. 595] _____

39. What are dissenting shareholder appraisal rights? [p. 593] _____

_____

_____

40. Describe a tender offer. [p. 594] _____

_____

41. What is meant by greenmail? [p. 596] _____

_____

42. What is required by the pro rata rule? [p. 595] _____

_____

43. What is prohibited by Section 14(e) of the Williams Act? [p. 595] _____

_____

44. What is the business judgment rule? [p. 597] _____

_____

_____

45. If a corporation places additional stock on the market, how does this impact a tender offer? [p. 596] _____

_____

Answers to Refresh Your Memory

1. election of directors and mergers (answers will vary) [p. 587]
2. director or officer [p. 587]
3. material omissions [p. 588]
4. 550 [p. 589]
5. surviving [p. 590]
6. consolidation [p. 591]
7. parent, subsidiary [p. 591]
8. secretary of state [p. 592]
9. short-form [p. 592]
10. hostile tender [p. 594]
11. Williams, tender [p. 595]

12. fair price [p. 595]
13. leveraged buyout [p. 595]
14. white knight merger [p. 596]
15. standstill [p. 596]

Critical Thought Exercise Model Answer

A merger involves the legal combination of two or more corporations in a manner that only one of the corporations continues to exist. When Blue Cab merged into Atlantic, Atlantic continued as the surviving corporation while Blue Cab ceased to exist as an entity. After the merger, Atlantic would be recognized as a single corporation, possessing all the rights, privileges, and powers of itself and Blue Cab Co. Atlantic automatically acquired all the assets and property of Blue Cab without the necessity of formality or deeds. The shareholders of Blue Cab receive stock or securities of Atlantic or other consideration as provided in the plan of merger. Additionally, Atlantic becomes liable for all of Blue Cab's debts and obligations. Lastly, Atlantic's articles of incorporation are deemed amended to include any changes that are stated in the articles of merger.

In a merger, the surviving corporation obtains the absorbed corporation's preexisting obligations and legal rights. If the merging corporation had a right of action against a third party, the surviving corporation can bring or maintain a suit after the merger to recover the merging corporation's damages. Atlantic will inherit Blue Cab's right to sue BAT and will be entitled to recover whatever damages Blue Cab was entitled to collect.

Answers to Practice Quiz

True/False

1. False   The proxy authorizes another person—the proxy holder—to vote the shares at the shareholders' meeting.
2. True   Shareholders who are injured by material misrepresentation can sue the wrongdoer and recover damages.
3. True   Insurgent shareholders may challenge the incumbent management in a proxy contest.
4. False   The SEC rules on whether a resolution can be submitted to shareholders.
5. True   Most shareholder resolutions have a slim chance of being enacted because large-scale investors usually support management.
6. False   A merger occurs when one corporation is absorbed into another corporation and ceases to exist.
7. True   Today, consolidations are not used very often because it is generally advantageous for one of the corporations to survive.
8. False   A corporation may sell, lease, or otherwise dispose of all or substantially all of its property in other than the usual and regular course of business.
9. True   If a parent corporation owns 90 percent or more of the outstanding stock of another corporation known as the subsidiary corporation, a short-form merger procedure may be followed to merge the two corporations.
10. True   The corporation that is proposed to be acquired in a tender offer situation is the target corporation.
11. True   A shareholder who has been injured by a violation of Section 14(e) can sue the wrongdoer for damages.
12. False   Most tender offerors purchase a bloc of stock in the target corporation before making an offer.

13. True   The business judgment rule protects the decisions of a board of directors.
14. False   Antitakeover statutes are aimed at protecting corporations from hostile takeovers.
15. True   The Exon-Florio law mandates the president of the United States to suspend, prohibit, or dismantle the acquisition of U.S. businesses by foreign investors if there is credible evidence that the foreign investor might take action that threatens to impair the "national security."
16. False   The Exon-Florio Law and the regulations adopted thereunder do not define the term "national security."
17. True   Selling a crown jewel is a tactic that makes the target corporation less attractive to the tender offeror.
18. True   Objecting shareholders are provided a statutory right to dissent to a short-form merger whereby they may obtain payment of the fair value of their shares.
19. True   Two consolidated corporations are called merged corporations and cease to exist.
20. False   In a share exchange, both corporations retain (not merge) their separate legal existence.

Multiple Choice

21. B   Answer B is the correct answer as this section promotes full disclosure during the proxy solicitation process. Answer A is a section relating to insider trading. Answer C is the section prohibiting fraud in the proxy solicitation process. Answer D relates to a section that prohibits short-swing profits in the sale of securities by insiders.
22. C   The proxy is sent to the corporation and states the shareholder's voting wishes.
23. D   Any person may be authorized to act as a proxy. Answers A, B, and C state choices that may be selected by a shareholder, but they are too restrictive because anyone can be chosen.
24. A   The disclosure must contain these two items. Answers B and C are incorrect because an analysis of the likelihood of success is subjective and is not required. Answer D is not correct because a correct answer is available.
25. D   Answers A, B, and C are all new rules that were adopted in 1992 by the SEC. Therefore, Answer D is the correct answer.
26. A   Answer A is the correct answer as the side that receives the greatest number of votes is the winner of a proxy contest. Answers B, C, and D are all incorrect as they are all nonsensical since the proxy contest hinges on the greatest number of votes which none of these answers address.
27. B   Consolidation is correct. This form of business combination is seldom used today. Answer A is not correct because one corporation continues to exist in a merger. Answers C and D are incorrect because both corporations continue to exist when there is a purchase of assets or share exchange.
28. D   Answer D is correct as answers A, B, and C all state what is required for an ordinary merger or share exchange.
29. D   Appraisal rights apply to mergers, a share exchange, or sale or lease of all or substantially all of the property of the corporation. Objecting shareholders are provided a statutory right to dissent and obtain payment of the fair value of their shares. Answers A, B, and C are partially correct, but D is the correct answer because all choices are correct.

30. D   In a Pac-Man or reverse tender offer, the target makes a tender offer for the tender offeror. Answer A is not correct because a flip-over allows stockholders to buy twice the value in stock to make the company too expensive to buy. Answer B is not correct because there has been no sale of a valuable asset by Harvest. Answer C is not correct because this was an act by Harvest management, not a strategy built into the articles of incorporation, bylaws, or contracts of Harvest.

Short Answer

31.   adopting a poison pill and issuing additional stock (answers will vary) See page 596 of your text for multiple strategies and tactics used by incumbent management in defending against hostile tender offers.

32.   persuasion of shareholders

33.   ESOP is an Employee Stock Option Plan which helps keep the corporation intact as the employees have a vested interest.

34.   A merger occurs when one corporation is absorbed into another corporation and ceases to exist. Title to all assets of the merged corporation passes to the surviving corporation without formality or deeds.

35.   In a share exchange, both corporations retain their separate legal existence. The parent corporation owns all the shares of the subsidiary corporation.

36.   A merger requires (1) the recommendation of the board of directors of each corporation and (2) an affirmative vote of the majority of shares of each corporation that is entitled to vote.

37.   The short-form procedure can be used if the parent corporation owns 90 percent or more of the outstanding stock of the subsidiary corporation. It is a simple procedure because the only approval that is needed is from the board of directors of the parent corporation.

38.   The pro rata rule applies.

39.   Shareholders who object to a proposed merger, for example, have a right to have their shares valued by a court and receive cash payment of this value from the corporation.

40.   A tender offer is an offer that an acquirer makes during a hostile takeover directly to a target corporation's shareholders in an effort to acquire the target corporation. The shareholders each make an individual decision about whether to sell their shares to the tender offeror.

41.   Greenmail is the purchase by a target corporation of its stock from an actual or perceived tender offeror at a premium.

42.   The pro rata rule requires that shares must be purchased on a pro rata basis if too many shares are tendered.

43.   Section 14(e) prohibits fraudulent, deceptive, or manipulative practices in connection with tender offers.

44.   It is a rule that protects the decisions of the board of directors, who act on an informed basis, in good faith, and in the honest belief that the action taken was in the best interests of the corporation and its shareholders.

45.   It impacts the tender offer, as the placing of additional stock on the market increases the number of outstanding shares that the tender offeror must purchase in order to gain control of the target corporation.

Chapter 39

LIMITED LIABILITY COMPANIES AND LIMITED LIABILITY PARTNERSHIPS

Chapter Overview

The main focus of this chapter is the formation, operation, and thorough explanation of the business entity called a limited liability company (LLC). A limited liability company is a hybrid company of sorts in that it has some of the desirable characteristics of general partnerships, corporations, and limited corporations. The interesting fact about the LLC is that the owners are allowed to manage the business and yet have limited liability. Further, it is allowed to be taxed as a partnership. Since it does offer so many advantages, it is a very favorable way for new business entrepreneurs to begin their ventures. This chapter also provides a further exploration of partnerships, with an emphasis on limited partnerships and their formation as well as the differentiation between limited and general partners. Additionally, this chapter discusses the limited liability partnership and the partners' liability if involved in the same.

Objectives

Upon completion of the exercises in this chapter, you should be able to:
1. Explain what comprises a limited liability company.
2. Explain the procedure for organizing a limited liability company.
3. Explain what is necessary to convert an existing business to an LLC.
4. Compare operating a business as an LLC as opposed to an S corporation.
5. Differentiate between a member-managed limited liability company and a manager-managed limited liability company.
6. Decide and discuss when members and managers owe fiduciary duties of loyalty and care to the limited liability company.
7. Discuss what is meant by a limited partnership.
8. Explain the difference between a limited and a general partner.
9. Explain the requirements for forming a limited partnership.

Practical Application

You should be able to recognize the benefits from conducting a newly organized business in the form of a limited liability company. Your previous studies of partnerships will aid you in reaching a decision as to the form your own business may want to take. If you are not planning on operating a business, not only is this chapter useful for general information but, it will give you insight on the choices available as well as why a company may choose to function in this manner from a tax, liability, and management perspective. For the student who wants to operate a business, the basic partnership explanations will be an invaluable tool in determining the type of business operation that would be best in light of an individual's circumstances.

Helpful Hints

It is important to keep in mind that the Uniform Limited Liability Company Act is responsible for codifying the limited liability company law. Further, its primary goal is to establish a comprehensive limited liability company law that is uniform throughout the United States. Since it is vital to this type of business, it is crucial to realize that it is your foundation toward learning this area of the law.

A limited liability company is much like a work of unique art that begins much like an ordinary piece of work, but develops into a creation that others would like to have too. As you go through the study tips section, keep in mind that as with all forms of business, a limited liability company will need to be organized with articles of organization, time limits set, capital contributions noted, its management set in place, and of course the duties of those operating under the company umbrella. Using your imagination to compare the characteristics of the limited liability company to an artistic endeavor will help to make the material enjoyable as well as manageable to learn.

Finally, it is helpful to review the previous study guide chapter on general partnerships, as it provides a solid foundation for this chapter to build upon. It is best to study this material in a methodical fashion in order for the information that is given to be of maximum benefit.

Study Tips

General Information for You to Remember

- It is important to remember that limited liability companies are created by **state law.**
- A large number of states have adopted the **Uniform Limited Liability Company Act** which sets forth the laws concerning formation, operation, and termination of the LCC.
- A limited liability company is referred to as an LLC and is a **separate legal entity** separate from its members.
- Limited liability companies can sue or be sued, enter into or enforce contracts, transfer and hold title to property, and be civilly as well as criminally liable under the law.
- Owners are called **members** and members usually are not personally liable to third parties for debts obligations and liabilities of an LLC beyond their capital contribution.
- Debts and obligations of the LLC are entirely those of the LLC.

Why Do Business as an LLC?

- If you were to **compare an LLC to an S Corporation**, you would learn that the S corporations have several undesirable restrictions concerning who can be shareholders, how many shareholders, and the percentage of stock that may be owned, whereas the LLC has none of these limitations.

- In **comparing an LLC to a general partnership**, members of the LLC have limited liability instead of personal liability for the obligations of the general partnership.

- Finally, in **viewing an LLC against a limited partnership**, the LLC allows all members to take part in management of the business with limited liability to its members. The limited partnership, however, requires at least one general partner who is personally liable for the partnership's obligations. Further, limited partners may not take part in the management of the business.

Formation of an LLC

A limited liability company may be organized for any lawful purpose. An example would be a real estate development company. Beware: an LLC cannot operate the practice of certain professions, such as doctors or lawyers. However, these professionals can conduct business as a limited liability partnership.

There are some important considerations to keep in mind when choosing a name for the LLC. They are as follows:

- The name must have the words **"limited liability company"** or limited company or the abbreviations L.L.C. or LLC or LC.
- Trademark issues must be explored so as to not violate federal law.
- The issue of similar names must be explored to determine if use of the name chosen is even a viable option for the new LLC.
- If the name is available, it may be reserved for 120 days while the organization process of the LLC is being completed.

Articles of Organization

An LLC can conduct business in all states, but may only be registered in one. An LLC is usually organized in the state that it will be transacting most of its business in.

Articles of organization must be delivered to the secretary of state's office for filing. If the articles are in **proper form**, the articles will be filed. The articles must contain the name and address of the initial LLC office, the name and address of the initial agent for service of process, the name and address of each organizer, and whether the LLC is a term LLC and, if yes, then the specifics of the term must be stated. Additionally, the articles must state whether the LLC is to be manager-managed and the identity and address(es) of the manager(s) given. Finally, the articles must indicate whether the members will be personally liable for the debts and obligations of the LLC.

Duration

An LLC is either an at-will LLC or a term LLC. The term LLC states how long the LLC will exist. An at-will LLC does not state a term of duration.

Capital Contribution

A member's capital may consist of money, real property, personal property, intangible property, services performed, and so on. A member's death will not excuse a member's obligation to contribute, nor will disability or the inability to perform.

Certificate of Interest

This acts like a stock certificate as it indicates a member's ownership interest in the LLC.

Operating Agreement

There are a variety of rights, duties, and rules that you need to be aware of as they pertain to the transacting of business by an LLC.

Operating Agreement – Members of an LLC may enter into an operating agreement to regulate the affairs of the company and the conduct of its business.

Conversion of an Existing Business to an LLC

Many businesses convert to operate as a limited liability company. They do so to obtain tax benefits as well as utilize the limited liability benefit. In order to convert, ULLCA at section 902 requires that there be a statement of terms contained in an agreement of conversion, that the agreement be approved by all parties and owners concerned, and that the articles of organization be filed with the secretary of state indicating the prior business name and form of operation.

Division of LLC's Profits and Losses

Generally speaking, a member has the right to an equal share in the LLC's profits. The members of the LLC may agree otherwise though.

Members' Distributional Interest

The ownership share of a member is called the distributional interest. A member's interest may be transferred.

Member-Managed and Manager-Managed LLCs

An LLC is considered member-managed unless it is deemed manager-managed in the articles of organization. In a member-managed LLC, all of the LLC member have agency authority to enter into contracts and bind the LLC. In a manager-managed LLC, however, only designated managers have agency authority to enter into contracts and bind the LLC and they also have equal rights in the management of the LLC business. Note that the contracts must be in the ordinary course of business or ones in which the LLC has authorized.

Compensation and Reimbursement

An LLC is required to reimburse members and manager for payments made on behalf of the LLC and to indemnify managers and members for liabilities incurred.

Fiduciary Duties of Loyalty and Care Owed to LLC

Regardless if a person is a member or a manager of an LLC, the duties of loyalty and care are fiduciary duties owed to the LLC. The duty of loyalty means that the parties must act honestly which means no usurping of LLC opportunities, no self-dealing, no competition with the LLC, and no making of secret profits. There is a limited duty of care owed to the LLC which means that a manager or member must not engage in a known violation of the law, grossly negligent conduct, reckless conduct, a known violation of the law, etc. Liability for ordinary negligence will be assessed against a member or manager of an LLC.

Dissolution of an LLC

A member may disassociate him or herself from the LLC by withdrawing from both a term and an at-will LLC. Wrongful disassociation from an at-will LLC occurs if the power to withdraw is absent from the operating agreement. Once a member is disassociated, he or she may not participate in the management of the LLC. Also, the member's duties of loyalty and care to the LLC end upon disassociation. Rightful disassociation requires the LLC's purchase of the disassociated member's distributional interest.

Notice of Disassociation

An LLC may give constructive notice of a disassociating member by filing a statement of disassociation with the secretary of state.

Continuation of an LLC

An LLC may be continued in two instances. The first situation is where the **members unanimously vote** prior to the expiration of the current LLC. The second situation is where there is **a simple majority vote** of the at-will LLC members.

Winding Up an LLC's Business

Winding up is "the process of preserving and selling the assets of the LLC and distributing the money and property to creditors and members." Assets of the LLC must be used to pay the **creditors first**, followed by any surplus left over to be distributed to the members in equal shares unless the operating agreement provides otherwise. After dissolution and winding up, articles of termination may be filed with the secretary of state.

Limited Liability Partnership

All partners are given limited liability. Professionals commonly use this type of partnership. A limited partnership must have a minimum of one general partner and one limited partner. Any person may be a limited partner. There is no tax paid at the partnership level.

Articles of Partnership

Limited liability partnerships must be created formally by filing articles of partnership with the secretary of state in which the LLP is organized. The LLP is a domestic LLP in the state in which it is organized. If an LLP does business in other states, it must register as a foreign LLP in the state(s) it wants to conduct business.

Liability Insurance Required

The use of an LLP as a means of conducting business is restricted in many states to certain types of professionals such as lawyers and accountants. Most state laws mandate that LLPs carry a minimum of one million dollars of liability insurance to cover negligence, wrongful acts, and other misconduct by employees and partners of the company.

Refresh Your Memory

The following exercise will enable you to refresh your memory on the rules and principles presented to you in this chapter. Read each question twice and place your answer in the blanks provided. Review the chapter material for any question you miss or are unable to remember.

1. The _____ of an LLP have limited liability.

2. Limited liability companies are creatures of _____ law, not _____ law.

3. An unincorporated business entity that combines the most favorable attributes of general partnerships, limited partnerships, and corporations is called a _____ _____ _____.

4. Owners of LLCs are usually called _____.

5. An LLC is taxed as a _____ unless it elects to be taxed as a _____.

6. An LLC has the same powers as an _____ to do all things necessary or convenient to carry on its business or affairs.

7. Managers of LLCs are not _____ liable for the debts, obligations, and liabilities of the LLC they manage.

8. A person who intentionally or unintentionally causes injury or death to another person is called a _____.

9. An LLC can be _____ in only _____ state, even though it can conduct business in all other states.

10. How is an LLC formed? _____ _____

11. An LLC is an _____ _____ unless it is designated as a _____ LLC.

12. What types of capital contribution can members give to an LLC? _____ _____

13. A document that evidences a member's ownership interest in an LLC is a _____.

14. If a company wants to change its existing business to an LLC, what type of agreement must it file in satisfying part of the requirements set forth in ULLCA Section 902? _____ _____

15. What part of the profits does a member of an LLC have a right to share in? _____ _____

Critical Thought Exercise

Hal, Mike, Sue, and Gail are college friends and have talents in the areas of e-commerce, marketing, product development, and business management. The four meet with a fifth friend, Karl, who is a second–year law student. They explain to Karl their idea for an Internet business that sends local cuisine from participating restaurants and caterers to students and military personnel who are away from home and miss their favorite food. Karl draws up the articles of organization as his contribution to being brought in as a member of the new limited liability company, "GoodGrub.com, LLC." Karl then decides that he does not have the time or energy to devote to the business. Karl declines the offer to join the LLC. Sue files the articles of organization with the secretary of state, but there is no mention of whether GoodGrub.com will be a manager-managed or member-managed LLC. It was originally anticipated that Hal would be the manager of the LLC but all four members begin to manage Good Grub.com and it is very successful. To keep up with demand and to expand their business into new markets, Hal and Gail secure a $200,000 loan from Jefferson Bank. When Hal is dividing up yearly profits, he gives each member 15 percent of the profits and invests the other 40 percent in the expansion efforts.

The resulting dispute over profits and quick expansion of the business leads to turmoil. GoodGrub.com is unable to meet its financial obligations. Mike, Sue, and Gail sue Hal for a full distribution of profits. Jefferson Bank sues GoodGrub.com, Hal, Mike, Sue, and Gail to recover the $200,000 loan.

Did Hal have the authority to withhold distribution of profits? Who is liable to Jefferson Bank?

Answer:

_____

_____

_____

_____

_____

_____

_____

_____

_____

_____

_____

_____

_____

_____

_____

_____

_____

_____

_____

_____

Practice Quiz

True/False

1. ____   An LLC is an unincorporated entity. [p. 605]

2. ____   A member's ownership interest in an LLC is called a distributional interest. [p. 612]

3. ____   In a member-managed LLC, each member has proportionate rights based on initial capital contribution in the management of the business of the LLC. [p. 613]

4. ____   A manager may be a member of an LLC or a nonmember. [p. 613]

5. ____   An LLC is a member-managed LLC unless it is designated as a manager-managed LLC. [p. 613]

6. ____   The designation of an LLC as member-managed or manager-managed is important in determining who has authority to bind the LLC to contracts. [p. 614]

7. ____   An LLC without a specified term of duration is called an at-will LLC. [p. 610]

8. ____   A term LLC is another name for an at-will LLC. [p. 610]

9. ____   Profits and losses from an LLC do not have to be distributed in the same proportions. [p. 612]

10. ____   An LLC provides unlimited liability to all members even though they participate in management of the business. [p. 613]

11. ____   An LLC is unique in that it is not bound to contracts that members or managers have properly entered into on its behalf in the ordinary course of business. [p. 615]

12. ____   An LLC may be continued an additional specified term by unanimous vote of all the members by filing an amendment to the articles of organization with the secretary of state. [p. 617]

13. ____   The articles of partnership for an LLP is a private document. [p. 618]

14. ____   The use of an LLP is unrestricted and any business can use it as a way to conduct business. [p. 618]

15. ____   Many states require LLPs to carry a minimum of $500 of liability insurance that covers negligence, wrongful acts, and misconduct by partners or employees of the LLP. [p. 618]

16. ____   An LLC is a manager-managed LLC unless it is designated as a member-managed LLC in the articles of organization. [p. 616]

17. ____   If Henrietta as a member of an LLC disassociates herself from a term LLC before the expiration of a specified term, her action will be considered wrongful. [p. 616]

18. ___ One way for the Tiny Toy Company to give notice of a member's disassociation is by filing a statement of disassociation with the secretary of state. [p. 617]

19. ___ When winding up the LLC, its assets must be applied to first pay off creditors. [p. 617]

20. ___ A member's distributional interest may not be transferred in whole or in part. [p. 616]

Multiple Choice

21. Which of the following is true with respect to a member's notice of disassociation from an LLC? [p. 617]
    a. The disassociating member has apparent authority to bind the LLC to contracts in the ordinary course of business with a couple of exceptions.
    b. An LLC can give constructive notice of a member's disassociation by filing a statement of disassociation with the secretary of state.
    c. The notice of disassociation is effective against any person who later deals with the disassociated member, whether the person was aware of the notice or not.
    d. all of the above

22. Which of the following does not need to be placed in the articles of organization of an LLC? [p. 610]
    a. the name and address of the initial agent for service of process
    b. the name and address of each organizer
    c. the name and address where the limited partnership will be primarily operating
    d. whether the LLC is a term LLC and if so, the term specified

23. A member's obligation to contribute capital is not excused by [p. 611]
    a. the member's death.
    b. the member's disability
    c. the member's inability to perform
    d. all of the above

24. Before Edward decides upon the way he wants to operate a business, he comes to you and asks about the powers that an LLC has. Which of the following best describes these powers? [p. 606]
    a. An LLC has the power to waive the distribution of assets upon winding up the LLC.
    b. An LLC has the power to own and transfer personal property.
    c. An LLC has the power to refuse reimbursement to members and managers for payments made on behalf of the LLC for business expenses.
    d. all of the above

25. What does a member's disassociation from an LLC terminate? [p. 616]
    a. the member's right to participate in management
    b. the member's right to act as an agent of the LLC
    c. the disassociating member's duties of loyalty and care to the LLC
    d. all of the above

26. If a motorcycle dealer is operating as a term LLC and wants to continue the LLC, which of the following applies to the continuation of the motorcycle dealer's LLC at the expiration of its term? [p. 617]
    a. The members of the motorcycle dealer's LLC may vote before the expiration date of the LLC for an additional specified term.
    b. The members must unanimously vote and file an amendment to the articles of organization with the secretary of state stating this fact.
    c. The LLC may continue as an at-will LLC utilizing a simple majority vote by the LLC members.
    d. all of the above

27. If Brenda wants to operate an LLC under the name of Brenda's Beautiful Babes, which of the following must she be aware of? [p. 610]
    a. She must be aware that LLCs have no restrictions on shareholders.
    b. She must be aware that the name she has chosen must contain the words limited liability company or an acceptable abbreviation as per the ULLCA code.
    c. She must be aware that the name she has chosen may not make a profit for her.
    d. She must be aware that trademark issues are not applicable to her.

28. Which of the following may Harry use as his capital contribution to the LLC that he is a member of? [p. 611]
    a. patents or other intangible property
    b. promissory notes
    c. services performed
    d. all of the above

29. If a general partnership wants to convert to operate as an LLC, which of the following requirements must be met? [p 612]
    a. There must be an agreement of conversion.
    b. The conversion must be approved by the parties or by a percentage of the owners.
    c. The articles of organization must be filed and state the prior form of business and its name before the conversion.
    d. all of the above

30. Which of the following apply to a limited liability partnership (LLP)? [p. 617]
    a. One general partner has to be personally liable for the debts and obligations of the partnership.
    b. All partners are limited partners who stand to lose only their capital contribution should the partnership fail.
    c. At least two partners are personally liable for the debts and obligations of the partnership beyond their capital contribution.
    d. all of the above

Short Answer

31. An LLC is liable for any _____ or _____ caused to anyone as a result of a wrongful act or omission by a member, a manager, an agent, or an employee of the LLC who commits the wrongful act while acting within the ordinary course of business of the LLC or with the authority of the LLC. [p. 608]

32. The certificate of interest acts the same as a _____ _____ issued by a corporation. [p. 611]

33. An operating agreement of the LLC may be _____ by the approval of all members unless otherwise provided for in the agreement. [pp. 611-612]

34 Losses from an LLC are shared _____ unless otherwise agreed. [p. 612]

35. If the LLC has chosen to be taxed as a partnership, the losses from an LLC flow to member's _____ income tax returns. [p. 612]

36. A member's distributional interest in an LLC is _____ property and may be transferred in _____ or in _____. [p. 612]

37. The transfer of an interest in an LLC does not entitle the transferee to become a _____ of the LLC or to exercise any _____ of a member. [p. 612]

38. What does the duty of loyalty owed to an LLC encompass? [p. 615] _____
_____

39. If a member of an LLC engages in a violation of the law, it would be breaching his/her duty of _____ to the LLC. [p. 615]

40. What effect does a member's disassociation from an LLC have on the member with respect to the LLC? [p. 617] _____
_____

41. How may an LLC terminate its existence after it has dissolved or wound up its operations? [p. 617]
_____

42. When does the existence of an LLC begin? [p. 610] _____

43. How may the articles of organization be amended in an LLC? [p. 610] _____
_____

44. What is an agreement of conversion? [p. 612] _____
_____

45. When starting a new LLC, the organizers must chose a name for the entity that contains the words _____ _____ _____ [p. 610].

Answers to Refresh Your Memory

1. owners [p. 605]
2. state; federal [p. 605]
3. limited liability company (LLC) [p. 605]
4. members [p. 606]
5. partnership; corporation [p. 606]
6. individual [p. 606]

7. personally [p. 608]
8. tortfeasor [p. 609]
9. organized; one [p. 610]
10. by delivering articles of organization to the office of the secretary of state of organization for filing [p. 610]
11. at-will term [p. 610]
12. A member's capital contribution may take the form of personal or real property, money, tangible or intangible property, etc. (Answers will vary.) [p. 611]
13. a certificate of interest [p. 611]
14. agreement of conversion [p. 612]
15. an equal share [p. 612]

Critical Thought Exercise Model Answer

GoodGrub.com could be either a member-managed or manager-managed LLC depending upon the wishes of its members. An LLC is a member-managed LLC unless it is designated as a manager-managed LLC in its articles of organization. The articles of organization do not specify whether the members named any member as a manager. Therefore, GoodGrub.com will be deemed a member-managed LLC. As a member-managed LLC, all members have agency authority to bind the LLC to contractual obligations. An LLC is only bound to contracts that are in the ordinary course of business or that have been authorized. As members, Hal and Gail have full authority to enter into the loan agreement with Jefferson Bank. Their action will legally obligate GoodGrub.com to repay the loan from GoodGrub.com assets.

The failure of GoodGrub.com to observe company formalities does not create personal liability for the members for the debts of the LLC. There is no mention of how the four members were running the company, but nothing in the facts would allow Jefferson Bank to seek repayment of the loan from the individual members.

Though an LLC will usually have a written operating agreement that regulates the affairs of the company and how the members will run the company, the agreement may be oral. Though Hal was the anticipated manager of GoodGrub.com, the facts state that all four members assumed a management role and the articles of organization did not specify a manager-managed LLC. All four members have the right to determine how the profits will be divided or reinvested. Any matter relating to the business of the LLC is decided by a majority vote of the members. Hal is obligated to acquiesce in the desires of the other three members as to how the profits should be divided.

Answers to Practice Quiz

True/False

1. True   An LLC is an unincorporated business entity.
2. True   A member's ownership interest in an LLC is called a distributional interest.
3. False   In a member-managed LLC, each member has equal rights in the management of the business of the LLC, irrespective of the size of his or her capital contribution.
4. True   A manager may be a member of an LLC or a nonmember.
5. True   An LLC is a member-managed LLC unless it is designated as a manager-managed LLC.
6. True   A manager must be appointed by a vote of a majority of the members.
7. True   An at-will LCC is one in which there is no specified term or duration.

8. False   These are two different terms with different meanings. An at-will LCC has no specified term or duration whereas a term LLC has a specified term or duration.
9. True   Profits and losses from an LLC do not have to be distributed in the same proportions.
10. False   An LLC provides **limited** liability to all members, even though they participate in management of the business.
11. False   An LLC is bound to contracts that members or managers have properly entered into on its behalf in the ordinary course of business.
12. True   An LLC may be continued for an additional specified term with the unanimous vote of all of the members and the filing of an amendment to the articles of organization with the secretary of state, stating this fact.
13. False   An LLP's articles of partnership is a public not a private document.
14. False   The use of LLPs are restricted to certain types of professionals, such as accountants, lawyers, and doctors.
15. False   Many states require LLPs to carry a minimum of $1 million of liability insurance that covers negligence, wrongful acts, and misconduct by partners or employees of the LLP.
16. False   An LLC is a member-managed LLC unless it is designated as a manager-managed LLC.
17. True   Disassociation from an LLC by a member prior to the expiration of the specified term is considered wrongful.
18. True   Constructive notice of a member's disassociation from an LLC is accomplished by filing a statement of disassociation with the secretary of state.
19. False   A member does have the right to an equal share in the LLC's profits.
20. False   A member's distributional interest may be transferred in whole or in part.

Multiple Choice

21. D   Answer D is the correct answer as answers A, B, and C all are correct statements regarding a member's disassociation from an LLC.
22. C   Answer C is the correct answer as the name and address of where a limited partnership will be operating is not relevant to the information that must be contained in the articles of organization of an LLC. Answers A, B, and D all provide information that does need to be placed in the articles of organization and therefore are all incorrect answers as per the question.
23. D   Answer D is the correct answer as a member's obligation to contribute capital to the LLC is not excused by all of the statements reflected in answers A, B, and C.
24. B   Answer B is the correct answer as it properly states one of the powers that Edward's LLC would have should he choose that form of business to operate under. Answer A is incorrect as it is a false statement. Answer C is incorrect as an LLC does not have the power to refuse reimbursement for expenses on behalf of the LLC. Answer D is incorrect based on the reasoning given above.
25. A   Answer A is the correct answer as it correctly states ULLCA Section 409 (d)'s requirement of good faith and fair dealing and what it encompasses. Answer B is incorrect as members are held to achieve the objectives of the LLC as per the duty of good faith and fair dealing. Answer C is incorrect as the duty not to usurp an LLC opportunity would come under the duty of loyalty. Answer D is incorrect based on the reasoning given above.
26. D   Answer D is the correct answer as a member's disassociation from an LLC terminates all of the things stated in answers A, B, and C.

27. B Answer B is the correct answer as under ULLCA Section 105 (a), Brenda must make sure that the proper words or abbreviations are included in the name that she has chosen. Answer A is inapplicable to Brenda's operation and concern for the name she has chosen. Answer C is incorrect as it is not relevant in terms of the name she has chosen for her LLC. Answer D is incorrect as trademark issues are applicable and important to her, especially when choosing a name for an LLC.

28. D Answer D is the correct answer as answers A, B, and C all state acceptable forms of capital contributions that Harry utilize.

29. D Answer D is the correct answer as answers A, B, and C all state requirements that must be met in order for a general partnership to be able to convert to an LLC.

30. B Answer B is the correct answer as it is the only true statement regarding an LLP. Answer A is incorrect as there does not have to be a general partner who is personally liable for the debts and obligations of the partnership. Answer C is incorrect as none of the partners are personally liable for the debts and obligations of the partnership beyond there initial contribution. Answer D is incorrect for the reasons given above.

Short Answer

31. loss; injury
32. stock certificate
33. amended
34. equally
35. individual
36. personal; whole; part
37. member; right
38. Only the designated managers have authority to bind the LLC to contracts in a manager-managed LLC.
39. care
40. A member's disassociation terminates that member's right to take part in the management of the LLC, act as an agent of the LLC, or conduct any of the LLC's business.
41. It may terminate its existence by filing articles of termination with the secretary of state.
42. It begins when the articles of organization are filed.
43. The articles may be amended by filing articles of amendment with the secretary of state.
44. It is a document that states the terms of converting an existing business to an LLC.
45. limited liability company

Chapter 40

FRANCHISES AND SPECIAL FORMS OF BUSINESS

Chapter Overview

Franchising has become an extremely important method of distributing goods and services to the public. Franchises account for 25 percent of all retail sales. This method of doing business can have risks for the franchisee, especially when the franchise contract is drafted solely by the franchisor. There, bulk of law controlling the area of franchises and franchise agreements comes from contract law (Chapters 9-17), sales (Chapters 18-21), and intellectual property law (Chapter 7). This chapter discusses the creation of a franchise, the rights and duties that arise in a franchise relationship, and the termination of a franchise.

Objectives

Upon completion of the exercises in this chapter, you should be able to:
1. Describe a franchise.
2. List the various forms of franchises.
3. Understand the disclosures required by state and federal disclosure rules.
4. Explain the rights and duties of the parties to a franchise agreement.
5. Explain the various forms of franchise fees.
6. Understand how intellectual property rights apply to franchises.
7. Describe the contract liability of franchisors and franchisees.
8. Understand the tort liability of franchisors and franchisees.
9. Describe the remedies available in conjunction with the termination of a franchise.
10. Describe international franchise formation.

Practical Application

You should be able to understand and analyze the problem areas in franchise formation. This will entail applying contract law principles to the special issues created in a franchise arrangement. Further, you will be able to comprehend the rights and liabilities associated with use of trademarks, service marks, patents, copyrights, trade name, and trade dress as they apply to franchises.

Helpful Hints

The biggest problem areas concerning franchises are in the areas of genuineness of assent, discharge, remedies, and intellectual property. It will be very helpful to review the pertinent chapters presented earlier in this test as part of the overall understanding of franchises.

Study Tips

The study of franchise law requires a basic understanding of the following concepts and principles:

franchise – a business arrangement that is established when one party licenses another party to use the franchisor's trade name, trademarks, patents, copyrights, and other property in the distribution and selling of goods and services.

distributorship franchise – the franchisor manufactures a product and licenses a retail franchisee to distribute the product to the public.

processing plant franchise – the franchisor provides a secret formula or process to the franchisee, and the franchisee manufactures the product and distributes it to retail dealers.

chain-style franchises – the franchisor licenses the franchisee to make and sell its products or distribute services to the public from a retail outlet serving an exclusive territory.

area franchise – the franchisor grants the franchisee a franchise for an agreed-upon geographical area within which the franchisee may determine the location of outlets.

Uniform Franchise Offering Circular (UFOC) – a uniform disclosure document that requires the franchisor to make specific presale disclosures to prospective franchisees.

FTC franchise rule – a rule set out by the FTC that requires franchisors to make full presale disclosures to prospective franchisees.

quality control standards – standards or performance and product quality set forth in the franchise agreement to preserve the franchisor's market name and reputation.

training requirements – employee standards that meet the franchisor's specifications.

covenant not to compete – an agreement by the franchisee to not compete with the franchisor for a period of time in a specified area after the termination of the franchise.

franchise fees – fees payable by the franchisee as set forth in the franchise agreement.

initial license fee – a lump-sum payment to obtain a franchise.

royalty fee – fee for use of franchisor's trade name, property, and assistance that is computed as a percentage of the franchisee's gross sales.

assessment fee – fee for advertising and administrative costs.

lease fee – payment for land or equipment leased from the franchisor.

cost of supplies – payment for supplies purchased from the franchisor.

breach of franchise agreement – aggrieved party can sue the breaching party for rescission of the agreement, restitution, and damages.

trademarks – a distinctive mark, symbol, name, word, motto, or device that identifies the goods or products of the trademark owner.

service mark – mark, symbol, name, word, motto, or device that identifies the service provided by the service mark owner.

trade secrets – ideas that make a franchise successful but that do not qualify for trademark, patent, or copyright protection.

tort liability – franchisors and franchisees are liable for their own torts.

independent contractor status – the franchisee is an independent contractor, preventing the franchisor from being liable for the franchisee's torts and contracts.

apparent agency – agency that arises when a franchisor creates the appearance that a franchisee is its agent when in fact an actual agency does not exist.

termination of franchise – the franchise agreement usually states reasons or conditions that allow the franchisor or franchisee to terminate the franchise agreement.

termination "for cause" – termination of franchise agreement for failure to fulfill the duties imposed by the agreement.

wrongful termination – termination of the franchise agreement when cause for such action does not exist.

Refresh Your Memory

The following exercises will enable you to refresh your memory of the principles presented in this chapter. Read each question carefully and place your answer in the blanks provided. Review the chapter material for any question you miss or are unable to remember.

1. A franchise is established when one party _____ another party to use the franchisor's name, trademarks, patents, copyrights, and other property.

2. The term franchise refers to

   _____

   _____

3. In a _____ _____ franchise, the franchisor provides a secret formula or process to the franchisee, and the franchisee manufactures the product and distributes it to retailers.

4. In a _____-_____ franchise, the franchisor licenses the franchisee to make and sell its products or distribute services to the public from a retail outlet serving an _____ territory.

5. A uniform disclosure document that state franchise administrators developed which requires a franchisor to make specific presale disclosures to prospective franchisees is a

   _____.

6. The FTC franchise rule requires franchisors to make full _____ disclosures to prospective franchisees.

7. The act which provides for the registration of trademarks and service marks associated with the federal Patent and Trademark Office in Washington, D.C., by franchisors and others is the _____ _____ _____.

8. The misappropriation of a trade secret is called _____ _____.

9. The franchisor's most important assets are its _____ and _____.

10. An initial license fee is a _____ payment for the privilege of being granted a franchise.

11. Most franchise agreements permit a franchisor to terminate the franchise _____ _____.

12. Which clauses in a franchise agreement are generally held to be void on the ground that they are unconscionable? _____

13. The franchisor deals with the franchisee as an _____ _____.

14. Franchisors are liable for their own _____ and _____.

15. What is a strategic alliance? _____

Critical Thought Exercise

Federal Foods, Inc., runs company stores and sells franchises for its restaurants, known as Yum-Me's. Under the franchise agreement with Federal, each franchisee agrees to hire and train all employees and staff in strict compliance with Yum-Me's standards and policies. Federal employs area supervisors who are responsible for reviewing and approving all personnel actions at any restaurant within the four restaurant chains owned by Federal. This includes comprehensive policies relating to employee hiring, training, discipline, and work performance. As part of the franchise agreement, Federal retains the right to terminate any franchise that violates the rules or policies of the franchisor. In practice, the area managers approve the hiring of whatever employees the franchisee desires and the policies that the franchisee desires to create and implement. The area managers inspect each franchise, dictate the food production method, and enforce customer relations policies that were created by Federal.

Ned, a crew leader at a Yum-Me's restaurant, has repeatedly harassed female employees and customers by making rude and explicit sexual remarks. The franchisee and the on-site manager have done nothing to correct Ned's behavior. Two female employees and three customers have filed suit in federal court against Federal based upon Ned's acts. Federal argues that a franchisor cannot be held liable for harassment by franchise employees. Who should prevail?

Answer:

_____

_____

_____

_____

_____
_____
_____
_____
_____
_____
_____
_____
_____
_____
_____
_____
_____
_____

Practice Quiz

True/False

1. ___ Strategic alliances are often used to enter foreign markets. [p. 623]

2. ___ Licensing permits one business to use another business's trademarks, service marks, brand names, and other intellectual property in selling goods or services. [p. 623]

3. ___ Generally the franchisor and the franchisee are established as the same corporation. [p. 623]

4. ___ The FTC franchise rule requires that franchisors make full presale disclosures to prospective franchisees. [p. 625]

5. ___ The area franchisee is called a chain-style franchise. [p. 624]

6. ___ Pepsi-Cola is a processing plant franchise. [p. 624]

7. ___ A fee for such things as advertising and promotional campaigns and administrative costs is a lease fee. [p. 627]

8. ___ The expansion into other countries through franchising means that U.S. franchisors can expand internationally without the huge capital investments. [p. 628]

9. ___ An apparent agency is formed when a franchisor leads a third person to believe that the franchisee is its agent. [p. 631]

10. ___ One disadvantage to franchising is that the franchisor can reach new lucrative markets. [p. 623]

11. ___ The FTC requires the registration of the disclosure document prior to its use. [p. 625]

12. ___ Area franchises are often used when a franchisor wants to enter a market in another country. [p. 624]

13. ___ The required notice that covers a franchisor's required disclosure statement must be in at least 12-point boldface type on the cover. [p. 626]

14. ___ Joint venturers often form a third corporation to operate the joint venture. [p. 633]

15. ___ Strategic alliances have the same protection as mergers, joint ventures, or franchising, and sometimes they are dismantled. [p. 635]

16. ___ A benefit to having a franchise is that the franchisee has access to the franchisor's knowledge and resources while running an independent business. [p. 623]

17. ___ Franchises are risky as consumers are never totally sure of uniform product quality. [p. 623]

18. ___ A wrongdoer who violates FTC disclosure rules is subject among other things to an injunction against further franchise sales as well as civil fines. [p. 626]

19. ___ Unreasonable covenants not to compete are void. [p. 627]

20. ___ Anyone who uses a trademark without permission may be sued for trademark infringement. [p. 626]

Multiple Choice

21. A franchise is established when [p. 623]
    a. the physical building to the franchise is complete.
    b. it has prepared its articles of incorporation.
    c. one party licenses another party to use the franchisor's trade name, trademarks, etc., and the other property in distribution and selling of goods and services.
    d. when a joint venture agreement has been prepared.

22. A business arrangement where one party allows another to use its name, trademark, or sell its products in its business is known as a [p. 623]
    a. sole proprietorship.
    b. partnership.
    c. franchise.
    d. joint venture.

23. Which of the following are types of franchises? [p. 624]
    a. a trade name
    b. distributorship
    c. a trademark
    d. copyright

24. An automobile dealership is [p. 624]
    a. a chain-style franchise.
    b. a distributorship franchise.
    c. a processing plant franchise.
    d. an area franchise.

25. The party to whom a franchise is granted is the [p. 623]
    a. franchisor.
    b. franchisee.
    c. principal.
    d. agent.

26. Bogart enters into an agreement whereby he receives an exclusive territory covering four states in which he is authorized to establish a plant to manufacture Fizzy Beer. After receiving Fizzy's secret formula, Bogart begins making beer. This is a [p. 624]
    a. processing plant franchise.
    b. chain-style franchise.
    c. distributorship.
    d. none of the above

27. For which type of franchise does the franchisee have the right to grant franchises to others within a geographical area? [p. 624]
    a. processing plant franchise
    b. chain-style franchise
    c. area franchise
    d. distributorship franchise

28. The FTC franchise rule requires franchisors to [p. 625]
    a. share profits with franchisees.
    b. supply advertising and administrative services to the franchisee.
    c. supply trademarks and secret formulas to the franchisee.
    d. make presale disclosures to prospective franchisees.

29. Which of the following items is considered to be a franchise fee? [p. 627]
    a. cost of supplies involved in payment for supplies purchased from franchisor
    b. a royalty for the continued use of the franchisor's trade name and property
    c. an initial license charge for the privilege of being granted a franchise
    d. all of the above

30. Which of the following remedies is generally available for breach of a franchise agreement? [p. 628]
    a. damages
    b. restitution
    c. rescission
    d. all of the above

Short Answer

31. A corporation owned by two or more joint ventures that is created to operate a joint venture is known as a [p. 633] _____

32. How are franchise fees paid? [p. 627] _____

_____

_____

33. How does a prospective franchisee obtain a franchise? [p. 626]

_____

_____

_____

34. List two hurdles that would convince a company to use franchising in a foreign market instead of company owned stores. [p. 628]

_____

_____

_____

35. Why are quality control standards important to the franchisor? [p. 627] _____

_____

36. Why are termination-at-will clauses in franchise agreements generally held to be void? [p. 627]

_____

_____

37. What is the purpose of an assessment fee and what does it cover? [p. 627]

_____

_____

38. What is the majority rule regarding whether or not a franchise agreement must be in writing? [p. 627]

_____

39. If Bob's Baked Goods, a franchise, holds a trade secret regarding its bountiful bagel recipe and Betty's Bagels uses the recipe to attract business, what may Bob's Baked Goods sue for? [p. 626]

_____

_____

40. What is a trade secret? [p. 626]

_____

_____

41. List two examples of information that must be disclosed in the Uniform Franchise Offering Circular. [p. 625]

_____

_____

42. Why is a franchisor normally not liable for the torts of a franchisee? [p. 628]

_____

_____

43. What is an apparent agency? [p. 631]

   _____

   _____

44. If the Walt Disney Corporation allows McDonald's to sell plastic figurines from its movies in McDonald's Happy Meals, this would be known as [p. 632]

   _____.

45. Who is liable for the debts and obligations of a joint venture partnership? [p. 633]

   _____

   _____

Answers to Refresh Your Memory

1. licenses [p. 623]
2. both the agreement between the parties and the franchise outlet [p. 623]
3. processing plant [p. 624]
4. chain-style; exclusive [p. 624]
5. Uniform Franchise Offering Circular [p. 625]
6. presale [p. 625]
7. Lanham Trademark Act   [p. 626]
8. unfair competition [p. 626]
9. name; reputation [p. 627]
10. lump-sum [p. 627]
11. for cause [p. 627]]
12. termination-at-will [p. 627]
13. independent contractor [p. 628]
14. contracts; torts [p. 628]
15. an arrangement between two or more companies in the same industry in which they agree to ally themselves to accomplish a designated objective [p. 635]

Critical Thought Exercise Model Answer

Liability for Ned's acts may be imputed to Federal because of an agency relationship that exists between Federal and the employees of the franchisee. An agency results from the manifestation of consent by one person to another so that the other will act on his or her behalf and subject to the control of the principal, and consent by the agent to so act. An agency agreement may be evidenced by an express agreement between the parties, or it may be implied from the circumstances and conduct of the parties. The principal's consent and right to control the agent are the essential elements of an agency relationship.

The franchise agreement in this case required adherence to comprehensive policies and rules for the operation of the restaurant. Federal enforces these rules and policies by sending area managers to inspect each franchisee. The area managers also approve the hiring and training of each employee. Federal controls the franchisee and the employees of Yum-Me's Restaurant by retaining the right to terminate the franchise agreement. Most importantly, the franchise agreement gave Federal the right to control the franchisees in the very parts of the franchisee's business that resulted in the injuries to the plaintiffs, these parts being the areas of employee training and discipline. Federal, the franchisor, may be held liable under an agency theory for the intentional acts of sexual discrimination by the employee of its franchisee.

Answers to Practice Quiz

True/False

1. True   Strategic alliances are often used to enter foreign markets.
2. True   Licensing permits one business to use another business's trademarks, service marks, and trade names.
3. False   Generally the franchisor and the franchisee are established as separate corporations.
4. True   The FTC franchise rule is a rule set out by the FTC that requires franchisors to make full presale disclosures to prospective franchisees.
5. False   An area franchise is called a subfranchisor not a chain-style franchise.
6. True   Pepsi and other soft drinks are processing plant franchises.
7. False   A fee for such things as advertising and promotional campaigns and administrative costs is an assessment fee not a lease fee.
8. True   The expansion into other countries through franchising means that U.S. franchisors can expand internationally without huge capital investments.
9. True   An apparent agency is created when a franchisor leads a third person into believing that the franchisee is its agent.
10. False Reaching new lucrative markets is an advantage, not a disadvantage for a franchise.
11. False The FTC does not require the registration of the disclosure document prior to use.
12. False The quality control standards in the franchise agreement provide protection.
13. True   The FTC notice must appear in at least 12-point boldface type on the cover of a franchisor's required disclosure statement to prospective franchisees.
14. True   Joint venturers often form a third corporation to operate the joint venture.
15. False Strategic alliances do not have the same protection as mergers.
16. True   One of the advantages to franchising is that the franchisee has access to the franchisor's knowledge and resources while running an independent business.
17. False Another advantage to franchising includes the fact that consumers are assured of uniform product quality.
18. True   If a franchisor violates FTC disclosure rules, the wrongdoer is subject to an injunction against further franchise sales, civil fines, and an FTC civil action on behalf of injured franchisees to recover damages from the franchisor that were caused by the violation.
19. True   Unreasonable covenants not to compete are void.
20. True   Anyone who uses a mark without authorization may be sued for trademark infringement.

Multiple Choice

21. C   Answer C is the correct answer as it correctly states when a franchise is established. Answer A is incorrect as it is not a legal reason of when a franchise is established. Answer B is incorrect as it is not a true statement as to when it is established. Answer D is incorrect as the establishment of a franchise is not dependent upon a joint venture agreement.
22. C   The property is used under a license. Answer A has no license arrangement with another business. Answer B is a single business entity, while a franchise involves two businesses. Answer D is not correct because a joint venture is not an ongoing business.
23. B   Answer B is the correct answer as it is a type of franchise whereby the franchisor manufactures a product and licenses a retail dealer to distribute the product to the public. Answers A, C, and D are incorrect as these are types of intellectual property.

24. B   Answer B is correct because in a distributorship franchise, the franchisor manufactures the product and the franchisee distributes the product within a geographical area. This is how automobiles are distributed. Answer A is not correct because the franchisee makes the product in a chain-style franchise and sells it at an outlet. Answer C is not correct because the automobile dealer is not given a secret formula from which to produce cars. Answer D is not correct because the dealership does not set up multiple dealerships within a geographical area as part of the franchise.

25. B   The franchisee receives the license from the franchisor. Answer A is not correct because the franchisor grants the franchise. Answers C and D are not correct because a franchise is not an agency relationship.

26. A   The processing plant franchise involves licensing a formula to allow the franchisee to manufacture and distribute a product to the franchisor's specifications. Answer B is not correct as a chain-style franchise makes and sells products from a retail outlet. Answer C is incorrect because a distributor does not make the product. Answer D is incorrect because Answer A is correct.

27. C   The area franchise gives the franchisee the rights to select the placement and number of franchises within its geographical area. Answers A, B, and D are incorrect because the franchisee in these franchises has no authority to grant an additional franchise to another.

28. D   The full disclosures must have cautionary language concerning risk and facts concerning anticipated profits. Answers A, B, and C are not requirements of the FTC rule, but may be part of the duties of a franchisor under specific franchise agreement.

29. D   Answer D is correct because Answer A lists a cost of supplies which are franchise fees; and Answer B describes a royalty fee; and Answer C is the initial license fee for a franchise. Therefore all of the answers given are correct.

30. D   Answers A, B, and C are all possible remedies a party may seek if there is a breach of the franchise agreement. Therefore, Answer D is the correct answer.

Short Answer

31. joint venture corporation
32. Franchise fees are usually stipulated in the franchise agreement.
33. The prospective franchisee must apply to the franchisor for a franchise.
34. Restrictions in some countries prohibit 100 percent ownership of a business by a foreign investor. Many companies lack the expertise and cultural knowledge to enter many foreign markets. The foreign franchisee would provide national ownership and knowledge of the business and cultural climate in a particular foreign market.
35. The franchisor's most important assets are its name and reputation. The quality control standards set out in a franchise agreement are intended to protect those assets.
36. The termination-at-will clauses are found to be unconscionable and void based on the money and effort the franchisee has spent on the franchise.
37. An assessment fee pays for advertising and promotional campaigns and administrative costs. It is billed either as a flat monthly fee or a percentage of gross sales.
38. The majority rule reflects that franchise agreements must be in writing as per the Statute of Frauds.
39. damages and to obtain an injunction to prohibit further unauthorized use of the trade secret
40. Trade secrets are ideas that make a franchise successful but that do not qualify for trademark, patent, or copyright protection.
41. description of the franchisor's business and balance sheets (answers will vary)
42. A franchisee is usually set up as an independent contractor in the franchise agreement. Because there is no agency relationship, the franchisor is not liable for the torts committed by the franchisee.

43. agency that results when a franchisor creates the appearance that a franchisee is its agent when in fact an actual agency does not exist
44. licensing
45. Each venturer is liable.

Chapter 41

INVESTOR PROTECTION AND ONLINE SECURITIES TRANSACTIONS

Chapter Overview

The stock market crash of 1929 motivated Congress to make investor security a priority. Up to this time, fraud and dealing on inside information was rampant. Congress passed two key pieces of legislation in an attempt to remedy the problem. The Securities Act of 1933 requires public disclosure of material information by companies and others who issue securities to the public. The Securities Exchange Act of 1934 was enacted to prevent fraud in the trading of securities, especially insider trading. Additional statutes have been passed by the states. These federal and state statutes are still the cornerstone that forms the protection for investors in securities. This chapter examines these protections.

Chapter Objectives

Upon completion of the exercises in this chapter, you should be able to:
1. Describe public offerings of securities and registration of those securities with the SEC.
2. Describe the exemptions from registration.
3. Explain insider trading violations of Section 10(b) of the Securities Exchange Act of 1934.
4. Discuss how tippers and tippees become liable for insider trading.
5. Understand how the SEC is addressing Internet stock fraud.
6. Describe criminal liability for violation of the federal securities laws.
7. Explain the meaning of short-swing profits that violate Section 16(b) of the SEC Act of 1934.
8. Describe investor protection under the Commodity Exchange Act.

Practical Application

This chapter has application from several viewpoints. The investor, which includes individuals, employee groups, and businesses, needs to know the protections that are available under federal and state law that prevent fraudulent loss of their investment. Those persons and businesses that issue securities, and the people who work for them, need to know the standards to which the federal government will hold them. Lastly, the unsuspecting investor needs to know what acts may make them part of a fraudulent or criminal transaction so that liability can be avoided. Unless each person familiarizes himself with federal securities law, there is an increased risk of financial loss, damage to his business, and exposure to criminal prosecution.

Helpful Hints

The securities laws are geared to regulating transactions involving the issuance and trading of securities. Focus on the individual transaction or related transactions and the information that was exchanged or withheld as to the particular transaction. It is the improper release or suppression of material information and trading upon that information that triggers the application of the securities laws.

Study Tips

The following terms and sections of the securities laws are key to understanding the material in this chapter. You should develop a working knowledge of these key terms and pay attention to how they are applied by the courts.

security – (1) An interest or instrument that is common stock, preferred stock, a bond, a debenture, or a warrant; (2) an interest or instrument that is expressly mentioned in securities acts; and (3) an investment contract.

Securities Exchange Act of 1934 – A federal statute that primarily regulates the trading in securities.

Securities Act of 1933 – A federal statute that primarily regulates the issuance of securities by a corporation, a general or limited partnership, an unincorporated association, or an individual.

Securities and Exchange Commission (SEC) – A federal administrative agency that is empowered to administer federal securities laws. The SEC can adopt rules and regulations to interpret and implement federal securities laws. Violations of these rules carry civil and criminal penalties.

registration statement – Document that an issuer of securities files with the SEC that contains required information about the issuer, the securities to be issued, and other relevant information.

prospectus – A written disclosure document that must be submitted to the SEC along with the registration statement and given to prospective purchasers of the securities.

prefiling period – A period of time that begins when the issuer first contemplates issuing securities and ends when the registration statement is filed. The issuer may not condition the market by engaging in a public relation campaign during this period.

waiting period – A period of time that begins when the registration statement is filed with the SEC and continues until the registration statement is declared effective. The issuer is encouraged to condition the market during this time.

posteffective period – The period that begins when the registration statement becomes effective and runs until the issuer either sells all of the offered securities or withdraws them from sale.

final prospectus – A final version of the prospectus that must be delivered by the issuer to the investor prior to or at the time of confirming a sale or sending a security to a purchaser.

exempt securities transactions – Transactions that are exempt from registration but must still comply with antifraud provisions of the federal securities laws.

nonissuer exemption – An exemption from registration that permits average investors from registering the resale of their securities because they are not the issuer, an underwriter, or a dealer in securities.

intrastate offerings exemption – An exemption from registration that permits local businesses to raise capital from local investors to be used in the local economy without the need to register with the SEC. The three requirements for this exemption are:

1. The issuer must be a resident of the state for which the exemption is claimed.
2. The issuer must be doing business in that state.
3. The purchasers of all securities must be residents of that state.

private placement exemption – An exemption from registration that permits issuers to raise capital from an unlimited number of accredited investors and no more than 35 nonaccredited investors without having to register the offering with the SEC. An accredited investor may be:
1. Any person with a net worth of at least $1 million.
2. Any person who has had an annual income of $200,000 for the previous two years and expects to make $200,000 in the current year.
3. Any corporation, partnership, or business trust with assets of $5 million.
4. Insiders of the issuers, such as officers and directors of corporate issuers and general partners of partnership issuers.
5. Institutional investors such as registered investment companies, pension plans, and colleges and universities.

small offerings exemption – An exemption from registration for the sale of securities not exceeding $1 million during a 12-month period.

restricted securities – Securities that were issued for investment purposes pursuant to the intrastate private placement, or small offering exemption. They cannot be resold for a limited period of time after their initial issue.

Rule 144 – Provides that securities sold pursuant to the private placement or small offering exemptions must be held for one year from the date when the securities are last sold by the issuer.

Rule 147 – Securities sold pursuant to an intrastate offering exemption cannot be sold to nonresidents for a period of nine months.

Rule 144A – The SEC rule permits qualified institutional investors to buy unregistered securities without being subject to the holding periods of Rule 144.

Section 24 of the Securities Act of 1933 – Imposes criminal liability of up to five years in prison for violating the act or the rules and regulations adopted thereunder.

SEC actions for violating 1933 act – the SEC may:
1. issue a consent order
2. bring an action seeking an injunction
3. request disgorgement of profits by the court

Section 12 of the 1933 act – Imposes civil liability against those who violate Section 5 of the act. Under Section 12, a purchaser may rescind the purchase or sue for damages.

Section 11 – A provision of the Securities Act of 1933 that imposes civil liability on persons who intentionally defraud investors by making misrepresentations or omissions of material facts in the registration statement or who are negligent for not discovering the fraud.

Section 10(b) – A provision of the Securities Exchange Act of 1934 that prohibits the use of manipulative and deceptive devices in the purchase or sale of securities in contravention of the rules and regulations prescribed by the SEC.

Rule 10b-5 – A rule adopted by the SEC to clarify the reach of Section 10(b) against deceptive and fraudulent activities in the purchase and sale of securities.

scienter – Means intentional conduct.

Regulation Fair Disclosure – Prohibits companies from leaking important information to securities professionals before the information is disclosed to the public.

insider trading – When an insider makes a profit by personally purchasing shares of the corporation prior to public release of favorable information or by selling shares of the corporation prior to the public disclosure of unfavorable information. **Insiders** are:
1. officers, directors, and employees at all levels of the company
2. lawyers, accountants, consultants, and other agents hired by the company to provide services or work to the company
3. others who owe a fiduciary duty to the company

tipper – A person who discloses material nonpublic information to another person.

tippee – The person who receives material nonpublic information from a tipper.

Liability Provisions of the Securities Exchange Act of 1934

Section 32 – Makes it a criminal offense to willfully violate the 1934 act or the rules or regulations adopted thereunder.

SEC actions – The SEC may enter into consent orders, seek injunctions, or seek disgorgement of profits by court order.

Insider Trading Sanctions Act – Permits the SEC to obtain civil penalty of up to three times the illegal profits gained or losses avoided by insider trading.

Section 16(a) – A section of the Securities Exchange Act of 1934 that defines any person who is an executive officer, a director, or a 10 percent shareholder or an equity security of a reporting company as a statutory insider for Section 16 purposes.

Section 16(b) – A section of the Securities Exchange Act of 1934 that requires that any profits made by a statutory insider on transactions involving short-swing profits belong to the corporation.

short-swing profits – Trades involving equity securities occurring within six months of each other.

Commodity Exchange Act (CEA) – Enacted in 1936 to regulate the trading of commodity futures contracts.

Commodity Futures Trading Commission Act amended the 1936 act significantly.

Section 4b of the CEA – Prohibits fraudulent conduct in connection with any order or contract of sale or any commodity for future delivery.

Commodity Futures Trading Commission – Five-member federal agency appointed by the president to regulate trading in commodities futures contracts.

Refresh Your Memory

The following exercises will enable you to refresh your memory as to the key principles and concepts given to you in this chapter. Read each question carefully and put your answer in the blanks provided. Review the chapter material for any question you miss or are unable to remember.

1. Give two examples of instruments or interests that are commonly known as securities.

   _____

   _____

2. A _____ _____ is a document that an issuer of securities files with the SEC that contains required information about the issuer, the securities to be issued, and other relevant information.

3. A _____ is a written disclosure document that must be submitted to the SEC along with the registration statement and given to prospective purchasers of the securities.

4. The _____ _____ is a period of time that begins when the registration statement is filed with the SEC and continues until the registration statement is declared effective.

5. Regulation A permits issuers to sell up to _____ million of securities to the public during a _____ month period, pursuant to a simplified registration process.

6. All defendants except the issuer may assert a _____ _____ defense against imposition of Section 11 liability.

7. Under Section 24 of the Securities Act of 1933, a violator may be fined up to $_____ or _____ up to _____ years or both.

8. Section 11 of the 1933 act provides for _____ liability for damages when a registration statement on its effective date _____ or _____ a material fact.

9. What may the SEC issue that in effect allows the defendant to agree not to violate securities laws in the future but does not admit to having violated securities laws in the past?

   _____

   _____

10. An issue of securities that does not involve a public offering is exempt from the registration requirements. This exemption is known as the _____ _____ exemption.

11. Section _____ is a provision of the Securities Exchange Act of 1934 that prohibits the use of _____ and deceptive devices in the purchase or sale of securities.

12. _____ means intentional conduct.

13. Why was the Uniform Securities Act adopted?

    _____

    _____

14. The Insider _____ _____ Act permits the SEC to obtain a civil penalty of up to three times the illegal gaines or losses avoided by insider trading.

15. Trades involving equity securities occurring within six months of each other are called _____-_____ profits.

Critical Thought Exercise

Jerry Dallas is a corporate officer for CompuGames (CG), the leading manufacturer of hand-held computer games. The profit margin of CG is greatly impacted by the cost of the microprocessor it purchases for its games from Mini-Micro. Dallas tells his girlfriend, Julie Profit, that she should watch for any announcement of a price increase of 20 percent or more by Mini-Micro and sell her stock in CG if there is such a large price increase. Profit has a friend, Louis Nooze, who works in the public relations department at Mini-Micro. She asks Nooze to tell her if he hears of an announcement of price increases by Mini-Micro. Two days before a 33 percent price increase is to be announced by Mini-Micro, Nooze gives the news to Profit. Profit calls her stockbroker and sells all her stock in CG. When the price increase is announced, CG stock falls from $38 per share to $22 per share. By selling her stock before the announcement by Mini-Micro, Profit realizes a profit of $800,000.

If a stockholder initiates a suit against Dallas, Profit, and Nooze, will any of these people be liable for realizing illegal profits based upon insider trading or misappropriation?

Answer:

_____

_____

_____

_____

_____

_____

_____

_____

_____

_____

_____

_____

_____

_____

_____

_____

_____

_____

Practice Quiz

True/False

1. ___ A security may consist of an investment contract. [p. 640]

2. ___ The Securities Act of 1933 is a federal statute that primarily regulates the trading in securities. [p. 642]

3. ___ Registration statements usually become effective 120 days after they are filed. [p. 642]

4. ___ The SEC has broad discretion and as such passes judgment on the merits of the securities offered. [p. 642]

5. ___ A prospectus is a confidential document that is filed only with the SEC. [p. 642]

6. ___ A prospectus is used as a selling tool by the issuer. [p. 642]

7. ___ The registration period for securities offerings is divided into three time periods. [p. 644]

8. ___ The prefiling period ends when the registration statement is filed. [p. 644]

9. ___ Sale of securities that should have been registered with the SEC but were not violates the Securities Act of 1933. [p. 644]

10. ___ The purpose of the intrastate offerings exemption is to prohibit local businesses from raising capital from local investors that then could be used in the local economy without the need to register with the SEC. [p. 647]

11. ___ The SEC permits companies to issue securities over the Internet. [p. 643]

12. ___ Securities issued by the government and common carriers are exempt from registration. [p. 649]

13. ___ Certain transactions in securities are exempt from registration, even if the type of security may not qualify as an exemption. [p. 647]

14. ___ The Securities Act of 1933 exempts securities transactions not made by an issuer, an underwriter, or a dealer from registration. [p. 647]

15. ___ The intrastate offerings exemption requires that the issuer be a resident of the state for which the exemption is claimed, but the purchasers may reside in any state. [p. 647]

16. ___ An accredited investor may under the private placement exemption include any person with a net worth of at least $1 million. [pp. 647-648]

17. ___ Restricted securities cannot be resold for a limited period of time after their initial issue. [p. 648]

18. ___ Securities sold pursuant to an intrastate offering exemption cannot be sold to nonresidents for a period of two years. [p. 648]

19. ___ A statutory insider is any person who is an executive officer, a director, or a 10 percent shareholder of an equity security of a reporting company. [p. 653]

20. ___ A tipper is not liable for the profits made by a tippee as long as the tipper does not buy or sell any security. [p. 652]

Multiple Choice

21. Which of the following are considered to be securities under the Howery test? [p. 641]
    a. limited partnership interests
    b. pyramid sale schemes
    c. investments in farm animals
    d. all of the above

22. The securities Act of 1933 primarily regulates [p. 645]
    a. short-swing profits.
    b. issuance of securities.
    c. insider trading.
    d. none of the above

23. Which of the following descriptions does not need to be contained in a registration statement? [p. 642]
    a. the securities being offered for sale
    b. the registrant's business
    c. the degree of competition in the industry
    d. the SEC's opinion as to the merits of the securities offered

24. The written disclosure document that must be submitted to the SEC and is given to all prospective investors to enable them to evaluate the financial risk of the investments is called a(n) [p. 642]
    a. registration statement.
    b. prospectus.
    c. tombstone advertisement.
    d. offering statement.

25. The time period of the registration process during which the issuer cannot tout the prospectus to potential purchasers is the [p. 644]
    a. prefiling period.
    b. waiting period.
    c. posteffective period.
    d. all of the above

26. Which of the following is a violation of the Securities Act of 1933? [p. 645]
    a. the use of a manipulative and deceptive device as per 10(b) of the act
    b. the use of fraudulent means in connection of a security
    c. selling securities pursuant to an unwarranted exception
    d. all of the above

27. An exemption from registration that permits local businesses to raise capital from local investors to be used in the local economy without the need to register with the SEC is the [p. 647]
    a. nonissuer exemption.
    b. intrastate exemption.
    c. private placement exemption.
    d. small offering exemption.

28. Which of the following does not apply to the Securities and Exchange Act of 1934? [p. 649]
    a. Its main concern is the regulation of subsequent trading.
    b. It provides for the registration of certain companies with the SEC.
    c. It provides for the regulation of securities exchanges, brokers, and dealers.
    d. It regulates the original issuance of securities.

29. Vista, Inc. issues stock after making a willful misrepresentation in its registration statement based upon misstatements of material fact concerning the financial health of Vista, Inc. Vista has huge debts that are recorded as assets in its financial statement, which was filed as part of the registration statement. Vista may be exposed to a penalty or remedy pursuant to [p. 645]
    a. Section 24 of the Securities Act of 1933.
    b. an SEC consent order.
    c. Section 11 of the Securities Act of 1933.
    d. all of the above

30. Lansing & Bismarck is a consulting firm that specializes in corporate reorganizations. Toji Bismarck learns that Superior Corp., a pharmaceutical company for whom he is doing temporary work, is about to announce that its scientists have developed a totally effective drug that will both prevent and cure lung cancer. Bismarck tells his wife, Sue, to buy the stock. Sue purchases $10 worth of Superior stock. Sue calls her brother, Ned, the next day. Ned purchases $50,000 worth of Superior stock that immediately climbs to $2.5 million when the drug discovery is announced. Sue's stock climbs to $500. Toji is liable for [p. 652]
    a. only the $490 profit made by Sue.
    b. all the profit made by both Sue and Ned, if Ned knew the tip was material inside information.
    c. all the profit made on both Sue's and Ned's trades, regardless of the tippee's knowledge.
    d. none of the profits made on the trades because Toji lacked scienter.

Short Answer

31. What is a security? [p. 640]

    _____

    _____

    _____

32. What descriptions must be contained within a registration statement? [p. 642]

    _____

    _____

    _____

33.   What is the due diligence defense? [p. 645]

_____
_____
_____

34.   What is the Small Corporate Offering Registration Form used for? [p. 645]

_____
_____
_____

35.   What are the three time requirements necessary to qualify for the intrastate offerings exemption? [p. 647]

_____
_____
_____
_____
_____

36.   What is an investment banker? [p. 643]

_____
_____
_____

37.   What is a nonissuer exemption from registration? [p. 647]

_____
_____
_____

38.   Who may be an accredited investor under the private placements or small offering exemptions? [p. 648]

_____
_____
_____
_____

39.   What are restricted securities? [p. 648]

_____
_____

40.   How can a small business raise $1 million or less from the public issue of securities? [p. 645]

_____
_____
_____

41.   What must a defendant show to establish a due diligence defense to a Section 11 violation? [p. 645]

_____
_____
_____

42.	What is prohibited by Section 10(b) of the Securities Exchange Act of 1934? [p. 649]

_____

_____

_____

43.	What is a tippee? [p. 652]

_____

_____

_____

43.	What is required by Section 16(b) of the Securities Exchange Act of 1934? [p. 653]

_____

_____

_____

45.	Violations of sections 10(b) and 10b-5 require scienter. What exactly is scienter? [p. 650]

_____

_____

_____

_____

Answers to Refresh Your Memory

1.	bonds, common stock (answers will vary) [p. 640]
2.	registration statement [p. 642]
3.	prospectus [p. 642]
4.	waiting period [p. 644]
5.	5; 12 [p. 644]
6.	due diligence [p. 645]
7.	$10,000; imprisoned; 5 [p. 645]
8.	civil; misstates; omits [p. 645]
9.	consent order [p. 645]
10.	private placement [p. 647]
11.	10(b); manipulative [p. 649]
12.	Scienter [p. 659]
13.	to coordinate state securities laws with federal securities laws [p. 654]
14.	Trading Sanctions [p. 653]
15.	short-swing [p. 653]

Critical Thought Exercise Model Answer

Under section 10(b) of the Securities Exchange Act of 1934 and SEC Rule 10b-5, persons may be sued and prosecuted for the commission of fraud in connection with the sale or purchase of any security. The 1934 Act prohibits officers and directors from taking advantage of inside information they obtain as a result of their position to gain a trading advantage over the general public. Section 10(b) of the 1934 act and SEC Rule 10b-5 cover not only corporate officers, directors, and majority shareholders but also any persons having access to or receiving information of a nonpublic nature on which trading is based. The key to liability under Section 10(b) and Rule 10b-5 is whether the insider's information is material. A significant change in a company's financial condition would be material information. The cost of an essential part from a supplier would create that significant change.

Jerry Dallas did not act upon inside information in this case, nor did he act as a tipper. The information he gave was general advice as to the strength of his company and the market factors that affected the price of its main product. All he did was advise Profit to watch for any announcements of a price increase from Mini-Micro. He did not provide any insider information regarding CG. Therefore, Dallas will not be liable for the profit realized by Profit.

To find liability for Nooze, his level of knowledge must be established. Though it appears that he is acting as a tipper, the information that he provided is not being used to trade on Mini-Micro stock. There is no information as to whether Profit told him the purpose of wanting to know when a price increase would occur. Under the tipper theory, however, liability is established when the inside information is obtained as a result of someone's breach of a fiduciary duty to the corporation whose shares are involved in the trading. In this case, Nooze owes no fiduciary duty to CG. There is no proof that his information leak hurt Mini-Micro in any way.

Under a theory of misappropriation, both Nooze and Profit may be liable. The misappropriation theory holds that if an individual wrongfully obtains inside information and trades on it for his or her own personal gain, then the person should be held liable because the individual stole information rightfully belonging to another. Profit and Nooze both knew that they were taking information that was material and belonged to Mini-Micro. Liability should be imposed upon Profit because she traded upon this stolen information. Though Nooze also misappropriated the information, there is a lack of evidence as to his knowledge that it would be used for making a trade of CG stock.

Answers to Practice Quiz

True/False

1. True   It may also be the typical stock, bond, debenture, or warrant.
2. False   The Securities Exchange Act of 1934 regulates the trading in securities.
3. False   Registration statements usually become effective 20 business days after they are filed.
4. True   The SEC does not pass judgment on the merits of the securities offered.
5. False   The prospectus must be given to prospective purchasers of the securities.
6. True   Securities offerings must be written in plain English.
7. True   It is divided into three time periods: prefiling, waiting, and posteffective.
8. True   The issuer may not condition the market during this period.
9. True   Sale of securities that should have been registered with the SEC but were not violates the Securities Act of 1933.
10. False The purpose of the intrastate offerings exemption is to permit local businesses to raise from local investors capital to be used in the local economy without the need to register with the SEC.
11. True   The SEC permits companies to issue securities over the Internet.
12. True   Securities issued by any government as well as those issued by common carriers are exempt from registration.
13. True   These transactions are still subject to the antifraud provisions of the federal securities laws.
14. True   Nonissuers, such as average investors, do not have to file a registration statement.
15. False The purchaser must reside in the same state as the issuer.

16. True Accredited investors also include persons who earn $200,000 for two consecutive years and expect to make $200,000 in the current year.

17. True Rule 144 provides that securities sold pursuant to the private placement or small offering exemption must be held for one year.

18. False Rule 147 requires that the securities be held for nine months.

19. True Section 16(a) of the 1934 act defines any person who is an executive officer, a director, or a 10 percent shareholder of an equity security of a reporting company as a statutory insider for Section 16 purposes.

20. False The tipper is liable for all profits made by the tippee.

Multiple Choice

21. D Answers A, B, and C have all been found to be securities under the Howery Act.

23. B Requirements that must be followed by issuers of securities are set forth in this act, such as registration requirements. Answer A is incorrect because short-swing profits are covered by Section 16(b) of the 1934 act. Answer C is incorrect because Section 10(b) of the 1934 act covers inside trading. Answer D is incorrect because choice B is available.

23. D The SEC does not pass upon the merits of the securities offered. Answers A, B, and C must be described in the registration statement.

24. B The prospectus discloses much of the contents of the registration statement and must have some parts written in plain English. Answer A is incorrect because it is a filing with the SEC that does not require the plain English clarity of a prospectus. Answer C is incorrect because it is only an advertisement telling potential investors where they can obtain a prospectus. Answer D relates to Regulation A offerings and requires much less disclosure.

25. A The issuer cannot condition the market and run a public relations campaign during this period. Answers B and C are incorrect because the issuer is expected or required to provide a prospectus during these periods. Answer D is incorrect because Answers B and C are incorrect.

26. C Answer C is the correct answer as selling securities pursuant to an unwarranted exception is a violation of the securities act of 1933, whereas Answers A, B, and D apply to violations of the Securities Exchange act of 1934.

27. B There is not limit on the dollar amount of capital that can be raised as long as the residence requirements are met. Answer A, C, and D are incorrect because they are not restricted to local activity.

28. D Answers A, B, and C are all correct statements, making Answer D the correct answer. If the issuer has taken these precautions, it will not lose its exemption from registration even if isolated transfers of stock occur in violation of the restricted periods.

29. D Answers A, B, and C are all possible sources of remedies or penalties for Vista's conduct. Therefore, Answer D is the correct answer. Section 24 imposes criminal sanctions, while Section 11 imposes civil liability. The SEC may also take actions that include filing suit and seeking an injunction, or requesting the court to order disgorgement of profits.

30. C Toji is liable as the tipper for all profits made by any tippee or remote tippee. Toji's liability is not dependant upon Ned's knowledge of the nature or source of the tip. Answer A is not correct because Toji is liable for the profits of remote tippees. Answer B is not correct because Ned's knowledge is not relevant to Toji's liability. Answer D is not correct because Toji should have known that his tip would be acted upon.

Short Answer

31. A security is (1) an interest or instrument that is common stock, preferred stock, a bond, a debenture, or a warrant; (2) an interest or instrument that is expressly mentioned in securities acts; and (3) an investment contract.

32. A registration statement must contain descriptions of (1) the securities being offered for sale, (2) the registrant's business, (3) the management of the registrant, (4) pending litigation, (5) how the proceeds will be used, (6) government regulation, (7) the degree of competition, and (8) any special risk factors.

33. The due diligence defense is a defense to a Section 11 action that, if proven, makes the defendant not liable.

34. It's a question and answer disclosure form that small businesses can complete and file with the SEC if they plan on raising $1 million or less from the public issue of securities.

35. (1) prefiling period; (2) waiting period; (3) posteffective period

36. These are independent securities companies.

37. Nonissuers, such as average investors, do not have to file a registration statement prior to reselling securities they have purchased. This is because the Securities Act of 1933 exempts securities transactions not made by an issuer, an underwriter, or a dealer from registration.

38. (1) any natural person with a net worth of at least $1 million; (2) any natural person who has an annual income of $200,000 for the past two years and expects to make at least $200,000 in the current year; (3) any corporation, partnership, or business trust with assets in excess of $5 million; (4) insiders of the issuers; (5) certain institutional investors

39. securities that were issued for investment purposes pursuant to the intrastate, private placement, or small offering exemption

40. It can use the simplified process afforded it under Regulation A by using the Small Corporate Offering Registration Form (SCOR), known as Form U-7.

41. The defendant must prove that after reasonable investigation, he or she had reasonable grounds to believe and did believe that, as the time the registration statement became effective, the statements contained therein were true and that there was no omission of material facts.

42. Section 10(b) prohibits the use of manipulative and deceptive devices in the purchase or sale of securities in contravention of the rules and regulation prescribed by the SEC.

43. A tippee is a person who receives material nonpublic information from a tipper.

44. Section 16(b) requires that any profits made by a statutory insider on transactions involving short-swing profits belong to the corporation.

45. Scienter is required for there to be a violation of Section 10(b) and 10b-5. Your chapter defines it as deliberate intentional conduct.

Chapter 42

ETHICS AND
SOCIAL RESPONSIBILITY
OF BUSINESS

Chapter Overview

This chapter provides a clear understanding of the moral principles that determine the conduct of individuals or a group. The five main theories of ethics are thoroughly discussed with case law providing an excellent example of each.

Objectives

Upon completion of the exercises in this chapter, you should be able to:
1. Discuss the meaning of ethics.
2. Define and compare the five main theories of ethics.
3. Discuss the principles of conduct that are necessary for international business.
4. Compare the traditional role of social responsibility of business to the modern trend.
5. Discuss the social responsibility of business.
6. Apply traditional ethics principles to technology such as the Internet.
7. Observe the differences in ethical standards from country to country.

Practical Application

You should be able to recognize the types of ethical behavior being utilized in business based upon your knowledge of the various ethical principles. Additionally, you will have a greater appreciation for the history of this area of the law.

Helpful Hints

It is important to become familiar with the key terms and phrases associated with ethics. Additionally, it is helpful to be familiar with a case example for the theory you are trying to remember. The study tips given below have been organized based on the cases presented in the text.

Study Tips

Ethics

Ethics is a set of moral principles or values that governs the conduct of an individual or a group.

Ethical Fundamentalism

A theory of ethics that says a person looks to an outside source for ethical rules or commands.

Utilitarianism

The concept behind this theory is that people have to choose or follow the rule that provides the greatest good to society.

Kantian Ethics

This theory of ethics is also referred to as duty ethics. In other words, **"do unto others as you would have them do unto you**." In terms of business under this theory, an obligated party must keep his or her part of the bargain as he or she has a moral duty to do so regardless of any detriment that the party may suffer.

Rawl's Social Justice Theory

Under this theory, each person in society is presumed to have entered into a social contract with society in an effort to promote peace and harmony. Those following this theory agree to abide by the rules as long as everyone else also keeps to the rules.

Ethical Relativism

Under this moral theory, individuals have to determine what is ethical using their own intuition or feelings as to what is right or wrong. Due to the subjectivity of what the moral standard is, an individual who adopts ethical relativism cannot be criticized for the way he or she feels. Most philosophers do not find this theory a satisfactory one when it comes to applying it to morals.

Business and Its Social Responsibility

More than ever we are looking at the impact as well as the social responsibility that businesses owe to society as a whole. Traditionally all that was viewed was a cost-benefit analysis and how a business's actions affected profits. Modernly, however, corporations are being held responsible for their actions. The four theories of social responsibility are the maximization of profits, the moral minimum, the takeholder's interest, and corporate citizenship, all of which are discussed individually.

Maximizing Profits

The traditional rule regarding a business and its social responsibility was that it should maximize its profits for the shareholders. Proponents of this theory affirm this philosophy by adding that a business should participate in activities that will increase its profits as long as it is without any fraud or deception.

Moral Minimum

This theory states that a business's social responsibility is met as long as it either avoids or corrects any social injury it causes. In other words, a corporation may make a profit, if it does not cause harm to others while doing so.

Stakeholder Interest

Businesses have to consider the impact their actions will have on their stockholders, employees, suppliers, customers, creditors, and the community as a whole. All of these individuals have a stake in the business.

Example of the stakeholder interest theory – As per your text, if employees of a business were seen only as a means to acquire wealth for the stockholders, this would not take into consideration the impact it would have on those employees.

Corporate Citizenship

This theory maintains that a business has a responsibility to do well. Under this theory, businesses are under a duty to help solve social problems that they had minimum or no association with. The rationale behind this theory is because of the social power society has given to businesses. Opponents of this theory tend to lean toward moderation as society will always have some sort of social problem that needs to be solved. Businesses have limits too.

Example of corporate citizenship – Corporations owe a duty to fund a cure for a local child suffering from a rare disease.

Sarbanes-Oxley Act

The Sarbanes-Oxley Act of 2002 makes certain conduct illegal and establishes criminal penalties for violations. Section 406 of the act requires a public company to disclose whether it has adopted a code of ethics for senior financial officers, including its principal financial officer and principal accounting officer. Many companies have included all officers as well as employees in the coverage of their code of ethics.

Refresh Your Memory

The following exercise will enable you to refresh your memory on the rules and principles presented to you in this chapter. Read each question twice and place your answer in the blanks provided. Review the chapter material for any question you miss or are unable to remember.

1. Ethics is a set of _____ principles or _____ that governs the conduct of an individual or group.

2. Opponents of ethical fundamentalism feel that this theory

_____

_____.

3. The ethical theory that would have an individual behave according to the imperative "Do unto others as you would have them do unto you" is known as _____ _____.

4. Rawls's social theory promulgates that

    _____

    _____

5. If June, a store clerk, observes a Brinks security man drop a bag of cash and her first instinct is to inform him of it, she would be applying the theory of _____

    _____.

6. If an oil company has an oil spill that causes damage to an entire town and the company offers to tear down the town and rebuild it, the company would be adhering to the _____ _____ theory.

7. The idea that businesses have a responsibility to do good is known as the _____ theory of ethics.

8. If the corporate citizenship theory were taken to its maximum limit, what might be the end result?

    _____

    _____

9. What theory would a corporation be violating if it looked at its employees entirely as a means of putting money into the shareholders' pockets?

    _____

10. Under the United Nations Code of Conduct, transnational corporation shall respect the national _____ of the countries in which they operate.

11. A corporation that views its employees, suppliers, and residents of the communities in which the businesses are located as being unimportant are utilizing the _____ _____ theory of ethics.

12. If George looks to the Bible for ethical rules or commands to guide him, he would be supporting the theory of _____ _____.

13. Corporations have some degree of _____ _____ for their actions.

14. Those following the theory that a corporation's duty is to make a profit while avoiding causing harm to others is known as the _____ _____ theory.

15. The corporate citizenship theory of social responsibility states that businesses have a _____ to do good for society.

Critical Thought Exercise

You are an employee in the public relations department of Preciso, the luxury European automobile manufacturer. Preciso's sales have skyrocketed since the handcrafted vehicles were introduced to the United States ten years ago. Preciso's president has announced that Preciso will stop buying wood products from endangered forests following the example last year of Challenger Motor Company. Preciso will immediately stop buying wood from Canada's Great Bear Forest in British Columbia and phase out purchases of other wood from endangered forests. Instead, Preciso would like to use a "manmade wood-like product" for the interior parts (steering wheels, door panels, shifter knobs, etc.) of the autos it designs and builds.

There is no law against using wood from endangered forests and it is highly profitable to include these rare woods as part of the interiors of Preciso's cars. Shareholders are furious with the decision and are considering suing the board of directors and the officers of Preciso for wasting profits.

You are asked by the president of Preciso to draft a speech that she will deliver to the annual shareholders meeting which will explain the ethical business decision that was made and persuade the shareholders to not pursue a suit against the company.

Answer:

_____
_____
_____
_____
_____
_____
_____
_____
_____
_____
_____
_____
_____
_____
_____
_____
_____
_____
_____
_____
_____
_____
_____
_____

Practice Quiz

True/False

1. ____ Many public companies have included all officers and employees in the coverage of their code of ethics. [p. 670]

2. ____ A theory of social responsibility whereby a corporation must consider the effects its actions have on persons other than its stockholders is called the moral minimum. [p. 668]

3. ____ When a person looks to an outside source such as the Koran or the Bible for ethical rules, he or she is utilizing ethical fundamentalism. [p. 661]

4. ____ Under Rawls's social justice theory, a person is presumed to have entered into a contract with all others in society to obey moral rules that are necessary for people to live in peace and harmony. [p. 665]

5. ____ Kantian ethics refers to an individual's own feelings as to what is right or wrong. [p. 663]

6. ____ Ethical standards are different in each country. [pp. 671-672]

7. ____ Under the maximizing profits theory, persons choose the alternative that would provide the greatest good to society. [p. 666]

8. ____ There is no international ethics code in existence because there are too many transnational values. [pp. 671-672]

9. ____ If a corporation pollutes the waters and then gives compensation to those whom it injures, it has met its moral minimum duty of social responsibility. [p. 668]

10. ____ The stakeholder interest theory is widely accepted, as it is an easy way to harmonize the conflicting interests of the stakeholders. [pp. 668-669]

11. ____ Proponents of the use of Kantian ethics say it is hard to reach a consensus as to what the universal rules should be. [p. 663]

12. ____ Ethical relativism would apply in the situation of one company making what it feels is an honest comparison to a competitor's product even though the comparison is invalid. [p. 666]

13. ____ It is unethical for a company to purposefully create partnerships in order to appear profitable and use these partnerships in an effort to borrow money to engage in speculative business dealings. [p. 661]

14. ____ Proponents of the corporate citizenship theory contend that the duty of a corporation to do good is unlimited and that business is responsible for helping solve social problems. [p. 670]

15. ___ Advertising dangerous products to youth in order to realize profits from all marketing channels is not considered unethical under today's ethical standards. [p. 668]

16. ___ As part of a transnational corporation's code of conduct, it must adhere to socio-cultural objectives and values of the countries in it they operates. [p. 672]

17. ___ Transnational corporations shall respect human rights and fundamental freedoms. [p. 672]

18. ___ The theory of ethical fundamentalism leaves little room for individuals to decide what is right and wrong on their own. [p. 661]

19. ___ The theory of utilitarianism is a favored moral theory as it assists in determining what "good" will result from different actions. [p. 662]

20. ___ The legislative and judicial branches of government have established laws that enforce the moral minimum of social responsibility on corporations. [p. 668]

Multiple Choice

21. A moral theory that states that people must choose the actions that will provide the greatest good to society is [p. 662]
   a. Kantian ethics.
   b. maximizing profits.
   c. utilitariansim.
   d. corporate social audit.

22. Which theory proposes a social contract theory of morality? [p. 665]
   a. stakeholder interest
   b. Rawls's social justice theory
   c. ethical relativism
   d. ethical fundamentalism

23. John lives in a rural area and has had little contact with other people. Larry wants to purchase John's tool shed. John tells Larry that there's nothing wrong with it, even though he knows that it has a leaky roof and has ruined some of his more expensive tools. Upon inspection Larry discovers a small hole in the roof of the tool shed and becomes angry at John because he thinks John was trying to trick him into buying it. What would John's best defense be in this situation? [p. 666]
   a. Rawls's distributive justice theory
   b. maximizing profits
   c. principles for international business
   d. ethical relativism

24. What do proponents of the corporate citizenship theory believe? [p. 670]
   a. Social power is a gift from society and should be used to good ends.
   b. Corporate funds are limited.
   c. Corporations say one thing and always do another.
   d. all of the above

25. Edward brought a $15.00 discount coupon off of his next oil change to Sam Slick's garage. Fred, an employee of Sam Slick's garage, convinces Edward to have a variety of other services performed, which in turn causes Edward's final bill to be over $500.00. What ethical theory would Sam Slick allege if his "bait and switch" scheme is questioned? [p. 666]
    a. utilitarianism
    b. ethical fundamentalism
    c. ethical relativism
    d. stakeholder interest

26. If a computer manufacturer decided to close one of its manufacturing plants in Burlington, Vermont, because the employees were not assembling the computers fast enough, which in turn was causing sales to drop, which ethical theory would this manufacturer be violating? [p. 662]
    a. stakeholder interest
    b. utilitarianism
    c. Kantian ethics
    d. all of the above

27. Under which ethical theory could an individual be considered to act unethically if he or she went to extremes in following the code of conduct promulgated by this theory? [p. 661]
    a. ethical fundamentalism
    b. maximizing profits
    c. corporate citizenship
    d. corporate audit

28. Fred Farmington calls himself a traditionalist in the way he conducts business. With this in mind, which of the following would best describe his ethical beliefs? [p. 667]
    a. social responsibility
    b. a cost-benefit analysis
    c. the economic and social impact of business
    d. the flip of a coin

29. Which view held that the interest of employees, suppliers, and residents of the communities in which the businesses are located are not important in and of themselves? [p. 667]
    a. the Milton Friedman law
    b. the Caux Round Table principles
    c. consumer protection laws
    d. maximizing profits

30. What is a *qui tam* lawsuit also known as? [p. 662]
    a. ethical relativism
    b. the Whistle-Blower statute
    c. international lawsuit
    d. "this for that"

Short Answer

31. Our values or moral principals that dictate the way we act are called _____.
    [p. 660]

32. If Judy looks to the Koran in order to determine how to act, which theory of ethics is she
    following? [p. 661] _____ _____

33. Which ethical theory doesn't necessarily choose what is good for the greatest number of
    people, but rather what provides the greatest good to society? [p. 662]

    _____

    _____

34. Individuals who use _____ _____ as a basis for their
    ethics decide what is ethical based on their own feelings. [p. 666]

35. If a winery uses a teenager sipping a glass of its wine while listening to a rock and roll
    concert in one of its ads, what responsibility would the wine company be breaching?
    [p. 667]

    _____

    _____.

36. The Environmental Safe Company promotes the safe dumping of toxic materials into our
    nation's waters. On one particular instance, Environmental caused the deaths of hundreds
    of sea lions. Its only response to the tragedy was that there are plenty of sea lines to mate
    with one another. Further, the population will be back in no time. If Environmental would
    have complied with the _____ _____ theory, it would have met its duty of
    social responsibility by cleaning up the waters where the toxic materials were dumped and
    provide for safe dumping in the future so that other marine life are saved. [p. 668]

37. Which theory says that a corporation must consider the effects its actions have on
    individuals other than its stockholders? [p. 668] The _____ _____ theory.

38. What is the code of conduct that includes the respect for national sovereignty as well as
    adherence to socio-cultural objectives and values called? [p. 671] The
    _____ code of conduct for _____.

39. The Allover Toys Corporation has recently heard about the homeless population in an
    Asian country. The company has decided it does not need to help since it does not have
    any ties to this country. Allover Toys is being criticized for breaching its ethical
    responsibility under the

    _____ _____ theory. [p. 670]

40. Give an example of a company in your area that may have breached its morally minimum
    duty of ethical responsibility. [p. 668]

    _____

41. If you extend a helping hand to a friend and, after doing so, expect that friend to do the
    same for you when you are in need of assistance, your ethical beliefs would be founded on
    _____. [p. 661]

42. A company that gives creditors incentive to extend credit to its unreliable customers so that the customers will buy from it would be exercising the _____ _____ theory of ethics. [p.668]

43. Compare the difference between ethical fundamentalism and ethical relativism. [pp. 661-666]

_____

_____

_____

44. If a senior officer of the XYZ Company breaches his responsibility to the company shareholders, what act might this officer be in violation of? [p. 670]

_____

45. What is the difference between what the law expects and the ethical standards society expects? [p. 660]

_____

_____

_____

Answers to Refresh Your Memory

1. moral; values [p. 660]
2. does not permit people to determine right from wrong for themselves [p. 661]
3. Kantian ethics [p. 663]
4. is presumed to have entered into a social contract with all others in society to obey moral rules that are necessary for people to live in peace and harmony [p. 665]
5. ethical relativism [p. 666]
6. moral minimum [p. 670]
7. corporate citizenship [p. 670]
8. Shareholders might be reluctant to invest in corporations. [p. 670]
9. the stakeholder interest [p. 668]
10. sovereignty [p. 671]
11. maximizing profits [p. 667]
12. ethical fundamentalism [p. 661]
13. social responsibility [p. 668]
14. moral minimum [p. 668]
15. responsibility [p. 670]

Critical Thought Exercise Model Answer

Traditionally, it was perceived that the duty to shareholders took precedence over all other duties owed by the corporation and that the primary duty and goal of a company was to maximize profits. However, as corporations have developed global markets and society has changed, corporations have come to realize that they have several other duties that must be fulfilled. Employers have an ethical duty to employees to provide a safe workplace, to pay a decent wage, and to provide employment opportunities to present and future employees. As society has changed, the corporation has had to take into account ethical concerns such as equal pay for equal work and the prevention of sexual harassment. The company has had to change its policies to comply with laws such as the Family and Medical Leave Act and the Americans with Disabilities Act. A corporation also has a duty to the persons who use its products. We must make a safe product that is economical and gives good value to consumers for their investment and faith in us. We have a duty to our suppliers to maintain good business relations and use good faith and fair dealing in our contracts with them. We have a duty to the community where our facilities and offices are located. What we do as a corporation affects the tax base of the community and the quality of the schools, services, and collateral businesses in the area. Lastly, we have a duty to society at large to be the most ethical citizen possible. This means complying with environmental protection laws, preservation of scarce natural resources, and being part of the solution to very big problems instead of a cause. This corporation is in a unique position because of our wealth and power. We have a responsibility to society to use that wealth and power in socially beneficial ways. We should promote human rights, strive for equal treatment of minorities and women in the workplace, preserve and protect the environment, and not seek profits at the expense of ethics. If a corporation fails to conduct its operation ethically or respond quickly to an ethical crisis, its goodwill and reputation, along with profits, will suffer. Instead of aiming for maximum profits, we should aim for optimum profits—profits that can be realized while staying within legal and ethical limits set by government and society. For all these reasons, we have a duty to refrain from using wood from endangered forests to decorate our product. The manmade products we will substitute are more economical and will not detract from the overall look. Conversely, if we are known as the company that abuses scarce resources, consumers will support our competitors who are concerned about their corporate ethics.

Answers to Practice Quiz

True/False

1. True   Many public companies have included all officers and employees in the coverage of their code of ethics.
2. False   The statement reflects the stakeholder interest not the moral minimum.
3. True   When an individual looks to an outside source for ethical rules or commands, the individual is said to be adhering to the theory of ethical relativism.
4. True   Under Rawls's social justice theory, a person is presumed to have entered into an implied social contract with all others in society to obey the moral rules that are needed for people to live in peace and harmony.
5. False   The question states the principle behind ethical relativism. Kantian ethics's basic premise is that people owe more duties that are based on universal rules.
6. True   Ethics derives its purpose based upon factors such as religion, history, and culture. Since these factors vary from country to country, the ethical standards also vary.
7. False   Utilitarianism provides the greatest good to society, not maximizing profits, which has its main focus on money versus society.
8. False   A group of leaders from many multinational corporations developed an international code of ethics that is based upon transnational values.
9. True   The moral minimum theory of corporate social responsibility asserts that a corporation's duty is to make a profit while avoiding harm to others. Compensation for the harm caused by the pollution meets the moral minimum as it acts as a corrective measure.
10 False   The stakeholder interest theory is criticized due to the difficulty in harmonizing the stakeholders' conflicting interests.
11. False   Critics say it's tough to reach a consensus as to what the universal rules should be.

12. True   Ethical relativism is based on an individual's own feelings of what is right or wrong. So, even though one company is making an invalid product comparison to that of its competitor, under this theory, it would not be unethical if the company making the comparison thought it was ethical to do so despite the lack of validity.

13. True   This is a classic example of what has happened to the Enron Corporation. It would be far-reaching to even apply ethical relativism to this situation in light of the fact that speculative business dealings were involved, which most business people should know are not the sort of ventures a secure company would engage itself in.

14. True   Those who promote the corporate citizenship theory contend that corporations owe a duty to promote the same social goals as individual members of society and that they should make the world a better place because of the social power placed upon them.

15. False   Advertising dangerous products such as cigarettes, for example, to youth so that a profit can be made is considered unethical especially under today's standards.

16. True   Not only do corporations have to have respect for national sovereignty and adhere to socio-cultural objectives and values in the countries that they operate in, but they must also respect human rights and fundamental freedoms as well as abstain from corrupt practices.

17. False   Even though Kantian ethics believes that people owe moral duties based upon universal rules, it is hard to reach an agreement as to what the rules should be.

18. True   Ethical fundamentalism involves looking to an outside source for commands or ethical rules. As such, this theory lacks flexibility to allow an individual the freedom to decide right from wrong.

19. False   Though the theory behind utilitarianism is that people must choose the actions or abide by the rule that provides the greatest good to society, it is difficult to predict the "good" that will come about as a result of different actions.

20. True   The legislative and judicial branches of government have established laws that enforce the moral minimum of social responsibility on corporations.

Multiple Choice

21. C   Answer C is correct as utilitarianism dictates that individuals must select the actions or abide by the rules that provide the greatest good to society. Answer A is incorrect as Kantian ethics dictates that people owe moral duties based upon universal rules. Answer B is incorrect as the maximizing profit theory bases its theory upon the maximum amount of profits that business can make for its shareholders regardless if it is good or bad for others with an interest. Answer D is incorrect as the corporate social audit involves checking on a corporation's moral health.

22. B   Answer B is correct, as Rawls's social justice theory believes that each person is presumed to have entered into an implied social contract with others to obey rules that are necessary for people to live in peace and harmony. Answer A is incorrect as the stakeholder interest theory contends that a corporation must consider the effects its actions have on other stakeholders. Answer C is incorrect as ethical relativism bases its theory upon an individual's feelings on whether the action he or she is taking is right or wrong. Answer D is incorrect as those following the theory of ethical fundamentalism look to an outside source for ethical guidelines.

23. D   Answer D is correct as actions that are usually viewed as unethical, such as fraud, would not be considered unethical if the perpetrator thought the action taken was ethical. Under ethical relativism, individuals must decide what is ethical based on their own feelings of what is right or wrong. Answer A is incorrect as in Rawls's distributive justice theory, fairness is the crux of justice. Answer B is incorrect as this theory is mainly concerned with the maximum amount of profits that can be made for the shareholders regardless of the effect it has on other interested parties. Answer C is incorrect as the Principles for International Business is a code of ethics that have been adopted by many multinational corporations wherein avoidance of illicit operations, including fraud, is clearly stated in one of its principles.

24. A   Answer A is correct as proponents feel corporations owe a debt to society to make it a better place and therefore their social power should be used to good ends. Answers B and C are incorrect as these are things that opponents feel. Answer D is incorrect for the reasons given above.

25. C   Answer C is correct as this moral theory leaves little room for criticism in that it is subjective in nature. If Sam truly believes that Edward should have the additional auto services even though Edward came in for a discounted oil change, then Sam has met his own moral standards based on what he feels are right or wrong. Therefore, ethical relativism would be Sam's best theory to allege. Answer A is incorrect as utilitarianism involves choosing the best alternative that would provide the greatest good to society. The greatest good would be the subject of debate depending on whom you were trying to do the greatest good for, Sam or Edward. Therefore this would not be the best answer. Answer B is incorrect as ethical fundamentalism involves looking to an outside source for what is right or wrong. By finding other automotive services to convince Edward of, some might contend that Sam was stealing or "ripping off" Edward in contradiction to an outside source's commandment for example of "Thou shall not steal." Answer D is incorrect as the stakeholder interest theory would favor Edward more as the social responsibility includes considering the interests of customers. Arguably, Edward's interests as a customer trying to save a little bit of money by using a coupon are not being considered.

26. A   Answer A is correct as the stakeholder interest theory would require that the computer manufacturer considers the effects of its actions on the other stakeholders. Since the amount of sales seems to be its main concern, it appears that the only value it sees in its employees is their ability to make money. The closing of the plant and its effects on unemployment do not appear to be a factor. Answer B is incorrect as closing the plant would not provide the greatest good to society, which is the premise underlying utilitarianism. Instead, closing the plant appears to be detrimental in nature. Answer C is incorrect as followers of Kantian ethics believe that people owe moral duties based upon universal rules. As such, even though the employees are not producing fast enough to create larger profits, the parties have a contract. Under Kantian ethics, this contract needs to be honored regardless of the drop in profits and the detriment suffered by the company's owners. Answer D is incorrect for the reasons stated above.

27. A   Answer A is correct as critics do not favor ethical fundamentalism since people take the outside source's meaning and guidelines literally which can make people go to extremes and act unethically despite the belief in an ethical principal. Answer B is incorrect as the theory of maximizing profits was the traditional view of social responsibility whereby business should maximize its profits for the shareholders and any other interests associated with the business is not important in and of themselves. Ignoring the other interests by itself does not necessarily constitute going to extremes that would qualify as being unethical. Answer C is incorrect as corporate citizenship involves a business's responsibility to do good and solve social problems regardless if the business caused the

problems or not. The solving of social problems hardly constitutes unethical behavior. Answer D is incorrect as the corporate audit involves a moral or values checkup of a business that would not be unethical in and of itself.

28. B   Answer B is correct as businesses used to make their business decisions mainly based upon a cost-benefit analysis. Answer A is incorrect as businesses made few if any decisions based on their social responsibility. Answer C is incorrect as the economic and social impact of a business's decision was not even a factor that went into deciding what they were going to do. Answer D is incorrect as this indicates that businesses just took their chances with little to no thought going into their business decisions.

29. D   Answer D is correct as the maximizing profits theory was the main philosophy businesses operated under and the effects that it had on anyone else were not even considered. Answer A is incorrect as Milton Friedman was an advocate of the maximizing profits theory as long as there was no deception or fraud involved. There is no Milton Freidman law per se. Answer B is incorrect, as the Caux Round Table principles specifically provide for the customers, employees, and shareholders by defining the responsibilities of business toward stakeholders. Answer C is incorrect as consumer protection laws are geared toward the concern of those associated with products which would include employees, suppliers, and residents of the communities in which the businesses are located.

30. B   Answer B is correct as the Whistle-Blower statue, also known as the False Claims Act, permits private parties to sue companies for fraud on behalf of the government. Answers B, C, and D are incorrect as they are nonsensical.

Short Answer

31.   ethics
32.   ethical fundamentalism
33.   utilitarianism
34.   ethical relativism
35.   social responsibility
36.   moral minimum
37.   stakeholder interest
38.   United Nations; transnational corporations
39.   corporate citizenship
40.   Answers will vary; however, the moral minimum states that a corporation's duty is to make a profit without causing harm to others.
41.   Kantian ethics
42.   shareholder interest
43.   The theory of ethical fundamentalism believes that a person looks to an outside source for his or her ethical guidelines, whereas the theory of ethical relativism believes that individuals determine what is ethical based on their own feelings about what is right or wrong.
44.   the Sarbanes-Oxley Act of 2002
45.   The law establishes a moral minimum and ethics demands more.

Chapter 43

ADMINISTRATIVE LAW

Chapter Overview

Administrative agencies that have been established to administer the law have a large and direct impact on the operation of the government, the economy, and businesses. Modernly, we have administrative rules and regulations that cover almost every aspect of a business's operation. The growth in the size of administrative agencies and the rules they create have been staggering. Administrative law functions at the federal, state, and local levels. Understanding the sources and effects of administrative law and being able to function in the administrative law environment are essential for a business if it is going to succeed.

Chapter Objectives

Upon completion of the exercises in this chapter, you should be able to:
1. Discuss government regulation and the source of its authority.
2. Differentiate between a regulation and a compensable taking of property.
3. Explain the functions of administrative agencies.
4. Understand the major provisions of the Administrative Procedure Act.
5. Understand the differences among substantive rules, interpretive rules, and statements of policy.
6. Determine the lawfulness of an administrative search.
7. Describe the process for administrative agency adjudication of disputes.
8. Explain how administrative agency decisions may be reviewed by the courts.
9. Understand when the Freedom of Information Act applies.
10. Describe the Government in the Sunshine Act.

Practical Application

Upon mastering the concepts in this chapter, you should understand the basis for the power of administrative agencies, the legality of administrative actions, procedures for challenging administrative action, and the effect of an administrative agency decision. The frontline contact between a business and the government is most often an administrative agency. The regulations and rules that control business behavior are generated and enforced by administrative agencies. The information in this chapter will make it easier for you to enforce your rights and meet your obligations under the law.

Helpful Hints

Administrative agencies only have the power granted to them by the branch of government that they serve. As such, administrative agencies are designed to implement the policy of the law as dictated by statute and the Constitution. The administrative agency must be in compliance with law before it can dictate the conduct of a business or individual. Focus on the parameters of administrative powers to understand when it is necessary to comply with an administrative agency rule or directive and when it is possible to challenge the authority of the agency to act.

Study Tips

It is wise to develop an understanding of the various powers possessed by agencies and the procedural steps that the agency and persons who come before the agency must adhere to. You should then look at the enforceability of agency decisions and a person's right to seek review of an agency decision. Lastly, you need to understand the rules and laws that govern access to agency controlled information.

The Administrative Agencies

The theory behind the creation of agencies is that they create a source of expertise in a particular field. Congress and the executive branch are unable to regulate the hundreds of individual industries and specialty areas that are part of our commerce and society. By delegating authority to the experts, the industries and commerce are regulated more efficiently.

Federal administrative agencies. The most regulation comes from federal administrative agencies that are either part of the executive branch or independent agencies created by Congress.

State administrative agencies. State agencies enforce state laws and regulations, such as corporations law, fish and game regulations, and workers' compensation law. Local (county and city) agencies closely regulate business, from redevelopment agencies to planning and zoning commissions.

Government Regulation

General government regulation. Business is subject to general government regulation that applies to many businesses and industries collectively.

Examples:
- Occupational Health and Safety Administration (OSHA) regulates workplace health and safety standards that apply to varied businesses, industries, and occupations. Equipment safety standards are applied equally to coal mines as they are to furniture factories. Work hour regulations apply equally to grocery stores and universities.
- National Labor Relations Board (NLRB) regulates the formation and operation of labor unions. The NLRB will supervise the election of union representatives for garment workers as well as hospital technicians or oil platform maintenance workers.
- Consumer Product Safety Commission (CPSC) establishes safety standards for products sold in this country, whether it is a toy for a child or a microwave oven.

Specific government regulation. Administrative agencies have been created by Congress and the executive branch to monitor specific industries.

Examples:

- Federal Aviation Administration (FAA) regulates only air travel and the airline industry.
- Federal Communication Commission (FCC) is responsible for regulating only federal communications such as radio, television, and telecommunications.
- Office of the Comptroller of the Currency (OCC) regulates national banks.

Administrative Law

Administrative law is a combination of substantive and procedural law. Each agency is empowered to administer a particular act or set of statutes. From this foundation, the agency enacts regulations to give effect to the statutes. Part of this body of law is the procedural rules that govern how the agency conducts its business. A prime example of the implementation of administrative law is the Securities and Exchange Commission. They are empowered to administer the Securities and Exchange Act of 1934 and the Securities Act of 1933. To do this, the SEC has developed the SEC Rules. Both sources of law work together to regulate the securities market. This body of law is substantive in nature, with the SEC Rules also providing some procedural guidance.

Federal administrative procedure is controlled mainly by the **Administrative Procedure Act (APA)**. This act set up procedures that federal administrative agencies must follow. Some of the APA rules provide for hearings, rules for conducting adjudicative actions, and procedures for rule making. **Administrative law judges (ALJ)**, who are employees of the agency, preside over administrative hearings and proceedings. The ALJ decides the case and issues a decision in the form of an order.

The power of the agency is restricted to those powers that are delegated to it by either the legislative or executive branch. This is the *delegation doctrine*. The agency has powers from all three branches as it can adopt a rule, prosecute a violation of the rule, and adjudicate any dispute.

Legislative Powers of Administrative Agencies

Rule Making

Agencies are delegated legislative powers that include the following **rule making** and licensing powers:

- *substantive rule making* – An agency can issue a substantive rule that is like a statute. The rule must be followed and carries civil and criminal sanctions, depending upon the purpose of the rule.
- *interpretive rule making* – An agency can issue interpretive rules that interpret existing statutes. These give notice of how the agency will apply a statute.
- *statements of policy* – These statements announce a proposed course of action that the agency intends to follow.
- *licensing powers* – Statutes often require the issuance of a government license before a person can take action of enter certain business markets. Most agencies have the power to determine whether an applicant will receive a license.

Executive Powers of Administrative Agencies

Executive powers are the powers that administrative agencies are granted, such as the investigation and prosecution of possible violations of statutes, administrative rules, and administrative orders. These powers are often exercised through the use of:

- *administrative subpoenas* – an order that directs the subject of the subpoena to disclose the requested information. Failure to comply with the subpoena may lead to a judicial order for compliance. Further failure to comply with the subpoena may cause the party to be held in contempt of court.

- *administrative searches* – are physical inspection of business premises. They are considered searches and must comply with the Fourth Amendment, which forbids an unreasonable search and seizure. An administrative search must satisfy the three criteria necessary to make reasonable warrantless inspections. According to the U.S. Supreme Court, these criteria are:
  1. the government has a substantial interest in regulating the particular industry
  2. regulation of the industry reasonably serves the government's substantial interest
  3. the statute under which the search is done provides a constitutionally adequate substitute for a warrant

Judicial Powers of Administrative Agencies

Many administrative agencies have the judicial authority to adjudicate cases in administrative proceedings. The administrative proceeding is initiated by serving a complaint on a respondent, who is the party that is accused by the agency of violating a statute or rule. The respondent must be accorded procedural due process, which requires that the respondent be given (1) proper and timely notice of the allegations or charges, and (2) an opportunity to present evidence in the matter.

At an administrative proceeding, an administrative law judge (ALJ) presides and makes rulings on fact and law without the use of a jury. Both sides have the right to be represented by an attorney, cross-examine witnesses, and produce their own evidence. The ALJ's decision is called an order, which may be reviewed by the agency. Any further appeal is to the appropriate federal of state court.

Judicial Review of Administrative Agency Actions

Most federal and state statutes provide for judicial review of administrative agency actions. If the statute does not contain authorization for judicial review, a party may rely upon the Administrative Procedure Act, which authorizes judicial review for federal administrative agency decisions. Before a petitioner can appeal an action of an administrative agency to a review court, the following conditions must be satisfied:

1. The case must be ripe for review. The **petitioner** must have standing to sue the agency.
2. The petitioner must have exhausted all administrative remedies. The party must follow agency appeal procedures before a court will agree that administrative remedies have been exhausted by the petitioner.
3. There must be an actual controversy at issue. Under the **final order rule,** the decision of the agency must be final before judicial review can be sought.

Disclosure of Agency Administrative Actions

Congress has passed several statutes to make administrative agencies more accountable by subjecting them to increased public scrutiny. These statutes aim to make agency actions and procedures more public in nature and protect people and businesses from overzealous actions by agencies. Four of these congressional acts are:

- **Freedom of Information Act.** Requires that federal administrative agencies disclose certain records and documents to any person upon request. No reason for the request need be given. There are exceptions to the act, such as documents that must remain confidential to preserve national security.
- **Government in the Sunshine Act.** Requires that every portion of every meeting of an agency be open to the public. The public must be given notice of the meeting and informed of the agenda. There are narrowly construed exceptions, such as meetings concerning future litigation and those where criminal acts of an agency target will be discussed.
- **Equal Access to Justice Act.** Enacted to protect persons from harassment by federal administrative agencies. A private person can sue to recover attorneys' fees and costs associated with repelling an unjustified agency action.
- **Privacy Act.** Requires that a federal agency maintain only that information about an individual that is relevant and necessary to accomplish a legitimate agency purpose. An individual has the right to inspect and correct the records.

Refresh Your Memory

The following exercises will enable you to refresh you memory of the key points given to you in this chapter. Read the question twice and place your answer in the blanks provided. Complete the entire exercise, and then review the chapter material you could not remember.

1. Administrative agencies are created by _____, _____, and _____ governments.

2. When Congress enacts a statute, it often creates an _____ agency to enforce and administer the statute.

3. Due to their importance, administrative agencies are casually referred to as the _____ _____ of government.

4. Who can create the federal administrative agencies?
   _____
   _____.

5. Give an example of a local administrative agency._____

6. Give an example of a specific administrative agency.
   _____

7. The National Labor Relations Board would be an example of an administrative agency that _____ and regulates an industry (_____ _____) collectively.

8. Who presides over administrative proceedings? _____ ____ _____.

9. Administrative agencies can issue so-called _____ rules that interpret existing statutory language.

10. What type of power would a new radio station rely upon if it wanted to operate its business in the town of Somewhere? _____.

11. Which amendment applies to administrative searches?

    _____

12. The decision of an administrative agency must be final before what can be sought?

    _____.

13. Federal administrative agencies can maintain only information about an individual that is _____ and _____ to accomplish a legitimate agency purpose.

14. The _____ ___ ____ _____ Act requires that certain federal administrative agency meetings be open to the public.

15. An _____ _____ is an order that directs the subject of the subpoena to disclose the requested information.

Critical Thought Exercise

Macey Resources runs a hazardous waste facility where large quantities of industrial waste are stored, neutralized, and packaged for burial once it is dehydrated. A state statute provides that any business that handles more than 5 gallons of hazardous materials in a calendar month is subject to inspection without notice or warrant. Macey's operation includes 300 acres of ponds and transfer machinery. If a pond is not properly maintained, the seepage into the ground water could contaminate a large area with a radius over 15 miles. Within this radius there are numerous housing developments, schools, hospitals, and recreational facilities, including a small lake that is used for fishing, water skiing, and swimming. Inspectors from the state and federal environmental protection agencies enter Macey's property without a warrant or any advance notice to inspect the facility and test for hazardous waste seepage outside the drying ponds. The inspectors find numerous violations of state and federal law, including falsification of documents pertaining to disposal of potentially lethal chemicals from a military base. Macey is cited for the violations and is prosecuted by the U.S. Attorney for criminal charges. Macey files motions in the appropriate courts to have the evidence seized by the inspectors suppressed based upon a violation of the Fourth Amendment and failure to procure an administrative search warrant. What is the likely result of such a motion by Macey?

Answer:

_____

_____

_____

_____

_____

_____

_____

_____

_____

_____

_____

_____

_____

_____

_____

_____

_____

_____

_____

_____

_____

_____

_____

Practice Quiz

True/False

1. ___ The establishment of safety standards by the Consumer Product Safety Commission for products sold to consumers is an example of specific government regulation. [p. 678]

2. ___ The Poultry Protection Act, as administered by the Department of Agriculture, is an example of general government regulation. [p. 679]

3. ___ The Administrative Procedure Act is an act that establishes certain administrative procedures that federal administrative agencies must follow in conducting their affairs. [p. 679]

4. ___ Administrative law is a combination of substantive and procedural law. [p. 678]

5. ___ If an administrative agency acts outside the scope of its delegated powers, it is an unconstitutional act. [p. 679]

6. ___ Administrative agencies are usually granted executive powers, such as the investigation and prosecution of possible violations of statutes. [p. 681]

7. ___ An administrative agency cannot issue an administrative subpoena without the approval of a trial court judge. [p. 681]

8. ___ Statements of policy announce a proposed course of action that an agency intends to follow in the future. [p. 680]

9. ___ In *Food and Drug Administration v. Brown and Williamson Tobacco Corporation*, the Supreme Court ruled that the FDA had the authority to regulate tobacco as a drug under the authority of the Food, Drug, and Cosmetics Act. [p. 680]

10. ___ The investigation and prosecution of violations of statutes, rules, and administrative orders is part of an agency's legislative powers. [p. 681]

11. ___ Tainted evidence from an administrative search is admissible. [p. 682]

12. ___ Most inspections by administrative agencies are considered searches that are subject to the Fourth Amendment of the U.S. Constitution. [p. 681]

13. ___ The Due Process Clause of the U.S. Constitution does not apply to administrative adjudication of cases. [p. 681]

14. ___ Substantive due process requires the respondent to be given proper and timely notice of the allegations or charges against him or her and an opportunity to present evidence on the matter. [p. 681]

15. ___ Substantive due process requires that the statute or rule that the respondent is charged with violating be clearly stated. [p. 681]

16. ___ The Equal Access to Justice Act protects persons from harassment by federal administrative agencies. [p. 685]

17. ___ The Freedom of Information Act is very private in nature as it closes all proceedings, rules, and regulations off to the general public, but the individuals involved may look at them. [p. 685]

18. ___ A federal administrative agency that proposes to adopt a substantive rule must in part publish a general notice of the proposed rule making in the *Federal Register*. [p. 679]

19. ___ If an agency requires formal rule making, it must conduct a trial-like hearing at which the parties may present evidence, engage in cross-examination, present rebuttal evidence, etc. [p. 679]

20. ___ Statements of policy may not be issued by administrative agencies. [p. 680]

Multiple Choice

21. Regulation of the formation and operation of labor unions in most industries by the NLRB is an example of [p. 678]
    a. general government regulation.
    b. specific government regulation.
    c. state government regulation.
    d. local government regulation.

22. The enforcement of the Horse Protection Act by the U.S. Department of Agriculture is an example of [p. 678]
    a.   general government regulation.
    b.   specific government regulation.
    c.   state fish and game regulation.
    d.   local government regulation.

23. Administrative procedures that federal administrative agencies must follow in conducting their affairs, such as notice and hearing requirements, rules for conducting agency adjudicative actions, and procedures for rule making, were established by the [p. 679]
    a.   Privacy Act.
    b.   Government in the Sunshine Act.
    c.   Equal Access to Justice.
    d.   Administrative Procedure Act.

24. Which of the following legislative powers announces a proposed course of action the agency plans to take in the future? [p. 683]
    a.   interpretive rule making
    b.   substantive rule making
    c.   statements of policy
    d.   licensing

25. The Government in the Sunshine Act opens most federal administrative agency meetings to the public except for which of the following? [p. 685]
    a.   if it concerns an agency's issuance of a subpoena
    b.   concerns day-to-day operations.
    c.   where a person is accused of a crime
    d.   all of the above

26. When administrative agencies interpret existing statutory language, they can issue [p. 683]
    a.   a substantive rule.
    b.   an interpretive rule.
    c.   a statement of policy.
    d.   a final order.

27. Executive powers give an administrative agency the authority to [p. 683]
    a.   adopt a substantive rule.
    b.   adjudicate a dispute over a rule or regulation.
    c.   investigate and prosecute a violation of a statute, rule, or order.
    d.   interpret a statute as it applies to an industry.

28. Which of the following are powers delegated to an administrative agency at its creation? [p. 679]
    a.   legislative power
    b.   executive power
    c.   judicial power
    d.   all of the above

29. If a business decides to challenge a physical inspection by an administrative agency what would be the business's best defense? [p. 681]
    a. that the administrative agency had no right to search the business
    b. that businesses and administrative agencies go hand and hand
    c. that the Statute of Frauds applies
    d. that the Fourth Amendment protects persons and businesses

30. Which of the following best demonstrates how a substantive regulation is like a statute? [p. 679]
    a. It has the force of law that must be followed by all covered persons and businesses.
    b. Violations may be prosecuted civilly or criminally.
    c. All substantive rules are subject to judicial review.
    d. all of the above

Short Answer

31. When Congress enacts some statutes, who administers them? [p. 678]

    _____

    _____

32. What are three requirements or procedural mandates contained in the Administrative Procedure Act? [p. 679] (1) _____

    (2) _____ (3) _____

33. The delegation doctrine says when an administrative agency is created, it is delegated _____. [.p 679]

34. Statutes often require the issuance of a government _____ before a person can enter certain types of industries (e.g., operation of banks, television stations, commercial airlines) or professions (doctor, lawyer, contractor). [p. 681]

35. Give an example of an industry that a statute would expressly provide for a nonarbitrary warrantless search. [p. 682] _____

36. List five circumstances under which a search by an administrative agency would be considered reasonable within the meaning of the Fourth Amendment. [p. 682]
    (1) _____
    (2) _____
    (3) _____
    (4) _____
    (5) _____

37. The party appealing the decision of an administrative agency is called the _____ [p. 683]

38. Where may decisions of state administrative agencies be appealed to? [p. 683]

    _____

39. The ALJ's decision from an adjudication states the reasons for the ALJ's decision and is issued in the form of an _____. [p. 679]

40. List three characteristics of an administrative proceeding wherein an administrative law judge presides: [p. 679] _____,

_____, _____

41. What did the Administrative Procedure Act (APA) of 1946 establish? [p. 679]

_____

_____

_____

42. Explain what *notice-and-comment rule making* means. [p. 679]

_____

_____

_____

43. The _____ Act requires agencies to publish quarterly indexes of certain documents. [p. 685]

44. A decision by an agency administrator to close meetings to the public because it could be embarrassing to the agency for the public to hear the business discussed may violate the _____ Act. [p. 685]

45. What does an administrative law judge decide regarding the cases he or she presides over? [p. 679]

_____

Answers to Refresh Your Memory

1.   federal; state; local [p. 677]
2.   administrative [p. 677]
3.   fourth branch [p. 677]
4.   the legislative or executive branch [p. 678]
5.   Answers will vary, however zoning commissions is one example. [p. 678]
6.   Answers will vary, but the FCC (Federal Communications Commission) is an example. [p. 678]
7.   enforces; labor unions [p. 678]
8.   administrative law judges [p. 679]
9.   interpretive [p. 679]
10.   licensing [p. 681]
11.   the fourth amendment [p. 681]
12.   judicial review [p. 681]
13.   relevant; necessary [p. 685]
14.   Government in the Sunshine [p. 685]
15.   administrative subpoena [p. 681]

Critical Thought Exercise Model Answer

Physical inspection of the premises of a business is often crucial to the implementation of lawful administrative regulation by the agency entrusted with monitoring certain commercial activity. Searches by administrative agencies are generally deemed to be reasonable within the meaning of the Fourth Amendment if the business is part of a highly regulated industry where searches are automatically considered to be valid (liquor), or where the business is engages in hazardous activity and a statute expressly provides for nonarbitrary warrantless searches (mines, nuclear power). Evidence from an unreasonable search and seizure may be inadmissible in court depending upon the reasonableness of the search in the particular case. An expectation of privacy in commercial premises is different from, and is less than, expectation in an individual's home. This expectation is made much less is commercial property employed in "closely regulated" industries. Because the owner of the highly regulated business has less of an expectation of privacy, searches that are conducted pursuant to a regulatory scheme do not require a search warrant. The expectation is removed almost totally when the activity is ultra hazardous and highly regulated. Macey, as an operator of a hazardous waste site, would be on notice that a search could take place at any time. He has impliedly waived his Fourth Amendment rights by engaging in this type of business.

Answers to Practice Quiz

True/False

1. False   This is an example of general government regulation.
2. False   Because the act regulates one particular industry, poultry, it is specific government regulation.
3. True   This correctly states the purpose of the APA.
4 True   Administrative law involves both substantive and procedural law.
5. True   If an administrative agency acts outside the scope of its delegated powers, it is an unconstitutional act.
6. False   Administrative agencies are usually granted executive powers such as the investigation and prosecution of possible violations of statutes.
7. False   There is no such requirement that a trial court judge must approve of an administrative subpoena before it is issued.
9. False   The Supreme Court ruled that Congress intended to exclude tobacco products from the FDA's jurisdiction. The Court stated that the FDA had exceeded its authority by misinterpreting the FDCA.
10. False   These acts are part of an agency's executive powers.
11. False   Tainted evidence is not admissible regardless of it being an administrative search.
12. True   The search must be reasonable under the Fourth Amendment to the U.S. Constitution.
13. False   The agency must afford a party procedural and substantive due process.
14. False   Notice, hearing, and the opportunity to present evidence are procedural due process rights.
15. True   It would violate substantive due process if the statute were vague or ambiguous.
16. True   A federal act that protects persons from harassment by federal administrative agency is the Equal Access to Justice Act.
17. False   The Freedom of Information Act is a federal act that gives the public access to documents in the possession of federal administrative agencies. There are many exceptions to disclosure.
18. True   The petitioner may appeal the final order of an administrative agency in most cases.

19. True   The petitioner must have standing to sue.
20. False   Statements of policy may be issued by administrative agencies.

Multiple Choice

21. A   Answer A is correct because the regulation is across numerous industries. Answer B is incorrect because the regulations apply to more than one industry. Answers C and D are incorrect because the NLRB is a federal agency.

22. B   Answer B is correct because the regulation applies to one specific industry. Answer A is incorrect because the act does not apply to numerous industries. Answers C and D are incorrect because they are not a form of federal regulation and the USDA is a federal agency.

23. D   Answer D is the act that set forth the specified procedural requirement for agencies. Answer A is not correct as it concerned the right of an individual to sue an agency for improper action. Answer B is incorrect because it concerned open meetings. Answer C is incorrect because it concerned the limitation upon the type of information that could be retained by agencies.

24. C   Answer C is correct as most administrative agency meetings are open to the public with the exceptions of interpretive rule-making meetings, substantive rule-making meetings, and licensing. Answers A, B, and D are incorrect for this reason. Note, though, that should the public want to attend a substantive rule-making meeting, public notice as well as participation are required.

25. D   Answer D is correct because all the choices are requirements for an agency to adopt a substantive rule. Answers A, B, and C would be incorrect because they are only part of the requirements that are covered by Answer D.

26. B   Answer B is correct because an interpretive rule is not a new law, it only interprets existing law. Answer A is incorrect because a substantive rule has the force of a new law. Answer C is incorrect because statements of policy do nothing more than announce a proposed course of action. Answer D is the ruling made by an ALJ at the conclusion of an adjudication.

27. C   Answer C is correct because investigation and prosecution are executive functions. Answers A and D are incorrect because they are legislative functions. Answer B is incorrect because it is a judicial function to adjudicate a dispute.

28. D   Answer D is correct because the legislative, executive, and judicial powers are all powers delegated to an administrative agency at its creation. Answers A, B, and C are all encompassed in Answer D.

29. A   Answer A is correct because the administrative process is not complete until the agency reviews the decision of the ALJ and issues a final order. Answer B is incorrect because a person must exhaust all administrative remedies before he/she can file suit in federal district court. Answer C is incorrect for the same reason that Answer B is incorrect with the addition that decisions of the federal district court may be appealed to the U.S. Court of Appeals. Answer D is incorrect because all levels of appeal must be exhausted before a party may petition for review to the U.S. Supreme Court.

30. D   Answer D is correct as both substantive regulations and statutes have the force of law that must be followed by all persons and businesses and there are both civil and criminal violations. Further, all substantive rules are subject to judicial review. Answers A, B, and C are collectively correct thereby making answer D the correct answer.

Short Answer

31. existing administrative agencies
32. notice and hearing requirements, rules for conducting agency adjudicative actions, procedures for rule making
33. certain powers
34. license
35. Answers will vary, however an example would be coal mines.
36. (1) The party voluntarily agrees to the search (2) The search is conducted pursuant to a validly issued search warrant (3) A warrantless search is conducted in an emergency situation (4) The business is part of a special industry where warrantless searches are automatically considered valid (5) The business is part of a hazardous industry and a statute expressly provides for nonarbitrary searches
37. petitioner
38. proper state court
39. order
40. Both the administrative agency and the respondent may be represented by counsel. Witnesses may be examined and cross-examined, evidence may be introduced, objections may be made, and such.
41. This act established certain administrative procedures that federal administrative agencies must follow in conducting their affairs.
42. Administrative judges preside over administrative proceedings.
43. Freedom of Information
44. Government in the Sunshine
45. questions of law and fact

Chapter 44

CONSUMER PROTECTION

Chapter Overview

Starting in the 1960s and continuing into the early 1980s, federal and state governments enacted numerous statutes in order to regulate the behavior of businesses that deal with consumers. The goal of the legislation was to promote product safety and prohibit abusive, unfair, and deceptive selling practices. This was a drastic change from earlier days when sales to consumers were governed by the principle of *caveat emptor*, which means "let the buyer beware."

This chapter presents the statutes, rules, and cases that allow consumers greater protection and have increased the ability of consumers to sue businesses for damages caused by their dangerous, fraudulent, and deceptive methods. Legal theories have developed in the areas of breach of warranty, negligence, and strict liability. Government mandates and regulation by administrative agencies have mushroomed in the area of consumer protection. These laws and regulations form the consumer protection laws that are examined in this chapter.

Objectives

Upon completion of the exercises in this chapter, you should be able to:
1. Discuss the authority and responsibilities of the Food and Drug Administration.
2. Describe the important regulations pertaining to food and food additives.
3. Describe the regulation of drugs, cosmetics, and medical devices.
4. Explain the FDA's food labeling regulations.
5. Describe the scope of the Consumer Product Safety Act and its effect on product safety.
6. Describe the regulation of packaging, labeling, and poison prevention labeling.
7. Explain the meaning of unfair and deceptive practices and efforts to prevent them.
8. Understand the key elements of consumer credit protection statutes.
9. Identify the protection provided to credit card users.
10. Discuss the conduct that is prohibited by the Equal Credit Opportunity Act.

Practical Application

Upon learning the main legislative protections for consumers in this chapter, you will understand the duties, obligations, and requirements placed upon businesses when they deal in the manufacture, sale, or distribution of consumer goods or services. This information will allow you to determine your specific rights and obligations whether you are a business that must comply with the law or a consumer who is seeking to enforce a protected right.

Helpful Hints

As with all law, your analysis of a situation must begin with the basic definitions and requirements as contained in the statutes. Once you have that foundation, your focus should turn to the act or nature of the product. By determining where the act or product fits in the legislative scheme of consumer protection, you can alleviate the illegality or enforce the mandates contained in a consumer law. Lastly, many of the statutes require a mental element in combination with the conduct. Examine the intent of the business employee to determine if the statute has been violated.

Study Tips

It is important that you become familiar with the following consumer protections if you are going to be able to analyze actual business situations where the statutes are implicated.

Food, Drug, and Cosmetic Act (FDCA)

This act regulates much of the testing, manufacture, distribution, and sale of foods, drugs, cosmetics, and medical products and devices in the United States. The **Food and Drug Administration (FDA)** administers the act. The FDA implements the FDCA as follows:

- **Regulation of Food** – The FDCA prohibits the shipment, distribution, or sale of *adulterated food*, which is any food that consists in whole or in part of any "filthy, putrid, or decomposed substance" that is unfit for consumption. The FDA allows certain amounts of contaminants up to the amount set by their "action levels." For example, tomato juice is allowed to have 10 fly eggs per 3 ½ ounces. Anything below the action level is considered safe to eat.

- **Nutritional Labeling and Education Act** – requires food manufacturers and processors to provide more nutritional information on virtually all foods and forbids them from making scientifically unsubstantiated heath claims. The law requires labels on food items with information on calories, fat, fiber, cholesterol, and other substances. The FDA regulations adopted to implement the act required information on serving size and nutrients. Definitions were developed for *light, low fat*, and *natural*.

- **Regulation of Drugs** – The FDA regulates the testing, licensing, manufacturing, distribution, and sale of drugs. The licensing process is long and thorough. Users of drugs must be provided with a copy of detailed directions that include any warnings and list possible side effects.

- **Regulation of Cosmetics** – The FDA regulations require cosmetics to be labeled, to disclose ingredients, and to contain warnings as to any carcinogenic ingredients. The FDA may remove from the market any product that makes a false claim of preserving youth, increasing virility, or growing hair.

- **Regulation of Medicinal Devices** – The FDA has authority under the Medicinal Device Amendment to the FDCA to regulate medicinal devices, such as heart pacemakers, surgical equipment, and other diagnostic, therapeutic, and health devices. The FDA is empowered to remove quack devices from the market.

- *Other acts and amendments* – The FDA has been empowered by numerous other acts and amendments to the FDCA to regulate pesticides, food additives, color additives, animal drugs and food, biological material (blood, vaccines), food service sanitation, and radiation products (X-ray machines, microwave ovens, etc.).

United Nations Biosafety Protocol for Genetically Altered Foods

The Biosafety Protocol was passed to resolve a dispute between exporters of genetically modified agricultural products and countries that desired to keep the products out of their country. As a compromise, the 138 countries that signed the protocol agreed to allow the importation of genetically engineered foods as long as they were clearly labeled with the phrase "May contain living modified organisms." This allows consumers to decide for themselves whether to purchase altered food products.

Product Safety

The federal government has enacted several statutes that regulate the manufacture and distribution of consumer products. Some of these are:
- The *Consumer Product Safety Act* regulates potentially dangerous consumer products and created the **Consumer Product Safety Commission (CPSC)**. The CPSC is an independent federal agency that is not attached to any department. It interprets the CPSA, conducts research on the safety of products, and collects data regarding injuries caused by products. The CPSC sets safety standards for consumer products and has the power to compel a manufacturer to recall, repair, or replace a hazardous product. Alternatively, the CPSC can seek injunctions and seize hazardous products. It can also seek civil and criminal penalties.
- *Fair Packaging and Labeling Act* requires the labels on consumer goods to identify the product, the manufacturer, processor, or packager of the product and its address; the net quantity of the contents of the package; and the quantity of each serving. The label must use simple and clear language that a consumer can understand. The act is administered by the Federal Trade Commission and the Department of Health and Human Services.
- *The Poison Protection Packaging Act* requires manufacturers to provide "childproof" containers and packages for all household products.

Unfair and Deceptive Practices

When sellers engage in unfair, deceptive, or abusive techniques, the **Federal Trade Commission (FTC)**, under the authority of the **Federal Trade Commission Act (FTC Act)**, is authorized to bring an administrative proceeding to attack the unfair or deceptive practice. If the FTC finds a violation under **Section 5 of the FTC Act**, it may order a cease-and-desist order, an affirmative disclosure to consumers, or corrective advertising. The FTC may sue for damages on behalf of consumers in either state or federal court. Improper acts by sellers that are addressed by the FTC include:
- *False and Deceptive Advertising* is prohibited under Section 5 when advertising
  1. contains misinformation or omits important information that is likely to mislead a "reasonable consumer" or
  2. makes an unsubstantiated claim (e.g., "This pain reliever works 50 percent faster on your headache than our competitors.").
- *Bait and Switch* is another type of deceptive advertising that occurs when a seller advertises the availability of a low-cost discounted item but then pressures the buyer into purchasing more expensive merchandise. Bait and switch occurs when the seller
  1. refuses to show consumers the advertised merchandise
  2. discourages employees from selling the advertised merchandise or
  3. fails to have adequate quantities of the merchandise available.

- ***Door-to Door Sales*** may entail overaggressive or abusive practices. These tactics are handled on a state level where laws give consumers a certain number of days to rescind door-to-door sales, usually three.
- ***Unsolicited Merchandise*** is handled under the **Postal Reorganization Act**. The act permits persons who have received unsolicited merchandise through the mail to retain, use, disregard, or dispose of the merchandise without having to pay for it or return it.
- ***Anti-Spam Statutes*** have been enacted by many states to prevent the sending of unsolicited commercial e-mail messages with misleading information in the subject line or transmission path. Courts have held that the benefits of the act outweigh any burden upon commerce.

Federal Consumer-Debtor Protection Laws

The federal government protects consumer-debtors (borrowers) from abusive, deceptive, and unfair practices by creditors (lenders) through a comprehensive scheme of laws concerning the extension and collection of credit. These laws include

- The ***Truth-in-Lending Act*** requires creditors to make certain disclosures when the creditor regularly
  1. extends credit for goods or services to consumers or
  2. arranges such credit in the ordinary course of its business.

  The TILA is administered by the Federal Reserve Board who adopted a laundry list of disclosures under **Regulation Z**. These disclosures include the finance charge, interest, points, annual percentage rate, due dates of payments, and late payment penalties.
- The ***Consumer Leasing Act (CLA)*** extended the TILA's coverage to lease terms in consumer leases.
- The ***Fair Credit and Charge Card Disclosure Act of 1988*** amended TILA to require disclosure of credit terms on credit and charge card solicitations and applications. The act requires, in tabular form, disclosure of
  1. the APR
  2. any annual membership fee
  3. any minimum or fixed finance charge
  4. any transaction charge for use of the card for purchases, and
  5. a statement that charges are due when the periodic statement is received by the debtor.
- The ***Equal Credit Opportunity Act (ECOA)*** prohibits discrimination in the extension of credit based on sex, marital status, race, color, national origin, religion, age, or receipt of income from public assistance programs.
- The ***Fair Credit Reporting Act (FCRA)*** is located under **Title VI** of TILA. It protects consumers who are subjects of a credit report by setting out guidelines for credit bureaus. The act gives consumers the right to request information on the nature and substance of their credit report, the sources of this information, and the names of recipients of the report.
- The Fair Debt Collection Practices Act protects consumer-debtors from abusive, deceptive, and unfair practices used by debt collectors. The practices prohibited by the FDCPA include:
  1. harassing, abusive, or intimidating tactics (threatening or abusive language)
  2. false or misleading representations (posing as police officer or attorney)
  3. unfair or unconscionable practices (threatening to take illegal action).

The debt collector may not contact the debtor:
1. at an inconvenient time
2. at inconvenient places
3. at the debtor's place of employment if the employer objects
4. if the debtor is represented by an attorney
5. if the debtor gives written notice that the debtor refuses to pay the debt or does not want to have any further contact with the debt collector.

Refresh Your Memory

The following exercises are intended to aid you in refreshing your memory in regards to the important concepts and rules contained in the consumer protection laws that have been presented in this chapter. Answer all the questions in the blanks provided before referring to the chapter material. Review the material for any question that you got wrong or were unable to remember.

1. The FDCA regulates the testing, _____, distribution, and _____ of food, drugs, _____, and medicinal products and devices in the United States.

2. What categorizes a food as being adulterated?
   _____
   _____.

3. The FDA has issued regulations that require cosmetics to be labeled, to disclose _____, and to contain warnings if they are _____.

4. The FDA may remove from commerce any cosmetics that contain unsubstantiated claims of _____ youth, _____ vitality, growing hair, and such.

5. Give three examples of health devices that the FDA may regulate.
   _____, _____, and
   _____

6. As part of its powers under the Consumer Product Safety Act, the CPSA is authorized to collect data regarding _____ caused by consumer products.

7. If a consumer product is found to be imminently hazardous, the manufacturer can be required to _____, repair, or _____ the product.

8. Which federal administrative agency is empowered to adopt rules and regulations to interpret and enforce the Consumer Product Safety Act? The _____ _____ _____ _____.

9. Helga, who is selling her 1978 Chrysler Cordova, tells Joe, an interested buyer, that "This is a great car!" Joe purchases the car and immediately thereafter the engine chugs down the road and the car barely moves. Tell Joe why Helga's statement would not be considered false and deceptive advertising.

    _____

    _____

10. Which act requires creditors to make certain disclosures to debtors in consumer transactions?

    _____

    _____

11. Advertising is false and deceptive is it contains _____ or omits important information that is likely to mislead a "_____ _____" or makes an unsubstantiated claim.

12. If a seller refuses to show a consumer merchandise that has been advertised, or discourages employees from selling the advertised merchandise, or fails to have adequate quantities of the merchandise available, this is known as _____ and _____.

13. Which act authorized the FCC to establish a national database of consumers who objected to receiving commercial sales calls?

    _____

    _____

14. What is Regulation Z?

    _____

    _____

15. The ECOA applies to all creditors who extend or arrange credit in the _____ _____ of their business.

Practice Quiz

True/False

1. ___ The FDCA prohibits the sale of adulterated food, but it does not regulate the misleading labeling of food. [p. 690]

2. ___ Ordinary household soap is exempted from the FDA's definition of cosmetics. [p. 693]

3. ___ Fruits, vegetables, and raw seafood must have a label to disclose the number of calories derived from fat and the amount of dietary fiber as well as a variety of other substances. [p. 691]

4. ___ The FDA may not withdraw approval of any previously licensed drug. [p. 691]

5. ___ Terms such as *low fat*, *light*, and *natural* have no standards that can be enforced by the FDA. [p. 691]

6. ___ The FDCA no longer allows any contaminants in food. [p. 691]

7. ___ An amendment to the TILA that requires disclosure of certain credit terms on credit and charge card solicitations and applications is the Consumer Leasing Act. [p. 696]

8. ___ Lemon laws establish an administrative procedure that is less formal than a court proceeding. [p. 693]

9. ___ Debt collection may take place round the clock. [p. 697]

10. ___ For purposes of debt collection, third parties can be consulted only for the purpose of locating the debtor. [p. 697]

11. ___ The United Nations-sponsored Biosafety Protocol stipulates that all genetically engineered foods are to be clearly labeled with the phrase "May contain living modified organisms." [p. 698]

12. ___ If a consumer finds an error regarding pertinent information in his or her credit file, the agency may be compelled to reinvestigate. [p. 697]

13. ___ Creditors in violation of the CLA are exempt from any penalties provided in TILA. [p. 696]

14. ___ If a business makes an unsubstantiated claim, such as "Our juice is 20 percent more nutritional than XYZ Juice," the FTC may pursue a violation of Section 5 of the FCT Act. [p. 693]

15. ___ The ECOA applies to all creditors who extend or arrange credit in the ordinary course of their business. [p. 696]

16. ___ Many states have enacted laws that give a consumer the right to rescind a door-to-door sales contract. [p. 694]

17. ___ If a creditor violates the ECOA, the consumer may bring a criminal action for false imprisonment. [p. 696]

18. ___ The Truth-in-Lending Act covers all businesses that extend credit to consumers, regardless of whether the extension of credit is a regular part of their business. [p. 695]

19. ___ The TILA has been extended to cover consumer leases. [p. 696]

20. ___ A debtor may not bring a civil action against a debt collector for intentional violation of the FDCPA. [p. 697]

Multiple Choice

21. Which of the following gives the FDA broad powers to license new drugs in the United States? [p. 691]
    a. New Labeling and Education Act
    b. Bait and Switch Act
    c. the Drug Amendment to the FDCA
    d. none of the above

22. Food is deemed adulterated if it consists in whole or in part of any [p. 690]
    a. filthy, putrid, or decomposed substance.
    b. food that is improperly labeled.
    c. food that does not contain the correct amount in the container.
    d. incorrectly colored or misshaped food.

23. The FDA has the authority to regulate the [p. 692]
    a. testing of drugs.
    b. manufacture of drugs.
    c. distribution and sale of drugs.
    d. all of the above

24. Which item is not regulated by the FDA under the FDCA? [p. 692]
    a. eye shadow
    b. lipstick
    c. face soap
    d. shampoo

25. Which of the following are exempt from the "Do-Not-Call" Registry? [p. 695]
    a. telemarketers
    b. charitable and political organizations
    c. customers
    d. all of the above

26. Which of the following administers the Truth-in-Lending Act (TILA)? [p. 695]
    a. an administrative judge
    b. the Federal Reserve Board
    c. the Telephone Consumer Protection Board
    d. any one of the above can administer it.

27. Which of the following applies to the FDA and food safety? [p. 691]
    a. The FDA has set ceilings, or "action levels."
    b. The FDA can mount inspections and raids to enforce its action levels.
    c. If the federal tolerance system has been violated, the FDA can seize the offending food and destroy it at the owner's expense.
    d. all of the above

28. In those states that allow rescission of door-to-door sales contracts, how many days does the consumer have to rescind a contract he or she may have entered into? [p. 695]
    a. one day
    b. fourteen days
    c. thirty days
    d. three days

29. Which unfair or deceptive sales practice is not regulated by the Federal Trade Commission Act? [p. 695]
    a. false and deceptive advertising
    b. bait and switch
    c. door-to-door sales
    d. mailing of unsolicited merchandise

30. If a consumer receives numerous telephone calls from a debt collector in the middle of the night, the consumer may bring an action against the debt collector for violating the [p. 697]
    a. Equal Credit Opportunity Act.
    b. Fair Credit Reporting Act.
    c. Fair Debt Collection Act.
    d. Fair Credit and Charge Card Disclosure Act of 1988.

Short Answer

31. Fiona was threatened by her Supercard charge card that if she did not pay the entire balance by close of business, she would be imprisoned for four years. Which act would best serve to protect her? [p. 697]

    _____

32. The _____ is empowered to regulate food, food additives, drugs, cosmetics, and medicinal devices. [p. 690]

33. What is required of food manufacturers and processors under the Nutrition Labeling and Education Act? [p. 691]

    _____
    _____
    _____

34. List three examples of "action levels." [p. 691] (1)_____
    (2) _____ (3) _____

35. List two things the FDA can do if it suspects there has been a violation of the Food, Drug, and Cosmetic Act? [p. 690]

    _____
    _____
    _____

36. What types of things does the FDA want food processors to establish standard definitions for? [p. 691]

    _____
    _____
    _____

37. Lemon laws state that if the dealer or manufacturer does not correct a recurring defect in a vehicle within _____ tries with a specified period of time (_____ years), the purchaser can rescind the purchase and recover a full refund of the vehicle's purchase price. [p.693]

38. Explain why the United States felt that trade barriers were being used against genetically modified foods and what the United States had to concede to get its exports into foreign countries. [p. 697]

    _____

    _____

    _____

39. What are three things that the Consumer Product Safety Commission is empowered to do? [p. 692]

    _____

    _____

    _____

40. Louise has challenged the accuracy of information contained in her credit file, and despite her complaint, and the credit card agency's investigation, the agency can't find an error. What can Louise do? [p. 697]

    _____

    _____

    _____

41. What is false and deceptive advertising under Section 5 of the FTC Act? [p. 693]

    _____

    _____

    _____

42. Many states have enacted statutes that permit consumers to rescind contracts made at home with _____-_____-_____ sales representatives within a _____-day period after signing the contract. [p. 694]

43. The Drug Amendment to the FDCA requires that users of prescription and nonprescription drugs receive proper directions for use of these drugs. What types of things are included in "proper directions for use?" [p. 691]

    _____

    _____

    _____

44. Who does the Truth-in-Lending Act apply to? [p. 695]

    _____

    _____

    _____

45. What types of phones can be registered under the Do-Not-Call Registry [p. 695]

    _____

    _____

    _____

Answers to Refresh Your Memory

1.   manufacture; sale; cosmetics [p. 690]
2.   If it consists in whole or in part of any "filthy, putrid, or decomposed substance" or if it is otherwise "unfit for food"[p. 690]
3.   ingredients, carcinogenic [p. 692]
4.   preserving; increasing   [p. 692]
5.   Answers will vary, however examples include surgical equipment and defibrillators and heart pace-makers. [p. 692]
6.   injuries [p. 692]
7.   recall; replace [p. 692]
8.   the Consumer Product Safety Commission [p. 692]
9.   because statements of opinion and sales talk are not false and deceptive advertising [p. 693]
10.   the Truth and Lending Act [p. 695]
11.   misinformation; "reasonable consumer" [p. 693]
12.   bait and switch [p. 693]
13.   the Telephone Consumer Protection Act of 1991 [p. 695]
14.   a regulation that sets forth detailed rules for compliance with TILA [p. 695]
15.   ordinary course [p. 695]

Answers to Practice Quiz

True/False

1. False   The FDCA prohibits the use of false or misleading labels on food products.
2. True   Ordinary soap is exempt from the FDA's definition of cosmetics.
3. True   This authority extends to drugs, cosmetics, and medicinal devices.
4. True   The FDA may withdraw approval of any previously licensed drug.
5. False   The Nutritional Labeling and Education Act lead to regulations that were adopted by the FDA that set standard definitions for these terms.
6. False   The courts have upheld the presence of some contamination in food as lawful under the federal FDCA.
7. False   It's the Fair Credit and Charge Card Disclosure Act, not the Consumer Leasing Act.
8. True   Lemon laws establish an administrative procedure that is less formal than a court proceeding.
9. False   Convenient hours are between 8a.m. and 9p.m.
10. True   Third parties can be consulted only for the purpose of locating the debtor.
11. True   The United Nations-sponsored Biosafety Protocol states that all genetically engineered foods are to be clearly labeled with the phrase "May contain living modified organisms."
12. True   If a consumer challenges the accuracy of pertinent information contained in the credit file, the agency may be compelled to reinvestigate.
13. False   Creditors who violate the CLA are subject to the civil and criminal penalties provided in the TILA.
14. True   The FTC may seek to halt any false advertising that makes an unsubstantiated claim.
15. True   The ECOA applies to all creditors who extend or arrange credit in the ordinary course of their business.
16. True   Consumers are usually allowed to rescind these contracts within three days.

17. False   The consumer may dispose of the property as he/she sees fit, without incurring any liability to the seller.
18. False   The TILA does not apply to a creditor unless it extends credit as a regular part of its business.
19. True   The Consumer Leasing Act extended the TILA's coverage to consumer leases.
20. False   A debtor may bring a civil action against a debt collector for intentionally violating the FDCPA.

Multiple Choice

21. C   Answer C is correct as the Drug Amendment to the FDCA enacted in 1962 gives the FDA broad powers to license new drugs in the United States. Answer A is incorrect as this applies to food manufacturers and processors and the requirement that they provide nutritional information without making unsubstantiated claims. Answer B is incorrect as there is no such act. Answer D is incorrect for the reasons given above.

22. A   Answer A is correct because it sets forth a type of substance that is unfit for human consumption. Answers B and C are incorrect because they do not relate to the quality of food. Answer D is incorrect because it involves defects that do not prevent the food from being fit for human consumption.

23. D   Answer D is correct because each of the choices lists a function of the FDFA in relation to the regulation of drugs. Answers A, B, and C would be incorrect individually because it would exclude other incorrect answers.

24. C   Answer C is correct because soap is expressly excluded from regulation under the FDCA. Answers A, B, and D are incorrect because they fit within the FDA's definition of cosmetics that includes substances and preparations for cleansing, altering the appearance of, and promoting the attractiveness of a person.

25. B   Answer B is correct as charitable and political organizations are exempt from the "Do-Not-Call" Registry. Answer A is incorrect as telemarketers are who the "Do-not-call Registry" is aimed at. Answer C is incorrect as customers are not who the law was designed to enforce the FTC's "Do-Not-Call" Registry against. Answer D is incorrect based on the reasons given above.

26. B   Answer B is correct as the Federal Reserve Board administers the Truth-in-Lending Act. Answer A is incorrect, as an administrative judge presides over administrative matters, not TILA. Answer C is incorrect as there is no such thing as the Telephone Consumer Protection Board. Answer D is incorrect based on the reasons given above.

27. D   Answer D is correct as all of the statements as per Answers A, B, and C's answers apply to the FDA foods safety. Therefore Answer D is correct.

28. D   In many states, the consumer has three days to rescind a contract that he or she has entered into. As such, Answers A, B, and C are all wrong.

29. D   Answer D is correct because the mailing of unsolicited merchandise is regulated by the Postal Reorganization Act. Answers A, B, and C are all incorrect because they are practices regulated by Section 5 of the FTC Act or by FTC regulations.

30. C   Answer C is correct because the FDCPA protects consumers from abusive, deceptive, and unfair practices used by debt collectors. Answer A is incorrect because that act prohibits discrimination in the granting of credit. Answer B is incorrect because it regulates the accuracy of information retained by credit bureaus. Answer D is incorrect because it pertains to required disclosure of credit terms on credit and charge card solicitations and applications.

Short Answer

31. the Fair Debt Collection Practices Act
32. FDA
33. They are required to provide nutritional information on virtually all food. This includes the number of calories derived from fat, amount of dietary fiber, saturated fat, cholesterol, and a variety of other substances.
34. (1) 35 fly eggs per 8 ounces of golden raisins (2) two rodent hairs per pound of popcorn (3) 20 insects per 100 pounds of shelled peanuts (4) 20 maggots per 3 ½ ounces of canned mushrooms (5) 10 fly eggs per 3 ½ ounces of tomato juice
35. seek search warrants, conduct inspections, obtain orders for seizure, recall and condemnation of products…answers will vary
36. light, low fat, natural
37. four; two
38. There was no evidence that the genetically altered foods were unsafe, but foreign countries were prohibiting the importation of these foods into their countries. The United States had to sign the Biosafety Protocol and agree that all genetically engineered foods would be clearly labeled with the phrase "May contain living modified organisms."
39. The CPSC is empowered to adopt rules and regulations to interpret and enforce the CPSA, conduct research on the safety of consumer products, and collect data regarding injuries caused by consumer products.
40. She may file a 100-word written statement of her version of the disputed information.
41. It is advertising that contains misinformation or omits important information that is likely to mislead a "reasonable consumer" or makes an unsubstantiated claim.
42. door-to-door; three
43. method and duration of use
44. The TILA covers only creditors who regularly (1) extend credit for goods or services to consumers or (2) arrange such credit in the ordinary course of their business.
45. wire connected and wireless

Chapter 45

ENVIRONMENTAL PROTECTION

Chapter Overview

With the great increases in population growth, urbanization, and all forms of industry, our desire for higher profits, more products, and technological advancement lead to damage to the environment on a worldwide basis. In an effort to curtail the damaging effects of pollution, the federal government and states have created environmental protection laws that apply to all businesses and individuals. This chapter examines the efforts of the government to contain the levels of pollution that is still being made, while cleaning up huge amounts of pollution and hazardous waste that have been dumped into the environment.

Objectives

Upon completion of the exercises in this chapter, you should be able to
1. Identify when an environmental impact statement is needed and what it must contain.
2. Describe the mandates of the Clean Air Act.
3. Discuss the effluent water standards of the Clean Water Act.
4. Understand what technologies must be installed to prevent air and water pollution.
5. Explain how environmental laws regulate the use of toxic substances.
6. Understand the environmental laws that regulate hazardous wastes.
7. Describe Superfund law and how it authorizes the government to recover the cost of cleaning up hazardous waste sites.
8. Discuss the scope of the Endangered Species Act and how it protects threatened species and their habitats.
9. Discuss the role of the Nuclear Regulatory Commission as well as the function of the Nuclear Waste Policy Act of 1982.

Practical Application

Upon mastering the concepts in this chapter, you will understand the theory and application of environmental protections laws. You will recognize when an action violates one of the laws and the remedies for the violation.

Helpful Hints

With all of the different regulations that have been enacted to curtail pollution and its effects upon the environment, it is helpful if you organize your analysis of any situation based upon the type of damage done or the segment of the environment that is at risk. This will lead you to the correct statute or regulation for guidance as to how the situation will be handled by the appropriate agency or the courts.

Study Tips

You should organize your study of environmental protection by looking at the areas of the environment that are protected. Examine the laws and cases within the areas of air, water, toxic and hazardous substances, nuclear waste, endangered species, and noise.

Under the common law, both an individual and the government could bring a suit for negligence. The individual could bring an action for private nuisance and the government could maintain an action against a polluter for public nuisance. This was a very ineffective way of controlling pollution. With the creation of the Environmental Protection Agency (EPA) by Congress in 1970, the federal government had a vehicle for implementing and enforcing federal environmental protection laws. The EPA can make rules, adopt regulations, hold hearings, make decisions, and order remedies for violation of federal environmental laws. The EPA can also initiate judicial proceedings against violators.

The National Environmental Policy Act became effective in January 1970. Under this act, an environmental impact statement must be prepared to assess the adverse impact that any legislation or federal action will have upon the environment. This study is required before the project or legislation can be approved. Each state has a similar statute.

Air Pollution

- The *Clean Air Act* provides comprehensive regulation of air quality in the United States. It directs the EPA to establish **national ambient air quality standards (NAAQS)** for certain pollutants. There are primary levels to protect humans and secondary levels to protect vegetation, climate, visibility, and economic values. The states are responsible for enforcing these levels. The Clean Air Act regulates both stationary (manufacturing plants) and mobile (automobiles) sources.
- *Nonattainment areas* are regions that do not meet air quality standards. Deadlines are established for areas to meet attainment levels. States must submit compliance plans that
  1. identify major sources of air pollution and require them to install pollution control equipment
  2. institute permit systems for new stationary courses
  3. implement inspection programs to monitor mobile sources.
  States that fail to develop and implement a plan are subject to the following sanctions:
  1. loss of federal highway finds
  2. limitations on new sources of emissions (prohibits new construction of industrial plants in the nonattainment area).
- The *Clean Air Act Amendment of 1990* allows companies to trade sulfur dioxide emissions (the pollutant that causes acid rain). Companies still face strict quotas, but they are free to satisfy their limits by buying pollution credits from other companies. These credits are actually traded on the Chicago futures market.
- *Toxic air pollutants* cause serious illness or death to humans. The EPA must identify toxic pollutants, set standards for these chemicals, and require stationary sources to install equipment to control emissions of toxic substances. These standards are set without regard to technological or economic feasibility.
- *Indoor air pollution* is a serious problem that is not regulated. Some buildings have air that is 100 times more polluted than the outdoor air. This is caused mainly by tightly sealed buildings and exposure to indoor chemicals and construction materials.

Water Pollution

Any person who wants to discharge pollution into water must obtain a permit from the EPA. This permit system is called the National Pollutant Discharge Elimination System (NPDES). The EPA can deny a permit or set restrictions as to amount and frequency of discharge.

- The *Clean Water Act* has been updated and amended several times from 1948 to 1987. Pursuant to the act, the EPA has established water quality standards that define which bodies of water can be used for drinking water, recreation, wildlife, and agricultural and industrial uses.
- The Clean Water Act authorizes the EPA to establish water pollution standards for **point sources** of water pollution, which are stationary sources of pollution such as paper mills, manufacturing plants, electric utility plants, and sewage plants. The EPA sets standards for technology that must be used and requires dischargers of pollution to keep records, maintain monitoring equipment, and keep samples of discharges.
- The Clean Water Act prohibits **thermal pollution** because it damages the ecological balance and decreases oxygen in a waterway.
- The Clean Water Act forbids the filling or dredging of **wetlands** unless a permit has been obtained from the Army Corps of Engineers. Wetlands include swamps, bogs, marshes, and similar areas that support birds, animals, and vegetative life.
- The *Safe Drinking Water Act* authorizes the EPA to establish national primary drinking water standards. The act prohibits dumping of waste into wells.
- The *Marine Protection, Research, and Sanctuaries Act* requires a permit for dumping waste and foreign material into ocean waters and establishes marine sanctuaries as far seaward as the Continental Shelf and in the Great Lakes and their connecting waters.
- The Clean Water Act authorizes the U.S. government to clean up **oil spills** within 12 miles of shore and on the Continental Shelf and to recover the cleanup costs from responsible parties.
- The *Oil Pollution Act of 1990*, which is administered by the Coast Guard, requires the oil industry to adopt procedures that can more readily respond to oil spills.
- The United Nations Conference on the Law of the Sea (LOS Convention) established a 200-mile exclusive economic zone (EEZ) for coastal nations. This convention grants sovereign rights to coastal nations to explore, exploit, conserve, and manage living resources in their EEZs. The coastal nations have the right to board and inspect ships, arrest a ship and its crew, and instigate legal proceedings against violators of its EEZ rights.

Toxic Substances

Many of the chemicals used for agriculture, mining, and industry contain toxic substances that cause birth defects, cancer, and other health-related problems. Because of the grave danger posed by these chemicals, the federal government has enacted legislation to regulate their use.

- The *Insecticide, Fungicide, and Rodenticide Act* requires pesticides, herbicides, fungicides, and rodenticides to be registered with the EPA. The EPA may deny, suspend, or cancel the registration if it finds that the chemical poses an imminent danger. The EPA sets standards for the amount of residue that is permitted on crops sold for human and animal consumption.
- The Toxic Substances Control Act requires manufacturers and processors to test new chemicals to determine their effect on human health and the environment before the EPA will allow them to be marketed. The EPA requires special labeling for toxic substances

and may limit or prohibit their manufacture and sale. A toxic substance that poses an imminent hazard may be removed from commerce.

Hazardous Waste

Solid waste may cause or significantly contribute to an increase in mortality or serious illness or pose a hazard to human health or the environment if it is not handled properly. These wastes consist of garbage, sewage, industrial discharge, and old equipment. If these wastes are mishandled they can cause air, water, and land pollution. They are regulated as follows:

- Congress enacted the ***Resource Conservation and Recovery Act*** to regulate the disposal of new hazardous waste. The act authorizes the EPA to regulate facilities that generate, treat, store, transport, and dispose of hazardous wastes. Any substance that is toxic, radioactive, or corrosive or can ignite is a hazardous material. Hazardous wastes are tracked and regulated from the moment they are created to the time of their final disposal or storage.
- The ***Comprehensive Environmental Response, Compensation, and Liability Act,*** which is known as the "**Superfund**," gave the federal government a mandate to deal with years of abuse and neglect in the disposal of hazardous waste. The EPA is required by the Superfund to:
  1. identify sites in the United States where hazardous wastes have been disposed, stored, abandoned, or spilled, and
  2. rank these sites regarding the severity of the risk they pose.

The sites with the highest ranking are put on a National Priority List. The sites on this list receive first priority for cleanup. Studies are conducted to determine the best method for cleaning up the waste site. The Superfund provides for the creation of a fund to finance the cleanup of sites. The EPA can order a responsible party to clean up a hazardous waste site. If the party fails to do so, the EPA can clean up the site and recover the cost from any responsible party under a theory of strict liability. The cost of cleanup can be recovered from:

  1. the generator who deposited the wastes
  2. the transporter of the wastes to the site
  3. the owner of the site at the time of disposal
  4. the current owner and operator of the site.

The Superfund contains a right to know provision that requires businesses to:

  1. disclose the presence of certain listed chemicals to the community
  2. annually disclosure emissions of chemical substances released into the environment, and
  3. immediately notify the government of spills, accidents, and other emergencies involving hazardous substances.

Nuclear Waste

Nuclear power plants create radioactive waste that maintains a high level of radioactivity for a very long period of time. Two federal agencies monitor and regulate nuclear energy in the United States.

- The Nuclear Regulatory Commission (NRC) regulates the construction and opening of commercial nuclear power plants. The NRC monitors the plants and may close an unsafe plant.

- The EPA sets standards for allowable levels of radioactivity in the environment and regulates the disposal of radioactive waste. The EPA also regulates thermal pollution caused by the nuclear power plants and emissions and uranium production.

Endangered Species

The Endangered Species Act protects endangered species and threatened species of animals. The EPA and the Department of Commerce designate critical habitats for each endangered and threatened species. Real estate or other development in these habitats is prohibited or severely limited. In addition to the Endangered Species Act, there are numerous other acts that protect migratory birds, eagles, horses, burros, marine mammals, and fish.

Noise Pollution

Noise pollution is created by planes, automobiles, manufacturing plants, construction equipment, audio equipment, and the like. Because noise pollution has a direct impact on human health, the federal government has addressed the need to decrease noise pollution.

- The Noise Control Act authorizes the EPA to establish noise standards for products sold in the United States. The EPA and Federal Aviation Administration jointly establish noise limitations for airplanes. The Department of Transportation and EPA regulate noise from trucks, railroads, and interstate carriers. The Occupational Safety and Health Administration (OSHA) regulates noise levels in the workplace.
- The Quiet Communities Act authorizes the federal government to provide financial and technical assistance to state and local governments to help control noise pollution.

Transborder Pollution

When another country is the source of pollution in an affected country, the countries must deal with transborder pollution. The regulation of this type of pollution depends upon the existence of a treaty between the offending and affected countries. The United States had several treaties with Canada and Mexico to address many transborder pollution issues. The whole issue of transborder pollution and regulation of global pollution is in its infancy.

Refresh Your Memory

The following exercise will enable you to refresh your memory of the principles given to you in this chapter. Read the question twice and place your answer in the blanks provided. If you do not remember the answer, go on to the next question and finish the exercise. After reviewing the chapter material again, retake this exercise.

1. What is the purpose of an environmental impact statement?

    _____

    _____

2. The _____ _____ _____ coordinates the implementation and enforcement of the federal environmental protection laws.

3.   What regulation does the United States have in regulating air quality?

_____

_____

4.   List the two national ambient air quality standard
      levels._____ and _____

5.   What are nonattainment areas?

_____

_____

6.   EPA officials suggest that air inside some buildings may be _____ times more
      polluted than outside air.

7.   Sick-building syndrome affects office buildings that are hazardous because of
      _____ and _____.

8.   List two types of things that can contribute to sick-building syndrome. _____
      and _____

9.   What two types of point sources does the EPA establish water pollution control standards
      for?_____ and _____

10.   What types of records are dischargers of pollutants required to keep?

_____

_____

11.   Define what wetlands are.

_____

_____

12.   Explain what is meant by the phrase national primary drinking water standards.

_____

_____

13.   _____ _____ pollutants cause serious illness or death to humans.

14.   The Resource Conservation and Recovery Act defines _____ _____ as a solid
      waste that may cause or significantly contribute to an increase in mortality or serious illness
      or pose a hazard to human health or the environment if improperly managed.

15.   The Endangered Species Act requires the EPA and the Department of Commerce to
      designate _____ _____ for each endangered and _____ species.

Critical Thought Exercise

The citizens of Marzville, Ohio, became concerned when they started noticing very high rates of death and birth defects in the community. The Friends of Marzville (FOM), an environmental group, investigated the situation and it was discovered that a hazardous waste disposal site in Marzville had polluted the ground water with very high levels of carcinogenic chemicals. Fast Dump, who had purchased the land from Wow Chemical Company, runs the disposal site. Wow Chemical had operated a chemical manufacturing facility at the site from 1951 to 1982. Wow Chemical dumped hundreds of thousands of gallons of chemicals and contaminated water into open pits and into a drainage pipe that emptied into the Marzville Creek, which in turn emptied into Marzville Lake. Fast Dump takes in solid and liquid waste from numerous sources, including Tripp Trucking, a hazardous waste transportation company who has the exclusive contract to haul all the hazardous waste for the huge, multinational petrol-chemical corporation, Chemkill.

What relief can FOM seek for the citizens of Marzville? Who may be liable for the horrible situation in Marzville and the massive cleanup that is needed?

Answer:

Practice Quiz

True/False

1. ___ A proposal to build a new federally funded highway needs to have an environmental impact statement. [p. 702]

2. ___ Primary levels for ambient air quality standards refer to those levels that are safe for vegetation, climate, matter, visibility, and economic values. [p. 703]

3. ___ Since the EPA establishes air quality standards, the states are not responsible for their enforcement. [p. 703]

4. ___ Automobile and other vehicle emissions are considered mobile sources of air pollution under the Clean Air Act. [p. 703]

5. ___ States must submit a state implementation plan that sets out how the state plans to meet the federal standards of the Clean Air Act. [p. 703]

6. ___ The intense monitoring of radioactive wastes have eliminated injuries and deaths that were formerly caused by the high levels of nuclear waste. [p. 709]

7. ___ Under the Endangered Species Act, taking is defined in part as an act intended to "harass, harm, pursue, or hunt an endangered animal." [p. 709]

8. ___ The government has not adopted any regulations governing indoor air quality. [p. 703]

9. ___ Vinyl chloride, benzene, and beryllium are the only chemicals that have not been listed as toxic by the environmental protection agency. [p. 707]

10. ___ Even though the EPA establishes air quality standards, the states are responsible for their enforcement. [p. 703]

11. ___ Thermal pollution upsets the ecological balance in a waterway by decreasing the oxygen content of the water. [p. 705]

12. ___ The Clean Water Act forbids the filling or dredging of wetlands unless a permit is obtained from the EPA. [p. 705]

13. ___ The Safe Drinking Water Acts authorizes the EPA to establish primary drinking water standards. [p. 705]

14. ___ There is no limitation or permit required for dumping wastes out in ocean waters. [pp. 706-707]

15. ___ The Kyoto Protocol was designed to encompass all environmental mishaps. [p. 711]

16. ___ Human error can cause radiation pollution [p. 709]

17. ___ Private industry often is required to prepare environmental impact statements for proposed developments. [p. 711]

18. ___ The secretary of commerce is empowered to enforce the provisions of the Endangered Species Act as to marine species. [p. 709]

19. ___ Sources of thermal pollution are exempt from the provisions of the Clean Water Act. [p. 705]

20. ___ Decisions of the EPA are final and not subject to appeal. [p. 703]

Multiple Choice

21. Which of the following are considered to be a category of a nonattainment area? [p. 703]
    a. marginal
    b. extreme
    c. moderate
    d. all of the above

22. Air pollution is caused by [p. 703]
    a. mobile sources.
    b. stationary sources.
    c. both mobile and stationary sources.
    d. none of the above.

23. Under the Clean Air Act, the EPA establishes primary and secondary levels of allowable pollution. These standards are called [p. 703]
    a. adverse impact.
    b. national ambient air quality standards.
    c. pollution credits.
    d. the National Pollutant Discharge Elimination System.

24. Under the Clean Water Act, which of the following bodies of water have quality standards attached to them? [p. 705]
    a. recreational water
    b. public drinking water
    c. water for industrial use
    d. all of the above

25. The mishandling and disposal of hazardous wastes can cause [p. 707]
    a. air pollution.
    b. water pollution.
    c. land pollution.
    d. all of the above

26. Which of the following are true regarding the Superfund? [p. 708]
    a. The Superfund is a surplus account for purifying water wherever it is needed.
    b. It provides for the creation of a government fund to finance the cleanup of hazardous waste sites.
    c. It is a large sum of money used to protect endangered species.
    d. all of the above

27. Under the Clean Water Act, dischargers of pollution are required to [p. 705]
    a. pay a "use fee" each time they discharge pollutants.
    b. keep records.
    c. maintain monitoring equipment.
    d. keep samples of discharges.

28. The Clean Water Act does not regulate [p. 707]
    a. thermal pollution.
    b. national primary drinking water standards.
    c. wetlands.
    d. oil spills.

29. The operator of a hazardous waste disposal site will have to clean up contamination caused by improper dumping of hazardous waste over 30 years ago by a previous owner of the waste site pursuant to the [p. 708]
    a. Toxic Substances Control Act.
    b. Insecticide, Fungicide, and Rodenticide Act.
    c. Resource Conservation and Recovery Act.
    d. Comprehensive Environmental Response, Compensation, and Liability Act.

30. Under the Endangered Species Act, a wildlife form may be declared threatened or endangered by [p. 709]
    a. the EPA.
    b. the Department of Commerce.
    c. the secretary of the interior.
    d. the Endangered Species Commission.

Short Answer

31. Congress created the Environmental Protection Agency to coordinate the implementation and _____ of the federal environmental _____ laws. [p. 702]

32. An environmental impact statement must address what five things? [p. 703]
    (1) _____   (2) _____
    (3) _____   (4) _____
    (5) _____

33. What are the two levels of ambient air quality standards protect? [p. 703]
    _____
    _____
    _____

34. What is a state implementation plan under the Clean Air Act? [p. 703]
    _____
    _____
    _____

35. Before a pesticide can be sold, what needs to be done? [p. 708]
    _____
    _____
    _____

36. What did the Marine Protection, Research, and Sanctuaries Act extend environmental protection to? [p. 706]_____

37. Who licenses the construction and opening of commercial nuclear power plants? [p. 709]

_____
_____
_____

38. What is the purpose of the Marine Protection, Research, and Sanctuaries Act? [p. 706]

_____
_____
_____

39. Which act requires manufacturers and processors to test new chemicals to determine their effects on human health and the environment and to report the results? [p. 707]

_____
_____
_____

40. Under the Oil Pollution Act of 1990, what is the oil industry required to do? [p. 707]

_____
_____
_____

41. What is radiation pollution? [p. 709]

_____
_____
_____

42. What type of facilities is the EPA authorized to regulate under the Resource Conservation and Recovery Act? [p. 708]

_____
_____
_____

43. A federal statute that protects endangered and threatened species of animals is the [p. 709]

_____
_____
_____

44. Who is responsible for controlling noise pollution in the workplace? [p. 705]

_____
_____
_____

45. What is thermal pollution? [p. 705] _____

Answers to Refresh Your Memory

1. to provide enough information about the environment to enable the federal government to determine the feasibility of the project. [p. 702]
2. Environmental Protection Agency [p. 702]
3. the Clean Air Act Amendments of 1990 [p. 703]
4. primary; secondary [p. 704]
5. regions that do meet air quality standards [p. 703]
6. 100 times [p. 704]
7. chemicals; construction [p. 705]
8. asbestos; radon (answers will vary) [p. 705]
9. mines; manufacturing plants [p. 705]
10. Dischargers of pollutants are required to keep records, maintain monitoring equipment, and keep samples of discharges. [p. 705]
11. Wetlands are areas that are inundated or saturated by surface water or ground water that support vegetation typically adapted for life in saturated soil conditions. [p. 705]
12. minimum quality of water for human consumption [p. 705]
13. Toxic air [p. 707]
14. hazardous waste [p 708]
15. critical habitats; threatened [p. 709]

Critical Thought Exercise Model Answer

Congress enacted the Comprehensive Environmental Response, Compensation, and Liability Act, also known as the "Superfund," which gave the federal government the authority and duty to deal with hazardous wastes that have been dumped, spilled, or abandoned in such a manner that a serious risk to public health has been created. The EPA is responsible for identifying the hazardous waste sites in need of cleanup and coordinating the studies to determine the best way to handle the situation. The EPA has the authority to clean up hazardous sites quickly to prevent explosion, contamination of drinking water, or other imminent danger. Because the drinking water of Marzville is contaminated, the city will be entitled to priority over other cleanup sites. The EPA can order a responsible party to clean up a hazardous waste site. If that party fails to do so, the EPA can clean up the site and recover the cost of cleanup. The Superfund imposes strict liability for all those involved in use of the site. The EPA can recover costs from (1) the generator who deposited the waste, (2) the transporter of the waste to the site, (3) the owner of the site at the time of the disposal, and (4) the current owner or operator of the site. Liability is joint and several, meaning that any party who is at fault even to the slightest degree will be responsible for the entire cleanup. In the Marzville situation, Wow Chemical is liable as the original owner at the time the chemicals were dumped. Chemkill is liable as a generator of waste, and Tripp Trucking is liable as the transporter of the waste to the facility. Lastly, Fast Dump is liable as the current operator. The Superfund law applies retroactively, so acts of dumping at the Marzville site that took place at the site prior to 1980 are still covered. Of course, the application of the Superfund law only applies to the cost of cleanup. Any party damaged by the hazardous waste dumping can still pursue his/her own suit under applicable tort theories.

Answers to Practice Quiz

True/False

1. True   The proposal to build a federally funded highway does require an EIS.
2. False   Primary levels refer to protecting human beings.
3. False   The federal government does have the right to enforce the standards if the states fail to do so.
4. True   Air pollution controls must be installed on these mobile sources.
5. True   Each state is required to prepare a state implementation plan that sets out how the state plans to meet the federal standards.
6. False   Radioactivity can cause injury and death to humans and other life and can also cause severe damage to the environment.
7. True   Taking is defined as an act intended to "harass, harm, pursue, hunt, shoot, wound, kill, trap, capture, or collect" an endangered animal.
8. True   No standards exist for this type of pollution.
9. False   So far, more than 200 chemicals have been listed as toxic, including asbestos, mercury, vinyl chloride, benzene, beryllium, and radionuclides.
10. True   Although the EPA establishes air quality standards, the states are responsible for their enforcement.
11. True   It also causes harm to fish, birds, and animals that use the waterway.
12. False The Clean Water Act forbids the dredging or filling of wetlands without a permit from the Army Corps of Engineers.
13. True   Under the Safe Drinking Water Act, the EPA establishes primary drinking water standards.
14. False The Marine Protection, Research, and Sanctuaries Act requires a permit for dumping waste into ocean waters.
15. False It is an international treaty to reduce greenhouse gases.
16. True   Human error can cause radiation pollution.
17. True   Many states require private industry to prepare EISs for proposed developments.
18. True   The secretary of commerce is empowered to enforce the provision of the act as to marine species.
19. False Sources of thermal pollution (such as electric utility companies and manufacturing plants) are subject to the provisions of the Clean Water Act and regulations by the EPA.
20. False Decisions of the EPA are appealable.

Multiple Choice

21. D   Answer D is correct as the answers given in Answer A (marginal), Answer B (extreme), and Answer C (moderate) are considered categories that nonattainment areas can be classified as.
22. C   Answer C is correct because both mobile sources (automobiles) and stationary sources (manufacturing facilities) are sources of air pollution. Answers A and B are only partially correct. Answer D is wrong because a correct answer is available.

23. B   Answer B is correct because ambient levels set the amount that exists overall that is unhealthy for humans, vegetation, etc. Answer A is incorrect because adverse impact relates to an environmental impact statement which is not a standard, but an individual report. Answer C is not correct because pollution credits refers to the amount of pollution that a business can use or trade. Answer D is incorrect because NPDES refers to water pollution, not air pollution.

24. D   Answer D is correct as the EPA has established water quality standards for many types of bodies of water, including recreational (answer A), public drinking water (answer B), and water for industrial use (answer C). Therefore, all of the answers are correct making Answer D the correct selection.

25. D   Answer D is correct because the mishandling and disposal of hazardous wastes can cause air, water and land pollution.

26. B   Answer B is correct as the Superfund is administered by the EPA whereby it provides for the creation of a government fund to finance the cleanup of hazardous waste sites.

27. A   Answer A is correct because a use fee is not part of the legislative scheme. Answers B, C, and D are incorrect because they are all requirements under the Clean Water Act.

28. B   Answer B is correct because national primary drinking standards are regulated by the Safe Drinking Water Act, not the Clean Water Act. Answers A, C, and D are not correct because they are all areas regulated by the Clean Water Act.

29. D   Answer D created the Superfund, which requires the current operator to pay cleanup costs for past improper dumping. Answers A, B, and C do not pertain to the cleanup of hazardous waste sites.

30. C   Answer C is empowered to declare a species either endangered or threatened. Answers A and B are required to designate critical habitats once a species is put on the endangered or threatened list, but the list is created by the secretary of the interior. Answer D does not exist.

Short Answer

31.   enforcement; protection
32.   (1) describe the affected environment (2) describe the impact of the proposed federal action on the environment (3) identify and discuss alternatives to the proposed action (4) list the resources that will be committed to the action (5) contain a cost-benefit analysis of the proposed action and alternative actions
33.   (1) primary – to protect human beings (2) secondary – to protect vegetation, climate, visibility, matter, and economic values
34.   The SIP sets out how the state plans to meet the federal air quality standard that is being required by the EPA for the state.
35.   They must be registered.
36.   the ocean
37.   the Nuclear Regulatory Commission
38.   It extended environmental protection to the ocean. It requires a permit for dumping wastes and other foreign materials into ocean waters and establishes marine sanctuaries.
39.   EPA
40.   to adopt procedures and contingency plans to readily respond to an clean up oil spills
41.   Radiation pollution is emissions from radioactive wastes that can cause injury and death to humans and other life and can cause severe damage to the environment.
42.   The EPA is authorized to regulate facilities that generate, treat, store, transport, and dispose of hazardous wastes.

43. Endangered Species Act
44. The Army Corps of Engineers is empowered to adopt regulations and conduct administrative proceedings to enforce the act.
45. Thermal pollution is heated water or material discharged into waterways that upsets the ecological balance and decreases the oxygen content.

Chapter 46

ANTITRUST LAW

Chapter Overview

After the Civil War, America changed from an agricultural to an industrialized nation. Freedom of competition took a huge blow with the formation of powerful business trusts that monopolized large segments of the country's economy. The anticompetitive practices of these large corporate enterprises resulted in monopolies in the oil, gas, sugar, cotton, and whiskey industries. Congress then stepped in and passed antitrust laws to limit the anticompetitive behavior of powerful trusts. The laws were written in general language, much like the Constitution, so that they could be applied to a broad range of activity and have the ability to respond to economic, business, and technological changes. This chapter examines the antitrust laws that strive to preserve freedom in the marketplace.

Objectives

Upon completion of the exercises in this chapter you should be able to
1. Explain the purpose of antitrust laws and describe the federal antitrust statutes.
2. Apply the rule of reason and the per se rule to identify unreasonable restraints of trade.
3. Describe horizontal and vertical restraints of trade that violate Section 1 of the Sherman Antitrust Act.
4. Explain acts of monopolization that violate Section 2 of the Sherman Antitrust Act.
5. Describe the scope of Section 7 of the Clayton Act as it relates to mergers.
6. Apply Section 5 of the Federal Trade Commission Act to antitrust cases.
7. Explain how antitrust laws prohibit unfair and deceptive conduct over the Internet.
8. Explain the exemptions from antitrust laws.

Practical Application

As seen in the application of antitrust laws in the case of *United States v Microsoft Corp.*, antitrust laws remain a vital part of the federal government's enforcement of freedom of competition. Whether it is the small investor, consumer, or business partners of large corporations, anticompetitive behavior can still damage many economic interests. When corporations are allowed to dominate large segments of the economy, their failure is more devastating because there is a void that is unfilled by an able competitor. The government will continue to examine each merger, acquisition, and anticompetitive contract through the scope of the federal antitrust laws. Our economy depends upon their existence and enforcement.

Helpful Hints

There can be no meaningful discussion of antitrust law until you understand the mandates of the major federal antitrust laws and the activities that trigger their application to the conduct of an individual, small business, or corporation. Examine each act individually and pay close attention to the type of conduct that it prohibits. Then focus on the types of activity that have triggered federal intervention in the past. This will make you better able to predict what type of behavior will be called into question in the future.

Study Tips

An organized examination of the individual antitrust laws and acts forbidden by the important sections is key to your understanding of antitrust law. You need to understand the general proposition or prohibition of each section and the specific practice or activity that violates the section.

Enforcement of Antitrust Laws

Government actions – Enforcement of antitrust laws is divided between the Antitrust Division of the Justice Department and the Bureau of Competition of the Federal Trade Commission (FTC). The Sherman Act is the only major act with criminal sanctions. The government may seek civil damages, including treble damages for antitrust violations. The courts can also order divestiture of assets, cancellation of contracts, liquidation of businesses, or any other reasonable remedy that will effectuate freedom of competition.

Private actions – Any private person who suffers antitrust injury to his or her business or property can bring a private civil action against the offenders. They may recover treble damages, costs of suit, and attorneys' fees.

Section 1 of the Sherman Antitrust Act

Section 1 outlaws restraints of trade. To determine the lawfulness of a restraint, the court applies the *rule of reason* and the *per se rule*.

Rule of Reason – The Supreme Court held that only unreasonable restraints of trade violate Section 1. The courts examine the following factors when trying to apply the rule of reason:
- The pro- and anticompetitive effects of the challenged restraint
- The competitive structure of the industry
- The firm's market share and power
- The history and duration of the restraint
- Other relevant factors

Per Se Rule – Some restraints are automatically a violation of Section 1 and no balancing of pro- and anticompetitive effects is necessary. Once a restraint is characterized as a per se violation, there is no defense or justifications for the restraint. If a restraint is not a per se violation, it is examined under the rule of reason.

Horizontal Restraints of Trade

A horizontal restraint of trade occurs when two or more competitors at the same level of distribution enter into a contract, combination, or conspiracy to restrain trade. These horizontal restraints include:
- *Price-Fixing* – Occurs where competitors in the same line of business agree to set the price of the goods or services they sell: raising, depressing, fixing, pegging, or stabilizing the price of a commodity or service. Price-fixing is a per se violation.
- *Division of Markets* – Occurs when competitors agree that each will serve only a designated portion of the market. It is a per se violation to enter into a market-sharing arrangement that divides customers, geographical area, or products.

- *Group Boycotts* – Occurs when two or more competitors at one level of distribution agree not to deal with others at another level of distribution.
- *Lawful Horizontal Agreements* – Some agreements at the same level are lawful, such as trade association rules, exchanging nonprice information, and participating in joint ventures. These horizontal restraints are examined using the rule of reason.

Vertical Restraints of Trade

A vertical restraint of trade occurs when two or more parties on different levels of distribution enter into a contract, combination, or conspiracy to restrain trade. The Supreme Court has applied both the per se rule and the rule of reason in determining the legality of vertical restraints of trade under Section 1. These vertical restraints include:

- *Resale Price Maintenance* – Occurs when a party at one level of distribution enters into an agreement with a party at another level to adhere to a price schedule that either sets or stabilizes prices.
- *Nonprice Vertical Restraints* – These restraints are examined using the rule of reason. They are unlawful if their anticompetitive effects outweigh their procompetitive effects. Nonprice vertical restraints occur when a manufacturer assigns exclusive territories to retail dealers or limits the number of dealers in a geographical area.

Defenses to Section 1 of the Sherman Trust Act

- *Unilateral Refusal to Deal* – A unilateral choice by one party to refuse to deal with another party does not violate Section 1 as long as there was no action by two or more parties in concert. This rule is known as the **Colgate doctrine**.
- Conscious Parallelism – This defense applies if two or more firms act the same but no concerted action is shown.
- Noerr Doctrine – Under this doctrine two or more persons may petition the executive, legislative, or judicial branch of the government or administrative agencies to enact laws or take other action without violating antitrust laws.

Section 2 of the Sherman Act

Section 2 prohibits the act of monopolization and attempts or conspiracies to monopolize trade. To prove a violation of Section 2, the act requires showing that the defendant possesses monopoly power in the relevant market and is engaged in a willful act of monopolization to acquire or maintain the power. The court will examine the following elements and defenses in determining the existence of a Section 2 violation:

- *Defining the Relevant Market* – This requires defining the relevant product or service market and geographical market. The relevant market generally includes substitute products or services that are reasonably interchangeable with the defendant's products or services. The relevant geographical market is defined as the area in which the defendant and its competitors sell the product or service.
- *Monopoly Power* – This is the power to control prices or exclude competition measured by the market share the defendant possesses in the relevant market.
- *Willful Act of Monopolizing* – A required act for there to be a violation of Section 2. Possession of monopoly power without such act does not violate Section 2.
- *Defenses to Monopolization* – Only two defenses to a charge of monopolization have been recognized:

1. innocent acquisition (acquisition because of superior business acumen, skill, foresight, or industry)
2. natural monopoly (a small market that can only support one competitor).

- Attempts and Conspiracies to Monopolize – A single firm may attempt to monopolize. Two or more firms are required for a conspiracy to monopolize.

Clayton Act Section 7

Section 7 provides that it is unlawful for a person or business to acquire stock or assets of another where, in any line of commerce or in any activity affecting commerce in any section of the country, the effect of such acquisition may be substantially to lessen competition or to tend to create a monopoly. In order to determine whether a merger is lawful under Section 7, the court must examine the following elements:

- *Line of Commerce* – Determining the line of commerce that will be affected by the merger involves defining the relevant product or service market. It includes products or services that consumers use as substitutes. If an increase in the price of one product or service leads consumers to purchase another product or service, the two products are substitutes for each other. The two products are part of the same line of commerce because they are interchangeable.
- *Section of the Country* – Defining the relevant section of the country consists of defining the relevant geographical market that will feel the direct and immediate effects of the merger.
- *Probability of a Substantial Lessening of Competition* – If there is a probability that a merger will substantially lessen competition or create a monopoly, the court may prevent the merger under Section 7.

In applying Section 7, mergers are generally classified as one of the following:

- *Horizontal Merger* – A merger between two or more companies that compete in the same business and geographical market. The court uses the presumptive illegality test for determining the lawfulness of horizontal mergers. Under this test the merger is illegal under Section 7 if:
  1. the merged firm would have a 30 percent or more market share in the relevant market and
  2. the merger would cause an increase in concentration of 33 percent or more in the relevant market.

Other factors are also considered such as the past history of the firms involved, the aggressiveness of the merged firms, the economic efficiency of the proposed merger, and consumer welfare.

- *Vertical Mergers* – A vertical merger is a merger that integrates the operations of a supplier and a customer. In a backward vertical merger, the customer acquires the supplier. In a forward vertical merger, the supplier acquires the customer. Vertical mergers do not increase market share but may cause anticompetitive effects.
- *Market Extension Mergers* – A merger between two companies in similar fields whose sales do not overlap. They are treated like conglomerate mergers under Section 7.
- *Conglomerate Mergers* – Are mergers between firms in totally unrelated businesses. Section 7 examines the lawfulness of such mergers under the following theories:

    The ***Unfair Advantage Theory*** holds that a merger may not give the acquiring firm an unfair advantage over its competitors in finance, marketing, or expertise.

    The ***Potential Competition Theory*** reasons that the real or implied threat of increased competition keeps businesses more competitive. A merger that would eliminate this perception can be enjoined under Section 7.

The ***Potential Reciprocity Theory*** says if Company A, which supplies materials to Company B, merges with Company C (which in turn gets its supplies from Company B), the newly merged company can coerce Company B into dealing exclusively with it.

- *Defenses to Section 7 Actions*
    The ***Failing Company Doctrine*** – Under this defense, a competitor may merge with a failing company if:
    1. there is no other reasonable alternative for the failing company
    2. no other purchaser is available
    3. the assets of the failing company would disappear from the market if the merger did not proceed.
    The ***Small Company Doctrine*** – Two small companies are permitted to merge if it would make them more competitive with a large company.
- *Hart-Scott-Rodino Antitrust Improvement Act* – Requires certain firms to notify the FTC and the Justice Department in advance of a proposed merger. Unless the government challenges the proposed merger within 30 days, the merger may proceed.

Section 3 of the Clayton Act – Prohibiting Tying Arrangements

Section 3 prohibits tying arrangements involving sales and leases of goods. Tying arrangements are vertical restraints where a seller refuses to sell one product to a customer unless the customer agrees to purchase a second product from the seller. The defendant must be shown to have sufficient economic power in the tying product market to restrain competition.

Section 2 of the Clayton Act – Price Discrimination

Section 2(a) prohibits direct and indirect price discrimination by sellers of a commodity of a like grade and quality where the effect of such discrimination may be to substantially lessen competition or to tend to create a monopoly in any line of commerce.
- *Elements of a Section (2)a Violation* – To prove a violation of Section 2(a), the plaintiff must show sales to two or more purchasers involving goods of like grade and quality that results in actual injury.
- *Indirect Price Discrimination* – This is a form of price discrimination (favorable credit terms, reduced shipping charges) that is less readily apparent than direct forms of price discrimination.
- *Defenses to Section 2(a) Actions* – There are three statutory defenses:
    Cost Justification A seller's price discrimination is not unlawful if the price differential is due to "differences in the cost of manufacture, sale, or delivery" of the product. Quantity or volume discounts are lawful to the extent they are supported by cost savings.
    Changing Conditions Price discrimination is not unlawful if it is in response to "changing conditions in the market for or the marketability of the goods." Reduction in price of winter coats would be lawful when the spring line of clothing comes out.
    Meeting the Competition A seller may engage in price discrimination to meet a competitor's price.

Section 5 of the Federal Trade Commission Act

Section 5 prohibits unfair methods of competition and unfair or deceptive acts or practices in or affecting commerce. Section 5 covers conduct that (1) violates any provision of the Sherman Act or the Clayton Act, (2) violates the spirit of those acts, (3) fills the gaps of those acts, and (4) offends public policy, or is immoral, oppressive, unscrupulous, or unethical, or causes substantial injury to competition or consumers.

Section 5 of the FTC Act and the Internet

Section 5 prohibits unfair and deceptive acts affecting commerce. When Internet site operators use deceptive methods to capture Internet traffic, such as disguising the true nature of their site, this practice violates Section 5. The FTC used Section 5 to shut down the "page-jacking" and "mouse-trapping" used by Internet porn sites.

Exemptions from Antitrust Laws

Statutory exemptions include labor unions, agricultural cooperatives, export activities of American companies, and insurance business that is regulated by a state. Other statutes exempt railroad, shipping, utility, and securities industries from most of the reach of antitrust law.

Implied exceptions are given by federal court decision. Two such exemptions include professional baseball and the airline industry.

State action exemptions are economic regulations, such as utility rates, mandated by state law. Though it is a form or price-fixing, the states and utilities are not liable for antitrust violations.

Refresh Your Memory

The following exercise will enable you to refresh your memory on the rules of law and principles presented to you in this chapter. Read each question twice and place your answer in the blanks provided. Review the chapter material for any question you miss or are unable to remember.

1. A government judgment against a defendant for an antitrust violation may be used as _____ evidence of liability in a private civil treble damage action.

2. Section 1 of the Sherman Act prohibits contracts, combinations, and conspiracies in _____ of trade.

3. The rule of reason requires a balancing of _____ and anticompetitive effects of the _____ restraint.

4. A _____ restraint of trade occurs when two or more competitors at the same _____ of distribution enter into a contract, combination, or conspiracy to restrain trade.

5. Horizontal _____ _____ occurs when the competitors in the same line of business agree to set the price of goods or services they sell.

6. Competitors that agree that each will serve only a designated portion of the market are engaging in _____ of markets, which is a _____ _____ violation of Section 1.

7. A group boycott occurs when two or more _____ at one level of distribution agree not to deal with others at a _____ level of distribution.

8. _____ _____ _____ is a per se violation of Section 1 that occurs when a party at one level of distribution enters into an agreement with a party at another level to adhere to a _____ schedule that either sets or stabilizes prices.

9. Section __ of the Sherman Act prohibits the act of monopolization and attempts or _____ to monopolize trade.

10. The _____ product or _____ market generally includes substitute products or services that are reasonably interchangeable with the defendant's products or services.

11. What are the two defenses to a charge of monopolizing that have actually been recognized? _____ and _____

12. What is predatory pricing?
   _____

13. Which test is used to determine the relevant product or service market?
   _____
   _____

14. Generally speaking, how is the geographical market identified?
   _____
   _____

15. What things might cause a court to prevent a merger?
   _____
   _____
   _____
   _____

Critical Thought Exercise

When the partners of The Four Brothers Pizza Shoppe terminated the partnership, they divided the greater Chicago area into four parts and agreed to restrict the geographical area within which each would advertise and deliver pizzas. Two years later one partner filed suit against the other three alleging in part that the restriction on advertising and delivery area was a per se violation of the Sherman Act. Was the agreement made as part of a breakup of a partnership that divided a city into geographical areas for advertising and delivery a violation of antitrust law?

Answer:

_____
_____
_____
_____
_____
_____
_____
_____
_____
_____
_____
_____

Practice Quiz

True/False

1. ____ A horizontal merger is a merger between two or more companies that compete in the same business and geographical market. [p. 727]

2. ____ The integration of the operations of a supplier and a customer is a vertical merger. [p. 727]

3. ____ A market extension merger is a merger between two companies in similar fields whose sales overlap. [p. 728]

4. ____ The unfair advantage theory holds that a conglomerate merger may give the acquiring firm an unfair advantage over its competitors in a finance, marketing, or expertise. [p. 728]

5. ____ Price discrimination happens if a seller offers favorable terms to its preferred customers without just cause. [p. 729]

6. ____ Labor unions are an example of an activity that is exempt from antitrust laws. [p. 731]

7. ____ The FTC act provides for a private civil cause of action for injured parties. [p. 731]

8. ____ Section 5 of the FTC is broader than the other antitrust laws. [p. 730]

9. ___ If two or more firms act the same, but no concerted action is shown, this is known as conscious parallelism. [p. 723]

10. ___ A unilateral refusal to deal is a violation of Section 1 of the Sherman Act. [p. 723]

11. ___ Section 16 of the Clayton Act prohibits the government or a private plaintiff from obtaining an injunction against anticompetitive behavior that violates antitrust laws. [p. 717]

12. ___ Nonprice restraints are unlawful if their anticompetitive effects outweigh their procompetitive effects. [p. 721]

13. ___ Setting minimum resale prices is not a per se violation of Section 1 of the Sherman Act. [p. 721]

14. ___ To prove a violation of Section 2 of the Sherman Act, the government need only prove that a defendant possesses monopoly power in the relevant market. [p. 723]

15. ___ The relevant geographical market, for Section 2 analysis, is defined as the area in which the defendant and its competitors sell the product or service. [p. 724]

16. ___ For an antitrust action to be sustained, the defendant must possess monopoly power in the relevant market. [p. 724]

17. ___ A single firm may not be found liable for monopolizing or attempting to monopolize. [p. 725]

18. ___ Monopoly power is the power to control prices or exclude competition measured by the market share the defendant possess in the relevant market. [p. 724]

19. ___ If ABC Beer, a beer that is sold nationally, desires to merge with Little Beer, which is sold in Ohio, Indiana, and Michigan, the relevant geographical market for this merger will be the entire United States because ABC is a national beer. [p. 719]

20. ___ The test for determining the lawfulness of horizontal mergers is the "substantial lessening of competition" test. [p. 724]

Multiple Choice

21. Section 1 of the Sherman Act is intended to prohibit certain [p. 717]
    a. criminals from illegal conduct.
    b. monopolization.
    c. concerted anticompetitive activities.
    d. all of the above

22. Courts analyze a price-fixing allegation under the [p. 719]
    a. rule of reason.
    b. per se rule.
    c. innocent acquisition rule.
    d. natural monopoly standard.

23. Which of the following is not a horizontal restraint of trade under the Sherman Act? [p. 721]
    a. Price-fixing
    b. Division of markets
    c. Resale price maintenance
    d. Group boycott

24. When two or more competitors at one level of distribution agree not to deal with others at another level of distribution, this is a restraint of trade known as [p. 720]
    a. price-fixing.
    b. division of markets.
    c. resale price maintenance.
    d. group boycott.

25. Which of the following applies to defining the relevant market when attempting to prove that the defendant is in violation of Section 2 of the Sherman Act? [p. 723]
    a. There must be a relevant product market.
    b. There must be a relevant geographical market.
    c. The plaintiff usually attempts to claim that its market share dictates a narrow definition of relevant product or market.
    d. all of the above

26. Section 2 of the Sherman Act prohibits [p. 723]
    a. restraint of trade.
    b. mergers.
    c. monopolization.
    d. tying arrangements.

27. The power to control prices or exclude competition measured by the market share the defendant possesses in the relevant market is [p. 724]
    a. price-fixing.
    b. a tying arrangement.
    c. the unfair advantage theory.
    d. monopoly power.

28. A conglomerate merger may be enjoined under the [p. 728]
    a. unfair advantage theory.
    b. potential competition theory.
    c. potential reciprocity theory.
    d. all of the above

29. The Robinson-Patman Act [p. 729]
    a. prohibits price discrimination.
    b. involves sellers of commodities of a like grade and quality.
    c. does not apply to the sale of services, real estate, or intangible property.
    d. all of the above

30. Price discrimination is allowed under Section 2 of the Clayton Act is the defendant can show [p. 730]
    a. a cost justification.
    b. changing conditions.
    c. it is just meeting the competition.
    d. all of the above

Short Answer

31. How is government enforcement of federal antitrust laws divided? [p. 716]

    _____

    _____

32. What factors does the court examine when applying the rule of reason? [p. 718]

    _____

    _____

33. What is the per se rule? [p. 718]

    _____

    _____

34. Explain the meaning of price-fixing. [p. 719]

    _____

    _____

35. A restraint of trade in which two or more competitors at one level of distribution agree not to deal with others at another level of distribution is known as
    _____. [p. 720]

36. Unreasonable restraints on trade violate which act? [p. 720]

    _____

37. Describe an example of a nonprice vertical restraint. [p. 721]

    _____

    _____

38. Pepsi and Coca-Cola decide not to deal with Foodman grocery store, a retailer. Why wouldn't this situation be considered a violation of Section 1 of the Sherman Act? [p. 723]

    _____

    _____

39. For the purpose of analyzing a Section 2 violation of the Sherman Act, what is a relevant geographical market? [p. 724]

    _____

    _____

40. How is monopoly power defined by the courts? [p. 724]

    _____

    _____

41.   What guidelines do the courts use in determining whether a defendant possesses monopoly power? [p. 724]

_____

42.   If a beverage company acquired a bottling process company, this would be a
_____ merger. [p. 727]

43.   If *I Am Mod*, a retail clothing chain, acquired a chain of stores across the country, this would be known as a _____ _____ merger. [p. 727]

44.   If two companies are proposing a merger, what must they do to comply with the Hart-Scott-Rodino Antitrust Improvement Act? [p. 728]

_____

_____

45.   If a doctor charges one patient $200 for the same procedure as she charges another patient only $55, is this price discrimination a violation of the Robinson-Patman Act? [p. 729]

_____

_____

Answers to Refresh Your Memory

1.   prima facie [p. 717]
2.   restraint [p. 717]
3.   pro; challenged [p. 718]
4.   horizontal; level [p. 718]
5.   price-fixing [p. 718]
6.   division; per se [p. 719]
7.   competitors; different [p. 720]
8.   resale price maintenance; price [p. 721]
9.   2; conspiracies [p. 723]
10.   relevant; service [p. 724]
11.   innocent acquisition; natural monopoly [p. 725]
12.   pricing below normal or average cost [p. 724]
13.   functional interchangeability test [p. 726]
14.   the geographical area that will feel the direct and immediate affects of the merger [p. 726]
15.   if the acquisition is likely to substantially lessen competition or create a monopoly [p. 726]

Critical Thought Exercise Model Answer

Society's welfare is harmed if rival businesses are permitted to join in an agreement that consolidates their market power or otherwise restrains competition. The types of trade restraints that Section 1 of the Sherman Act prohibits are generally divided into horizontal and vertical restraints. A horizontal restraint is any agreement that in some way restrains competition between rival businesses competing in the same market. These agreements include price fixing, group boycotts, and horizontal market division. It is a per se violation of Section 1 of the Sherman Act for competitors to divide up territories or customers. The effect of the agreement between the four former partners is to say, "That will be your market and this will be mine." The agreement to limit advertising and delivery to different geographical areas was intended to be, and was in practice, an agreement to allocate markets so that the per se rule of illegality applies.

Answers to Practice Quiz

True/False

1. True   A horizontal merger is a merger between two or more companies that compete in the same business and geographical market.
2. True   A vertical merger is a merger that integrates the operations of a supplier and a customer.
3. False A market extension merger is a merger between two companies in similar fields whose sales do not overlap.
4. False The unfair advantage theory holds that a conglomerate merger may not give the acquiring firm an unfair advantage.
5. True   Price discrimination occurs if a seller offers favorable terms to their preferred customers.
6. False Division of markets is a per se violation of Section 1.
7. True   The FTC provides for a private civil cause of action for injured parties.
8. True   Section 5 is broader than the other antitrust laws.
9. True   If two or more firms act the same, but no concerted action is shown, there is no violation of Section 1 of the Sherman Act. This is known as conscious parallelism.
10. False A unilateral refusal to deal is not a violation of Section 1 because there is no concerted action with others.
11. False Section 16 of the Clayton Act permits the government or a private plaintiff to obtain an injunction against anticompetitive behavior that violates antitrust laws.
12. True Nonprice restraints are unlawful under this analysis if their anticompetitive effects outweigh their procompetitive effects.
13. False Setting minimum prices is a per se violation of Section 1 of the Sherman Act as an unreasonable restraint on trade.
14. False It must also be proven that the defendant engages in a willful act of monopolization to acquire or maintain the power.
15. True This may be a national, regional, state, or local area, depending on the circumstances.
16. True Monopoly power is the power to control prices or exclude competition.
17. False A single firm may be found liable for monopolizing or attempting to monopolize.
18. True The power to control prices or exclude competition measured by the market share the defendant possesses in the relevant market is monopoly power.
19. False The relevant geographical market is the area that will feel the direct and immediate effects of the merger. The area of the three states is the geographical market.
20. False The presumptive illegality test is applied to horizontal mergers.

Multiple Choice

21. C   Answer C is correct as Section 1 of the Sherman Act was intended to prohibit certain anticompetitive activities. Answer A is too vague and is therefore incorrect. Answer B refers to the act of monopolization and is therefore incorrect. Answer D is incorrect based on the reasons given above.
22. B   There is no justification or defense to price-fixing. Answer A is incorrect because it requires a balancing test that allows for justification. Answers C and D relate to Section 2 violations.
23. C   Answer C is a vertical restraint. Answers A, B, and D are incorrect because they are all horizontal restraints of trade under Section 1.

24. D Answer D is correct because it correctly defines a boycott. Answers A, B, and C are not correct because they do not involve a refusal to buy or sell goods or services.
25. D Answer D is the correct answer as it must be shown that there was a relevant product or service market as well as geographical market; additionally that plaintiff's relevant market share should be narrowly construed. As such, Answer D encompasses all that Answers A, B, and C contained.
26. C Section 2 prohibits the act of monopolization and attempts or conspiracies to monopolize. Answer A is prohibited by Section 1 of the Sherman Act. Answer B is prohibited by Section 7 of the Clayton Act. Answer D is prohibited by Section 3 of the Clayton Act.
27. D Answer D is correct because monopolization power is controlling the two key aspects of the market: prices and competition. Answer A is a restraint of trade, not a part of analyzing a monopoly. Answer B relates to a violation of the Clayton Act, not Section 2 of the Sherman Act. Answer C is relates to conglomerate mergers.
28. D All three choices are correct theories under which a conglomerate merger may be enjoined.
29. D Answer D is correct as the Robinson-Patman Act prohibits price discrimination by sellers of commodities of a like grade and quality. Further, it doesn't apply to the sale of services, real estate, or intangible property. Answer D reflects all of the statements contained in Answers A, B, and C.
35. D Answers A, B, and C are all correct statements of a defense to price discrimination under Section 2 of the Clayton Act; therefore Answer D is correct.

Short Answer

31. between the Antitrust Division of the Department of Justice and the Bureau of Competition of the FTC
32. The court will examine the following factors: The pro- and anticompetitive effects, the competitive structure of the industry, the firm's market share and power, the history and duration of the restraint, and other relevant factors.
33. a rule that is applicable to those restraints of trade considered inherently anticompetitive
34. Price-fixing occurs when competitors in the same line of business agree to set the price of the goods or services they sell. It is accomplished by raising, depressing, fixing, pegging, or stabilizing the price of a commodity or service.
35. group boycott
36. Section 1 of the Sherman Act
37. It includes a situation where a manufacturer assigns exclusive territories to retail dealers or limits the number of dealers that may be located in a certain territory.
38. There is no violation of Section 1 because each of the manufacturers acted on its own.
39. It is the area in which the defendant and its competitors sell the product or service. This may be a national, regional, state, or local area, depending on the circumstances.
40. the power to control prices or exclude competition
41. Market share above 70 percent is monopoly power. Market share under 20 percent is not monopoly power.
42. backward vertical merger
43. forward vertical merger
44. They are required to notify the FTC and the Justice Department in advance of a proposed merger.
45. No, because Section 2 of the Clayton Act does not apply to the sale of services.

Chapter 47

PERSONAL PROPERTY
AND BAILMENT

Chapter Overview

Property would have little if any value if the law did not protect the rights of owners to use, sell, dispose of, control, and prevent others from trespassing upon their property. Property may be either real property (buildings and land) or personal property. In this chapter we examine the types of personal property, the methods of acquiring ownership in personal property, and property rights in mislaid, lost, and abandoned property. The chapter then discusses bailment of property, situations where possession of (but not title to) property is delivered to another party for transfer, safekeeping, or use. The typical rental of equipment is a bailment.

Objectives

Upon completion of the exercises in this chapter, you should be able to
1. Define personal property.
2. Describe the methods for acquiring ownership in personal property.
3. Describe how ownership rights are transferred by gift.
4. Understand how title to personal property is acquired by purchase, production, accession, and confusion.
5. Apply the rules relating to lost, mislaid, and abandoned property.
6. Define ordinary bailments and list the elements of a bailment.
7. Describe the rights and duties of bailors and bailees.
8. Explain bailee liability for lost, damaged, or destroyed property.

Practical Application

Businesses are constantly transferring ownership of personal property or creating personal property for sale. Additionally, temporary use of property, whether by borrowing or renting, is a common commercial practice. The material in this chapter has valuable application to everyday business practices. Knowledge of the rights and duties relating to ownership and bailment of personal property helps anyone to make informed and reasoned choices when deciding how to deal with a personal property issue.

Helpful Hints

Once it is determined that something is personal property, it is wise to focus on the treatment of the property to determine who has rights in it and what duties may have arisen in regards to the property. The circumstances under which possession of property is accomplished from person to person or business to business will determine who may ultimately be responsible for damage to or loss of the property. The law differentiates the rights of people depending upon how they came into possession of the property and the circumstances surrounding the acquisition of possession.

As you study this material, look at the status of the property as it changes possession. This will guide you in applying the correct law to solve a personal property issue.

Study Tips

In order to answer questions or resolve disputes relating to personal property, it is wise to examine personal property from the perspective of creation and acquisition, transfer by gift, temporary or permanent loss, and rights and duties associated with bailments. The following terms and rules of law are essential to that understanding.

Acquiring Ownership in Personal Property

The methods for acquiring personal property are:
- *By Possession* – Property can be acquired by capturing it.
- *By Purchase or Production* – The most common way to obtain property is to purchase it. Production is another common method. A manufacturer who turns raw materials into a product acquires ownership of the product.
- *By Gift* – A gift is a voluntary transfer of property without consideration. The person making the gift is the donor and the person receiving the gift is the donee. The three elements of a valid gift are:
  1. **Donative intent.** For a gift to be effective, the donor must have intended to make a gift.
  2. **Delivery.** Delivery must occur for there to be a valid gift. Delivery can either be physical or constructive (giving title documents to a car).
  3. **Acceptance.** This is usually not a problem unless the gift is refused.
  Gifts *inter vivos* are made during a person's lifetime while a gift *causa mortis* is made in contemplation of death. Gifts *causa mortis* can be revoked up until the time of death.
  Uniform Gift to Minor Acts allow adults to make irrevocable gifts to minors. The custodian of the gift has broad discretionary powers to invest the money or securities for the benefit of the minor.
- *By Will or Inheritance* – If a person who dies has a valid will, the property is distributed to the beneficiaries, pursuant to the provisions of the will.
- *By Accession* – Accession occurs when the value of personal property increases because it is added to or improved by natural or manufactured means.
- *By Confusion* – Confusion occurs if two or more persons commingle fungible goods. The owners share ownership in the commingled goods to the amount of the goods contributed.
- *By Divorce* – Parties obtain property rights in the property of the marital estate.

Mislaid, Lost, and Abandoned Property

People find property belonging to others and ownership rights to the property differs depending on whether the property was mislaid, lost, or abandoned. These are the rules that apply to property in those categories.
- *Mislaid Property* – Property is mislaid when the owner places it somewhere and forgets it. The owner will probably return when it is discovered that the property was mislaid. The owner of the property where it was found has the right to take possession against all except the rightful owner. The owner of the premises becomes an

involuntary bailee and must take reasonable care of the property until it is reclaimed. The typical situation for this is when a patron leaves their glasses or jacket at a business.

- *Lost Property* – Property is lost when the owner negligently, carelessly, or inadvertently leaves it somewhere. The finder of the property takes title against the world except the true owner. The finder must make efforts to return the property.
- *Abandoned Property* – Property is classified as abandoned if the owner discards the property with the intent to relinquish his rights in it or he gives up all attempts to locate lost or misplaced property.
- **Estray Statutes** – Most states have an estray statute, which dictates what the finder of lost or misplaced property must do to acquire title to the property. This usually includes turning the property over to the police, giving notice that the property was found, and waiting for a time period to pass. The finder can then claim ownership.

Bailments

A bailment is a transaction where the owner transfers his or her personal property to another to be held, stored, delivered, or for some other purpose. Title to the property remains with the owner. The owner of the property is the bailor and the party who received the property is the bailee.

- There are three essential elements that must be present to create a bailment:
  1. Only personal property can be bailed.
  2. There must be delivery of possession which also involves two elements:
     (i) The bailee has exclusive control over the personal property.
     (ii) The bailee must knowingly accept the personal property.
  3. There must be a bailment agreement, which may be either express or implied.

Ordinary Bailments

There are three classifications of ordinary bailments. The importance of these categories is that they determine the degree of care owed by the bailee in protecting the bailed property. The three categories are:

- **Bailments for the sole benefit of the bailor** are gratuitous bailments that benefit only the bailor. The typical gratuitous bailment involves the bailee watching the bailor's property as a favor without compensation. The bailee only owed a duty of slight care. As long as the bailee is not grossly negligent, no liability will be incurred for loss or damage.
- **Bailments for the sole benefit of the bailee** are gratuitous bailments for the sole benefit of the bailee. This is the typical "borrowing the lawnmower" situation. The bailee owes a duty of great care. The bailee is responsible for even the slightest negligence.
- **Mutual benefit bailments** are made for the benefit of both the bailor and bailee. The bailee has a duty of reasonable care, making the bailee liable for any goods that are lost, damaged, or destroyed because of his or her negligence. This is the typical paid storage or valet parking situation.

Special Bailments

Special bailees include common carriers, innkeepers, and warehouse companies. In addition to the rules applicable to ordinary bailees, they are subject to the special liability rules contained in Article 7 of the Uniform Commercial Code (UCC).

- **Common Carriers** – These bailees offer transportation to the public. They include airlines, railroads, bus companies, trucking companies, and public pipeline carriers. The delivery of goods to a common carrier creates a mutual benefit bailment. Unlike an ordinary bailment, common carriers are held to a duty of strict liability. If goods are lost, damaged, or stolen, the common carrier is liable even if it was not at fault. The liability of airlines for lost luggage is limited to $1,250 per piece of luggage for a domestic flight.
- **Warehouse Companies** – These bailees contract for the storage of goods for compensation. They are held to a duty of reasonable case. They are not liable for the negligence of others that causes loss or damage.
- **Innkeepers** – An innkeeper owns a facility that provides lodging for compensation. Under common law, innkeepers are held to strict liability for the loss or damage to the property of guests. Most all states have innkeepers statutes that limit the liability of innkeepers. To limit their liability, the innkeeper must provide a safe and make guests aware of its availability for their use.

Duration and Termination of Bailments

Bailments usually end at a specified time or when a certain purpose has been achieved.

Documents of Title

A document of title generally serves as a receipt for the goods, establishes the terms of the bailment contract, and evidences title to the goods. It is evidence that the holder of the receipt is entitled to receive, hold, and dispose of the document and the goods that it covers.

- **Warehouse Receipts** – This is a written document issued by a warehouseman. It contains the terms of the bailment. The warehouse has a lien on the goods until all expenses incurred have been satisfied.
- **Bill of Lading** – This document of title is issued by a carrier when goods are received for shipment. Bills of lading are issued by common carriers, contract carriers and others engaged in the business of transporting goods. A through bill of lading provides that connecting carriers may be used to transport the goods. The original carrier is liable to the bailor for loss or damage caused by the connecting carrier.

Refresh Your Memory

The following exercise will enable you to refresh your memory of the principles presented to you in this chapter. Read each question twice and place your answer in the blanks provided. Complete the entire exercise, and then review the chapter material for any question you miss or are unable to remember.

1.   Concurrent ownership means _____.

2. The most common method of acquiring title to personal property is by _____ the property from its owner.

3. A gift is _____.

4. A gift *inter vivos* is a gift made during a person's _____ that is an _____ transfer of ownership.

5. Acts that establish procedures for adults to make gifts of money and securities to minors would fall under the _____ _____ to _____ Act and _____ _____ _____ to _____ Act.

6. _____ occurs when the value of personal property increases because it is added to or improved by natural or _____ means.

7. Property is _____ when its owner voluntarily places the property somewhere and then inadvertently forgets it.

8. The finder of _____ property obtains title to the found property against everyone except the _____ owner.

9. _____ statutes permit the finder of lost or misplaced property to obtain title to the property if they follow the procedure set forth in the statute.

10. Anyone who finds _____ property acquires title to it.

11. If Brenda delivers her Corvette to Jason's Storage for safekeeping, Jason would be considered the _____.

12. Using the example in the previous question, Brenda is the _____.

13. Bailments for the sole benefit of the bailor are _____ bailments for which the bailee owes only a duty of _____ care.

14. Common carriers are held to a duty of _____ _____.

15. A _____ _____ _____ is a document of title that is issued by a carrier when goods are received for transportation.

Critical Thought Exercise

Tom Cruel, chairman of the Central Republican Committee for Rashaw County, was transporting a valuable painting in his trunk to a friend's home where it was to be displayed during a fundraiser. Cruel stopped at the country club for lunch and left his Mercedes in the care of a parking attendant who worked for Jiffy Parking Service, Inc. The attendant left the key box unattended while taking a break. The car and its contents were stolen. The car was recovered by police using a global positioning system, but the trunk was empty upon its return. Cruel was missing the painting worth $30,000, a golf bag and clubs valued at $1,400, and a CD case containing 120 music compact discs worth an estimated $1,500. Cruel has filed suit against Jiffy

for the value of all the items taken from the trunk, including the painting. Is Jiffy liable to Cruel?
If so, for which stolen items must it pay damages to Cruel?

Answer:

_____

_____

_____

_____

_____

_____

_____

_____

_____

_____

_____

_____

_____

_____

_____

_____

_____

_____

Practice Quiz

True/False

1. ____   Personal property may be acquired or transferred with a minimum of formality [p. 739]

2. ____   Title to personal property is rarely accomplished by will or inheritance. [p. 741]

3. ____   The laws give custodians broad discretionary powers to invest money or securities for the benefit of the minor. [p. 741]

4. ____   The owner of the premises where the property is mislaid is entitled to take possession of the property against all including the rightful owner. [p. 743]

5. ____   The Uniform Gift to Minors Act is used by adults whenever they want to give a gift of any type of personal property to a minor. [p. 741]

6. ____   If a person dies without a will, his/her property will be distributed to the beneficiaries. [p. 741]

7. ____   A business owner who has an addition built on his building acquires ownership by confusion. [p. 742]

8. ___ If an improvement is made to the owner's property by mistake and the improvement cannot be removed, the owner obtains title to the improvement but must pay for it. [p. 742]

9. ___ Confusion occurs if two parties divorce. [p. 742]

10. ___ Anyone who finds abandoned property acquires title to it. [p. 745]

11. ___ In a bailment for the sole benefit of the bailor, the bailee owes only a duty of slight care to protect the bailed property. [p. 747]

12. ___ Federal law requires common carriers who take advantage of limiting their liability to a stated dollar amount as per their bail agreement to offer shippers the chance to pay a premium and declare a higher value for the goods. [p. 749]

13. ___ If an owner of mislaid or lost property gives up any further attempts to locate the property, the property is abandoned. [p. 743]

14. ___ Many states require the finder of lost property to conduct a reasonable search to find the rightful owner. [p. 744]

15. ___ A bailment is different than a sale or a gift because title to the goods does not transfer to the bailee. [p. 746]

16. ___ Tangible or intangible personal property can be bailed. [p. 746]

17. ___ To have a delivery, the property must be put in the possession of the bailee, but the bailee does not have to knowingly accept the personal property. [p. 746]

18. ___ Innkeeper statutes allow innkeepers to avoid liability for loss caused to guests' property if a safe is provided in which the guests' valuable property may be kept and the guests are aware of the safe's availability. [p. 750]

19. ___ Warehousers are not liable for loss or damage to their bailed property caused by their own negligence. [p. 748]

20. ___ The bailee in a gratuitous bailment owes a duty of ordinary care. [p. 747]

Multiple Choice

21. Which of the following applies to personal property? [p. 739]
    a. A seller may remove personal property from real estate prior to its sale.
    b. Personal property is real property.
    c. Minerals are considered personal property.
    d. Since crops can be removed from land, they are personal property.

22. Which of the following is a method of acquiring ownership in personal property? [pp. 739-740]
    a. By possession
    b. By purchase or production
    c. By gift
    d. all of the above

23. Ella, while visiting her cousin Abby, volunteered to help Abby with some painting. Ella did not want to get paint on her $3,000 diamond tennis bracelet, so she took it off and set it down where the two ladies were working. Upon finishing the job for the day, Ella could not locate her tennis bracelet. After Ella left Abby's house, Abby found the bracelet. What duty does Abby have to Ella? [p. 743]
    a. She has no duty, as "finders keepers, losers weepers."
    b. She already fulfilled her duty by helping Abby look for the bracelet.
    c. She has a duty to return it to Ella, the rightful owner.
    d. none of the above

24. When a person cuts a car in half, adds a middle section, and creates a limousine, he has acquired ownership to the limousine by [p. 742]
    a. purchase or production.
    b. gift.
    c. confusion.
    d. accession.

25. Marissa was in a hurry as she departed a bus she was on and, as such, she left her leather back pack sitting on the seat. Paul, a new passenger on this same bus saw the back pack and decided to keep it. Later that day, Hal, the bus driver saw Marissa and told her that Paul had her back pack. When approached by Marissa, Paul refused to give it back to her telling her that he found it and he was going to keep it. What legal choices does Marissa have against Paul? [p. 744]
    a. She doesn't have any choices, as she was irresponsible in leaving the backpack in the first place.
    b. She can offer Paul a small amount as a reward for its return.
    c. She may have a cause of action for the tort of conversion and have him charged with larceny as well.
    d. none of the above

26. If Sue put her purse on the top of her car and it is blown off the roof as she drives to work, the purse is [p. 743]
    a. mislaid property.
    b. lost property.
    c. abandoned property.
    d. intangible property.

27. When a co-worker leaves their car at your house while on vacation, this is a [p. 747]
    a. bailment for the sole benefit of the bailor.
    b. bailment for the sole benefit of the bailee.
    c. mutual benefit bailment.
    d. gift.

28. A bailment cannot exist without [p. 746]
    a. personal property.
    b. delivery of possession.
    c. a bailment agreement.
    d. all of the above

29. Which of the following creates a mutual benefit bailment? [p. 749]
    a. Barbara asks Jerry to care for her cat while she is vacationing.
    b. Lyla asks Tilly if she can borrow her crock pot for a party she is hosting.
    c. The Santa Lula Transit System has been asked to deliver a crate of oranges to the Santa Lula School District Office.
    d. all of the above

30. Bailments without a fixed term are called [p. 749]
    a. open ended bailment
    b. bailments at will
    c. bailments for a fixed term
    d. none of the above

Short Answer

31. What type of property allows the finder to acquire title to it, even against its original owner? [p. 745]

    _____
    _____

32. When must a bailment be in writing? [p. 746]

    _____
    _____

33. What three elements must be shown to prove a valid gift? [p. 740]
    (1) _____
    (2) _____
    (3) _____

34. Is a heating system considered a fixture or personal property and why? [p. 739]

    _____
    _____

35. Most states have an estray statute that permits a finder of lost or misplaced property to clear title to the property (and become the new owner) if [p. 744]

    _____
    _____
    _____

36. John, who owns fifty Kennedy half dollars, and Marge, who owns thirty Kennedy half dollars, both place their coins in the center of John's dining room table. They both soon realize that they cannot tell whose money is whose. What term is used to describe the situation and how many coins does each now own? [p. 742]

    _____
    _____
    _____

37. What is a bailment for the sole benefit of the bailor? [p. 747]

    _____
    _____
    _____

38. What must a bailee do at the termination of a bailment? [p. 748]

    _____
    _____
    _____

39. If Pricilla borrows Sheila's automatic mixer for a recipe she is making, but leaves it laying in the sink only to rust from water constantly being ran over it, what type of bailment is this? [p. 747]

    _____
    _____
    _____

40. Using the facts in the previous question, what duty did the bailee owe and what is her liability if any to the bailor? [p. 747]

    _____
    _____
    _____

41. What type of duty does the bailee have in a mutual benefit bailment? [p. 748]

    _____
    _____
    _____

42. When are warehouses liable for loss or damage to the bailed property? [p. 748]

    _____
    _____
    _____

43. Under common law, what standards were innkeepers held to when a transient guest suffered a loss? [p. 750]

    _____

44. What must an innkeeper do to take advantage of an innkeeper's statute? [p. 750]

    _____
    _____
    _____

45. Identify who the consignor, consignee, and common carrier are if Busco, a public trucking company, accepts goods from Doug that are to be delivered to Samantha. [p.749]

_____

_____

_____

Answers to Refresh Your Memory

1. property owned concurrently by two or more persons [p. 739]
2. purchasing [p. 740]
3. a voluntary transfer of property without consideration [p. 740]
4. life time; irrevocable [p. 740]
5. Uniform Gift to Minors Act; Revised Uniform Gift to Minors Act [p. 742]
6. Accession; manufactured [p. 742]
7. mislaid [p. 743]
8. lost; true [p. 743]
9. Estray [p. 744]
10. abandoned [p. 745]
11. bailee [p. 745]
12. bailor [p. 745]
13. gratuitous; slight [p. 747]
14. strict liability [p. 747]
15. bill of lading [p. 749]

Critical Thought Exercise Model Answer

For liability to be created, a bailment must exist. A bailment is created when personal property is delivered into the possession of a bailee by a bailor for a stated purpose for some period of time. The bailee has the right of exclusive possession, but the bailor retains ownership of the bailed property. Delivery may be accomplished by actual physical delivery of the property or constructive delivery of an item that gives control of the property, such as delivery of a car key to a parking lot attendant. By delivering his car key to the employee of Jiffy Parking, Cruel created a bailment agreement. Mutual benefit bailments are bailments that benefit both parties. The bailee (Jiffy) owes a duty of reasonable care to protect the bailed goods. The bailee is liable for any goods that are lost, stolen, damaged, or destroyed because of his or her negligence. The law presumes that if bailed property is lost, damaged, destroyed, or stolen while in the possession of the bailee, it is because of lack of proper care by the bailee. The typical commercial bailment where someone pays to have his property watched for a fee is this type of bailment. A bailee accepts responsibility for unknown contents of a bailed automobile when the presence of those contents is reasonably foreseeable based on the factual circumstances surrounding the bailment of the automobile. It cannot be said that a country club parking attendant should reasonably foresee the presence of a valuable painting in a member's car trunk. Unless the bailee accepts possession of the property, either expressly or impliedly, there can be no bailment. Therefore, Jiffy Parking had no duty of care to protect the painting in the trunk. The other items lead to a different result. It is quite foreseeable that a club member would have golf clubs in his trunk. Additionally, car owners often have cases to carry an assortment of music for them to play in their car. Jiffy Parking will be liable to Cruel for $2,900, the cost of the golf clubs and compact discs.

Answers to Practice Quiz

True/False

1. True   Personal property may be acquired or transferred with a minimum of formality.
2. False   Title to personal property is frequently acquired by will or inheritance.
3. True   The laws give custodians broad discretionary powers to invest the money or securities for the benefit of the minor.
4. False   The owner of the premises where the property is mislaid is entitled to take possession of the property against all except the rightful owner.
5. False   This statute applies only to gifts of money or stock.
6. False   If a will does not exist, the property is distributed to the heirs by statute.
7. False   Accession occurs when the value of personal property increases because it is added to or improved by natural or manufactured means.
8. False   The owner does not have to pay for the improvement.
9. False   Confusion occurs if two or more persons commingle fungible goods.
10. True   The finder of abandoned property acquires title to that property.
11. True   In a bailment for the sole benefit of the bailor, the bailee owes only a duty of slight care to protect the bailed property.
12. True   Federal law requires common carriers who take advantage of limiting their liability to offer shippers the opportunity to pay a premium and declare a higher value for the goods.
13. True   Anyone who finds this property acquires title to it.
14. True   Many states require the finder to conduct a reasonable search to find the rightful owner.
15. True   Instead, the bailee must follow the bailor's directions concerning the goods.
16. True   Real property cannot be bailed.
17. False The bailee must knowingly accept the personal property.
18. True.   Innkeepers statutes allow innkeepers to avoid liability for loss caused to guests' property if a safe is provided in which the guests' valuable property may be kept and the guests are aware of the safe's availability.
19. False Warehousers are liable only for loss or damage to the bailed property caused by their own negligence.
20. False The bailee only owes a duty of slight care.

Multiple Choice

21. A   Answer A is correct as a seller may remove personal property from real estate before it is sold. Answer B is incorrect as it is a false statement. Answer C is incorrect as minerals are real property. Answer D is also incorrect as crops are considered real property as well.
22. D   Answer D is correct because all three choices are methods for acquiring personal property.
23. C   Answer C is correct as Ella as an involuntary bailee has a duty to take reasonable care of the bracelet till it is returned to Abby, its rightful owner. Answer A is incorrect as it is a false statement as Abby has a duty as per the law regarding mislaid property. Answer B is incorrect as Ella's status as an involuntary bailee does have duties regarding mislaid property. Answer D is incorrect based on the reasons given above.

24. D   When goods are improved by manufacture, this is accession. Answer A is incorrect because production is from scratch, and the limousine was added to an already existing piece of property. Answer B is incorrect because there is no indication that the limousine was given to the new owner. Answer C is incorrect because this is not a fungible good that has been commingled.

25. C   Answer C is correct as a finder who refuses to return lost property knowing who its owner is may be liable for the tort of conversion as well as for the crime of larceny. Answer A is incorrect as her negligence does not have a bearing on the end result. Answer B is incorrect as it is a false statement that is not a legally recognized choice. Answer D is incorrect based on the reasons given above.

26. B   Sue has negligently let the purse be blown off and it is now in an unknown location. Answer A is incorrect because Sue did not intentionally place her purse in the road. Answer C is incorrect because she did not intend to relinquish her ownership interest in the purse. Answer D is not correct because the purse is tangible property.

27. A   The co-worker is the bailor and is the only one receiving a benefit from this bailment. Answer B is incorrect because there is no benefit to the bailee in this situation. Answer C is incorrect because there is no benefit for the bailee, nor is there any compensation involved. Answer D is not correct because the co-worker did not intend to pass title by leaving the car.

28. D   Answers A, B, and C are essential elements of a bailment. Answer D is therefore correct.

29. C   Answer C is correct as the delivery of goods to a common carrier creates a mutual benefit bailment. Answer A is incorrect as this is a benefit for the sole benefit of the bailor, Barbara. Answer B is incorrect as this is a sole benefit for the sole benefit of the bailee, Fred. Answer D is incorrect based on the reasons given above.

30. B   Answer B is correct as bailments without a fixed term are called bailments at will. Answer A is incorrect as there is no such thing as an open ended bailment. Answer C is incorrect as that is why it is called a bailment at will, because it doesn't have a fixed term. Answer D is incorrect based on the reasons given above.

Short Answer

31.   abandoned property
32.   if it is for more than one year
33.   (1) donative intent (2) delivery (3) acceptance
34.   fixture as it is permanently affixed to a building. Personal property can be removed, as it is more portable.
35   (1) The finder reports the found property to the appropriate government agency and turns over possession. (2) Post notices describing the lost property. (3) A specified time passes without the rightful owner claiming the property.
36.   The goods are said to be commingled and each has an ownership interest in proportion to the amount each contributed before the commingling took place. So, John owns fifty and Marge owns 30 of the Kennedy half dollars.
37.   A gratuitous bailment is one that only benefits the bailor.
38.   The bailee is obligated to do as the bailor directs with the property. Usually, the bailee is obligated to return the identical goods bailed.
39.   a benefit for the sole benefit of the bailee (Sheila)
40.   Sheila owed a duty of great or utmost care and is liable to Pricilla for the automatic mixer.
41.   duty of reasonable or ordinary care
42.   Warehousers are liable only for loss or damage to the bailed property caused by their own negligence. They owe a duty of reasonable care.

43. strict liability
44. The innkeeper can avoid liability if a safe is provided in which the guests' valuable property may be kept and the guest was aware of the safe's availability.
45. Busco is the common carrier; Doug is the shipper or consignor; and Samantha is the consignee.

Chapter 48

REAL PROPERTY

Chapter Overview

In the Western world, we have come to value real property more than most any other possession. To the ownership of land attaches wealth and influence in Western society. More importantly, the privacy rights associated with property ownership are assigned great personal worth and psychological value. Even in the face of government power, we proclaim, "A man's home is his castle." In this chapter we focus on the legal rights associated with ownership, occupation, use, and transfer of real property.

Chapter Objectives

Upon completion of the exercises contained in this chapter, you should be able to
1. Explain the different types of ownership interests in real property.
2. Describe ownership interests in surface, subsurface, and air rights.
3. Describe a life estate.
4. Identify and explain the future interests of reversion and remainder.
5. Explain the different types of joint tenancy.
6. Describe the difference between separate property and community property.
7. Understand how property can be acquired by adverse possession.
8. Explain recording statutes.
9. Distinguish between easements appurtenant and easements in gross.

Practical Application

Upon mastering the concepts in this chapter, you should be able to recognize how a piece of real property is held by the owner and what affect that has upon its use, transfer, and value. As an example, real estate that has an easement attached to it is worth less because another party has the right to use the property for their own purposes as specified in the easement. When the property is transferred to another owner, that owner may have to accept the easement, depending on whether legal requirements have been met.

Helpful Hints

There are many rules created by common law, statute, and current case law. A logical order can be created to this large volume of law if you focus on the creation of the right in the land, its transfer, and perfecting the right by giving notice to the rest of the world. When you are faced with a real property problem, you need to know how the person or company obtained its interest in the real property, what rights go with that interest, if any other party claims a joint interest in the same property, and how that interest is protected or sold to another. Unlike personal property that is usually not granted to a beneficiary until a will becomes effective, the transfer of an interest in real property may be dictated by the language and conditions contained in the deed. It is often necessary to look backwards in the line of owners to determine who will own the interest in the future.

Study Tips

The following outline will help you create a mental checklist of the main issues and rights involved in ownership and transfer of rights in real property. This "checklist" is constantly trying to answer the following questions:

- Is this real or personal property?
- In what form is the real property currently owned?
- Does anyone hold a future interest in this land?
- Is anyone a co-owner of this real property?
- Was there a legal transfer of an ownership interest?
- Was the transfer of the ownership interest property recorded by deed?
- Does anyone own a nonpossessory interest in this real property?
- Is any legal action being taken against the real property?

Nature of Real Property

Real property is the land itself and any buildings, trees, soil, minerals, timber, plants, and other things that are permanently affixed to the land. Any building or permanent structure that is built upon the land becomes part of the real property. The owner of the property also owns the **subsurface rights** to any minerals, oil, gas, or other commodity that may be under the surface. These subsurface rights may be sold separate from the rest of the real property. **Plant life and vegetation** growing on the surface of land are considered real property. Both natural and cultivated plants are part of the real property. They become personal property if the owner severs them from the land. Items that are permanently affixed to the land or a building become part of the real property if they cannot be removed without causing substantial damage to the realty. A regular refrigerator would remain personal property and may be removed when the realty is sold. A built-in commercial refrigerator becomes a *fixture* and is sold with the realty.

One other type of property is the air space above the surface of realty. This space may be sold or leased separate from the realty like a subsurface right.

Estates in Land

The ownership right one possesses in real property is called an estate in land. An estate is defined as the bundle of legal rights that the owner has to possess, use, and enjoy the property. The type of estate an owner possesses is determined by the deed, will, lease, or other document that created or transferred ownership rights.

- A *freehold estate* is an estate where the owner has a present possessory interest in the real property. Two types of freehold estates are estates in fee and life estates.
- A *fee simple absolute* is a type of ownership of real property that grants the owner the fullest bundle of legal rights that a person can hold in real property.
- A *fee simple defeasible* grants the owner all the incidents of a fee simple absolute except that it may be taken away if a specified condition occurs or does not occur.
- A *life estate* is an interest in land for a person's lifetime. Upon that person's death, the interest will be transferred to another party. Note that a life tenant is treated as the owner of the property during the duration of the life estate.

Concurrent Ownership

The forms of co-ownership or concurrent ownership are
- *Joint Tenancy* – Upon the death of one owner, the property passes to the other joint tenants automatically. This is called the right of survivorship.
- *Tenancy in Common* – The interest of a surviving tenant in common passes to the deceased tenant's estate and not to the co-tenants.
- *Tenancy by the Entirety* – This form can only be used by married couples. This also has a right of survivorship, but unlike a joint tenancy, one tenant cannot sell their interest in the realty.
- *Community Property* – Nine states recognize community property rights. Upon the death of one spouse, one-half of the community assets automatically pass to the surviving spouse. The other half passes by will or by the state's intestate statute.
- *Condominium* – A form of ownership in a multiple-dwelling building where the purchaser has title to an individual unit and owns the common areas as a tenant in common.
- *Cooperative* – A form of ownership of a multiple-dwelling building where a corporation owns the building and the residents own shares in the corporation.

Future Interests

A person may be given the right to possess property in the future rather than in the present. The two forms of future interests are:
- *Reversion* – A right of possession that returns to the grantor after the expiration of a limited or contingent estate.
- *Remainder* –The right of possession returns to a third party upon the expiration of a limited or contingent estate.

Transfer of Ownership of Real Property

An owner may transfer his/her interest in realty by one of the following methods:
- *Sale* – This is the passing of title from a seller to a buyer for a price. It is also called a conveyance.
- *Tax Sale* – The government may obtain a tax lien against property for unpaid property taxes. If the lien remains unpaid, a tax sale is held to satisfy the lien.
- *Gift, Will, Inheritance* – These forms of transfer involve granting title to another without the payment of any consideration.
- *Adverse Possession* – When a person openly possesses the property of another, he/she may acquire title if certain statutory requirements are met. The owner must have notice that his or her land is being wrongfully possesses and take no steps to eject the adverse possessor.

Deeds and Recording Statutes

Deeds are used to convey property by sale or gift. The seller or donor is called the *grantor*. The buyer or recipient is the *grantee*. A *warranty deed* has the greatest number of warranties or guarantees. The *quitclaim deed* provides no protection for the buyer, granting only whatever interest the grantor possesses.

A ***recording statute*** provides that copies of the deed and other documents, such as mortgages and deeds of trust, may be filed with the *county recorder's office* to give constructive notice of the ownership to the world. Recording statutes are intended to prevent fraud and to establish certainty in the ownership and transfer of property.

A seller has the obligation to transfer ***marketable title*** to the grantee. Marketable title means that the title is free from encumbrances, defects in title, or other defects that would affect the value of the property.

Nonpossessory Interests

Nonpossessory interests exist when a person holds an interest in another person's property without actually owning any part of the property. The three nonpossesory interests are

- **Easements** – An easement is a given or required right to make limited use of someone else's land without owning or leasing it.
  Easements may be **expressly** created by
  1. *grant* – where the owner gives another party an easement across his or her property
  2. *reservation* – where an owner sells his or her land but keeps an easement on the land
  Easements may be **implied** by
  1. *implication* – where an owner subdivides a piece of property with a well, path, road, or other beneficial appurtenant that serves the entire parcel, or by
  2. *necessity* – where a landlocked parcel must have egress and ingress
- There are two types of easements
  1. Easements Appurtenant – A situation created when the owner of a piece of land is given an easement over an adjacent piece of land.
  2. Easements in Gross – An easement that authorizes a person who does not own adjacent land the right to use another's land. Examples include easements granted for power lines, telephone lines, gas lines, and cable lines.
  The easement holder owes a duty to maintain and repair the easement.
- **Licenses** – A license grants a person the right to enter upon another's property for a specified and usually short period of time. A ticket to a football game gives you a license to use a seat in the stadium for a period of time.
- **Profit** – Grants a person the right to remove something from another's real property.

Refresh Your Memory

The following exercise will enable you to refresh your memory on the rules of law and principles presented to you in this chapter. Read each question twice and put your answer in the blanks provided. Review the chapter material for any question that you miss or are unable to remember.

1. _____ is the most common form of real property.

2. The owner of land possesses _____ rights or _____ rights, to the earth located beneath the surface of the land.

3. Plant life that is severed from the land is considered_____ property.

4. List two forms of co-ownership:_____ and _____.

5. What happens if Joan, who is a joint tenant of lake front property with Maurice, sells her interest to Cody?

   _____.

6. A form of co-ownership of a multiple-dwelling building in which a corporation owns the building and the residents own shares in the corporation is known as a

   _____.

7. The buyer or recipient of real property is called the _____.

8. A writing that describes a person's ownership interest in a piece of real property is a

   _____.

9. What is the purpose of having a recording statute?_____

   _____

   _____.

10. The land that benefits from the easement is called the _____ estate.

11. What duties does an easement holder have? _____

12. A _____ a'pendre gives the holder the right to remove something from another's real property.

13. A given or required right to make limited use of someone else's land without owning or leasing it is an _____.

14. A document that grants a person the right to enter upon another's property for a specified and usually short period of time is a _____.

Critical Thought Exercise

Jim Lewis and Dale Tingle decided to form a partnership for the purpose of entering the restaurant business. Prior to forming the partnership, Lewis and Tingle purchased a large Victorian house in Sacramento with the idea that they would convert the first floor into a restaurant and the upper floors into office space. Lewis contributed $90,000 to the purchase and Tingle contributed $10,000. Lewis and Tingle took title as joint tenants with the right of survivorship. The partnership was formed five months later and the Sacramento property was converted into a restaurant and offices as planned. When Lewis and Tingle purchased another house in Davis, California, they took title as tenants in common. Tingle contributed $100,000 as the down payment for the Davis property. When the partnership was dissolved, the court ordered that both properties be sold. Lewis was given a reimbursement for the Sacramento property in the amount of $80,000. The Davis property was sold for $320,000 and the proceeds of the sale were divided equally between Lewis and Tingle. Did the court divide the proceeds from the sale of the two properties properly?

Answer:

_____
_____
_____
_____
_____
_____
_____
_____
_____
_____
_____
_____
_____
_____
_____
_____
_____
_____
_____

Practice Quiz

True/False

1. ___ Buildings constructed on land are personal property. [p. 755]

2. ___ Subsurface rights may not be sold separately from surface rights. [p. 755]

3. ___ Natural plants such as trees are real property, but cultivated plants such as a corn crop are personal property. [p. 755]

4. ___ A life tenant is treated as the owner of the property during the duration of the life of the estate. [p. 757]

5. ___ Property that Ted acquired from his Uncle Walter's estate while Ted was married to Louise is considered Ted's separate property. [p. 758]

6. ___ A freehold estate is one where the owner has a future possessory interest in realty. [p. 756]

7. ___ A fee simple absolute is the highest form of ownership of real property. [p. 756]

8. ___ A sale and a conveyance are not the same thing. [p. 761]

9. ___ If a person dies without a will, his or her property is distributed through a court created will. [p. 763]

10. ___ The most distinguished feature of a joint tenancy is the co-owner's right to survivorship. [p. 757]

11. ___ A remainder is a right of possession that returns to the grantor after the expiration of limited or contingent estate. [p. 760]

12. ___ If the right of possession returns to a third party upon the expiration of a limited or contingent estate, it is called a remainder. [p. 760]

13. ___ Picture Me Cable has an easement in gross on Bill's property.

14. ___ Each time a property is transferred or refinanced, a new title insurance policy must be obtained. [p. 763]

15. ___ Adjacent land is defined as two estates that abut one another. [p. 765]

16. ___ Just because the elements for a cause of action for adverse possession have been met does not mean that the adverse possessor will obtain clear title to the property he or she has been on. [p.765]

17. ___ A condominium is a form of co-ownership of a multiple-dwelling building where a corporation owns the building and the residents own shares on the corporation. [p. 759]

18. ___ An estate where the owner has a present possessory interest in the real property is a freehold estate. [p. 756]

19. ___ A mortgage can exceed the duration of a life estate. [p. 757]

20. ___ An easement would be considered to be a nonpossessory interest in another person's property. [p. 765]

Multiple Choice

21. Which of the following is real property? [p. 755]
    a. The tables and chairs in a restaurant
    b. A portable hot tub
    c. A camper in which a family is living
    d. An in-ground swimming pool

22. The rights to natural gas under Sue's home are her [p. 755]
    a. easement rights.
    b. profit.
    c. personal property.
    d. subsurface rights.

23. Which of the following would be considered part of real property? [p. 756]
    a. Throw rugs
    b. A dining room table that weighs 350 pounds
    c. Carpeting
    d. A large fern in a massive ceramic pot

24. If a grantor conveys property "to Ann Brown for life," the grantor's retained interest in the property is called a [p. 757]
    a. reversion.
    b. remainder.
    c. life estate.
    d. tenancy in common.

25. Which of the following applies to the concept of adverse possession? [p. 764]
    a. A lessee can claim title to property.
    b. The adverse possessor need not occupy the property.
    c. The adverse possessor can take the property by force from the owner.
    d. Most states say that wrongful possession must last between 10 and 20 years.

26. Larry conveys Blackacre to "Jim Smith and Greg Brown, as tenants in common." Jim Smith has a will that leaves his entire estate to Ned Green. If Smith dies, his interest in Blackacre will pass to [p. 757]
    a. Smith's heirs under the state's intestate statute.
    b. Green.
    c. Brown.
    d. none of the above

27. The owner of a condominium [p. 759]
    a. has title to his/her individual unit.
    b. owns the common areas as tenants in common with the other owners.
    c. may sell or mortgage his/her unit without the permission of the other owners.
    d. all of the above

28. With regard to adverse possession, the requirement that possession be hostile and adverse refers to [p. 764]
    a. the occupancy needing to be continuous.
    b. the occupancy needing to put the true owner on notice.
    c. the occupancy needs to be without the express or implied permission of the owner.
    d. the occupancy must be plant crops or build a structure on the premises.

29. Gus has a home on a 10-acre parcel that he subdivides into two 5-acre parcels. Gus builds a new house on the subdivided parcel. The only way for the new homeowner to get to the main road is to drive across Gus's parcel. The new homeowner has acquired an [p. 765]
    a. easement by express grant.
    b. easement by implication.
    c. license.
    d. profit a'pendre.

30. Charlotte has failed to pay taxes on her 3,000-square-foot house in Connecticut. What may the government do in this situation? [p. 763]
    a. Obtain a lien on the property for the amount of the taxes
    b. Rent the property if the taxes remain unpaid for the time allotted by statute
    c. Absolutely nothing
    d. Satisfy the tax amount out of any homeowner policy that Charlotte may have

Short Answer

31. Things such as radio towers, bridges, and grain silos are considered _____ property. [p. 755]

32. _____ parcels may be sold or leased above owner's land. [p. 756]

33. During a marriage, neither spouse can _____, _____, or _____ community property without the consent of the other spouse. [p. 758]

34. What determines whether or not community property law applies? [p. 758]

35. How can title to real property be transferred? [p. 761]

36. What does every state have that enables it to provide copies of deeds and other documents concerning interests in real property? [p. 761]

37. Where would such things as mortgages, liens, and easements be filed? [p. 761]

38. What is a joint tenancy and how should it be created in a deed? [p. 757]

39. What must a cooperative owner do before selling his or her share or before subleasing his or her unit? [p. 759]

40. What is a reversion? [p. 760]

41. Why don't reversions need to be expressly stated? [p. 760]

42. What can a person do who is concerned about his or her ownership rights in a parcel of real property? [p. 762]

43. What effect does recording a deed to real estate have? [p. 762]

44. What is a marketable title? [p. 763]

_____
_____
_____

45. When is a gift considered made? [p.763]

_____
_____

Answers to Refresh Your Memory

1. Land [p. 755]
2. subsurface; mineral [p. 755]
3. personal [p. 755]
4. community property; tenancy in common (answers will vary) [p. 757]
5. The joint tenancy is terminated and Maurice and Cody are now tenants in common. [p. 757]
6. cooperative [p. 759]
7. grantee [p. 761]
8. deed [p. 761]
9. to prevent fraud and establish certainty in ownership transfers [p. 761]
10. dominant [p. 765]
11. to maintain and repair the easement [p. 765]
12. profit [p. 766]
13. easement [p. 765]
14. license [p 765]

Critical Thought Exercise Model Answer

The deed to the Sacramento property created a joint tenancy in the real estate. When a joint tenancy is created, each tenant acquires an equal right to share in the enjoyment of the land during his or her life. A joint tenancy confers equivalent rights on the tenants that are fixed and vested at the time the tenancy is created. These do not change just because an additional agreement is executed to form a partnership. Once a joint tenancy is established between two people and a partition action is undertaken to divide the property, each person owns a one-half interest and they are entitled to one-half of the total proceeds without reimbursement for an unequal down payment. When parties hold property as tenants in common, each tenant's share is fully divisible and fully transferable to a purchaser or an heir upon death. The Davis property was subject to equitable adjustments for the large down payment made by Tingle. When the property is sold, the court must determine the percentage of equity that is attributable to the original down payment. Tingle will be entitled to a substantially greater share of the proceeds from the Davis property. However, the court may consider the Davis property as just one asset in the partnership. The adjustments to the division of the proceeds will consider the partnership contributions and assets as a whole.

Answers to Practice Quiz

True/False

1. False   Buildings constructed on land are real property.
2. False   Owners may sell mineral rights, oil rights, etc., without selling their surface land.
3. False   All plant life and vegetation are considered real property.
4. True   A life tenant is treated as the owner of the property during the duration of the life estate.
5. True   Property that is acquired through gift or inheritance either before or during marriage remains separate property.
6. False   A freehold estate is a present possessory interest in realty.
7. True   This is because it grants the owner the fullest bundle of legal rights that a person can hold in real property.
8. False   A sale and conveyance are the same thing.
9. False   The property is distributed via an intestacy statute.
10. True   The most distinguished feature of a joint tenancy is the co-owner's right of survivorship.
11. False   This is a reversion, not a remainder.
12. True   The person who is entitled to the future interest is called a remainderman.
13. True   An easement in gross authorizes a person who does not own adjacent land the right to use another's land. Examples of easements in gross include those granted to run power, telephone, and cable television lines across an owner's property. Picture Me Cable therefore has an easement in gross.
14. True   Each time a property is transferred or refinanced, a new title insurance policy must be obtained.
15. False   Adjacent land is defined as two estates that are in proximity to each other but do not necessarily abut each other.
16. False   If the elements of adverse possession are met, the adverse possessor acquires clear title to the land.
17. False   This is the definition of a cooperative.
18. True   An estate where the owner has a present possessory interest in the real property is a freehold estate.
19. False   A mortgage cannot exceed the duration of the life estate.
20. True   An easement is a nonpossessory interest in another's real estate.

Multiple Choice

21. D   An in-ground pool cannot be removed without causing substantial damage to the property. Answers A, B, and C are all portable and their movement or removal will not damage the land.
22. D   The owner of land owns the rights to whatever is under the surface of his or her land, including minerals, gas, and oil. Answer A is incorrect because an easement is a right to use or cross another person's land. Answer B is not correct because a profit is the right to remove something from another person's land. Answer C is not correct because gas and minerals are a form of real property until they are removed from the land.

23. C   Answer C is correct as the occupancy needs to be without express or implied permission which is exactly what the hostile and adverse requirement is. Answer A is incorrect as this goes toward the continual and peaceful requirement. Answer B is incorrect as this refers to the open, visible, and notorious requirement. Answer D is incorrect as this answer is referring to the actual and exclusive requirement whereby the adverse possessor must physically occupy the premises.

24. A   A reversion is a right of possession that returns to the grantor at the expiration of a limited estate. The life estate in Ann Brown is a limited estate. Answer B is not correct because the remainder is an interest held by a third person, not the grantor. Answer C is not correct because the grantor will obtain the property in fee simple absolute. Answer D is incorrect because this is a form of co-ownership, not a future interest.

25. A   Answer A is the correct answer as the government may obtain a lien for Charlotte's failure to pay taxes. Answer B is incorrect as there is no indication the government may rent the property for failure to pay taxes; however, the government may sell the property in question. Answer C is incorrect as it is a false statement, since the government does in fact have a remedy. Answer D is incorrect as Charlotte's possession of a homeowner's policy has nothing to do with the government's remedy of collecting on the back taxes on her property.

26. B   Green will receive the interest in Blackacre because Smith's interest may be passed through a will. Answer A is incorrect because Smith has a will and did not die intestate. Answer C is incorrect because a tenancy in common does not have a right of survivorship. Answer D is incorrect because B is a correct answer.

27. D   Answer D is correct because Answers A, B, and C are all rights of a condominium owner.

28. B   A quitclaim deed provides the least amount of protection for the buyer (and, is thus, best for Fred) because the grantor conveys only whatever interest he or she has in the property. Answer A is not correct because a warranty deed contains the greatest number of warranties. Answer C is incorrect because it involves a lawsuit when there is a dispute over the title to a parcel of real estate. Answer D is incorrect because even a gift must be deeded.

29. B   It is implied by Gus's action that he would allow the new owner to have a driveway across his property. Answer A is incorrect because Gus never expressly granted the right to cross his land to the new owner. Answer C is not correct because a license is usually for a short specified period of time. Answer D is incorrect because nothing is being removed from Gus's land.

30. A   If the owner is not satisfied with the government's offer for compensation, the owner may bring an action to have a court determine the amount of compensation. Answer B is not correct because it is an action to settle ownership of property, not the compensation to be paid by the government. Answer C is not correct because it concerns ownership rights in Germany. Answer D relates to compensation for taking something (timber) from the owner's land.

Short Answer

31. real
32. Air
33. sell, transfer, gift
34. location
35. sale, tax sale, gift, will, inheritance, adverse possession
36. recording statutes
37. county recorder's office
38. It is a form of co-ownership that includes the right of survivorship. It is created when the property is conveyed "to Mike and Sue as joint tenants, with the right of survivorship."
39. obtain approval of other owners
40. A reversion is a right of possession that returns to the grantor after the expiration of a limited or contingent estate.
41. because they arise automatically by law
42. bring a quiet title action
43. The deed gives constructive notice to the world of the owner's interest in the property.
44. It is title that is free from any encumbrances or other defects that are not disclosed but would affect the value of the property.
45. A gift is made when the deed to the property is delivered by the donor to the donee or to a third party to hold for the donee.

Chapter 49

LANDLORD-TENANT RELATIONSHIP
AND LAND USE REGULATION

Chapter Overview

The average business does not have the resources to buy land and build its store, offices, manufacturing facilities, or other commercial facilities. Renting or leasing real property is a necessary part of doing business. This chapter covers law in the areas of contracts and real property that relate to the landlord-tenant relationship. It also discusses the regulation of land use by the government.

Objectives

Upon completion of the exercises in this chapter, you should be able to
1. Recognize the various types of tenancy.
2. Identify the landlord's duties under a lease.
3. Discuss a tenant's duties under a lease.
4. Describe how federal law in the areas of fair housing and disabilities regulates real estate.
5. Explain how tort liability arises for landlords and tenants.
6. Describe how a lease can be terminated.
7. Explain how restrictive covenants restrict the use of land.
8. Describe public and private nuisances.
9. Understand how zoning laws regulate the use of land.
10. Describe the acquisition of property by the government by the use of eminent domain.

Practical Application

Upon learning the objectives in this chapter, you should understand the duties and rights of landlords and tenants in the common leasing of real property. Failure to meet the duties imposed at common law and by statute may cause a tenant to lose his/her tenancy. A landlord who violates his/her duties is subjected to damages and sanctions. A businessperson who is leasing a storefront or commercial building must understand the restrictions on the use of the building and what affirmative tasks must be undertaken to keep him/her out of breach of contract.

Helpful Hints

It is important that you learn the terminology associated with the rights and duties that arise from the landlord-tenant relationship. In each lease of real property, whether you are the landlord or the tenant, you must understand your obligations and know how those obligations are created in a written lease. You must also understand the obligations that are created by statute and remain in effect even if they are not included in the lease. As you examine each right and duty, determine the type of land use that is proper and improper in each situation.

Study Tips

A landlord or tenant can have obligations created by the lease, by statute, or by common law doctrines such as negligence. Examine each of these areas individually to discover the specific rights and duties that are created for the landlord and tenant.

Landlord-Tenant Relationship

This relationship is created when the owner of a freehold estate transfers a right to exclusively and temporarily possess the owner's property. The tenant receives a leasehold estate. The types of tenancy are:

- *tenancy for years* – a tenancy created when the landlord and the tenant agree on a specific duration for the lease.
- *periodic tenancy* – a tenancy created when a lease specifies intervals at which payments are due but does not specify how long the lease is for.
- *tenancy at will* – a lease that may be terminated at any time by either party.
- *tenancy at sufferance* – a tenancy created when a tenant retains possession of property after the expiration of another tenancy or a life estate without the owner's consent.

Duties Owed by the Landlord

The landlord has the following duties:

- *duty to deliver possession*
- *duty not to interfere with the tenant's right of quiet enjoyment* – the law implies a covenant of quiet enjoyment in all leases. The landlord may not interfere with the tenant's quiet and peaceful possession, use, and enjoyment of the leased premises.
- *duty to maintain the leased premises* – the landlord must comply with the requirements imposed by building and housing codes. Under an implied warranty of habitability, the leased premise must be fit, safe, and suitable for ordinary residential use.

Duties Owed by the Tenant

A tenant owes the landlord the duties agreed to in the lease and any duties imposed by law. These include:

- *duty not to use leased premises for illegal or nonstipulated purposes.*
- *duty not to commit waste* – waste occurs when a tenant causes substantial and permanent damages to the leased premises that decreases the value of the property and the landlord's reversionary interest in it.
- *duty not to disturb other tenants* – a landlord may evict the tenant who interferes with the quiet enjoyment of other tenants.

Tort Liability of Landlords and Tenants

Landlords and tenants owe a duty of reasonable care to third parties not to negligently cause injury to them. The landlord also owes this duty to the tenant.

Transferring Rights to Leased Property

Landlords may sell, gift, devise, or otherwise transfer their interests in leased property. The new landlord cannot alter the terms of an existing lease.

The tenant may transfer his or her rights under a lease to another by way of an assignment. The new tenant is the assignee and is obligated to perform the duties that the assignor had under the lease. The assignor remains responsible for his or her obligations under the lease unless released by the landlord.

If a tenant transfers only some of his or her rights under the lease, it is a sublease. The sublessor is still responsible under the lease and the sublessee does not obtain any rights under the original lease.

Land Use Control

Land use control is the collective term for the laws that regulate the possession, ownership, and use of real property. Forms of land use control include:

- *private nuisance* – a landowner or tenant who is affected in the use and enjoyment of real property by the use of adjoining or nearby property may bring a private nuisance action for damages.
- *restrictive covenants* – this is a private agreement between landowners that restricts the use of their land. They are often used by residential developers and condominium buildings to establish uniform rules for all occupants.
- *public nuisance* – this is a nuisance that affects or disturbs the public in general.
- *zoning* – zoning ordinances are local laws that are adopted by municipalities and local governments to regulate land use within their boundaries. Zoning ordinances are adopted and enforced to protect the health, safety, morals, and general welfare of the community. A landowner may obtain a variance that permits a type of building or use that would not otherwise be allowed by a zoning ordinance.

Civil Rights Act

The **Civil Rights Act** is a federal statute that prohibits racial discrimination in the transfer of real property. Many states and local communities have enacted statutes as well as ordinances that prohibit discrimination in the sale or lease of real property.

Fair Housing Act

A federal statute that makes it unlawful for a party to refuse to rent or sell a dwelling to any person because of his or her race, color, national origin, sex or religion.

Title III of the Americans with Disabilities Act

A federal statute that prohibits discrimination on the basis of disability in places of public accommodation by private entities.

Refresh Your Memory

The following exercise will enable you to refresh your memory of the principles given to you in this chapter. Read the questions twice and place your answer in the blanks provided. Review the chapter material for any question you miss or are unable to remember.

1. When the owner of a freehold estate transfers a right to exclusively and temporarily possess the owner's property, a _____ relationship is created.

2. The tenant's interest in property is called a _____ _____.

3. A tenancy for years terminates _____, without _____, upon the expiration of the sated term.

4. When the landlord and tenant agree on a specific duration for the lease, it is a tenancy _____ _____.

5. A _____ tenancy may be terminated by either party at the end of any payment interval.

6. A lease that may be terminated at any time by either party is a tenancy _____ _____.

7. A _____ at _____ is not really a true tenancy but merely the _____ of property without right.

8. Which covenant prevents the landlord from interfering with the tenant's quiet and peaceful possession? _____

9. Give two examples of things that have been held to breach the implied warranty of habitability.
    _____ and _____.

10. The implied warranty of _____ provides that the leased premises must be fit, safe, and suitable for ordinary residential use.

11. If Kali assigns her rights under a lease that she has with Chad to Edwin, what rights does Edwin now have?
    _____

12. What is a rent control ordinance?
    _____

13. An _____ is a transfer by the tenant of his or her rights under a lease to another.

14. What is an argument against rent control?
    _____
    _____

15.   A _____ is an exception that permits a type of building or use in an area that would not otherwise be allowed by a zoning ordinance.

Critical Thought Exercise

The city of Peaceful Meadows has numerous historical districts and expensive housing. The architecture is classical with almost no use of neon signs in commercial areas. As the city grows and new commercial areas are developed on streets that intersect with the interstate freeway on the edge of town, the city council is becoming increasingly alarmed with the increase in large electric signs and the typical glass and metal construction used by fast food restaurants and chain stores. Peaceful Meadows passes a zoning ordinance that forbids electrical signs over five feet by eight feet in size and limits the use of neon to the face of opaque signs that must be mounted flush with the ground. The style of the signs must be in conformance with the classical architecture of Peaceful Meadows. Three large chain restaurants desire to place 70-foot tall signs on the property where they are constructing restaurants near the freeway. They also desire to build their restaurants in the style that they always use in other communities because these "cookie-cutter" plans are efficient and economical to build. The Planning Commission of Peaceful Meadows rejects the permits for all signage and building plans proposed by the three restaurants. The restaurants apply for a variance to allow them to avoid the restrictive zoning law. These variance applications are also denied. The restaurants file suit and allege that the zoning ordinance creates an undue hardship and prevents then from making a reasonable use of their land. They also complain that the zoning ordinance is unfairly applied to them due to the numerous other restaurants that already have very tall signs and cheap unsightly construction.

Is aesthetic zoning lawful as used by the city of Peaceful Meadows?

Answer:

_____
_____
_____
_____
_____
_____
_____
_____
_____
_____
_____
_____
_____
_____
_____
_____
_____
_____

Practice Quiz

True/False

1. ___ The Fair Housing Act makes it unlawful for a party to refuse to rent or sell a dwelling to any person because of his or her race, color, national origin, sex, or religion. [p. 781]

2. ___ Lola, an opera singer, sings at all hours of the night in her apartment building. Consequently, John, Lola's neighbor, has lost sleep night after night. Lola has done nothing wrong as she has a right to sing in her own apartment. [p. 775]

3. ___ A net lease is where the tenant is responsible for paying rent, property taxes, and utilities. [p. 774]

4. ___ In a tenancy for years, property is leased for a specific duration of time. [p. 772]

5. ___ A tenancy for years terminates when one party gives notice to the other party. [p. 772]

6. ___ A month-to-month tenancy is a type of tenancy for years. [p. 772]

7. ___ The death of either party to a tenancy at will terminates the tenancy. [p. 773]

8. ___ A periodic tenancy automatically terminates at the end of the payment interval. [pp. 772-773]

9. ___ George has lived in an apartment building that Iris owns for nearly ten years. Over the course of time, paint has chipped off of the walls. Iris can now recover damages from George for waste. [p. 775]

10. ___ A legal relationship is lacking between a landlord and a sublessee. [p. 778]

11. ___ A tenant owes a duty of reasonable care to persons who enter upon leased premises. [p. 776]

12. ___ A periodic tenancy does not terminate upon the death of either party. [pp. 772-773]

13. ___ Because a tenant at sufferance has no legal right to possession of the property, most states allow the landlord to take immediate possession of the property without the need for court process. [p. 773]

14. ___ Jayme rented a 3,000-square-foot home from Miguel, who decided to use the leased premises as a restaurant. Since Miguel has used the premises lawfully, the landlord has no recourse against him. [p. 775]

15. ___ Housing codes mandate that property owners maintain and repair leased premises. [p. 774]

16. ___ If the city of Zoonie enacts a new zoning ordinance whereby a formerly commercial business area is now zoned residential and Pete is operating a hardware store, his use will be nonconforming; however, he will still allowed to continue his business. [p. 780]

17. ___ The law implies a covenant or quiet enjoyment in all leases. [pp. 773-774]

18. ___ If a tenant does not leave premises he or she is leasing at the end of its duration, then he or she could be subjected to an unlawful detainer action. [p. 773]

19. ___ The Fair Housing Act prohibits racial discrimination, in the transfer of real property. [p. 781]

20. ___ When the government decides that it wants to use a private individual's property, the Due Process Clause requires that the government allow the owner to make a case for keeping the property. [p. 782]

Multiple Choice

21. Bula lives in a ten-story convalescent apartment building that is outdated. She feels it has not complied with the Americans with Disabilities Act and wants to know which of the following would be considered to be a reasonable accommodation to ask for under this act. [p. 781]
    a. Installation of a railing next to the entrance of Bula's apartment building
    b. Wheelchair accessible ramps to enter Bula's apartment building
    c. Signs written in Braille in the elevators inside of Bula's apartment building
    d. all of the above

22. Larry leases a storefront in the mall and agrees to pay $1,600 per month, due by the tenth of each month. This tenancy is a [p. 772]
    a. tenancy for years.
    b. periodic tenancy.
    c. tenancy at sufferance.
    d. tenancy at will.

23. Larry rents a storefront in the mall for the Christmas season through December 31st. As of January 5th, Larry has not moved out of the store. This tenancy is a [p. 772]
    a. tenancy for years.
    b. periodic tenancy.
    c. tenancy at sufferance.
    d. tenancy at will.

24. Angela has been renting an apartment from Joel under a five-year lease. The five-year anniversary mark came and went and Angela continued to stay in the apartment. Joel is upset and tells Angela that he doesn't appreciate the fact that she is a holdover tenant under a tenancy at sufferance. Angela isn't sure what Joel is talking about and wants to know which of the following best describes what a tenancy at sufferance is. [p. 773]
    a. It is not a true tenancy, but a possession of property without a right.
    b. It is a trespasser.
    c. It is a tenant that is liable for the payment of rent during the period of sufferance.
    d. all of the above

25. Kyle, a landlord, has always rented his apartments to female schoolteachers. Kyle believes that schoolteachers, especially women, are neat and quiet and make the best tenants. Does Kyle have the right to discriminate against others in favor or female schoolteachers in this manner? [p. 781]
    a. Yes, because Kyle owns the premises and is free to contract with whomever he pleases.
    b. Yes, because Kyle is free to rent his freehold estate to anyone he desires.
    c. No, because there is no proof that schoolteachers are neat.
    d. No, because Kyle is prohibited by the Civil Rights Act from discriminating against tenants on the basis of their sex.

26. A landlord's promise that he or she will not interfere with the tenant's quiet and peaceful possession, use, and enjoyment of the leased premises is a(n) [p. 773]
    a. implied warranty of habitability.
    b. duty to deliver possession.
    c. warranty of title.
    d. covenant of quiet enjoyment.

27. The Country Inn rents efficiency suites by the day, week, and month. The Inn has staircases and steps leading into all suites as part of its Victorian architecture. The Inn tells all disabled persons that it is unable to accommodate physical handicaps. The policy of the Country Inn [p. 781]
    a. is lawful because private businesses do not have to accommodate handicapped persons.
    b. is lawful because an owner may design their hotel to fit their own style and budget.
    c. is unlawful because the Americans with Disabilities Act prohibits discrimination on the basis of disability in places of public accommodation operated by private entities.
    d. is unlawful because it violates the Fair Housing Act.

28. Dave rents a storefront for his laundromat and the apartment underneath the store. The apartment is below street level and Dave's bathroom floods when the washing machines are in heavy use. The failure of the landlord to rectify this plumbing problem is a breach of the [p. 775]
    a. duty to deliver exclusive possession.
    b. covenant of quiet enjoyment.
    c. implied warranty of habitability.
    d. duty to not commit waste.

29. A transfer by a tenant of part of his or her interest under a lease to another is [p. 778]
    a. a delegation.
    b. a sublease.
    c. an assignment.
    d. a breach of contract.

30. Sue purchases a lot in a housing development. Her deed contains a building height restriction that prohibits any structure taller than one story. Sue builds a two-story house on her lot. The building of this house by Sue is a [p. 780]
    a. private nuisance.
    b. violation of the restrictive covenant.
    c. public nuisance.
    d. variance.

Short Answer

31. If Karissa subleases her apartment to Mayada, what type of relationship does Mayada now have with Karissa's landlord? [p. 779]

    _____

32. What may a landlord recover if his or her tenant has allowed the carpeting in the rented premises to be destroyed by the tenant's four large dogs? [p. 775]

    _____
    _____

33. When can a periodic tenancy be terminated? [p. 773]

    _____
    _____

34. What factors are considered in deciding whether a barrier to accessibility for a disabled person must be removed by the owner of an old building that was built before the ADA was enacted? [p. 782]

    _____
    _____
    _____
    _____

35. What is the implied warranty of habitability? [p. 775]

    _____
    _____

36. What may Kerri, a tenant, do if Joe, her landlord, fails to maintain or repair leased premises and it affects the tenant's use and enjoyment of the premises? [p. 774]

    _____
    _____

37. What is meant by the term net, net, net lease? [p. 774]

    _____
    _____
    _____
    _____

38. What are four of the most common types of commercial leases? [p. 773]

    _____
    _____
    _____
    _____

39. What level of care must a tenant use towards a visitor to the leased premises? [p. 776]

    _____
    _____

40. John, a real estate broker, listed a house in one of the wealthiest cities of Somewhere. He used to live in the particular neighborhood where this listing is and has decided to sell only to Asians. Marla, an African American, qualified for the house and feels that there may be some discrimination going on. What may she base a cause of action on should she decide to sue? [p. 781]

_____

_____

_____

_____

41. What remedy does the landlord have if a sublessee fails to pay rent? [p. 778]

_____

_____

42. What is land use control? [p. 780]

_____

_____

_____

43. Who are the parties to an assignment? [p. 777]

_____

_____

44. What is the purpose of a zoning ordinance? [p. 780]

_____

_____

45. Compare a variance to a nonconforming use. [p. 780]

_____

_____

Answers to Refresh Your Memory

1. landlord tenant [p. 771]
2. leasehold estate [p. 771]
3. automatically; notice [p. 772]
4. for years [p. 772]
5. periodic [p. 773]
6. at will [p. 773]
7. tenancy at sufferance; possession [p. 773]
8. covenant of quiet enjoyment [p. 773]
9. unchecked rodent infestation; leaking roofs [p. 775]
10. habitability [p. 775]
11. all of the rights Kali had under the lease [p. 777]
12. an ordinance that stipulates what amount of rent a landlord can charge for residential housing [p. 779]
13. assignment [p. 777]
14. Rent control is merely a regulatory tax that merely transfers wealthy from landowners to tenants. [p. 779]
15. variance [p. 780]

Model Answer to Critical Thought Exercise

Municipalities may enact zoning ordinances pursuant to their police power as reserved to them by the Tenth Amendment. Zoning ordinances may (1) designate the type of land use allowed in an area (residential, commercial, industrial), (2) restrict the height, size, and locations of buildings, and (3) establish aesthetic requirements or restrictions for signs and exteriors of buildings. The owner who wishes to use his land for a use different from that contained in a zoning ordinance may request a variance. The landowner must prove that the ordinance causes an undue hardship by preventing the owner from making a reasonable use or return on investment. Zoning laws are applied prospectively, allowing uses in existence at the time the ordinance is passed to continue. Modifications or renovations often trigger a requirement that the nonconforming use be terminated. A city's planning commission may legally act to protect the character and stability of its neighborhoods. The city may consider what effect any variance may have upon surrounding properties and the overall zoning plan for the city. If a zoning ordinance is enacted pursuant to the city's police power to protect its residents' health, safety, and welfare, then it will be deemed a lawful exercise of constitutional power. The ordinance in Peaceful Meadows was enacted to preserve the quality of the community and to protect the value and use of property in the city. The ordinance only required that the restaurants conform to aesthetic requirements. The ordinance did not prevent the building of the restaurants or the use of signs to announce the location of the restaurants. The restaurants were not deprived of the use of their land and may still obtain a reasonable return on their investment. The zoning ordinance in Peaceful Meadows does not create an undue hardship and is therefore lawful in both design and application.

Answers to Practice Quiz

True/False

1. True — The Fair Housing Act, a federal statute, makes it unlawful for a party to refuse to rent or sell a dwelling to any person because of his or her race, color, national origin, sex or religion.
2. False — A landlord may evict a tenant who interferes with the quiet enjoyment of other tenants.
3. True — In this arrangement, the tenant is responsible for paying rent, property taxes, utilities, and insurance.
4. True — This may be for a week, month, year, or other period of time.
5. False — A tenancy for years terminates automatically, without notice, upon the expiration of the stated term.
6. False — This is a periodic tenancy.
7. True — The death of either party terminates a tenancy at will.
8. False — A periodic tenancy is terminated at the end of an interval with proper notice given by either party.
9. False — Chipped paint is part of ordinary wear and tear.
10. False — No legal relationship is formed between the sublessee and the landlord.
11. True — A tenant owes a duty of reasonable care to persons who enter upon leased premises.
12. True — This is not a true tenancy, but merely possession of the property without right.
13. False — The owner must go through unlawful detainer proceedings to regain possession.
14. False — If the tenant utilizes the leased premises for unlawful purposes, the landlord may terminate the lease, evict the tenant, and sue for damages.

15. True   Building or housing codes, as they are sometimes called, are statutes that impose specific standards on property owners to maintain and repair leased premises.
16. True   This is part of the landlord's duty to deliver exclusive possession.
17. True   The landlord may not interfere with the tenant's quiet and peaceful possession, use, and enjoyment of the leased premises.
18. True   An unlawful detainer action is available to a landlord when he or she has a holdover tenant at the end of a lease term.
19. False   The Civil Rights Act prohibits racial discrimination in the transfer of real property.
20. True   The Due Process Clause of the U.S. Constitution requires the government to allow the owner
            to make a case for keeping of his or her property. Further, the Just Compensation clause of the Fifth Amendment requires the government to compensate the property owner when it uses the power of eminent domain.

Multiple Choice

21. D   Answer D is correct as railings, wheelchair ramps, and Braille signs in elevators (hence answers A, B, and C, respectively) are all reasonable under the Americans with Disabilities Act.
22. B   This tenancy has no expiration date and rent is payable in set intervals. A is incorrect because the lease has no expiration date. C is incorrect because the tenant is not a trespasser. D is incorrect because the periodic rent payments will require adequate notice for termination.
23. C   By staying past the expiration of the lease, Larry has become a trespasser and now has a tenancy at sufferance. A is incorrect because the tenancy for years expired on December 31st. B is incorrect because the lease has a termination date. D is incorrect because even a tenancy at will involves mutual consent for the tenant to occupy the premises.
24. D   Answer D is correct as it encompasses all of the answers that pertain to a tenancy at sufferance, which are Answers A, B, and C.
25. D   The Fair Housing Act makes it unlawful for a party to refuse to rent or sell a dwelling to any person because of his or her race, color, national origin, sex, or religion. Answers A, B, and C are incorrect because the mandates of the Fair Housing Act control the renting of property.
26. D   The covenant is broken if the landlord interferes with the tenant's use and enjoyment of the property. Answer A is incorrect because it relates to maintaining that the premise it is a safe, fit, and suitable condition. Answer B is incorrect because it relates only to the duty to turn over possession and does not relate to continued use. Answer C is incorrect because it relates to the landlord's right to transfer possession, not interference with possession.
27. C   The ADA requires facilities to be designed, constructed, and altered in compliance with accessibility requirements. Answer A is incorrect because the ADA applies to private businesses. Answer B is incorrect because the ADA has design and construction guidelines that must be followed. Answer D is incorrect because accommodations for disabilities are not covered by the Fair Housing Act.
28. C   Leased premises must be fit, safe, and suitable for ordinary use. The flooding of the bathroom makes the apartment unusable. Answer A is incorrect because possession has been delivered but the condition of the premises is not suitable. Answer B is incorrect because there is no outside interference with possession or use of the premises. Answer D is not correct because waste applies to damage by tenants.

29. C   Answer B is correct as a sublease only transfers part of the rights under the lease. A is not correct because a delegation only transfers the duty under a contract. Answer C is not correct as an assignee acquires all the rights that the assignor had under the lease. Answer D is incorrect because a tenant may assign their rights under a lease unless it is expressly prohibited in the lease.

30. B   A restrictive covenant is an agreement between private landowners that restricts the use of their land. The height restriction was implemented by private agreement. Answer A is not correct because the house is not a nuisance since it does not make entry onto another's land. Answer C is not correct because there is no harm caused to others. Answer D is not correct because the restrictive covenant was contained in a private agreement and no government permission was sought for an exception to a zoning law.

Short Answer

31.   No legal relationship, as Mayada has no rights under the sublease.
32.   damages from the tenant for the waste
33.   payment at the end of any payment interval
34.   With respect to existing buildings, architectural barriers must be removed if such removal is readily achievable. In determining when an action is readily achievable, the factors to be considered include the nature and cost of the action, the financial resources of the facility, and the type of operations of the facility.
35.   a warranty that provides that the leased premises must be fit, safe, and suitable for ordinary residential use
36.   The tenant may (1) withhold from his or her rent the amount by which the defect reduced that value of the premises to him or her, (2) repair the defect and deduct the cost of repairs from the rent due for the leased premises, (3) cancel the lease if the failure to repair constitutes constructive eviction, or (4) sue for damages for the amount the landlord's failure to repair the defect reduced the value of the leasehold.
37.   The tenant is responsible for paying rent, property taxes, utilities, and insurance.
38.   Gross lease, net lease, double net lease, and triple net lease
39.   The tenant owes a duty of reasonable care to persons who enter upon the leased premises.
40.   Civil Rights Act
41.   Because there is no legal relationship between the landlord and the sublessee, the landlord must seek the rent from the sublessor.
42.   Zoning ordinances are adopted and enforced to protect the health, safety, morals, and general welfare of the community.
43.   The assignee and assignor.
44.   an exception that permits a type of building or use in an area that would not otherwise be allowed by a zoning ordinance
45.   A variance is an exception that permits a type of building or use in an area that would not otherwise be allowed by a zoning ordinance. A nonconforming use is one that uses buildings that already exist in a zoned area that are permitted to continue even though they do not fit within new zoning ordinances.

Chapter 50

INSURANCE

Chapter Overview

The potential risk of loss that a business or individual faces due to death, fire, or injury may be staggering. Insurance is a crucial part of business planning. This chapter examines the insurance contract, types and uses of insurance, defenses used by insurance companies to avoid liability, and secondary liability for losses. The businessperson should understand the types of insurance coverage that are necessary for the proper protection of personal and business assets.

Objectives

Upon completion of the exercises in this chapter, you should be able to:
1. Describe the essential parts of an insurance contract.
2. Understand the meaning of an insurable interest.
3. Describe various types of life, health, and disability insurance.
4. Describe the parameters of fire and homeowner's coverage.
5. Explain uninsured motorist and no-fault insurance.
6. Understand the various forms of business insurance.
7. Explain the coverage provided by various types of business insurance.

Practical Application

Even the most successful business has limited resources. This chapter will help you develop a greater understanding of the role that insurance plays in the overall business plan and estate planning of the individual. By understanding the coverage provided by different insurance products, you can make an informed decision as to the type and amount of insurance that is needed to achieve business and personal goals that have been set. Just as important is an understanding of your rights as an insured and the potential defenses that an insurance company will use to avoid paying a claim.

Helpful Hints

You should examine insurance products and incorporate them into any business plan and personal estate plan. When a businessperson is making a decision as to the type and amount of coverage needed, he or she must first determine the asset or risk for which protection is needed. The coverage must then be matched to that risk. The needs of a business will vary depending upon the type of business activity, product produced or sold, importance of key personnel, and exposure to liability based upon the risk created by the business to its employees and members of the general public.

Study Tips

In order to accomplish their business goals, each businessperson should understand the important points contained in the following outline. This laundry list of insurance terms and principles is indispensable.

Regulation of the Insurance Industry

Each state has enacted statutes that regulate the insurance industry that operates within the state. State regulation covers all aspects of insurance company incorporation, licensing, oversight, termination of business, and the licensing of agents and brokers.

Insurance Contracts

- The *insurance contract* is a form of third-party beneficiary contract, as was discussed in Chapter 15. The insurance contract, or *policy*, is purchased by the *insured* who pays premiums to the insurance company or *insurer*. The policy is usually sold by an *agent* who works for the insurance company or by an *insurance broker* who represents several insurance companies and is the agent of the insured.
- *Mandatory provisions* are required by statute and must be included in each policy. If mandatory provisions are omitted from the contract, they will still be implied. Examples of these provisions include coverage for certain losses and how limitations on coverage must be worded in the contract.
- The *effective date of coverage* is the first date when the insurer becomes obligated to pay for any loss suffered by the insured. This effective date may be when the application and first premium are paid, when a physical exam is passed, or when a broker obtains the insurance.
- Modification of an insurance contract by the parties is usually accomplished by adding an *endorsement* to the policy or by executing a document called a *rider*.
- A person must have an insurable interest in anything he or she insures. For life insurance, a person must have a familiar relationship or an economic benefit from the continued life of another. For property insurance, anyone who would suffer a monetary loss from the destruction of the property has an insurable interest in that property.
- Coverage is limited by deductible clauses and exclusions from coverage.

Life Insurance

- *Life insurance* is a form of insurance where the insurer must pay a specific sum of money to a named **beneficiary** upon the death of another. There are numerous life insurance products, including whole life, limited-payment life, term life, universal life, and endorsement and annuity. The amount of **premiums** for a policy depends upon factors such as availability of a cash or surrender value, and the period over which premiums will be paid.
- *Key-person life insurance* is often purchased by business owners to finance **buy-sell agreements** upon the death of one of the owners of the business. If an insured owner dies, the insurance proceeds are paid to the deceased's beneficiaries. The deceased's interest in the business then reverts to the other owners of the business according to the terms of the buy-sell agreement. This allows a business to continue upon the death of an owner and prevents the beneficiaries from selling off the assets of the business.
- A *double indemnity clause* stipulates that the insurer will pay double the amount of the policy if death is caused by accident or criminal agency.
- *Exclusions from coverage* in many policies include death caused by military actions, executions by government, accidents in private aircraft, and suicide within one or two years.

Health and Disability Insurance

- *Health insurance* can be purchased to cover the costs of medical treatment. Plans vary from health maintenance organizations with low deductibles and copayments to self-funded plans that have high deductibles, but have greater freedom in choosing doctors and much lower monthly premiums.
- *Disability insurance* provides a monthly income to an insured who is unable to work due to a nonwork-related disability.

Fire and Homeowners' Insurance

- A standard *fire insurance policy* protects real and personal property against loss resulting from fire and certain related perils. Most policies provide for replacement cost insurance that pays the cost to replace the damaged or destroyed property at its current cost.
- A *homeowners' policy* covers personal liability in addition to the risks covered by the fire insurance policy. The homeowners' policy covers losses from a much wider range of causes, including negligence and theft.
- A *residence contents broad form* policy covers losses incurred by renters for damage or destruction to their possessions.

Automobile Insurance

Many states have mandatory automobile insurance statutes. Proof of insurance is required to be kept on file with the state department of motor vehicles. The basic types of automobile insurance are:
- *Collision insurance* insures the owner's car against the risk of loss or damage. The premium varies depending upon the amount of deductible paid towards any loss by the car owner.
- *Comprehensive insurance* insures an automobile from loss or damages from causes other than collision, such as fire, theft, hail, falling objects, earthquakes, floods, and vandalism.
- *Liability insurance* covers damages that the insured causes to third parties. This coverage usually has a limit for injury to each person in an accident, a limit for the total bodily injury for all persons injured, and a limit for property damage.
- *Medical payment coverage* covers medical expenses for the driver and his or her passengers who are injured in an accident.
- *Uninsured motorist coverage* provides coverage to the driver and passengers who are injured by an uninsured motorist or hit-and-run driver.
- *No-fault automobile insurance* has been enacted in some states. Under this system, a driver's insurance company pays for any injuries he or she suffered in an accident, no matter who caused the accident. Claimants may not sue to recover damages from the party who caused the accident unless the injured party suffered serious injury.

Business Insurance

The owner of real property and a business should purchase several types of insurance in addition to liability and fire insurance. These additional types of insurance include:
- *Business interruption insurance* that pays for lost revenues during the period a business is rebuilding after a fire or some other event.
- *Workers' compensation insurance* pays for injuries and lost wages of employees who are injured on the job. This insurance is mandatory in most states.
- *Fidelity insurance* covers the employer against losses caused by employee theft or fraud.

- *Directors' and officers' liability insurance* protects directors and officers from liability for their negligent actions that they take on behalf of the corporation.
- *Product liability insurance* protects against losses incurred by manufacturers and sellers for injuries caused by their defective products.

Other Types of Insurance

Some special types of insurance that a particular business or individual may desire include:
- *Professional malpractice insurance* which covers the injuries caused by professionals, such as doctors, lawyers, accountants, and architects, resulting from the negligent performance of their duties.
- *Title insurance* protects against defects in title and liens and encumbrances that are not disclosed on the title insurance policy. A lender often requires this insurance before it will fund a loan.
- *Credit insurance* may be purchased by either the creditor or debtor to protect against the debtor's inability to pay a debt. It usually consists of credit life insurance or credit disability insurance.
- *Marine insurance* protects owners and shippers against loss or damage to their ships and cargo.
- *Group insurance* is an insurance that is sold to all the members of a single group, often all the employees of one employer, union, or professional association.
- *Umbrella insurance* coverage pays only if the basic policy limits of a liability policy have been exceeded. This insurance is inexpensive and often extends coverage to $5 million.

Performance of Insurance Contracts

The parties to an insurance contract are obligated to perform the duties imposed by the contract. The duties of the insured are:
- *Duty to pay premiums* – the insured must pay the agreed-upon premiums. Many policies include a grace period during which an insured may pay an overdue premium.
- *Duty to notify insurer* – the insured must notify the insurer after the occurrence of an insured event.
- *Duty to cooperate* – the insured must cooperate with the insurer in investigating claims made against the insurer.

The duties of the insurer are:
- *Duty to defend* – the insurer has a duty to defend against any suit brought against the insured that involves a claim within the coverage of the policy.
- *Duty to pay insurance proceeds* – the insurer's primary duty is to pay legitimate claims up to the policy limit.

Defenses of the Insurer

The most common defenses that may be raised by the insurer to avoid liability are:
- *Misrepresentation and concealment* – the insurer may avoid liability if: 1) the applicant makes a material misrepresentation in the application that is relied upon by the insurer in deciding whether to issue the policy, or 2) the applicant concealed material information from the insurer. Many states have enacted incontestability clauses that prevent insurers from contesting the statements in an application after a number of years.

- *Breach of warranty* – the insured may be required to make affirmative or promissory warranties that certify that facts or conditions are true, such as there being no known structural defects in a building, or that facts will continue to be true while the policy is in effect. The breach of these promises by the insured will relieve the insurer of liability.

Subrogation

If an insurance company pays a claim to an insured for liability or property damage caused by a third party, the insurer succeeds to the right of the insured to recover from the third party.

Refresh Your Memory

The following exercise will enable you to refresh your memory on the important principles presented to you in this chapter. Read each question twice and place your answer in the blanks provided. Review the chapter material for any question you miss or are unable to remember.

1.   Under an insurance contract, the insurance company is the _____ who underwrites the insurance coverage.

2.   An insurance _____ is an independent contractor who represents a number of insurance companies.

3.   Insurance may be modified by the insured and insurer by adding an _____ to the policy.

4.   Before a person can purchase insurance, they must have an _____ _____ in the insured item or person.

5.   A deductible clause provides that insurance proceeds are payable only after the _____ has paid a certain amount of the damage or loss.

6.   Life insurance that is issued for a limited period of time with premiums payable and coverage effective only during this term is called _____ insurance.

7.   _____ is a right that says if an insurance company pays a claim to an insured for liability or property damage caused by a third party, the insurer succeeds to the right of the insured to recover from the third party.

8.   The standard fire insurance policy protects the homeowner from loss caused by fire, _____, smoke, and _____ damage.

9.   An _____ _____ prevents insurers from contesting statements made by insureds in applications for insurance after the passage of a stipulated number of years.

10.   A copay clause is also known as a _____ clause.

11.   _____ insurance is a form of property insurance that insures an automobile from loss or damage from causes other than collision.

12.   _____ protects the insured while driving other automobiles, such as rental cars.

13. _____ _____ insurance reimburses a business for loss of revenue incurred when the business has been damaged or destroyed by fire or some other peril.

14. The insurer had a duty to _____ against any suit brought against the insured that involves a claim within the coverage of the policy.

15. _____ _____ life insurance is paid for by a business that insures against the death of owners and other key executives and employees of the business.

Critical Thought Exercise

The five partners in the law firm of Higgins & Ford, LLP, purchased a $500,000 life insurance policy on the life of each partner from Celestial Insurance. The firm was listed as the beneficiary. On the application forms, the relationship pf the beneficiary to the insured was listed as "business/family association." The period of contestability was two years. Three years after the policy on the life of Victor Ford was purchased, Mr. Ford died in an automobile accident. Celestial refused to pay on the policy and filed suit in a federal district court against Higgins & Ford, seeking to have the policy declared void *ab initio* (from the beginning) on the ground that the law firm lacked an insurable interest.

Does the misleading statement regarding the relationship with the insured by the beneficiary or the lack of a personal relationship with Victor Ford prevent Higgins & ford from having an insurable interest?

Answer:

_____
_____
_____
_____
_____
_____
_____
_____
_____
_____
_____
_____

Practice Quiz

True/False

1. ____ The party who pays a premium to a particular insurance company for insurance coverage is the insured. [p. 787]

2. ____ An insurance broker is an independent contractor who usually represents a number of insurance companies. [p. 787]

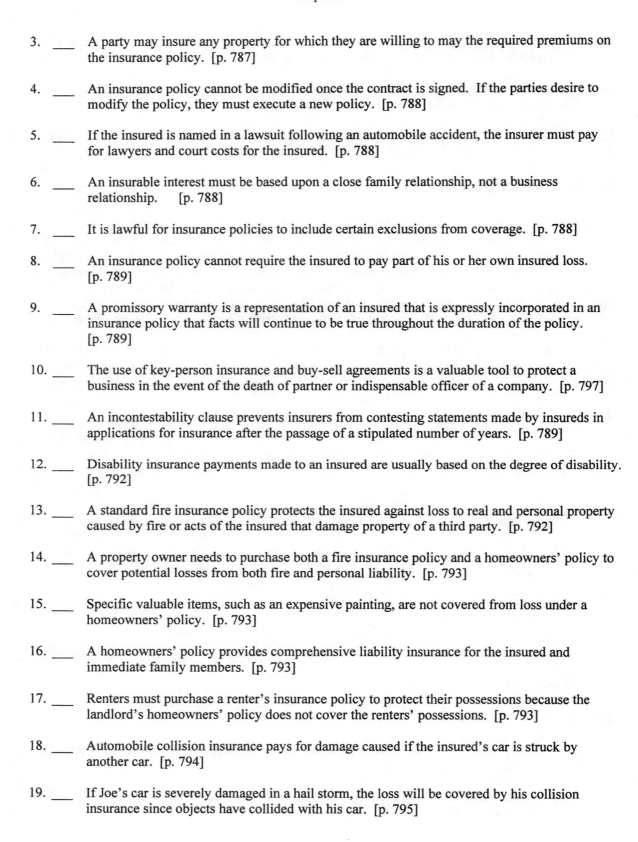

3. ___ A party may insure any property for which they are willing to may the required premiums on the insurance policy. [p. 787]

4. ___ An insurance policy cannot be modified once the contract is signed. If the parties desire to modify the policy, they must execute a new policy. [p. 788]

5. ___ If the insured is named in a lawsuit following an automobile accident, the insurer must pay for lawyers and court costs for the insured. [p. 788]

6. ___ An insurable interest must be based upon a close family relationship, not a business relationship. [p. 788]

7. ___ It is lawful for insurance policies to include certain exclusions from coverage. [p. 788]

8. ___ An insurance policy cannot require the insured to pay part of his or her own insured loss. [p. 789]

9. ___ A promissory warranty is a representation of an insured that is expressly incorporated in an insurance policy that facts will continue to be true throughout the duration of the policy. [p. 789]

10. ___ The use of key-person insurance and buy-sell agreements is a valuable tool to protect a business in the event of the death of partner or indispensable officer of a company. [p. 797]

11. ___ An incontestability clause prevents insurers from contesting statements made by insureds in applications for insurance after the passage of a stipulated number of years. [p. 789]

12. ___ Disability insurance payments made to an insured are usually based on the degree of disability. [p. 792]

13. ___ A standard fire insurance policy protects the insured against loss to real and personal property caused by fire or acts of the insured that damage property of a third party. [p. 792]

14. ___ A property owner needs to purchase both a fire insurance policy and a homeowners' policy to cover potential losses from both fire and personal liability. [p. 793]

15. ___ Specific valuable items, such as an expensive painting, are not covered from loss under a homeowners' policy. [p. 793]

16. ___ A homeowners' policy provides comprehensive liability insurance for the insured and immediate family members. [p. 793]

17. ___ Renters must purchase a renter's insurance policy to protect their possessions because the landlord's homeowners' policy does not cover the renters' possessions. [p. 793]

18. ___ Automobile collision insurance pays for damage caused if the insured's car is struck by another car. [p. 794]

19. ___ If Joe's car is severely damaged in a hail storm, the loss will be covered by his collision insurance since objects have collided with his car. [p. 795]

20. ___ Automobile liability insurance covers damages that a third party causes to the insured. [p. 795]

21. ___ Workers' compensation insurance compensates employees for injuries received during the period of time that they are employed by the employer who has purchased the insurance. [p. 797]

22. ___ A shipper may purchase marine insurance to cover the risk of loss of goods being shipped on the vessel of a different owner. [p. 796]

23. ___ Damage caused by a hit-and-run driver is covered by the owner's liability insurance. [p. 795]

24. ___ Insurance that protects employers against dishonesty and defalcation of employees is called business interruption insurance. [p. 798]

25. ___ Key-person insurance is often used to fund buy-sell agreements among the owners of a business. [p. 797]

Multiple Choice

26. The regulation of the insurance industry was granted to the states and insurance companies were exempted from federal antitrust laws by [p. 787]
    a. the Commerce Cause of the U.S. Constitution.
    b. the federal insurance code.
    c. insurance company self-regulation.
    d. the McCarran-Ferguson Act.

27. Which of the following statements is accurate? [p. 787]
    a. Insurance brokers work for an individual insurance company.
    b. Insurance brokers are independent contractors who represent a number of insurance companies.
    c. Insurance agents represent multiple insurance companies.
    d. Insurance agents and brokers are both independent contractors.

28. A modification to an insurance policy is called a(n) [p. 788]
    a. exclusion.
    b. endorsement.
    c. warranty.
    d. coinsurance clause.

29. Stan is a partner in a very successful law firm, is married, and has two children. Who has an insurable interest that would allow them to purchase life insurance if Stan is the insured? [p. 788]
    a. Stan's wife
    b. Stan's children
    c. Stan's partners in the accounting firm
    d. all of the above

30. The type of life insurance that has a cash value that grows at a variable interest rate is [p. 791]
    a. universal life.
    b. whole life.
    c. term life.
    d. limited-payment life.

31. Small businesses, such as partnerships, limited liability companies, and close corporations, often purchase _____ life insurance on the owners of the business as part of buy-sell agreements. [p. 797]
    a. whole
    b. key-person
    c. universal
    d. term

32. Sue's children are playing baseball in the street and break the windshield of a passing car, which then crashes into a store and burns. This damage will likely be covered by [p. 793]
    a. standard fire coverage.
    b. a personal articles floater.
    c. personal liability coverage.
    d. residence contents broad form coverage.

33. Jill's automobile is stolen from the parking lot at the local mall. Her loss will be covered if she has purchased [p. 795]
    a. automobile collision insurance.
    b. automobile comprehensive insurance.
    c. automobile liability insurance.
    d. automobile medical payment coverage.

34. Rick has a $500,000 automobile insurance policy that includes collision, comprehensive, and liability insurance. If Rick is worried that in the future he may be liable for damages of $2,000,000 because of an incident caused by his negligent driving, he would be well advised to purchase a(n) [p. 796]
    a. title insurance policy.
    b. credit insurance policy.
    c. group insurance policy.
    d. umbrella insurance policy.

35. Which of the following is not a duty of an insured under an insurance contract? [p. 788]
    a. Duty to pay insurance proceeds
    b. Duty to pay premiums
    c. Duty to cooperate
    d. Duty to notify insurer

Short Answer

36. What is reinsurance? [p. 787]

    _____

    _____

37. What is an insurable interest? [p. 787]

    _____

    _____

38. What is the difference between universal and term life insurance? [p. 791]

    _____

    _____

    _____

39. Explain the two duties owed by an insurer to their insured. [p. 788]
    (1) _____
    (2) _____

40. What is a double indemnity clause? [p. 791]

    _____
    _____

41. What is the difference between health insurance and disability insurance? [p. 792]

    _____
    _____
    _____

42. Personal liability coverage under a homeowners' policy will cover what types of losses? [p. 793]

    _____
    _____

43. What is a personal articles floater? [p. 793]

    _____
    _____

44. List four standard types of coverage that an automobile owner may purchase. [p. 795]
    (1) _____ (2) _____
    (3) _____ (4) _____

45. What is business interruption insurance? [p. 797]

    _____
    _____

46. Why may a manufacturing business located in Denver, Colorado, want to purchase marine insurance? [p. 796]

    _____

47. Kyle has automobile liability insurance that pays up to $500,000 per accident and an umbrella policy with an additional $2,000,000 of coverage. If Kyle's negligence causes an accident in which injuries to other persons total $1,500,000, how will the losses be paid? [p. 796]

    _____
    _____

48. How does no-fault insurance work? [p. 795]

    _____
    _____

49. What is replacement cost insurance? [p. 793]

    _____
    _____

50. Explain how the doctrine of subrogation is applied. [p. 790]

_____

_____

_____

_____

Answers to Refresh Your Memory

1.   insurer [p. 787]
2.   broker [p. 787]
3.   endorsement [p. 788]
4.   insurable interest [p. 787]
5.   insured [p. 788]
6.   term [p. 791]
7.   Subrogation [p. 790]
8.   lightning; water [p. 793]
9.   incontestability clause [p. 789]
10. coinsurance [p. 789]
11. Comprehensive [p. 795]
12. Drive-other coverage or D.O.C. [p. 795]
13. Business interruption [p. 797]
14. defend [p. 788]
15. Key-person [p. 797]

Critical Thought Exercise Model Answer

A person must have an insurable interest in anything he or she insures. If there is no insurable interest, the contract is treated as a wager and cannot be enforced. In the case of life insurance, a person must have a close family relationship or an economic benefit from the continued life of another to have an insurable interest in that person's life. An insurable interest may be based upon a business relationship. Higgins & Ford not only had a business relationship with Ford, but as a partner in the firm, Higgins & Ford derived an economic benefit from the continued life of Victor Ford. His death created an economic loss for Higgins & Ford, especially if his partnership interest was subject to attachment by creditors. Because the policy was not void *ab initio* and because the period for contesting the policy had passed under the contestability clause, Celestial may not now challenge the terms of the policy or the extent of Higgins & Ford's insurable interest.

Answers to Practice Quiz

True/False

1. True   The insured purchases the insurance and pays the premiums to the insurer (insurance company).
2. True   The insurance broker is an independent contractor, while the agent works exclusively for one insurance company.
3. False   There is a requirement that a person who purchases insurance have a personal interest in the insured item or person, called an insurable interest.
4. False   The insurer and insured can agree to modify the contract either by adding an endorsement to the policy or by execution of a document called a rider.
5. True   These costs are part of the insured's duty to defend.

6. False   An insurable interest may also be based upon a business relationship, such as the creditor who has an insurable interest in a debtor.

7. True   Standard fire policies might exclude coverage for damage caused by the storage of flammable liquids or a medical insurance policy might exclude coverage for preexisting undisclosed medical conditions.

8. False   This is a coinsurance clause or copay clause. The insured usually pays a small copay or percentage of the loss and the insurer pays the balance.

9. True   The promissory warranty may be that the insured will not conduct certain activities on the premises or engage in certain dangerous activities.

10. True   The proceeds of the insurance policy are used to pay the beneficiaries of the deceased and the ownership interest of the deceased reverts to the other partners or owners.

11. True   If the insured fails to reveal a material fact in the application, the insurer will normally be able to avoid paying for a loss. With the passage of a two-to-five-year period, this right to challenge the insured's claim is lost.

12. True   The monthly payments provide income to an insured who is disabled.

13. False   A standard fire insurance policy does not carry personal liability coverage.

14. False   A homeowners' policy includes both personal liability and fire coverage.

15. True   A personal articles floater is needed in addition to the homeowners' policy to cover specific valuable items.

16. True   A homeowners' policy covers the insured and family members for damages and injury caused on the insured's property and while away from home.

17. True   A renter must purchase residence contents broad form coverage to cover their personal property.

18. True   Coverage applies even if the insured's car is parked at the time of the collision.

19. False   Incidents like fire, theft, storms, falling objects, vandalism, floods, earthquakes, and riot are covered by comprehensive insurance, not collision insurance.

20. False   Liability insurance covers damages that the insured causes to third parties.

21. False   This insurance covers employees who are injured within the scope of their employment.

22. True   Shippers may also purchase marine insurance to cover the risk of loss to their goods during shipment. Owners may purchase marine insurance to cover their ships and its cargo.

23. False   This would be covered by uninsured motorist coverage, which is required to be included in a policy by many states.

24. False   Fidelity insurance protects employers against dishonesty and defalcation of employees.

25. True   If an insured owner dies, the insurance proceeds are paid to the deceased's beneficiaries, and the deceased's interest in the business then reverts to either the other owners or the business.

Multiple Choice

26. D   This act was passed by Congress to expressly remove the insurance from federal regulation under the Commerce Clause. Answer A is incorrect because the Commerce Clause favors federal regulation. Answer B is not correct because there is no federal insurance code. Answer C is incorrect because the government regulates the insurance industry, not by the industry itself.

27. B   The insurance broker is the agent for the insured and sells insurance for different companies. Answer A is not correct because a broker is not an employee of any one insurance company. Answer C is not correct because an agent works for one company exclusively. Answer D is incorrect because an insurance agent is not an independent contractor.

28. B The modification can be done by either an endorsement to the policy or by executing a rider. Answer A in not correct because an exclusion is a condition that prevents coverage. Answer C is incorrect because a warranty is a promise or affirmation as to a condition that must be met or prevented by the insured. Answer D is incorrect because this is a copay clause, not a modification.

29. D Each of the parties has an insurable interest because they have a close family relationship or an economic benefit from the continued life of Stan. Answers A, B, and C are not correct because they disregard other correct choices.

30. A Universal life combines features of both term and whole life. Answers B, C, and D are not correct because they do not involve an investment portion that is invested at a variable interest rate.

31. B Combined with a buy-sell agreement, this insurance protects the business in the event of the death of an owner. Answers A, C, and D are types of life insurance, but they are not the category of insurance that the question calls for. The key-person insurance may be one of the other three choices, (i.e., the company could buy whole life on a company owner.)

32. C Liability coverage protects against injury or damage caused by the insured or his immediate family to the person or property of third parties. Answer A is not correct because fire insurance does not protect against injury to the property of third parties unless the insured property is damaged first. Answer B is not correct because it protects against loss or damage to the insured's property. Answer D is not correct because this protects against the loss or damage to the insured's personal property when the insured is a renter.

33. B Comprehensive coverage protects against noncollision losses such as damage or loss from theft, storms, earthquakes, and vandalism. The other types of coverage do not specifically protect against loss from theft.

34. D An insurer will issue an umbrella policy if the insured has purchased a stipulated minimum amount of coverage on another policy, usually a homeowners' policy. Answer A is incorrect because it pertains to protection against defects in the title to real estate. Answer B is not correct because if protects a creditor against default by a debtor. Answer C is incorrect because it provides health insurance coverage for members of a single group.

35. A The duty to pay insurance proceeds is a duty owed by the insurer to the insured. Answers B, C, and D are all duties owed by the insured.

Short Answer

36. when insurers spread the risk of loss by selling a portion of the policy's risk and right to receive premiums to another insurance company

37. An insurable interest is a personal interest in the item or person based upon a family, economic, or ownership interest in the person or property.

38. Term life insurance is effective for a limited period of time and only pays the face value of the policy while universal life combines features of whole life and term life, giving a set face value that is increased by an investment portion of the premium with no set time for expiration of the policy, as in whole life.

39. (1) The insurer must defend the insured in any suit, including paying for a lawyer and the costs associated with the suit.
(2) The insurer has a duty to pay legitimate claims up to the policy limit.

40. a clause that stipulates that the insurer will pay double the amount of the policy if death is caused by accident

41. Health insurance pays for the costs of medical treatment, surgery, and hospital care, while disability insurance pays for lost income and provides a monthly payment when the disabled person cannot work.

42. personal injury of third persons, property damage caused by the insured or family members, medical expenses resulting from the acts of the insured or family members

43. It is an addition to a homeowners' policy that covers specific valuable items such as jewelry, paintings, antiques, and collectibles.

44. (1) collision insurance (2) comprehensive insurance
(3) liability insurance (4) medical payment coverage

45. (1) business interruption insurance (2) workers' compensation insurance (3) fidelity insurance
(4) directors' and officers' liability insurance (5) product liability insurance

46. If the business engages in shipping of goods by ship or other vessel, the marine insurance will cover the risk of loss to their goods during shipping. Marine inland insurance may be purchased for shipping that uses inland waters such as rivers and lakes.

47. If Kyle has automobile insurance that pays up to $500,000 for each insured event and an umbrella policy with $2 million of coverage, and Kyle causes $1,500,000 in damages to persons in an accident, the liability policy will pay the first $500,000 of the damages and the umbrella policy will cover the remaining $1.0 million in damages.

48. A driver's insurance company pays for any injuries or death he or she suffered in an accident, no matter who caused the accident.

49. insurance that pays the cost to replace the damage or destroyed property up to the policy limits

50. If an insurance company pays a claim to their insured for liability or property damage caused by a third party, the insurer succeeds to the right of the insured to recover from the third party.

Chapter 51

LIABILITY OF ACCOUNTANTS

Chapter Overview

Accountants can be held liable to both clients and third parties for breach of contract, misrepresentation, and negligence when they fail to properly perform their duties. These duties may include both auditing of financial statements and rendering opinions based upon those audits. Accountants also prepare statements for clients, give tax advice, prepare tax filings, and provide consulting services. In addition to the liability exposure for the common law actions already noted, an accountant may be subjected to liability under securities laws and the tax codes. The material in this chapter will help you examine the liability of accountants and other professionals.

Objectives

Upon completion of the exercises in this chapter, you should be able to
1.   Define audit and explain the different types of auditor's opinions.
2.   Explain the source of an accountant's liability for breach of contract and fraud.
3.   Describe an accountant's liability for malpractice.
4.   Explain liability under the *Ultramares Doctrine*.
5.   Describe the foreseeability standard and accountant liability under the Restatement (Second) of Torts.
6.   Outline liability that may be imposed on accountants under the securities laws.
7.   Identify accountants' potential criminal liability.
8.   Explain the protection of accountants and their clients for their communications.
9.   Explain professionals' privilege concerning working papers.

Practical Application

This material will help you determine the duty of care owed by an accountant to a business, thereby allowing you to make an initial determination of whether or not an accountant has fulfilled their duties as required by law. By understanding the conduct that triggers liability for accountants, you will be able to question decisions and procedures that could have far reaching implications for the client and the accountant. Businesses that understand accountant liability will have a better understanding of when they can exercise their business judgment based upon representations and decisions made by their accountants. Likewise, accountants need to be aware of the situations that require them to investigate the information supplied to them by the client.

Helpful Hints

Until you understand the duties that are imposed upon an accountant, you will be unable to determine if they have met their duty of care to the client. Additionally, if you do not understand the duties imposed by statute, you will not know when the accountant has placed the client in jeopardy of civil or criminal liability. In this chapter, focus on the standards that are set and what degree of performance fulfills that standard. Make special note of the trouble areas where mistakes are often made that create liability.

Study Tips

Commence your study of accountant liability by closely examining the following standards, types of auditor's opinions, theories of common law liability, theories establishing liability to third parties, sources of statutory liability, and privileges related to accountants' work.

Accounting Standards

Certified public accountants must comply with:
- Generally accepted accounting principles (GAAPs) pertaining to preparation and presentation of financial statements, and
- Generally accepted auditing standards (GAASs) pertaining to audits

Audits and Auditor's Opinions

Audits are the verification of a company's books that must be performed by an independent CPA.
Auditors render an opinion about how fairly the financial statements:
- present the company's financial position
- result of operations
- change in financial position

The types of auditor's opinions are:
- *Unqualified opinion* – The most favorable opinion that the auditor can give. Represents the auditor's finding that the three areas of examination are correct and in conformity with consistently applied generally accepted accounting principles.
- *Qualified opinion* – States that the financial statements are fairly presented except for a departure from generally accepted accounting principles, a change in accounting principles, or a material uncertainty. The irregularity is noted in the auditor's opinion.
- *Adverse opinion* – Determines that the financial statements do no fairly represent the three areas of examination. Usually issued when the auditor determines that the company has materially misstated items on its financial statements.
- *Disclaimer of opinion* – Expresses an inability to draw a conclusion as to the accuracy of the company's financial records. Generally issued when the auditor lacks sufficient information about the financial records to issue an overall opinion.

Theories of Common Law Liability

- *Breach of contract* – An accountant can be held liable for breach of contract and resulting damages when he or she fails to perform as agreed in their *engagement*, or contract.
- *Fraud* – May be found when there is an actual intent to misrepresent a material fact to a client, if the client relies on the misrepresentation. Constructive fraud may be shown if the accountant commits gross negligence in the performance of his or her duties.

- *Negligence* – While performing his or her duties, an accountant must use the care, knowledge, and judgment generally used by accountants in the same or similar circumstances. Failure to fulfill this duty is negligence. An accountant's violation of GAAPs and GAASs is *prima facie* evidence of negligence. An accountant can be held liable for malpractice if he or she reveals confidential information or the contents of working papers without the permission of the client or pursuant to court order.

Theories of Liability to Third Parties

- *Ultramares doctrine* – Liability will be imposed only if the accountant is in privity of contract, or a privity-like relationship with a third party. A relationship would occur where a client employed an accountant to prepare financial statement to be used by a third party, such as by a bank to evaluate a client's loan application.
- *Restatement rule* – Liability will be imposed only if the third party's reliance is foreseen, or known, or if the third party is among a limited class of intended, or known, users. This is the rule followed in most states.
- *"Reasonably foreseeable user"* – Liability will be imposed on the accountant if the third party's use of the client's financial statements was reasonably foreseeable.

Sources of Statutory Liability – Civil

- Securities Act of 1933, Section 11(a) – An accountant who makes misstatements or omissions of material facts in audited financial statements required for registration of securities or fails to find such misstatements or omissions may be liable to anyone who acquires the securities covered by the registration agreement. Accountants can assert a due diligence defense and rely upon a reasonable belief that the work was complete and correct. A willful violation of this section is a criminal offense.
- Securities Exchange Act of 1934, Sections 10(b) and 18 – Accountants are held liable for any manipulative or deceptive practice in connection with the purchase or sale of any security under Section 10(b). Only intentional conduct and recklessness, but not ordinary negligence, violates this section. Under Section 18(a), the accountant may be liable for any false or misleading statements in any application, report, or document filed with the SEC. The accountant can defend against a section 18(a) violation by showing that he or she acted in good faith when making the filing, or the plaintiff in a suit had knowledge of the false or misleading statement when the securities were purchased or sold.

Sources of Statutory Liability – Criminal

- Securities Act of 1933, Section 24 – It is a criminal offense to:
  1. willfully make any untrue statement of material fact in a registration statement
  2. omit any material fact necessary to ensure that the statements made in the registration statement are not misleading, or
  3. willfully violate any other provision of the Securities Act of 1933
- Securities Exchange Act of 1934, Section 32(a) – It is a criminal offense for any person willfully and knowingly to make or cause to be made any false or misleading statement in any application, report, or other document required to be filed with the SEC.
- Racketeer Influenced and Corrupt Organization Act – Securities fraud is defined as a racketeering activity for which two or more occurrences qualify as a pattern of racketeering.

- 1976 Tax Reform Act – imposes criminal liability on an accountant for:
    1. aiding or assisting in the preparation of a false tax return
    2. aiding and abetting an individual's understatement of tax liability
    3. negligently or willfully understating a client's tax liability or recklessly or intentionally disregarding IRS rules or regulations
    4. failing to provide a taxpayer with a copy of the return, failing to sign the return, failing to furnish the appropriate tax identification numbers, or fraudulently negotiating a tax refund check

Accountant Privileges

- **Accountant-Client Privilege** – It is not recognized by the federal courts, but has been enacted in approximately 20 states where it says that an accountant cannot be called as a witness against a client in a court action.
- **Accountants' Work Papers** – These often include a wide array of notes, memos, calculations, and plans concerning audits, work assignments, data collection, client's internal controls, reconciling reports, research, comments, opinions and information regarding the affairs of the client. Under federal law these papers are subject to discovery. Some states provide work product immunity for accountants, much the same as lawyers, whose work papers on strategy, research, opinions, and trial preparation are not discoverable in a lawsuit involving the client.
- **Ownership of Work Papers** – The accountant is an independent contractor, making the work papers of the accountant his or her property. The accountant does owe the client some rights and duties in regards to these papers, including:
    1. the right to review them upon reasonable notice
    2. the duty to transfer the papers upon the client's request
    3. the duty not to transfer the papers without the client's permission

Refresh Your Memory

The following exercises will enable you to refresh your memory as to the key principles and concepts given to you in this chapter. Read each question carefully and put your answer in the blanks provided. Review the chapter material for any question you miss or are unable to remember.

1. A person who is not a certified accountant is referred to as a _____.

2. When an accountant has been found liable for actual or constructive fraud, what may the client recover?
   _____

3. What are the two uniform standards of professional conduct that a certified public accountant must comply with?_____
   and _____

4. What is an audit?
   _____

5. An accountant's negligence is also known as _____ _____.

6. For purposes of assigning negligence to an accountant, the accountant's actions are measured against those of a "_____ accountant" in similar _____.

7. The _____ doctrine says that an accountant is not held liable for negligence to a party unless they are in _____ _____ _____.

8. Give two examples of opinions that an auditor may give. _____ _____.

9. If an accountant engages in _____ or constructive fraud, a third party who relies on the accountant's fraud and is injured may bring a tort action against the accountant.

10. Section 18(a) of the Securities and Exchange Act of 1934 imposes liability on any person who makes _____ or _____ statements of material fact in any application, report, or document filed with the SEC.

11. The Private Securities Litigation Reform Act of 1995 replaced joint and several liability with _____ liability.

12. Section 10(b) of the Securities Exchange Act of 1934 prohibits any manipulative or _____ practice in connection with the purchase or sale of any _____.

13. Section 10 A of the Securities and Exchange Act imposes duties on auditors to _____ and report _____ acts committed by their clients.

14. Section 24 of the Securities Act of 1933 makes it a criminal violation to willfully make any _____ statement of _____ fact in a registration statement filed with the SEC.

15. States whose laws provide _____ _____ _____ are referring to the fact that an accountant's work papers cannot be discovered in a court case against the accountant's client.

Critical Thought Exercise

BGT Technologies, Inc., issued stock in a public offering that violated federal securities laws due to material misrepresentations and multiple acts of fraud. When it was discovered that BGT has substantially overstated its assets and failed to report debts owed to foreign banks, the SEC commenced an investigation. Kyle Sawyer was a partner in Jones Bateman, an independent certified public accounting firm. Sawyer was responsible for the BGT account and prepared numerous documents as part of the public offering. The documents filed by Sawyer contained the material misrepresentations. The SEC filed a suit against Sawyer and Jones Bateman, charging them with aiding and abetting the securities fraud perpetrated by BGT. Jones Bateman and Sawyer argue that they relied upon the information supplied to them by BGT to prepare the SEC filings. Jones Bateman did not verify or investigate the debt being carried by BGT. Jones Bateman argues that it should not be liable for aiding and abetting the securities fraud by BGT. What is the likely result when the matter is litigated?

Answer:

_____
_____
_____
_____
_____
_____
_____
_____
_____
_____
_____
_____
_____
_____
_____
_____
_____
_____
_____

Practice Quiz

True/False

1. ____ GAAPs are the standards for the preparation and presentation of financial statements. [p. 803]

2. ____ Pursuant to federal securities law, state laws, and stock exchange rules, an audit must be performed by an independent CPA. [p. 804]

3. ____ As part of an audit, a CPA must review the client's financial records, but need not do any independent investigation. [p. 804]

4. ____ An adverse opinion is generally issued by an auditor when the financial statements are fairly presented except for a departure from generally accepted accounting principles. [p. 804]

5. ____ A limited partner whose negligent or intentional conduct causes injury is personally liable for his or her own conduct. [p.804]

6. ____ Actual fraud occurs when the accountant acts with "reckless disregard" for the truth or consequences of his or her actions. [p. 805]

7. ____ Under the rule known as the foreseeability standard, accountants are not held liable to third parties for their negligence. [p. 809]

8. ___ Under the *Ultramares* doctrine, the accountant is liable only for negligence to third parties who are in privity of contract or a privity-like relationship with the accountant. [p. 806]

9. ___ In states that have enacted the accountant-client privilege, an accountant can be called as a witness against a client in a court action. [p. 813]

10. ___ Section 101 of the Uniform Securities Act makes it a criminal offense for accountants and others to willfully falsify financial statements and other reports. [p. 813]

11. ___ There is an implied civil private cause of action for violations of 10(b) and 10b-5. [p. 810]

12. ___ There is no accountant-client privilege under federal law. [p. 813]

13. ___ Accountants are considered to be experts, and the financial statements they prepare are considered an *expertised portion* of the registration statement. [p. 810]

14. ___ If an accountant is held to be liable along with four other defendants, the accountant may have to pay the entire judgment because he or she would have joint and several liability. [p. 811]

15. ___ Third parties may sue accountants for breach of contract. [p. 810]

16. ___ Accountants are rarely defendants in Section 10(b) and Rule 10b-5 actions. [p. 811]

17. ___ The Private Securities Litigation Reform Act of 1995 replaced joint and several liability of defendants with proportionate liability. [p. 811]

18. ___ Though some professions may be able to use a due diligence defense to liability, accountants may not. [p. 810]

19. ___ An investor who uncovers fraud may recover the difference between the price he or she paid for the security and the value of the security at the time of the lawsuit provided he or she proves that he or she relied on the misstatement or omission. [p. 810].

20. ___ The Department of Justice determines whether criminal charges will be brought when the SEC finds evidence of fraud or other willful violation of federal securities laws, or other federal laws. [p. 812]

Multiple Choice

21. Standards for the preparation and presentation of financial statements are found in [p. 803]
    a. GAAPs.
    b. GAASs.
    c. *Greenstein, Logan & Company v. Burgess Marketing, Inc.* 744 S.W.2d 170 (1987).
    d. The *Ultramares* doctrine.

22. Standards that specify the methods and procedures that must be used to conduct audits are found in [p. 803]
    a. GAAPs.
    b. GAASs.
    c. *Greenstein, Logan & Company v. Burgess Marketing, Inc.* 744 S.W.2d 170 (1987).
    d. The *Ultramares* doctrine.

23. To comply with the standards for the methods and procedures that must be used to conduct an audit, an auditor must [p. 804]
    a. review the financial records of the company that is being audited.
    b. check the accuracy of the financial records of the company that is being audited.
    c. conduct a sampling of inventory to verify the figures contained in the client's financial statements.
    d. all of the above

24. An auditor's opinion that is the most favorable one an auditor can give is a(n) [p. 804]
    a. unqualified opinion.
    b. qualified opinion.
    c. adverse opinion.
    d. disclaimer of opinion.

25. An auditor's opinion that is usually issued when the auditor determines that the company has materially misstates certain items on its financial statement is a(n) [p. 804]
    a. unqualified opinion.
    b. qualified opinion.
    c. adverse opinion.
    d. disclaimer of opinion.

26. An auditor's opinion which states that the financial statements are fairly presented except for a departure from generally accepted accounting principles, a change in accounting principles, or a material uncertainty, is a(n) [p. 804]
    a. unqualified opinion.
    b. qualified opinion.
    c. adverse opinion.
    d. disclaimer of opinion.

27. A few states have followed this theory of liability to third parties for negligence by accountants. [p. 809]
    a. The *Ultramares* doctrine
    b. Section 552 of the Restatement (Second) of Torts
    c. The foreseeability standard
    d. GAAPs

28. Third parties cannot sue accountants for breach of contract because they are not [p. 806]
    a. covered by the *Ultramares* doctrine.
    b. covered by Section 552 of the Restatement (Second) of Torts.
    c. covered by the foreseeability standard.
    d. in privity of contract.

29. When an accountant has been found liable for constructive fraud, this means [p. 805]
    a.   the accountant acted precisely and deliberately.
    b.   the accountant is liable for breach of contract.
    c.   the accountant is not liable.
    d.   the accountant acted with "reckless disregard" for the truth or consequences of his or her actions.

30. The Sarbanes-Oxley Act of 2002 did which of the following? [p. 813]
    a.   It provided work product immunity.
    b.   It allowed accountants to generate substantial work papers for their services.
    c.   It created the Public Company Accounting Oversight Board
    d.   It gave auditors a right to an opinion.

Short Answer

31. What is the difference between actual and constructive fraud? [p. 805]

_____
_____
_____

32. What effect would something other than an unqualified opinion have on a company that is being audited? [p. 804]

_____
_____
_____

33. When does an auditor give a *disclaimer of opinion*? [p. 804]

_____
_____
_____

34. Who is an accountant liable to under the foreseeability standard? [p. 809]

_____   _____

35.   What does proportionate liability mean under the Private Securities Litigation Reform Act of 1995? [p. 811]

_____

36. What professional repercussions may an accountant face if he or she violates any of the provisions that are stated in the 1976 Tax Reform Act? [p. 812]

_____
_____
_____

37. Describe the *Ultramares* doctrine. [p. 806]

_____
_____
_____

38. What conduct produces liability for accountants under Section 11(a) of the Securities Act of 1933? [p. 810]

_____
_____
_____

39. What is the common law rule regarding accountant-client privilege? [p. 813]

_____
_____
_____

40. What is a limited liability partnership? [p. 804]

_____
_____
_____

41. What are the two ways an accountant or other defendant can defeat the imposition of liability under Section 18 (a) of the Securities Exchange Act of 1934? [p. 811]

_____
_____
_____
_____

42. What three things create criminal liability for an accountant under Section 24 of the Securities Act of 1933? [p. 812]
    (1) _____
    _____
    (2) _____
    _____
    (3) _____
    _____

43. Because securities fraud falls under the definition of racketeering activity, accountants are vulnerable to prosecution under the _____ _____ _____
    _____ _____ ____ (RICO). [p. 812]

44. Name three specific acts for which an accountant may incur criminal liability under the 1976 Tax Reform Act. [p. 812]
    (1) _____
    (2) _____
    (3) _____

45. Name three rights or duties owed by an accountant to a client concerning work papers. [p. 813]
    (1) _____
    (2) _____
    (3) _____

Answers to Refresh Your Memory

1.   public accountant [p. 803]
2.   any damages proximately caused by that fraud [p. 805]
3.   generally a verification of a company's books and records [p. 804]
5.   accountant malpractice [p. 806]
6.   reasonable; circumstances [p. 806]
7.   *Ultramares*, privity of contract [p. 806]
8.   foreseeability standard [p. 809]
9.   actual [p. 805]
10. false; misleading [p. 811]
11. proportionate [p. 811]
12. deceptive, security [p. 810]
13. defect; report [p. 811]
14. untrue; material [p. 812]
15. work product immunity [p. 813]

Critical Thought Exercise Model Answer

It has been a much-debated issue whether accountants may be held liable in private actions for aiding and abetting violations of securities laws such as Section 10(b) and Rule 10b-5. The case of *Central Bank v. First Interstate Bank* in 1994 saw the United States Supreme Court rule that private parties could not bring actions against accountants for aiding and abetting violations of Section 10(b) of the 1934 Act. The ruling in *Central Bank* was addressed by Congress when it passed the Private Securities Litigation Reform Act of 1995. The act imposed a new statutory duty on accountants. An auditor must use adequate and thorough procedures in any audit performed by them to detect any illegal acts of the customer for whom the audit is being prepared. Any illegality must be disclosed to the company's board of directors, the management audit committee, or even the SEC it the circumstances warrant such action. The act makes aiding and abetting a violation of the Act of 1934 a violation in itself. The Private Securities Litigation Reform Act of 1995 precluded the extension of the ruling in Central bank to SEC actions. Thus, the SEC action against Jones Bateman would be allowed under a theory of aiding and abetting the SEC violations by BGT.

Answers to Practice Quiz

True/False

1.   False   GAAPs are the standards for the preparation and presentation of financial statements.
2.   True   The CPA can have no internal relationship with the client.
3.   False   The CPA must investigate the financial position of the company, take a sampling of the inventory, and verify information from third parties.
4.   False   The adverse opinion is issued when the auditor determines that the company has materially misstated certain items on its financial statements.
5.   True   A limited partner whose negligent or intentional conduct causes injury is personally liable for his or her own conduct.
6.   False   This is a definition of constructive fraud.
7.   False   A few states have adopted a rule known as the foreseeability standard for holding accountants liable to third parties for negligence.

8. True   Under this doctrine, the accountant must be aware of the use of the work by the third party.
9. False   An accountant cannot be called as a witness against a client in a court action.
10. True   This is a correct definition of privity of contract.
11. True   The courts have implied a civil private cause of action.
12. True   There is no accountant-client privilege under federal law.
13. False   The accountant has special skill and knowledge.
14. False   The accountant would only have to pay for his/her proportionate degree of liability.
15. False   Third parties usually cannot sue accountants for breach of contract because the third parties are merely incidental beneficiaries who do not acquire any rights under the accountant-client contract.
16. False   Accountants are often defendants in Section 10(b) and Rule 10b-5 actions.
17. True   The Private Securities Litigation Reform Act of 1995 replaced joint and several liability with proportionate liability which limits a defendant's liability to its proportionate degree of fault.
18. True   Accountants can assert a due diligence defense to liability.
19. False   The plaintiff may recover the difference between the price he or she paid for the security and the value of the security at the time of the lawsuit. The plaintiff does not have to prove that he or she relied on the misstatement or omission.
20. True   If the SEC finds evidence of fraud or other willful violation of federal securities laws, or other federal law, the Department of Justice determines whether actual criminal charges will be brought.

Multiple Choice

21. A   Answer A is correct because GAAPs are the generally accepted accounting principles which deal with the preparation of financial statements. Answer B is not correct because GAASs deal with preparation of audits. Answer C is not correct because it is a case that dealt with the failure to follow GAAS. Answer D is incorrect because it is a negligence doctrine.
22. B   Answer B is correct because GAASs are the standards that specify the method and procedures for conducting audits. Answer A is incorrect because it pertains to preparation of financial statements. Answer C is incorrect because it is a case that dealt with the failure to follow GAAS. Answer D is incorrect because it is a negligence doctrine, not a source of accounting standards.
23. D   Answer D is correct because Answers choices A, B, and C are all necessary steps in an audit.
24. A   Answer A is correct because this opinion states that the company's financial statements fairly present the company's financial position. Answer B is incorrect because a qualified opinion notes an exception, departure from accounting principles, or a material uncertainty. Answer C is incorrect because it gives the opinion that there is a material misstatement in the financial records. Answer D is not correct because the auditor renders no opinion due to lack of sufficient information.
25. C   Answer C is issued by the auditor when a material misstatement is found in the financial records of the company. Answer A is incorrect because an unqualified opinion would not be issued if there were anything materially wrong with the financial records. Answer B is incorrect because it only notes a potential problem, not a material misstatement. Answer D is incorrect because no opinion is issued due to a lack of sufficient information.

26. B Answer B is correct because an exception, departure, or uncertainty prevent the opinion from being unqualified, but the problems are not serious enough to require an adverse opinion. Answer A is not correct because an unqualified opinion notes no problems. Answer C is incorrect because it reveals a material misstatement in the financial records, not just an exception to or departure from accounting principles. Answer D is incorrect because a disclaimer is made when no opinion is possible due to a lack of sufficient information.

27. C Answer C is correct because this is the theory applied in a few of the states. Answers A and B are not correct because they are applied in a majority of states. Answer D is not correct because GAAPs are used to show negligence, not to extend liability to third parties.

28. D Answer D is correct because there must be a contractual relationship, or privity, before a party can maintain an action for breach of contract. Answer A, B, and C are incorrect because they state negligence theories and are unrelated to breach of contract.

29. C Answer C is the correct choice pursuant to Section 10A, which has a three-tier reporting requirement. If the first step is unsuccessful, the auditor must then go to the board of directors. Answer A is wrong because the auditor does not have to report to the SEC until other options are exhausted. Answer B is incorrect because the board of directors does not have to be informed unless the management fails to take timely and appropriate remedial action. Answer D is incorrect because the auditor must act to remedy the illegality by following the mandates of Section 10A.

30. D Answer D is correct as it states what constructive fraud is, "a reckless disregard or the truth or consequences of an individual's actions." Answer A is incorrect, as the answer implies that the fraud was intentional. Constructive fraud implies negligence. Answer B is incorrect as fraud is a tort-based cause of action, not a contract-based one. Answer C is incorrect as it is completely erroneous since the question states that the accountant has been found liable.

Short Answer

31. Actual fraud is intentional, whereas constructive fraud is sometimes categorized as "gross negligence."

32. An example of an adverse effect for issuing more than an unqualified opinion is that a company may not be able to sell its securities to the public, merge with another company, or obtain loans from banks.

33. This opinion is generally issued when the auditor lacks sufficient information about the financial records to issue an overall opinion.

34. to any foreseeable use of the client's financial statements

35. It means that the defendant's liability is proportioned to his or her degree of fault.

36. Accountants who have violated the provisions of the 1976 Tax Reform Act can be enjoined from further federal income tax practice.

37. The *Ultramares* doctrine provides that an accountant is not liable for negligence to third parties unless the plaintiff was either in privity of contract or a pritivy-like relationship with the accountant. Privity of contract would occur if a client employed as accountant to prepare financial statements to be used by an identified third party for a specific purpose that the accountant was made aware of.

38. The accountant is liable for making misstatements or omissions of material fact in a registration statement or failing to find such misstatements or omissions.

39. An accountant may be called to testify against his or her client.

40. a special form of partnership in which all partners are limited partners

41. First, the defendant can show that he or she acted in good faith. Second, he or she can show that the plaintiff had knowledge of the false or misleading statement when the securities were purchased or sold.

42. (1) willfully make any untrue statement of material fact in a registration statement filed with the SEC, (2) omit any material fact necessary to ensure that the statements made in the registration statement are not misleading, or (3) willfully violate any other provision of the Securities Act of 1933 or rule or regulation adopted thereunder

43. Racketeer Influenced and Corrupt Organizations Act

44. (1) willful understatement of a client's tax liability, (2) negligent understatement of tax liability, or (3) wrongful indorsing a client's tax refund check

45. (1) right to review the work papers with reasonable notice, (2) duty to transfer the papers upon the client's request, and (3) duty to not transfer the papers without the client's permission

Chapter 52

WILLS, TRUSTS, AND LIVING WILLS

Chapter Overview

Wills and trusts are the two main ways that a person disposes of their assets prior to or upon their death. These assets may include business ownership, intellectual property, stocks and bonds, real estate, and personal property. A person who dies intestate, or without a will, will have his or her estate distributed according to a state statute. A trust may be created before death so that property may be held and managed for the benefit of another.

Objectives

Upon completion of the exercises in this chapter, you should be able to:
1. Describe the requirements for making a valid will.
2. Understand how a will can be revoked.
3. Describe holographic and noncupative wills.
4. Explain the types of gifts that can be contained in a will.
5. Understand the principles of abatement and ademption.
6. Explain *per stirpes* and *per capita* distribution of an estate.
7. Describe the effect of simultaneous death of beneficiaries.
8. Explain the effect of the execution of mutual wills.
9. Describe the application of an intestacy statute.
10. Explain the probate process.
11. Describe the formation and functioning of a trust.

Practical Application

When a businessperson acquires assets, it is wise to know how those will be distributed upon their death. The fruits of years of hard work may be wasted if a person does not take adequate steps to preserve their estate and ensure that the estate will be distributed as they wish. As discussed in Chapter 50, insurance, especially key-person insurance, is an integral part of the estate planning process. A business may have to be dissolved if the owners do not take estate planning into account.

Helpful Hints

The main purpose of entering into business is to acquire wealth and provide the necessities of life for yourself, family, and others that depend upon you. Regardless of the amount of current assets held by a person, everyone should have an estate plan. It may be as simple as a will or may involve complex estate planning with the use of trusts, tax consultation, and use of joint tenancy. If an estate plan is in place, it will provide the distribution of assets as desired by the businessperson even if the assets grow or change. Periodic updates of the estate plan are advisable.

Study Tips

In order to make informed judgments involving estate planning, the individual should understand the following principles OF law relating to wills and trusts.

Requirements for Making a Will

A will is a declaration of how a person wants his or her property distributed upon death. The person who makes this testamentary disposition of property is called the testator or testatrix. The persons designated to receive the property are the beneficiaries.

Every state has a Statute of Wills that sets forth the requirements for a valid will. They are

- Testamentary capacity – the testator must be of legal age and of sound mind
- Writing – the will must be in writing except for noncupative wills
- Testator's signature – the will must be signed at the end

Attestation by Witnesses

Wills must be attested to by two or three objective and competent persons. The person need not live in the same state, but all the parties must be present when the will is attested to by all witnesses and signed by the testator.

Changing the Will

Wills may be changed by a codicil, a separate document that must be executed with the same formalities as a will. The codicil must incorporate by reference the will it is amending by referring to the testator by name and the date of the previous will. The codicil and will become one document that is read as a whole.

Revoking a Will

Any act that shows a desire to revoke a will shall be deemed a revocation. Making a new will, burning, tearing, or crossing out the pages are all forms of revocations. Wills may also be revoked by operation of law, such as when people get divorced or a spouse is convicted of the murder of the other spouse.

Special Types of Wills

- *Holographic wills* are entirely handwritten by the testator, dated, and signed. They need not be witnessed.
- *Noncupative wills* are oral wills made before witnesses during a final illness. They are sometimes call deathbed wills.

Types of Testamentary Gifts

- A gift or real property is a *devise.*
- A gift of personal property is a *bequest* or *legacy.*
- *Specific gifts* are specifically named items of personal property, such as a ring.
- *General gifts* do not specify the source, such as a cash gift.

- *Residuary gifts* are established by a residuary clause that leaves the portion of the estate left over after all distributions and costs are satisfied.

Ademption and Abatement

- *Ademption* – the beneficiary receives nothing when the testator leaves a specific gift and that gift is not in the testator's estate when he or she dies.
- *Abatement* – if the testator's estate is not large enough to pay all of the devises and bequests, the doctrine of abatement applies. If the will has general and residuary gifts, the residuary gift is abated first. If the will only has general gifts, each gift is reduced proportionately.

Per Stirpes and Per Capita Distribution

When the will leaves the estate to the testator's lineal descendants, it will be distributed either per stipres or per capita.
- *Per stirpes* – the lineal descendants inherit by representation of their parents.
- *Per capita* – the lineal descendants equally share the property of the estate without regard to the degree of relationship to the testator. Children share equally with grandchildren.

Videotaped and Electronic Wills

Electronic wills and videotaped wills do not have any legal force by themselves. A written will is still required. The videotaped or electronically recorded will can be used to supplement the written will to show that the testator had testamentary capacity.

Reciprocal Wills

Reciprocal wills arise where two or more testators execute separate wills that make testamentary dispositions of their property to each other on the condition that the survivor leave the remaining property on his or her death as agreed by the testators.

Undue Influence

A will may be invalidated if it was made as a result of undue influence upon the testator. Undue influence occurs when one person takes advantage of another person's mental, emotional, or physical weakness and unduly persuades that person to make a will. The persuasion by the wrongdoer must overcome the free will of the testator.

Murder Disqualification Doctrine

Most state statutes and court decisions provide that a person who murders another person cannot inherit the victim's property.

Intestate Succession

If a person dies without a will, or a will fails for some legal reason, the property is distributed to his or her relatives pursuant to the state's intestacy statute. Relatives who receive property under these statutes are called heirs. If there are no heirs, the property escheats (goes) to the state.

Probate

Probate is the process of a deceased's property being collected, debts and taxes being paid, and the remainder being distributed. A personal representative must be appointed to administer the estate. If the person is named in a will, they are called an executor. If the court appoints the representative, they are an administrator. A probate proceeding is administered and settled according to the state's probate code. Almost half of the states have adopted most or all of the Uniform Probate Code.

Living Wills

People who do not want their lives prolonged indefinitely by artificial means should sign a living will that stipulates their wishes before catastrophe strikes and they become unable to express it themselves.

Trusts

A trust is a legal arrangement established when one person, the settlor or trustor, transfers title to property to another person to be held and used for the benefit of a third person. The property held in trust is called the trust corpus or trust res. Trusts often give any trust income to an income beneficiary and the corpus is distributed to a remainderman upon termination of the trust. There are several kinds of trusts.
- **Express trust** – A trust created voluntarily by the settlor. Express trusts are either:
  - *inter vivos trust* – a trust that is created while the settlor is alive
  - *testamentary trust* – a trust created by will
- **Implied trust** – A trust that is implied by law or from the conduct of the parties. These trusts are either:
  - *constructive trust* – an equitable trust that is imposed by law to avoid fraud, unjust enrichment, and injustice
  - *resulting trust* – a trust created by the conduct of the parties
- **Charitable trust** – created for the benefit of a segment of society or society in general
- **Spendthrift trust** – designed to prevent a beneficiary's personal creditors from reaching his or her trust interest
- **Totten trust** – created when a person deposits money in a bank in their own name and holds it as trustee for the benefit of another

Refresh Your Memory

The following exercises will enable you to refresh your memory as to the key principles and concepts given to you in this chapter. Read each question carefully and put your answer in the blanks provided. Review the chapter material for any question you miss or are unable to remember.

1. A person who makes a will is called the _____ or _____.

2. The action of a will being witnessed by two or three objective and competent witnesses is called _____.

3. A separate document that must be executed to amend a will is called a _____.

4. A holographic will is entirely _____ by the testator, dated, and signed.

5. A gift in a will of personal property is a _____ or _____.

6. If Lou leaves his 1944 Mercedes to his nephew in his will, but the car had been sold before Lou died, the nephew will receive nothing under the principle of _____.

7. When distribution of property takes place _____ _____, the lineal descendants equally share the property of the estate.

8. A will may be invalidated if it was made as a result of _____ _____ upon the testator.

9. If a person dies without a will and has no surviving relatives, their property _____ to the state.

10. If an executor is not named in the will, the court will appoint an _____ or _____.

11. A _____ trust is created by will.

12. Property held in trust is called the trust _____ or trust _____.

13. An _____ _____ trust is an express trust created while the settlor is alive.

14. A _____ trust is created by a will.

15. A _____ _____ receives the assets of a living trust upon the death of the grantor.

Critical Thought Exercise

Fanny York was unmarried and had no children. Her will made the following bequests: (1) all of the stock she owned in AOL to her friend, Betsy Petersen, (2) all of her stock in Lucent Technologies to her great niece, Molly Burke, (3) her entire doll collection to be sold and the proceeds to be held in trust for the benefit of her two cats, Elmo and Fred, and (4) the residue to Teen Recovery. When the value of her stocks dropped sharply in 2002, York sold the stock and placed the proceeds in separate bank accounts. A piece of paper with Petersen's name is put inside the savings book for the account started from the proceeds from the sale of the AOL stock. Another savings book has a piece of paper with Burke's name on it. The balance of this account came from the sale of the Lucent stock. When York dies in November 2002, Teen Recovery requests that the entire estate, including the proceeds from both savings accounts, be granted to it.

Teen Recovery also requests that the proceeds from the sale of the dolls be given to it because the cats are not human and should not be considered a legitimate heir.

Should the probate court give the proceeds from the bank accounts to Burke and Petersen? Should the court uphold the trust for the benefit of Elmo and Fred?

Answer:

_____
_____
_____
_____
_____
_____
_____
_____
_____
_____
_____
_____
_____
_____

Practice Quiz

True/False

1. ____ An attestation is a declaration of how a person wants his or her property distributed upon death. [p. 819]

2. ____ The persons designated to receive the property under a will are the beneficiaries. [p. 818]

3. ____ The testator's signature must appear at the end of the will. [p. 819]

4. ____ The signatures of the witnesses to a will are called the codicil. [p. 819]

5. ____ A will may be changed by a codicil without revoking the entire will. [p. 819]

6. ____ If the testator tears a will, the will is revoked. [p. 819]

7. ____ When a husband and wife get divorced, their wills are entirely revoked by operation of law. [p. 821]

8. ____ Holographic wills must be witnessed like a formal written will. [p. 821]

9. ____ If a second will is executed by the testator that does not revoke the prior will, the second will automatically controls. [p. 819]

10. ___ The birth of a child does not revoke or change a will, but does entitle the child to receive his or her share of the parents' estate, as determined by state statute. [p. 821]

11. ___ A gift of real estate by a will is called a devise. [p. 822]

12. ___ A general gift is an item of personal property, such as your great-grandmother's ring. [p. 822]

13. ___ Ademption is applied if the property the testator leaves is not sufficient to satisfy all the beneficiaries named in a will. [p. 824]

14. ___ When a testator leaves his or her property to descendants per stirpes, all living descendants at the time of the testator's death receive an equal share. [p. 823]

15. ___ A beneficiary may not renounce a gift once it has been lawfully made in a legal will. [p. 822]

16. ___ When two people who would inherit property from each other die simultaneously, each deceased person's property is distributed as though he or she survived. [p. 821]

17. ___ If two or more testators execute the same instrument as their will, the document is called a reciprocal or mutual will. [p. 821]

18. ___ There is no such thing as a valid oral will. [p. 821]

19. ___ A will may be found to be invalid if it was made as a result of undue influence on the testator. [p. 821]

20. ___ The process of a deceased's property being collected, debts and taxes being paid, and the remainder of the estate being distributed is intestate succession. [p. 822]

21. ___ Nancy dies in an automobile accident and has not left a will. Her estate will be distributed pursuant to the state's intestacy statute. [p. 825]

22. ___ Heirs receive the testator's estate after a will has been validly probated. [p. 825]

23. ___ A Totten trust is designed to prevent a beneficiary's personal creditors from reaching his or her trust interest. [p. 828]

24. ___ The property and assets held in a trust are called the beneficiary income. [p. 826]

25. ___ The settlor is the person who creates the trust by transferring the res to the trustee. [p. 826]

Multiple Choice

26. Fred executes a valid will. Fred is the [p. 818]
    a. testator.
    b. executor.
    c. beneficiary.
    d. administrator.

27. Betty receives $10,000 under Dan's will when it is probated. Betty is a(n) [p. 818]
    a. testator.
    b. executor.
    c. beneficiary.
    d. administrator.

28. Which of the following is not a requirement to form a valid will? [p. 818]
    a. The testator must have testamentary capacity.
    b. The will must be in writing.
    c. The testator must sign the will.
    d. An attorney must prepare the will for it to comply with the Statute of Wills.

29. A will that meets the requirements of the Statute of Will is called [p. 819]
    a. a holographic will.
    b. a formal will.
    c. a noncupative will.
    d. none of the above

30. Steve executes a separate instrument to amend a will so that his baseball card collection is not given to Vince but to Martha. This instrument is called a(n) [p. 819]
    a. trust.
    b. holographic will.
    c. codicil.
    d. attestation.

31. Which of the following will not revoke a will? [p. 819]
    a. Divorce
    b. A child being born after the will has been executed
    c. A subsequent will that revokes all prior will and codicils
    d. The testator burning the will in her fireplace

32. A gift of $20,000 left to Bob in Laurie's will is a [p. 822]
    a. general bequest.
    b. general devise.
    c. specific bequest.
    d. specific devise.

33. Carl leaves a Ming vase to Opal in his will, but the vase is no longer in the estate when Carl dies. Opal receives nothing under the principle of [p. 824]
    a. abatement.
    b. ademption.
    c. intestacy.
    d. per capita distribution.

34. When 88-year-old Juan leaves all of his property to Ed Rush, the lawyer who drafted his will and ignored numerous blood relatives, a probate court will likely invalidate the will [p. 821]
    a. under the murder disqualification doctrine.
    b. because of the lack of proper attestation.
    c. because of undue influence.
    d. unless it is a holographic will.

35. Zeke sets up a trust in his will that will come into existence when Zeke dies. This is a(n) [p. 828]
    a. charitable trust.
    b. Totten trust.
    c. *inter vivos* trust.
    d. testamentary trust.

Short Answer

36. The three main requirements of a valid will are: [p. 818]

    _____

    _____

37. Nancy and Karl witness Ron executing his will. They then sign the will as witnesses. This is called _____. [p. 819]

38. What is a codicil and what is required for a valid codicil? [p. 819]

    _____

    _____

39. Describe three of the ways that a will may be revoked. [p. 819]

    _____

    _____

40. Explain what is required for Hank to execute a valid holographic will. [p. 821]

    _____

    _____

41. What is a general gift? [p. 822]

    _____

    _____

42. Explain when the doctrine of abatement applies. [p. 824]

    _____

    _____

43. Explain per stirpes distribution. [p. 823]

    _____

    _____

    _____

44. What is the purpose of a videotaped will? [p. 822]

    _____

    _____

45. Describe how undue influence may occur in the execution of a will. [p. 821]

    _____

    _____

46. Explain the possible distribution of a person's estate if they have not executed a valid will. [p. 825]

_____

_____

47. What is the purpose of a living trust? [p. 829]

_____

_____

48. What are lineal descendants? [p. 823]

_____

49. How is a trust terminated? [p. 828]

_____

_____

50. Dave steals $50,000 from his employer. What type of trust may be applied to the funds stolen by Dave? [p. 828]

_____

_____

Answers to Refresh Your Memory

1. testator or testatrix [p. 818]
2. attestation [p. 819]
3. codicil [p. 819]
4. handwritten [p. 821]
5. bequest, devise [p. 822]
6. ademption [p. 824]
7. per capita [p. 823]
8. undue influence [p. 821]
9. escheats [p. 825]
10. administrator or administratrix [p. 822]
11. settler or trustor [p. 826]
12. corpus, res [p. 826]
13. *inter vivos* [p. 827]
14. testamentary [p. 828]
15. remainder beneficiary [p. 829]

Critical Thought Exercise Model Answer

If a testator leaves a specific gift of property to a beneficiary, but the property is no longer in the estate of the testator when he or she dies, the beneficiary receives nothing. This is called the doctrine of ademption. When York sold the stock and opened the two savings accounts, this was an ademption. The stock was a specific gift. Though York may have been trying to preserve the value of the bequest by selling the stock when their values fell significantly, there isn't sufficient proof that York wanted to create a separate gift of money. Petersen and Burke may argue that by putting their names with the savings books, York created Totten trusts for them. However, there is no indication that York held the funds in trust for them. The trust that is to be created for the benefit of the two cats is lawful. In addition to people, trusts may be created for the benefit of animals, groups, social causes, the environment, or any other lawful purpose. As long as a trustee is named and there is a way of fulfilling the testator's wishes, courts have upheld trusts that were created for the care and maintenance of pets. The court should find that the specific gifts to Petersen and Burke were revoked by the sale of the stock and the funds in the accounts are now part of the residue that goes to Teen Recovery.

Answers to Practice Quiz

True/False

1. False upon — A will is the declaration of how a person wants his or her property to be distributed upon death.
2. True — Beneficiaries receive property under a will made by the testator.
3. True — The will must be signed at the end to prevent fraud.
4. False — The witnesses' signatures are called the attestation clause.
5. True — The codicil must be executed with the same formalities as a will.
6. True — The will may be revoked by any act that shows an intent to revoke the will.
7. False — Those portions not disposing of property to the spouse remain valid.
8. False — A holographic will need not be witnessed.
9. False — Any conflicting provisions are controlled by the second will, but the wills are read together.
10. True — The newborn is entitled to receive his or her share of the parents' estate as determined by state statute.
11. True — It is called a devise while a gift of personal property is called a bequest or legacy.
12. False — This is a specific gift. A general gift is usually money.
13. False — This is the definition of abatement. Ademption is when a specific gift no longer exists at the time of death and the beneficiary receives nothing.
14. False — All descendants receive an equal share regardless of their degree of relationship to the testator under distribution per capita. Children must share equally with all relatives.
15. False — A beneficiary may always renounce a gift and this often occurs when the beneficiary cannot afford liens or mortgages against the property.
16. True — It is a question of inheritance that is decided by the Uniform Simultaneous Death Act.
17. False — The document is a joint will.
18. False — Noncupative wills are oral wills made before a witness during the testator's last illness. They are sometimes called deathbed wills.
19. True — The undue influence is usually established by circumstantial evidence surrounding the making of the will.
20. False — This process is called settlement of the estate or probate.
21. True — The property is distributed pursuant to the state's intestacy statute to the heirs then living.
22. False — Heirs receive property under a state's intestacy statute when a person dies without a will.
23. False — A spendthrift trust is designed to prevent the beneficiary's personal creditors from reaching his or her trust interest.
24. False — The property held in a trust is called the trust corpus or trust res.
25. True — The trustee has legal title to the trust corpus, and the beneficiary has equitable title.

Multiple Choice

26. A   A few states still maintain the additional designation of testatrix for a female testator. Answer B is not correct as the executor is the person named in the will to serve as personal representative for the administration of the will. Answer C is not correct because the beneficiary receives the property upon disbursement. Answer D is incorrect because the administrator is the personal representative who is appointed when an executor is not named in the will.

27. C   The beneficiary may be a person, organization, or institution. Answers A, B, and D are incorrect as defined in Question 26.

28. D   A person may prepare his/her own will. Answers A, B, and C are all requirements to form a valid will.

29. B   The requirements for a formal will must be followed without exception. Answers A and C do not meet all the formal requirements, lacking either attestation or a writing. Answer D is not correct because a correct Answer, B, is available.

30. C   A codicil must be executed with the same formalities as a will. Answer A is not correct because a trust is a legal arrangement for holding property by one person for the benefit of another. Answer B is not correct because it is an informal will in the testator's own handwriting. Answer D is incorrect because the attestation is the action of a will be witnesses, not an amendment to the will.

31. B   The birth of a child after a will has been executed does not revoke the will but does entitle the child to receive his or her share of the parents' estate as determined by state statute. Answer A is not correct because divorce revokes any disposition of property to the former spouse. Answer C is not correct because a properly executed subsequent will revokes a prior will if it specifically states the testator's intention to do so. Answer D is not correct because any act that demonstrates an intent to revoke the will serves as a revocation.

32. A   General gifts do not identify the specific property from which the gift is to be made, such as a cash amount that can be paid from any source. Answer B is not correct because a devise is related to real property. Answer C is not correct because a specific gift refers to a specifically named piece of property. Answer D is not correct because a specific devise is a gift of a particular piece of real property, not cash.

33. B   The gift lapses and is not granted from other estate assets. Answer A is not correct because abatement is a method for dividing an estate that does not have enough assets to satisfy all the gifts and taxes. Answer C is not correct because intestacy applies when there is no will. Answer D is not correct because per capita distribution is a method for dividing the estate equally among all the living descendants.

34. C   The large benefit to the beneficiary with such an easy opportunity to exert influence is strong evidence of undue influence. Answer A is incorrect because no one was murdered. Answer B is not correct because the presence or lack of an attestation clause does not prevent undue influence. Answer D is not correct because undue influence can be used whether there is a formal will or a holographic will.

35. D   The danger of waiting until death to create a trust by will is that the trust will be deemed invalid if the will that creates the trust is invalid. Answers A and B are forms of *inter vivos* trusts that are created during the settlor's lifetime. Answer D is incorrect for the same reason, as it is created during the settlor's lifetime, not upon his or her death.

Short Answer

36. testamentary capacity, a written will, testator's signature
37. attestation
38. A separate document that must be executed to amend a will. It must be executed with the same formalities as a will.
39. (1) divorce (2) an act by the testator that destroys the will (3) execution of a subsequent will that expressly revokes all former wills and codicils
40. The will must be entirely in the testator's own handwriting, dated, and signed by the testator.
41. A gift in a will that does identify the specific property from which the gift is to be made. A gift of an amount of money would be a general gift.
42. when the testator's estate is not large enough to pay all the devises and bequests
43. In per stirpes, the lineal descendants (grandchildren and great-grandchildren of the deceased) inherit by representation of the parent. They split what their deceased parent would have received. If their parent is alive, they receive nothing.
44. The videotaped will is not valid by itself, but it can be used to supplement the written will to demonstrate the testamentary capacity of the testator. It helps defeat challenges to the will.
45. Undue influence occurs when one person takes advantage of another person's mental, emotional, or physical weakness and unduly persuades that person to make a will.
46. If a person dies without a will, their property is distributed to his or her relatives, called heirs, under the state's intestacy statute. If there are no surviving relatives, the deceased's property goes to the state.
47. People who do not want their lives prolonged indefinitely by artificial means may execute a living will that stipulates their wishes before catastrophe strikes and they become unable to express it themselves because of an illness or an accident.
48. children, grandchildren, great-grandchildren, etc.
49. A trust is irrevocable unless the settlor reserves the right to revoke it. Usually a trust contains a specific termination date or provides that it will terminate upon the happening of an event.
50. The property or money that an embezzler takes may be invested in another business or piece of real estate. If so, a court may impose a constructive trust under which the embezzler, who hold title to the property, is considered a trustee who is holding the property in trust for the rightful owner.

Chapter 53

FAMILY LAW

Chapter Overview

There are a variety of legal issues that surround the area of family law. This chapter addresses a wide gamut of topics including premarital issues involving such things as the promise to marry, the engagement, and prenuptial agreements. Further, though many people have a romantic notion regarding marriage, there are certain state law requirements that must be met before a couple may get married. Once two individuals are married, issues concerning children and parents' rights, duties, and liabilities may also present themselves.   These issues, along with topics such as paternity, adoption and foster care are also investigated in your text. Finally, a discussion on the ways to terminate a marriage, the division of assets and debts, spousal and child support as well as child custody, are thoroughly examined.

Objectives

Upon completion of the exercises in this chapter, you should be able to:
1.   Identify premarital issues.
2.   Understand when a court will enforce a prenuptial agreement.
3.   Describe the general requirements for marriage.
4.   Discuss the basic rights and duties of a parent.
5.   Describe what a paternity action is.
6.   Identify the procedure for adoption.
7.   Understand what is involved with foster care.
8.   Explain the two legally recognized ways to terminate a marriage.
9.   Discuss the division of assets and debts upon termination of a marriage.
10.   Discuss the issues of spousal support, child support, and child custody.

Practical Application

This chapter will reinforce the concept that marriage is not to be entered into lightly. The responsibilities as well as life altering consequences a divorce may have are to be taken very seriously. This chapter will better enable you to understand the importance of not only making an educated decision on whom you marry, but also the potential issues that you might have to deal with should the marriage go awry.

Helpful Hints

A majority of people marry for love and companionship. However, many do not recognize the importance of planning before, during, and after the termination of a marriage. In the unfortunate event that a marriage is terminated, it is helpful to be aware of how assets and debts will be divided as well as the various issues that surround child custody. This chapter methodically takes you through the stages of a relationship from a legal viewpoint.

Study Tips

In order to make informed judgments involving marriage and family law, the individual should understand the following.

Premarital Issues

❖ In the 19th century, **promises to marry** were actionable as a breach of contract, in the event that someone did not fulfill the promise to do so. Modernly however there is no such cause of action. The groom, though, may be responsible for costs incurred in the planning of the wedding should he decide to back out of the marriage.

❖ The **engagement** of a couple refers to the period of time prior to the actual marriage of a couple. A proposal accompanied by a ring is the traditional way in which an engagement takes place.
   <u>What if the engagement is broken off?</u>
   If the prospective groom breaks the engagement, the prospective bride may keep the engagement ring.
   If the prospective bride breaks the engagement, she must return the ring to the prospective groom.

❖ **Prenuptial agreements** are often considered prior to marriage. A prenuptial agreement is a contract entered into prior to marriage that specifies how property will be distributed upon the termination of the marriage or death of a spouse.
   <u>What are the requirements of a prenuptial agreement?</u>
   Each party must make full disclosure of his or her assets and liabilities.
   Each party should be represented by his or her own attorney.
   Prenuptial agreements should be entered into voluntarily.
   The agreement must reflect a fair distribution of assets.

• **Special mention of the antenuptial agreement should be made.** An antenuptial agreement is made during the marriage whereby the parties agree on the distribution of property in the event of dissolution or death. The same requirements for a prenuptial apply to an antenuptial agreement.

Marriage

Simply stated, a marriage is a legal union between a man and woman as per the requirements of the state in which the marriage takes place.

Marriage Requirements

Most states require the following:
❖ The parties be a man and a woman.
❖ The parties be of a certain age (usually 18 years of age).
   - Younger parties may marry if emancipated, that is, not supported by his or her parents and provides for himself or herself.
   - All states provide that persons under a certain age like 14 or 15 cannot be married.
   - Marriages between people who are related by blood are prohibited, except in those states allowing cousins to be married.
❖ Neither party may be married to someone else.
❖ A marriage license must also be procured.

❖ Some states require a marriage ceremony.

❖ Most states require a spouse to **financially support** the other spouse and their children, which includes food, shelter, clothing, and medical care.

❖ Several states allow **common law marriages**, that is, a marriage in which the parties have not obtained a valid marriage. The requirements for this type of marriage area: 1) the parties are eligible to marry; 2) the parties voluntarily intend to be husband and wife; and 3) the parties must live together; and 4) hold themselves out to be husband and wife. ***A court decree of divorce must be obtained to end a common law marriage.**

❖ Same sex marriages are allowed in several states, whereby gay partners may enter into "civil unions." Under the **Defense of Marriage Act,** states may not be forced to recognize same-sex marriage performed in other states.

Parents and Children

Parents have certain obligations to their children. They must provide food, shelter, clothing, and medical care until a child reaches the age of 18 or becomes emancipated. Parents may be legally responsible beyond the age of 18 if their child has a disability.

Parental rights include:
- The right to control the behavior of a child.
- The right to select the schools for their children and the religion they will practice.
- Parents may use corporal punishment as long as it does not get to the level of child abuse.

* Parental neglect is present when a parent fails to provide a child with the necessities of life or other basic needs.

Paternity Actions

❖ If there is a question as to the child's father, a paternity action may be filed to determine the father's identity.

❖ The majority of paternity actions are filed by the mother against a man whom she claims is the child's father.

❖ Paternity actions are sometimes brought by the government where the mother is receiving welfare payments.

❖ A male will sometimes bring a paternity action to prove that he is not the father or to prove that he is in fact the father.

Parent's Liability for a Child's Wrongful Act

Generally, parents are not liable for the children's negligent acts, unless their negligence caused the child's act. Almost half of the states have child liability statutes whereby the parents are financially liable for the intentional torts of their children. Liability, however, is limited to a specific dollar amount.

Adoption

Adoption happens when a person becomes the legal parent of a child who is not his or her biological child. The two main ways to become adoptive parents are by agency adoption and independent adoptions. An **agency adoption** occurs when a person adopts a child from a social service organization of a state. *Open-adoption* procedures are used whereby the biological and the adoptive parents are introduced prior to adoption. Further, the biological parents may screen the prospective adoptive parents to assure suitability for the child. Further, adoptive and biological parents remain in contact with each other with the biological parents having visitation rights to see the child.

An **independent adoption** occurs when there is a private arrangement between the biological and adoptive parents. A lawyer, doctor, or private adoption agency often introduces the parties.

Court approval of the adoption must occur in both agency and independent adoptions before the adoption is legal. The decision will be based on what is in the best interests of the child. Preference is usually given to couples, however, single parents may adopt as well. Homosexual adoptions are allowed depending on the state. Court approved adoptions are subject to a probation of six months to a year. This time period allows a government social worker the time to investigate whether the adoptive parents are properly caring for the adoptive child.

Marriage Termination

There are two methods to terminate a marriage:

Annulment

- ❖ An annulment is an order of the court declaring that the marriage did not exist.
- ❖ Most annulments are rarely granted.
- ❖ Grounds for annulment are: lack of capacity or the marriage was never consummated.
- ❖ Children born of a marriage that is annuled are considered to be legitimate.
- ❖ Some of the same issues such as child support and custody, spousal support, and property settlement must be agreed upon by the couple or decided by the court.

Divorce

Divorce is a legal proceeding whereby the court issues a decree that legally orders a marriage terminated.

- ❖ In the 1960s, states began to recognize no-fault divorce. All one would need to state is that the couple had irreconcilable differences.
- ❖ Divorce proceeding:
    - One party files a petition for divorce within the state stating the basic information of parties' names, date and place of marriage, minor children names of and the reason for the divorce.
    - The petition must be served on the other spouse.
    - The spouse being served has a certain time frame in which to answer the petition.
    - The parties can conduct discovery to obtain evidence to support their claims.
    - A typical waiting period is 6 months before a divorce is final. This gives the parties time to reconcile should they decide to do so.
    - Restraining orders are issued if there is a showing that one party is likely to injure the other party.
    - *Pro se* divorce is where parties represent themselves. This is usually done for simple divorces.
    - **Settlement** of divorce cases – About 90 percent of divorce cases are settled before trial. Some divorce parties use mediation, as it is mandatory in some states. A mediator is a go-between.

Division of Assets

When a marriage is terminated, the parties must reach a settlement regarding their assets and debts. If the parties cannot reach a settlement, the court will order a division of assets.

Separate Property

Separate property includes property owned by a spouse prior to marriage, and inheritances as well as gifts received during the marriage. Each spouse retains his or her own separate property upon dissolution of the marriage. However, if separate and marital property is commingled during the marriage or if the owner of separate property places the other spouse's name on the title to property, then the property is considered to be a marital asset.

Marital Property

Marital property is property acquired during the course of the marriage using income from the spouses that was earned during the marriage. Marital property is also separate property that has been converted to marital property. The two theories of distribution are as follows:

1. **Equitable Distribution** – The court may order the fair distribution of property which does not necessarily mean an equitable distribution. Several factors are considered before the property can be distributed. They are: length of the marriage, occupation of each spouse, standard of living during the marriage, wealth and income-earning ability of each spouse, which party is awarded custody of the children, health of the individuals, and any other relevant factors in the case.
2. **Community Property** – This theory states that all property acquired during the marriage using income earned during the marriage is considered marital property regardless of which spouse earned the income. Those states having community property laws divide property equally between the individuals.

Division of Marital Assets

Each spouse is responsible for his or her own debts acquired prior to marriage. Joint debts, or those that were incurred during marriage are the joint responsibility of each spouse. Additionally, each spouse is jointly liable. If a debt is not paid by the spouse to whom the court has distributed the debt, the third-party creditor may recover payment of the debt from the other spouse. Thereafter the spouse who ultimately paid the debt may seek recourse against the nonpaying spouse.

Spousal Support, Child Support, and Child Custody

<u>Spousal Support</u> – Spousal support is also called alimony. Either spouse may collect alimony over a specified period of time. The temporary nature enables this to be called rehabilitation alimony or temporary alimony. The amount of the alimony is based on the needs of the individual who will receive the alimony and the income and ability of the other individual to pay. Spousal support terminates if the former spouse dies, remarries, or becomes self-sufficient. Permanent alimony is also known as lifetime alimony. This is awarded only if the individual to receive alimony is of an older age and if that person has been a homemaker who has little opportunity to obtain job skills. Permanent alimony lasts until the person dies or remarries.

Child Support – The noncustodial parent is obligated to contribute to the expenses of paying for the financial support of his or her natural and adopted children, included of which are food, shelter, clothing, medical expenses, and other necessities of life. If the parents cannot come to an agreement regarding the amount of child support, the court will award an amount to be paid to the custodial parent. The court considers the following factors when making its award of child support: number of children, needs of the children, net income of the parents, standard of living of the children prior to the dissolution of the marriage, any special medical needs of the children. Child support payments usually continue until the child reaches the age of majority or its equivalent via emancipation or graduation from high school.

Half of the states have a formula to compute the amount of child support to award. The formula is based upon a percentage of the noncustodial parent's income. Deviation from the formula is allowed where a child has a disability or requires special educational assistance. Child support awards can be modified if the noncustodial parent's income or job situation changes or if the child's needs change.

Family Support Act

The federal law states that all original or modified child support orders require automatic wage withholding from a noncustodial parent's income. The rationale for this act is to prevent noncustodial parents from failing to pay their required support payments.

Child Custody

Traditionally the mother always got custody of a child. However, modernly, fathers are taking a more active role in the raising of their children. As such, the court has several factors it looks at to determine the child custody issue. They are as follows:

- ❖ The ability of each parent to provide for the emotional needs of the child.
- ❖ The ability of each parent to provide for the needs of the child, such as education.
- ❖ The ability of each parent to provide for a stable environment for the child.
- ❖ The ability of each parent to provide for the special needs of a child if the child has a disability and requires special care.
- ❖ The desire of each parent to provide for the needs of the child.
- ❖ The wishes of the child. This factor is given more weight the older the child is.
- ❖ The religion of each parent.
- ❖ Other factors the court deems relevant.

Custody may always be modified and is therefore not permanent. The parent who is awarded custody has legal custody of the child. Day-to-day decisions regarding the child are then made by the custodial parent. Custody will not be awarded to a parent where there has been signs of abuse. As such, another relative or foster care will be awarded custody.

Joint Custody – Most states allow joint custody whereby both parents are responsible for making major decisions concerning the child, such as education, religion, and other major matters. Joint physical custody is also sometimes awarded whereby the child spends a certain amount of time being raised by each parent. Joint custody is awarded only if the child's best interests are served and if the child remains in the same school while in the physical custody of each parent.

Visitation Rights – The noncustodial parent usually has visitation rights to see his or her child. Limited visitation as per the agreement of the court is allowed. If the safety of the child is an issue, the court will order supervised visitation. This sort of visitation is implemented if there has been child abuse or if there is a chance that the noncustodial parent will kidnap the child.

Refresh Your Memory

The following exercises will enable you to refresh your memory as to the key principles and concepts given to you in this chapter. Read each question carefully and put your answer in the blanks provided. Review the chapter material for any question you miss or are unable to remember.

1.   At common law, if a man proposed marriage and the woman accepted and then the man backed out, the woman would be able to bring a lawsuit based on _____ ___ _____.

2.   As a prelude to getting married, many couples go through a period of time known as an _____..

3.   If the prospective groom breaks off the engagement, who gets to keep the engagement ring? _____ _____.

4.   What does the modern rule, which is an objective rule, say with regard to broken engagements and the issue of who gets to keep the engagement ring? _____ _____

5.   What is a prenuptial agreement? _____ _____

6.   An _____ _____ is one the parties enter into during the marriage, setting forth the distribution of property upon death or termination of the marriage.

7.   A _____ _____ marriage is one in which the parties have not obtained a valid marriage license nor have they participated in a legal marriage.

8.   If there is ever a question as to who is the true father of a child, a _____ action may be filed to determine the father's identity.

9.   _____ _____ occurs when a parent fails to provide a child with the necessities of life or other basic needs.

10. Parents have an obligation to provide _____, _____, _____, medical care, and other necessities to their children until a child reaches the age of 18 or until _____.

11. The Defense of Marriage Act bars _____-_____ from enjoying _____ _____.

12. When does the government initiate a paternity lawsuit?

    _____

    _____

13. _____ occurs when a person becomes the legal parent of a child who is not his or her biological child.

14. What are the two main ways by which persons can become adoptive parents?

    _____ and _____ adoption.

15. What are the two legally recognized ways to terminate a marriage? _____

    and _____.

Critical Thought Exercise

Marissa and Hank, both eighteen years old, decided to get married; however, Hank did not want a traditional marriage ceremony. The couple told all of their friends that they were married and even had a celebration party at their new apartment. Marissa was pregnant at the time of the couple's celebration; however, Hank did not know this fact. After ten months of living together, the couple had acquired a brand new SUV, the down payment of which Marissa put down from a graduation gift of money that her generous parents had given to her. Additionally both Marissa and Hank bought a boat, a new computer, and two Old English Sheepdogs from their earnings at the local Burger King. It should be noted that Marissa had to quit working after two months of marriage, as her ankles became as big as watermelons from standing on her feet all day. The couple also has approximately $28,000 of debt together.

After four months of marriage, Marissa revealed to Hank that she was pregnant and due in three months. Hank became suspicious that maybe the baby she was carrying wasn't his and left Marissa. Marissa now wants a divorce, plus the SUV and all of the other assets the two have accumulated. Further, she wants full custody of their unborn child and child support and alimony as well. She also wants Hank to pay off their debt since she is no longer working and he has a job now as manager of Burger King making $58,000 a year. Marissa plans on moving back in with her parents and going back to school. Marissa's mother and sister will be able to help with the baby. What advice can you give her regarding her situation with Hank?

Answer:

_____

_____

_____

_____

_____

_____

_____

_____

_____

_____

_____

_____

_____

_____

Practice Quiz

True/False

1. ____ If parents do not have joint custody, the noncustodial parent will not have visitation rights. [p. 844]

2. ____ The awarding of custody to a custodial parent is permanent. [p. 844]

3. ____ Alimony is usually awarded temporarily. [p. 843]

4. ____ In community property states, marital property is divided equally between individuals. [p. 842]

5. ____ The fair distribution of property means the equitable distribution of property. [p. 841]

6. ____ *Pro se* divorces are also called "do-it-yourself" divorces. [p. 840]

7. ____ Approximately forty percent of divorce cases are settled between the parties prior to trial. [p. 841]

8. ____ A divorce proceeding is commenced when one spouse leaves the other spouse. [p. 840]

9. ____ Traditionally, a married person who sought a divorce had to prove that the other person was at fault for causing a major problem with continuing the marriage. [p. 840]

10. ____ A no-fault divorce means that neither party is to blame for the divorce. [p. 840]

11. ____ An annulment is an order of the court declaring the validity of a common law marriage. [p. 839]

12. ____ If Jody's parents die and she has no relatives to take care of her, nor are there any other arrangements for her care, then the state in which Jody, a twelve-year-old, lives is responsible for her. [p. 839]

13. ____ In an open-adoption procedure, the biological and adoptive parents never have the opportunity to meet. [p. 839]

14. ____ Approximately half of the states have statutes making parents liable for the intentional torts of their children. [p. 838]

15. ____ Several states have provided that gay partners can enter into "civil unions" that grant gay partners rights similar to those of heterosexual partners. [p. 836]

16. ____ Many states have a father's registry where a male may register as the father of a child. [p. 836]

17. ____ Some states allow parties to a marriage to be married to multiple individuals. [p. 835]

18. ___ An antenuptual agreement is one in which spouses sign an agreement in advance of their marriage. [p. 835]

19. ___ One of the current trends in the law is to recognize a breach of a promise-to-marry lawsuit. [p. 834]

20. ___ If the prospective bride breaks off an engagement to be married, she gets to keep the engagement ring. [p. 834]

Multiple Choice

21. Which of the following represents the modern rule and trend regarding broken engagements? [p. 835]
    a. The prospective bride gets to keep the engagement ring.
    b. The prospective bride must sell the engagement ring and split the proceeds with the prospective groom.
    c. The prospective bride must return the engagement ring regardless of who broke off the engagement.
    d. none of the above

22. In which situation will the court refuse to enforce a prenuptial agreement? [p. 835]
    a. Where one of the parties was not represented by an attorney
    b. Where one of the parties failed to make full disclosure of his or her assets and liabilities
    c. Where the terms of the agreement are unfair and unconscionable
    d. all of the above

23. In order for Marie and Jeff to have their marriage declared annulled, which of the following would assist them? [p. 839]
    a. One of the parties must lack capacity to consent.
    b. One of the parties was intoxicated at the time of the marriage.
    c. The marriage was never consummated.
    d. any of the above

24. Which of the following is not necessary for a common law marriage? [p. 836]
    a. That the parties are eligible to be married
    b. That the parties must live together
    c. That the parties hold themselves out as husband and wife
    d. That the parties submit blood test results to the administration

25. Which of the following is considered to be a joint marital debt? [p. 842]
    a. Automobiles
    b. Clothing
    c. Medical expenses
    d. all of the above

26. Which of the following require wage withholding from a noncustodial parent's income? [p. 843]
    a. The Alimony Act
    b. The Family Support Act
    c. The Surrogacy Act
    d. none of the above

27. Jasmine has filed for divorce against Al and wants to know which of the following would be considered her separate property. [p. 841]
    a. A ruby ring she inherited from her great aunt Abbey
    b. A silver vase given to her by her friend Sue for her birthday
    c. A posturpedic queen sized bed she had before she and Al got married
    d. all of the above

28. Chad wants to know which of the following the court will examine when making an equitable distribution of property upon the dissolution of his marriage to Maggie. [p. 841]
    a. How many relationships prior to the parties marriage were there?
    b. Health of the spouses
    c. What jobs did each of the spouses hold prior to marriage?
    d. What plans do each of the spouses have with respect to children after the dissolution of this marriage?

29. After being married to Devin for twenty-seven years, Helga has decided to divorce Devin. The couple have a lot of belongings and want to know what qualifies as community property. [p. 842]
    a. Helga's license to practice medicine in the state of New York
    b. Devin's stock option in the XYZ Corporation where he works
    c. Helga and Devin own a grocery store in a very desirable location.
    d. all of the above

30. Karen wishes to seek modification of the child support she is receiving for her handicapped son Marty. Which of the following is a good reason to grant the modification? [p. 843]
    a. Karen's ex-husband Waldo has lost his job.
    b. Karen's work schedule has become such that she has to hire an aide to help Marty off of the school bus and stay with him for two hours a day until Karen gets home.
    c. Karen feels Waldo hid some of his assets when it came time to determine the amount of child support and wants to redo her kitchen in her home.
    d. none of the above

Short Answer

31. States prohibit marriages between persons who are [p. 835]
    _____.

32. A person under the age of 18 who is not supported by his or her parents and who provides for himself or herself is said to be [p.835]
    _____

33. When a person adopts a child from a social service organization of a state, it is an [p. 838]
    _____.

34. An order of the court declaring that the marriage did not exist is an [p. 839]
    _____.

35. List a couple of the things that the court will consider when approving an adoption. [p. 839]
    _____
    _____

36. What is the type of divorce in which the parties represent themselves? [p. 840]

    _____

37. A legal proceeding whereby the court issues a decree that legally orders a marriage terminated is a _____. [p. 840]

38. What is the primary means of caring for children under the state's jurisdiction? [p. 839]

    _____

    _____

39. What type of testing is used to prove or not prove that an individual is the father of a child? [p. 837]

    _____

40. Give an example of separate property. [p. 841]

    _____

    _____

41. What are the two theories of distribution that are used when dividing marital assets upon termination of a marriage? [p. 841]

    _____

    _____

42. How do many states determine the amount of child support to be paid to the custodial parent? [p. 843]

    _____

43. What does joint custody mean? [p. 844]

    _____

    _____

    _____

45. The parent who is awarded custody has [p. 844] _____.

Answers to Refresh Your Memory

1. breach of contract [p. 834]
2. engagement [p. 834]
3. the prospective bride [p. 834]
4. The prospective bride must return the engagement ring. [p. 835]
5. are contracts that specify how property will be distributed upon termination of the marriage or death of a spouse [p. 835]
6. antenuptial agreement [p. 835]
7. common law ceremony [p. 836]
8. paternity [p. 837]
9. Child neglect [p. 837]
10. food, shelter, clothing; emancipation [p. 837]
11. same-sex [p. 837]
12. if the mother is receiving welfare benefits [p. 837]
13. Adoption [p. 838]

Critical Thought Exercise Model Answer

Since the facts indicate that Marissa and Hank have not followed the traditional way of getting married by obtaining a marriage license, taking a blood test, and being part of a marriage ceremony, it would appear that the couple has a common law marriage. This is especially evident as both Marissa and Hank are eligible to marry since they are both of legal age (18), and further their intent to be married has been expressed by telling their friends that they were married. The fact that they have an apartment together is indicative that they live together and the fact that the couple is having a party to celebrate their marriage satisfies the requirement that they hold themselves out as husband and wife. Since Marissa now wants a divorce, she will need to file a petition for the same and eventually get a decree of divorce to end her common law marriage to Hank.

The fact that Marissa is pregnant is not so much an issue as who the father may be. In order to ease his suspicious mind, he may want to file a paternity action to determine the identity of the father as well as help assist in whether or not he indeed must pay child support. However, it must be noted that most states presume that the husband of a wife who bears a child is the legal father of the child. If the child is shown to be Hank's, the court will consider the fact that it is apparently the couple's first child, the baby will be an infant that presumably needs its mother, the standard of living the couple had before their marriage terminated, since the baby is not yet born, as well as other factors like the home the baby will be raised in. Hank's income will be used in computing the amount of child support. As for custody of the unborn child, a variety of factors will be considered including each parent's ability to provide for the emotional and financial needs of the child and whether or not the child will be in a stable environment. Since Marissa's mother and sister will be available to help care for the couple's baby, the baby will presumably be in a stable environment. In all likelihood, Hank will be granted either joint custody or at a minimum visitation rights if the child Marissa is carrying is determined to be his.

As for spousal support, it is obvious from Hank's $58,000 a year salary that he is financially better off than Marissa, who has decided to go back to school. Marissa will probably get temporary alimony from Hank until she is able to obtain the necessary education to enter into the job force. The amount of alimony is based on the needs of the individual who will receive the alimony and the income and ability of the other individual to pay. Arguably Marissa will need alimony to care for the newborn especially since she does not have a job.

In terms of dividing the couple's assets, hence the SUV, boat, computer, and two Old English Sheepdogs, it must be determined whether or not these items are separate or marital property. Arguably the down payment on the SUV is separate property since it appears it was a gift from Marissa's parents, which, according to the law, gifts are separate property. However, even though the facts are silent as to whether Marissa and Hank were making payments together once they declared their relationship to be a marital one, it would seem that they probably were. As such the SUV may be paid for with commingled funds, in which case, Marissa needs to ask for her down payment out of the SUV, provided that the status of the SUV has not been completely changed to where it is the couple's community property. As for the boat, computer, and dogs, these are community property since the couple acquired these items during their marriage. As such, if Marissa and Hank do not reach an agreement as to how these will be divided, then the court will order a division of these assets.

As for the couple's debt of $28,000, the court may equally distribute these debts upon termination of their marriage. Note too that if a debt is not paid by the spouse to whom the court has distributed the debt, the third-party creditor may recover payment of the debt from the other spouse

Answers to Practice Quiz

True/False

1. False   If the parents do not have joint custody of a child, the noncustodial parent is usually awarded visitation rights.
2. False   The awarding of custody to a custodial parent is not permanent.
3. True   Alimony is usually awarded for a specific period of time. This is called temporary alimony or rehabilitation alimony.
4. True   In community property states, marital property is divided equally between the individuals.
5. False   The fair distribution of property does not necessarily mean the equal distribution of property.
6. True   Most states permit *pro se*, commonly called "do-it-yourself," divorces.
7. False   Approximately 90 percent of divorce cases are settled between the parties prior to trial.
8. False   A divorce proceeding is commenced by a spouse filing a petition for divorce with the proper state court.
9. True   Traditionally, a married person who sought a divorce had to prove that the other person was at fault for causing a major problem with continuing the marriage.
10. True   In a no-fault divorce, neither party is blamed for the divorce.
11. False   An annulment is an order of the court declaring that a marriage did not exist.
12. True   A child may become the responsibility of the state under several circumstances. The first is if a child's parents or parent dies and there are no relatives to take the child or no other arrangements have been made for the care of the child.
13. False   In an open-adoption, the biological and adoptive parents are introduced prior to the adoption.
14. True   About half of the states have enacted child liability statutes that make the parents financially liable for the intentional torts of their children.
15. True   Several states have provided that gay partners can enter into "civil unions" that grant gay partners rights similar to those of heterosexual marriage partners.
16. True   Most states have a father's registry where a male may register as the father of a child.
17. False   One of the requirements of marriage is that neither party is currently married to someone else.
18. False   This describes a prenuptial. An antenuptial agreement is one where the parties enter into an agreement during the marriage, setting forth the distribution of property upon death or termination of the marriage.
19. False   Today, most courts do not recognize a breach of a promise-to-marry lawsuit. The denial of such lawsuits is based on current social norms.
20. False   If the prospective bride breaks off the engagement, she must return the engagement ring to the prospective groom.

Multiple Choice

21. C   Answer C is correct as it aptly states the modern trend of abandoning the fault rule and adopting the objective rule, in that if an engagement is broken off, the prospective bride must return the engagement ring regardless of who broke off the engagement. Answer A is incorrect as under the fault rule, if a prospective groom broke off the engagement, the prospective bride would keep the engagement ring. This is not the modern trend. Answer B is incorrect as there is no such law that says the bride must sell the ring and split the proceeds. Answer D is incorrect based on the reasoning given above

22. D   Answer D is correct as answers A, B, and C all correctly state situations whereby the court will refuse to enforce prenuptial agreements.

23. D   Answer D is correct as lack of capacity (answer A), intoxication at the time of marriage (Answer B), and lack of consummation of the marriage (answer C) are all reasons that will assist Marie and Jeff is they are trying to annul their marriage.

24. D   Answer D is the correct answer as answers A, B, and C are necessary for a common law marriage. Answer D, however, is only necessary if a couple is marrying under state law requirements. As such, answer D is not required for a common law marriage.

25. D   Answer D is correct as automobiles, clothing, and medical expenses (hence answers A, B, and C, respectively) are all considered to be joint marital debt.

26. B   Answer B is correct as the Family Support Act provides that all original or modified child support orders require automatic wage withholding from a noncustodial parent's income. Answers A and C are incorrect as these acts do not exist. Answer D is incorrect for the reasons given above.

27. A   Answers A, B, and C all reflect what would be considered Jasmine's separate property, as inheritances, gifts, and property owned by a spouse before marriage are considered separate property.

28. B   One of the factors the court will look at is the health of the spouse. Answers A, C, and D are irrelevant in determining an equitable distribution of property and therefore are incorrect.

29. D   Answer D is correct as professional licenses, stock options, and the value of a business are all considered community property as expressed in answers A, B, and C.

30. B   Answer B is correct as Marty needs special care (an aide) as a handicapped individual. Answer A is incorrect as this is what Waldo would assert to decrease the amount of child support he would have to pay. Answer C is incorrect as, without proof, there is no grounds to seek modification. Answer D is incorrect for the reasons given above.

Short Answer

31. closely related
32. emancipated
33. agency adoption
34. annulment
35. home environment, financial resources, and family stability of adoptive parents (answers will vary)
36. *pro se* divorce
37. divorce
38. foster care
39. DNA testing
40. property owned by a spouse prior to marriage (answers will vary)
41. equitable distribution and community property

42. The states use a formula usually based on the noncustodial parent's income.
43. It means both parents are responsible for making major decisions concerning the child.
44. if there is a history of child abuse or if there is a strong possibility that the noncustodial parent may kidnap the child
45. legal custody

Chapter 54

INTERNATIONAL AND
WORLD TRADE LAW

Chapter Overview

This chapter explores the federal government's power under the Foreign Commerce and Treaty Clauses of the U.S. Constitution as well as the sources of international law. It also details the functions and governance of the United Nations. Various economic organizations including the North American Free Trade Agreement are also examined. The other international facets that are discussed include international intellectual property rights provided by Internet treaties, sovereign immunity, the World Trade Organization's dispute resolution procedure, and the arbitration of international disputes.

Objectives

Upon completion of the exercises in this chapter, you should be able to:
1. Recognize the function of the federal government's power under the Foreign Commerce and Treaty Clauses of the U.S. Constitution.
2. Differentiate between the different sources of international law.
3. Discuss the functions and importance of the United Nations.
4. Be familiar with the North American Free Trade Agreement and other regional economic organizations.
5. Discuss how the World Trade Organization's dispute resolution procedure works.
6. Discuss the doctrine of sovereign immunity.
7. Discuss how international disputes are arbitrated.

Practical Application

You should be able to appreciate the importance of the Foreign Commerce and Treaty Clauses of the U.S. Constitution as well as the impact of sovereign immunity. Further, you should be familiar with the names and functions of the various regional organizations. Finally, you should be able to state how international disputes are arbitrated and how the World Trade Organization's dispute resolution procedure works.

Helpful Hints

One of the most helpful tools to understanding the importance of this chapter is to focus on the fact that the chapter involves the international spectrum of business. The study tips below are organized first by sources of international law, then by regional organization, followed by procedure for resolving international disputes. It is very beneficial to understand the functions of the various organizations in order to better understand the cases discussed in this chapter.

Study Tips

Background information – A legislative source of international law does not exist. A separate court for interpreting international law does not exist. Further, a world executive branch that could enforce the international laws is also nonexistent. International law is very important with the increase in technology and transportation that is bringing businesses all over the world closer together.

The United States and Foreign Affairs

The Foreign Commerce Clause allows Congress to regulate commerce with foreign nations. Then Treaty Clause gives the president the power to make treaties as long as two-thirds of the senators present agree. States cannot unduly burden foreign commerce. State and local laws cannot conflict with treaties, as treaties are part of the Constitution.

Sources of International Law

- **Treaties and conventions** – These are like legislations that published by the United Nations and whose subject matter involves human rights, commerce, dispute settlements, foreign aid and navigation.
- **Treaty defined** – An agreement or contract between two or more nations, formally signed and ratified by the supreme power of each nation.
- **Conventions defined** – Treaties that are sponsored by international organizations and are signed by several signatories.
- **Customs** – A separate source of international law which defines a practice followed by two or more nations when interacting with one another. Requirements for a practice to become a custom include a repetitive action by two or more nations over a long period of time and acknowledgment that the custom is followed. Special note: Customs that have been followed for a considerable amount of time may become treaties.
- **General Principles of Law** – Many countries depend on general principles of law that are used in civilized nations in order to resolve international disputes. These principles may be derived from statutes, common law, regulations, or other sources.
- **Judicial Decisions or Teaching** – This fourth source of law refers to the judicial teachings and decisions of scholars from the nations in dispute. Note: There is no precedent for international courts.

The United Nations

- **The United Nations** – A very important international organization dedicated toward maintaining peace and security in the world, espousing economic and social cooperation, and protecting human rights. A legislative body called the **General Assembly, the Security Council, and the Secretariat governs it**. The General Assembly adopts resolutions and the council's duty is to maintain peace and security internationally. The United Nations is made up of several agencies including the United Nations Educational, Scientific, and Cultural Organization, the United Nations International Children's Emergency Fund, and the International Monetary Fund, the World Bank International Fund for Agricultural Development.

Regional International Organizations

- **The European Union** – This international regional organization used to be referred to as the European Community or Common Market. It represents more than 300 million people and is made up of several countries of Western Europe. The European Commission acts solely in the best interests of the union. Customs duties have been abolished among member nations and customs tariffs have been enacted for European Union trade with the rest of the world.
  NAFTA (North American Free Trade Agreement) – A three-country free-trade zone which eliminated or reduced most of the duties, tariffs, quotas, and other trade barriers among Mexico, the United States and Canada. There is a safety provision in the agreement whereby a country can reimpose tariffs if an import surge from one of the other nations hurts its economy or workers.
- **Asian Economic Communities** – Several Asian countries have created the Association of South East Asian Nations (ASEAN). China and Japan are not members of this association; however, Japan has given financing for the countries that comprise this organization. China may one day become a member of ASEAN.
- **Latin, Central, and South American Economic Communities** – There are several Latin American and Caribbean countries that have founded many regional organizations to further economic development and cooperation. They are the Central American Common Market, the Mercosur Common Market, the Caribbean Community, and the Andean Common Market.
- **African Economic Communities** – The economic communities that have been formed in Africa include the Economic and Customs Union of Central Africa, the East African Community, the Organization of African Unity, and the Economic Community of West African States.
- **Middle Eastern Economic Communities** – The Organization of Petroleum Exporting Countries is the best-known Middle Eastern economic organization. The Gulf Cooperation Council was formed to develop an economic trade area.

Regional Courts

Note that there are several treaties that have created *regional courts* to handle disputes among member nations. The problem arises where the regional courts do not have the ability to enforce their judgments.

World Trade Organization (WTO)

- **Basic Information** – The WTO was created as part of the Uruguay Round of trade negotiations concerning the General Agreement on Tariffs and Trade. It is located in Switzerland.
- **Function of the WTO** – The function of the WTO is to hear and decide trade disputes between nations that are members. A three-member panel hears the dispute, which then generates a report that is given to the dispute settlement body. The WTO has expunged the blocking ability of member nations. There is, however, an appellate body to appeal the dispute settlement body. Only issues of law, not fact, may be appealed.

- **Findings of Trade Agreement Violations** – If a violation of a trade agreement is found, the offending nation may be ordered to stop participating in the violating practice, as well as to pay damages to the other party. If the violating nation does not comply with the order, retaliatory trade sanctions by other nations may be assessed against the offending nation.
- **WTO Jurisdiction** – The WTO is also known as the "Supreme Court of Trade." Its jurisdiction involves the enforcement of comprehensive and important world trade agreements.

Ways to Resolve International Disputes

International arbitration is a nonjudicial method of resolving disputes whereby a neutral third party decides the case. The arbitrator will issue an award, not a judgment. The award-winning party may attach property of the losing party regardless of which country the property is located in.

International Criminal Court

A nation may criminally prosecute a business or individual that commits crimes within its jurisdiction or that violate the nation's laws. If the wrongdoer takes refuge in another country, the person may be sent back to the country that wants to prosecute him or her. Extradition is necessary in order to punish the perpetrator.

National Courts to Decide International Disputes

- **General Facts** – National courts of individual nations hear the bulk of disputes involving international law.
- **Judicial Procedure and the Problems Nations Face** – The main problems a party seeking judicial resolution of an international dispute faces are which court will hear the case and which law will be applied. Most cases are heard in the plaintiff's home country. However, many international contracts provide for a forum-selection clause as well as a choice of law clause. Dispute resolution becomes more difficult and often impossible without these two clauses.
- The **act of state doctrine** – This act proclaims that judges of one country cannot question the authority of an act committed by another country that occurs within that country's own borders.
- The **doctrine of sovereign immunity** – This doctrine states that countries are granted immunity from suits in courts in other countries.
- The **Foreign Sovereign Immunities Act** – This act provides a qualified or restricted immunity in two situations. The first instance in which a foreign country is not immune from lawsuits in the United States courts is if the foreign country has waived its immunity, either explicitly or by implication. The second instance is if the action is based upon a commercial activity carried on in the United States by the foreign country or carried on outside the United States but causing a direct effect in the United States.

International Arbitration

The parties to an international contract may agree to settle disputes between them by mandatory arbitration. **Arbitration** is a nonjudicial method of dispute resolution whereby a neutral third party decides the case. The parties thereafter agree to be bound by the decision. Arbitration is quicker, less expensive, informal, and more private than litigation.

An **arbitration clause** should state the arbitrator, the means of selecting the arbitrator, and the law that the arbitrator will be applying. An arbitrator issues an **award**, not a judgment. An arbitrator cannot enforce the award it renders. As such the winning party must petition the court to enforce the award.

Jewish Law and the Torah

In addition to abiding by the criminal and civil laws of their host countries, the Jews also obey the legal principles of the Torah. The Torah is an exhaustive set of religious and political rules that are formulated from Jewish principles. The base of the Torah is to determine the truth.

Islamic Law and the Koran

Saudi Arabia has Islamic law as its only law. It is mainly used in matters involving divorce, marriage, and inheritance, with some criminal law. One main characteristic of Islamic law is that it prohibits the making of unjustified or unearned profit.

Hindu Law – Dharmasastra

The Hindu law is religious based, using scholarly decisions that have been handed down from century to century. It embodies the doctrine of proper behavior. Note, that outside of India, Anglo-Hindu law applies in many countries with Hindu populations.

Refresh Your Memory

The following exercise will enable you to refresh your memory on the rules and principles presented to you in this chapter. Read each question twice and place your answer in the blanks provided. Review the chapter material for any question you miss or are unable to remember.

1. The doctrine of proper behavior is called _____.

2. Islamic law prohibits _____, or the making of unearned or unjustified profit.

3. The most notable consequence of riba is that _____ is forbidden.

4. The Islamic law system is derived from the _____.

5. Beis Din is Hebrew for _____ of _____.

6. A nonjudicial method of dispute resolution is known as _____.

7. A clause contained in many international contracts that stipulates that any dispute between the parties concerning the performance of the contract will be submitted to an arbitrator or arbitration panel for resolution is known as an _____ clause.

8. Which act exclusively governs suits against foreign nations in the United States, whether in federal or state court?

    _____

9. Under this doctrine, countries are granted immunity from suits in courts in other countries. Which doctrine is it?

    _____

10. The act of _____ states that judges of one country cannot question the validity of an act committed by another country within that other country's own borders.

11. A _____ _____ _____ designates which nation's court has jurisdiction to hear a case arising out of contract.

12. Give an example of a problem a party seeking judicial resolution of an international dispute may face.

    _____

    _____

13. Commercial disputes between private litigants that don't qualify to be heard by international courts have their international law disputes heard by _____
    _____.

14. One of the primary functions of the WTO is to _____, and decide _____ disputes between member nations

15. The WTO has been referred to as the "_____ _____ of _____."

Critical Thought Exercise

Scientists at Cornell University engaged in genetic engineering and created a pear called the New York Sweetie that is resistant to bruising, browning, and insect infestation. The Sweetie grows approximately 30 percent larger than known pears and has both a higher water and sugar content, making the Sweetie highly desired by consumers worldwide. The only pear that can compete with the quality of the Sweetie is the Favlaka Beauty, grown exclusively in Favlaka. Favlaka is a large European nation with a population of over 300 million people. The country of Favlaka is a member of the European Union and the World Trade Organization. The residents of Favlaka consume over $1.2 billion worth of pears each year. All pears that are eaten on Favlaka are grown in Favlaka or a neighboring EU country. Favlaka will not allow the importation of fruit that has undergone any genetic engineering. The Favlaka Pear Cartel argues that the introduction of genetically engineered pears into their markets jeopardizes the Favlakan pear industry and the health of all Favlakans. They fear that future crops will become susceptible to insect infestation and attacks by mold and fungus. The United States Pear Growers argue that there is no scientific evidence that the NY Sweetie will cause damage to any other variety of pear or humans when it is grown or consumed. They further argue that the actions of the Favlakan government is banning the Sweetie are unfair trade practices under WTO agreements. It is argued that the Favlakan government is only motivated by the goal of preventing international competition for the Favlakan Beauty.

In what forum should this dispute be resolved? What procedure should be used to resolve this international dispute? What law should control the issues in this case? How should the WTO rule in this case?

Answer:

_____
_____
_____
_____
_____
_____
_____
_____
_____
_____
_____
_____
_____
_____
_____
_____
_____
_____
_____
_____
_____
_____

Practice Quiz

True/False

1. ____ On an international level, the Constitution gives most of the power to regulate affairs to the federal government. [p. 849]

2. ____ The president is the agent of the United States dealing with foreign countries. [p. 849]

3. ____ International tribunals are of little importance in deciding international disputes. [p. 850]

4. ___ Courts and tribunals that decide international disputes often count on general principles of law that are recognized by civilized nations. [p. 851]

5. ___ A fourth source of law to which international tribunals can refer is judicial decisions and teachings of the most qualified scholars of the various nations involved in the dispute. [p. 851]

6. ___ A treaty is a consistent and recurring action by two or more nations over a considerable period of time. [p. 851]

7. ___ One of the goals of the United Nations is to promote economic and social cooperation. [p. 851]

8. ___ The General Assembly is composed of 15 member nations, 5 of which are permanent members and 10 other countries chosen by the members of the General Assembly to serve two-year terms. [p. 852]

9. ___ The International Court of Justice (ICJ) is also called the World Court. [p. 853]

10. ___ The EU treaty creates open borders for trade by providing for the free flow of capital, labor, goods, and services among member nations. [p. 854]

11. ___ The World Bank restricts money to developing countries. [p. 854]

12. ___ The China-U.S. trade agreement was a prelude to China's trade agreements with other countries. [p. 859]

13. ___ WTO appeals are limited to issues of law, not fact. [p. 859]

14 ___ The World Trade Organization has also been called the "Supreme Court of Trade." [p. 858]

15. ___ In the United States, commercial disputes between U.S. companies and foreign governments or parties may not be brought in federal district court. [p. 860]

16. ___ An arbitrator issues a judgment. [p. 863]

17. ___ The Foreign Sovereign Immunities Act governs suits against foreign nations in the United States, whether in federal or state court. [p. 863]

18. ___ The rabbi-judges sitting as Beis Din are more concerned with the truth than its adversarial process. [p. 863]

19. ___ Islamic law prohibits the making of unearned or unjustified profit. [p. 863]

20. ___ To resolve tension between Shari'a and the practice of modern commercial law, the Shari'a is often ignored in commercial transactions. [p. 863]

Multiple Choice

21. What types of matters are treaties and conventions concerned with? [p. 851]
    a. Statutes banning state governments from purchasing goods and services
    b. Human rights, foreign aid, navigation, commerce, and dispute settlement
    c. Consistent and recurring action by two or more nations over a long period of time
    d. General principles of law that are recognized by civilized nations

22. Custom is often defined as [p. 851]
    a an agreement between two nations.
    b. a principle of law that is common to the national law of the parties in dispute.
    c. a practice followed by two or more nations when dealing with each other.
    d. a goal to maintain peace and security in the world.

23. Which of the following are sources of international law? [p. 851]
    a. Custom
    b. Judicial decisions and teachings
    c. General principles of law
    d. all of the above.

24. What is the main function of the International Monetary Fund? [p. 853]
    a. To create open borders for trade by providing for the free flow of capital, labor, goods, and services among member nations.
    b. To eliminate barriers among Mexico, the United States, and Canada
    c. To provide an alternative to litigation
    d. To promote sound monetary, fiscal, and macroeconomic policies worldwide by providing assistance to needy countries

25. Which fact describes the appellate body of the World Trade Organization? [p. 859]
    a. Panels composed of three members of the appellate body hear appeals.
    b. The appeals court is made up of seven professional justices.
    c. Appeals are limited to issues of law, not fact.
    d. all of the above

26. Under the doctrine of sovereign immunity, [p. 861]
    a. a foreign country has waived its immunity, either explicitly or by implications.
    b. the foreign sovereign is subject to suit in the United States.
    c. a nation's right to nationalize private property is recognized by international law.
    d. countries are granted immunity from suits in courts in other countries.

27. Which of the following is not a true statement? [p. 853]
    a. Nations must obey international law enacted by other countries or international organizations.
    b. There is no world executive branch to enforce international laws.
    c. There is no individual world court that must interpret international laws.
    d. There is no individual legislative source of international law.

28.   Which of the following applies to the act of state doctrine? [p. 861]
   a.   A country has absolute authority over what transpires within its own territory.
   b.   Judges of one country cannot question the validity of an act committed by another country within the other country's own borders.
   c.   The case of *United States v. Belmont* applies this to doctrine.
   d.   all of the above

29.   Which of the following does not apply to the Jewish law and Torah? [p. 863]
   a.   Jewish law is based on ideology and theology of the Torah.
   b.   The legal principles of the Torah coexist with the secular laws of the Jews' home countries.
   c.   The rabbinical judges are actively involved in the cases.
   d.   The Shari'a forms the basis of family law but coexists with other laws.

30.   Which of the following applies to the international criminal court (ICC)? [p. 860]
   a.   The ICC has authority to prosecute individuals of war crimes.
   b.   The ICC has complementary jurisdiction with the national courts of a country.
   c.   If a nation is unwilling or unable to prosecute, the ICC can then prosecute the accused national.
   d.   all of the above

Short Answer

31.   What type of law is Hindu law? [p. 864]

32.   What countries make up the European Union? [p. 854]
   _____
   _____

33.   What are the two constitutional provisions that give power to the federal government to regulate international affairs? [p 849] The _____ _____ Clause and the _____ Clause.

34.   What is the name of the international organization that was created by a multinational treaty to promote social and economic cooperation among nations and to protect human rights? [p. 859] _____ _____

35.   What is the General Agreement on Tariff's and Trade? [p. 858]
   _____
   _____

36.   What is one of the most well-known oil producing and exploring economic organizations? [p. 858]
   _____

37.   Which two countries do not belong to any significant economic community? [p. 857]
   _____ and _____

38. Which large industrialized country in Latin American and the Caribbean have entered into a free trade agreement with all the countries of Central America as well as Chile, Columbia, and Venezuela? [p. 857] _____

39. What regional international organization that comprises many countries of Western Europe was created to promote peace and security as well as economic, social, and cultural development? [p. 854]

_____

40. What types of things does the World Bank provide funds for? [p. 854]

_____

_____

41. What are the benefits of having an arbitrator decide a dispute that arises between parties to a contract? [p. 862]

_____

_____

_____

42. What type of immunity does the United States have to foreign governments? [p. 861]
_____ or _____

43. What does the International Criminal Court have authority to prosecute individuals for? [p. 860]

_____

_____

_____

44. If the Free Trade Area of the Americas were created, what would it eliminate or reduce? [p. 857]

_____

_____

_____

45. Give two United Nations autonomous agencies that deal with a variety of economic and social problems. [p. 853]
_____ and _____

Answers to Refresh Your Memory

1. Dharmasastra [p. 864]
2. riba [p. 863]
3. the payment of interest on loans [p. 863]
4. Koran [p. 863]
5. house of judgment [p. 863]
6. arbitration [p. 862]
7. Foreign Sovereign Immunity Act of 1976 [p. 861]
9. the doctrine of sovereign immunity [p. 861]
10. state doctrine [p.861]

11. forum-selection clause [p. 860]
12. One problem is determining which nation's court will hear the case. [p. 860]
13. national courts [p. 860]
14. hear; trade [p. 859]
15. Supreme Court of Trade [p. 858]

Critical Thought Exercise Model Answer

Both Favlaka and the United States are members of the United Nations (UN) and signatories to the General Agreement on Tariffs and Trade that created the World Trade Organization (WTO). The World Court in The Hague is the judicial branch of the UN. One of the functions of the WTO is to hear and decide trade disputes between member nations. Any member nation that believes a trade agreement has been breached can initiate a proceeding that is first heard by a three-member panel of the WTO. The panel issues a report that is referred to a dispute settlement body of the WTO. A seven-member appellate body hears any appeal from the dispute settlement body. The dispute between Favlaka and the United States involves a trade barrier imposed by Favlaka. A nation may protect its food sources and livestock from foreign threats that are scientifically proven to exist. A member nation cannot create a barrier that favors its domestic sources of goods over foreign sources for the sole purpose of economic advantage. Favlaka will have to show that the threat of crop destruction from the NY Sweetie is real. According to the facts, there is no scientific proof that the NY Sweetie poses any danger to the Favlaka Beauty. This issue has been decided before. Japan tried to prevent the importation of American apples into Japan by creating apple-testing regulations that acted as a form of tariff or trade barrier. The WTO ruled that the lack of scientific evidence that the American apples posed any threat to the Japanese crops meant that the apple-testing regulations were without merit and improperly impeded entry of foreign-grown apples. The situation with Favlaka is very similar. A judge would likely be compelled to follow the same reasoning and order Favlaka to receive the NY Sweetie for sale in its country.

Answers to Practice Quiz

True/False

1. True   On the international level, the Constitution gives most of the power to the federal government.
2. True   The president is the agent of the United States in dealing with foreign countries.
3. False   The sources of international law are those things that international tribunals rely on in deciding international disputes.
4. True   Courts and tribunals that decide international disputes frequently rely on general principles of law.
5. True   A fourth source of law to which international tribunals can refer is judicial decisions and teachings of the most qualified scholars of the various nations involved in the dispute.
6. False   This refers to practice that has become a custom, not a treaty.
7. True   One of the goals of the UN is to promote economic and social cooperation.
8. False   The Security Council, not the General Assembly, is composed of 15 member nations, 5 of which are permanent members.
9. True   The International Court of Justice is also called the World Court.
10. True   The EU treaty creates open borders for trade by providing for the free flow of capital, labor, goods, and services among members nation.

11. False   The World Bank provides money to developing countries to fund projects for humanitarian purposes and to relieve poverty.

12. True   The China-U.S. trade agreement was a prelude to China's trade agreements with other countries.

13. True   WTO appeals are limited to issues of law, not fact.

14. True   Many refer to the World Trade Organization as the "Supreme Court of Trade" because of the power given to it to peaceably solve trade disputes among its more than 130 member nations.

15. False   In the United States commercial disputes between U.S. companies and foreign governments or parties may be brought in federal district court.

16. False   An arbitrator issues an award, not a judgment.

17. True   The act exclusively governs suits brought against foreign nations regardless if it is brought in the United States federal or state court.

18. True   Due to the active involvement of the rabbi-judges, the Beis Din is more concerned with the truth than the adversarial process.

19. True   Making a profit from providing services or the sale of goods is allowed. However, making a profit from unearned or unjustified profit is not.

20. True   To resolve tension between Shari'a and the practice of modern commercial law, the Shari'a is often ignored in commercial transactions.

Multiple Choice

21. B   Answer B is correct as their provisions address such things as the settlement of disputes, human rights, foreign aid, navigation, and commerce. Answer A is incorrect as treaties and conventions both involve agreements often involving trade versus abolishing the purchase of goods and services. Further, treaties and conventions involve agreements between nations, not states. Answer C is incorrect as this indicates one of the two elements necessary to show that a practice has become a custom. Answer D is incorrect as this refers to what courts and tribunals depend on to resolve international disputes, not what treaties and conventions center around.

22. C   Answer C is correct as consistent and recurring action by two or more nations over a significant period of time as well as recognition of the custom's binding effect is what is needed to show a custom exists between two or more nations. Answer A is incorrect as this is the definition of a treaty. Answer B is incorrect as a custom is not a principle of law, but rather a practice. Answer D is incorrect as this states one of the goals of the United Nations.

23. D   Answer D is correct as custom, judicial decisions and teachings, and general principles of law are all sources of international law. Therefore, Answers A, B, and C are all correct thereby making answer D the correct choice.

24. D   Answer D is correct as answer A describes the function of the European Union while Answer B which is also incorrect, describes the purpose of NAFTA and Answer C (also incorrect) describes arbitration. Therefore answer D is the correct answer.

25. D   Answer D is correct as answers A, B, and C all are correct statements of fact that describe the appellate body of the World Trade Organization.

26. D   Answer D is correct as countries are granted immunity from suits in other countries. Answer A is incorrect as this states an exception when a foreign country is not immune from lawsuits in U.S. courts. Answer B is incorrect as this is making reference to commercial activity being carried on by a foreign country that would be subject to suit in the United States. Answer C is incorrect as it is referring to nationalization not sovereign immunity.

27. A   Answer A is correct as nations do not have to obey international law enacted by other countries or international organizations. Answers B, C, and D are all true statements and therefore they are not the correct answers.

28. D   Answer D is correct as answers A, B, and C all apply to the act of state doctrine. The act of state doctrine is a doctrine that states that judges of one country cannot question the validity of an act committed by another country within that other country's borders. It is based on the principle that a country has absolute authority over what transpires within its own territory.

29. D   Answer D is correct as the Shari'a is Islamic law, not Jewish Law and the Torah. Answers A, B, and C all apply to Jewish Law and the Torah.

30. D   Answers A, B, and C all apply to the International Criminal Court thereby making answer D correct.

Short Answer

31. religious law
32. many countries of Western Europe, including, France, Italy, Belgium, Luxembourg, Germany, The Netherlands, Denmark, the United Kingdom, Ireland, Greece, Spain and Portugal
33. the Foreign Commerce Clause and the Treaty Clause
34. the United Nations
35. a multilateral treaty that establishes trade agreements and limits tariffs and trade restrictions among its more than 130 member nations.
36. OPEC
37. Japan and China
38. Mexico
39. 854 European Union
40. build roads, construct dams and water projects (answers will vary)
41. Arbitration is faster, less formal, less expensive and more private than litigation.
42. qualified or restricted
43. genocide, war crimes, and crimes against humanity
44. The FTAA would eliminate or reduce trade barriers among countries.
45. UNESCO (United Nations Educational, Scientific, and Cultural Organization), UNICEF (United Nations International Children's Emergency Fund), IMF (International Monetary Fund), the World Bank, and IFAD (International Fund for Agricultural Development).